Indian Epigraphy

Indian Epigraphy

D.C. SIRCAR

SINCE 1901

MOTILAL BANARSIDASS
PUBLISHING HOUSE

*3rd Reprint: Delhi, **2026***
First Edition: Delhi, 1965

Also available at:
MOTILAL BANARSIDASS PUBLISHING HOUSE

- 4637/20, F-2, Hari Sadan, First Floor, Ansari Road, Darya Ganj Delhi–110 002 *Tel.*: (+91-11) 4559 7999
- 1st Floor, 1/2 Rathnavilas Road, Basvanagudi, Next to Pai Vista Convention Hall, South End Circle, Bengaluru–560004 (India) *Tel.*: +91-80-41275911

MLBD Cataloging-in-Publication Data
Indian Epigraphy
by D.C. SIRCAR
Includes Various appendices,
Index and xxxvi b/w plates
I. Indian Epigraphy II. Sircar, D.C.

ISBN: 978-93-5903-741-7 (Hardcover)
ISBN: 978-93-5903-742-4 (Paperback)

Printed & Published by
Rajendra P Jain *for*
Motilal Banarsidass Publishing House
A-44, Naraina Industrial Area, Phase I, New Delhi–110 028 (INDIA)
Email: naraina@mlbd.in Website: www.mlbd.in
Tel.: (+91-11) 4751 1592

Dedicated to the Memory of

G. Bühler, F. Kielhorn, J. F. Fleet, E. Hultzsch

and other Savants to whose writings the Author owes his little knowledge of Indian Epigraphy.

CONTENTS

SECTION III

CHAPTR III

WRITING MATERIALS

SECTION I

SECTION II

SECTION III

CHAPTER IV

PREPARATION AND PRESERVATION OF RECORDS

CHAPTER VII

DATING AND THE ERAS

Section I

DATES IN INDIAN EPIGRAPHS

Section II

SOME CURRENT RECKONINGS

Section III

OBSOLETE RECKONINGS

Section IV

HIJRĪ AND ITS INDIAN MODIFICATIONS

PREFACE

It was during my student days about thirty five years ago that I felt the want of suitable books for the study of inscriptions in the post-graduate classes of Indian Universities. While I was preparing my *Select Inscriptions bearing on Indian History and Civilisation* on behalf of the University of Calcutta nearly twenty-five years back, it was also my aspiration to write an introductory volume dealing with Indian epigraphy and palaeography. But the subjects appeared to me so vast and complicated that I soon became doubtful about my competence to undertake it.

In 1954, the University of Calcutta requested me to revise the *Select Inscriptions* for a second edition. While revising the work and correcting the proofs of the revised edition, the old desire to write a text book on Indian epigraphy and palaeography again seized me, and I planned a small work on the subjects. Soon I completed some short chapters on Indian palaeography together with a few on certain connected topics of epigraphy in the lines of G. Bühler's *Indische Palaeographie* and G. H. Ojha's *Bhāratīya Prācīn Lipimālā*. It was only then that I realised that Indian epigraphy required a more elaborate treatment in a separate volume.

In the present work, I have tried to discuss various aspects of Indian epigraphy. But a satisfactory treatment of the subject requires so much width of reading and depth of knowledge and the number of inscriptions in the various Indian languages is so large that I have failed to do full justice to many of the topics owing principally to my limited knowledge and want of leisure. It is a matter of regret that various pre-occupations stood in my way to devote as much time as a comprehensive work on Indian epigraphy demands. There are again topics on each of which it is possible to write a detailed monograph, and it has been necessary to be brief for want of space. Nevertheless, I hope that the book will be of some help to the students of early Indian history and culture. The readers are requested to point out to me whatever serious flaws they may notice in the plan of the work and its execution so that I may consider them for the betterment of the work in a future edition.

While my work on this volume was progressing, I also felt the necessity of a glossary of interesting words occurring in Indian inscriptions and began to compile one. At first I wanted to append it to the present volume. But, when the glossary was ready, it was found to be too big for an appendix. I have therefore arranged for its publication as a separate volume under the name of *Indian Epigraphical Glossary*. My *Indian Palaeography*, which was taken up earlier as indicated above, is also being published as a separate volume.

Parts of the present book had been written before I left the post of Government Epigraphist for India in the Epigraphical Branch of the Department of Archaeology, Government of India, about the middle of 1961, and I am happy to record my feelings of gratitude to the members of the Branch for the help they rendered me in various ways. My thanks are due to Dr. S.K. Maity of the University of Jadavpur, who prepared the Index with the assistance of his pupils. I am also grateful to the Department of Archaeology for the photographs that have been used for illustrating the volume as well as to the authorities of the periodicals in which a few of its sections appeared either in English or in translation.

It is unfortunate that misprints and other blemishes have crept into the work in spite of my best efforts. For these, I crave the indulgence of the readers. I should also mention that some of the points of discussion have been repeated in different contexts for the benefit of average students.

Some errors and misprints have been corrected in the *Addenda et Corrigenda*.

University of Calcutta, D. C. SIRCAR
8th June, 1964.

ABBREVIATIONS

ABORI =*Annals of the Bhandarkar Oriental Research Institute*, Poona.

Allan's Catalogue (Gupta) =*British Museum Catalogue of the Coins of the Gupta Dynasties and of Śaśāṅka, King of Gauḍa*, by J. Allan, London, 1914.

Anc. Ind. Hist. Trad. =*Ancient Indian Historical Tradition* by F. E. Pargiter, Delhi reprint, 1962.

An. Rep. Arch. Dept., Gwalior =*Annual Report of the Archaeological Department*, former Gwalior State.

An. Rep. Arch. Surv. Ind. =*Annual Report of the Archaeological Survey of India.*

An. Rep. Ind. Ep. =*Annual Report on Indian Epigraphy*, New Delhi.

An. Rep. Mys. Arch. Dept. =*Annual Report of the Archaeological Department*, Mysore State.

ARASI =*Annual Report of the Archaeological Survey of India.*

Arch. Surv. Mayur. =*Archaeological Survey of Mayurbhanj*, Vol. I, by N. N. Vasu.

A. R. Ep. =*Annual Report on* [*Indian* or *South Indian*] *Epigraphy.*

A. R. Mys. Arch. Dept. =*Annual Report of the Archaeological Department*, Mysore State.

ASI, AR =*Annual Report of the Archaeological Survey of India.*

ASIR, A. S. I. Reports =Alexander Cunningham's *Archaeological Survey Reports.*

ASR =Alexander Cunningham's *Archaeological Survey Reports.*

ASSI =*Archaeological Survey of South India*, Vol. I, etc.

ASWI *Archaeological Survey of Western India*, Vol. I, etc.

BDCRI =*Bulletin of the Deccan College Post-Graduate and Research Institute*, Poona.

BEFEO =*Bulletin de l'Ecole Francaise d'Extreme Orient*, Hanoi and Paris.

Bhandarkar's List =*A List of Inscriptions of Northern India in Brāhmī and its Derivative Scripts, from about* 200 *A. C.*, Appendix to *Epigraphia Indica*, Vols. XIX-XXIII.

Bhār. Vid. =*Bhāratīya Vidyā*, Bombay.

Bomb. Gaz. =*Bombay Gazetteer.*

BSOAS =*Bulletin of the School of Oriental and African Studies*, University of London.

Bull. Baroda Mus. =*Bulletin of the Baroda Museum.*

Camb. Hist. Ind. =*Cambridge History of India.*

C H I =*Cambridge History of India.*

CII =*Corpus Inscriptionum Indicarum.*

Com. Vol. =Commemoration Volume.

Corp. Ins. Ind. =*Corpus Inscriptionum Indicarum.*

DHNI =*Dynastic History of Northern India* by H.C.Ray, Vols. I-II, Calcutta.

E. Hist. Ind. =*Early History of India* by V. A. Smith, 4th edition, 1924.

Ep. Birm. =*Epigraphia Birmanica*, Rangoon.

Ep. Carn. =*Epigraphia Carnatica*, Bangalore.

Ep. Ind. =*Epigraphia Indica*, New Delhi.

Ep. Indo-Mosl. =*Epigraphia Indo-Moslemica.*

Ep. Zeyl. =*Epigraphia Zeylanica*, Colombo.

Hist. Beng. =*History of Bengal* published by the Dacca University.

Hist. Ins. S. Ind. =*The Historical Inscriptions of Southern India* by R. Sewell, Madras, 1932.

Icon. Bud. Brahm. Sculp. Dac. Mus.=*Iconography of the Buddhist and Brahmanical Sculptures in the Dacca Museum* by N. K. Bhattasali, Dacca, 1929.

Ind. Ant. =*Indian Antiquary*, Bombay.

Ind. Cult. =*Indian Culture*, Calcutta.

IHQ =*Indian Historical Quarterly*, Calcutta.

Imp. Gaz. Ind. =*Imperial Gazetteer of India.*

Ins Beng. =*Inscriptions of Bengal*, Vol. III, by N. G. Majumdar, Rajshahi, 1929.

JAHRS =*Journal of the Andhra Historical Research Society*, Rajahmundry.

=*Journal of the Asiatic Society*, Calcutta; *JASB*=*Journal of the Asiatic Society of Bengal*; *JASB*, NS=*Journal of the Asiatic Society of Bengal*, New Series; *JRASB*=*Journal of the Royal Asiatic Society of Bengal.*

JBBRAS =*Journal of the Bombay Branch of the Royal Asiatic Society.*

JBORS =*Journal of the Bihar and Orissa Research Society*, Patna; *JBRS*=*Journal of the Bihar Research Society.*

JNSI =*Journal of the Numismatic Society of India.*

Journ. Am. Or. Soc. =*Journal of the American Oriental Society.*

Journ. As. =*Journal Asiatique*, Paris.

Journ. Bhār. Iti. Saṁś. Maṇḍ.=*Journal of the Bhāratīya Itihās Saṁśodhak Maṇḍal*, Poona.

Journ. Bomb. Hist. Soc. =*Journal of the Bombay Historical Society.*

Journ. G. Ind. Soc. =*Journal of the Greater India Society.*

Journ. Ind. Hist. =*Journal of Indian History.*

Journ. Or. Inst. =*Journal of the Oriental Institute*, Baroda.

Journ. Or. Res. =*Journal of Oriental Research*, Madras.

JRAS =*Journal of the Royal Asiatic Society of Great Britain and Ireland*, London.

JUPHS =*Journal of the U. P. Historical Society*, Lucknow.

Kielhorn's Southern List =*A List of the Inscriptions of Southern India from about A.D.* 500 by F. Kielhorn, Appendix to *Epigraphia Indica*, Vol. VII.

Lüders' List =*A List of Brāhmī Inscriptions from the earliest times to about A.D.* 400 by H. Lüders, Appendix to *Epigraphia Indica*, Vol. X.

Mem. ASB =*Memoirs of the Asiatic Society of Bengal.*

Mem. ASI =*Memoirs of the Archaeological Survey of India.*

Mys. Arch. Rep. =*Annual Report of the Archaeological Department*, Mysore State.

N. Ind. Ant. =*New Indian Antiquary.*

Or. Hist. Res. Journ. =*Orissa Historical Research Journal*, Bhubaneswar.

PHAI, Pol. Hist. Anc. Ind. =*Political History of Ancient India* by H. C. Raychaudhuri, Calcutta.

Proc. ASB =*Proceedings of the Asiatic Society of Bengal.*

Proc. Hist. Rec. Comm. =*Proceedings of the Historical Records Commission.*

Proc. IHC =*Proceedings of the Indian History Congress.*

Proc. Trans. A.I. Or. Conf. =*Proceedings and Transactions of the All-India Oriental Conference.*

Purāṇa Text =*The Purāṇa Text of the Dynasties of the Kali Age* by F. E. Pargiter, Delhi reprint, 1962.

Quart. Journ. Myth. Soc. =*Quarterly Journal of the Mythic Society*, Bangalore.

Rājatar. =Kalhaṇa's *Rājataraṅgiṇī*, edited and translated by Aurel Stein.

Rapson's Catalogue = *ritish Museum Catalogue of the Coins of the Andhras*, etc., by E.J. Rapson, London, 1908.

Rep. Dir. Arch. Surv., Burma=*Report of the Director of Archaeological Survey*, Burma.

SII =*South Indian Inscriptions.*

Smith's Catalogue =*Catalogue of the Coins in the Indian Museum*, Calcutta, Vol. I, by V. A. Smith, 1906.

Sour. Med. Hist. Dek. =*The Sources of the Medieval History of the Dekkan* by G. H. Khare, Poona.

Stud. Geog. Anc. Med. Ind. =*Studies in the Geography of Ancient and Medieval India* by D. C. Sircar, 1960.

Stud. Hist. Cult. Geog. Ethn. Guj.=*Studies in the History, Culture, Geography and Ethnology of Gujarat* by H. D. Sankalia.

Suc. Sāt., *Suc. Sāt. L. Dec.* =*The Successors of the Sātavāhanas in the Lower Deccan*, by D. C. Sircar, Calcutta, 1939.

Trav. Arch. Ser. =*Travancore Archaeological Series.*

Trans. Arch. Soc. S. Ind. =*Transactions of the Archaeological Society of South India*, Madras.

Univ. Cey. Rev. =*University of Ceylon Review.*

V. G. =*Verspreide Geschriften.*

Whitehead's Catalogue =*Catalogue of the Coins in the Punjab Museum, Lahore*, by R. B. Whitehead, Vol. I.

Wilson's Glossary =*A Glossary of Judicial and Revenue Terms*, by H. H. Wilson, 1855.

LIST OF PLATES

[Nos. I—XII, XIV—XIX, XXIII—XXXV are from *Ancient India*, No. 9. For Nos. XIII and XX—XXII, see *Epigraphia Indica*, Vol. XXX, Articles Nos. 8, 16 and 40. No. XXXVI appears in *Epigrahia Indica*, Vol. XXXVI.]

SYSTEM OF TRANSLITERATION

आ=ā,	ई=ī,	ऊ=ū,
ऋ=ṛ,	ॠ=ṝ,	ऌ=ḷ,
ॡ=ḹ,	ए (long)=e,	ए (short)=ĕ,
ओ (long)=o,	ओ (short)=ŏ,	ङ=ṅ,
च=c,	ञ=ñ,	ट=ṭ,
ड=ḍ,	ण=ṇ,	श=ś,
ष=ṣ,	ड़=d̤,	ळ=l̤,

Dravidian palatal alveolar *n*=n̤

Dravidian palatal alveolar *r*=r̤

Dravidian cerebral voiced fricative (i.e. voiced *ṣ*) =ḷ̤

anusvāra=ṁ, visarga=ḥ,

upadhmānīya=h̤, jihvāmūlīya=ḣ

CHAPTER I

INSCRIPTIONS AND THEIR EVIDENCE

1. *Indian Inscriptions*

Epigraphy is the study of inscriptions, and 'inscription' literally means any writing engraved on some object. In India, rocks as well as lithic, metallic, earthen or wooden pillars, tablets, plates and pots, as also bricks, shells, ivory plaques and other objects were generally used for incising inscriptions. Often writing in relief such as we find in the legends on coins[1] and seals,[2] which are usually produced out of moulds or dies, and also records painted on cave walls or written in ink on wooden tablets are regarded as inscriptions, although these writings are not actually engraved. As is usually the case with inscriptions in the Perso-Arabic script, the letters of certain late medieval records in the indigenous Indian alphabets are generally not engraved but are formed by scooping out the space around them.

Inscriptions may greatly vary in point of length. Sometimes an epigraph contains only a mark or one single word or expression, indicating the name of an individual, often a pilgrim at a holy religious establishment engraving his name on a wall or stone to commemorate his visit, or standing as the

1. Thousands of early Indian coins have been discovered at various places in different parts of India. The earliest of these bear no legend. The fashion of mentioning the name of the issuing authority in the coin-legend was popularised in India by the foreign rulers beginning with the Indo-Greeks who conquered wide areas of North-Western India about the beginning of the 2nd century B.C. Most of the indigenous Indian coins bearing legends have to be assigned to later dates. See *The Age of Imperial Unity*, ed. Majumdar, p. 159.

2. Hundreds of seals have been discovered in various ancient sites in different parts of North India. They are mostly of clay and steatite, though some of them are of ivory and other objects including metal. Royal seals affixed to copper-plate grants for the purpose of authentication were made of bronze or copper. Some of the seals bear only emblems and others only legends, while the majority bear both emblems and legends. See Chapter V, ii, 6, below.

label of a sculptured scene from the epics or the Jātakas.[1] Somewhat longer inscriptions may record the dedication of the images of deities[2] or commemorate such events as the fall of a hero in battle or such curious social customs as the self-immolation of a widow[4] and the head-offering of a devotee.[5] In some cases, however, an inscription may embody a *kāvya* in many cantos or a drama in several acts. The Udaipur Rājasamudra inscription,[6] called the *Rājapraśasti-kāvya,* falls in the first category, while the Ajmer *Lalitavigraharāja* and *Harakelināṭaka* inscriptions[7] are instances of the second type. The Kudumiyamalai (Pudukottai, Madras State) inscription[8] contains a unique seventh century work on musical notations.

Epigraphic records may be broadly classified under two groups: (1) those engraved by or on behalf of the ruling authority, and (2) those incised on behalf of private individuals or organizations. The largest number of epigraphs of the second category record donations made in favour of religious establishments or installation of images for worship. They are usually incised on the object that were donated or installed, and are, as a rule, small. In some cases, however, they mention the king during whose reign the grant was made or the installation took place. Innumerable dedicatory inscriptions, big and small, are engraved on the walls, etc., of reputed religious establishments and centres of pilgrimage, such as the temples at Bhubaneswar, Draksharama, Srikurmam, Simhachalam, Srirangam, Kanchipuram, Lalgudi and other places.[9] The majority of the donations recorded in these epigraphs were made by pilgrims, some of whom were kings, chiefs or royal officers. In certain cases, people are known to have made donations in favour

1. Some of the Barhut inscriptions belong to this class. The marks and names of masons fall in the category of very small inscriptions.
2. See, e.g., *Ancient India*, No. 9, Plate CX, Nos. 1-2.
3. Loc. cit., No. 3, Plate CXI, No. 1.
4. Ibid., Plate CXII, No. 1.
5. Ibid., Plate CXI, No. 1.
6. *Ep. Ind.*, Vols. XXIX-XXX, Appendix, pp. 1 ff.
7. *Ind. Ant.*, Vol. XX, pp. 201 ff.
8. *Ep. Ind.*, Vol. XII, pp. 226 ff.
9. *SII*, Vol. IV, Nos. 99 ff. and 1006 ff.; Vol. V, Nos. 1150 ff.; Vol. VI, Nos. 678 ff. and 692 ff.; *Ancient India*, No. 9, Plate CVIII; etc.

of such temples *in absentia*.[1] Pilgrims visiting the temples in the course of pilgrimage often carried with them a written eulogy with a view to getting it engraved on a temple wall after having made the desired donations.[2]

Eulogistic compositions, called *praśasti*, were sometimes composed and engraved on stone tablets or pillars to commemorate public works like the excavation of a tank or step-well or the construction of a temple by a royal or ordinary personage or a group of individuals. The ruler of the country is usually mentioned in such works composed on behalf of private persons or officials. Even private records, therefore, often offer valuable information for the reconstruction of political and cultural history as well as for other allied subjects such as topography. The Uttiramerur (Chingleput District, Madras) inscriptions[3] throw very welcome light on the village administration in Southern India during the tenth century.

By far the most important are, however, the records incised by or on behalf of the ruling authority. These inscriptions may be classified under such heads as: (1) royal edicts (e. g. the rock and pillar edicts[4] of the Maurya emperor Aśoka), (2) epigraphs commemorating particular achievements of a king in a eulogistic *kāvya* or *praśasti*,[5] (3) grants in favour of learned

1. Cf. *Ep. Ind.*, Vol. XXXI, pp. 100-01.
2. Cf. ibid., Vol. XXXIII, p. 43, note 2.
3. *An. Rep. Arch. Surv. Ind.*, 1904-05, pp. 131 ff.
4. Most of these edicts have several versions. There are also other cases of inscriptions having several versions. See *Ep. Ind.*, Vol. XXXIII, pp. 147 ff.
5. The Junagadh rock inscription of Rudradāman I and the Allahabad pillar inscription of Samudragupta fall in this class. See *Select Inscriptions*, pp. 169ff.; 254 ff. In later epigraphs, the word *praśasti* often occurs about the end of the records to indicate the composition. In some cases, the word *pūrvā* is used instead of *praśasti* and it has been suggested that *pūrvā* and *praśasti* are synonyms (cf. *Ep. Ind.*, Vol. XXX, p. 123). But *pūrvā* really means 'the above', i.e. the above-quoted or above-mentioned thing in the feminine gender, and is often used with reference not only to *praśasti* but also to *tithi* or the lunar day. It has to be noticed that *pūrvā* is not recognised in the lexicons as a synonym of *praśasti* or *tithi*, even though it is very often found in epigraphic literature. The subject of the eulogies was generally called the *kīrti* of the person concerned. The word *kīrti* means 'fame', but is here used to indicate any performance (e.g., a temple, an image, a grant of land and the like) calculated to render the person responsible for it famous. The words *kīrtana* and *kīrtanā* are also sometimes used in the same sense. See *CII*, Vol. III, pp. 212-13, note; *Ep. Ind.*, Vol. XXVIII, p. 184; Vol. XXXIII, p. 170 (text line 2).

Brāhmaṇas, religious institutions or deserving individuals and officials, and (4) miscellaneous.

Some of the epigraphic records, especially those of the eulogy type, were composed by poets of great ability and their compositions are of a high order. Mention may be made in this connection of Hariṣeṇa of the Allahabad pillar inscription (c. 360 A.D.)[1] of Samudragupta, Kubja of the Talagunda inscription (c. 460 A. D.)[2] of Śāntivarman, Vatsabhaṭṭi of the Mandasor inscription of 473 A.D.,[3] Vāsula of the Mandasor inscription (c. 532 A.D.)[4] of Yaśodharman, Ravikīrti of the Aihole inscription (634 A. D.)[5] of Pulakeśin II, Chittapa of the Bhilsa inscription (c. 1050 A. D.),[6] Vācaspati of the Bhubaneswar inscription (c. 1100 A. D.)[7] of Bhavadeva-bhaṭṭa, and Umāpatidhara of the Deopada inscription (c. 1130 A. D.)[8] of Vijayasena. Some of the authors of the epigraphic *kāvyas* are known only from the inscriptions, their other works being lost. It should be pointed out in this connection that private records were often composed by people of indifferent education and generally contain numerous errors of orthography and language. But epigraphs like the Chhoti Sadri inscription[9] of Gauri and the Vasantgadh inscription[10] of Pūrṇapāla show that sometimes even the Pandits at the kings' courts possessed very poor knowledge of the Sanskrit language.

The epigraphs recording royal grants of land were generally engraved on copper plates and there gradually developed a tendency to introduce in the copper-plate grants an elaborate eulogy of the donor and his ancestors. Fairly detailed information about a king and his ancestors is often found in the elaborate *praśastis* on stone or copper plates, which are therefore of inestimable value for the reconstruction of ancient and medieval

1. *Select Inscriptions*, pp. 254 ff.
2. Ibid., pp. 450 ff.
3. Ibid., pp. 288 ff.
4. Ibid., 393 ff.
5. *Ep. Ind.*, Vol. VI, pp. 1 ff.
6. Ibid., Vol. XXX, pp. 215 ff.
7. Majumdar, *Ins. Beng.*, Vol. III, pp. 25 ff.
8. Ibid., pp. 35 ff.
9. *Ep. Ind.*, Vol. XXX, pp. 120 ff.
10. Ibid., Vol. IX, pp. 10 ff.

Indian history, especially because most of the facts supplied by them are in many cases not known from any other source. But, as indicated above, private records also often offer valuable information for the reconstruction of political and cultural history and on allied subjects.

Excluding coins and seals bearing legends which are not inscriptions in the real sense, the largest number of Indian epigraphic records belong to the category of stone inscriptions. Most of the early *praśastis* are incised on stone—rocks, tablets or pillars, though, in the later period, they were also incorporated in royal charters engraved on copper plates as already indicated above.

A few words may be added here about certain characteristics of Indian inscriptions though we shall have occasion to discuss many of them in detail separately. At the beginning of an inscription generally and also at its end occasionally, there is an auspicious symbol or word or a passage in adoration to a deity. The word *siddham* and *svasti* at the beginning of inscriptions are commonly found, though *siddham* gradually came to be represented by a symbol found at the beginning of numerous inscriptions. Among other auspicious symbols, occasionally we have the *svastika*,[1] the trident-on-wheel called *triratna*,[2] the *śrīvatsa*,[3] the tree-in-railing,[4] and certain unidentified symbols[5] in early inscriptions.[6]

Generally separation of words or their groups is not observed in inscriptions. In certain cases, some letters are found to be separated from others; but this was done without any system and probably according to the will of the scribe or engraver. Often the end of an epigraph was indicated by punctuation marks and occasionally the end of a sentence or section

1. *ASSI*, Vol. I, Plate 69; *ASWI*, Vol. IV, Plate 49, Nos. 5-7, 9, 11, 13-14, etc.

2. *ASWI*, Vol. IV, Plate 49, Nos. 8, 10, 15, etc. It is sometimes called *nandipada* (Rapson's Catalogue, p. clxxv).

3. See this together with the *svastika* symbol at the beginning of the Hathigumpha inscription of Khāravela (*Select Inscriptions*, Plate facing p. 208).

4. This occurs at the end of the Hathigumpha inscription (ibid., Plate facing p. 209).

5. *ASWI*, Vol. IV, Plate 44—Bhaja No. 7; Plate 45—Kuda Nos. 1, 6, 16; Plate 46—Kuda Nos. 20, 22, 24, 26.

6. See also *Ep. Ind.*, Vol. XXXIII, p. 247 and Plate facing p. 251.

or the first or second half of a stanza was also likewise marked. At the end of a section, sometimes we have the representation of a lotus,[1] a floral design,[2] a circle[3] and other symbols.[4] In the upper part of a number of medieval inscriptions, there are such representations as the Śiva-liṅga, Nandin (Śiva's bull), a cow-with-calf, sun and moon, etc. Only in some cases an omission was indicated by a cross or *kākapāda* (or *haṁsapāda*) symbol and the omitted letter or letters were engraved in the margin.[5] Letters wrongly engraved were occasionally erased by chiselling or the cancellation was indicated by one or more strokes.[6]

Often, the names of the author, the writer and the engraver of a record were mentioned.[7] The dates of the epigraphs sometimes record the year [of the regnal reckoning of a ruler or of an era], season, month, day, fortnight, *tithi*, etc.[8]

The practice of engraving eulogies on pillars or tablets of stone and charters on copper plates was not popular with the foreigners professing Islam, who conquered wide areas of India during the medieval period. They were used to the writing of books on history and issued their many *farmāns* generally on paper. It was the Muhammadans who were responsible for the popularity of paper in India as a writing material. The increase in the popularity of the practice of writing on paper gradually led to the decline of the custom of engraving inscriptions on stone and copper. Another factor contributing to the decline is that the number of independent Hindu rulers, who would have followed the old convention, gradually became fewer and fewer. Indeed we have copper-plate charters issued by the kings of Tripura and Assam as late as the 18th century[9]

1. *Ep. Ind.*, Vol. XVIII, Plate facing p. 96.
2. Ibid., Vol. II, Plate facing p. 120, text line 33.
3. See ibid., Vol. XIV, Plate facing p. 185.
4. See, e.g., ibid., Vol. XXX, Plate facing p. 124, text line 17.
5. See ibid., Vol. XII, Plate facing p. 12, text line 1; Vol. II, Plate facing p. 276, text lines 8, 11 and 20.
6. See ibid., Vol. I, Plate facing p. 254, text lines 1, 5; *Ind. Ant.*, Vol. XIX, Plate facing p. 58, text line 16.
7. See, e.g., the Arthuna inscription (1080 A.D.) of Paramāra Cāmuṇḍarāja (Bhandarkar's List, No. 145), which was composed by the poet Candra, written by the Vālabhya-Kāyastha Āsarāja and engraved by Cāmuṇḍaka.
8. See *Ep. Ind.*, Vol. I, pp. 381 and 384; Vol. VIII, p. 42.
9. See *A. R. Ep.*, 1957-58, Nos. A 3-5.

and the engraving of pilgrims' records at holy places is popular even today in accordance with the old custom. The final blow to the practice of incising eulogies on stone was delivered by the introduction of the printing press and to that of engraving charters on copper plates by the system of registering documents introduced by the British administration.

2. *Reconstruction of Early Indian History*

For the ancient and medieval periods of Indian history, the study of inscriptions has a special importance. No doubt India contributed to the civilization of the world in all periods of history; but her more significant contributions to world culture were made in the early period. The study of early Indian history has, therefore, great importance to the student of the history of human civilization. Unfortunately, unlike Greece, Rome or China, ancient India has no history, because the Indians of antiquity did not care to leave written accounts of all their achievements. Ancient India did not produce a Herodotus, Thucydides or Tacitus to leave for posterity a genuine and comprehensive history of the achievements of her sons. Therefore, the information gathered from various sources, such as the literary, epigraphic, numismatic, archaeological and monumental records, has to be utilized to reconstruct this lost history of the most glorious days of India. Of all such sources for the reconstruction of early Indian history, epigraphic records are the most important, for they provided material for the major part of what we now know about the achievements of the Indians of old.

Writing in 1839, Elphinstone observed in his famous *History of India* that in Indian history 'no date of a public event can be fixed before the invasion of Alexander and no connected relation of the national transactions can be attempted until up to the Muhammadan conquest'.[1] In 1866 Cowell accepted the truth of Elphinstone's dictum in regard to the whole of the so-called Hindu period of Indian history,

1. Cf. M. Elphinstone, *History of India*, ed. E. B. Cowell, 5th ed. (London, 1866), p. 11.

for he pointed out that 'it is only at those points where other nations came into contact with the Hindus that we are able to settle any details accurately.'[1] But the activities of a multitude of scholars working in the various branches of ancient Indian history led to the gradual discovery and accumulation of an unexpected wealth of material for its reconstruction. The achievements of ancient Indian rulers recorded in inscriptions on stone and copper plates were undoubtedly the most important of this.

As early as 1837, the necessity of arranging epigraphical records systematically for the reconstruction of the ancient history of India was pointed out by James Prinsep, to whom goes the credit of first placing the study of Indian archaeology on a sound and critical foundation. Many inscriptions appeared in periodicals like the *Asiatic Researches* and the *Journal of the Asiatic Society* (both published by the Asiatic Society, Calcutta, established in 1784), the *Indian Antiquary* (started by J. Burgess in 1872) and others such as the *Madras Journal of Literature and Science*, the *Journal of the Royal Asiatic Society* (London), the *Journal of the Bombay Branch of the Royal Asiatic Society* and the *Transactions of the Literary Society of Bombay*.[2] The creation of the post of Archaeological Surveyor by the Government of

1. Loc. cit.; cf. V. A. Smith, *E. Hist. Ind.*, 4th ed., 1924, p. 1.

2. For a short account of the early phase of epigraphical studies, especially in South India, see J. F. Fleet, *Dynasties of the Kanarese Districts*, 2nd ed. (Bombay, 1882), pp. ii ff. Between 1783 and 1821, Colin Mackenzie collected from various parts of the old Madras Presidency innumerable manuscripts together with transcripts of numerous inscriptions on stone and copper. Walter Elliot collected the impressions of a large number of inscriptions and published a paper on 'Hindu Inscriptions' in the *Journal of the Royal Asiatic Society* (London), First Series, Vol. IV, pp. 1 ff., and its revised version later in the *Madras Journal of Literature and Science*, Vol. VII. pp. 193 ff. Manuscripts of his *Carnátaka Désa Inscriptions*, Vols. I-II, are preserved in the library of the Edinburgh University and the Royal Asiatic Society, London. In 1885 the Mysore Government published a photographic collection of 150 inscriptions and next year Theodore Hope edited photographic copies of 64 inscriptions in a volume entitled *Inscriptions in Dharwar and Mysore*, for the Committee of Architectural Antiquities of Western India. Some more inscriptions were inserted by him in his *Architecture in Dharwar and Mysore*. A limited edition of these collections, edited by J. F. Fleet, was published in 1878 by the India Office under the title *Pali, Sanskrit and Old-Canarese Inscriptions from the Bombay Presidency and Parts of the Madras Presidency and Mysore*. In 1879 Rice published his *Mysore Inscriptions*. Later he published his *Inscriptions of Sravana-Belgola* and *Inscriptions in the Mysore District* and several volumes of the *Epigraphia Carnatica*.

India in 1861 encouraged official and unofficial search for inscriptions and their study and publication.

Out of the numerous epigraphic records discovered respectively till the seventies and eighties of the 19th century, Alexander Cunningham, the first Director General of the Archaeological Survey of India (1871-85)[1], collected those of Aśoka in a volume,[2] and J. F. Fleet edited the inscriptions of the Gupta age[3] as Epigraphist to the Government of India (1883-86). E. Hultzsch, as Epigraphist to the Government of Madras (1886-1903), published the first volume of his *South Indian Inscriptions* in 1890.[4] About a year earlier, J. Burgess, Cunningham's successor as Director General of the Archaeological Survey of India, started an official journal entitled *Epigraphia Indica* exclusively for the publication of inscriptions.[5]

1. He earlier served as Archaeological Surveyor to the Government of India from the end of 1861 to 1865, when his Report on the Archaeological Survey, Vols. I-II, were prepared. As Director General, he prepared Vols. III, V, IX-XI, XIV-XVII and XX-XXI of the said Reports. Vols. IV, VI-VIII, XII-XIII, XVIII-XIX and XXII-XXIV of the Reports were written by Cunningham's assistants under his guidance. See Sastri's edition of Cunningham's *Geography of Ancient India*, pp. liii-liv, and *Ancient India*, No. 9, pp. 10-11.

2. A. Cunningham, *Inscriptions of Aśoka* (*CII*, Vol. I, Calcutta, 1877; revised edition, edited by E. Hultzsch, 1925).

3. J. F. Fleet, *Inscriptions of the Early Gupta Kings and their Successors* (*CII*, Vol. III, Calcutta, 1888). Vol. II, Part i, of the same series, edited by Sten Konow, was published in 1929 and Vol. IV, edited by V. V. Mirashi, in 1955. Several other volumes of the same type were published by non-official organisations in different parts of the country. Mention may be made of *Inscriptions of Bengal* (one volume edited by A. K. Maitreya and another by N. G. Majumdar), Varendra Research Society, Rajshahi; P. N. Bhattacharya's *Kāmarūpaśāsanāvalī*, Rangpur Sāhitya Parishad; *Bhavnagar Inscriptions*; P.C. Nahar's *Jainalekhasaṁgraha*; etc.; also P. Sreenivasachar's *Inscriptions in the Telingana Districts*; A. S. Gadre's *Important Inscriptions of the Baroda State*, Vol. I; etc.

4. Vol. II and Parts i-ii of Vol. III were also edited by Hultzsch, while Parts iii-iv of Vol. III, were edited by H. Krishna Sastri. The latest Volume of the series so far published is Vol. XIII.

5. The first volume of *Epigraphia Indica* (completely published by 1892 although the first fasciculus appeared in October 1888) was edited by J. Burgess with the assistance of E. Hultzsch, Epigraphist to the Government of Madras, and A. Führer, Archaeological Surveyor, North-Western Province and Oudh. The second volume was also edited by Burgess assisted by Führer. After these two volumes, which were published as a sort of supplement to the *Corpus* volumes, the *Epigraphia Indica* became a regular periodical. The next four volumes (1894 to 1901) were edited by Hultzsch as Epigraphist to the Government of Madras, and the seventh and eighth ones (1902-1906), together with a few parts of the ninth (1907-1908), by the same scholar as Professor in the University of Halle, Germany. The later parts of the ninth volume were edited by Sten Konow as Government Epigraphist for India. Sten Konow's successor in the said post was Rao Bahadur V. Venkayya,

The Government of Madras was publishing notices of inscriptions examined by its officers in an annual report from 1887 till 1921, the name of the publication being later changed to *Annual Report on South Indian Epigraphy*. In half a century, nearly 25,000 inscriptions on temple walls and other monuments and about 500 copper-plate grants were reviewed in this periodical.[1] With the increase in the number of epigraphic records discovered and studied, several lists of inscriptions were published for the benefit of the students of history. The earliest such work is F. Kielhorn's *Inscriptions of Northern India*, published in 1898-1899 as an Appendix to the *Epigraphia Indica*, Vol. V.[2]

About the beginning of the present century, V. A. Smith published his celebrated work entitled *Early History of India*, in which an attempt to 'sort and arrange the accumulated stores of knowledge' in a somewhat connected account of the political and cultural history of ancient India was made for the first time. The book was revised and enlarged in subsequent editions published in 1908, 1914 and 1924, the last one appearing shortly after the author's death. The importance of the discovery and study of new inscriptions in the reconstruction of ancient Indian history and the progress made year after year becomes perfectly clear from a comparative study of the successive editions of Smith's work and H. C. Raychaudhuri's *Political History of Ancient India* first published in 1923 and revised in 1927,

followed eight years after his death (1912) by Rao Bahadur H. Krishna Sastri. During the interval between Venkayya's death and Krishna Sastri's appointment, some volumes and parts of the journal were edited from abroad by Sten Konow and F. W. Thomas. A volume of the journal consists of 8 parts published quarterly in 2 years. Its publication was stopped for several years during the Second World War. For the career of the *Epigraphia Indica*, see ibid., Vol. XXXIV (pertaining to the years 1961-1962), Appendix, pp. i ff.

1. From 1945-46, the scope of the publication was widened and its name was changed to *Annual Report on Indian Epigraphy*.

2. The work as revised by D.R. Bhandarkar appeared as Appendix to the *Epigraphia Indica*, Vols. XIX-XXIII. Other lists of the kind are Kielhorn's *Inscriptions of Southern India*, published as an Appendix to *Ep. Ind.*, Vol. VII; H. Lüders' *List of Brāhmī Inscriptions*, published as an Appendix to *Ep. Ind.*, Vol. X; V. Rangacharya's *Inscriptions of the Madras Presidency*, Vols. I-III, 1919; N. G. Majumdar's *List of Kharoṣṭhī Inscriptions*, *JASB*, 1924; R. Sewell's *The Historical Inscriptions of Southern India*, 1932; A. V. Naik's *Inscriptions of the Daccan*, *BDCRI*, Vol. IX, 1947-48; C. R. K. Charlu's *List of Inscriptions noticed in the Annual Reports* and their *Subject Index*; H. N. Dvivedi's *Gvāliyar Rājyake Abhilekh*, etc.

1931, 1938, 1950 and 1953. But, though much progress has been made, there are still innumerable gaps in the early period of Indian history, and numerous problems still await solution by further discoveries and studies.

The work of the reconstruction of the early period of Indian history was inaugurated by European scholars in the 18th century. Later on, Indians also became interested in the subject. The credit for the decipherment of early Indian inscriptions, written in the Brāhmī and Kharoṣṭhī alphabets, which paved the way of epigraphical and historical studies in India, is due to scholars like Prinsep, Lassen, Norris and Cunningham. Indian epigraphic studies also owe a great debt to many other European savants like G. Bühler, E. Senart, F. Kielhorn, E. Hultzsch, L. Rice, W. Elliot, J.F. Fleet and L.D. Barnett as well as to Indian scholars like Bhagwanlal Indraji, R.L. Mitra, R.G. Bhandarkar, R. D. Banerji, P. N. Bhattacharya, D. R. Bhandarkar, H. P. Sastri, V. Venkayya, H. Krishna Sastri, N. G. Majumdar, N. P. Chakravarti and others. Amongst the above European scholars, the most outstanding contributions to Indian epigraphic studies are those of Bühler, Kielhorn, Fleet and Hultzsch. Among Indian epigraphists, the contributions of D.R. Bhandarkar and N. G. Majumdar are conspicuous while Venkayya and Krishna Sastri were good in dealing with South Indian inscriptions.[1]

The great part played by inscriptions, including legends on coins and seals, in the reconstruction of the history of ancient

1. The study of inscriptions and coins formed the major and most important item of the archaeologists' work in India till the beginning of the 20th century. Even later, in the first quarter of the present century, when the study of excavated antiquities began to receive due attention, most officers of the Department of Archaeology, Government of India, were dealing with inscriptions and coins. This seems to be the reason why epigraphy, which in India is at least as great a subject as pure archaeology and is easily separable from the latter, was made the responsibility of a small branch of the Department while provision was not at all made for numismatics. The effect of this policy manifested itself in the following quarter of the century when more and more emphasis was laid by the Department on the study of prehistoric antiquities, so that the study of inscriptions came ultimately to be confined mainly to the Epigraphical Branch while the study of coins by the Departmental officers practically ceased. Indian epigraphical and numismatic studies would have thrived if the Government would have placed them in the charge of a separate Department of their own. There is a rumour that Hultzsch and Sten Konow resigned from the posts they held in the Department of Archaeology as a result of the said policy.

India can be demonstrated by an example. No imperial ruler named Budhagupta was known till the first quarter of the 19th century. A stone inscription mentioning Suraśmicandra, a viceroy of king Budhagupta, was discovered at Eran in the Sagar District of Madhya Pradesh in 1838.[1] The record, bearing a date in the Gupta year 165 corresponding to 484-85 A. D., states that Mātṛviṣṇu, ruler of Eran, was subordinate to Budhagupta's viceroy governing a province lying between the rivers Kālindī (Yamunā) and Narmadā. Thus we came to learn that a king named Budhagupta held sway over the Malwa region in 484-85 A.D. Some silver coins of Budhagupta were discovered in 1894, and they were found to have been issued in the Gupta year 175 corresponding to 494-95 A. D.[2] It was thus further learnt that Budhagupta, king of Malwa, reigned for about ten years between 484 and 495 A.D. In 1914-15 two inscriptions belonging to Budhagupta's reign were discovered at Sarnath near Banaras[3] and were found to be dated in the Gupta year 157 (476-77 A. D.). Thus we came to learn that king Budhagupta was not a local ruler of the Malwa region, but that his dominions included considerably large portions of the U. P. It was also clear that he ruled not for about ten years but at least for about eighteen years between 476 and 495 A.D. The extension of Budhagupta's dominions from Malwa in the west to Banaras in the east led to the suspicion that he might have belonged to the Imperial Gupta house of Magadha. This possibility was nearly proved in 1919-20, when two copper-plate inscriptions[4] of the same king were found at Damodarpur in the Dinajpur District of North Bengal. These indicated the inclusion of the northern part of Bengal within the vast empire of Budhagupta. But, even then, we were in the dark about the exact position of Budhagupta in the genealogy of the Imperial Guptas of Magadha. In 1943, however, the study of the legend on a damaged clay seal[5] of Budhagupta, discovered at Nalanda (Patna District,

1. *CII*, Vol. III, pp. 88 ff.
2. J. Allan, *Catalogue of Coins of the Gupta Dynasties*, etc. (London, 1914), pp. lxii and 153.
3. *An. Rep. Arch. Surv. Ind.*, 1914-15 (1920), p. 125.
4. *Ep. Ind.*, Vol. XV (1919-1920), pp. 134 ff.
5. *IHQ*, Vol. XIX (1943), pp. 119 ff. and 272 ff.

Bihar), proved that he was the son of Pūrugupta, grandson of Kumāragupta I Mahendrāditya, great-grandson of Candragupta II Vikramāditya and great-great-grandson of the mighty Samudragupta of the Imperial Gupta dynasty of Magadha. Thus, after the lapse of more than a century from 1838 to 1943, fairly complete information about the position of an ancient Indian monarch named Budhagupta was available to the students of early Indian history. Unfortunately, however, many facts associated with the reign of this ruler have still to be recovered. But this gathering of information bit by bit is of absorbing interest to all investigators in the field of Indian historical research. The students of Indian history, who studied the Eran inscription in 1838, Budhagupta's coins in 1894, the Sarnath inscriptions in 1914-15, the Damodarpur plates in 1919-20 and the Nalanda seal in 1943, must have felt like 'some watcher of the skies when a new planet swims into his ken.'

There is a popular belief that all important inscriptions have already been discovered and studied and utilised for the reconstruction of early Indian history. That this is a wrong notion is very clearly demonstrated by the articles appearing in the pages of the *Epigraphia Indica* during the past few years.[1]

3. *Historical Perspective*

Fleet observed, "It is indeed very questionable whether the ancient Hindus ever possessed the true historical sense in the shape of the faculty of putting together genuine history on broad and critical lines."[2] A study of such epigraphs as the Hathigumpha inscription[3] (first century B. C.) of Khāravela, Junagadh rock inscription[4] (150 A. D.) of Rudradāman, Aihole inscription[5] (634 A. D.) of Pulakeśin II and official records of

1. In the present quarter of the 20th century, circumstances have so developed that suitably qualified and serious students are not easily available for conducting research work in subjects like epigraphy mainly because they are attracted by other avenues of life. The study of Indian inscriptions and coins is no longer popular among European scholars.

2. *Imp. Gaz. Ind.*, Vol. II, p. 5.

3. *Ep. Ind.*, Vol. XX, pp. 71 ff.

4. Ibid., Vol. VIII, pp. 36 ff.

5. Ibid., Vol. VI, pp. 1 ff.

such royal families as the Coḷas, Eastern Cālukyas and Imperial Eastern Gaṅgas side by side with chronicles like Kalhaṇa's *Rājataraṅgiṇī* (c. 1150 A.D.) and works like Bāṇa's *Harṣacarita* (first quarter of the 7th century) and Bilhaṇa's *Vikramāṅkadeva-carita* (close of the 11th century) would suggest that the observation can only be regarded as partially justifiable.

It has to be remembered in this connection that many inscriptions as well as literary works of a historical character are lost. We know that, of no less than twelve chronicles dealing with the ancient history of Kashmir, including the works of Nīlamuni, Helārāja, Chavillākara, Padmamihira, Suvrata and Kṣemendra (11th century), which were available to Kalhaṇa in the 12th century, only a part of Nīlamuni's chronicle has so far been discovered. It is well known that the Indian climate is not favourable for the preservation of manuscripts, written on leaves, birch-bark sheets and similar other perishable materials. Even first rate dramas of poets like Rāmila and Saumilla, which were widely popular in the days of Kālidāsa (4th-5th century A.D.), have not come down to us. Fortunately some of the documents were engraved on lasting materials like stone and metal and a large number of these has been discovered.

It is clear from the reference to numerous earlier chronicles in the *Rājataraṅgiṇī* (12th century) that works dealing with the activities of the ancient kings of Kashmir began to be written at a very early date, long before the secluded vale came into close contact with history-minded foreigners like the Musalmans. That chronicles at least of the *Vaṁśāvalī* type were prepared and preserved at the courts of various royal families ruling over other parts of India is also suggested by several factors. In the 11th century, Al Bīrūnī referred to the 'pedigree' of the Śāhīs of Afghanistan and North-Western Bhāratavarṣa, written on silk, which is stated to have been preserved at the fortress of Nagarkot in the Punjab. What he says about the Śāhīs seems to indicate that this was a dynastic account of the Śāhī kings from the foundation of Kuṣāṇa power about the beginning of the Christian era down to the fall of the Brāhmaṇa Śāhīs in the 11th century. From about the 6th and 7th centuries

A.D., official charters of most of the imperial families ruling over various parts of India began to incorporate historical accounts from their foundation to the date of the records. In many cases, such an account covers several centuries and it is impossible to believe that it could have been prepared without the help of earlier written records. It has to be noticed, for instance, that the reference to the 18 years' duration of Kubja-Viṣṇuvardhana's rule is found only in the Eastern Cālukya charters of the time of his distant descendants who ruled three centuries later.[1] That the practice of preparing dynastic annals was popular from very old times is suggested by the inclusion of many such accounts of ancient ruling families in the Purāṇas. It is well known that the Puranic *Vaṁśāvalīs* quote the names of the rulers of a family in a chronological order often with the duration of the rule of each king and his relation with his predecessor. Achievements of particular monarchs (e. g. the foundation of the city of Puṣpapura or Pāṭaliputra by Udayin of Magadha during the fourth year of his reign)[2] are mentioned only occasionally. Kālidāsa's *Raghuvaṁśa*, which is essentially a chronicle of the traditional rulers of the Ikṣvāku house, based on legends and dynastic accounts as those contained in the Purāṇas, would, however, suggest that the composition of bigger chronicles on the achievements of imperial families was not quite unknown or unpopular in ancient India.

While describing the ideal historian in his *Rājataraṅgiṇī*,[3] Kalhaṇa pays homage to the genius of a gifted poet, which immortalises the glory of the author as well as the subject of his narration and without which it is impossible to vivify before the reader's eyes the events of the bygone age. It is further said that the poet should possess divine perception so as to be able to show, through intuition, his awareness of the existences he is going to reveal to his readers. Above all, Kalhaṇa praises the poet of merit whose language, like that of the judge, has discarded love and hatred, i.e. bias or prejudice, in recounting the

1. Cf. *SII*, Vol. I, p. 39, text lines 6-7.
2. Cf. *Vāyu Purāṇa*, ch. 99, verse 319.
3. I, verses 4 ff.

events of the past. The qualities of a historian emphasised here are the ability to see the facts in their proper perspective by linking one of them with others by means of intuition and to describe them in a pleasant and impartial manner so that the narrative becomes intelligible and agreeable to the readers and the presentation of facts true to the author's knowledge and belief. Kalhaṇa's conception of history may fall short of the modern western stadards; but the concluding sections of the *Rājataraṅgiṇī* would hardly suffer from a comparison with earlier historical works written in different parts of the world, especially those of the contemporary Muslim chroniclers.

The author of the *Rājataraṅgiṇī*[1] had before him no less than twelve works of earlier authors; but he justifies his attempt to write a new chronicle by pointing out that the earlier works were defective, apparently because their authors did not strictly follow the principles postulated and followed by him. The sources consulted by Kalhaṇa to free his own composition from mistakes are referred to in a stanza saying, "By a scrutiny of the ordinances of former kings regarding religious foundations and grants, laudatory inscriptions as well as written records, all wearisome errors have been set at rest." Similarly, the author of the Kumbhalgadh inscription[2] of 1450 A.D. had before him both written and oral traditions of the Rajput bards, although he claims to quote the genealogy of the kings of Mewar after having examined numerous old inscriptions of the *praśasti* type. These authors therefore utilised epigraphic evidence for checking the details of the chronicles, as historians have to do in other countries for which written history is available. Unfortunately, modern writers on the early history of most parts of India are not as fortunate as the authors of the *Rājataraṅgiṇī* and the Kumbhalgadh inscription were. No early work even of the type of bardic chronicles is available for most of the other areas of India. Historians therefore have to depend often almost entirely on informations supplied by inscriptions, including legends on coins and seals.

1. I, verses 9 ff.
2. *Ep. Ind.*, Vol. XXIV, p. 324.

We have no doubt what may be called historical *kāvyas* on the careers of some ancient Indian monarchs, such as Bāṇa's *Harṣacarita* on the early life of the Puṣyabhūti king Harṣavardhana (606-47 A. D.) of Thanesar and Kanauj, Sandhyākaranandin's *Rāmacarita* on the career of Rāmapāla (c. 1077-1120 A.D.) of Eastern India and Bilhaṇa's *Vikramāṅkadevacarita* on the life of Cālukya Vikramāditya VI (1076-1126 A.D.) of Kalyāṇa. But the number of such works so far discovered is meagre. Another class of semi-historical works is represented by Viśākhadatta's dramas, *Mudrārākṣasa* (on the life of Candragupta Maurya, c. 322-298 B.C.) and *Devīcandragupta* (on the career of the Gupta emperor Candragupta II, 376-414 A. D.), written in the 6th or 7th century A.D. Unfortunately, not only is their number few, but, in the absence of corroborative evidence from other sources, it is often extremely difficult to distinguish their historical substratum from imaginary elements. Kālidāsa's *Mālavikāgnimitra*, Bhāsa's *Pratijñāyaugandharāyaṇa*, etc., are similar works written on the bases of historical traditions, although they obviously contain a good deal of what is legendary and imaginary. But even such compositions are not many. More important from the historian's point of view are casual references to historical personages and events in works like Patañjali's *Mahābhāṣya*, Rājaśekhara's *Viddhaśālabhañjikā*, *Bālabhārata* (*Pracaṇḍa-Pāṇḍava*), etc., and others. Works of the type of Pampa's *Vikramārjunavijaya* (Kannaḍa), and Jayaṅkoṇḍan's *Kaliṅgattuparaṇi* (Tamil) dealing with the achievements of the Cōḷa-cālukya king Kulottuṅga I (1070-1120 A. D.) are of some importance.

4. *Merits of Epigraphical Evidence*

The great importance of inscriptions lies in the fact that they generally offer information about personages and events of Indian history, about which nothing is known from any other source. Only in some cases, we have recorded traditions about such subjects, the details of which can be compared with epigraphic information. Such a comparison very often shows that the details of the traditions are mostly wrong. There are cases of a personage or an event or a subject being merely referred to vaguely in some source and inscriptions clothing them with interesting details.

Among the merits of epigraphic records as a source of Indian history, the formost is the fact that their authors in most cases described contemporary events. In describing the ancestors of his royal patron, the court poet had sometimes to deal with past events and personages. But the material for the description of events of the near past was easily available to him. As regards the distant past, sometimes he depended on recorded or unrecorded tradition. There are also instances (e. g. in the Kumbhalgadh inscription) to show that the author of an epigraphic record tried to ascertain the correct facts with the help of old documents either in his patron's archives or elsewhere. The author of the Junagadh inscription of 150 A. D., while recounting the early history of the Sudarśana lake, says that it was created by *Rāṣṭriya* Puṣyagupta during the reign of Candragupta Maurya (c. 322-298 B. C.), and that *Yavanarāja* Tuṣāspha endowed it with irrigation canals on behalf of Aśoka Maurya (c. 272-232 B.C.). It appears that some genuine records about the lake, belonging to the 4th and 3rd centuries B.C., were available for consultation to the author of the Junagadh inscription in 150 A.D.

As already indicated above, from the early medieval period, inscriptions of the imperial families generally incorporated a historical account of the particular dynasties from their foundation down to the date of the records. The Aihole inscription of 634 A.D. gives a fairly clear and trustworthy, if not satisfactorily elaborate, account of the rise and early history of the Cālukyas of Bādāmi covering a period of about one century. The story begins with Jayasiṁha-vallabha, founder of the Cālukya dynasty, and his son Raṇarāga. Raṇarāga's son Pulakeśin I, who made Vātāpipurī his capital, established the greatness of the family by performing an Aśvamedha sacrifice. His son and successor Kīrtivarman I subdued neighbouring powers like the Nalas, Mauryas and Kadambas. He was succeeded by his younger brother Maṅgaleśa who extended his power in the north by conquering Revatīdvīpa and defeating the Kalacuri king Buddharāja. His attempt to appoint his own son as his successor led to a civil war between the king and his nephew Pulakeśin II, son of Kīrtivarman I. The whole kingdom fell into a chaotic condition; but ultimately Pulakeśin II succeeded in killing his uncle and gaining the throne. Soon after his accession, Pulakeśin II had to face the invading forces of Appāyika and Govinda who had reached as far as the northern bank of the Bhīmarathī. He succeeded in winning over Govinda and driving out Appāyika. Next, in the south, he subdued the Kadambas of Vanavāsī on the Varadā and their neighbours like the Gaṅgas and Āḷupas and, in the north, the Lāṭas, Mālavas and Gurjaras. Then he defeated Harṣa in the region of the Revā (Narmadā) and became the undisputed lord of the three Mahārāṣṭras. Later, in the course of a *digvijaya* in the east, he subdued [South] Kosala and Kaliṅga, conquered Piṣṭapura and Lake Kuṇāla and defeated the Pallava king of Kāñcī. He next crossed the Kāverī, made friends with the Coḷas, Pāṇḍyas and Keralas, and defeated the Pallavas once again before his return to Vātāpi.

This account of early Cālukya history by the author of the Aihole inscription may be compared with many similar accounts of various imperial families (e.g. the Pālas, Rāṣṭrakūṭas and others) found in their epigraphic records. It has to be noticed that the treatment of the subject in the inscriptions is not as elaborate as in works like the *Rājataraṅgiṇī*. This is mainly because their space was considerably limited. Often the authors of inscriptions had to recount the history of several centuries for being engraved only on a few copper plates. Another defective feature of the account is that, although the Aihole inscription quotes the date of its incision on the occasion of the construction of a Jain temple as the Kali year 3735 corresponding to Saka 556, it gives no date for any of the past events described nor does it quote the duration of the reign of any of the past rulers. Such defects are, however, less prominent in the official charters of some other families. Thus the grants of the Eastern Cālukyas quote the reign-period of each of the past rulers in some cases in years, months and days,[1] while those of the Eastern Gaṅgas quote, in addition to the reign-periods of most of the rulers in years only, the exact date of the coronation of a few of the issuer's predecessors.[2]

Another important characteristic of inscriptions is that their texts are generally free from variant readings as they were not usually liable to modification like those of literary works which were copied and recopied by people in later times. Casual references to historical events or personages found in epigraphic records are generally more useful than similar mention in literary works. This is because such works are usually known from late copies and the date of their composition is very often uncertain while an inscription can be assigned to a definite period on palaeographic grounds even when it does not bear a date in any era.

Although Kalhaṇa's extraordinary impartiality in describing the events of the reign of the contemporary king Jayasiṁha and of the latter's father and uncle cannot be expected in the official *praśastis* composed by court poets, some inscriptions are known to describe facts which could not have been quite palatable to the patrons of the authors. Attention in this connection may be drawn to the later charters of the Cālukyas of Bādāmi (such as the Kendur plates)[3] describing Cālukya Vijayāditya having been captured by the enemies as well as to the Dubi plates[4] of the Bhauma king Bhāskaravarman of Prāgjyotiṣa giving a vivid description of the discomfiture and capture of the brothers Supratiṣṭhitavarman and Bhāskaravarman, soon after the death of their father, by the Gauḍa invaders who carried off the princes to their own country and released them afterwards apparently on their acceptance of Gauḍa supremacy.

An important feature of epigraphic evidence is that many of the knotty problems of early Indian chronology have been solved by inscriptions dated in eras. Of course the use

1. Cf. *SII*, Vol. I, pp. 39 ff., 44 ff., 47 ff., 53 ff.
2. See, e.g., *Ep. Ind.*, Vol. XXVIII, pp. 235 ff.
3. Ibid., Vol. IX. p. 200.
4. Ibid., Vol. XXX, pp. 287 ff.

of popular eras in the dating of documents was originally unknown in India and even royal charters used to be dated in the regnal reckoning of the kings who issued them. But the Vikrama Saṁvat of 58 B. C. was introduced by the Scytho-Parthians and the Śaka era of 78 A. D. by the Kuṣāṇas and there are numerous inscriptions dated in these eras as well as others introduced later (e.g. the Traikūṭaka-Kalacuri era of 248 A.D., the Gupta-Valabhī era of 319 A.D., the Eastern Gaṅga era of about 497 A.D., the Harṣa era of 606 A.D., the Bhauma-Kara era of about 831 A.D., the Cālukya-Vikrama era of 1076 A.D., etc.).

There are some inscriptions mentioning past events with reference to particular dates. Thus an inscription[1] from Mandasor tells us how a temple of the Sun-god was built in the said locality in [Vikrama] Saṁvat 493 (436 A.D.), Pauṣa-sudi 13, when Bandhuvarman was ruling over the area as a feudatory of the Gupta emperor Kumāragupta I and how the same temple was repaired in [Vikrama] Saṁvat 529 (473 A.D.), Phālguna-sudi 2. Of course, in areas where the use of an era was not popular, a past event was usually associated with the regnal reckoning of bygone monarchs. Thus the Madras Museum plates[2] of the 16th regnal year of Uttama-coḷa refer to two earlier events respectively of the 22nd regnal year of Parakesarin (Parāntaka I) and the 9th regnal year of Kampavarman.

We have also inscriptions containing a record of events happening at different dates arranged in a chronological order. The Siron Khurd (Siyāḍoṇī) inscription[3] in 46 lines records twentyseven donations made at different dates between Vikrama Saṁvat 960 and 1025 by some subordinates and subjects of the Gurjara Pratīhāra emperors of Kanauj in favour of the Brahmanical deities worshipped at the locality. Some of the records of these donations are undated while a few of the dated records refer to the reigns of the Gurjara Pratīhāra monarchs. But there is little doubt that the records were arranged in strict chronological order. The dates, Vikrama Saṁvat 960 (903 A.D.) and

1. *CII*, Vol. III, p. 81.
2. *SII*, Vol. III, p. 264 ff.
3. *Ep. Ind.*, Vol. I ,p. 162.

964 (907 A.D.), are associated with the reign of Mahendrapāla, successor of Bhoja, and Vikrama Saṁvat 1005 (948 A.D.) with that of Devapāla, successor of Kṣitipāla. The inscription was drawn up by people who were apparently endowed with a sense of chronological order. Similarly, in the Nagari plates[1] of Eastern Gaṅga Anaṅgabhīma III (c. 1211-38 A.D.), we have not only an account of the predecessors of the donor for many generations together with the duration of their rules and the date of the coronation of one of them in the Śaka era, but also the description of seven grants made by the king within a period of about one year quoting the exact date of each one of them.

Chronological representation of the events of a particular reign is also noticed in inscriptions. Thus the Hathigumpha inscription of the thirteenth regnal year of Khāravela first tells us how he was made a *Yuvarāja* in his sixteenth year and was installed as *Mahārāja* in his twentyfifth year and then recounts his achievements in each one of the thirteen years of the reign beginning from the first regnal year. The inscriptions of the Imperial Coḷas similarly quote the achievements of the kings in a strict chronological order although the events are not specifically assigned to particular years. It has been noticed, e.g., that a record of the 6th regnal year of Rājendra-coḷa copies the account of his exploits found in a record of the 5th year of his reign and adds to it his activities during the current year, while a record of his 7th year quotes what is given in the previous year's record with the addition of that year's success.[2]

With reference to the introduction of popular eras in ancient India, it may be noticed that even in earlier times there appears to have been a tendency to regard the dates of the death of the Buddha and of Mahāvīra and that of the battle of Kurukṣetra as some sort of epochs of eras. But the Buddhist and Jain *Nirvāṇa* reckonings were nothing like popular eras and often particular events were placed in a century of such a reckoning.

1. Ibid., Vol. XXVIII, p. 235.

2. See *SII*, Vol. IV, No. 327; Vol. V, No. 578; *A. R. Ep.*, 1908. No. 587; *SII*, Vol. II, No. 82. Cf. Nilakanta Sastri, *The Colas*, 2nd ed., p, 195; *The Pandyan Kingdom*, p. 144.

Thus the *Milindapañha* places Milinda, the Yavana or Greek king of Śākala, 500 years (i.e. in the 6th century) after the Buddha's *prarinirvāṇa*. As regards the date of the battle of Kurukṣetra, there were several different traditions: (1) about the beginning of the Kali-yuga in 3102 B.C., (2) 653 years after the beginning of the Kali-yuga, i.e. 2449 B.C., and (3) 1015 or 1050 years before the accession of Mahāpadma Nanda (4th century B.C.), i.e. about the middle of the second millennium B.C. The third of these dates was arrived at by the Puranic chroniclers by adding together the durations of the reigns of a succession of kings from Parikṣit down to the predecessor of Mahāpadma Nanda. The above reckonings are certainly not of much use for purposes of chronology; but they appear to show that the Indians of old were not absolutely devoid of a chronological sense.

5. *Demerits of Epigraphic Evidence*

Although inscriptions have contributed largely to the reconstruction of the lost history of ancient and early medieval India, their evidence is not free from defects. Some of these are briefly discussed below.

It has to be admitted that only some of the inscriptions can be regarded as truly historical documents. No doubt many of them deal with historical events and personages; but history is often shadowed in them by poetical, eulogistic and conventional elements. Most records therefore give the impression that references to historical events in them are incidental. Their evidence is thus often indirect and leaves many things to be surmised and inferred. It is only rarely that we get in inscriptions fairly full and satisfactory information regarding an event or a person. As already pointed out, the authors of inscriptions always suffered from a limitation of space and their treatment of history was never elaborate. Sometimes the genealogical section of the inscriptions quotes the names of past rulers with the barest detail or without any details at all.

We have seen above how the use of popular eras in dating documents was unknown in ancient India, how even royal records were dated in the regnal reckoning of the rulers of the land, and how eras were introduced and popularised in the country by foreign rulers. But, even after the popularity of the eras had been well established in wide areas of the country, documents of many parts were not endowed with verifiable dates. Moreover, a large number of records of all ages and of all parts of the land are altogether undated. In many cases, the details of the dates quoted in dated records contain errors owing to mistakes in the calculation of astronomical data either by the persons responsible for the records or by the astronomers on whom they depended.[1] Although, therefore, dated inscriptions have solved many of the knotty problems of chronology in ancient and medieval Indian history, a number of problems still remain unsolved owing to the said defects of epigraphic records. In the absence of a date in a known era, an epigraph can only be approximately referred to a period, but not to a definite date.

A tendency is often noticed in ruling families from the early medieval age to fabricate a respectable genealogy. The process began with the elaboration of the genealogy on the basis of the *gotra* name of a royal family. The Pallavas of Kāñcī claimed to have belonged to the Bhāradvāja-gotra which offered them the opportunity to trace their descent, through a number of mythical and imaginary personages, from the sage Bharadvāja, famous in the epics and the Purāṇas, and through him to the god Brahman, the creator.[2] Among royal families of the early medieval period, it was a fashion to claim descent from the solar, lunar, Yādava and other dynasties, well-known from ancient Indian literature.[3] Many of the rulers claiming such respectable descent belonged really to aboriginal families. Legends were often fabricated to explain the name of a royal family, sometimes with reference to an eponymous hero.[4]

1. Cf. *IHQ*, Vol. XXVIII, pp. 342 ff.

2. Cf. *SII*, Vol. I, p. 9; *Ep. Ind.*, Vol. XVIII, p. 150; etc.

3. Note the cases of the Gurjara-Pratīhāras, Rāṣṭrakūṭas and Imperial Gaṅgas claiming descent respectively from the solar, Yādava and lunar dynasties.

4. Note the cases of families like Pallava, Paramāra, Pratīhāra, etc.

In some cases, the fabricated element in the genealogy can be easily detected. In the records of Vajrahasta III (1038-70 A.D.) and Rājarāja I (1070-78 A.D.) and also in the earlier epigraphs of Anantavarman Coḍagaṅga (1078-1147 A.D.), Vajrahasta III of the Imperial Gaṅga dynasty of Orissa is represented as the grandson's great-grandson of a king named Guṇamahārṇava (Guṇārṇava) of the Ātreya-gotra. But, in the later records of the family, including inscriptions belonging to the later years of Anantavarman Coḍagaṅga himself, the origin of the family is traced to the god Viṣṇu through his navel-born son Brahman, his mind-born son Atri, his eye-born son Candra (the Moon), his son Budha, his descendants Purūravas, Āyus, Nahuṣa, Yayāti and Turvasu—all known from epic and Puranic literature, and a host of apparently imaginary personages standing between Turvasu and Guṇārṇava who was the progenitor of the family according to the earlier account, but is here represented as Guṇārṇava II. Names of Kolāhala, founder of Kolāhalapura in the Gaṅgavāḍi-viṣaya in Mysore, and his successors, some of whom are said to have migrated to Kaliṅga, are inserted before the reference to Guṇārṇava obviously in an attempt to connect the Gaṅgas of Orissa with those of Mysore, even though the latter claimed the Kāṇvāyana-gotra. The genealogy was fabricated on the basis of the *gotra* claimed by the Eastern Gaṅgas; but it also exhibits their eagerness to claim descent from the lunar dynasty and some connection with the god Viṣṇu, to whom Anantavarman Coḍagaṅga transferred his allegiance from Śiva during the latter part of his career.[1]

The authors of the *praśastis* were mostly attached to royal courts and eager to exaggerate the achievements of their patrons and the latters' ancestors. Such exaggeration often mars considerably the value of inscriptions of the *praśasti* type as a source of history. A few illustrations will make the point sufficiently clear.

According to the Mahakuta pillar inscription,[2] the Cālukya

1. See *Ep. Ind.*, Vol. XXVIII, pp. 237 ff.
2. *Ind. Ant.*, Vol. XIX, p. 7.

king Kīrtivarman I (566-98 A.D.) of Bādāmi defeated the rulers of Vaṅga, Aṅga, Kaliṅga, Vaṭṭūra, Magadha, Madraka, Kerala, Gaṅga, Mūṣaka, Pāṇḍya, Dramila, Choḻiya, Āluka and Vaijayantī. It is impossible to believe that Kīrtivarman I actually came into conflict with such far off lands as Vaṅga, Aṅga, Magadha and Madraka, especially in view of the fact that, in the Aihole *praśasti* of his own son Pulakeśin II who can hardly be expected to have concealed any of his father's glorious achievements, Kīrtivarman I is credited with military success only against the Nalas, Mauryas and Kadambas, all of whom were neighbours of the Cālukyas of Bādāmi. The real basis of the tall claim made on behalf of Kīrtivarman I in the Mahakuta pillar inscription seems to be imagination.

The Candella king Dhaṅga (c. 950-1002 A.D.) is described in a stanza of an inscription at Khajuraho[1] (Chhatarpur District, Madhya Pradesh), which implies that the monarch crushed many kings, including the rulers of Kāñcī, Andhra, Rāḍhā and Aṅga, and had the queens of all the defeated rulers imprisoned in his capital. There is little doubt that the claim is an exaggeration. In the first place, it is doubtful if Dhaṅga at all came into collision with all the four kings mentioned in the record, even if the rulers of Aṅga and Rāḍhā are regarded as merely viceroys of the contemporary Pāla emperor of Eastern India. Secondly, even if Dhaṅga actually fought with the four kings, it is more doubtful that he succeeded in defeating all of them. Thirdly, even if he was victorious in all the four cases, it is difficult to believe that he succeeded in carrying off the queens of all his adversaries. Fourthly, even granting that Dhaṅga actually captured the queens of his enemies, he would normally be expected to have placed the ladies in his harem or in the charge of his favourite subordinates rather than in the prison.[2]

Gross exaggerations are, however, less conspicuous in the description of kings found in records of the earlier period. For this reason, in spite of the fact that there is always an amount of exaggeration in the royal *praśastis* composed by the court

1. *Ep. Ind.*, Vol. I, p. 145.
2. See my *Studies in the Geography of Ancient and Medieval India*, pp. 1 ff.

poets of Indian monarchs, the earlier the king is the greater is our reliance on his claims. Vague claims are generally less reliable than definite statements involving the mention of the personal names of adversaries. Whatever be the nature and amount of exaggeration, there is undoubtedly a very considerable amount of truth in the claims put forward in records like the Allahabad pillar inscription[1] of Samudragupta and the Tirumaḷai rock inscription[2] of Rājendra-coḻa. The manner in which the personal names of adversaries are mentioned in epigraphs like the Deopada inscription[3] of Vijayasena (c. 1095-1158 A.D.) of Bengal appears, however, to be too poetic and artificial and therefore suspicious. But there is no doubt that the kings so named were contemporaries of the Sena monarch.

In some cases, the poets are found more eager to display their skill in rhetoric rather than in the accuracy of their statements. The Candella king Yaśovarman (middle of the 10th century A.D.), who was a feudatory of the Gurjara Pratīhāra emperor of Kanauj, is described in a Khajuraho inscription[4] as a subduer of the Gauḍas, Khaśas, Kośalas, Kaśmīras, Mithilas, Mālavas, Cedis, Kurus and Gurjaras, though during the period in question neither were Kośala, Mithilā and Kuru separate states nor was the Candella king likely to have had anything to do with them. It seems that the lure of alliteration (cf. *kośalaḥ Kośalānām*, *śithilita-Mithilaḥ*, *Kuru-taruṣu marut*, etc.) carried the poet far away from historical accuracy.[5]

The authors of the *praśastis* were reluctant to take notice of the defeat and discomfiture of their patrons and their ancestors. Such unpalatable facts were often completely suppressed, and at times they were only vaguely and euphemistically referred to. Powerful feudatories were sometimes described deli-

1. *CII*, Vol. III, pp. 1 ff.
2. *Ep. Ind.*, Vol. IX, p. 299.
3. Ibid., Vol. I, p. 305.
4. Ibid., p. 126.
5. Note the poet's eagerness to exhibit his knowledge of the *Kāmaśāstra* in a verse ascribed to Mayūra (Tripathi, *History of Kanauj*, p. 121), in which the words *aṅga*, *kuntala*, *cola*, *madhyadeśa* and *kāñcī* are used in the description of the king's enjoyment of the earth, conceived as a lady, in two senses; e.g. *aṅga* refers to the seizure of 'the body' [of the lady] as well as of the Aṅga country. Cf. *Bhār. Vid.*, Vol. XV. No. 3, p. 26.

berately in ambiguous language that can be interpreted as applicable both to a paramount sovereign and to a subordinate ruler.[1] In medieval inscriptions, the evidence of which can be checked with that of various sources, we have instances not only of an indecisive battle described as a victory but even of a defeat represented as a victory. *Rāṇā* Kumbhā of Mewar fought an indecisive battle with the Sulṭān of Malwa, but went back to Chitor to raise a *kīrti-stambha* bearing a *praśasti*[2] in commemoration of his victory over the Sultān ! *Rāṇā* Udayasiṁha is represented in an inscription[3] as having shadowed the glory of Akbar, even though wide areas of his dominions, including the capital city of Chitor, had passed to the Mughals.

The description of kings in the *praśastis* often contain claims that are conventional and therefore of little historical value. One of these conventions is the representation of an imperial ruler either as the conqueror or as the ruler of the entire 'earth' meaning the *Cakravarti-kṣetra* or 'the sphere of influence of a paramount ruler.'[4] This 'earth' was conceived as identical with ancient Bhāratavarṣa; but sometimes it was regarded as conterminous with either Āryāvarta (for North Indian kings) or Dakṣiṇāpatha (for South Indian monarchs). We know that the Pāla king Devapāla (9th century) ruled over Bengal and Bihar; but he is sometimes described in inscriptions as the ruler of the entire land bounded by the Himalayas in the north, Setubandha-Rāmeśvara in the south, the Bay of Bengal in the east and the Arabian Sea in the west, although sometimes the southern boundary is given as the Vindhyas instead of Setubandha. In the Nagpur *praśasti*[5] of the Paramāras, king Lakṣmavarman (c. 1087-97 A.D.) is represented as the conqueror of the Gauḍas, Aṅgas and Kaliṅgas in the east, the Coḻas and Pāṇḍyas in the south in the region of the river Tāmraparṇī

1. Cf. *Ep. Ind.*, Vol. XXVIII, p. 186.
2. Bhandarkar's List, No. 797.
3. *Ep. Ind.*, Vol. XXIV, p. 68.
4. See *JRASB*, Vol. V, 1939, pp. 407 ff; my *Studies in the Geography of Ancient and Medieval India*, pp. 2 ff.
5. *Ep. Ind.*, Vol. II, pp. 186-88.

and the bridge of Rāma, and the Turuṣkas (Muhammadans) on the banks of the Vaṅkṣu (Oxus) in the north. There is little doubt that the description is a modification of Raghu's *digvijaya* as described in Kālidāsa's *Raghuvaṁśa*. It is impossible to think that the Paramāra king had any opportunity to encamp on the banks of the Oxus and to have come into contact with the Turuṣkas there. This exploit reminds us of the mythological Raghu's advance as far as the banks of the same river inhabited by the Hūṇas in the age of Kālidāsa. Similar is the case often with titles assumed by some medieval Indian monarchs. King Kapilendra (c. 1435-66 A.D.) of Orissa called himself *Gauḍeśvara-Navakoṭi-Karnāṭa-Kalavargeśvara*, i.e. lord of Gauḍa as well as of Karnāṭa-nine-crores and Kalavarga (Gulbarga). The claim is, however, tall enough even for the mighty Kapilendra. But it is more interesting to note that petty Oriya rulers, who claimed to be his descendants, continued to assume the same title till recent times. But such instances are not too many, although the same description is often noticed to have been applied to royal residences situated in different localities.[1]

We often see that a mere present from the ruler of a distant land could be pompously represented by the court poet as tribute, and contact of any kind with a king put up as his subordination to the poet's patron or his ancestors.[2]

Often illiterate and semi-literate stone-cutters or goldsmiths were entrusted with the task of engraving records on stone or copper plates, and this fact accounts for the numerous errors noticed in a large number of epigraphs, especially those engraved on behalf of private individuals. There are many instances of indifferently drafted and badly engraved records even among royal charters, particularly those issued by minor ruling families. Mistakes committed by the scribes and engravers of inscriptions often lead to difficulties of interpretation and to controversies. Some of the controversies are due to ambiguity of expression from which many epigraphic passages suffer. As we have already noticed, in several cases such ambiguity

1. Cf. the description of the *jayaskandhāvāras* in the charters of the Pālas.
2. Cf. *The Classical Age*, ed. Majumdar, p. 245 and note 3.

was purposely resorted to in the description of feudatories aspiring for an independent status.

There are often discrepancies in the same account quoted in different records of a family. Thus the date of the accession of the Eastern Gaṅga king Kāmārṇava (1147-56 A.D.) is quoted correctly in the Dasgoba plates[1] of 1198 A.D. and the Nagari plates[2] of 1230-31 A.D. as the Śaka year counted by *nanda* (9), *ṛtu* (6), *vyoman* (0) and *candra* (1), which according to the *vāmagati* principle would yield Śaka 1069, corresponding to 1147 A.D. But all the later charters of the family, so far discovered, wrongly read *veda* (4) in the place of *nanda* (9) and thus make the date five years earlier. This mistake must have crept into the later records of the Gaṅgas exactly as errors usually creep into manuscripts in the process of copying.

Ep. Ind., Vol. XXXI, pp. 259 ff.
Ibid., Vol. XXVIII, p. 242.

APPENDIX

Indo-Muslim Epigraphy[1]

1. *Study of the Subject*

The contributions of the pioneers in the study of Indo-Muslim epigraphy since the middle of the 19th century can be assessed from the list of published inscriptions compiled by J. Horovitz[2] about half a century ago. A large number of Arabic and Persian inscriptions were received by the Asiatic Society of Calcutta from officials in various parts of India and these were deciphered and published in the Society's journal by H. Blochmann. The *Asiatic Researches* and *Journal of the Asiatic Society of Bengal* did valuable work in this direction, which was followed by other periodicals such as the *Indian Antiquary, Journal Asiatique* and *Journal of the Royal Asiatic Society of Great Britain and Ireland.* Among books published in the last century and dealing specially with inscriptions, mention may be made of the *Corpus Inscriptionum Bhavnagari* which is a collection of fiftyone inscriptions from Kathiawar and Gujarat, published in 1889 by the former State of Bhavnagar.

A few such inscriptions were published in the *Epigraphia Indica,* a publication of the Department of Archaeology, which was, however, meant primarily to deal with epigraphs in the Sanskritic and Dravidian languages. A biennial supplement to the *Epigraphia Indica* to deal specially with Indo-Muslim inscriptions was later conceived and its issue for 1907-1908 was

1. See Z. A. Desai's survey in *Ancient India,* No. 9, pp. 224 ff.

2. *Epigraphia Indo-Moslemica,* 1909-1910, pp. 30-44. For the notices and copies of some inscriptions, see also Sangin Beg, *Sairu'l Manāzil* (published about 1835); Sayyid Ahmad Khan, *Āthāru'ṣ Ṣanādīd* (1846), J. H. Ravenshaw, *Gaur: its Ruins and Inscriptions* (London, 1878); Saiyid Muhammad Latif, *Lahore: its History, Architectural Ruins and Antiquities* (Lahore, 1892) and *Agra: Historical and Descriptive* (Calcutta, 1896); Muhammad Akbar Jahan, *Aḥsanu's Siyar* (Agra, A. H. 1320); Raziuddin Bismil, *Kanzu'l Tawārikh* (Badaun, A. H. 1319); and M. Nur Ahmad Chishti, *Taḥqīqāt-i-Chishtī* (Lahore, A. H. 1324

publisled under the editorship of E. Denison Ross. Its next issue for 1909-1910 was, however, published under the independent title *Epigraphia Indo-Moslemica* which was edited by J. Horovitz who was appointed Government Epigraphist for Muslim Inscriptions. The next issue of the periodical was edited by Ghulam Yazdani who succeeded Horovitz in the said honorary post and successfully ran the series for about quarter of a century, bringing out in all fourteen issues and one supplement, the last issue being for 1939-1940. The fifteenth issue was published as the one for 1941-1950 due to the conditions created by World War II. In 1946, the post of Assistant Superintendent for Epigraphy for Arabic and Persian inscriptions was created and the issue for 1941-1950 was published under the editorship of Muhammad Ashraf Husain who had been appointed to the post. The issues for 1951-1952 and the following years are being published under the new name *Epigraphia Indica: Arabic and Persian Supplement.*

The prominent Indian contributors to the said periodical of the Department of Archaeology, besides Yazdani, are Zafar Hasan, M. Nazim, Shamsuddin Ahmad, Ramsingh Saksena and Khwaja Muhammad Ahmad. Most of the inscriptions published in it came from the former Hyderabad State and Bombay Presidency, though many inscriptions were found also in other parts of the country.[1] From time to time, the Archaeological Survey published inscriptions in its series of Memoirs. A monograph on the Qurānic and non-historical epigraphs in the protected monuments in Delhi, edited by M. Ashraf Husain, and another on the inscriptions of Bijapur, edited by M. Nazim, were published as Memoirs Nos. 47 and 49 in 1936.

Amongst epigraphical works recently published by scholars unconnected with the Department of Archaeology, mention may be made of *Important Inscriptions of the Baroda State*, Vol. II, edited by G. Yazdani and R. G. Gyani and a monograph containing fiftynine inscriptions, mostly from Ahmedabad,

1. Cf. J. Cumming, *Revealing India's Past*, London, 1939, p. 220; V S Bendrey, *A Study of Muslim Inscriptions* Bombay, 1944, p. 22.

with facsimiles of 46 out of them, edited and published by M. A. Chaghtai in the *Bulletin of the Deccan College Research Institute*, Vol. III, No. 2, 1942.[1] A few inscriptions studied by different scholars have also appeared in Indian periodicals like the *Journal of the Asiatic Society of Bengal*, *Indian Historical Quarterly* and *Oriental College Magazine* (Lahore). V. S. Bendrey's *Study of Muslim Inscriptions* (Bombay, 1944) deals specially with the inscriptions published in the *Epigraphia Indo-Moslemica* from 1907 to 1938 and contains summaries of epigraphs, arranged chronologically, with four appendices. The introductory portion of the work explains the principles on which a methodical study of epigraphical material should be based and contains suggestions to be followed by the students of Indo-Muslim epigraphy.

2. *Nature of the Records*

Indo-Muslim inscriptions in Arabic and Persian are available in India from the last decade of the 12th century A.D. The earliest epigraphs were found in the Quṯb premises at Delhi, the Arhai Din ka Jhonpra at Ajmer and the tomb of Shāh Ni'matu'llāh Shahīd at Hansi. The number of records of the subsequent centuries is large ; but it is the largest in the 16th and 17th centuries. Later inscriptions in Arabic and Persian are not so numerous. Punjab, Uttar Pradesh, Bengal, Bombay and Hyderabad are comparatively rich in Indo-Muslim inscriptions, while Madras is the poorest. Among single places yielding a large number of inscriptions mention may be made of Bijapur, Delhi, Ahmedabad, Fatehpur Sikri and Agra, Ajmer, Gulbarga, Hansi, Gaur, Biharsharif, and Pandua and Malda.

Indo-Muslim inscriptions are generally found on mosques, tombs and similar religious buildings and give the date of their construction or repairs often with the names of the reigning monarch and the builder or repairer. There are some deeds of endowment made in favour of mosques and other religious

1. The article has been separately printed under the title *History of Muslim Monuments of Ahmedabad through their Inscriptions*, Poona, 1942.

institutions for their maintenance. Occasionally we find them removed from their original places. Epitaphs sometimes appear on mosques and inscriptions relating to mosques on graves. Another kind of Indo-Muslim epigraphs are those recording the construction or repairs of forts, bastions, fort-walls, gateways, roads, granaries, etc. There are also some administrative records containing orders or mandates proclaiming the abolition of taxes and prohibition of undesirable practices or relating to the amelioration of public grievances. A few inscriptions appear on stones indicating boundaries or on slabs commemorating the visit of eminent personages or their halt at particular places. Some such stone slabs of Akbar's time, mostly carved by Mīr Muḥammad Ma'ṣum Nāmbī of Bakkar, commemorate the Mughal emperor's expedition to and conquest of Khandesh and the Deccan as well as his halts at various places in the course of his journeys. Some inscriptions are also found on slabs attached to tanks, wells, schools, palaces, gardens, bridges, caravansarais, etc.

Besides stone inscriptions and, of course, also the legends on coins, there are inscriptions on arms, seals, signets, vases, vessels, precious stones, etc. A few inscriptions on guns and swords have been published. The Muslim rulers did not generally engrave their records on copper plates, though a few copper-plate inscriptions are also available.[1]

3. *Language*

The majority of Indo-Muslim inscriptions are written in Persian. Many of them are in Arabic and some partly in Arabic and partly in Persian. There is another kind of bilingual records which are written in Arabic or Persian on the one hand and Sanskrit or a regional language like Marāṭhī, Kannaḍa or Telugu on the other.[2] Inscriptions in more languages than

1. For a copper-plate record of the time of Farrukhsiyar, see *A. R. Ep.*, 1952-53, No. A 15.

2. For some bilingual records, see *A. R. Ep.*, 1952-53, Nos. A 15 (C-87); B 55-A, 192-A(C-78), 623-A(C-107), 566-A(C-160); 1954-55, Nos. B 89-A(C-90); 513(C-136), 517 (C-155), 521(C-71). The language of one such record is Hindī written in both Persian and Devanāgarī characters

two are also known.[1]

The earliest Indo-Muslim inscriptions are in Arabic except the epigraph in the Quwwatu'l Islām mosque at Delhi, which is written in Arabic and Persian. Its date is 1191-92 A.D., though it may have been set up some years later. Arabic continued to be the language of Indo-Muslim epigraphy till the latest decades of the 13th century. But, with the rise of the Khaljis, from about the beginning of the 14th century, Persian is found more frequently in epigraphical records and its popularity gradually increased, though Arabic was not totally ousted since religious inscriptions continued to be written in that language. Arabic was more popular than Persian in Bengal. With the establishment of Mughal rule in India in the 16th century, Persian began to be generally used in State records as well as in inscriptions and, in the first half of the 18th century, it ousted Arabic almost completely. There is an Urdū inscription of the middle of the 18th century.[2]

With few exceptions, the Arabic inscriptions are in prose. Of the versified records in Arabic, one dated 1313-14 A.D. from Tribeni (Hooghly District, West Bengal) is the earliest of its kind in India. It also provides the earliest chronogram among Indo-Muslim inscriptions.[3] Earlier Persian inscriptions are generally in prose. The earliest dated inscription in Persian verse is the Hansi epigraph[4] of 'Alāu'ddīn Khaljī. Versified Persian inscriptions became more common at a later date. The majority of the inscriptions are not good literary compositions and exhibit grammatical inaccuracy and disregard for the rules of prosody.

(*Important Inscriptions of the Baroda State*, Vol. II, pp. 10-11; *IHQ*, Vol .XXI, p. 66).

1. For an inscription in Persian, Sanskrit and Gujarātī, see *Bull. Baroda Mus.*, 1953-55, pp. 73 ff.

2. *Ep. Indo-Mosl.*, 1909-1910, p. 31. A chronogram, supposed to be in old Urdū, giving the date of the erection of a mosque at Ahmedabad, is found in an inscription dated 1555-56 A.D. See ibid., 1935-1936, p. 51. For some versified Urdū inscriptions of the 19th century, see *A. R. Ep.*, 1953-54, Nos. C 36, 53, 63, 65.

3. *Ep. Indo-Mosl.*, 1917-1918, pp. 33-34

4. Ibid., p. 19. For a fragmentary inscription from Mathura, see ibid., 1937-1938, p. 60.

4. *Palaeography and Calligraphy*

As in other parts of the Muslim world,[1] Arabic and Persian epigraphy in India is interesting from the historical and paleographic points of view. It exhibits a diversity of scripts often beautifully executed and ingeniously ornamented. As specimens of extraordinary calligraphy, some of the inscriptions can favourably compete with certain records on paper.

The scripts principally used in the Muslim epigraphs are Kūfic, Nasta'līq, and Naskh including its variety called Thulth. Each of these writings was executed with its distinctive conventional style which varied according to the period and locality as well as the ingenuity of particular calligraphists.[2] We have only a few inscriptions in Kūfic which was written in a simple and an ornamental style.[3] The inscriptions of the pre-Mughal period are mostly written in Naskh.[4] The characters are vigorous, rigid and also bold at times. The Naskh script, as used in such areas as those under the Sulṭāns of Bengal and Gujarat, developed an individuality of its own. The decorative Tughrā style of Bengal, which is also noticed in a large number of records from Gujarat, exhibits distinctive ornamentation.[5] In this style of writing, the elongated shafts and curves of the letters are arranged so as to form different motifs. The arrangement of the curved letters across the arrow-headed ones representing the motif of bow and arrow is commonly found, so that some scholars prefer to call it 'the bow-and-arrow style'. A slightly modified form of this motif is that of the arches or railings.[6] Another motif represents the parade or march of an army with raised banners, 'the flags being either conspicuous or disturbed by the

1. Cf. ibid., 1913-1914, Appendix C, p. 46. For illustrations of a few inscriptions from foreign countries, see M. Ziauddin, *Moslem Calligraphy*, Calcutta, 1936.

2. See *Ancient India*, No. 9, Plates CXIII and CXIV.

3. Cf. ibid., Plate CXIII-A. Kūfic took its name from the town of Kūfa on the Euphrates, which was famous for its copyists (D. C. Phillott, *Higher Persian Grammar*, p. 35).

4. For its different forms, cf. *Ancient India*, No. 9, Plates CXIII-B and CXIV-C.

5. See ibid., Plate CXIV-A.

6. *Ep. Indo-Mosl.*, 1935-1936, Plate XXXVI-a.

intervention of a row of knotted ropes representing the halters sometimes hung below banner heads, the cluster of letters at the foot of the straight-drawn vertical lines presenting the thick mass of soldiers which in old times formed an interwoven group during a march'.[1]

In the Tughrā style, sometimes the letters look like the outlines of birds and animals, the forms being intended to serve as a security against evil. The lion and tiger, which are the symbols of the valour of 'Alī, 'the Lion of God', are often found carved on forts in the Deccan, which were rebuilt in the 15th and 16th centuries by the Muslim kings of the Shiite faith. Such inscriptions generally contain a prayer comprising a religious text or a passage quoted from the holy Qurān, the Nād-ī-'Alī being a frequent quotation.[2]

Nasta'līq is seen in inscriptions from the first half of the 16th century A.D. It is a beautiful combination of the Naskh (the ordinary hand) and the Ta'līq or the 'hanging' writing which is the elegant court hand of the Persians.[3] During the following two centuries, it almost entirely replaced Naskh, although the latter's artistic variety known as Thulth was used for religious epigraphs in Arabic exactly as Kūfic was employed in the earlier period.

Inscriptions in beautiful Thulth and Nasta'līq have been found in all parts of the country.[4]

5. *Historical Importance*

From the historical point of view, the Indo-Muslim inscriptions are not as important as the epigraphs in the Sanskritic and Dravidian languages, bacause there is no dearth of historical works dealing with the activities and achievements of the Muslim monarchs. Moreover, State documents of the Muslim rulers,

1. Ibid., 1923-1924, p. 18 and Plate VII.
2. Ibid., 1935-1936, p. 44, Plate XXX-a.
3. D. C. Phillott, op. cit., p. 36.
4. Cf. *Ancient India*, No. 9, Plates CXIII-C and CXIV-B. The Shikasta or 'broken' hand is the name of the cursive writing, in which the dots are omitted and the letters are joined together so that it is difficult to read (D. C. Phillott, op. cit., p. 36).

such as *farmāns* and *sanads*, were written generally on paper. Nevertheless, inscriptions as well as coins sometimes supply valuable data for the reconstruction of political, social and religious history. In some cases, they supply the missing links in the chronology of rulers[1] and throw light on events and personages unknown from literary sources.[2] At times they also correct anachronism or incongruity and settle the dates of historical events in cases where the information from literary sources happen to be confusing or conflicting.[3] Although, in most of the cases, they merely corroborate the statements in historical works, sometimes they offer details left out in the chronicles and provide links in the reconstruction of the succession of public officials and the history of noble families.[4] Often they give the correct names of places and persons, thus correcting the wrong or conflicting spellings found in the manuscripts of the chronicles.[5] The inscriptions on buildings are important to the student of the history of architecture.

1. That Kaikā'ūs, son of Nāṣiruddīn Bughrā Khān, actually ruled over Bengal is not indicated by the Persian historians and is only known from inscriptions (*Ep. Indo-Mosl.*, 1917-1918, pp. 8-15). Inscriptions have shown that Mahmūd Tughlaq was a ruling king in A.H. 795 (1392-93 A.D.) and did not begin to rule in the following year as stated in the chronicles (ibid., 1919-1920, pp. 12-15; 1933-1934, Supp., pp. 22-23). Cf. also the evidence of a Sanskrit inscription referring to Muḥammad bin Tughlaq (believed to have ascended the throne in 1325 A.D.) but dated June 3, 1324 A.D. (*Ep. Ind.*, Vol. XXXV, p. 141).

2. Cf., e.g., *Ep. Indo-Mosl.*, 1925-1926, p. 7.

3. See, e.g., ibid., 1939-1940, pp. 11-12.

4. Cf., e.g., ibid., 1917-1918, pp. 33-34.

5. Cf. *A. R. Ep.*, 1952-53, pp. 18 ff.

CHAPTER II

LANGUAGE OF INSCRIPTIONS

The earliest records in a foreign language discovered in India are those written in Aramaic and belonging to about the 3rd century B.C. They are found in the north-western region, now in West Pakistan. The coins of the Indo-Greeks and other foreign rulers of Noth-Western Bhāratavarṣa bear legends in the Greek language. A bilingual Greek and Aramaic inscription of the Maurya king Aśoka (c. 272-232 B.C.) has recently been discovered in Afghanistan which formed in ancient times a part of the Uttarāpatha division of Bhāratavarṣa. Coins issued by the rulers of foreign countries with legends in their own languages, e.g. those of the Roman emperors, have also been discovered in India. Most of the medieval Indian records of the Muslim rulers are written in Arabic and Persian. Among medieval and modern inscriptions, there are some written in Tibetan, Burmese and many other languages including those of Europe. The language of the legends on the prehistoric seals from Mohenjodaro and other places has not been determined.[1]

Section I

Prakrit and Sanskrit

The earliest epigraphic records of the indigenous rulers of India are written in the Prakrit language. Originally the epigraphic language of the whole of India was mainly Prakrit and Sanskrit is first noticed in the inscriptions of North India from about the second half of the 1st century B.C. Sanskrit gradually ousted Prakrit from the field of Indian epigraphy in all parts of the country. In North India, the establishment

1. See the section on foreign alphabets used in Indian records in our *Indian Palaeography* to be published shortly. The Indian records are mostly written in the Kharoṣṭhī and Brahmī alphabets and the derivatives of the latter, which are also dealt with in the said work.

of Sanskrit in the place of Prakrit in inscriptions was nearly complete by the end of the 3rd century A. D. But the suppression of Prakrit in the epigraphs of South India took place as late as the second half of the 4th century.[1]

The pillar edicts of Aśoka and the same king's rock edicts at Dhauli, Jaugada and Erragudi are written in the so-called Magadha dialect, some of its main characteristics being the representation of *ra* by *la*, of all the three sibilants by *sa* and of reduplicated consonants by single letters as well as the avoidance of conjuncts to a considerable extent. But the language of Aśoka's inscriptions in the western half of Northern India, viz. at Girnar, Sopara, Shahbazgadhi and Mansehra, is characterised by the retention of *ra* and the occasional change of *la* to *ra*. The Shahbazgadhi and Mansehra edicts often exhibit especially the tendency of using conjuncts as in Sanskrit. The minor rock edicts of Aśoka discovered in South India and the rock edicts at Kalsi exhibit the influence of both of the dialects in a more or less conspicuous degree. The language of Aśoka's rock edicts found in North-Western Bhāratavarṣa is closer to Sanskrit in comparison with that of his other records.[2]

The inscriptions of North-Western Bhāratavarṣa, belonging to the age of the Indo-Greeks, exhibit linguistic peculiarities similar to those of the Shahbazgadhi and Mansehra inscriptions of Aśoka.[3] It is interesting to note in this connection that the Besnagar (Bhilsa or Vidisa District, Madhya Pradesh) inscription of Heliodorus, who hailed from Taxila in the Rawalpindi District of West Pakistan and was an envoy of the Indo-Greek king Antialcidas (last quarter of the 2nd century B. C.) at the court of king Bhāgabhadra of Vidiśā, exhibit some influence of Sanskrit and literary Prakrit.[4]

1. Cf. *Suc. Sāt.*, p. 87, note 3; pp. 166 and 168; *Ep. Ind.*, Vol. XXIX, pp. 170-171.

2. See *IHQ*. Vol. XV, p. 40; *Ep. Ind.*, Vol XXXII, pp. 4-5, 29-30. The Sopara fragment of Rock Edict IX exhibits the change of Sanskrit *la* to *ra* in Prakrit in all cases.

3. See the Bajaur casket inscriptions (*Select Inscriptions*, pp. 102 ff.).

4. See ibid., pp. 90-91 (cf. the words *putreṇa* and *Takhkhasilākena* for *putena* and *Takhasilākena* expected in early inscriptional Prakrit).

Some of the inscriptions of the Scytho-Parthian and Kuṣāṇa rulers of North-Western Bhāratavarṣa are written in a mixture of Prakrit and Sanskrit and some of the earliest epigraphs in Sanskrit are also noticed amongst the records of the foreign rulers of Śaka nationality. Thus a few Mathura inscriptions[1] of the time of Śaka Śoḍāsa (first quarter of the 1st century A.D.) contain stanzas in Classical Sanskrit and in ornate metres like *Śārdūlavikrīḍita* and *Bhujaṅgavijṛmbhita*, while the Junagadh inscription[2] (150 A.D.) of Śaka Rudradāman is a good composition in Sanskrit prose in the Classical *kāvya* style. It appears that Sanskrit was patronised at the courts of the foreign rulers of North-Western Bhāratavarṣa whence its popularity spread gradually over other parts of the country. One of the earliest authors of works in Classical Sanskrit was Aśvaghoṣa who, according to tradition, lived in the 1st and 2nd centuries A.D. first at Pāṭaliputra in Bihar and later at the court of the Kuṣāṇa king Kaniṣka at Puruṣapura (Peshawar). It has, however, to be noted that, in spite of the occasional use of Sanskrit noticed in the inscriptions of the time of the Śaka rulers belonging to the 1st and 2nd centuries A. D., some of their West Indian epigraphic and numismatic records of the following two centuries exhibit the use of Sanskrit with an admixture of Prakrit.[3]

Essentially, the popularity of Sanskrit at the courts of the rulers either of foreign or indigenous extraction was due to the influence of grammarians. Classical Sanskrit was codified as a result of the efforts of a number of early grammarians, the most outstanding amongst them being Pāṇini (5th century B.C.) who was an inhabitant of Śālātūra in Gandhāra (i.e. the Rawalpindi-Peshawar region) in North-Western Bhāratavarṣa. Gradually Pāṇini's *Aṣṭādhyāyī* eclipsed all the other works of earlier authors. The well-known story[4] of the association of the grammarian Śarvavarman, author of the *Kātantra* (*Kaumāra* or *Kālāpa*), with the court of king Sātavāhana (probably Simuka

1. *Ep. Ind.*, Vol. II, p. 200, No. 7; Vol. XXIV, pp. 194 ff.
2. *Select Inscriptions*, pp. 169 ff.
3. Ibid., pp. 175 ff. As in palaeography, so in epigraphy, West India was thus allied to South India at least partially.
4. Cf. Keith, *A History of Sanskrit Literature*, p. 431.

Śātavāhana who flourished in the second half of the 1st century B.C.) shows that indigenous Indian kings patronised Sanskrit grammarians. But the fact that the records of the kings of the Śātavāhana family are all in Prakrit indicates that the influence of the grammarians at the Indian courts was acting rather slowly. We have, however, some inscriptions in Sanskrit (slightly influenced by Prakrit) belonging to Indian rulers who flourished about the second half of the 1st century B.C., that is to say, some time before Śaka Śoḍāsa, the Sanskrit records of whose age have been referred to above. One of the earliest such inscriptions from Western India is the Ghosundi-Hathibada (Chitorgadh District, Rajasthan) epigraph[1] (in duplicate) of king Gājāyana Sarvatāta while the earliest such record in East India is the Ayodhya (Fyzabad District, U. P.) inscription[2] of Dhanadeva, both of whom flourished in the said age. It is interesting to note that, whereas the grammarian Patañjali, author of the *Mahābhāṣya* on Pāṇini's grammar, is known to have taken part in one of the two Aśvamedhas celebrated by Puṣyamitra Suṅga,[3] the sixth ancestor of Dhanadeva, Sarvatāta was also the performer of an Aśvamedha sacrifice.

The Sanskrit language as used in the early inscriptions shows that the influence of the grammar of Pāṇini was not fully established even in the central part of India, which was the home of its great commentator, Patañjali (2nd century B.C.) of Gonarda (between Ujjayinī and Vidiśā),[4] as late as the 3rd century A.D. This is indicated by Prakritic forms occurring in Sanskrit epigraphs, e.g. *khānāpita* (for *khānita* preferred by the Paninean school) noticed in a *Śārdūlavikrīḍita* stanza in the Kanakhera (near Sanchi) inscription[5] (3rd century A.D.) of Śaka Śrīdharavarman.

1. *Select Inscriptions*, pp. 91-92.

2. Ibid., p. 96. The Pabhosa cave inscriptions (ibid., pp. 97-98) of about the end of the 1st century B.C. are written in an admixture of Sanskrit and Prakrit.

3. Cf. Raychaudhuri, *Pol. Hist. Anc. Ind.*, 1938, pp. 315-16.

4. *JAHRS*, Vol. IX, Part 3, pp. 1 ff.; my *Studies in the Geography of Ancient and Medieval India*, pp. 206ff.

5. *Select Inscriptions*, pp. 180-81. Cf. *bandhāpita* and a few other cases of Prakritism in a Sanskrit inscription dated 181 A.D. belonging to the Śakas of Western India (ibid., p. 176).

Of the 2nd century epigraphs of Eastern India, the Kailvan (Patna District, Bihar) inscription[1] (186 A.D.) of Ārya-Viśākhamitra is written in a mixture of Prakrit and Sanskrit, while the language of the epigraphs[2] of the kings of Kauśāmbī flourishing in the second and third centuries A.D. are written in Sanskrit slightly influenced by Prakrit. But the Jagatpur (Dehradun District, U.P.) brick inscriptions[3] of Śīlavarman, who seems to have flourished about the end of the 3rd century A.D., are written in Sanskrit verse. By the time of the rise of the Guptas of Pāṭaliputra (near Patna in Bihar) in the 4th century A.D., Sanskrit is found to be holding the field of North Indian (excluding West Indian) epigraphy. The Guptas were great patrons of Sanskrit literature. The celebrated dramatists Bhāsa and Kālidāsa flourished in their age and the great epics and some sections of the Purāṇas appear to have reached their final form in the first half of the 4th century.

The earliest Sanskrit inscriptions in South India are a few records of the time of the Ikṣvāku king Ehuvula Śāntamūla (close of the 3rd and first half of the 4th century A.D.), which have been discovered at Nagarjunikonda.[4] But that Prakrit continued to enjoy popularity at the courts of South Indian kings till the latter half of the 4th century A.D. is clearly indicated by numerous inscriptions. As we have seen above, the earliest form of inscriptional Prakrit indicated reduplicated consonants by single letters. This characteristic is noticed in the Śātavāhana inscriptions[5] of the 2nd century A.D. and in the records[6] of the time of the Ikṣvāku king Vīrapuruṣadatta who flourished about the third quarter of the 3rd century A.D. But many of the records[7] of the age of Vīrapuruṣadatta's

1. *Ep. Ind.*, Vol. XXXI, pp. 229 ff.

2. See ibid., Vol. XVIII, pp. 159-60; Vol. XXIII, pp. 248-49; Vol. XXIV, pp. 147-48; *Ind. Cult.*, Vol., III, pp. 177 ff.; etc. Some of their inscriptions exhibit greater influence of Prakrit (cf. *Ep. Ind.*, Vol. XXIV, pp. 253 ff.). But the Prakrit inscriptions at Bandhogadh exhibit little Sanskrit influence, though the later records there are in Sanskrit (ibid., Vol. XXXI, pp. 167 ff.).

3. *Indian Archaeology*, 1953-54, ed. A. Ghosh, p. 11.

4. *Ep. Ind.*, Vol. XXXIII, pp. 147 ff.; Vol. XXXV, pp. 11 ff.

5. See *Select Inscriptions*, pp. 191 ff.

6. Cf. ibid., pp. 219 ff. Some of their silver coins have legend in a Dravidian variety of Prakrit. See Rapson's Catalogue, pp. xc-xci.

7. See., e.g., ibid., pp. 229 and 230-31.

son Ehuvula Śāntamūla, which may be assigned to the close of the 3rd century and the first half of the 4th, are written either in the old inscriptional Prakrit or in a language which may be regarded as literary Prakrit in so far as they use reduplicated consonants. The language of the latter group of records is nearer Sanskrit than that of the former group. The Basim plates[1] of Vākāṭaka Vindhyaśakti II (middle of the 4th century A.D.) are written partially in this language, a portion of the record being couched in Sanskrit.

The same story is told by other records of the Deccan such as those of the Śālaṅkāyanas of Veṅgī in the Telugu-speaking area. The earliest inscriptions of the Śālaṅkāyana dynasty are in Prakrit of the literary type.[2] They may be assigned to the 4th century. The 5th century records of the family are, however, written in Sanskrit.[3] It is also interesting to note that the Mattepad plates[4] of Dāmodaravarman, who probably ruled over the Guntur region about the close of the 4th century A.D., are written partly in Sanskrit. The latest inscription written in literary Prakrit and discovered in the Kannaḍa-speaking region is the Chandravalli epigraph[5] of the Kadamba king Mayūraśarman who flourished about the middle of the 4th century A.D. But the Halsi plates[6] of his great-grandson Kākusthavarman, who flourished in the first half of the 5th century, are written in Sanskrit. Thus the suppression of Prakrit by Sanskrit in South Indian epigraphy may be assigned to the second half of the 4th century A.D.

The language of the Prakrit charters of the Pallavas of Kāñcī belonging to the 4th century A. D. tells us the story of the supercession of Prakrit by Sanskrit in the southern-

1. Cf. *Select Inscriptions*, pp. 406 ff.
2. See, e.g., *Ep. Ind.*, Vol. XXXI, pp. 1 ff.
3. Cf., e.g., ibid., pp. 7 ff.
4. Ibid., Vol. XVII, pp. 327 ff.
5. *Select Inscriptions*, p. 449. The Malavalli charter, probably issued by the same Kadamba king, is written in literary Prakrit, but contains a *maṅgala* passage in Sanskrit. See *Ep. Carn.*, Vol. VII, Sikarpur 264; *The Successors of the Sātavāhanas*, pp. 248 ff.
6. *Ind. Ant.*, Vol. VI, p. 23. The Talagunda pillar inscription describing a pious deed of the same king is really a *kāvya* in Classical Sanskrit, composed by a poet named Kubja. See *Select Inscriptions*, pp. 450 ff.

most areas of the country, the tale being similar to that of the progress of Sanskrit in the epigraphy of the Telugu- and Kanaḍa-speaking areas. Thus the Mayidavolu and Hirahadagalli plates[1] of Śivaskandavarman (middle of the 4th century) are written in literary Prakrit; but the legend on the seals affixed to them is in Sanskrit. A *maṅgala* passage at the end of the Hirahadagalli plates is also written in the Sanskrit language. The Gunapadeya plates[2] of the time of Skandavarman, who flourished about the last quarter of the fourth century, are likewise written in literary Prakrit, but have two of the imprecatory and benedictory stanzas in Sanskrit at the end of the document. The later grants[3] of the Pallava kings who flourished in the 5th and 6th centuries are written in Sanskrit.

Some of the early Prakrit inscriptions such as the Hathigumpha inscription[4] of Khāravela (close of the 1st century B.C.) and the Nasik cave inscription[5] of the 19th regnal year of Puḷumāvi (middle of the 2nd century A.D.) are written in the *kāvya* style. The Piprawa vase inscription[6] of the 3rd century B.C. appears to contain a Prakrit stanza.

There are some medieval Jain inscriptions in Prakrit; e.g. the Ghatiyala inscription[7] of Pratīhāra Kakkuka, dated 862 A.D. Specimens of Prakrit are also found in a few medieval records[8] in Sanskrit. An inscription[9] in characters closely resembling those of the Dhar inscriptions of the time of Paramāra Bhoja (c. 1000-55 A.D.) contains specimens of various kinds of Prakrit speech. The Dhar inscriptions[10] referred to above contain the text of the Prakrit poem entitled *Kūrmaśataka* ascribed to Bhoja.

1. *Select Inscriptions*, pp. 433 ff.
2. Ibid., pp 43 ff.
3. See, e.g., ibid., pp. 445 ff.
4. Ibid., pp. 206 ff.
5. Ibid., pp. 196 ff.
6. Ibid., p. 84.
7. Bhandarkar's List, No. 31.
8. Cf. e.g., verse 12 (in Prakrit) in the Banaras plates (*Ep. Ind.*, Vol. II, pp. 305 ff.) of the Kalacuri king Karṇa, dated 1041 A.D.
9. *Bhār. Vid.*, Vol. XVII, Nos. 3-4, 1957, pp. 130 ff. and Plate.
10. *Ep. Ind.*, Vol. VIII, pp. 243 ff. and Plates.

Section II

DRAVIDIAN LANGUAGES

1. *Tamil* (*Tamiḻ*)

The earliest use of a regional language in Indian inscriptions is noticed in certain small records discovered in the Tamil country. Their language is believed to be Tamil and they belong to the early centuries of the Christian era probably to the 2nd and 3rd centuries A.D.[1] From the 6th century A.D., Tamil began to be used along with Sanskrit in the copper-plate grants of the Pallava kings and from that time its use in inscriptions increased gradually. The charters of the Imperial Pallavas discovered in the Telugu-speaking area are written in Sanskrit, while those of their grants which were meant for the Tamil-speaking region are written partly in Sanskrit and partly in Tamil. To the first group belong the Vunnaguruvayapalem plates[2] of Parameśvaravarman I (c. 669-700 A. D.) and the Reyuru plates[3] of Narasiṁhavarman II (c. 700-25 A.D.). Both these records are written in early Telugu-Kannaḍa script. The Kuram plates[4] of Parameśvaravarman I, the Kasakudi and Tandantottam plates[5] of Nandivarman II Pallavamalla (c. 730-96 A.D.) and the Bahur plates[6] of Nṛpatuṅgavarman (9th century A.D.) are written in the Sanskrit and Tamil languages in Grantha and Tamil characters respectively. The Udayendiram plates[7] of Nandivarman II Pallavamalla are, however, written in Sanskrit.[8]

The copper-plate charters of the early Coḻa kings are

1. See *Proc. Trans. A.-I. Or. Conf.*, 1920, pp. 327-48; ibid., 1924, pp. 275-300; *Ancient India*, No. 2, pp. 109 ff.; etc. Cf. *A. R. Ep.*, 1911-12, Plate facing p. 50; 1917-18, Plate I facing p. 7.
2. *Ep. Ind.*, Vol. XXXII, pp. 91 ff.
3. Ibid., Vol. XXIX, pp. 89 ff.
4. *SII*, Vol. I, pp. 144 ff.
5. Ibid., Vol. II, pp. 346 ff.; pp. 520 ff.; see also pp. 507 ff.
6. *Ep. Ind.*, Vol. XVIII, pp. 5 ff.
7. *SII*, pp. 365 ff.
8. The recently published Pallavankoyil plates of Pallava Siṁhavarman (third quarter of the 6th century) are written in Sanskrit and Tamil. See *Trans. Arch. Soc. S. Ind.*, 1958-59, pp. 41 ff.

generally written partly in Sanskrit and partly in Tamil like the second group of Pallava grants referred to above. Mention may be made in this connection of the larger Leiden plates[1] of Rājarāja I (985-1016 A.D.), the Tiruvalangadu plates[2] of Rajendra-coḷa I (1012-43 A.D.) and the Anbil plates[3] (c. 960 A.D.) of Sundara-coḷa. But the Tirukkalar copper-plate grant[4] of Rājendra-coḷa I is written in Tamil and so are the Tirukkalar plates of Rājādhirāja I, Kulottuṅga I, Rājarāja II and Kulottuṅga III written in Tamil only.[5] The Tirunelveli plate[6] (1021 A.D.) of Bhāskara Ravivarman of Kerala is written in the Tamil language and the Vaṭṭeḻuttu script excepting the passage *Oṁ namo Nārāyaṇāya namaḥ* at the end, which is in the Sanskrit language and in the triangle-headed North Indian alphabet. The smaller Leiden plates[7] of Kulottuṅga I (1070-1120 A.D.) are also written completely in Tamil. Thus Tamil was more frequently used alone in Coḷa official charters from the 11th century A. D. Early Pāṇḍya charters are written in Sanskrit and Tamil; but, unlike the Pallava and Coḷa grants, the Tamil part is written in the Vaṭṭeḻuttu alphabet instead of the Tamil script.[8] Later Pāṇḍya documents, such as the copper-plate grant[9] of Vīra-pāṇḍya, dated Śaka 1392 (1470 A.D.), are, however, written in Tamil.

The early copper-plate grants of the subordinate families, e.g., the Udayendiram plates[10] of the Gaṅga-Bāṇa chief Pṛthvīpati II Hastimalla who was a feudatory of Coḷa Parāntaka I (907-53 A.D.), are similarly written partly in Sanskrit and partly in Tamil. But late medieval rulers like the Nāyakas of Tanjavur and Madurai issued their charters either in Telugu (some-

1. *Ep. Ind.*, Vol. XXII, pp. 213 ff.
2. Ibid., Vol. III, pp. 383ff.
3. Ibid., Vol. XV, pp. 44 ff.
4. *SII*, Vol. III, pp. 465 ff.
5. Ibid., pp. 469 ff.
6. *Ep. Ind.*, Vol. XVI, pp. 339 ff. and Plate.
7. Ibid., Vol. XXII, pp. 267 ff. See also *SII*, Vol. III, pp. 465 ff.
8. See the two Pāṇḍya grants from Sinnamanur (*SII*, Vol. III, pp. 441 ff.).
9. *A. R. Ep.*, 1946-47, No. A 30.
10. *SII*, Vol. II, pp. 375 ff.

times Telugu and Sanskrit) or in Tamil while the grants of the Setupatis of Ramanathapuram are generally only in Tamil.[1]

There are also some Tamil charters of the Vijayanagara kings, one of them being issued by Mallikārjuna in Śaka 1340 (1418 A.D.) and two others by Sadāśiva in Śaka 1468 (1546 A.D.).[2] The majority of the private records of the Coḷa-Pāṇḍya age and later epochs are written in Tamil.

2. *Kannada* (*Kanarese*)

Among the other languages of the Dravidian group, Kannaḍa appears in inscriptions from the 6th century A.D. An inscription of Cālukya Maṅgaleśa (598-610 A. D.) outside the Vaiṣṇava cave at Badami is one of the earliest records in the Kannaḍa language.[3] The Halmidi inscription[4] of about the end of the 6th century is also written in Kannaḍa while there is a Kannaḍa endorsement at the end of the Aihole inscription[5] (634 A. D.) which may be slightly later than the main record. The copper-plate grants issued by the Cālukyas of Badami are written in Sanskrit, though most of the stone inscriptions of their age, both official and private, are in Kannaḍa. The introductory part of an inscription[6] (699 A.D.) of Cālukya Vinayāditya is written in Sanskrit. But its latter part containing the details of the grant is in Kannaḍa which is called *Prākṛta-bhāṣā* in the epigraph.

Similar is the case with most of the official records of later

1. For the Tamil records of the Nāyakas of Tanjavur, see *A.R. Ep.*, 1946-47, Nos. A 13-14; for their Telugu grants, cf. ibid., 1949-50, Nos. A 29-30. For the Tamil charters of the Nāyakas of Madurai, see ibid., 1946-47, Nos. A 41, 43; 1948-49, No. A 1; and for their Telugu grants, ibid., 1950-51, No. A 10. For the Tamil copper-plate grants of the Setupatis, see ibid., 1946-47, Nos. A 25-27, 29-31, 39, 42, 46, 48; etc.

2. See ibid., 1949-50, No. A 46, and 1956-57, Nos. A 51-52. For certain Tamil grants of the later rulers of Vijayanagara extraction, see ibid., 1946-47, No. A 19; 1949-50, Nos. A 18-25, 27-28; 1956-57, Nos. A 50, 53; etc. For certain miscellaneous copper-plate grants written in the Tamil language and belonging to the late medieval period, see ibid., 1952-53, Nos. A 8-10; 1953-54, No. A 19; 1957-58, Nos. A 7, 30; etc.

3. *Ind. Ant.*, Vol. X, p. 59.

4. *A. R. Mys. Arch. Dept.*, 1936, pp. 72-81.; *IHQ*, Vol. XVII, p. 134.

5. *Ep. Ind.*, Vol. VI, pp. 1 ff.

6. Cf. *Karnatak Inscriptions*, p. 3.

imperial dynasties of the Kannaḍa-speaking area, such as the Rāṣṭrakūṭas, the Later Cālukyas, the Kalacuris and the kings of Vijayanagara. Among the copper-plate grants of the time of the Rāṣṭrakūṭas, a few like the British Museum plates[1] (804 A.D.) of Govinda III are written in the Kannaḍa language. The Haldipur plates[2] of the Pallava chief Gopāla, who seems to have flourished in the 8th century A.D., are written partly in Sanskrit and partly in Kannaḍa. The Kalas inscription[3] (930 A.D.) of the time of Govinda IV contains good specimens of Kannaḍa poetry in various metres.

A few copper-plate grants of the Vijayanagara kings, who generally used the Sanskrit language and Nandināgarī characters for their charters, are written either in Sanskrit and Kannaḍa or in Kannaḍa only.[4] Late rulers like the chiefs of Keladi and Mysore generally used Kannaḍa for their official charters.[5]

Private stone inscriptions of the age of the medieval dynasties are, in the majority of cases, written in Kannaḍa, although some of them have a portion written in Sanskrit.

3. *Telugu (Tĕlugu, Tĕnugu)*

The official charters of the early ruling families of the Telugu-speaking area belonging to the 5th and the following centuries are written in Sanskrit, grants written in Telugu appearing only from about the 9th century A.D. A number of stone inscriptions dating from the close of the 6th century A.D. are, however, written in Telugu.

The earliest Telugu inscriptions are those belonging to the Telugu-Coḍas of Renāṇḍu, which have been discovered in the

1. *Ind. Ant.*, Vol. XI, p. 125. For the Rāṣṭrakūṭa charters in Sanskrit, see, e.g., *Ep. Ind.*, Vol. XVIII, pp. 235 ff.
2. *Ep. Ind.*, Vol. XXI, pp. 173 ff.
3. Ibid., Vol. XIII, pp. 329-33.
4. A few grants of Harihara (*A. R. Ep.*, 1956-57, No. A 63, dated 1414 A.D.), Virūpākṣa (ibid., No. A 8 dated 1465 A.D.) and Vijayabhūpati (ibid., 1952-53, No. A 12, dated 1714 A.D.) are written partly in Sanskrit and partly in Kannaḍa.
5. For the charters of the Keladi chiefs, see ibid., 1951-52, No. A 8; 1954-55, Nos. A 7-8; etc., and for those of the Mysore chiefs, cf. ibid., 1947-48, Nos. A 1-2; 1952-53, No. A 11; etc. For miscellaneous late copper-plate grants in Kannaḍa, see ibid., 1953-54, Nos. A 20-21; etc.

Anantapur and Cuddapah Districts and assigned to the period between the 6th and 8th centuries A.D. Some of the earliest amongst them, written completely in Telugu, are the Kalamalla and Erragudipadu inscriptions[1] of Erikal Muturāju Dhanañjaya who flourished about the close of the 6th and the beginning of the 7th century A.D. The Pottadurti-Malepadu inscription[2] is another early epigraph in Telugu belonging to the Telugu-Coḍa family. Records like the Bhairavakonda inscription[3] of the time of Vikramāditya, probably belonging to the same royal house and flourishing about the middle of the 8th century, are written in Telugu, with an admixure of Sanskrit. Most of the private records of the following centuries are in Telugu.

Of the copper-plate grants of the Telugu-Coḍa family, the Malepadu plates[4] of Puṇyakumāra and the Madras Museum plates[5] of Śrīkaṇṭha-coḍa are written in Sanskrit; but the Madras Museum plates[6] of Balliya-coḍa, who seems to have flourished about the middle of the 9th century, are writen in Telugu. This is the earliest copper-plate grant in Telugu so far discovered.

The copper-plate grants of the early Cālukya kings of Veṅgī are written in Sanskrit; but a few charters like the Ahadanakaram plates[7] of Viṣṇuvardhana IV or V are written partly in Sanskrit and partly in Telugu. The stone inscriptions of the Cālukya age are generally written in Telugu. Thus the Vipparla inscription of the time of Jayasiṁha I and the Lakshmipuram inscription of the reign of Maṅgi-yuvarāja, both of the 7th century A.D., are in Telugu.[8] There are also some Telugu inscriptions of the 7th and 8th centuries quoting regnal years of the Cālukya kings of Badami,[9] whose copper-plate grants found in the Telugu-

1. *Ep. Ind.*, Vol. XXVII, pp. 221 ff.
2. *Vyāsasaṁgrahamu*, pp. 301 ff.
3. *Ep. Ind.*, Vol. XXXIII, pp. 79ff.; cf. Vol. XXVII, p. 269, note 1.
4. Ibid., Vol. XI, pp. 337 ff.
5. *Journ. Ind. Hist.*, Vol. XV, pp. 255 ff.
6. Ibid., p. 257.
7. *Ind. Ant.*, Vol. XIII, pp. 185 ff.
8. *A. R. Ep.*, 1900, para. 35.
9. See, e.g., the Dimmagudi inscription (*A. R. Ep.*, 1920, No. 864) of the time of Vikramāditya and the Kondupalli inscription (ibid., No. 359) of the reign of Vijayāditya.

speaking area, however, are all written in Sanskrit. Among the 10th century copper-plate grants in Telugu, mention may be made of the Madras Museum plates[1] (Śaka 893 for 891) of Bhuvanatrinetra.

The stone inscriptions of the medieval rulers of the Telugu-speaking area, e.g. the Eastern Gaṅgas, Cālukyas, Chindas, Telugu-Coḍas, Kākatīyas, Reḍḍis, Gajapatis, the Vijayanagara kings, the Qutub Shāhīs of Golkonda and others, are generally written in Telugu, while the copper-plate grants of some of these rulers so far known are written in Sanskrit although often they contain a section in Telugu especially in the description of the boundaries of the gift lands.

Some of the copper-plate grants of the Reḍḍis, e.g., the charters of Komaragiri dated 1385 and 1403 A.D., are written partly in Sanskrit and partly in Telugu.[2] The Vijayanagara kings generally used Sanskrit in their charters; but there are a few of their copper-plate grants in Telugu; e.g., some of Kṛṣṇadevarāya and Acyutarāya.[3] Among late medieval rulers, the Nāyakas of Madurai and Tanjavur sometimes used Telugu in their charters, in some cases along with Sanskrit.[4]

4. *Malayāḷam and Tulu*

Tamil was exclusively the epigraphic language of the Malayāḷam-speaking area till the 14th century A.D. and inscriptions in Tamil were engraved in that region in the Vaṭṭeḻuttu alphabet. But Malayāḷam influence is noticed in a few records of the 13th century such as the Suchindram inscription

1. *Ep. Ind.*, Vol. XXVIII, p. 69.

2. *A. R. Ep.*, 1946-47, No. A 4.

3. See ibid., Nos. A 9-10 (of Kṛṣṇadevarāya); 1953-54, No. A 17. No. A 5 of 1852-53 and No. A 34 of 1957-58 referring themselves to Bukka and Harihara respectively, though in Telugu, were apparently forged at a much later date. For Telugu charters of later rulers of the family, see ibid., 1948-49, No. A 26. A few such records are written in both Sanskrit and Telugu (cf. ibid., 1956-57, No. A 61; *Ep. Ind.*, Vol. XVI, pp. 88 ff.).

4. See *A. R. Ep.*, 1949-50, Nos. A 29-30 (Telugu and Sanskrit); 1950-51, No. A 10 (Telugu); 1952-53, No. A 13 (Telugu). For some other Telugu copper-plate grants issued by late chiefs, see ibid., 1953-54, No. A 7; 1956-57, No A 4; etc. For a Telugu grant issued by an officer of the Mughals, see ibid., 1952-53, No. A 15 (dated 1714 A.D. during the reign of Farrukhsiyar).

of the Kollam year 403 (1228-29 A.D.).[1] One of the earliest epigraphs in the Malayāḷam language is the Attingal inscription[2] of 1452 A.D. written in Vaṭṭeḻuttu characters. Another 15th century epigraph in that language is the Tonnal inscription[3] of 1474 A.D., only the first two lines of which are in Sanskrit written in Grantha. Of the 16th century epigraphs in the Malayāḷam language, mention may be made of the Tripunitura inscription[4] of 1584 A.D. Out of later records, we may refer to the Parur inscriptions[5] of 1624 A. D., Manambur inscription[6] of 1635 A. D., Veṭṭikkavila inscription[6] of 1648 A. D. and Verapoli copper-plate grants[7] of 1718, 1760 and 1780 A.D.

The Tulu language, spoken in the South Kanara District of Mysore State and written in the Malayāḷam alphabet, has no literature and alphabet of its own. A few late medieval inscriptions written in the Tulu language and Malayāḷam characters, have been discovered.[8] The palaeography of these epigraphs is comparable to that of an inscription[9] of Kulaśekhara Aḻvar who may possibly be identified with the Āḷupa ruler Kulaśekhara Āḷupendra IV flourishing in the first half of the 15th century.

1. *A. R. Ep.*, 1958-59, No. B. 464.
2. *Trav. Arch. Ser.*, Vol. VI, p. 80, No. 64.
3. Ibid., pp. 34-35, No. 23.
4. Ibid., p. 196, No. 146.
5. Ibid., Vol. I, pp. 299 ff.
6. Ibid., Vol. VI, p. 82, No. 67.
6. Ibid., pp. 196 ff., Nos. 148-50.
7. See *A. R. Ep.*, 1929, No. B 462; 1931, No. B 371; 1935-36, No. B 111.
9. Ibid., 1929, No. B 506.

Section III

NEO-INDO-ARYAN LANGUAGES

In the tracts where the Neo-Indo-Aryan languages are spoken, Sanskrit was in general use in the early medieval period in preference to the regional languages. Independent Hindu rule was ousted by the Muhammadans from wide areas of the region in question. But, wherever in this area independent or semi-independent Hindu rulers flourished during the late medieval period, we notice occasional use of the regional languages in their official charters. Private records of the said period were often written in the regional languages in many parts of the country.

There are many bilingual epigraphs in Sanskrit and one of the regional languages. Some records are written in more than one regional language.[1] There are also inscriptions written in more than two languages.[2]

1. *Marāṭī*

Among the Neo-Indo-Aryan languages, Marāṭhī appears first in epigraphic records.[3] One of the earliest specimens of the Marāṭhī language is found in the Marmuri copper-plate grant[4] (974 A.D.) of the Cālukya prince Iṟiva-beḍaṅga Satyāśraya. Certain private records of the 11th century, such as the Dive Agar plate[5] of 1060 A.D. and the Sravana-Belgola epigraph[6] of c. 1118 A.D., are written in Marāṭhī. In this connection, reference may also be made to the Ambe-Jogai (1144 A.D.), Ranjali (1148 A.D.), Chiplun (1156 A.D.), Tera (1163 A.D.), Savargaon (1164 A.D.), Parel (1186 A.D.),

1. See, e.g., *A.R. Ep.*, 1949-50, No. B 397 in Hindī and Oriya; 1955-56, No. B 117 in Tamil and Oriya (*Ep. Ind.*, Vol. XXXII, pp. 229 ff.).

2. Cf. an inscription in Persian, Sanskrit and Gujarātī in *Bull. Baroda Mus.*, 1953-55, pp. 73 ff., and another in Sanskrit, Telugu and Oriya in *Ep. Ind.*, Vol. XXXIII, pp. 275 ff.

3. See A. Master, 'Some Marathi Inscriptions, A.D. 1060-1300' in *BSOAS*, Vol. XX, pp. 418 ff.; cf. S. G. Talpule, *An Old Marāṭhī Reader*, Poona, 1960, pp. 83 ff.

4. *Journ. Bomb. Hist. Soc.*, Vol. II, p. 214.

5. *Ep. Ind.*, Vol. XXVIII, pp. 121 ff.

6. *Ep. Carn.*, Vol. II, Sorab No. 974. Cf. *Ep. Ind.*, Vol. VII, p. 109.

Patan (1206 A.D.), Navasem (1239 A.D.) and Ranebennur (1252 A.D.) stone inscriptions.[1] The earliest Marāṭhī literary work is the *Jñāneśvarī* (the popular name of the *Bhāvārthadīpikā* by Jñānadeva), a commentary on the *Gītā*, which was composed much later than some of the above records in 1296 A.D.[2] The Velapur stone inscriptions[3] of 1300 A.D. are slightly later than the date of the composition of the said work.

The popularity of Marāṭhī in the epigraphic field increased with the rise of the Yādavas who patronised the language and used it in some of their charters. Yādava grants like the Tasgaon[4] (1250 A.D.) and Nandgaon[5] (1254-55 A.D.) plates of Kṛṣṇa are written partly in Sanskrit and partly in Marāṭhī. The same is the case with certain Śilāhāra grants, e.g., the Kaseli plate[6] of 1279 A.D.

A number of epigraphs of the time of the 'Adil Shāhī Sulṭāns are written in Marāṭhī.[7] Among bilingual inscriptions written in Marāṭhī and another language, mention may be made of the Kandarpur plate[8] of the Yādava king Jaitugi (1191-1210 A.D.) and the Lepakshi (Anantapur District) temple inscription[9] of the 16th century, both in Kannaḍa and Marāṭhī, the Cuddapah Telugu-Marāṭhī inscription[10] of 1689 A.D. and several Persian and Marāṭhī inscriptions.[11] The Dabhoi inscription[12] of 1652 A.D. records the purport of a *farmān* of Muḥammad 'Adil Shāh of Bijapur. Two of the three Marāṭhī inscriptions,[13]

1. Cf. *BSOAS*, Vol. XX, 1957, pp. 417 ff.; *A. R. Ep.*, 1933-34, No. B 117.
2. Talpule speaks of the *Jyotiṣaratnamālā* of 1050 A. D. and the *Līlācaritra* of 1278 A.D.
3. See *BSOAS*, op.cit., pp. 433-34. The date of a Bhandak inscription in old Marāṭhī has been tentatively read as Śaka 1308 (1386 A.D.). See *Ep. Ind.*, Vol. XXVI, p. 183.
4. *Ep. Ind.*, Vol. XVIII, pp. 208 ff. See also *Sāmanta* Jaitra's grant of 1202 A.D. (*BSOAS*, Vol. XX, pp. 428 ff.).
5. *Ep. Ind.*, Vol. XXVII, pp. 9 ff.
6. Cf. *BSOAS*, Vol. XX, pp. 432-33.
7. See *A. R. Ep.*, 1952-53, No. B 60 (Śaka 1520); 1954-55, No. B 106 (Śaka 1515).
8. *Journal of the Oriental Institute*, Vol. VI, p. 134.
9. *A. R. Ep.*, 1937-38, No. 15.
10. *Journal of the Oriental Institute*, Vol. VI, p. 136.
11. See, e.g., *Ep. Indo-Mosl.*, 1939-1940, p. 30, No. 2.
12. Ibid., 1933-1934, p. 9.
13. Ibid., 1937-1938, pp. 1 ff.

discovered in the Bidar District and containing dates in the Shāhūr years 979 (1579 A.D.), 1001 (1601 A.D.) and 1010 (1609 A.D.), have their Persian counter-parts. The first of them mentions 'Alī Barīd (1542-79 A.D.).

There are several copper-plate grants in Marāṭhī issued by Marāṭhā rulers such as the chiefs of Tanjavur.[1]

2. *Hindī and its Dialects and Allied Languages*

A number of Hindī inscriptions, mostly on images and hero or *satī* stones, were discovered in the former Gwalior State now merged in Madhya Pradesh.[2] The earliest of these records is on a Jain image from the Shyopur region and the date in it has been tentatively read as V. S. 1078 (1022 A.D.).[3] The Bhonrasa (old Gwalior State) inscription of 1483 A. D. referring to Sulṭān Ghiyāṣuddīn of Malwa is written in Persian and Hindī.[4] Among Hindī records of the time of the Gond rulers of Madhya Pradesh, reference may be made to a grant (1550 A.D.) of Dalpat Shāh, son of Saṁgrām Shāh[5]. The Damoh inscription[6] of the time of Muḥammad Shāh II of Malwa is dated in 1512 A.D.

There are many official and private records of the late medieval period, which are written in Hindī or one of its dialects.[7] Among the dialects of Hindī, some late medieval copper-plate grants issued by the Hindu rulers of the Kumaun-Garhwal region in the Himalayas are written in the local dialect.[8]

1. *A. R. Ep.*, 1930-31, p. 4, Nos. A 3-4. Some grants of the Marāṭhās of Tanjavur are written in Sanskrit and Tamil (cf. *A. R. Ep.*, 1945-46, No. A 15; 1946-47, Nos. A 20-23) and some in Tamil only (ibid., 1946-47, Nos. A 17-18). For a Marāṭhī copper-plate of Amṛtarāva Raghunātha, see *JBORS*, Vol. V, pp. 216 f.
2. H. N. Dvivedi, *Gvāliyar Rājyake Abhilekh*, Nos. 36, 44, 50, 52, 62, etc.
3. See also *An. Rep. Arch. Dept.*, Gwalior State, V. S. 1992, No. 39.
4. *Ep. Indo-Mosl.*, 1937-1938, p. 25.
5. *Journ. Bhār. Iti. Saṁs. Maṇḍ.*, Vol. XXVI, pp. 51 ff. See also the Dantewara (old Bastar State) inscription of 1702 A.D. in *Ep. Ind.*, Vol. XII, pp. 245 ff.
6. *Ep. Ind.*, Vol. XV, pp. 291 ff.
7. Cf. ibid., Vol. IX, p. 166; *IHQ*, Vol. VII, pp. 410 ff.; etc. See also *A. R. Ep.*, 1952-53, No. A 30.
8. *A. R. Ep.*, 1948-49, Nos. A 7-10. Muslim writers ascribe a poem in Hindī to Candella Vidyādhara (first quarter of the 11th century). See Ray, *DHNI*, Vol. II, p. 692.

Rājasthānī was used by the rulers of the various states in Rajasthan in writing their official charters.[1] An early charter in this dialect is the copper-plate grant of Guhila Mokalasiṁha of Mewar, which is dated in V. S. 1431 (1375 A.D.).[2] Numerous private records in Rājasthānī belonging to the late medieval period are found in different parts of Rajasthan.[3]

There are a few copper-plate grants[4] of the rulers of Sambalpur, which are written in a dialect of Hindī. Late medieval private records in the various dialects of this language have been discovered in large numbers.[5]

Very few inscriptions in the Nepālī language have so far been published. A few short Punjabi and Hindī epigraphs were found near Baku, U. S. S. R.

3. *Gujarātī*

The language of a number of inscriptions, discovered in Kathiawar and belonging to the second half of the 14th century, is an admixture of Sanskrit and Gujarātī while, from about the middle of the 15th century, we have inscriptions in the Gujarātī language written in the Nāgarī alphabet slightly modified by the later Gujarātī or Boḍiyā script.[6] Some of the earliest private records entirely written in the Gujarātī language, so far discovered in Kathiawar, are the Khambhad and Kutiyana inscriptions[7] of 1474 A.D., the Gosa inscription[8] of 1480 A.D., and the Khodu inscription[9] of 1488 A.D.

1. *A. R. Ep.*, 1954-55, No. A 71; 1957-58 Nos. A 40-52.
2. See ibid., 1957-58, No. A 51.
3. Ibid., 1952-53, Nos. B 157, 296-405; 1954-55, Nos. B 450-51, 473-75, 477-81, 484, etc. See also *Ep. Ind.*, Vol. XXX, pp. 191 ff.; etc.
4. *A. R. Ep.*, 1953-54, Nos. A 15-16 (dated V. S. 1747 and 1838).
5. Ibid., 1952-53, Nos. B 157, etc.; 1953-54, Nos. B 105, 108, 132-36, etc.; 1954-55, Nos. B 185, 187, 191-92, 195, 202, 228-39, 241-42, 244-48, etc.
6. See D. B. Diskalkar, 'Inscriptions of Kathiawad' in *N. Ind. Ant.*, Vols. I-III (December 1938-March 1941); cf. op. cit., December 1938, pp. 587 and 588. For inscriptions in the mixed language, see loc. cit.: the Than inscription (No. 36) of 1376 A.D., the Nagichana inscription (No. 37) of 1377 A.D., the Phulka inscription (No. 50) of 1391 A.D., etc.
7. Diskalkar, op. cit. (*N. Ind. Ant.*, June 1940), p. 122.
8. Ibid., pp. 123-24.
9. Ibid., p. 125.

There is a large number of similar late medieval private inscriptions in Gujarātī,[1] while many of them are bilingual being written partly in Sanskrit[2] or Persian[3] and partly in Gujarātī. Records like the Sathod (Baroda District) inscription[4] of 1369 A.D. are trilingual being written in Persian, Gujarātī and Sanskrit. Most of the private Gujarātī inscriptions are found engraved on hero or *satī* stones called *pāliyā* in Gujarātī.

Among later inscriptions in the Gujarātī language mention may be made of the Borsad (1496 A.D.), Lasundra (1522 A.D.), Junraj (1620 A.D.), Sojitra (1627 and 1781 A.D.), Lal Darwaja (1782 A.D.) and Juna (1782 and 1794 A.D.) inscriptions.[5]

4. *Kashmiri (Kaśmīrī) and Allied Dialects*

We have few epigraphic records in Kashmiri so far discovered and published. There are some written in an admixture of Sanskrit and Kashmiri.[6]

The charters issued by the early rulers of Chamba are written in Sanskrit[7] while those of the later rulers are mostly in the local dialect. There are also numerous private records in this dialect.

A large number of the official and unofficial records published recently by Dr. B. Ch. Chhabra in the *Antiquities of Chamba State*, Part II, are bilingual being written in Chambyālī (called *Bhāṣā* in the records) and Sanskrit. The bilingual charters of the Chamba rulers generally begin and end in Sanskrit while their middle portion constituting the deed proper is written in the local dialect.[8]

1. See Diskalkar, op. cit. ; *A. R. Ep.*, 1949-50, Nos. B 50-51; etc.
2. Cf. *Ep. Ind.*, Vol. XXIV, p. 225 (cf. text lines 21-22). For some inscriptions in a mixture of Gujarātī and Sanskrit, see ibid., Vol IX, pp. 24 ff.
3. See *A. R. Ep.*, 1952-53, No. B 433-A; etc.
4. *Bull. Baroda Mus.*, 1953-55, pp. 73 ff.
5. See A. V. Pandya's 'Some Newly Discovered Inscriptions from Gujarāt' in *Vallabh Vidyanagar Research Bulletin*, No.2, Inscriptions Nos. 21-24, 26, 28-30.
6. Cf. Vogel, *Antiquities of Chamba State*, Part I, p. 251 (No. 48).
7. See, e.g., ibid., pp. 159 ff., pp. 182 ff., for the Sanskrit grants. For a private record in the local dialect, see op. cit., p. 251 (No. 49).
8. B. Ch. Chhabra, op. cit., p. 13.

5. *Oriya* (*Oḍiyā*)

In Orissa, the influence of the Oriya language in inscriptions written in Sanskrit appears as early as the 10th century.[1] Records, both private and royal, written entirely in Oriya appear in the 13th century.[2] A few official charters of the later members of the Eastern Gaṅga dynasty such as the Puri plates[3] of Narasiṁha IV (c. 1378-1402 A.D.) are written partly in Sanskrit and partly in Oriya. Similar is the case with Gajapati charters like the Veligalani grant of Kapileśvara (c. 1435-66 A.D.),[4] which has a section in Oriya, its other sections being written in Sanskrit and Telugu. But we have the same king's stone inscriptions, together with a number of records of his successors, in the Jagannātha temple at Puri, which are all written wholly in Oriya.[5] Some official charters of the Gajapati kings and many issued by the later rulers of Orissa are written entirely in Oriya.[6] Private inscriptions in Oriya belonging to the late medieval period are numerous.[7]

1. See the Madras Museum plates of the time of Narendradhavala (*Ep. Ind.*, Vol. XXVIII, pp. 44 ff.).

2. See, e.g., the Puri inscriptions of the time of Anaṅgabhīma III (ibid., Vol. XXX, pp. 197 ff.). For the Kapilas inscriptions of Narasiṁha I, one in Sanskrit and another in Oriya and the Sonepur inscription (1268 A.D.) of Bhānu I, see ibid., Vol. XXXII, pp. 325 ff.; Vol. XXXIII, pp. 41 ff.

3. Ibid., Vol. XXVIII, pp.302ff. For a private record of the same king's reign written completely in Oriya, see ibid., Vol. XXIX, pp. 105 ff. For another private record of the reign of Narasiṁha IV in Oriya and Tamil, cf. ibid., Vol. XXXII, pp. 229 ff.

4. Ibid., Vol. XXXIII, pp. 275 ff.; *JAS*, Letters, Vol. XXIII, pp. 13ff. For private records of his time written in Oriya, see *Or. Hist. Res. Journ.*, Vol. I, No. 2, p. 9.; *A. R. Ep.*, 1953-54, No. B 92; etc.

5. See *JASB.*, Vol. LXII, Part i, 1893, pp. 90 ff.; LXIV, Part i, 1895, pp. 149 ff. See also *A. R. Ep.*, 1955-56, No. B 353.

6. For a Gajapati charter completely written in Oriya, see the Balasore copper axe-head inscription of Puruṣottama (*Ind. Ant.*, Vol. I, p. 355; *JBORS*, Vol. IV, p. 363). For later copper-plate grants and stone inscriptions, see, e.g., *JAHRS*, Vol. III, pp. 1 ff.; *A. R. Ep.*, 1951-52, No. A 20; 1952-53, Nos. A 23-26; 1953-54, Nos. A 3-4 and B 422 ff.; etc., and 1957-58, Nos. A 40-41; etc. The Warangal inscription (1460 A. D.) of Raghudeva, the Gajapati viceroy of Rajahmundry, is written in the Oriya language, but in Telugu characters (*Ep. Ind.*, Vol. XXXIII, pp. 125 ff.).

7. For various official and private Oriya records of the medieval period, mostly of the age of the Gaṅgas and Gajapatis, see *SII*, Vol. V, Nos. 1006, 1119, 1152, 1161; Vol. VI, Nos. 697, 700-03, 720, 748-49, 778, 793, 895, 903, 908-09, 927, 940, 1078, 1089, 1110; etc.

6. *Bengali (Vaṅgālī) and Maithili*

In the Bengali-speaking area, Sanskrit was more popular than the regional language for official purposes. It has been suggested that lines 29-51 of the Bhatera copper-plate grant[1] are written in the Sylhet dialect of the Bengali language. But the language is really Sanskrit influenced by the local dialect as in the case of 13th century inscriptions of Bengal and also of various other localities. The date of the epigraph has been read as Pāṇḍava 4328 (1245 A.D.) or Kali 4151 (1049 A.D.), the first of which is more probable.

Official and private records of the medieval period such as the Tripura plate[2] (1488 A.D.) and Maharani inscriptions[3] of the reign Vijayamāṇikya, the Dhurail inscription[4] (1533 A.D.) of the time of Maḥmūd Shāh, the Muhammadpur stone inscription[5] (1703 A.D.) of Sītārāma-rāya, etc., are written in Sanskrit. The coins of the Tripura kings and other ruling families of the Bengali-speaking area and its neighbourhood, also have legends in the Sanskrit language.[6]

Epigraphic records were written during the late medieval period in this area mostly in Sanskrit and only rarely in Bengali.[7] Thus a few copper-plate grants, such as those issued by king Govindamāṇikya (15th century) of Tripura,[8] are principally written in Bengali, although many of the charters issued by the Tripura kings including the successors of Govindamāṇikya, e.g. Kṛṣṇamāṇikya (17th century), are written mainly in Sanskrit.[9]

1. *Ep. Ind.*, Vol. XIX, pp. 277 ff.
2. *JAS*, Letters, Vol. XVII, pp. 73 ff.
3. *IHQ*, Vol. XXXII, pp.99ff., where another Sanskrit epigraph of the same area and age has been noticed.
4. *A. R. Ep.*, 1953-54, No. B 436.
5. Ibid., No. B 433.
6. See Smith's Catalogue, pp. 307 ff.
7. *A. R. Ep.*, 1949-50, Nos. B 3-4.
8. See ibid., 1951-52, Nos. A 13 ff.
9. See ibid., Nos. A 18-19. For a copper-plate grant and a stone inscription of the time of Vijayamāṇikya (16th century), both in Sanskrit, see *JAS*, Letters, Vol. XVII, pp. 73 ff.; *IHQ*, Vol. XXXII, pp. 99 ff. For another copper-plate grant belonging to the Tripura kings, Rāmamāṇikya and Ratnamāṇikya, both of the 18th century, see *A. R. Ep.*, 1952-53, No. A 28.

Similar was the condition in Mithila or North Bihar. Very few epigraphs in the Maithilī language have so far been published, one such being an inscription dated 1665 A.D.[1]

7. *Assamese* (*Asamīyā*)

The Ahom kings of Assam originally issued copper-plate charters in the Ahom language.[2] But, when their Hinduization was more or less complete, they adopted Sanskrit and Assamese as their official languages. The charters of the later Ahom rulers are written partly in Sanskrit and partly in Assamese. They are dated in the Śaka era. The coins of the early rulers have legends in the Ahom language and alphabet while the legends on the coins of the later kings are in Sanskrit in Assamese-Bengali characters exactly as their epigraphic records are.[3]

Among the Sanskrit-Assamese copper-plate grants known to us, mention may be made of those (1) of Śivasiṁha and his queen Ambikā granted in 1732 A.D. and renewed by Rājeśvarasiṁha in 1760 A.D., (2) of Lakṣmīsiṁha issued in 1775 A.D., and (3) of Gaurīnāthasiṁha issued in 1892 A.D.[4] The stone inscriptions of the time of the later Ahom kings are generally in Sanskrit.[5]

1. See R. K. Choudhary, *Select Inscriptions of Bihar*, p. 138. For a paper document in Sanskrit and Maithilī, see *Proc. Hist. Rec. Comm.*, Mysore, 1942, pp. 87 ff. For the Sanskrit legend on the coins of a late medieval ruler of Mithilā, see *JNSI*, Vol. XX, pp. 192 ff.

2. I saw one such record with the Pāṇḍās of the Kāmākhyā temple near Gauhati. For an Ahom pillar inscription of the 16th century, see *ASIR*, Vol. XXIV, pp. 157-58; *A. R. Ep.*, 1957-58, No. B 75.

3. See Smith's Catalogue, pp. 298 ff., for the coins of Śukleṅmuṅ (1539-52 A. D.), Śupātphā *alias* Gadādharasiṁha (1681-95 A. D.) and Śuneñphā *alias* Pramathasiṁha (1744-51 A.D.) with legends in Ahom and those of Śuseṅphā (Cuceṅphā) *alias* Svarganārāyaṇa Pratāpasiṁha (1611-49 A.D.), Rudrasiṁha (1696-1714 A.D.) and others with legends in Sanskrit.

4. Cf. *A. R. Ep.*, 1957-58, Nos. A 3-5.

5. See ibid., Nos. B 62 ff.

CHAPTER III

WRITING MATERIALS

Section I

MATERIALS FOR WRITING OR SCRATCHING

1. *Palmyra Leaves*

Palmyra[1] leaves, separated from the lengthwise joint in the middle and cut at both ends according to the required size,[2] were used for writing letters as well as manuscripts of literary works in Sanskrit and other languages.[3] That sometimes royal charters written on palmyra leaves were issued to the donees is clearly established by the Kurud plates[4] of the 6th century. The originals of some of the documents later copied on copper plates or stone must have been written on palmyra leaves.

For writing manuscripts of important works, the leaves were seasoned in the following way. They were at first dried, then soaked or boiled in water for a considerable time and again dried. Both sides of the leaves were then rubbed with conch - or cowrie-shells or a smooth piece of stone. Excluding certain parts of the Punjab-Kashmir region, palmyra leaves were in general use throughout India.

In North India, the general practice was to write on the leaves with pen and ink, while, in the South, the letters were

1. This is *tāla* (*tāḍa*) and *tālī* (*tāḍī*) respectively called *Borassus flabel liformis* and *Coryfa umbraculifera* (or *taliera*). Rājaśekhara's *Kāvya-mīmāṁsā* (G.O.S. ed., p. 50) suggests that *tāḍi-patra* and birch-bark was used for writing with pen and ink while the *loha-kaṇṭaka* or iron needle was used to write on *tāla-dala*.

2. The size of the leaves in manuscripts varies between one and three feet in length and between one and a quarter and four inches in breadth.

3. In the 11th century Al-Bīrūnī said, "The Hindus have in the south of their country a slender tree like the date and coconut palms, bearing edible fruits and leaves of the length of one yard and as broad as three fingers one put beside the other. They call these leaves *tārī* (Sanskrit *tālī* or *tāḍī*) and write on them" (Sachau, *Alberuni's India*, Part I, p. 171).

4. *Ep. Ind.*, Vol. XXXI, pp. 263 ff., pp. 267-68.

incised on the leaves with a sharp-pointed needle and were made black by besmearing ink on the writing.

The leaves for writing a particular book were cut to the same length and a wooden plate each was placed at the top and the bottom of the leaves arranged according to order. A hole was made about the middle of the leaves of a manuscript (and sometimes also of the covers) for a string to pass through. The string was meant for binding the material about the middle of the packet and it string prevented the leaves from moving away from their proper places.[1] Sometimes, manuscripts of several books were preserved together in the same way. When the leaves of the manuscripts were considerably long in size, two holes were made instead of one, one of them about the middle of the left half and another about the middle of the right half. The availability of paper as a cheap writing material gradually pushed palmyra leaves out of use. Early Buddhist literature refers to *paṇṇa* or *parṇa* (i.e. leaf) as a popular writing material.[2] The reference is no doubt to palmyra leaves.

In the 7th century, the Chinese pilgrim Hiuen-tsang spoke of the general use of palmyra leaf as a writing meaterial throughout the country.[3] The popularity of this material is also indicated by the fact that the birch-bark sheets of the Bower manuscripts as well as such early copper plates as the Taxila plate[4] of Patika (21 A.D.) are cut according to the shape of a palmyra-leaf sheet. According to a Buddhist tradition, the canon was written on palmyra leaves immediately after the Buddha's death.[5]

1. Al-Bīrūnī says, "They (i.e. the Indians) bind a book of these (i.e. palmyra) leaves together by a cord on which they are arranged, the cord going through all the leaves by a hole in the middle of each.........They write the title of the book at the end of it and not at the beginning" (Sachau, loc. cit. and p. 182).The string holding the leaves of a manuscript together was called *sūtra* or *śarayantraka* (cf. *Vāsavadatta*, Hall's ed., p. 250).

2. Bühler, *Indian Palaeography*, p. 94.

3. Beal, *Si-yu-ki*, Vol. II, p. 225.

4. See *CII*, Vol. II, Part i, pp. 23 ff., Plate V, 1. The size of the plate is 14 inches by 3 inches and it weighs 3½ ounces. See also the Kalwan copper plate measuring 8.85 inches by 2.65 inches and weighing 879 grains (*Ep. Ind.*, Vol. XXI, pp. 251 ff.).

5. Beal, *Life of Hiuen Tsiang*, p. 117. Cf. also the story regarding Saṅghabhadra's 'dotted manuscript of the Vinaya' (*JRAS*, 1896, pp. 436 f.).

Some of the earliest palmyra-leaf manuscripts have been discovered outside India. A few works copied on palmyra leaves in the early centuries of the Christian era were discovered in Central Asia,[1] while the Horiuzi (Japan) manuscript of the Buddhist work entitled *Uṣṇīṣavijayadhāraṇī* is believed to have been written in India in the 6th century A.D.[2]

Among the early palm-leaf manuscripts found in Nepal, mention may be made of the *Skanda Purāṇa* (supposed to have been copied about the 7th century A. D.), the *Parameśvara Tantra* copied in the year 252 (probably of the Harṣa era and corresponding to 859 A.D.) and the *Laṅkāvatāra* copied in the Newari year 28 (906-07 A.D.).[3] Manuscripts of the 11th and later centuries on palmyra leaves have been discovered in numbers in Gujarat, Rajasthan, Nepal and other regions, while those written in the South Indian style with sharp-pointed needle are generally not earlier than the 15th century. The hot climate of the South is likely to have led to the destruction of earlier manuscripts on palmyra leaves.

Even about the beginning of the present century, in the rural areas of some parts of India, e. g. Bengal, small boys in the primary schools used to practise their knowledge of the alphabet on palmyra or plantain leaves.

2. *Birch and Aloe Bark*

Sanskrit *bhūrja-patra* (literally, 'the birch leaf') is in reality a sheet of the required size cut out of the inner bark of the Bhūrja or birch tree grown in the Himalayas. In the 11th century, Al-Bīrūnī said, "In Central and Northern India, people use the bark of the *tūz* tree, one kind of which

1. *JASB*, Vol. LXVI, p. 218, Plate VII, 1, etc. For palm-leaf manuscripts from Turfan, which contain parts of Aśvaghoṣa's Sanskrit drama entitled *Sāriputraprakaraṇa*, see N. P. Chakravarti, *India and Central Asia*, p. 31. As regards various other manuscripts from Central Asia, see ibid., pp. 35ff. for the manuscript of the Sanskrit *Udānavarga*, pp. 39 ff. for that of Kumāralāta's *Kalpanāmaṇḍitikā*, and pp. 41 ff. for the Bower manuscripts.

2. *Annecdota Oxoniensia*, Aryan Series, Vol. I, Part iii, Plates I-IV.

3. H. P. Sastri, *Catalogue of Palm-Leaf and Selected Paper Mss.*, I, Introduction, p. 52, p. 140, and Plate. For the *Kiraṇatantra* copied in 924 A.D., see Vol. II, p. 99. See also *Mem. ASB*, Vol. V, Plates XXXVI ff.

is used as a cover for bows. It is called *bhūrja*. They take a piece one yard long and as broad as the outstretched fingers of the hand, or somewhat less, and prepare it in various ways. They oil and polish it so as to make it hard and smooth, and then they write on it.........Their letters and whatever else they have to write they write on the bark of the *tūz* tree."[1]

Q. Curtius seems to refer to the Indian practice of writing on birch bark when he says that, at the time of Alexander's invasion, the Indians used the tender bark of tree for writing.[2] A synonym of *bhūrja* is *lekhana*, i.e. 'writing' or 'a written document', while it is also recognised in the sense of other words meaning 'a written document'. The use of birch bark is supposed to have started in the north-west, although copper plates of the central, eastern and western regions of India, cut to the shape of birch-bark sheets, suggests the spread of the custom in early times. In North India, letters were generally written on birch-bark sheets.

As in the palmyra-leaf manuscripts, the sheets in the manuscripts written on birch bark also had a hole or two for a string or two to pass through. Generally, space was left, while writing on the sheets in ink, for the perforation to be made afterwards. Some Kashmirian manuscripts written on birch-bark sheets during the Mughal age were bound with leather like the contemporary Arabic and Persian manuscripts. The introduction of cheap paper led to the disappearance of birch bark as a writing material, though it is still used in some areas for writing spells for insertion in talismans.

Among the earliest birch-bark manuscript so far discovered, we may count the Khotan copy of the Prakrit *Dhammapada* written in Kharoṣṭhī characters of about the 2nd or 3rd century A.D., the manuscripts of the Sanskrit Buddhist work *Saṁyuktāgamasūtra* copied about the 4th century A.D., the Bower manuscripts (the sheets of which have a hole in the midd e for a string to pass through) and the Bakhshali manuscript of a mathematical work copied about

1. Sachau, *Alberuni's India*, Part I, p. 171.
2. Bühler, *Indian Palaeography*, p. 6.

the 8th century A.D.[1] But the majority of birch-bark manuscripts are of the 15th and later centuries.

The originals of many of the royal charters and other records later copied on copper plates or stone were apparently written on birch-bark sheets.

The inner bark of the Aguru or Aloe tree (*Aquilaria agallocha*), called Sãci in Assam, was the most popular material for writing manuscripts in the north-eastern corner of India.[2] The sheets of this bark, made specially ready for writing, were called *Sãci-pāt* (literally, 'the Sãci leaf') in Assamese. A large number of manuscripts written on this material have been discovered in Assam and some of them have found their way to the libraries and museums of the Western countries.[3] A manuscript of the Sundarakāṇḍa of the *Rāmāyaṇa*, written on aloe-bark sheets in the Bengali-Maithili-Assamese characters of about the 15th century, is preserved in the Bibliothéque Nationale, Paris. It is believed that some of the bark sheets of the manuscript contain a layer of wood with them.[4]

3. *Cloth*[5] *and Hide*

Pieces of cotton cloth (called *paṭa* or *kīrpāsika-paṭa* in Sankrit), cut according to the required size, were used for writing after applying on it a paste of rice or wheat powder and making its faces smooth by rubbing them with conch-or cowrie-shell, etc. The Bhaḍlī or Gurḍe astrologers of Rajasthan are stated to have prepared illustrated almanacs on such cloth sheets, which they explained to the public for earning their livelihood.[6] The mercantile community of the Mysore region are stated to have prepared their account books with such sheets of cloth seasoned with a paste made out of the powder of tamarind seeds and afterwards blackened

1. For some manuscripts dating from the 6th century, cf. N. Dutt, *Gilgit Manuscripts*, Vol. I, Intr.
2. See *JASB*, 1894, p. 109.
3. *Journ. As.*, 1958, pp. 85 ff.
4. Cf. ibid., Plate IX, p. 86.
5. Cf. P. K. Gode in *Prof. M. Hiriyanna Comm. Vol.*, Mysore, 1952, pp. 1-7 of offprint.
6. Ojha, *Bhāratīya Prācīn Lipimālā*, p. 146.

with charcoal.[1] These books, called *Kaḍitam* or *Kaḍatam*, are said to have been written with chalk or steatite pencil so that the writing became white or black. Such account books of several centuries are preserved in the Sringeri Maṭha.[2] A copy of Śrīprabha-sūri's *Dharmavidhi* (with Udayasiṁha's commentary), preserved in a Jain library at Anhilwada Patan, is written on 93 sheets of cloth, each of them 13 inches long and 5 inches broad.[3]

About the last quarter of the 4th century B.C., Nearchus seems to have noted that the Indians used to write letters on well-beaten cotton cloth.[4] According to the *Life of Hiuen Tsiang* by Hwui Li, king Harṣa 'wrote some letters on fine white cotton stuff and sealed them with red wax (or a composition)' and they were handed over to the official guides (called *Mahattaras*) of the Chinese pilgrim for presenting them to the authorities of the countries through which the pilgrim would pass.[5] The *Harṣacarita* (Ucchvāsa V) mentions a *lekha* or letter brought to Harṣa by a person, which is stated to have been 'tied in his forehead-wrap of rags of deep indigo blue', i.e. in his blue turban.

A stone inscription of about the first quarter of the 8th century A.D. refers to itself as a *kraya-cīrikā*, i.e. 'a deed of purchase written on a piece of cloth'.[6] The original document must have been later engraved on the stone.

According to Yājñavalkya (I, 319), the royal charters were written on cloth (*paṭa* explained as *kārpāsika-paṭa* by the commentator Vijñāneśvara) or copper plate (*tāmra-paṭṭa*). Some of the Śātavāhana charters later engraved on

1. Al-Bīrūnī says, "They (i.e. the Hindus) use black tablets for the children in the schools and write upon them along the long side, not the broad side, writing with a white material from the left to the right" (Sachau, *Alberuni's India*, Part I, p. 182).

2. *An. Rep. Mys. Arch. Dept.*, 1916, p. 18.

3. Peterson's 5th Report, 1916, pp. 18, 113. The manuscript is dated 1351-52 A.D.

4. Cf. Bühler, *Indian Palaeography*, p. 6.

5. Beal's trans., p. 190.

6. *Ep. Ind.*, Vol. XXVI, p. 246; *JBORS*, June 1944, pp. 198 ff.

cave walls refer to themselves as *paṭikā*.[1] It is however difficult to determine whether this word is derived from *paṭa* (cloth) or is an inscriptional Prakrit form standing for *paṭṭikā* derived from *paṭṭa* (plate).

Al-Bīrūnī says that he was told about the existence of a pedigree[2] of the Shāhī royal family of Kabul in the fortress of Nagarkot and this is stated to have been 'written on silk'. Bühler noticed a list of Jain Sūtras written in ink on a piece of silk in a Jain library at Jaisalmer.[3] Some fragmentary records on silk were discovered from Central Asian sites.[4]

Parchment was in general use as a writing material in early and medieval times in Western Asia and Europe. But it was rarely used in India, if at all. Reference to hide as a writing material is however found in Buddhist literature,[5] while Subandhu's *Vāsavadattā* speaks of *ajina* (skin of an antelope or tiger) as a writing material.[6] Some leather documents have been discoverd from such Central Asian sites as Niya and Endere.[7]

4. *Paper*

It is generally believed that the Chinese first made paper in 105 A.D.[8] Indians must have known paper through the Chinese travellers and I-tsing seems to refer to Indian paper,[9] though it was certainly not a popular writing material.

1. *Select Inscriptions*, pp. 192, 201.
2. Sachau, *Alberuni's India*, Part II, p. 11.
3. Bühler, *Indian Palaeography*, p. 93.
4. See N. P. Chakravarti, *India and Central Asia*, p. 75.
5. Bühler, op. cit., p. 95.
6. Hall's ed., p. 182. A blank piece of parchment was found among the manuscripts in a library at Jaisalmer. The Petersburg collections are said to possess some pieces of leather with writing in Indian characters, which were secured from Kashgarh. See Bühler, loc. cit., pp. 95-96.
7. N. P. Chakravarti, *India and Central Asia*, pp. 23-24.
8. See P. K. Gode's 'Migration of Paper from China to India' in K. B. Joshi's *Paper Making as a Cottage Industry*, pp. 205 ff. Al-Bīrūnī says, "It was in China that paper was first manufactured. Chinese prisoners introduced the fabrication of paper in Samarkand, and thereupon it was made in various places, so as to meet the existing want" (Sachau, *Alberuni's India*, Part I, p. 171). The Arabs are supposed to have begun to use paper from the middle of the 8th century A. D. (Wayriffe, *Arabica and Islamica*, p. 11; cf. Barnett, *Antiquities of India*, p. 229).
9. See Gode, loc. cit.

There is no doubt that the practice of writing on palmyra leaves and birch bark was much more popular, even though the word *śaya*, Sanskritized from Chinese *tsie* meaning 'paper', occurs in Sanskrit-Chinese lexicons of the 8th century A.D., which also recognise *kakali* or *kakari* no doubt Sanskritized forms of *kāghaz*.[1]

In writing manuscripts of books on paper, the sheets were generally cut according to the size of palmyra-leaf or birch-bark sheets and perforation for the string was made in the same way as in the leaf and bark manuscripts. For writing the manuscripts of important works, sometimes a paste, prepared by boiling rice or wheat powder in water, was applied to both sides of the paper sheets and, when it was dried, the sheets were rubbed with conch-or cowrie-shell, etc., to make the surface smooth.

The earliest paper manuscript discovered in Gujarat was copied in 1223-24 A. D.[2] M. A. Stein[3] refers to a Kashmirian manuscript of the *Śatapatha Brāhmaṇa* on paper which was copied in 1089 A.D. Some manuscripts, written on paper, covered with a layer of gypsum, in North Indian characters of about the 5th century A.D. or a slightly earlier date, were discovered near Yarkhand in Central Asia.[4] But they may have been written outside India.

5. *Wood*

Wooden slabs or planks with four legs were used in some parts of India in the schools before the introduction of slates. Some mud or chalk was applied to the surface of the wooden slate on which brick powder was evenly spread. Figures of sums were then written with the help of a blunt

1. P.C. Bagchi, *Deux Lexiques Sanskrit-Chinois*, Tome I, p. 287.
2. Bühler's *Catalogue of Mss.*, Vol. I, p. 238, No. 147.
3. *Catalogue of Jammu Mss.*, 1894, p. 8. The *Bulletin of the Ramavarma Research Institute*, Vol. VI, Part ii, July 1938, p. 125, contains the statement: "Paper Mss. begin with the date 1236 Saṁvatsara, i.e. 1180 A. D." But the statement is doubtful.
4. *JASB*, Vol. LXII, p. 8; Vol. LXVI, pp. 213 ff. For some paper documents from Central Asia, see also N. P. Chakravarti, *India and Central Asia*, pp. 24-25.

stick, called *bartanā* or *barthā* in Rajasthan. The astrologers and merchants of Rajasthan made their rough calculations on such wooden 'slates' which were also used in some other parts of India even down to recent times.[1]

The *phalaka*, mentioned in the Jātaka stories in connection with young learners in elementary schools, was apparently wooden slabs or planks while the *Vinayapiṭaka* refers to the early use of wooden boards or bamboo chips as writing material.[2] Bamboo chips called *śalākā*, with the names of the bearers incised on them, served as passports to Buddhist monks. Kātyāyana and Daṇḍin speak respectively of plaints written on boards with *pāṇḍu-lekha* (chalk) and of royal declarations written on a varnished board.[3] A large number of wooden sheets with Kharoṣṭhī writings have been discovered in Central Asia. They are mostly of the nature of letters.[4] Some of these wooden records are wedge-shaped (called *kīla-mudrā* in the documents themselves) and some are rectangular tablets.[5]

There are also some Indian records engraved on wooden subjects, e.g., the pillars from Kirari, the ceiling rib of a Bhaja cave,[6] etc., which properly form the subject of the following section.

1. Ojha, *Bhāratīya Prācīn Lipimālā*, p. 146.

2. Bühler, *Indian Palaeography*, pp. 5, 93.

3. Loc. cit. Manuscripts on varnished boards are common in Burma. The Bodleian Library, Oxford, is said to possess a manuscript on wooden boards, which was secured from Assam. They may however really be sheets of Aloe bark with a layer of wood attached to them (cf. *Journ. As.*, 1958, p. 86). Poor people of U. P. copied religious works on black boards with chalk (R.L. Mitra in Gough's *Collection and Preservation of the Records of Ancient Sanskrit Literature*, 1878, p. 18).

4. See A. M. Boyer, E. J. Rapson, E. Senart and P. S. Noble, *Kharoṣṭhī Inscriptions*, Part I (1920), Part II (1927), Part III (1929); *Select Inscriptions*, pp. 234 ff.

5. See N. P. Chakravarti, *India and Central Asia*, pp. 21 ff.

6. *Ep. Ind.*, Vol. XVIII, pp. 152 ff.; *Indian Archaeology*, 1955-56, Plate XLIV.

Section II

MATERIALS FOR ENGRAVING OR EMBOSSING

1. *Stone*

Stone was used from the earliest times for engraving writing for the purpose of making it *cira-sthitika* or everlasting.[1] Inscriptions were often engraved on rocks, stone pillars or slabs, stone images or their pedestals and stone articles such as jars or their covers, etc.

Sometimes epigraphs were incised without making the surface of the stone sufficiently smooth; but often, especially when an inscription of the eulogy (*praśasti*) type was engraved, the stone was carefully dressed and made very smooth by chiselling and sometimes it was even made shiny by rubbing it with smooth pieces of stone. A record was often composed by a poet or learned man or a high royal officer and was written with ink or chalk on the surface of the stone by a calligraphist, sometimes only a few lines at a time, and ultimately the letters were engraved by an artisan with the help of a chisel. To ensure the straightness of the lines, straight lines were sometimes drawn on the stone with the help of a ruler and chalk or a pointed instrument or of a string dipped in ink or dye as even now used by the carpenters for drawing straight lines on wooden blocks for splitting them into planks.

Generally stone slabs were at first inscribed and then fixed into their proper place in the foundations or walls of temples, step-wells, etc. Such slabs had often raised or lined borders. Stone slabs bearing carefully engraved inscriptions, such as the *Lalitavigraharāja* and *Harakelināṭaka* inscriptions

1. Various kinds of stones were used for engraving inscriptions. We have inscriptions on blocks of basalt or trap, columns of sandstone, prisms of crystal, etc. Precious stones were sometimes used for making seals or medals. For a cornelian seal, see *CII*, Vol. II, Part i, pp. 7-8. Among stone inscriptions, we have official and private records, royal proclamations, treaties between kings, agreements between private individuals, grants and donations, poetical effusions, etc.

in the Ajmer Museum, show that sometimes a break or damage in the stone was covered up with metal.

A single slab of stone was generally used for engraving an inscription; but in some cases it was incised on several slabs, especially when it was a big eulogy or a book. *Rāṇā* Kumbhā's inscription[1] in the Kumbhasvāmin or Māmādeva temple at Kumbhalgadh is written on five stone slabs while the *kāvya* entitled *Rājapraśasti*, written in 24 cantos by an Āndhra poet named Raṇachoḍa on the occasion of the excavation of the Rājasamudra tank by *Rāṇā* Rājasiṁha of Mewar, was engraved on no less than 24 slabs.[2] The *Rājapraśasti* slabs were fixed into the embankment of the said tank. Among other such works incised on stone slabs, mention may be made of Paramāra Bhoja's Prakrit poem entitled *Kūrmaśataka*[3] and Madana's *Pārijātamañjarī* (or *Vijayaśrīnāṭikā*).[4] The *Harakelināṭaka* by the Cāhamāna king Vigraharāja IV (1153-64 A. D.) and the *Lalitavigraharājanāṭaka* by his court poet Someśvara were similarly engraved on stone slabs.[5] A Digambara Jain work called *Unnataśikhara Purāṇa*, composed in 1170 A.D., was engraved on the flat surface of a rock at Bijolia in the Bhilwara District of the Udaipur Division of Rajasthan.[6]

Inscribed and uninscribed pillars of stone, found in different parts of India, are innumerable. They were raised for various purposes in all the ages of Indian history. Amongst the inscribed pillars, the earliest belong to the days of the Maurya emperor Aśoka (c. 272-232 B.C.).[7] These are called *stambha* or *śilā-stambha* (i.e. stone pillar) in the epigraphs they bear. There are some pillars which may be classified as *dhvaja-stambha*[8] or flag-staff (often standing before a temple and bearing inscriptions in some cases), *jaya-stambha* or

1. See *Ep. Ind.*, Vol. XXIV, pp. 304ff.
2. Ibid., Vols. XXIX-XXX, Appendix, pp. 1-123.
3. *Ep. Ind.*, Vol. VIII, pp. 243 ff.
4. Ibid., pp. 101 ff.
5. See Bhandarkar's List, No. 289 and note.
6. Ibid., No. 1854; Ojha, *Bhāratīya Prācīn Lipimāla*, p. 150, note 6.
7. See *CII*, Vol. I, pp. xv ff.
8. Cf., e.g., the Eran pillar inscription of 484 A.D. (ibid., Vol.III, pp. 88 ff.).

victory-pillar[1] (often bearing the eulogy of a conqueror) and *kīrti-stambha* or fame-pillar[2] (often bearing the eulogy of a person who performed a pious deed calculated to render him famous). Certain memorial pillars known as hero-stones[3] (often with inscriptions recording the death of warriors while fighting against enemies) and *satī*-stones[4] (often bearing epigraphs recording the death of widows burning themselves in fire) are found in large numbers in the southern and western regions of India, though they are also known from other parts of the country. Besides these, we have also other kinds of inscribed pillars bearing small inscriptions. Some of these are votive pillars set up in religious establishments by pious men, especially pilgrims, for acquiring religious merit. They are also generally called *stambha* in the records incised on them. Instances of such votive pillars are numerous in the inscriptions discovered in the ruins of old Buddhist *stūpas* like those at Barhut, Sanchi and Nagarjunikonda.[5] There is yet another class of memorial pillars similar to the hero- and *satī*-stones. The erection of such pillars in honour of one's dead relatives is referred to in several records of the early centuries of the Christian era,[6] which mention the object on which they are engraved as *yaṣṭi*. Sometimes the memorial pillar bore the representation of the person in whose memory it was raised. Such a pillar was called *chāyā-stambha* (image-

1. The Eran and Mandasor pillars bearing the inscriptions respectively of Samudragupta and Yaśodharman fall in this class. Cf. *Select Inscriptions*, pp. 260 ff.; 393 ff. A *jaya-stambha* could sometimes be regarded as a *kīrti-stambha*.

2. The Talagunda pillar bearing a *praśasti* of the Kadamba king Kākusthavarman, who excavated a tank near a Śiva temple, belongs to this category. Cf. ibid., pp. 450 ff.

3. See, e.g., *Ep. Ind.*, Vol. XXXI, pp. 323 ff.

4. See, e.g., Hiralal's List, p. 46 (No.78), p.53 (No. 95), etc. In many cases, the inscriptions on the pillars record both the death of a hero and the self-immolation of his widow (cf. ibid., p. 49, No 83). The *satī*-stones are called *māsti* (*mahāsatī*) in Kannaḍa (*A. R. Ep.*, 1951-52, Nos. B69-70, 85); cf. Gujarātī *paliyā*.

5. See Barua and Sinha, *Barhut Inscriptions*; *Ep. Ind.*, Vol II, pp. 95 ff.; Vol. XX, pp. 1 ff.; etc. Cf. *JRASB*, Letters, Vol. XV, 1949 pp. 6-8.

6. See, e.g., *Select Inscriptions*, pp. 35-36, 167-68. They are also called *gotra* for *gotra-śailikā* (*Ep. Ind.*, Vol. XXXIII, p. 172).

pillar).[1] Sacrificial pillars were called *yūpa*. We have a number of inscribed *yūpas* of the early period.[2]

We have also inscriptions on various other objects of stone besides a large number of images and seals.[3]

2. *Earthen Objects*

Among inscriptions on bricks, mention may be made of a number of Buddhist Dhāraṇīs and Sūtras incised on such material as well as royal epigraphs recording achievements like the celebration of the Aśvamedha.[4] Bricks bearing inscriptions of the latter class were apparently fixed into structures like the platform constructed for the performance of the horse-sacrifice.

Sometimes votive records were also engraved on lumps of clay, which were later baked and burnt. Clay seals and sealings, both burnt and unburnt, have been discovered in various sites of North India in large numbers.[5] These seals belonged to private individuals, offices and officials, religious institutions, etc. Earthen pots were often inscribed, generally before being burnt. A large number of potsherds bearing inscriptions have been discovered.[6] Some such pots were meant for being dedicated in favour of religious institutions or were specially made for some particular purpose such as interring

1. Cf. *A.R. Ep.*, 1957-58, No. B 26. While arranging for the burning of a perpetual lamp before a deity, sometimes the lamp was placed in the hands of the image of a dead person made for the purpose. Such lamps were called *chāyā-dīpa* (*SII*, Vol. V., No. 1205).

2. See *Select Inscriptions*, pp. 92-93.

3. For an inscription of votive character on a stone vase, see *Indian Archaeology*, 1955-56, Plate XLIV.

4. For Buddhist works on bricks, see Cunningham, *ASR*, Vol. I, p. 47; Vol. V, p. 102; etc. See also *CII*, Vol. II, Part i, p. 137. For the brick inscriptions referring to the horse-sacrifice performed by kings Devīmitra, Dāmamitra and Śilavarman, see *Ep. Ind.*, Vol. XXX, pp. 118ff.; Vol. XXXIII, pp. 99 ff.; *Indian Archaeology*, 1953-54, Plate XV. For other interesting brick inscriptions, cf. *Ep., Ind.*, Vol. XXI, pp. 193ff.; Vol. XXIV, pp. 20ff.; *A. R. Ep.*, 1951-52, No. B262; 1952-53, Nos. B477, 499-500, 508, 513-14.

5. See, e.g., *Mem. ASI*, No. 66. For terracotta plaques and tablets, see *CII*, Vol. II, Part i, p. 177; *Indian Archaeology*, 1955-56, Plate XLIII; *A. R. Ep.*, 1952-53, No. B489.

6. See, e. g., *CII*, Vol. II, Part i, pp. 173 ff.; *Ep. Ind.*, Vol. XXVIII, pp. 125 ff.

the relics of a *Satī*.[1] As indicated above, the letters were generally either embossed or scratched on moist clay before the earthen material was baked.[2]

Inscribed bricks were sometimes fixed into brick-made pillars.

3. *Shells and Other Non-Metallic Objects*

Some inscribed conch-shells were discovered in the ruins of a Buddhist establishment at Salihundam in the Srikakulam District of Andhra Pradesh.[3] The inscriptions are votive in character.

Seals made of ivory plaques and bearing legends are also known. There are *mantras* engraved on tortoise shells.

Inscriptions were sometimes engraved on wooden objects such as beams and pillars,[4] to which reference has already been made.

4. *Copper*

Among metals, copper was the most popular writing material in ancient and medieval India.

Official charters, especially grants made by kings and subordinate rulers (called *tāmra-patra*, *tāmra-śāsana*, *tāmra*, etc.) were generally engraved on copper plates which served the donees as title-deeds. Fa-hien's statement[5] that, about 400 A.D., Buddhist monasteries in India possessed copper-plate grants some of which dated from the Buddha's time may not be trustworthy; but the practice of issuing copper-plate grants is certainly very old.[6]

Many North Indian royal families incised their charters on one or both sides of single copper plates while most

1. Cf. *JAHRS*, Vol. XIX, pp. 203 ff.
2. Cf. *Proc. ASB*, 1896, pp. 9 ff.; see *Ep. Ind.*, Vol. XXX, pp. 85ff. and Plate.
3. See *Indian Archaeology*, 1953-54, Plate XVII.
4. For inscribed beams, see *ibid.*, 1955-56, Plate XLIV, A.; *A.R.Ep.*, 1952-53, No. B322. For inscribed pillars of wood, see *Ep. Ind.*, Vol. XVIII, pp. 152ff.
5. Beal, *Si-yu-ki*, Vol. I, p. xxxviii.
6. The Sohgaura plate is really a bronze plaque cast from a mould. For details of copper-plate grants, see below.

of the royal families of South India engraved their charters on a number of plates held together by a copper ring passing through holes made in the left or upper margin of the plates. Certain West Indian royal families incised their documents on the inner side of two plates strung often on two rings. Some North Indian royal families like the Bhauma-Nārakas of Assam had their grants engraved on many plates.[1] Royal grants were sometimes engraved on peculiar objects of copper.[2]

The plates, which were small, medium or big in size, were generally oblong in shape. The royal seal, previously fashioned from a mould, was usually fixed to the upper or left margin of single plates and on the joint of the ring holding several plates together. The seals were generally of bronze and were so cast from moulds that the emblems and legends on them appeared on a counter-sunk surface. On plates having the seal fixed at the top, the lines were incised breadthwise, while those having the seal at the left margin had the lines engraved lengthwise. Similarly, the writing on multiplate charters is lengthwise or breadthwise according as the ring holding them passes through holes made in the left or top margin of the plates.

When the holes were made in the upper margin, it was often in the upper margin of the obverse of the plates and in the lower margin on their reverse. When two rings were used to hold the plates together, they generally passed through holes in the upper margin of the plates. For the protection of the writing, the rims of the plates were sometimes thickened or raised and generally the outer sides of the first and last plates of a set were kept blank.

1. See Bhāskaravarman's charters from Nidhanpur and Dubi both engraved on no less than six plates (P. N. Bhattacharya, *Kāmarūpaśāsanāvalī*, pp. 1 ff. ; *Ep. Ind.*, Vol. XXX, pp. 287 ff.).

2. Cf. the Balasore copper axe-head grant of Gajapati Puruṣottama (Bhandarkar's List, No. 1753).

3. According to Bāṇa's *Harṣacarita* (Nirnaysagar Press ed., p. 227), the state seal of king Harṣa was made of gold. The royal seals on cheaper material like bronze or clay were prepared for various purposes. The moulds were probably of metal or burnt clay.

The engraving was done sometimes from a draft. Often the text was written on the plates with ink or was scratched with a needle and the letters were cut according to their shapes thus drawn by means of a chisel. Sometimes, especially in certain South Indian records, the engraving looks like scratching and it is possible that, in such cases, the surface of the plate was covered with a layer of a substance like mud and the writing was done, when it was in a semi-dried condition, by means of a graver. The engraving of the letters in some early epigraphs like the Kalwan plate[1] is done by dots instead of continuous strokes.

Mistakes in the grants engraved were generally left uncorrected. But, in certain cases, the wrong letters were rubbed off or beaten in by hammering and the correct letters were re-engraved on the erasures. In some of the medieval copper-plate grants, the corrections were engraved in the margins of a plate occasionally with indications of the omission or correction.

Occasionally old or rejected copper plates were utilized for engraving fresh charters. Although they were often thoroughly refashioned, in some cases the old writing was beaten in by hammering and the new text was re-engraved. In the latter case, traces of the older writing are often still noticeable. We have a number of such palimsests.[2]

The plates of copper were fashioned with hammer by the brazier and some of them still exhibit traces of hammering. A number of the plates are small, thin and light while others are big, thick and heavy. The Taxila plate of Patika is so thin that it was found bent double and it weighs only 3½ ounces. The size of a plate depended on factors like the length of the writing to be engraved (i.e. the nature of the draft used in a particular area), the size of the letters in the copy prepared by the clerk, etc. The smiths made the plates according to the size of the clerks' drafts received by them. When the drafts were written on palmyra leaves, the

1. *Ep. Ind.*, Vol. XXI, p. 259 and Plate.
2. See, e.g., ibid., Vol. XXV, Plate facing p. 191.

plates were narrow and long, while, for copying drafts on birch bark, the plates required to be much broader, sometimes almost square. The plates used by the Vijayanagara kings were shaped like stone stelae. The copper-plate grants of the kings of the Maitraka dynasty of Valabhī clearly show how the size of the documents increased with the increase in the length of the eulogies. The eulogies in the records of the later members of the family had to mention a much larger number of predecessors.

Some inscriptions engraved on copper plates are not grants. A few such records are the *yantras* of the Brāhmaṇas and Jains, engraved on copper plates of various shapes and sizes. The practice of engraving books on copper plates is also known. According to a tradition recorded by Hiuen-tsang, Kaniṣka caused the Buddhist religious texts to be engraved on copper plates.[1] There is also a story that Sāyaṇa's commentary on the Vedas was engraved on copper plates.[2] Whether these traditions are genuine or not, we have actually the Tāllapāka-ṅvari works in Telugu engraved on many copper plates preserved at Tirupati.[3]

We have a number of copper statues bearing inscriptions on their bases. Objects of general use made of copper were often inscribed[4] and the custom is still prevalent. Such inscriptions were usually either votive or indicative of the ownership of the objects. There are also small Buddhist texts engraved on copper plaques or seals.[5]

5. *Gold and Silver*

There are references in Buddhist literature to family

1. See Beal, *Si-yu-ki*, Vol. I, p. 155; Watters, *On Yuan Chwang's Travels in India*, Vol. I, p. 271. Cf. the Kasia copper plate containing the *Nidānasūtra* in Sanskrit and deposited by a person in the local *Nirvāṇacaitya* (Bhandarkar's List, No. 1754).
2. Cf. Burnell, *Elements of South Indian Palaeography*, p. 86.
3. *A. R. Ep.*, 1912, No. 568.
4. See the Taxila copper vase and ladle inscriptions (*CII*, Vol. II, Part i, pp. 87 ff.), the Jamalgarhi lamp inscription (ibid., p. 116), the Palatu Dheri jar inscriptions (ibid., p. 120), the Wardak (Khawat) vase inscription (ibid., pp. 165 ff.), etc. For an inscribed copper cauldron, see *Ep. Ind.*, Vol. XVI, p. 15.
5. See *Indian Archaeology*, 1954-55, Plate XLIX. ; *A. R. Ep.*, 1956, No: B120.

records of rich merchants, royal orders and religious regulations being engraved on golden plates[1] while Burnell refers to the practice of engraving royal letters and land grants on such plates.[2] We have some gold records including a plate bearing a votive inscription in Kharoṣṭhī discovered in the ruins of Taxila.[3] But gold is too precious a metal to be generally used for such purposes.

Among the few inscriptions on silver plates,[4] mention may be made of the Bhattiprolu[5] and Taxila[6] inscriptions. The Jains sometimes write certain *yantras* on plates of silver, which are found in some Jain temples.[7] But, being a precious metal, silver was rarely used for such purposes.

The engraving of the owner's name on silver objects is old.[8]

6. *Bronze, Iron and Other Metals*

Many bronze images bear inscriptions, in most cases on the pedestal. An inscribed bronze casket was discovered

1. See Bühler, op. cit., p. 95; Ojha, op. cit., p. 5, notes 6-8. Gold plates with Buddhist Dhāraṇīs inscribed on them have been discovered outside India (cf. *Bulletin of the Archaeological Survey of the Republic of Indonesia*, No. 4, 1958, p. 3).

2. *Elements of South Indian Palaeography*, pp. 90, 93.

3. Cf. Cunningham, *ASR*, Vol. II, pp. 129-30, Plate LIX; *CII*, Vol. II, Part i, pp. 83 ff. A few Buddhist records engraved on gold plates have been discovered in India and Burma. See *Select Inscriptions*, pp. 462 ff. The British Museum is stated to possess some manuscripts on gold-plated palmyra leaves (Bühler, op. cit., p. 95). A book of 24 thick golden leaves bound together by a copper wire was found from the Dhāmdaha tank (Dacca District, East Bengal) and was melted down (Bhattasali, *Icon. Bud. Brahm. Sculp Dac. Mus.*, p. x). For the gold jars, bowl, pendant and palanquin of a deity with inscriptions, see *A. R. Ep.*, 1952-53, Nos. B 345-48

4. See Burnell, *Elements of South Indian Palaeography*, p. 87; Rea, *Mem. Arch. Surv. Ind.*, No. 15, p. 13, Plate XXII; *Journ. Pali T. Soc.*, 1883, pp. 134 ff. In the British Museum, there are manuscripts on silver-plated palmyra leaves (Bühler, *Indian Palaeography*, p. 95).

5. Bühler, op. cit., p. 95.

6. *Ep. Ind.*, Vol. XIV, p. 295; *CII*, Vol. II, Part i, pp. 70 ff.; *Select Inscriptions*, pp. 129-30. This is the Taxila silver scroll inscription of 79 A.D., which is very thin and measures only $6\frac{1}{4}$ inches by $1\frac{3}{8}$ inches. Silver inscriptions from Taxila include cups, plate with three legs, a circular plate, a silver sieve, a disc, etc. See *CII*, Vol. II, Part i, pp. 97 ff., p. 151.

7. Ojha, *Bhāratīya Prācīn Lipimālā*, p. 152, note 5.

8. See the Taxila silver vase inscription of 34 A.D. (*Select Inscriptions*, p. 131).

at Manikiala.[1] The early inscription known as the Sohgaura copper plate is really written on a small bronze plaque.[2] The seals affixed to the copper-plate grants are generally made of bronze. They often bear a legend along with the royal emblems and were cast in moulds and later affixed to the plates on the copper rings on which the plates were strung or on the plates themselves when the charters were incised on single plates.

Canons of the late medieval period often bear inscriptions.[3] The Mehrauli (near Delhi) iron pillar bears an inscription[4] of king Candra who is probably identical with Candragupta II (376-413 A.D.) of the Imperial Gupta dynasty of Magadha. A huge iron trident in the Acaleśvara temple on Mount Abu bears an inscription[5] of Vikrama 1468, Phālguna-sudi 15.

The bells in many temples bear inscriptions recording their gift in favour of the temples in question.[6] The practice of incising the owner's name on bell-metal utensil is well known, although it cannot be regarded as a popular material for engraving.[7]

Inscribed plates or plaques of brass, etc., were sometimes nailed on the doors of temples.[8]

1. *CII*, Vol. II, Part i, p. 150.

2. *JAS*, Letters, Vol. XVIII, pp. 1 ff. The plate, which was not fashioned by hammering as in the case of most copper plates, was cast in a mould of sand. The letters and emblems were previously scratched into the mould with a pointed instrument. They therefore appear on the plate in relievo.

3. Cf. Bhandarkar's List, Nos. 1141-43, 1148-49, 1152-53, etc.

4. *Select Inscriptions*, pp. 275 ff.

5. Cf. Ojha, op. cit., p. 154.

6. There are incribed bells, e.g., in the Bodhagaya and Tripurāsundarī (Udaypur, Tripura State) shrines.

7. Amongst other rare metals used for writing, mention may be made of tin and lead. A Buddhist manuscript on tin sheets is preserved in the British Museum (Bühler, op. cit., p. 96) while lead coins sometimes bearing legends were issued by the kings such as those of the Śātavāhana dynasty.

8. Cf. *A.R. Ep.*, 1953-54, No. B135.

Section III

INK AND PEN

1. *Ink*

Ink for writing is called *maṣi*, *maṣī*, *masi* or *masī* and *melā* in Sanskrit. It was prepared with lamp-black or charcoal mixed in water with gum, sugar, etc. The ink was put in pots called in Sanskrit *masī-bhājana*, *melāmandā*, *melāndhu*, *melāndhukā*, *maṣimaṇi*, *maṣi-pātra*, *maṣi-bhāṇḍa*, *maṣi-kūpikā*, etc.

Writing ink was generally of two kinds, viz. lasting and washable, the first of which was used in copying manuscripts and the second for writing things like letters and the account-books of shop-keepers. Cheap ink was made of lamp-black mixed with catechu, gum, etc.

For preparing lasting ink, the resin of the pipal tree was ground nicely and mixed with water kept for sometime in an earthen pot. It was then boiled on fire and a quantity of nicely ground borax and *lodhra* was mixed with it while boiling. This thing was ultimately strained through cloth. To the liquid thus prepared[1] was mixed lamp-black, made by burning sesame oil in lamps, in order to make the colour of the liquid sufficiently black. This process of preparing black ink was prevalent in Rajasthan till recent times.[2]

The ink for writing manuscripts on birch-bark sheets was made by boiling the powder of the burnt husk of almond in cow's urine.[3] Writing in this ink could not be washed away with water.

Among coloured inks, red ink was the most popular. Often *alakta*, referred to above, was used for writing. Another kind of red ink was made of vermilion mixed with gum in

1. This was called *alakta* used by women for dying certain parts of their body especially the feet and the lips.

2. See Ojha, op. cit., p. 155.

3. Bühler's Kashmir Report, p. 30.

water. Red ink was used to write particular expressions and passages (e.g. colophons of chapters) in a manuscript, on which the copyist wanted to put special stress.

By mixing green colour with gum in boiling water, people prepared green ink. Similarly yellow ink was made from the yellow orpiment. Such special inks were used as red ink was done. For deleting a letter or a group of letters, often it was covered with yellow orpiment or encircled by a line or endowed with one or more small vertical strokes above the letter or letters. These marks were sometimes made in coloured ink. Coloured ink is mentioned in the Puranic sections dealing with the donation of manuscripts.[1] Chalk, red lead or minium (*hiṅgula*) was generally used as a substitute for ink.[2]

Gold and silver powder was mixed with gum in boiling water in order to prepare golden and silvery ink respectively. Such costly inks were used generally by painters. But sometimes they were used in writing letters and manuscripts on behalf of rich people.[3]

The writing on cloth and birch bark referred to by Nearchus and Curtius suggests that ink was used by the Indians in the 4th century B.C. The word *lipi*, from the root *lip*, found in Pāṇini's grammar (c. 5th century B. C.) and the inscriptions of Aśoka (c. 272-232 B.C.), points to the same conclusion. A pre-Christian record written in ink has been found on a relic vessel from the ruins of Andher.[4] One of the earliest manuscripts written in ink is the Kharoṣṭhī *Dhammapada* from Khotan. Several records painted in ink on stone have been discovered in different parts of India.[5]

2. *Pen and Other Instruments*

Lekhanī (literally 'the instrument for writing') is a

1. Hemādri's Dānakhaṇḍa, pp. 549 ff. See R. L. Mitra, *Notices of Sans. Mss.*, p. 3, Plate 1.
2. Bühler, op. cit., p. 98.
3. See Ojha, *Bhāratīya Prācīn Lipimālā*, p. 156, note 1.
4. Cunningham, *Bhilsa Topes*, p. 349, Plate XXX, 6; cf. pp. 295-308.
5. Cunningham, *ASR*, Vol. XXI, p. 119, Plate XXX; *Ep. Ind.*, Vol. XXVIII, p. 275; Vol. XXXI, p. 168; etc.

general name for the stilus, pencil, brush, pen, etc.[1] *Varṇikā*, mentioned in early Indian literature, was a wooden pen, pointed at the end without a slit. It was used by young learners at the elementary schools. *Iṣikā* or *iṣīkā* was originally a pen made of reed or bamboo branch. It was used by the copyists of manuscripts. The *varṇa-vartikā* mentioned in the *Daśakumāracarita* (Ucchvāsa II) may have been a kind of brush. The word *kalama* may have been adopted in Sanskrit from Greek through Arabic. But it is recognised as a Sanskrit word in the Sanskrit-Chinese lexicons of the 8th century A. D.[2]

For scratching letters on palmyra leaves, iron pens with sharp points were in use especially in the southern parts of the country. Sometimes ornamental designs at the end of chapters in palmyra-leaf manuscripts written in ink were drawn with such iron pens. The prevalent Sanskrit name for the instrument is *śalākā* (Marāṭhī *salaī*). Rājaśekhara's *Kāvyamīmāṁsā*[3] refers to it as *loha-kaṇṭaka* or iron needle used to write on *tāla-dala* whereas *lekhanī* and *masī-bhājana* are mentioned in connection with writing on *tāḍi-patra* and birch birk. The work also mentions other writing materials as *phalaka* (a board) and *khaṭikā* (a piece of chalk), both preserved in a small box, and refers or the practice of writing on well-cleaned *bhittis* meaning floors or walls.

A kind of ruler (called *kāmbī* or *kambā* in Rajasthan) was used for drawing straight lines in order to keep the lines of writing straight. Another instrument for drawing straight lines used by the copyists of manuscripts was called *rekhā-pāṭī* or *samāsa-pāṭī* which was a piece of wood or cardboard with strings fixed at equal distances.[4]

1. Cf. however the information from the *Kāvyamimāṁsā* referred to below.

2. P.C. Bagchi, *Deux Lexiques Sanskrit-Chinois*, Tome I, p. 287.

3. G. O. S. ed., p. 50.

4. See Ojha, op. cit., pp. 157-58. For its probable predecessors, see *Annecdota Oxoniensia*, I, iii, p. 66; *Anzeiger d. W. Akademie*, 1897, No. VIII.

CHAPTER IV

PREPARATION AND PRESERVATION OF RECORDS

1. *Writing and Engraving*

The practices of writing the letters of a record with ink on a softer material and of scratching or engraving them on a hard substance were both popular in ancient India. The royal charters were generally written at first on a perishable material and then engraved usually on copper plates and occassionally on stones.

In ancient and medieval India, specialised learning in various branches of the sciences and arts and in the sacred lore was more or less the monopoly of the Brāhmaṇa community. But secular learning of the three R's was available to the upper classes among the non-Brahmanical communities, members of which sometimes acquired proficiency in Sanskrit and produced poetical works of considerable merit.[1] Literate people of these classes often took the writer's profession and, as a result, the communities of professional writers gradually came into being even in the early period.

The common expression for the writer of a document or the copyist of a manuscript was *lekhaka* which also indicated a professional clerk.[2] Often people of the Brāhmaṇa community also adopted this profession. Among copyists of manuscripts there are many Brāhmaṇas. Buddhist and Jain monks are known to have copied works of their religious literature.

1. See the poems composed by the Māthura-Kāyastha brothers Jayasiṁha and Śivanābhaka in *Ep. Ind.*, Vol. XXXII, pp. 336 ff.; Vol. XXXIII, pp. 31 ff., pp. 65 ff.

2. Cf. the word *lipikara* in the inscriptions of Aśoka (*Select Inscriptions*, p. 40, text line 6; p. 53, note 9) and the designation *rāja-lipikara* sometimes occurring in early inscriptions (*Ep. Ind.*, Vol. II, p. 102).

In copper-plate grants, the writer is generally called *Kāyastha*[1] and *Karaṇika*[2] or *Karaṇin*[3] (i.e. an officer belonging to the *Karaṇa*[4] meaning 'the office of administration'). The epigraphic records sometimes mention the *Karaṇika-Brāhmaṇa*[5] and *Karaṇa-Kāyasthsa.*[6] While early legal authorities[7] mention Karaṇa as a tribe, medieval lexicons[8] recognise *Kāyastha* and *Karaṇa* as synonymous terms meaning a 'scribe' or 'a member of the writer class.' These facts may suggest that the tribal people called Karaṇa adopted, in some parts of India, the profession of scribes while the Kāyasthas were originally a professional class of accountant-scribes, the whole group of writers being later crystallised into a sort of caste called Kāyastha or Karaṇa. The Persian word *dabir*, 'writer', is found in Indian epigraphs as *dibira* or *divira.*[9] It was probably introduced into the western areas of India, which once came under the influence of the Śakas and the Sassanians of Iran.

1. The *Kāyasthas* first occur in the inscriptions of the Gupta age (cf. *Select Inscriptions*, p. 284; etc.). Vijñāneśvara explains the word occurring in the *Yājñavalkyasmṛti* (I, 336) as *gaṇako lekhakaś=ca*, i.e. an accountant-scribe, for which see also the *Mahābhārata*, 11, 5, 72. The word *kāya-stha* literally means 'one who stays in the body [of another]'. An officer who sat beside his master in discharging his duties and was generally the chief intermediary between his master and the latter's clients may have been called *Kāyastha* because he was staying in the person of his master as it were. See *Bhār. Vid.*, Vol. X, 1949, pp. 280 ff.

2. *Ep. Ind.*, Vol. I, pp. 81, 129, 16?, etc. Kielhorn explains *Karaṇika* as 'a writer of a *karaṇa* (a legal document)'. The *Karaṇika* is the same as *Karaṇattāṉ* (Sanskrit *Karaṇastha*?) of Tamil inscriptions (*Ep. Ind.*, Vol. XXV, p. 132), mentioned along with *Kaṇakku* (Sanskrit *Gaṇaka*), i.e. the present day *Karaṇam* (accountant-scribe) of South India.

3. *Ind. Ant.*, Vol. XII, p. 122; *Harṣacarita*, Nirnayasagar Press ed., p. 227.

4. *Ep. Ind.*, Vol. XXIV, p. 128.

5. Bhandarkar's List, No. 350.

6. See *Ind. Ant.*, Vol. XVII, p. 13; Bendall, *Cat. Sans. Budh. Mss.*, p. 70, No. 1364.

7. *Manusmṛti*, X, 20; *Yājñavalkyasmṛti*, I, 92.

8. Cf. *Vaijayantī*, p. 78, l. 147 (*Karaṇa*, writer of the king); p. 137, l. 4 (*Karaṇa*, writer); p. 137, l. 45 (*Kāyastha*, writer). The Karaṇa community of Orissa is similar to the Kāyasthas of Bengal and elsewhere in North India. For the mention of the Karaṇas in the early medieval inscriptions of Orissa, see *Ep. Ind.*, Vol. XXIV, p. 175, text line 15.

9. *CII*, Vol. III, p. 122 (Khoh plate of 496 A. D.); *Ind. Ant.*, Vol. VI, p. 10; etc.

As regards private records on stone, their text was usually prepared by a professional writer and a copy of it was given to the engraver who was generally a mason called a *sūtradhāra*, *śilākūṭa*, *rūpakāra*, *śilpin*, etc. The mason at first dressed the stone and drew the letters on it with ink, etc., under the supervision and guidance of the writer and then engraved the letters. Sometimes the professional writer himself copied the text of the document on the stone for the guidance of the engraver. We have some records, the letters of which are painted on stone, the intention of engraving them at a later date remaining unmaterialised.[1] The amount of carelessness noticed in a large number of private epigraphs on stone however indicates that often incompetent masons engraved the records without getting the letters drawn previously on the stone.

For royal records, a learned man of the court was engaged to prepare a fair copy of the text on a sheet of birch bark, etc., or to write it on the stone slabs or copper plates with ink or a pointed instrument. The copy of the document was written on a sheet of the size of the stone on which it had to be engraved. The text of a copper-plate grant was generally prepared by a high officer of the king, although the eulogistic poems appearing in medieval grants were composed by the court poets.

The practice of writing the text of a document on the plates first in ink is clearly indicated by a copper plate discovered at Kasia (Gorakhpur District, Uttar Pradesh), which bears 13 lines of writing of which only the first is incised while the remaining 12 are written in black ink.[2] This was meant to facilitate the work of engraving and also to ensure the correctness of the inscription. In many of the cases, the writing was done by a professional scribe of the court and the engraver incised the letters according to the drawing, although some-

1. See *Ep. Ind.*, Vol. XXXI, p. 168; above, p. 81.

2. *An. Rep. Arch. Surv. Ind.*, 1910-11, p. 74. This inscription must have been first written out in ink on the plate and then the plate was given to the engraver to cut the written letters into the metal.

times, especially in the case of minor ruling families, the engravers themselves wrote the text on the plates or engraved the text on the plates without previously drawing the letters on them.

The Deopada stone inscription[1] of king Vijayasena of Bengal is known to have been engraved by a renowned artist named Śūlapāṇi who was the head of a guild of the artisans of Varendra (North Bengal) and enjoyed the feudatory title of *Rāṇaka*. The neat and beautiful incision of the inscription excites the readers' admiration. The Talagunda inscription,[2] which is a *praśasti* composed by Kubja, the court poet of the Kadamba king Śāntivarman of the Kannaḍa country, was written on the stone slab by the poet himself so that the engraver succeeded in performing his work neatly without committing mistakes. The number of inscriptions carelessly written and engraved is, however, by far larger than those written and engraved carefully.

On some early copper plates the letters are formed by means of dots instead of continuous strokes.[3] The engraving on some copper-plate grants from South India is so shallow that the letters appear to have been scratched on them by a sharp-pointed needle, as on the palmyra leaves, probably after putting a layer of mud on the plates.[4]

According to Kalhaṇa's *Rājataraṅgiṇī*,[5] the officer-in-charge of the preparation of documents at the Kashmirian court was called *Paṭṭopādhyāya* (i.e. a professional teacher in charge of the preparation of title-deeds), who belonged to the *Akṣapaṭala* department which Stein understands as the Accountant General's office and Bühler as the Record office or the Daftar or Court of Rolls.[6] In inscriptions, a similar

1. *Ep. Ind.*, Vol. I, pp. 307 ff.
2. Ibid., Vol. VIII, pp. 31 ff. and Plate. See verse 34 of the record.
3. See the Taxila and Kalwan plates (ibid., Vol. IV, pp. 55 f. and Plate; Vol. XXI, p. 259 and Plate); above, p. 76.
4. Cf. ibid., Vol. XXVII, Plates between pp. 128 and 129, 130 and 131; above, p. 76.
5. V, verses 397 f.
6. Cf. Bühler, *Indian Palaeography*, p. 102; below, p. 99.

royal officer is sometimes mentioned as *Dharmalekhin*, *Śāsanika*, *Śāsanādhikārika*, *Śāsanādhikārin*, etc.[1]

Often illiterate or semi-literate stone-cutters or goldsmiths were entrusted with the task of engraving records on stone or copper plates, and this fact accounts for the numerous errors noticed in a large number of epigraphs, especially those engraved on behalf of private individuals.[2] We have also many instances of badly engraved records even among royal charters, particularly those issued by minor ruling chiefs.[3] The Banaras plate[4] of Kalacuri Karṇa (c. 1040-71) offers an instance of an imperial charter written and engraved by irresponsible and incompetent persons. But the grant was made when the king was stationed at Prayāga (Allahabad) in the course of a tour of pilgrimage and it is possible that the work of engraving the charter was entrusted to a local artisan who could not read the writing of the draft properly. Usually, however, powerful kings had in their service trained and competent engravers who performed their work creditably. The minor errors noticed in the records of imperial ruling families are due generally to the scribes and not to the engravers.

The name of the person who engraved the copper-plate grants is often mentioned in medieval records. The word for 'engraved' is generally *utkīrṇa* and rarely *utkīlita*, etc. These engravers were artisans styled the *pitalahāra*, *lohakāra* or *ayaskāra*, i.e. a brazier, blacksmith or coppersmith,[5] the *sūtradhāra*, i.e. a mason,[6] the *hemakāra* or *sūnāra*, i.e. a goldsmith,[7]

1. *Ind. Ant.*, Vol. XVI, p. 208; Vol. XX, p. 315; *Ep. Ind.*, Vol. XI, pp. 115, 314; Vol. XXVIII, p. 189; etc.
2. See, e.g., *Ep. Ind.*, Vol. XXVIII, pp. 44 ff., p. 145; *JBRS*, Vol. XXXVII, Parts 3-4, pp. 7 ff.; Vol. XLI, Part 2, pp. 1 ff.; etc. According to the *Mitākṣarā* on the *Yājñavalkyasmṛti* (II, 89), a royal deed had to be written in correct and elegant language, although documents of ordinary people were not required to be written in correct Sanskrit and could be written in local dialects.
3. See, e. g., *Ep. Ind.*, Vol. XXVIII, pp. 112 ff.; pp. 276 ff.; pp. 290 ff.; pp. 324 ff.; etc.
4. Ibid., Vol. II, pp. 305 ff.
5. See ibid., Vol. IV, p. 170; *Ind. Ant.*, Vol. XVII, pp. 227, 230, 236; etc.
6. *Ind. Ant.*, Vol. XV, p. 360.
7. *Ep. Ind.*, Vol. III, p. 314; *Ind. Ant.*, Vol. XVIII, p. 17.

the *śilpin*, *vijñānin* or *vijñānika*, i.e. an artisan,[1] etc. In the inscriptions of the Ganjam-Srikakulam region, the engraver is often mentioned as the *akṣaśālin*, *ākṣaśālika*, *arkaśālin akhasāle*, etc. This refers to the goldsmith caste now called Akasāle in the Telugu- and Kannaḍa-speaking areas.

There were manuals for the guidance of the clerks for the preparation of documents. Kṣemendra Vyāsadāsa's *Lokaprakāśa* shows how different kinds of bonds, bills of exchange (*huṇḍi*), etc., were to be drafted while the *Lekhapañcāśikā* indicates how private letters as well as land-grants, treaties, etc., should be drawn.[2] One such work entitled *Lekhapaddhati* containing numerous specimens of letters and documents of various kinds has been published in the Gaekwad Oriental Series. The *praśast-āvali* works of Mithilā deal with the epistolary art and contain forms of communications to be addressed to feudatory and imperial rulers, both indigenous and foreign, as well as to one's feudatories, learned men, private citizens, etc. They also contain specimens of private communications. A notable work of this class is the *Patrakaumudī* ascribed to Vararuci.[3]

In the schools, pupils generally copied their text books from their teachers' copies. Rich men used to engage professional scribes for copying manuscripts for them. These manuscripts were generally written with great care.

2. *Illustration and Ornamentation*

Some medieval inscriptions contain illustrations of the artificial arrangement of the letters of verses in *bandhas* known as *padma-bandha*, *sarpa-bandha*, etc.[4] In a few cases, the lotus symbol is found without letters in it.[5] Sometimes the letters of an inscription, especially the signs above and below the letters,

1. Cf. *Ind. Ant.*, Vol. XVII, p. 234; Vol. XVI, p. 208.
2. See Bühler, *Indian Palaeography*, p. 102.
3. K.P. Jayaswal, *A Descriptive Catalogue of Manuscripts in Mithila*, Vol. II, pp. 12-13, Nos. 71 ff., 85ff. Another work of the same kind is Dalapati's *Yāvanapáripāṭyanukrama* (*Itihāsa*, Bengali, Vol. IX, pp. 71-72). Cf. below, p. 106.
4. See, e.g., *Ep. Ind.*, Vol. XXXI, Plate facing p. 85; cf. Plates facing pp. 28-29. See also ibid., Vol. XXXIV, Plate facing p. 82; Sreenivasachar, op. cit., Part II, Plate 49; Part III, Plates 22, 31.
5. Sreenivasachar, op. cit., Part II, Plate 47.

are given an ornamental shape.[1] In some cases, this was done in respect of only some of the letters.[2]

Sometimes the contents of the inscription are indicated by an engraved or sculptured representation. Thus the symbols of the sun and the moon or the stars are found incised on numerous medieval records in order to indicate that the epigraphs record grants made for as long a time as the sun and the moon or the stars would endure.[3] Similarly the engraved representation of a female or a sow under a donkey on inscribed stone slabs indicates the curse that the father of a violator of the grant recorded would become a donkey and his mother a sow or that his mother would be molested by a donkey.[4]

The sculptured representation of one or more females with the right hands raised upwards or only of hands raised upwards (i.e. pointing to heaven) indicated that the inscriptions in question recorded the commitment of *Satī* by a lady or several ladies who went to heaven as a result of the meritorious act.[5] Inscriptions recording the deaths of heroes in battle generally bear sculptures depicting a warrior sometimes as dead or as engaged in fighting.[6] In many cases, the *Satī*- and hero-stones bearing such representations do not bear any inscription apparently because the meaning of the representations was easily understood.

Some other kinds of memorial inscriptions also bear sculptured representations of the persons concerned.[7] An interesting class of these records depicts devotees offering their heads to a god or goddess.[8]

Besides the above kinds of ornamentation, some medieval records, especially copper plates, sometimes bear the repre-

1. See Ojha, op. cit., Plates XV and XXI.
2. Ibid., Plates XX and XXI.
3. See, e.g., *Ep. Ind.*, Vol. XXXII, Plate facing p. 170; Sreenivasachar, op. cit., Part II, Plate 43. In the medieval records of the Andhra region, a figure of the Śivaliṅga is sometimes added to the above symbols. See Sreenivasachar, op. cit., Plate 52; ibid., Part III, Plates 28-29.
4. See, e.g., *Ep. Ind.*, Vol. XII, Plate facing p. 28; Vol. XXXV, p. 187.
5. See, e.g., *Ancient India*, No. 9, Plate CXII, No. 1.
6. See, e. g., *Ep. Ind.*, Vol. XXX, Plate facing p. 279.
7. Cf. *SII*, Vol. IX, Part i, Plate facing p. 20. For inscribed *chāyā-stambhas*, see *Ep. Ind.*, Vol. XXXIV, p. 20. Cf. above, pp. 72-73.
8. See, e.g., *Ancient India*, No. 9, Plate CXI.

sentation of the royal crest instead of the regular seal[1] or the royal coat of arms.[2] Mention need not be made here of inscriptions which are labels to sculptures or are incised on the pedestals of images.

Manuscripts were sometimes illustrated.

3. *Omission, Correction and Pagination*

In both manuscripts and inscriptions, a letter omitted by 'the scribe through oversight was generally written above or below the line near the spot of omission with or without any indication.[3] Often letters or groups of them thus omitted were engraved in the margin and, in such cases, generally the number of the line, in which the matter written above or below the record would ha e to be read, was indicated by mentioning its number counted in the first case from the top and in the latter from the bottom.[4] Sometimes the place of omission is indicated by a sign.[5]

In line 31 of the Kalsī inscription (Rock Edict XII) of Aśoka, the passage *ti apaśalahā vā*, wrongly written originally, is struck out by cancellation strokes and the correction *pala-pāśaṁḍa-galahā va* is incised above the line.[6] On copper plates, such passages are generally rubbed off by chiselling or beaten in by hammering and the correction re-engraved on the erasure.[7] But a letter or a group of them, when detected to have been wrongly engraved, was sometimes altered to other letters without erasing the former.[8] Old and invalid copper-plate records coming into the possession of the Government were no doubt melted in order to fashion new plates for fresh use.

1. See, e. g., *Ep. Ind.*, Vol. XXXI, Plate facing p. 72; Vol. XXXII, Plate facing p. 156.
2. See *JAS*, Letters and Science, Vol. XXIII, pp. 13ff., Plate B.
3. See, e. g., *Ep.Ind.*, Vol. XXXI, p. 116, note 4; p. 120, note 1; p. 123, note 3.
4. See, e.g., ibid., p. 122, note 2; p. 125, note 4; p. 126, notes 1, 4-7; p. 127, notes 2-3.
5. See, e.g., the cases cited in the previous note.
6. Hultzsch, op. cit., p. 42, note 14. For cases of scoring off on the copper plates, see, e.g., *Ep. Ind.*, Vol. XXXI, p. 117, notes 1 and 3; p. 118, note 2; p. 119, notes 2, 3-4; p. 120, note 2; p. 123, notes 2, 4; p. 125, note 6; p. 126, note 2.
7. See , e.g., *JAS*, Letters, Vol. XX, 1954, pp. 209 ff.; above, p. 76.
8. cf. *Ep. Ind.*, Vol. XXXIV, p. 163, note 6.

But occasionally the entire writing of an inscription on copper plates was beaten in by hammering and a totally new record was re-engraved on them. This kind of palimsests is often met with.[1] In manuscripts, wrong passages were often covered with turmeric paste and the erasure was either kept blank or the correction was re-written on it.

In later inscriptions and manuscripts, the spot of omission was indicated often by a small upright or inclined cross, generally called *kāka-pāda* or *haṁsa-pāda*.[2] Instead of the cross, the *svastika* symbol was also used.[3]

In South Indian manuscripts, the cross was used also as an indication of intentional omission which, as well as defective passages in the original quoted in the commentaries, were marked elsewhere in the country by dots or short strokes above or beneath the line.[4] The symbol of an ear-ring (*kuṇḍala*) or a *svastika* was sometimes used to mark unintelligible passages.[5] A globular mark was sometimes engraved below a letter to indicate that it was wrongly engraved and should not be taken into account.[6] A similar practice is referred to in Śrīharṣa's *Naiṣadhīya*[7] which speaks of a circle being drawn round a letter as a mark of cancellation.

The leaves of a manuscript, not their pages, were given consecutive numbers. The number of a leaf was usually put on its reverse except in the southern areas where it was generally written on the obverse of the leaf.[8] In royal charters engraved on more than two copper plates, the numbering of the plates is sometimes noticed. Such multiplate royal records were more popular in the central and southern regions of India and only in some cases the plates are numbered. Some-

1. See, e.g., *Ep. Ind.*, Vol. XXV, Plate facing p. 191; Vol. XXIII, Plate facing p. 106; above, p. 76.
2. See, e.g., ibid., Vol. III, p. 52, Plate 2, line 1; p. 276, line 11.; above, p. 6.
3. See, e.g., *Ind. Ant.*, Vol. VI, p. 32, Plate 3.
4. See Bühler, op. cit., p. 91.
5. Loc. cit.; cf. Bühler's Kashmir Report, p. 71; Kielhorn, *Mahābhāṣya*, Vol. II, p. 10, note.
6. See *Ep. Ind.*, Vol. XXVIII, p. 262 and Plate, text line 12 (cf. the mark below *pa* at the end of the line).
7. See I, 14.; cf. *Journ. Or. Inst.*, Vol. III, pp. 267-68.
8. See Bühler, *Indian Palaeography*, p. 92.

times they bear the numbers on the obverse as in the case with the southern manuscripts;[1] but the first plate, with its obverse often blank, bears the number on the reverse.[2] In rare cases, the obverse and reverse of a plate in multiplate records are both numbered as in the case of a modern book.[3]

4. *Auspicious Symbols*

A *maṅgala*, i. e. a benediction or an auspicious word, at the beginning, in the middle and at the end of a composition was believed to ensure its completion and preservation. The auspicious word *siddham* is found at the beginning of numerous early records.[4] This word was in later times generally indicated by a symbol of varying shape. The symbol was sometimes followed by the auspicious word *svasti* which, in some cases, stands singly at the beginning of epigraphic records.[5] Sometimes the *maṅgala*: *siddhir=astu*, having the same import as *siddham*, as also a bigger *maṅgala* sentence beginning with *svasty=astu*, is found at the end of the documents.[6] In some cases again a symbol, which is apparently a variant of the *siddham* sign, appears at the end of a document and, in rare cases, also in the body of its text especially at the end of a section of it.[7] Besides the *siddham* symbol, various other auspicious symbols also appear in inscriptions.

Al-Bīrūnī regarded the auspicious symbol at the beginning of inscriptions as indicating the *praṇava* or the sound *Om*.[8] N. K. Bhattasali challenged the authority of Al-Bīrūnī and

1. See, e. g., *Ep. Ind.*, Vol. I, pp. 1 ff.; Vol. III, pp. 156, 300; *Select Inscriptions*, Plates between pp. 408 and 409.

2. See, e.g., *Ep. Ind.*, Vol. XXXI, Plates between pp. 4 and 5.

3. See, e.g., ibid., Vol. VI, pp. 86 ff. and Plates.

4. See, e.g., *Select Inscriptions*, pp. 157, 160, 164, 165, 169, 176, 191, 193, 196, 200, 203, 204, 205, etc. For the contractions *sdha* and *sdhi*, see ibid., pp. 150, 156.

5. See, e.g., ibid., p. 331, text line 1; p. 403, text line 1; *Ep. Ind.*, Vol. XXVIII, Plate facing p. 62, text line 1; etc.

6. See, e. g., *Select Inscriptions*, p. 297, text line 24; p. 385, text line 41; p. 409, text line 30; p. 327, text line 9; p. 397, text line 8; p. 441, text line 55; p. 455, text line 15.

7. See, e. g., *Ep. Ind.*, Vol. III, p. 129, Plate, text line 24; *Select Inscriptions*, p. 457.

8. Sachau, *Alberuni's India*, Part I, p. 173.

suggested that the symbol indicates *siddham* or *siddhir=astu*.[2] There is no doubt that the symbol stood for the word *siddham* found at the beginning of numerous early inscriptions. But there is evidence to show that sometimes the symbol was pronounced as *Oṁ siddhiḥ*[2] and Al-Bīrūnī seems to have confused this *Oṁ siddhiḥ* with *Om*. Instances of such confusion are also noticed in Indian epigraphs like the Baud plates[3] of Raṇabhañja which begin with the symbol followed by the word *siddhiḥ* and the Belabo plate[4] of Bhojavarman, which has the symbol followed by *Oṁ siddhiḥ* at the beginning. The symbol was generally used till recent times in the eastern areas with the sign of nasalisation placed above the Bengali figure for 7 or as the figure 4 as found in medieval inscriptions from Bengal.[5] The sign is called *piḻḻaiyār śuḻi* (Gaṇeśa's curl) in Tamil.[6]

The *svastika* (of both the *vām-āvarta* and *dakṣiṇ-vārta* types) and taurine symblols are found in Aśoka's separate edicts at Jaugaḍa.[7] The triskele symbol, which is a modification of the *svastika*, is found at the beginning of the Eṟṟaguḍi and Rājula-Maṇḍagiri M. R. Edicts of Aśoka.[8] The *svastika* is also found at the beginning and the end of many other records generally belonging to dates earlier than the 3rd century A.D.[9] While occurring at the beginning of a document, it is sometimes placed before, and rarely after, the word *siddham*[10] (*sidha*, *sidhaṁ*, etc. in Prakrit and sometimes in contractions like

1. *Ep. Ind.*, Vol. XVII, p. 352.
2. Certain medieval charms, composed in the form of royal charters, have *Oṁ siddhiḥ* at the beginning, which is apparently the pronounced form of the symbol at the commencement of numerous inscriptions including copper-plate grants. See *Proc. IHC*, 1939, pp. 471 ff. See also below, p. 95.
3. *IHQ*, Vol. X, p. 475.
4. Majumdar, *Ins. Beng.*, Vol. III, p. 19.
5. Cf. *Proc. IHC*, 1939, p. 471; *IHQ*, Vol. XXXIII, p. 103 and Plate facing p. 102; P. N. Bhattacharya, *Kāmarūpaśāsanāvalī*, p. 55. See below p. 96,
6. *Ep. Ind.*, Vol. XVII, p. 352, note. See below, p. 96.
7. See *Corp. Ins. Ind.*, Vol. I, Plate facing p. 116.
8. *Ep. Ind.*, Vol. XXXI, Plates facing pp. 221, 216; Vol. XXXII, Plate facing p. 6.
9. See, e.g., ibid. Vol. VII, Plate III (No. 6) facing p. 76; Plate VII (No. 16) facing p. 88; etc.
10. Ibid., Plate III (No. 6) facing p. 76, and Plate IV (No. 10) facing p. 78.

dha or *sdhi*). At the beginning of the Hāthigumphā inscription, the *svastika* appears beneath a crown-like symbol called *śrīvatsa*, while the inscription ends with the 'tree-within-railing' symbol.[1] Other symbols found in some cases are the trident or *triratna* resting on the *dharma-cakra*,[2] and the lotus.[3] The *praṇava*, generally represented by a symbol, is sometimes found at the beginning of medieval inscriptions.[4]

In early medieval epigraphs and manuscripts, a circle, with a smaller circle or dot (or dots) inside, sometimes indicates fullstop. As the circle with a central dot is the old Brāhmī letter *tha*, modified forms of the same letter came to be used in later times.[5] In some medieval records, the symbol stands midway between *tha* and *cha*,[6] and this confusion led to the growth of the popular use of the letter *cha* as the concluding mark at the end of literary or epigraphic records and sections thereof.[7] *Cha* is recognised in this capacity in early medieval works like Śrīharṣa's *Naiṣadhīya*[8] and Hemacandra's *Ekākṣarakoṣa*.[9] Sometimes the auspicious word *śrī* also appears in the same way at the end of documents.[10]

In the inscriptions of the Gupta age, the auspicious word *siddham* at the beginning of epigraphs was sometimes repre-

1. Cf. *Select Inscriptions*, Plate facing pp. 208 and 209; above, p. 5, notes 3-4.

2. Above, p. 5, note 2.

3. See, e.g., *Ep. Ind.*, Vol. XVIII, Plates facing pp. 96, 150, 151; Vol. XIX, p. 81, text line 41; Plate facing p. 60, text lines 6, 16, 20; Vol. XXX, p. 219, text line 11; Vol. XXXI, p. 128, text lines 205 and 212; *Corp. Ins. Ind.*, Vol. III, No. 63.

4. See, e.g., *Ep. Ind.*, Vol. XXXI, Plate facing p. 165. The symbol usually looks like *õ, oṁ, auṁ*, etc., as written in the East Indian (Bengali) script.

5 See, e.g., ibid., Vol. XVIII, p. 298, text line 30; Vol. XIX p. 81, text line 41; Plate facing p. 331, text line 21; Vol. XXX, p. 125, text line 17; Vol. XXXI, p. 166, text line 20 (not *śrī* ; but cf. p. 16). The same symbol is found in some old Jain manuscripts as a circle with a globular mark at the centre and drawn under a horizontal line. See *Journ. Or. Inst.*, Baroda, Vol. III, No. 4, June 1954, p. 368.

6. See *Ep. Ind.*, Vol. XVIII, p. 80, text line 38.

7. Ibid., Vol. XXIII, pp. 140-41 (text lines 4 and 15); Vol. XXV, p. 63 (text line 94), p. 221 (text line 141); etc. It is really not a variety of the *siddham* symbol (as stated in op. cit., Vo. XXX, p. 218).

8. XVI, 98; cf. *Journ. Or. Inst.*, Vol. III, p. 368.

9. Cf. verse 13.

10. See, e.g., *Ep. Ind.*, Vol. XXXI, p. 16, text line 26. Medieval South and West Indian records often end with *maṅgalaṁ mahā-śrīḥ* sometimes preceded by *śubhaṁ bhavatu*. They begin with *svasti jayaś=-c=ābhyudayaś=ca*.

sented by a crescent-like curved stroke opening towards the left.[1] This mark resembles the symbol or mark of interpunctuation at the end of many of Aśoka's edicts at Kalsī. It has been pointed out that some scholars regard it as standing for the *praṇava*, i.e. the auspicious syllable *om*, even though the sign occurs in typical Buddhist epigraphs and the Buddhists did not attach any importance to the *praṇava*.[2] We have seen above that, though this view is supported by a statement of Al-Bīrūnī,[3] there is some evidence to show that the symbol was read as *siddham* or *siddhir=astu*.[4] The suggestion seems to be supported by the fact that some medieval inscriptions begin with the symbol followed by a *namaskāra* passage like *Oṁ namaḥ*, *Oṁ namaḥ Śivāya*, *Oṁ namo Nārāyaṇāya*, *Oṁ namaḥ śrī-Viśveśvarāya*, etc.,[5] and also by the *maṅgala*: *Oṁ svasti*.[6] We have explained the confusion of the symbol with the *praṇava* by the fact that sometimes it was read as *Oṁ siddhiḥ*.[7]

The symbol was gradually modified to the shape of a stroke slanting towards lower right with its top curved or looped inwards to the right[8] or slanting towards lower left with its top curved or looped inwards to the left.[9] Sometimes the lower end of the stroke exhibits an ornamental downward flourish[10] or upward bend.[11] Both the *vām-āvarta* and *dakṣiṇ-āvarta* types were used in some cases in records of the same

1. See, e.g., *Corp. Ins. Ind.*, Vol. III, Nos. 11 (Plate VI A), 20 (Plate XII B); etc.

2. Ibid., p. 46, note 3.

3. See Sachau, *Alberuni's India*, Part I, p. 173.

4. Cf. *Ep. Ind.*, Vol. XVII, p. 352; *Proc. IHC.*, 1939, pp. 471 ff.

5. See, e. g., Majumdar, *Ins. Beng.*, Vol. III, pp. 46, 61, 71, 85, 94, 101, 109, 121, 133, 143; *Ind. Ant.*, Vol. XI, p. 242; *Ep. Ind.*, Vol. II, p. 305; Vol. XXXIV, p. 81.

6. See, e.g., *Ep. Ind.*, Vol. XXIX, Plate facing p. 192, text line 1.

7. In rare cases, the symbol is followed by the word *siddhiḥ* or *Oṁ siddhiḥ* as we have already noticed above (p. 93). Cf. also the text of the *mantra* (in the shape of a royal charter) beginning with the *maṅgala*: *Oṁ siddhiḥ* । *guru-pādebhyo namaḥ* । *svasti* । (*Proc. IHC*, 1939, p. 472).

8. See, e.g., *Ep. Ind.*, Vol. XXVII, Plate facing p. 328, text line 1; Vol. XXVIII, Plate facing p. 50, text line 1; Plate facing p. 112.

9. See, e.g., ibid., Vol. XXVIII, Plate facing p. 66, text line 1; Plate facing p. 84. text line 1; Plate (B) facing p. 183.

10. See, e. g., ibid., Vol. XXVIII, Plate facing p. 50; Vol. XXIX, Plate facing p. 88; Vol. XXXI, Plate facing p. 266.

11 See, e. g., ibid., Vol. XXXI, Plate facing p. 72.

locality and also of the same age.[1] In the medieval inscriptions of Eastern India, the symbol resembles the Bengali numerical figure 7 (a vertical stroke with its top curved towards the left and ending in an inward bend)[2] and it was used in the central parts of Bengal with the addition of a sign called *candra-bindu* or *ānunāsika* above. But, in the easternmost areas of Bengal, the same symbol was written with the lower end curved considerably towards the right and was called *āñjī*,[3] and the Bengali alphabet with this symbol at the head was called *āñjī-ka-kha*.[4] In Western India, however, the symbol appearing in medieval inscriptions looks like a numerical figure[5] and often a globular mark looking like a cypher is placed after it.[6] In South Indian records of the early and medieval periods, the symbol is often a *vām-āvarta* spiral,[7] sometimes resembling the representation of a conch-shell, which is called *piḻḻaiyār-śuḻi* or Gaṇeśa's curl and is first taught to the children before they begin to learn the alphabet.[8]

Certain Nepal inscriptions exhibit auspicious symbols representing the conch-shell, the lotus, the bull, the fish, the sun-wheel and the stars.[9] In the medieval epigraphs of the Andhra region, the lotus symbol is sometimes found about the beginning.[10]

The Kailvan (Patna District, Bihar) inscription[11] of about the second century A.D. exhibits four symbols between the beginning and the end of a circular line of writing. These are a long-necked pitcher, a double *svastika* (one of the *vām-*

1. See, e. g., the Valgudar (Monghyr District, Bihar) inscriptions illustrated in *Ep. Ind.*, Vol. XXVIII, Plate facing p. 145.
2. See, ibid., Vol. XXX, Plates facing pp. 186, 236. Cf. above, p. 93.
3. *IHQ*, Vol. XXXIII, p. 103.
4. P. N. Bhattacharya, *Kāmarūpaśāsanāvalī*, p. 55.
5. See, e. g., *Ep. Ind.*, Vol. XXXI, Plate facing p. 72.
6. See, e.g., ibid., Vol. III, Plate (middle) facing p.306; Vol. XXXI, Plate facing p. 14, text line 1; Vol. XXX, Plate facing p. 191.
7. See, e. g., ibid. Vol. XXXI, Plate facing p. 233.
8. Ibid., Vol. XVII, p. 352, note. Cf. above, p. 93.
9. *Ind. Ant.*, Vol. IX, pp. 163 ff. For the conch-shell in other records, see *Ep. Ind.*, Vol. XXV, Plate facing p. 236; and for the lotus, see *JAS*, Letters, Vol. XVIII, 1952, pp. 77 ff., Plate II.
10. Cf. P. Sreenivasachar, *A Corpus of Inscriptions*, Part II, Plates 37, 41.
11. *Ep. Ind.*, Vol. XXXI, Plate facing p. 231.

āvarta and the other of the *dakṣiṇ-āvarta* type), and another looking like a sacrificial altar. At the end of the Guakuchi copper plate grant[1] of king Ratnapāla of Assam, there are the representations of a bird (Garuḍa) carrying a snake, the lotus, the conch-shell and the discus, all connected with the god Viṣṇu.

5. *Preservation of Copper-plate Grants*

Copper-plate grants were very valuable documents for the donees and their descendants, since their loss or destruction rendered the revenue-free holdings, created by them, ordinary rent-paying lands unless fresh charters were issued in the place of the old ones. There are instances of charters written on plam leaves or engraved on copper plates being destroyed by fire and the re-issue of copper-plate grants by the later rulers of the territories in question.[2] The donees therefore preserved the documents received from the donors generally with special care.

Monks dwelling in artificial caves sometimes engraved the texts of the copper-plate grants, received by them in respect of rent-free lands, on the walls of the caves.[3] In the ruins of the ancient city of Valabhī at modern Wala in Kathiawar, copper-plate charters have been found immured in the walls or foundations of the houses of the donees or their descendants, while in many places the charters have been dug out from the fields, to the donation of which they refer, usually hidden in small caches made of bricks.[4]

Sometimes several documents were preserved together. An urn containing four sets of copper plates was dug out from the ground near the foot of a tree at the village of Andhavaram in the Srikakulam District of Andhra Pradesh.[5] The

1. P. N. Bhattacharya, *Kāmarūpaśāsanāvalī*, Plate facing p. 140.

2. See the Kurud plates of Narendra (*Ep. Ind.*, Vol. XXXI, p. 267) and the Dubi and Nidhanpur plates of Bhāskaravarman (ibid., Vol. XXX, p. 290). See below, p. 106.

3. See *Proc. IHC*, Lahore, 1940, pp. 54 ff.; below. p. 106.

4. Cf. Bühler, *Indian Palaeography*, pp.99-100.

5. *Ep. Ind.*, Vol. XXVIII, pp. 175 ff.

grants were issued by different rulers of different ages to different donees and may have been interred in the ground when the owners left the village at one time on an occasion like pilgrimage. The sets of plates were suspended by means of an iron rod passing through their seal-rings,which was inserted across the deliberately broken rim of the urn having a wide circular mouth. The urn was covered by a hemispherical lid and the plates, kept inside it in paddy-husk, were found in a good state of preservation.[1]

Sometimes the plates were preserved in a specially made stone casket or coffer. Thus the Kalegaon plates[2] of Yādava Mahādeva were found inside a stone box made of two slabs of stone firmly joined together. The upper slab measures 22 inches by 15½ inches by 7 inches and has a hollow (4½ inches in depth) curved in the inner surface of it while the lower slab measures 24 inches by 16½ inches by 7 inches with a similar hollow (1½ inches deep) in its upper surface. The set of three plates, each measuring 15 inches by 11 inches by ¼ inch and together weighing 1075 tolas, was found inside the box which was dug out of the ground.

There are instances of copper-plate grants being discovered at localities far away from their places of issue. Thus the Kamauli plate[3] of Vaidyadeva is a record which was issued by a ruler of Assam in respect of a gift of land in favour of a Brāhmaṇa, but was discovered at a place near Banaras. It is possible that the donee or one of his descendants in this case settled at Banaras at a later date, although it is difficult to determine whether he was still enjoying the gift land or had sold it out. If the land had been sold out, the plate was only of some sentimental value to him. It is also not impossible that he went to Banaras on pilgrimage and carried the plate

1. For the preservation of copper plates in paddy-husk, see also *Ep. Ind.*, Vol. XXVII, p. 268 and note 2. The interment of copper-plate grants may be compared to that of coins. In the pre-British days, life and property were generally insecure and hiding one's valuables under the earth was a common practice because there were no banks of the modern type.

2. See ibid., Vol. XXXII, pp. 31-32.

3. See Bhandarkar's List, No. 1636.

with him as a valuable possession, but could not return home owing to sudden death.

The originals of the grants from which the plates were prepared, probably written on perishable material, must have been preserved in the records office of the kings. As we have seen, an officer called *Akṣapaṭalika*, very often mentioned in inscriptions, is regarded by some as an Accountant and by others as a Record-keeper,[1] though he may have served in both the capacities. The store-room of original grants in a king's *Akṣapaṭala* department is probably called the *phalaka-vāra* (literally, 'the store-house of plates') in a Nasik inscription[2] of the 2nd century A. D.

A smaller officer called *Pustapāla* or *Pustakapāla*, literally 'the keeper of books (i.e. records)', is mentioned in such records as those of the Bhuama-Karas of Orissa.[3] Another officer mentioned in the records of the same area is the *Peṭapāla*, *Peṭṭapāla*, *Peḍāpāla*, etc. (literally 'the keeper of the boxes [containing records]') who apparently served under the *Pustapāla*.[4]

6. *Treatment of Letters*

The custom of wrapping up letters in cloth and of sealing the packet is referred to in the Jātakas.[5] According to Bāṇa's *Harṣacarita*,[6] the *lekhahāraka* or *lekhahāra* (i.e. letter-carrier) tied each packet separately to a strip of cloth and wound the cloth round his head. Ordinary letters written on palm leaf or birch bark were folded, the ends of the leaves or sheets being split and joined and the whole being tied up with a thread.[7]

1. Stein, *Rājatar.*, trans., V, 249, 397 and notes; above, p. 86.
2. Cf. *Select Inscriptions*, p. 160.
3. Cf. *Ep. Ind.*, Vol. XXIX, p. 88, text line 29. For the earlier mention of the *Pustapāla* in Bengal records of the Gupta age, see *Select Inscriptions*, p. 285, text line 10; etc.
4. Bhandarkar's List, No. 2041 (*Peṭapāla*); *Ep. Ind.*, Vol. XXVIII, p. 216, text line 29 (*Peḍāpāla*); Vol. XV, p. 5, text line 34 (*Peṭṭapāla*), etc.
5. Fausböl, *Jātaka*, Vol. II, pp. 173 ff.
6. Nirnayasagar Press ed., pp. 58, 167. See also p. 66 above.
7. Cf. Bühler, *Indian Palaeography*, p. 100.

A number of royal seals, both metallic and earthen, belonging to kings, who had their capitals far away from Bihar, have been discovered at Nalanda in the Patna District of Bihar.[1] It appears that these seals accompanied the letters of the kings in question, which were addressed to the head of the Buddhist establishment at Nalanda. It also seems that the seals were either tied up with the letters or were carried by the letter-carriers separately in order to prove to the addressee the genuineness of the letter he received. A person carrying a verbal message also carried a seal or a ring bearing the name of the sender of the message, which had to be shown to the person to whom the message was to be delivered.[2] This sort of token was generally called *abhijñāna*. Some of the Nalanda seals are big and heavy and could not have been carried by the letter-carriers on their heads along with the letters, since they came from a great distance. These therefore should better be regarded as *abhijñānas* carried by the messengers separately.

7. *Preservation of Manuscripts*

Manuscripts were preserved in a library called *Bhāratī-bhāṇḍāgāra* or *Sarasvatī-bhāṇḍāra* (literally, 'the store-house of the goddess of learning'). Books written on palmyra leaves or on bark or paper sheets had wooden covers on the top and bottom and the whole was tied up with a string. Often this string passed through the leaves or sheets and sometimes also the covers through holes made in them and was wound round the cover and knotted. These practices are referred to by Al-Bīrunī[3] and Bāṇa.[4] In Nepal, the covers of important manuscripts were often made of embossed metal and manuscripts were wrapped up in dyed or embroidered cloth.[5] In Jain libraries, palmyra-leaf manuscripts were often

1. Cf. *Mem. ASI*, No. 66, pp. 64 ff.
2. See *Rājatar.*, VI, verses 33-36.
3. Sachau, *Alberuni's India*, Part I, p. 171; cf. above, p. 62 and note 1.
4. Nirnayasagar Press ed., p. 95, referring to *sūtra-veṣṭana* of a manuscript. See above, p. 62, note 1, for *sūtra* or *śarayantraka*.
5. Bühler, *Indian Palaeography*, p. 99.

kept in small sacks of cloth, the sacks being preserved in small boxes of white metal. We have noticed above that, in Kashmir, manuscripts were sometimes bound in leather and kept on shelves in accordance with Muhammadan practice.

In the libraries attached to colleges, royal courts and monasteries, the manuscripts were generally preserved in boxes of wood or cardboard under the charge of a librarian. The collections of such libraries were often catalogued. Individual scholars are also known to have sometimes possessed good collections of manuscripts.

Among royal libraries, mention may be made of the celebrated collection of the Paramāra king Bhoja (c. 1000-55 A.D.). In the first half of the 12th century, the Caulukya king Siddharāja Jayasiṁha (c. 1094-1144 A.D.) conquered Malwa and carried away the books of Bhoja's library to Anhilwada where they were apparently amalgamated with the Caulukya collection of manuscripts. The Caulukya royal library at Anhilwada is often mentioned in the 13th century works. The Caulukya-Vāghelā king Vīsaladeva (Viśvamalla, c. 1244-62 A.D.) is stated to have supplied a copy of Śrīharṣa's *Naiṣadhīya* to Vidyādhara for writing his commentary on it and also a copy of Vātsyāyana's *Kāmasūtra* to Yaśodhara who composed the *Jayamaṅgalā* commentary on it. A copy of the *Rāmāyaṇa* in Vīsaladeva's collection is known to be preserved now in the library of the University of Bonn, West Germany.[1]

As regards libraries of individual scholars, it is interesting to note that, in the early years of the 7th century, Bāṇa in his *Harṣacarita* mentions his *pustaka-vācaka* or 'the reader of books' and describes the latter's manipulation of a manuscript of the *Vāyu Purāṇa*.[2] There were numerous collections of manuscripts pertaining to individual scholars or families of scholars in all parts of the country. One of the biggest such libraries of the medieval age was the collection of manuscripts made by

1. See Bühler, *Indian Palaeography*, p. 99.
2. Nirnayasagar Press ed., p. 95.

Kavīndrācārya Sarasvatī (16th-17th century) at Banaras. A manuscript of Vāmana's *Kāvyālaṅkāra* in Kavīndrācārya's collection bears the seal of Prince Salīm (the earlier name of the Mughal emperor Jahāngīr, 1605-27 A. D.). Some of the works mentioned in the old catalogue of manuscripts in Kavīndrācārya's library are not available now.[1]

According to the Purāṇas, it was a sacred duty of rich men to make donations of books to temples and other institutions.[2] Such donations were obligatory on the followers of the Buddhist and Jain creeds.[3] There is evidence to show that both local scribes as well as copyists hailing from the neighbouring territories were employed for the purpose of copying manuscripts.[4]

1. M. Krishnamachariar, *History of Classical Sanskrit Literature*, pp. 390 b-c.
2. See Hemādri's *Dānakhaṇḍa*, pp. 544 ff.
3. Cf. Bühler, op. cit., p. 99.
4. Cf. *IHQ*, Vol, XXX, p. 387; see also above, p. 88.

CHAPTER V

COPPER-PLATE GRANTS

Section I

ROYAL CHARTERS AND CONNECTED PROBLEMS

1. *Rāja-śāsana*

The word *śāsana* means a *rāja-śāsana* or royal charter, and *tāmra-śāsana* 'a royal charter engraved on [a plate or plates of] copper'.[1] Ancient Indian authorities classify *rāja-śāsana* under three heads, viz. (i) *dāna-śāsana* recording gifts, (2) *prasāda-śāsana* recording various kinds of favour, and (3) *jaya-patra* declaring the victory of one of the parties in a dispute.[2] Most of the records of ancient Indian rulers so far discovered however belong to the first category.

Revenue-free lands granted by ancient Indian rulers in favour of persons, deities or religious establishments were usually endowed with a deed engraved on durable *tāmra-paṭṭa*, i.e. 'a plate or plates of copper',[3] although we also know that such documents were sometimes incised even on stone. By *lakṣaṇā*, a *tāmra-śāsana* was sometimes called *tāmra-paṭṭa*.[4] Often again the word indicating the deed or charter (e.g. *tāmra-śāsana*) was applied, by *lakṣaṇā*, to indicate the land granted by means of such a charter.[5] But, besides *tāmra-śāsana*, this modified sense of revenue-free land was in many cases indi-

1. The deeds of gift were often called *dāna-patra*, *tāmra-patra*, *śāsana-patra*, etc. The word *patra* in these compounds suggests that the records were written on *bhūrja-patra* (birch-bark sheets) or *tāla-patra* (palmyra leaves) and only some of them were later engraved on copper plates.

2. Cf. *Kṛtyakalpataru* (G. O. S.), Vyavahāra-khaṇḍa, pp. 157-60.

3. In the place of *paṭṭa*, we have also the use of the words *paṭṭaka*, *paṭṭikā*, *phalaka*, *phalī*, *patra*, *patraka*, *patrikā*, etc., in the same sense.

4. Cf., e. g., *tāmra-paṭṭa-dharmeṇa* in *Select Inscriptions*, p. 352, etc.

5. Cf. ibid., p. 353, text line 24, etc.

cated either by *tāmra*[1] or by *śāsana*.[2] The word *śāsana* in this sense is widely used not only in the medieval records of Orissa but even in modern Oriya. Numerous villages in Orissa still bear names ending with the word *śāsana*, indicating that originally they were gift villages. In early records of different parts of India, rent-free holdings under the possession of gods and Brāhmaṇas were usually called *deva-deya* or *deva-dāya* and *brahma-deya* or *brahma-dāya* respectively. In the southern part of India, the word *agrahāra* was more popular in the sense of a rent-free village in the possession of Brāhmaṇas.

Works of a few of the early writers on law, such as Viṣṇu[3] and Yājñavalkya,[4] give us some idea about the *rāja-śāsanas* or charters recording grants of land, property, etc., made by kings. According to Viṣṇu, "[The king] should grant land to Brāhmaṇas. For the information of future kings, he should also give the donees of the grant a charter written on cloth or copper-plate endowed with his own seal and with a description of the boundaries of the land, of his own ancestors and of the measurement of the area. He should not confiscate land granted by others...The king should kill persons who prepare spurious charters, and also those preparing spurious documents."[5] According to Yājñavalkya "After granting land or making a *nibandha*, the lord of the soil (i.e. the king) should have a document prepared for the information of noble kings of the future. He would then cause the preparation of a lasting charter writt n on cloth or copper-plate, adorned with his own seal on the outer side,

1. See, e. g., *IHQ*, Vol. XXIII, p. 240, text line 33; *Ep. Ind.*, Vol. XXVIII, p. 308, p. 311 (text line 9-10), etc. See also *tāmraka* in the same sense (*Ep. Ind.*, Vol. IV, pp. 128, 131).

2. See, e. g., *Inscriptions of Bengal*, Vol. III, p. 74, text line 43, etc. Cf. words like *paṭṭa* or *paṭṭikā* in the same sense (*Ep. Ind.*, Vol. XXIV, p. 298, note; Vol. XVII, p. 330, note).

3. In the matter of the *rāja-śāsanas*, Viṣṇu agrees with Yājñavalkya, although the former is assigned to a later date (cf. *Camb. His. Ind.*, Vol. I, p. 279).

4. The *Yājñavalkyasmṛti* is assigned by scholars to a date about the fourth century A.D. (ibid., pp. 279 f.)

5. See III, 57-59; V, 9-10,

with his own signature and date and with a description of himself and his ancestors and the amount of the gift and the boundaries of the gift land."[1] As regards the preparation of a document, Vyāsa says that it should be written first by chalk on a slab or on the ground and, after the elimination of all errors, should be finally written on a leaf (or, metal tablet).[2]

The *Mitākṣarā*, a medieval commentary on the *Yājñavalkyasmṛti* by Vijñāneśvara, also furnishes some valuable information regarding the preparation of royal charters. According to this work, the passage 'on cloth or copper-plate' and the word 'date' in the original should be explained respectively as 'on cotton cloth, copper plate or copper tablet' and 'the expired year of the Śaka kings and the [regnal] year [of the donor], the solar and lunar eclipses, etc.'

The information drawn from the above sources may be summed up as follows : (1) After making a grant of land, etc., the king caused the preparation of a *lekhya* or document for the guidance of future kings of the land. (2) It was then written on a piece of cloth or engraved on copper plates or a copper tablet, and thus was made a permanent charter. (3) It contained a description of the king and three of his immediate predecessors and of the land granted together

1. Cf. II, 318-20.

2. Vyāsa quoted in the *Śabdakalpadruma* says: *Pāṇḍu-lekhyena phalake bhūmau vā prathamaṁ likhet* । *ūn-ādhikan=tu saṁśodhya paśchāt=patre niveśayet* ॥ The same authority as quoted in the *Kṛtyakalpataru* (op. cit., pp. 157-58) says: *Rājñā tu svayam=ādiṣṭaḥ sandhivigraha-lekhakaḥ* । *tāmra-paṭṭe paṭe v=āpi pralikhed=rāja-śāsanam* ॥ *Sthānaṁ vaṁś-ānupūrvi ca deśaṁ grāmam=upāgatān* । *Brāhmaṇāṁś=ca tathā c=ānyān=mānyān=adhikṛtān likhet* ॥ *Kuṭumbino=tha kāyastha-dūta-vaidya-mahattarān* । *Mleccha- cāṇḍāla-paryantān=sarvān=sambodhayann=iti* ॥ *Mātā - pitror=ātmanaś=ca puṇyāy=āmuka-sūnave* । *dattaṁ may=āmukīyāya dānaṁ sabrahmacāriṇe* ॥ *Candr-ārka-sama-kālīnaṁ putra-pautr-ānvay-āgatam* । *anācchedyaṁ=anāhāryaṁ sarv-ābhāvya-vivarjitam* ॥ *Dātuḥ pālayituḥ svargaḥ hartur=narakam=eva ca* । *jñātaṁ may=eti likhitaṁ tadā vyakt-ākṣarair=yutam* ॥ *Abda-māsa-tadardh-āho rāja-mudr-āṅkitaṁ tathā* । *anena vidhinā lekhyaṁ rāja-śāsanakaṁ likhet* ॥ The word *ābhāvya* means 'tax', although it is wrongly quoted and explained in the *Kṛtyakalpataru*.

3. As regards the marking of boundaries, Manu (VIII, 250-51) says, *Aśmano=sthīni go-bālāṁs=tūṣān=bhasma- kapālikāḥ* । *karīṣam=iṣṭak-āṅgārāñ=charkarā bālukās=tathā* ॥ *Yāni c=aivaṁ-prakārāṇi kālād=bhūmir=na bhakṣayet* । *tāni sandhiṣu sīmāyām=aprakāśāni kārayet* ॥ According to Yājñavalkya (II, 151), *Nayeyur=ete sīmānaṁ sthal-āṅgāra - tuṣa - drumaiḥ* । *setu-valmīka- nimn-āsthi-caity-ādyair=upalakṣitām* ॥ while according to Bṛhaspati, *prakṣipya kumbheṣv=etāni sīm-ānteṣu nidhāpayet*. See *Select Inscriptions*, pp. 345 (text line 19), 363 (text lines 15-16), etc.

with its boundaries and measurement; it was also endowed with the king's seal, signature and date. (4) There is no explicit statement regarding the donee by Yājñavalkya, though it is supposed that the donee is implied in his language and that his name should also be written in the charter. (5) A high official was entrusted with the drafting of a document according to the *Mitākṣarā*. As will be seen below, the above characteristics are noticeable in the copper-plate charte s discovered in different parts of India, though the paucity of early charters may suggest that many of them were written on cloth which is an easily perishable material.

Very interesting light on the nature of the *rāja-śāsana* is also thrown by the section entitled *lekhya-prakaraṇa* in Yājñavalkya's work, though the verses deal with bonds. Vijñāneśvara points out that, of the two kinds of documents called *śāsana* and *jānapada*, the section deals with the latter, although he admits that there was no great difference between the two varieties. From this section we learn that the year, the month, the fortnight, the day, the names [of both the parties], the case, *gotra*, *sabrahmacārika*, the fathers' names [of both the parties] and similar other details were specified in the documents. It is also said that a duplicate document could be prepared when the original one was left in a distant land or was illegible, lost, damaged, stolen, broken, burnt or torn.[1] The *jānapada* documents were evidently not written on durable material. Ancient Indian authorities also dealt with the problem of spurious charters and the ways of distinguishing such documents from genuine records.[2]

Treatises like the *Lekhapaddhati* and *Lokaprakāśa*[3] quote some specimens of different types of documents as they were written in the late medieval period respectively in Gujarat and Kashmir.

1. We have some instances of the issue of a duplicate *rāja-śāsana* (cf. the Nidhanpur plates of Bhāskaravarman in *Kāmarūpaśāsanāvalī*, pp. 1 ff.). See *Ep. Ind.*, Vol. XXX, p. 290; Vol. XXXI, p. 267; above, p. 97.

2. Cf. *Kṛtyakalpataru*, op.c it., pp. 161 ff

3. See Gaekwad Oriental Series, No. XIX and Appendix IV in the work. See also the *Patrakaumudī* noticed by Jayaswal in *A Descriptive Catalogue of Manuscripts in Mithila*, Vol. II, pp. 12-13. Cf. above, p. 88.

Metallic plates or tablets, especially of copper, are known to have been used in India for writing documents since very early times. The Sohgaura (Gorakhpur District., U.P.) inscription[1] of the 3rd century B. C. which is written on a bronze tablet, the Taxila copper-plate inscription[2] (21 A.D.) of Patika and the Kalawan (near Taxila) copper plate inscription[3] of 77 A. D. are some of the early instances of this practice.[4] But these are not copper-plate charters of the proper type described above.

The earliest copper-plate charters of the usual type, so far discovered, come from the southern areas of India. They are the Prakrit charters of the Pallava kings of Kāñcī, viz. the Mayidavolu and Hirahadagalli plates of Śivaskandavarman,[5] both assignable to the middle of the 4th century A.D. The Gunapadeya plates[6] of Pallava Skandavarman's time and the Kondamudi plates[7] of Jayavarman, both from the Guntur District of Andhra Pradesh, the Basim (Akola District, Bombay State) plates[8] of Vākāṭaka Vindhyaśakti II and the earliest charters[9] of the Śālaṅkāyanas of Veṅgī should have to be assigned to the same century. In the north, the Dhanaidaha (Rajshahi District, North Bengal) plate,[10] issued in the Gupta year 113 (433 A. D.) during the reign of the Gupta emperor Kumāragnpta I, is one of the earliest copper-plate grants as yet discovered. But a recently discovered plate of Īśvararāta, a ruler of the Kathiawad region, appears to belong to the end of the 4th century A.D.[11]

1. *Select Inscriptions*, pp. 85-86.
2. Ibid., pp. 120-21.
3. Ibid., pp. 127-28. Cf. above, p. 74.
4. For early inscriptions on vases of copper and silver and other metallic objects, see ibid., pp. 84, 109, 129 f., 131, etc. See also above, pp. 74 ff.
5. *Select Inscriptions*, pp. 433 ff.; 437 ff., *Suc. Sāt. L. Dec.*, pp. 165ff.
6. *Select Inscriptions*, pp. 443 ff.
7. *Ep. Ind.*, Vol. VI, p. 315; *Suc. Sāt. L. Dec.*, pp. 41 ff.
8. *Select Inscriptions*, pp. 406 ff.
9. *Ep. Ind.*, Vol. IX, pp. 51 ff.; Vol. XXXI, pp. 1 ff.; *Suc. Sāt. L. Dec.*, pp. 63 ff.
10. *Select Inscriptions*, pp. 280 ff. Samudragupta's Gaya and Nalanda plates (ibid., pp. 262 ff.) are spurious.
11. See *Ep. Ind.*, Vol. XXXIII, pp. 303 ff.

But some of the West Indian cave inscriptions belonging to the Kṣaharāta and Śātavāhana rulers of the 2nd century A.D. were undoubtedly copied on the cave walls from original *rāja-śānsanas* on cloth or copper plate.[1] Thus the Nasik cave inscriptions[2] of Gautamīputra Śātakarṇi (c. 106-30 A. D.), dated in his regnal years 18 and 24, another epigraph[3] at the same place belonging to the reign of Nahapāna and dated in 120 A.D. and several others of the same type engraved on the walls of the excavated caves in Western India are copies of original *rāja-śāsanas*. These records resemble the known specimens of early copper-plate grants and generally agree with the specifications of the ancient legal writers discussed above.[4] The records of Gautamīputra Śātakarṇi actually refer to themselves respectively as a *paṭikā* (regarded as standing for Sanskrit *paṭṭikā* meaning a copper-plate grant)[5] and a *lekhya* (document) while the epigraph of Nahapāna's reign refers either to the engraving of the document on *phalakas* (plates or tablets [of copper]) or to the preservation of such documents in the store-house of *phalakas*.

The above Kṣaharāta and Śātavāhana records and others of the same type in the caves of Western India are thus *rāja-śāsanas* originally engraved on copper plate. The system of engraving royal charters on copper plates is therefore not later than the beginning of the second century A.D. It is possible to think that it was the ascetic donees, and not the donors, who were responsible for copying the charters on the walls of the caves in which they lived either for a considerable period of time or only for the rainy season. The aim was evidently to have a charter which, unlike copper-plate grants, could not be lost. The copying therefore may not have been

1. *Proc. IHC.*, *Lahore*, 1940, pp. 52 ff.
2. *Select Inscriptions*, pp. 191 ff.; 193 ff.
3. Ibid., pp. 157 ff.; cf. above, p. 99 and note 2.
4. The minor differences that are noticed in this regard are also found in the charters of different ages, of different parts of the country and of different ruling families. See the Section on the structure of the *rāja-śāsanas* below.
5. The word *paṭikā* may also be derived from *paṭa* meaning 'cloth', though its derivation from Sanskrit *paṭṭikā* is generally accepted by scholars. See above, p. 67.

done exactly when a charter was issued and the records may have been engraved on the walls several at a time without special regard to their chronological order. Their nature thus seems to resemble that of the medieval votive inscriptions engraved on the walls of temples of renown.[1]

We have many later instances in which royal grants were copied on temple walls or stone slabs. Among such records found in North India, the Shergaḍh stone inscription,[2] originally affixed to the wall of the local temple of the god Somanātha, is a careful copy of a regular charter of the Paramāra king Udayāditya (c. 1060-87 A.D.) of Malwa recording the grant of a village made by the king in favour of the said deity. Of the many well-known instances from South India, mention may be made of the Gadag inscription[3] (1192 A.D.) of the Hoysala king Vīra-Ballāla II, the Belgaum inscriptions[4] (1204 A.D.) of Raṭṭa Kārtavīrya IV and others.

2. *Other Types of Śāsanas*

Sometimes *rāja-śāsanas* were characterised by different names. Thus the Motupalli inscription[5] (1244-45 A.D.) of the Kākatīya king Gaṇapati calls itself *abhaya-śāsana*, i.e. an edict [assuring] safety'. It is stated, 'Formerly kings used to take away by force the whole cargo, viz. gold, elephants, horses, gems, etc., carried by ships and vessels which, after they had started from one country for another, were attacked by storms, wrecked and thrown on shore. But we, out of mercy, for the sake of glory and merit, are granting everything besides the fixed duty (*kḷpta-śulka*) to those who have incurred the great risk of sea voyage with the thought that wealth is more valuable than even life." The fixed duties are enumerated in the record and the stone pillar bearing the document is styled a *śāsana-stambha*.

1. *Ep. Ind.*, Vol. XXX, p. 19, note 7; p. 159; Vol. XXXIII, p. 239.
2. Ibid. Vol. XXIII, pp. 132-36.
3. Ibid., Vol. VI, pp. 89 ff.
4. Ibid., Vol. XIII, pp. 16 ff.; pp. 27 ff.
5. Ibid., Vol. XII, pp. 189,

Similarly a stone inscription[1] (1531 A. D.) of the Vijayanagara king Acyutarāya, found in the Viṣṇupāda temple at Gayā, is called his *dharma-śāsana* since it records how a person visited Gayā on behalf of the king and performed the *śrāddha* ceremony of the king's dead ancestors. Although it is called an edict for religion (i.e. religious merit), it is not a *śāsana* in the real sense of the term. It is so called because in the late medieval period any royal record was a *śāsana*. A similar stone inscription[2] (1521 A. D.) of king Kṛṣṇadevarāya, the predecessor and brother of Acyutarāya, recording the king's performance of a pilgramage to Gayā through a proxy, is styled a *vijaya-śāsana* (a document relating to victory) although this *vijaya* can only be regarded as *dharma-vijaya*, i.e. success relating to religion or religious merit.

Early Orissan epigraphy knows of a type of *śāsanas* called *kraya-śāsana*. The Madras Museum plates[3] (10th century) of the time of king Narendradhavala of Orissa record a *kraya-śāsana* which literally means 'a charter of purchase' and is similar to an ordinary 'sale deed'. The expression also indicates 'land sold or purchased by means of a *kraya-śāsana*.' The inscription does not record any royal charter, although it refers to a village originaly sold by a king. According to it, a person named Seḍā sold a village to three other persons on receipt of an amount of *rūpyaka* or silver.[4] It has been called a *śāsana* or charter apparently because the village was originally purchased by Seḍā from a king named Śilābhañja. A private deed of purchase or sale has been called a *kraya-cīrikā* in the Mangraon inscription and a *kraya-lekhya* in Bṛhaspati's work while *cīrikā* and *cīṭhikā* are both used in the sense of 'a private document' in the *Lekhapaddhati*.[5]

1. Ibid, Vol. XXXIII, pp. 113ff.
2. Ibid., pp. 110ff.
3. Ibid., Vol. XXVIII, pp. 40 ff.
4. See *JRAS*, 1952, pp. 4 ff. The amount is specified as *pla* 10 *ā mā* 2 *gu* 4. *Pla* is a contraction of the well-known weight *pala* (320 *ratis*) while *ā-mā* stands for *ādya-māṣa* (5 *ratis*) and *gu* for *guñjā* (or *rati*).
5. See *Ep. Ind.*, Vol. XXVI, p. 246 and note 8. For various kinds of private documents, see A. Thakur in *ABORI*, Vol. IX, pp. 49ff.

It is interesting to note that the Madras Museum plates, specifically called a *kraya-śāsana*, quote the usual imprecatory and benedictory verses meant for the *tāmra-śāsanas* or charters recording revenue-free gifts of land. This is because, as the *Mitākṣara*[1] explains, the Indians of old extolled the gift of land and rather deprecated the sale of landed property, which they also preferred to represent as a gift. This attitude of the ancient Indians was responsible for the representation even of a sale of land in the form of a gift in the record referred to above.

The Chicacole plates[2] of the Gaṅga king Madhukāmārṇava has the passage: '[the amount of] 150 *Rūpyas* [is paid] to the donor.' This shows that the donor received from the donee 150 silver coins. The charter thus records what was actually a *kraya-śāsana*, although the *vaiśy-āgrahāra* created by means of the document may have been made a rent-free holding.

There was another kind of *śāsana* called *kara-śāsana*,[3] a number of which have been traced among the early epigraphs of Orissa and Andhra Pradesh. The expression *kara-śāsana* means 'a charter recording a revenue-paying grant'. Thus it can refer to a piece of land either sold, the purchaser being allowed to enjoy some privileges, or given away subject to the payment of a small rent regularly.

In the Bengal Asiatic Society's plate[4] of Gayāḍatuṅga, we have : 'Toro-grāma is made a *kara-śāsana* at nine *palas* of silver', while the Talcher plate[5] of the same king speaks of the fixation of *tṛṇodaka* for the gift land at four *palas* of silver without using the word *kara* or *kara-śāsana* in the context.

1. *Mitākṣarā* on the *Yājñavalkyasmṛti*, II, 114 : *sthāvarasya vikraya-pratiṣedhāt......dāna-praśaṁsāc=ca vikraye='pi kartavye sa-hiraṇyam=udakaṁ dattvā dāna-rūpeṇa sthāvara-vikrayaṁ kuryāt.*

2. *JAHRS*, Vol. VIII, pp. 180 ff.; *JBORS*, Vol. XVIII, pp. 293 ff. Cf. *JRAS*, loc. cit.

3. See *JRAS*, 1952, pp. 4-10. The inscriptions referred to in this section were mostly wrongly read and interpreted by previous writers.

4. *JASB*, N. S., Vol. V, 1909, pp. 348 ff.

5. *Archaeological Survey of Mayurbhanj*, Vol. I, pp. 152-54; *JASB*, N.S., Vol. XII, 1916, pp. 293-94.

The expression *tṛṇodaka* (literally, '[tax for] grass and water') has here the technical sense of a cess due to the king even when the gift land was declared to be revenue-free.[1] There is also no doubt that the village, granted by the second of the two charters to several Brāhmaṇas, was subject to the payment of an annual cess at the rate of four *palas* of silver. Similar is the case with the Talcher plate[2] of the Śulkī king Kulastambha, which says that the gift village was made a rent-free holding, though elsewhere *tṛṇodaka* is stated to have been fixed for it at two *palas* of silver. Thus, although the village was made a revenue-free holding, a cess styled *tṛṇodaka* was levied at the annual rate of two *palas* of silver. Five *palas* of silver appear to be mentioned as the *tṛṇodaka* for the gift village in the Narasinghpur plate[3] of Devānanda.

The use of this special term *tṛṇodaka* in preference to the usual *kara* points to the eagerness of the ancient Indian rulers to represent even a rent-paying holding as a rent-free one, as indicated by the *Mitākṣarā* quoted above. It seems that the land was given away (and not sold) to the party and that this transaction had to be distinguished from an ordinary sale of land. This may explain the use of the word *tṛṇodaka* for *kara*.

The Jurāḍā grant[4] of Neṭṭabhañja shows that a village was made a rent-free gift, though its *rājakīya-pratyāya* (i.e. the dues payable to the king) was fixed at the rate of four *palas* of silver, while another four *palas* of silver were also due for the taxes called *khaṇḍapāla-muṇḍamola*.

The Angul plate[5] of the Bhauma-Kara queen Dharmamahādevī seems to state that the queen granted the village of Śakembā in favour of a Brāhmaṇa as a *tāmra-śāsana*, i.e. a revenue-free gift, and that she also gave to the same Brāhmaṇa

1. It is actually mentioned in a list of taxes in the Sonepur plates of Kumāra Someśvara (*Ep. Ind.*, Vol. XII, pp. 239 ff.).

2. *Archl. Surv. Mayur.*, op. cit., pp.157-160; *Ep. Ind.*, Vol. XII, pp. 156-59.

3. *IHQ*, Vol. XXIX, p. 300.

4. *Ep. Ind.*, Vol. XXIV, pp. 15-20.

5. B. Misra, *Orissa under the Bhauma Kings*, pp. 50 ff.

a part of another village called Deśalā, which was subject to the annual payment of three *palas* of silver. The Ganjam plates[1] of Gaṅgā Pṛthvīvarman of Śvetaka do not use the expression *kara-śāsana* but clearly state that the gift village was made a rent-paying holding at the fixed rate of four *palas* of silver to be paid every year by the donee as rent. The Patna plates[2] of the Somavaṁśī king Mahābhavagupta I Janamejaya similarly state that a village was granted by the king as a *kara-śāsana* with its annual rent fixed at eight *palas* of silver. The Chicacole plates of the Gaṅga king Anantavarman record a grant, for which the dues payable to the king (apparently, annually) were ten *māṣakas* (i.e. one-fourth *pala*) probably of silver.

The Adava-Kannayavalasa plates[3] of the Māṭhara king Prabhañjavarman record the gift of a locality as an *agrahāra*, but state at the same time that the annual rent (*kara*) was fixed for it at two hundred *paṇas* probably of cowrie-shells. The same amount is mentioned in the Bobbili plates[4] of Acaṇḍavarman as the annual dues payable for a rent-free *agrahāra*.

The records discussed above come from the ancient country of Kaliṅga covering parts of Orissa and of Andhra Pradesh. As instances of the grant of a rent-paying village outside the said area, reference may be made to the recently published Bhaturiya inscription[5] of Rājyapāla of Bengal and Bihar and the Nesarikā grant[6] of Govinda III.

Many of the *kara-śāsanas* discussed above quote the imprecatory and benedictory stanzas meant for rent-free gifts. The reason for this is indicated by the *Mitākṣarā* passage quoted above.

Some of the copper-plate records of the Gupta age discovered in Bengal were issued by the district officers. These

1. *Ep. Ind.*, Vol. IV, pp. 192-201.
2. Ibid., Vol. III, pp. 340-44. For another *kara-śāsana* of the same king, see *JPASB*, Vol. I, pp. 12-13.
3. *Ep. Ind.*, Vol. XXX, pp. 114-15.
4. *IHQ*, Vol. XXIX, p. 299. The king's name is not Caṇḍavarman.
5. *Ep. Ind.*, Vol. XXXIII, pp 150ff.
6. Ibid., Vol. XXXIV, p. 140

were official records but not royal charters in the strict sense. They record the purchase of plots of State land for the purpose of creating rent-free holdings in favour of gods and Brāhmaṇas. With this end in view, a person had to apply to the district authorities and the record-keepers of the district office had to certify about the availability of land at the price offered by the applicant. The price was then accepted and the creation of the rent-free holding sanctioned. In many cases, such holdings were created out of fallow land in the possession of the State.[1]

3. *Creation of Rent-Free Holdings*

As indicated above, some charters[2] record the sale of Government land (often fallow land) to an applicant paying the usual price and the Government's acceptance of his proposal to create a rent-free holding out of the purchased land in favour of Brāhmaṇas or religious institutions. In such a transaction, it was believed, according to an ancient Indian convention, that five-sixths of the religious merit for the creation of the revenue-free holding would go to the purchaser of the land and one-sixth of it to the king of the country, whose government alone could create such a holding.[3]

There is another kind of charters which, instead of speaking of the sale of the land that was created into a rent-free holding by the king in favour of Brāhmaṇas or religious institutions, merely state that the particular holding was created at the request of a certain officer or feudatory of the king or some other persons. In spite of the absence of any reference to sale in such records, some of them appear to be based on a transaction involving sale.[4] Thus the Nalanda plate[5] of Devapāla records a grant of five villages by the Pāla king to

1. See *Select Inscriptions*, pp. 280ff., 283ff., 324ff., 328 ff., 337ff., 342ff.

2. Ibid., pp. 337 ff., 342 ff., etc.

3. Cf. ibid., p. 344, text line 13; p. 348, text line 16; etc. Cf. *tapaḥ-ṣāḍbhāgam=ākṣayyam* in the *Abhijñānaśakuntala*, Act II, verse 13.

4. As we have seen, sale of land was generally represented in ancient India as a gift. See above, p. 111, note 1.

5. Bhandarkar's List, No. 1613.

a Buddhist monastery at Nalanda at the request of *Māhārāja* Bālaputradeva who was the lord of Suvarṇadvīpa (Sumatra) and was responsible for establishing the monastery. The five villages were apparently purchased by Bālaputradeva from Devapāla as otherwise the whole of the religious merit accruing to the pious act of endowing the monastery with a rent-free holding for its maintenance would go to Devapāla and nothing at all to Bālaputradeva.[1] This was no doubt an undesirable position for the king of Sumatra. If he really purchased the villages, as he no doubt did, five-sixths of the merit would be his and only one-sixth would go to Devapāla according to the convention referred to above.

But as regards the land made into a rent-free holding at the request of an officer or feudatory of the king, it was no doubt in many cases lying within their *jāgīr*, i.e. fief or estate. In the case of land forming part of *jāgīrs* which royal officers of ancient India enjoyed temporarily,[2] their occupants lost the rent of or income from the land in question so long as they were in their possession. But the king's loss of revenue was greater as the land remained rent-free when the *jāgīr* reverted to him or was later allotted to some other officer. It therefore seems that the occupants of *jāgīrs* had to compensate the king's loss at least partially for the creation of revenue-free holdings within their fiefs, as otherwise they could scarcely expect the full share of merit accruing to the pious act. We have also cases[3] where a king is found to ratify the rent-free holdings created in their *jāgīrs* by members of the royal family.

But it appears that a number of the grants of rent-free lands issued by the kings were really made on behalf of persons whose names are not mentioned in the documents. This seems to be suggested by the fact that, in a few cases, even

1. Cf. R. D. Banerji, *Bāṅgālār Itihās*, Vol. I, B. S. 1330, p. 210.

2. Cf. Watters, *On Yuan Chwang's Travels in India*, Vol. I, p. 177.

3. See the cases of such holdings created by Princes Sūryasena and Puruṣottamasena and ratified by king Viśvarūpasena in his Vaṅgīya Sāhitya Pariṣat plate (N. G. Majumdar, *Inscriptions of Bengal*, Vol. III, p. 147; *JAS*, Letters, Vol. XX, pp. 206-07).

though the grants are recorded in the king's name, an endorsement at the end of the documents says that they were made by others and in reality there is a contradiction between the facts as stated in the charter proper and the endorsement. An important document of this type is the Bangaon plate[1] of Vigrahapāla, which purports to record the grant of a village by the Pāla king in favour of a Brāhmaṇa, although in an endorsement at the end it is summarily stated that the grant was made by an officer of the king named Ghaṇṭīśa out of his own *jāgīr*.

Another interesting fact is that the indication of a particular grant being actually made by one of the king's officers or feudatories but represented as one made by the king is not clear in the documents, though some of them appear to suggest the fact in a vague way. There are many records which introduce a person without any ostensible relation with the charter stated to have been granted by the king. Such an introduction is often found at the end of the documents exactly in the position of the endorsement in the Bangaon plate of Vigrahapāla III, referred to above. In a few cases, such an enigmatic name is also met with in the body of the charter without any justification for its introduction. Since it is inexplicable why a person without anything to do with the grant should be mentioned in a royal charter at all, it seems that they might have been the real donors of the grants in question and that this fact was intended to be rather vaguely indicated in the said way. It also appears that there was an amount of reluctance on the part of the Government to admit such a fact.

The Mehar plate[2] of Dāmodara records a grant of lands in favour of a number of Brāhmaṇas. But at the end of the king's description in verse, there is one stanza introducing Gaṅgādharadeva who was the officer in charge of the royal elephant force. The introduction of this person cannot be explained unless it is supposed that he was the real donor of

1. *Ep. Ind.*, Vol. XXIX, pp. 48ff. Cf. Vol. XXXIII, p. 63, text line 10.
2. Ibid., Vol. XXVII, pp. 182 ff.

the grant although the king was not eager to mention the fact explicitly in the document.[1]

The Andhavaram plates[2] of the Eastern Gaṅga king Indravaraman record the grant of a village as an *agrahāra* or rent-free holding in favour of several Brāhmaṇas. The king is clearly mentioned as the donor. But the record is stated in the end to have been written under orders of Lokārṇavadeva, the vanquisher of many foes. The charter was issued in the Gaṅga year 133. But, instead of describing it as the usual *pravardhamāna-vijaya-rājya-saṁvatsara* or *Gāṅgeya-vaṁśa-pravardhamāna-vijaya-rāyjya-saṁvatsara* as we find in other Gaṅga records, the inscription in question calls it *Tumburu-vaṁśa-rājya-saṁvatsara*. This reminds us of the Santa-Bommali plates[3] issued by a Kadamba feudatory of a Gaṅga king, which describe the Gaṅga era as *Gaṅga-Kadamba-vaṁśa-pravardhamāna-vijaya-rājya-saṁvatsara* even though the Kadambas had nothing to do with the establishment of the era. It appears that the grant recorded in the Andhavaram plates of Gaṅga Indravarman was really made by his feudatory Lokārṇava of the Tumburu dynasty. Unless such was the case, it is difficult to explain why he was introduced as ordering for the writing of the document and why the Gaṅga era is described only in this record as associated with the Tumburu dynasty.[4]

There is a stanza about the end of a charter issued by the Śailodbhava king Sainyabhīta Mādhavarman II Śrīnivāsa.[5] The verse seems to refer to a ruler named Varamora or Varanara who is described as *varadīkṛta-lokanātha-sakha*. It appears that *lokanātha* mentioned in the passage quoted above is no other than the Śailodbhava king himself and Varamora or Varanara was his feudatory who was the real donor of the grant. The word *varadīkṛta* means, '[the king] who was made the giver of boons [by Varamora or Varanara]' and refers to the

1. Ibid., Vol. XXX, pp. 52-53.
2. Ibid., pp. 37 ff.
3. Bhandarkar's List, No. 2053.
4. *An. Rep. Ind. Ep.*, 1951-52, p. 5.
5. *Ep. Ind.*, Vol. XXIV, pp.128 ff.; Vol. XXXIII, p. 52.

favour shown by the king to the feudatory by agreeing to the creation of the rent-free holding recorded in the inscription no doubt at the feudatory's request.

There is an endorsement at the end of the Balangir Museum plates[1] of the 8th regnal year Mahāśivagupta Yayāti I. It speaks of Prince Durgarāja as the son of Svabhāvatuṅga who seems to be identical with Mahāśivagupta Yayāti himself. The introduction of the prince is really inexplicable unless he was the real donor of the grant which was ratified by his father. Similarly the enigmatic endorsement at the end of the Mahada plates[2] of the Telugu-Coḍa king Someśvaradevavarman of South Kosala appears to show that Yaśogaja, described in it as a ruling chief born in the family of the donor, was the real donor of the grant which was ratified by the king. If this was not the case, the endorsement is quite meaningless.

In this connection, reference may be made to the epithet *dāpaka* applied to a person in a number of copper-plate grants of the Imperial Paramāras. The word is generally understood by scholars in the sense a *Dūtaka* or executor.[3] Since, however, the epithets *dāpaka* and *dūta* are sometimes both applied to the same person,[4] it is difficult to support the suggestion. It is not impossible that the *dāpaka* was the real donor whose grant was ratified by the king.

Rent-free holdings in the possession of gods, Brāhmaṇas and others were generally called *agrahāra*, *sarva-mānya*, *sarva-namasya*, *namasya-vṛtti*, etc. Sometimes particular names were applied to such holdings in order to indicate the special character of a gift. Thus the Garra plates[5] (1205 A.D.) of Candella Trailokyavarman refer to the rent-free holding granted to the son of one who died while fighting the Turuṣkas (Muhammadans) on the king's behalf as a *mṛtyuka-vṛtti* (literally 'death-grant'). In the inscriptions of the Śāta-

1. *JAS*, Letters, Vol. XIX, pp. 117 ff.
2. *Ep. Ind.*, Vol. XXVIII, pp. 283 ff.
3. *CII*, Vol. III, p. 291, note.
4. Cf. *Ep. Ind.*, Vol. XXII, p. 76, text lines 67 ff. (verse 39).
5. Ibid., Vol. XVI, pp. 272 ff.

vāhanas, the expression *bhikṣu-hala* is used to indicate a rent-free holding to be enjoyed by the Buddhist monks while the privileges of the donees are collectively styled as *parihāras*.[1] The same records[2] show that sometimes an *akṣaya-nīvī* or permanent endowment was created by means of land instead of a sum of money.[3]

1. Cf. *Select Inscriptions*, p. 201.
2. Ibid., p. 200, text line 2.
3. For the technical terms, see below.

Section II

SPECIMENS OF RĀJA-ŚĀSANA

1. *Form*

There are various kinds of copper-plate records. Sometimes they contain official orders or the record of the construction of a monastery, etc. The *yantras* of the Jains and the Brāhmaṇas are also engraved on copper plates of various sizes—big, small or medium, and triangular, rectangular or round.[1] But the most important among copper-plate records are those issued by kings in respect of the grants they made for the purpose of attaining religious merit. These also greatly vary in size and shape. As regards shape, the plates were usually rectangular though some of them resemble squarish blocks of stone, or stone stelae.[2] Among rectangular plates, there are some which are somewhat longer or broader in the middle than at the ends or at the ends than in the middle.[3] They have either rounded or angular corners. In rare cases, royal charters were written on peculiarly shaped lumps of copper such as an axe-head, as we have seen above.

Copper plates of small size resembling palmyra leaves or bark sheets were originally employed in writing royal documents recording grants of land. Thus the Kanas plate[4] of Lokavigraha measures $4\frac{17}{20}''$ in length and $2\frac{1}{2}''$ in height while the Kesaribeda plates[5] of Arthapati are each $7\frac{2}{5}''$ long and $1\frac{1}{2}''$ high. These resemble sheets cut out of palmyra leaves. As regards copper-plate records resembl-

1. Ojha, *Bhāratīya Prācīn Lipimālā*, p.153 and note 9. See above, pp. 74ff.
2. Cf. *Ep. Ind.*, Vol. XXVIII, Plates between pp. 310 and 311. See ibid., Vol. XIV, Plates between pp. 348 and 349.
3. Cf. ibid., Vol. XXIX, Plate facing p. 168 and Plates between pp. 40 and 41; Vol. XXXI, Plates between pp. 306 and 307.
4. Ibid., Vol. XXVIII, p. 329.
5. Ibid., p. 12. The smallest plate in the Rajputana Museum, Ajmer, is $4\frac{1}{2}$ inches by 3 inches and weighs twelve *tolās* (Ojha, op. cit., p. 153, note 6). Cf. above, pp. 75-76.

ing bark sheets, reference may be made to the charter[1] of Viṣṇuṣeṇa, which is engraved on plates measuring 17.2 inches by 7.3 inches.

The shape of the plates is generally oblong or rectangular and the corners are usually rounded off. The earlier records, especially those written on more than one plate, have thin sheets. But the bigger plates of later days were often thick and the borders of the inscribed faces of the sheets in multi-plate documents were in many cases slightly raised in order to avoid friction so that the writing might not be rubbed out. For the protection of the writing, the charters of the Candella kings, when written on more plates than one, generally had narrow copper bands fixed with copper rivets on the margins of the inscribed sides of the plates.[2]

Single plates had the royal seal affixed to the left or top margin while, in the case of records engraved on more sheets than one, the plates were strung on copper ring and the seal was soldered on its joints.[3] The ring passed through holes made in the plates in the left or the top margin. The seal was usually of bronze, but occasionally of copper, and it was cast from a mould. The royal emblem or the legend or both are noticed in relief on the counter-sunk surface of the seal. The seals were affixed to the single plates by means of knobs passing through holes made in the plate.

Sometimes the plates of the early rulers were slightly bigger in size when only one was used in writing a charter than when several of them were employed. Small records often mentioned the donor alone as in the records of Lokavigraha and Arthapati referred to above; but, in some cases, the name of his father was added.[4] In many cases, however, the donor is found to be introduced as the son and grandson or the son, grandson and great-grandson of particular rulers[5] and is also

1. *Ep. Ind.*, Vol. XXX, pp. 163 ff. and Plates.
2. Cf. ibid., Vol. XXXII, p. 119.
3. Cf. above, p. 75.
4. See, e. g., *Ep. Ind.*, Vol. XXIII, p. 251, text lines 9 ff.
5. See, e. g., *Select Inscriptions*, pp. 445 f. and pp. 456 f. for four generations and pp. 378 and 407 for three generations.

often mentioned along with a large number of his ancestors.[1] But such details are not generally found in single-plate records of smaller size. An elaborate description of the achievements of the donor and his ancestors does not usually find place in the earliest copper-plate inscriptions.

Some kings of the Kathiawar region issued charters incised on the inner sides of two plates, their outer sides being kept blank.[2] The majority of the multi-plate documents of the early period were, however, written on three plates. The records of the Somavaṁśī kings of Orissa speak of such charters as *triphalī-tāmraśāsana*,[3] i.e. a deed written on three plates or tablets of copper. The outer sides of the first and third plates of these records are usually uninscribed. This practice was no doubt meant for the preservation of the writing. We have stated above how, for the same purpose, the borders of the inscribed sides of the plates were sometimes slightly raised.

One of the biggest of the three-plate records is the Paithan epigraph[4] (1272 A.D.) of the Yādava king Rāmacandra. The plates are each 20½ inches by 15 inches and together weigh 2,300 *tolās*. They are strung on two rings weighing 457 *tolās*, one of which bears the royal seal with the emblem of Garuḍa. The total weight of the charter is thus 2,757 *tolās* (about 70 lbs.). There are altogether one hundred and eighteen lines of writing on the plates.

A tendency to introduce an elaborate eulogy of the donor and his ancestors in the copper-plate grants gradually developed. This is specially noticed in the charters issued by imperial rulers. As a result of this, even those dynasties which engraved their charters on single plates (e. g. the Pālas and Senas of Eastern India) had to use plates of a bigger size. Thus, the Monghyr plate[5] of Devapāla measures 18¾ inches by 13⅞ inches and the Naihati plate[6] of Ballālasena 15

1. See ibid., pp. 371, 375, 419-20, etc.
2. See, e. g., the Maitraka charters in *Ep. Ind.*, Vol. XXXI, pp. 299 ff.; cf. above, p. 75.
3. Cf. ibid., Vol. III, pp. 346 ff.
4. *Ind. Ant.*, Vol. XIV, pp. 314 ff.
5. *Ep. Ind.*, Vol. XVIII, pp. 304 ff.
6. Ibid., Vol. XIV, pp. 159 ff.

inches by $13\frac{5}{8}$ inches. Such epigraphs often contain about seventy lines of writing. The weight of a single plate (19 inches by 13 inches), without any seal, bearing an inscription (in twentyfour lines of writing) of the Gāhaḍavāla king Govindacandra (c. 1114-55 A. D.) on only one of its faces, is $372\frac{1}{2}$ *tolās*.[1] The Daulatpura plate[2] of Pratīhāra Bhoja I (c. 836-85 A. D.), together with the seal affixed to it, measures $29\frac{1}{2}$ inches by $16\frac{1}{2}$ inches and weighs 1580 *tolās*. A single-plate charter[3] issued by the Ahom king Gaurīnāthasiṁha of Assam in 1792 A. D. measures 24 inches in length and $17\frac{1}{5}$ inches in breadth.

Among the early dynasties that used more than one copper plate for their documents, we may mention the Pallavas of South India, the Vākāṭakas of Berar, the Maitrakas of Valabhī and the Bhaumas of Prāgjyotiṣa. The Nidhanpur inscription[4] of the Bhauma king Bhāskaravarman (first half of the 7th century) was originally written at least in about one hundred and seventy lines on as many as six or seven plates. The records of the Eastern Gaṅga emperors of medieval Orissa were usually incised on six or seven plates which, together with the seal-ring, generally weigh more than one thousand *tolās*. One of the Puri copper-plate inscriptions[5] of Gaṅga Narasiṁha IV, who ascended the throne about 1378 A. D., contains no less than two hundred and seventy-eight lines of writing. But the biggest copper-plate inscriptions so far discovered belong to the Coḷa dynasty of the Tanjore-Tiruchirapalli area of South India. The Leiden inscription[6] of Rājarāja I (985-1016 A.D.) has four hundred and forty-three lines of writing engraved on twentyone plates. The Tiruvalangadu inscription,[7] dated in the sixth regnal year of Rājarāja's son Rājendra I (1016-43 A. D.), is written on

1. *Ep. Ind.*, Vol. XXXV, p. 207.
2. Cf. Ojha, loc. cit.
3. *A. R. Ep.*, 1957-58, No. A 3.
4. P. N. Bhattacharya, *Kāmarūpaśāsanāvalī*, pp. 1 ff.
5. *JASB*, Vol. LXIV, Part i, pp. 136 ff.
6. *Ep. Ind.*, Vol. XXII, pp. 213 ff.
7. *SII*, Vol. III, pp. 383 ff.

thirtyone plates which, together with the massive seal-ring, weigh 7,980 *tolās* (about 200 lbs.) and bear eight hundred and sixteen lines of writing. But the biggest copper-plate charter so far discovered is the Karandai inscription of the eighth regnal year of the same Coḷa monarch.[1] It is engraved on no less than fifty-five plates which measure 16½ inches by 9½ inches each and together weigh, even without seal-ring, 8645 *tolās* (about 216 lbs.). The weight of one of the two seal-rings found with the plates is 753 *tolās*. The inscription contains upwards of two thousand and five hundred lines of writing. The first three plates, containing one hundred and thirtyone lines, give the genealogy of the Coḷas up to Rājendra I and record the gift of a village in favour of certain Brāhmaṇas. The next twentytwo plates contain a eulogy (in one thousand and fortyone lines) of the king as well as a description of the boundaries of the gift village and the names of the officials and other persons associated with the grant. The last thirty plates quote (in one thousand three hundred and sixtyseven lines) the names of the donees together with those of their *gotras*, places of residence, etc. The number of donees thus enumerated is no less than one thousand and seventythree.

We know that, while describing the boundless liberality of a king, a poet sometimes speaks of the dearth of copper that resulted from the issue of innumerable copper-plate grants by the former.[2] Considering the great bulk of the copper charters of the Coḷa monarchs, we have to admit that the statement, hyperbolic though it is, may not, at least in some cases, be entirely without foundation.

In this connection, it has also to be noticed that sometimes old or rejected copper plates were utilised for the preparation of fresh charters. Often they were melted to make a sheet of copper and smaller sheets were cut out of it for parti-

1. *Jour. Or. Res.*, Vol. XIX, p. 148.

2. Ballāla's *Bhojaprabandha* (Nirnayasagara Press, 1932), p.34, verse 162 : *Asya śrī-Bhojarājasya dvayam=eva sudurlabham* । *śatrūṇāṁ śṛṅkhalair=lohaṁ tāmraṁ śāsana-patrakaiḥ* ॥

cular charters. In such cases, the old writing is completely lost even though sometimes traces of hammering are noticeable on the plates. But, in some cases, the old writing was merely beaten in by hammering and the text of the new document was written on the erasure. In such records, traces of the old writing are often visible under the later writing. We have a number of palimsests of this kind.[1] In certain cases, only a part of the old writing is beaten in by hammering or erased by chiselling.[2]

Late copper-plate grants like those of the Ahom kings of Assam and the rulers of Chamba are generally written on one side of a single plate, though the size of the plate varies according to the requirement in individual cases. The donor's seal is usually engraved on such plates. The copper-plate grant of the Chamba rulers is provided with a handle to its proper right and the plate thus puts on the appearance of a *takhtī* or wooden board used formerly by school children. A hole is sometimes noticed in the centre of this handle probably for hanging it on to a peg with a string. The predilection for engraving only on one side of the plate is much in evidence in certain cases where the writing runs on into all the margins not excluding the handle, and the size of the letters in the concluding part of a record gradually diminishes.[3]

The seal engraved on these charters has the shape of a rosette or some other ornamental design, the space in the centre being occupied by a legend containing the name of the donor. Sometimes the seal is replaced by the word *sahī* which has been compared to the word *dṛṣṭa* found in early charters and taken to mean 'correct'.[4] The word, however, also means 'a signature'[5] and may really stand for the donor's

1. Cf. *Ep. Ind.*, Vol. XXXI, pp. 202 ff. and Plates; above p. 76.
2. Ibid., Plates IVa and IVb facing pp. 307 and 308.
3. B. Ch. Chhabra, *Antiquities of Chamba State*, II, pp. 1-2.
4. Ibid., p. 75. In East Indian charters of the early medieval period, we have often the contraction *ni* which is generally taken to indicate *nibaddha* (i.e. registered), but may also stand for *nirikṣita* meaning 'seen' (i.e. approved), the same as *dṛṣṭa*. See below, p. 127 and note 2, pp. 149-50.
5. See Wilson's Glossary, s. v.

signature on the original document. In certain late medieval copper plates of the Orissa region, the word *śrī* is found to stand for the donor's signature.[1]

Late Orissan charters are also generally written on both sides of a single plate. But a peculiarity is that the first few lines mentioning the donor's name are engraved on the obverse, then the writing of the major part of the document is continued on the reverse and finally the closing lines are engraved on the lower part of the obverse, to be read now from the opposite side.

2. *Classification of Contents*[2]

The contents of royal charters, which were generally engraved on copper plates but sometimes also on stone slabs, may be divided into three broad sections, viz. (a) Preamble, (b) Notification and (c) Conclusion. But the grants of different ages, different royal families, different rulers of the same family and different categories of rulers often exhibit differences and there may be omissions and alterations in the details in each one of the sections.

The Preamble generally comprises the following items: (1) invocation, (2) the place of issue, (3) the name of the donor with his titles and ancestry, and (4) the address in respect of the grant. The Notification similarly comprises: (1) specification of the gift, (2) the name of the donee, (3) the occasion of the grant, (4) the purpose of the grant, and (5) the boundaries of the gift land. The Conclusion likewise contains: (1) an exhortation in respect of the grant, (2) the names

1. In the charters of the Senas of Bengal, we have the contractions *śrī-ni* probably standing for *śrī-nirīkṣita* (i.e. seen or approved by the illustrious [king]). In Orissan charters, sometimes the king is mentioned as *śrī-hasta* or *śrī-caraṇa* (cf. *Ep. Ind.*, Vol. XXVIII, p. 304; Vol. XXXIII, p. 292, text lines 181, 183; below, p. 150).

2. See B. Ch. Chhabra, 'Diplomatic of Sanskrit Copper-plate Grants' in *The Indian Archives*, Vol. V, 1951, pp. 1 ff., especially pp. 6 ff. The author uses the word 'diplomatic' in the sense of 'a critical study of diplomas' and 'diploma' in that of 'documentary source of history'. The Roman 'diploma' (from a Greek verb meaning 'to double') was so called because it was formed of two sheets of metal, which were shut together like the leaves of a book. Similar is the case with the grants of some West Indian rulers, which were incised on the inner side of two plates of copper with two rings passing through holes in their upper margin holding them together (cf. above, pp. 75, 122).

of the officials responsible for the preparation of the document, and (3) the date and authentication of the record.

The language in which these items are indicated is generally similar in different charters of the same king and of the kings of the same family. Some medieval copper-plate grants are, however, entirely written in verse and do not follow such stereotyped drafts.[1]

3. *Preamble*

Generally a charter opens with a *maṅgala* or auspicious invocation.[2] Early records[3] often begin with the auspicious word *siddham* which means the same thing as *siddhir=astu*, 'Let there be success.'[4] Sometimes the word *svasti* was used instead of *siddham*.[5] Later on, *siddham* began to be expressed by a symbol[6] which was often followed by the word *svasti*.[7] Medieval records sometimes show *Oṁ* at the beginning generally along with the *siddham* symbol and other invocatory passages.[8]

1. Cf. *Ep. Ind.*, Vol. III, pp. 24 ff., 120 ff., 151 ff., 240 ff.

2. Before this, some early copper-plate grants, especially of certain South Indian royal families (e. g. the Vākāṭakas, Pallavas, etc.), have the word *dṛṣṭam* (Prakrit *diṭhaṁ* or *diṭṭhaṁ*) meaning, '[It has been] seen', to indicate that the original of the document on the plates had been examined by the proper authorities who found it allright. See *Select Inscriptions*, pp. 406, 412, 419, 433, 357, etc. In some early medieval charters of East India, e. g. those of the Pālas, the letter *ni* is found about the beginning or the end of the first line of writing or at its both ends. See *Ep. Ind.*, Vol. XV, p. 295, note 4; Vol. XXIX, pp. 2, 9, 49. This letter may be taken to be an abbreviation of *nibaddha* meaning 'registered', or, as we have seen, *nirīkṣita* which means 'seen' or 'approved' exactly as the word *dṛiṣṭa* found in a similar position in certain South Indian grants referred to above. See *JAS*, Letters, Vol.XX, pp. 216-17. Cf. also above, pp. 92 ff., p. 125, note 4; below, pp. 149-50.

3. See, e. g., *Ep. Ind.*, Vol. I, p. 5; Vol. XXVI, p. 151; etc.

4. The antiquity of the use of this word is proved by Patañjali's *Mahābhāṣya* on the first *vārttika* (*siddhe śabd-ārtha-sambandhe*) of Kātyāyana on Pāṇini's *Aṣṭādhyāyī*. Patañjali says that Kātyāyana employs the word *siddha* at the very outset for the auspicious completion of his scientific treatise. See Chhabra, loc. cit.

5. See, e. g., *Ep. Ind.*, Vol. XVII, p. 336.

6. Al-Bīrūnī is wrong in stating that the symbol stands for the *Praṇava* or the auspicious sound *Oṁ* (Sachau, *Alberuni's India*, Part I, p. 173). The mistake is clear from its use by the Buddhists who had no regards for the *Praṇava* (cf. *Proc. IHC*, 1939, pp. 471 ff.; above, pp. 92-93,95).

7. See, e. g., ibid., Vol. XXVI, p. 317; Vol. XXVII, p. 199. Sometimes we have *siddhiḥ* instead of *svasti* (ibid., Vol. XII, p. 323).

8. Cf. ibid., Vol. XV, p. 282 (symbol followed by *Oṁ namaḥ Śivāya*, etc.).

Gradually the invocation became more and more elaborate, and it ran from mere symbols and words to more or less big sections in prose and verse in praise of the favourite deities of the grantors or the writers of the document. Thus the charters of the Early Western Gaṅgas begin with the symbol denoting *siddham*, followed by a passage hailing the god Viṣṇu in the words: *jitaṁ bhagavatā gata-ghana-gagan-ābhena Padmanābhena.*[1] A still more elaborate type of invocation is illustrated by records like the Rewah plates of Trailokyamalla, which begin with *Oṁ namaḥ Śivāya Gaṇapataye namaḥ*, followed by three invocatory verses, the first in praise of the god Kṛṣṇa, the second of the god Śiva and the third of the goddess Sarasvatī.[2] Sometimes the same stanza is found in many records of the same family or area[3] and such a verse may be borrowed from a well-known work.[4] In the charters of some dynasties, e. g., the Pālas of Bengal and Bihar and the Imperial Gaṅgas of Orissa, an invocatory stanza as well as the genealogy of the donor in verse was copied by him from his predecessors' grants. As in the case of most dynasties, this invocatory verse refers to the deity worshipped by the donor's family. But in charters like those of the Early Kadambas of Banavasi, the different grants of the same ruler often begin with invocation to different deities. In such cases, the deity referred to in the invocation seems to have been worshipped by the particular scribe who drafted a charter.[5]

The name of the place, from which a grant was issued,

1. See, e. g., the Sasanakota plates of Mādhavavarman I (ibid., Vol. XXIV, pp. 234 ff.).

2. Ibid., Vol XXV, p. 5.

3. The verse *Labhate sarva-kāryeṣu pūjayā gaṇanāyakaḥ | vighnaṁ nighnan=sa vaḥ pāyād=apāyād=Gaṇanāyakaḥ* || in praise of Gaṇanāyaka is found in most of the grants of the Śilāhāras of the Northern Konkan as well as some other rulers of the same region. See, e. g., *Ep. Ind.*, Vol. XXV, p. 55; Vol. XXXII, p. 66, text lines 1-2; p. 74, text lines 1-2; etc.

4. The verse *Caturmukha-mukh-āmbhoja-vana-haṁsa-vadhūr=mama | mānase ramatāṁ nityaṁ sarva-śuklā Sarasvatī* || in praise of Sarasvatī is quoted from Daṇḍin's *Kāvyādarśa* (cf. ibid., Vol., XXV, p. 5) while the stanza *Namas=tuṅga-śiraś-cumbi-candra-cāmara-cārave | trailokya-nagar-ārambha-mūla-stambhāya Śambhave* || in praise of Śambhu, quoted from the *maṅgala* in Bāṇa's *Harṣacarita*, is found in numerous epigraphs especially from South India (cf., e. g., *Ind. Ant.*, Vol. XIII, p. 92).

5. See *Suc. Sāt. L. Dec.*, pp. 260, 265, etc.

was sometimes mentioned after the *maṅgala* or invocation. Charters were generally issued from the capital of the donor and, in such cases, the place of issue was often omitted as it was taken for granted. Sometimes the place of issue happens to be a royal camp, either in the course of a military expedition or of a pilgrimage, and it was specifically mentioned in the charter.[1] In some cases, the place of issue is mentioned in connection with the donor's name, either before or after it, and not immediately after the *maṅgala* or invocation at the beginning of a document.[2]

As in the case of invocation, so too in mentioning the place of issue, we have in later records sometimes an elaborate description of the city or camp instead of a mere mention of its name. Thus, while the Sasanakota plates[3] of the early Western Gaṅga king Mādhavavarman I omit this item altogether, the Prince of Wales Museum plates[4] of Gurjara Dadda III have merely : 'from the prosperous [city of] Bharukaccha' without any embellishment and the Chittagong plate[5] of Kāntideva has only: 'from the glorious and victorious campresidence at the city of Vardhamāna.' Similarly, Mādhavavarman's Ipur plates[6] have : 'from the victorious camp [pitched] at Kuḍavāḍa', after the donor's name and not after the *maṅgala* or invocation. An elaborate mention of the place of issue is illustrated by records like the Sonepur plates of the Somavaṁśī king Mahābhavagupta I Jaṇamejaya of South Kosala, in which the invocation is followed by a long

1. See Bāṇa's *Kādambarī*, N. S. Press, p. 225, for the issue of grants by kings while on their marches. The Banaras copper-plate grant of Kalacuri Karṇa (Bhandarkar's List, No. 1223) was issued when he was on a pilgrimage at Prayāga in connection with his father's annual *Śrāddha* ceremony.

2. Cf. the *siddham* symbol followed by *svasti Valabhītaḥ* at the beginning of the Bhamodra-Mohota plate of Maitraka Droṇasiṁha and *Gahilū-grāma-samāvāse* in line 15 of the Mahoba plates of Candella Paramardin (*Ep. Ind.*, Vol. XVI, p. 18 and p. 12); also *śrī-Vikramapura-samāvāsita-śrīmaj-jaya-skandhāvārāt* before the king's name in the prose passage after the versified introduction in the records of the kings of Bengal (iibid Vol. XXXIII, p. 139, text lines 17-18).

3. Ibid. Vol. XXIV, p. 238.

4. Cf. ibid., Vol. XXVII, pp. 197 ff.

5. Ibid., Vol. XXVI, p. 317.

6. Ibid., Vol. XVIII, p. 336.

prose passage in nine lines of writing, describing the city of Ārāma.[1]

The mention of the name of the donor in the preamble of a grant is an important source of historical information. In the earlier charters, only the name of the donor is mentioned, with or without a royal title, and occasionally the name of his father and, in some cases, also of his grandfather are mentioned in his description. In certain early records like those of the Sātavāhanas, the king is mentioned only with a metronymic like *Gautamī-putra* indicating his birth from a lady born in a family belonging to a particular *gotra*.[2]

The above bare outline gradually expanded into elaborate genealogies and strings of epithets in later records. We have often racy and ornate descriptions, in prose or verse or in a mixture of both, in the introduction of the donor, which cover a considerable part of his charter. The military exploits of the donor and his ancestors received special attention of the court poets who composed the said section called *praśasti* or eulogy and often attributed vague and imaginary achievements to the personages described. Physical charms and qualities of head and heart, sometimes real but often imaginary, were generally made the subjects of description. Thus while the Śātavāhana charters usually introduce the king's name with a metronymic but with or without any royal epithet, eleven out of the twenty four lines of writing on the Sasanakota plates, referred to above, are devoted to the introduction of the donor. After the invocation, the Jāhnaveya family and the Kāṇvāyana *gotra*, to which king Mādhavavarman I claimed to have belonged, and his father Koṅgaṇivarman are gradually introduced. This is followed by the donor's own name, the intervening spaces being filled up with epithets describing the father and the son. Some of these epithets

1. *Ep. Ind.*, Vol. XXIII, p. 250.

2. See *Select Inscriptions*, pp. 191ff. This was apparently done to distinguish the ruler in question from his namesakes as well as his step-brothers born of his father's other queens. For the absence of *gotr-āntara* (the change of the wife's *gotra* to that of her husband) in some forms of ancient Indian marriage, see *Proc. IHC*, 1945, pp. 48 ff.

are of little importance to the student of history, e. g. when the father is described as 'one who has produced lands [inhabited by] good people by the conquests born of the impetuosity of his own arms.' The description of king Kāntideva and his parents in the Chittagong plate consists of six ornate verses followed by a prose passage, while Dadda's charter describes in ornate prose, in about 14 lines out of a total of about 30, not only his father or parents, but also some of his distant ancestors.

The charters of imperial dynasties like the Eastern Gaṅga, Kalacuri, Rāṣṭrakūṭa, Coḷa, Cālukya, Paramāra and Pāla, contain an elaborate genealogical description in connection with the introduction of the donor. Thus the Asankhali plates[1] (1303 A. D.) of Gaṅga Narasiṁha II of Oṛissa have 212 lines of writing, 165 of which are covered by an elaborate genealogical description introducing the donor. It consists of 105 stanzas in various metres and a passage in prose between verses 6 and 7. Of the many ancestors mentioned (some of whom are mythical or imaginary), the achievements of 10 beginning with Vajrahasta III (1038-70 A. D.) are specially dealt with. The same introductory section is not only found in the other charters of the same king, but the verses are mostly copied from the grants of his ancestors.[2] The real grant begins in line 165 with the word *svasti*. The introductory composition of this nature was often kept ready for adding the grant portion at a later date. We have several copper-plate grants with only the introductory portion engraved on them.[3] Important historical information is generally scattered here and there in these descriptions which are, as indicated above, in most part full of vague praises for the king and his ancestors. Records like those of the imperial branch

1. *Ep. Ind.*, Vol. XXXI, pp. 109 ff.

2. The stanzas describing the end of the rule of the donor's predecessor and those dealing with the donor himself were newly composed and added to those found in the charters of the predecessor.

3. See, e. g., the Chittagong plate of Kāntideva and the Kedarpur plate of Śrīcandra (*Ep. Ind.*, Vol. XXVI, pp. 313 ff.; Vol. XVII, pp. 188 ff.) which illustrate the practice of keeping such blanks in readiness in the office.

of the Eastern Gaṅga dynasty of Orissa give the duration of the different kings' rules in years in round numbers[1] while those of the Eastern Cālukya kings give it more accurately sometimes mentioning months and days.[2]

The order in respect of a grant was often addressed to subordinates and officials as well as to the inhabitants of the area where the donated land or village was situated. In early charters sometimes the item is altogether absent or only the governor or the villagers are addressed in respect of the grants.[3] But the list of state officials is generally more or less lengthy in some of the later records especially of Northern India. Such big lists often include subordinate rulers, fief-holders, officers of the revenue department as well as those of the police, the judiciary and the military department and some members of the royal household.

While issuing the order in respect of a grant, the king often shows the courtesy of greeting the addressees and enquiring after their welfare. The expressions indicating the command is generally *samādiśati* or *ādiśati*; but sometimes other words like *bodhayati*, *mānayati*, *kuśalayati*, etc., are added to it. According to the legal etiquette of those days, the donor is usually described as *kuśalin*, 'in good health'. The implication is that the donation was made when the donor was in his full senses and was not under the influence of any disease or intoxicant and that therefore the deed issued in favour of the donee should have to be recognised as a valid document.

The item of address is absent in charters like the Sasanakota plates referred to above and the Parbatiya plates[4] of king Vanamālavarman of Assam, who flourished in the 9th century A.D. The Ipur plates contain an address only to the residents of the village granted and the expressions *kuśalī* and *viditam=astu vaḥ* are missing in the record. The persons addressed in Dadda's grant include the subordinate rulers

1. See *Ep. Ind.*, Vol. XXVIII, pp. 249 ff.
2. *SII*, Vol. I, pp. 53 ff.
3. Cf. *Select Inscriptions*, pp. 445 ff., 456 ff., 433 ff., 458 ff. See also Appendix below, pp. 161 ff.
4. *Ep. Ind.*, Vol. XXIX, pp. 145 ff.

and chiefs and the donor's own officers, but not the villagers. In certain Sātavāhana and Early Pallava records, the order is issued to the governor of the district in which the gift land was situated.[1] The above-mentioned Chittagong plate of Kāntideva has : 'the illustrious Kāntideva, being in good health, informs the future kings of the Harikelā *maṇḍala* as follows, for their own good : "Be it known to you".' Passages like *viditam=astu vaḥ, viditam=astu bhavatām, astu vaḥ saṁviditam, matam=astu bhavatām,* etc., calling attention to the notification that follows immediately, are of frequent occurrence.[2] In the Svalpavelura grant of the Gaṅga king Anantavarman,[3] the fairly long list of officers is headed by the Brāhmaṇas and the expressions used are : 'being in good health, duly honours and commands', while the Baripada Museum plate of Devānanda[4] has : 'duly honours, intimates to, enquires after the health of, and commands'. The persons addressed in these cases include both officials and villagers.

A very long list of officials and non-officials addressed by the donor in connection with a grant is found in the early medieval charters of some parts of Northern and Eastern India such as those issued by the Pāla and Sena kings of Bengal and Bihar. Thus the Anulia plate[5] of Lakṣmaṇasena has twenty-five entries in the list while the Bangadh plate[6] of Mahīpāla I has no less than fortyfour including those of peoples like Gauḍa, Mālava, Khasa, Hūṇa, etc., who were probably mercenaries in the Pāla army, not to mention certain other classes including the Brāhmaṇas, Medas, Andhras and Caṇḍālas.[7]

1. See, e.g., *Select Inscriptions*, pp. 191 ff., 193 ff., 433 ff., etc.
2. Some times, *c=ānyat*, 'and another thing', intervenes between *samājñāpayati* and *viditam=astu* (cf. *Ep. Ind.*, Vol. XXVI, p. 204, text lines 17-18).
3. *Ep. Ind.*, Vol. XXIV, p. 135.
4. Ibid., Vol. XXVI, p. 79.
5. N. G. Majumdar, *Ins. Beng.*, Vol. III, pp. 86-87.
6. A. K. Maitreya, *Gauḍalekhamālā*, pp. 96-97.
7. The officials and others referred to in the Pāla records are : *rājan* (subordinate king) ; *rājanyaka* (subordinate chief); *rājaputra* (possibly, nobleman) ; *rājāmātya* (minister or executive officer); *mahāsāndhivigrahika* (minister for peace and war); *mahākṣapaṭalika* (accountant and record-keeper) ; *mahāsāmanta* (feudatory); *mahāsenāpati* (general) ; *mahāpratihāra* (officer in charge of palace-gates, etc.) ; *mahākārtākṛtika*; *dauḥsādhasādhanika* (emergency officer) ; *mahādaṇḍanāyaka* (commander, etc.) ; *mahākumārāmātya* (minister of the rank of a prince of the royal blood) ; *rājasthān-oparika* (viceroy); *dāśāparā-*

4. *Notification*

As indicated above, the items in notification, which is the central theme of a charter, are: (1) the specification of the gift, (2) the name of the donor, (3) the occasion and purpose of the grant, and (4) the boundaries of the gift land. These items, however, do not always appear in the records in the said order, neither do all charters have all the five of them. The recorded details in different grants sometimes differ widely.

The gift generally consists of a plot of land or a field or a village or several plots, fields or villages. The name and location of the gift land are often indicated with reference to the district and other territorial divisions such as *grāma*, *viṣaya*, *maṇḍala*, *bhukti*, *vīthī*, *pattalā*, etc. The area of a plot of land is usually specified in the current land measure called *hala*, *nivartana*, *pādāvarta*, *kulyavāpa*, *droṇavāpa* *āḍhavāpa*, *nālikāvāpa*, *kalasikā:āpa*, *ṭimpira*, etc. It is difficult to determine the exact area of these land measures with reference to particular ages and localities, though the words ending in *vāpa* give some vague indication. Thus *droṇa-vāpa* no doubt meant originally an area of land on which one *droṇa* measure of the seeds of the principal crop could be sown.[1]

In connection with the measurement of land, sometimes particular measuring rods are mentioned and its length, occasionally according to the length of the forearm of an individual, is vaguely or specifically indicated. Thus the land granted by means of the Barrackpur plate[2] of Vijayasena is

dhika (police magistrate); *cauroddharaṇika* (prefect of the police); *dāṇḍika-dāṇḍapāśika* (police officers); *śaulkika* (customs officer); *gaulmika* (officer in charge of police-station, etc.); *kṣetrapa* (officer in charge of the royal lands); *prāntapāla* (warden of the marches); *koṭṭapāla* (governor of a fort); *khaṇḍarakṣa* or *aṅgarakṣa*; those in charge of elephants, horses, camels, navy and army; those in charge of foals, mares, cows, she-buffaloes, goats and sheep; *dūta*, *preṣaṇika*, *gamāgamika*, *abhitvaramāṇa*; head of a district; head of a village; ferry-man; *cāṭa*, *bhaṭa* and other servants of such nationalities as Gauḍa, Mālava, Khasa, Hūṇa, Kulika, Karṇāṭa and Lāṭa; and other non-mentioned subjects and servants of the king. See *Ep. Ind.*, Vol. XXIX, p. 5, note 1; also below, Chapter VIII, Section iii.

1. See *Bhārata Kaumudi*, Part II, pp. 943 ff. One of the reasons for the difference was that the cubit was measured according to the length of the forearm of an individual and, consequently, the length of the measuring rod differed. See below, Chapter VIII, Section vi.

2. N. G. Majumdar, *Ins. Beng.*, Vol. III, p. 63, text line 33.

stated to have been measured according to the standard measuring rod (*nala*) used in the Samataṭa country, while one of the Faridpur plates of Dharmāditya states that the gift land was measured with a rod, the length of which was determined according to that of the forearm of the pious Śivacandra.[1] The measurement of the gift land was sometimes entrusted to a high officer of the king.[2]

The party, in whose favour the grant was made, sometimes consisted of a single person and sometimes of a number of persons. Some of the royal charters record grants of land to hundreds of donees often specifying the allotment to each one of them. The Chammak plates[3] of Vākāṭaka Pravarasena II record the grant of a village to 49 Brāhmaṇas without specifying their shares. The donees in this case were probably entitled to enjoy equal shares of the gift village. The Brāhmaṇa donees of the Nidhanpur plates[4] of Bhāskaravarman are more than 200 in number and their shares in the land are carefully specified. The largest list of donees is probably found in the Karandai plates[5] of Rājendra-coḷa I, which enumerate the names, etc., of no less than 1073 Brāhmaṇas. The donees were generally Brāhmaṇas whose names are often mentioned along with those of their fathers[6] and occasionally also with those of their grandfathers[7] and great-grandfathers as well as those of their *gotras*, *pravaras*, *caraṇas* and the Vedic *śākhās* to which they belonged.[8] In some cases, later inscriptions mention the place from which a donee's family originally hailed.[9] The list of donees sometimes throws welcome light on the social history of the country.[10]

1. *Select Inscriptions*, p. 356, text line 17.
2. Cf. *Ep. Ind.*, Vol. XXVIII, p. 188.
3. *Select Inscriptions*, pp. 418 ff. Sometimes the donees are mentioned as a group and not individually (*Ep. Ind.*, Vol. XXXI, pp. 5, 9).
4. P. N. Bhattacharya, *Kāmarūpaśāsanāvalī*, pp. 33 ff.
5. *Journ. Or. Res.*, Vol. XIX, 1950, p. 148.
6. See, e. g., *Ep. Ind.*, Vol. XXXII, p. 160.
7. See, e. g., ibid., Vol. XXIII, p. 205.
8. Cf. N. G. Majumdar, *Ins. Beng.*, Vol. III, pp. 5, 21, etc.
9. *Ep. Ind.*, Vol. XXIX, p. 12, text line 41; p. 56, text line 39.
10. Thus the list in the Nidhanpur plates show how the second part of personal names was stereotyped as family designations at a fairly early

When a religious institution like a temple was the recipient of a grant, the name of the deity (sometimes together with that of the priest or priests) is mentioned.[1]

Though gifts were made for acquiring religious merit, some grants do not specifically mention either the purpose or the occasion on which they were made. But most of the donations are known to have been made on occasions like a *saṅkrānti*, an eclipse of the sun or of the moon, a religious festival, or a visit to a sacred spot such as a temple or a confluence of rivers.[2] In a number of cases, the donor is stated to have made the grant after taking a ceremonial bath in the waters of a holy river.[3] Similarly, the grant is sometimes stated to have been made to the donee in the name of the family-deity of the king.[4]

A gift of land was sometimes made at the request of the donor's mother, wife or some other relative and, in some cases, also of an official or subordinate or a different ruler.[5] There are cases of grants made in return for a service done by the donee or his ancestors for the donor. Such donees sometimes belonged to communities other than the Brāhmaṇa. Thus the Pedda-Bammidi plates[6] of Gaṅga Vajrahasta III record the grant of a village to a non-Brāhmaṇa for his satisfactory military service, while the Garra plates[7] of Candella Trailokyavarman record the grant of land as *mṛtyuka-vṛtti* (literally, 'death-grant') in favour of a noble whose father died fighting the Muhammadans on the king's behalf. The gifts were

date in East India where the Brāhmaṇas were then enjoying cognomens now prevalent only among the non-Brāhmaṇa classes. Cf. *IHQ*, Vol. XIX, pp. 17-18; Vol. XXIII, p. 236.

1. See, e.g., *Ep. Ind.*, Vol. XXXI, p. 189.

2. Cf. ibid. Vol. XXVIII, p. 64 and note 3; etc.; *Garuḍa Purāṇa*, Pūrva-khaṇḍa, Ch. 51, verse 29: *Ayane viṣuve c=aiva grahaṇe candra-sūryayoḥ* | *saṅkrānty-ādiṣu kāleṣu dattaṁ bhavati c=ākṣayaṁ* See below, p. 145.

3. Cf. the expression *vidhivad=Gaṅgāyāṁ snātvā* in the Pāla charters (*Ep. Ind.*, Vol. XXIX, p. 8, text line 46).

4. Cf. *bhagavantaṁ Buddha-bhaṭṭārakam=uddiśya* (ibid., Vol. XXXIII, p. 140, text line 37).

5. See above, pp. 114 ff.

6. *Ep. Ind.*, Vol. XXXI, pp. 305 ff.

7. Ibid., Vol. XVI, pp. 272 ff.

generally sanctified by the libation of water,[1] although this ritual is not mentioned in some of the charters.

The purpose of a grant, which was generally the accretion of merit to the donor and his parents, is specifically mentioned in many cases. A number of early charters are stated to have been issued for ensuring the longevity, strength, glory and prosperity of the donor. In some cases, a grant is known to have been made in order to enable the donee to perform his daily rites if he was a Brāhmaṇa, for the maintenance of the worship of a deity, for conducting repairs to a temple, or for feeding monks, etc., as the case may be, the expenses involved being met from the income derived from the gift land. Sometimes, however, no such specification was made and the donee was to enjoy the gift as he pleased. The donee's and his descendants' rights and privileges, including exemptions and immunities in respect of the gift land, are often clearly stated. In some cases, as already indicated above, the donee had to pay certain taxes while he was rarely allowed to enjoy the fines from thieves and some other transgressors of law.[2]

In cases where the plot of land or the village granted happened to have its boundaries well known to the villagers, the limits were not specifically defined, though mention was sometimes made of the fact that it went with its wellknown boundaries. In other cases, the boundaries of the gift land are properly defined. Natural land-marks generally resorted to were hillocks, brooks, trees or groves. Often boundaries were demarcated by erecting posts or pillars[3] or by interring husks, charcoal, etc., in the ground.[4] Where a large area was involved, such records as those of the Coḻa and Pāṇḍya kings of South India sometimes speak, in connection with the

1. Cf. *Agni Purāṇa*, Ch. 209, verses 49-50:
Dravyasya nāma gṛhṇīyād = dadān = īti tathā vadet ı
toyaṁ dadyāt = tato haste dāne vidhir = ayaṁ smṛtaḥ ıı

2. Cf. also below, Chapter VIII, Section v.

3. The Mallasarul plate (*Select Inscriptions*, p. 363, text lines 15-16) speaks of the demarcation of boundaries with posts or pillars having the representations of lotuses and rosary. See also *Ep. Ind.*, Vol. XXXI, p. 12 and note 1; etc.

4. See, e. g., *Select Inscriptions*, p. 345 (Baigram plate, line 19) and note 1.

determination of boundaries, of a *kariṇī-bhramaṇa.* A high official, seated on a she-elephant and followed by a number of subordinates, took a ride round the gift land and the subordinates marked off the boundary and noted down the details as the procession proceeded.[1]

For a simpler notification we may refer to the Sasanakota plates,[2] in which we have: "On the 10th day of the bright fortnight in the month of Phālguna in the first year of his own [reign] with his extensive sovereignty ever on the increase, [the illustrious Mādhavavarman] has given to Dhāraśarman of the Vatsa *gotra* and the Taittirīya *caraṇa* , for his own welfare, the village named Velputtoru in the district of Paru, as a gift for the Brāhmaṇa, carrying all the [customary] exemptions, with the libation of water." The notification in Dadda's grant,[3] which is a lengthier one, begins with the statement of purpose which is 'the increase of the glory and merit in this world and the next' for the donor and his parents. This is followed by the name of the district and of the village granted, together with the specification of the privilege to be enjoyed by the donee, which included the collection of various taxes in cash and kind. The gift is stated to have been a perpetual one to be enjoyed by the donee and his descendants. Then come the names of the donee, his father, his *gotra* and the place of his origin, etc., as well as a reference to the libation of water. The occasion of the gift, which was omitted from this place, is recorded towards the end. It was the Rathasaptamī, the 7th day of the bright fortnight of Māgha, on which day, the gift of vehicles was supposed to be specially meritorious. It is thus interesting in this connection to note that the gift of land is stated in this case to have been accompanied with that of an elephant and a chariot. Boundaries are specified in the notification of such records as the Chevūru

1. See, e.g., *Ep. Ind.*, Vol. XXV, pp. 67-68. Jājuka, an ancient king of Kānyakubja, is said to have granted to a Brāhmaṇa, by means of a *śāsana*, as much land in the Jodhpur region of Rajasthan as he could traverse in 4 *praharas* on horse-back (cf. Bhandarkar's List, No. 200).

2. *Ep. Ind.*, Vol. XXIV, p. 238.

3. Ibid., Vol. XXVII, pp. 200-01.

grant of Amma I,[1] which records a gift made in favour not of a Brāhmaṇa but of a warrior who received a village along with certain distinctions, as a reward for his meritorious services and devotion to the king, on the occasion of the *anna-prāśana* ceremony of a prince.[2]

The privileges to be enjoyed by the donees are not exactly the same in the records of different ages and areas. But an idea may be formed from their specification in certain early and medieval records. Thus the Early Pallava grants speak of the following immunities (*parihāra*): 'not to be dug for salt' (*a-lavaṇa-khātaka*); 'to be treated as different from other parts of the district' (*a-rāṣṭra-sāṁvinayika*); 'free from the obligation of the supply of bullocks by the villages successively for royal officers on tour' (*a-paramparā-balīvarda*); 'free from the entry of royal agents' (*a-bhaṭa-praveśa*); 'free from the obligation of supplying boiled rice, pots, fire-wood, cot and shelter to royal officers on tour' (*a-kūra-collaka-vināśi-khaṭvā-saṁvāsa*); 'free from the obligation of supplying milk and curds, grass and wood, and myrobalan, vegetables and flowers' (*a-dugdha-dadhi-grahaṇa, a-tṛṇa-kāṣṭha-grahaṇa, a-harītaka-śāka-puṣpa-grahaṇa*); 'free from the obligation of paying various levies, etc.' (*a-kara-viṣṭi-koñjalla*); etc.[3] The Vākāṭaka inscriptions similarly speak of: 'free from payment of taxes' (*a-kara-dāyī*); 'free from the entry of royal agents' (*a-bhaṭa-cchātra-prāveśya*); 'free from the obligation of supplying flowers and milk' (*a-puṣpa-kṣīra-sandoha*); 'free from the obligation of supplying free passage (or, ferry), camping, hide-seats and charcoal' (*a-cār-āsana-carm-āṅgāra, a-pār-āsana°*); 'not to be dug for salt and other objects' (*a-lavaṇa-klinna-kreṇi-khanaka*); 'together with hidden treasure and deposits' (*sa-nidhi, s-opanidhi*); 'together with fixed and occasional

1. *Ep. Ind.*, Vol. XXVII, p. 46.

2. The ceremony is observed during the sixth month after the child's birth (cf. *Manusmṛti*, II, 34). For grants made on the occasions of the birth-day and the naming ceremony of a prince, see Bhandarkar's List, Nos. 368-69.

3. Cf. *Suc. Sāt. L. Dec.*, pp. 186 ff., 192-93. The exemptions are sometimes referred to as of 'eighteen kinds', in which 'eighteen' really means 'all'. See also below, Chapter VIII, Section v.

taxes' (*sa-klpt-opakḷpta*) ; 'for so long as the moon and sun endure'; 'for transmission to sons and grandsons'; etc.[1] According to the charters of the Pālas, the privileges of the donees were: 'upto the boundaries, grass and pasture lands [of the gift village]' (*sva-sīmā-tṛṇayūti-gocara-paryanta*); 'with the ground' (*sa-tala*); 'with the space [above the ground]' (*s-oddeśa*); 'with the mango and *madhūka* trees' (*s-āmra-madhūka*); 'with the waters and dry land' (*sa-jala-sthala*); 'with the pits and saline spots' (*sa-gart-oṣara*); 'with the tax from temporary tenants, etc.' (*s-oparikara*); 'with the *daś-āpacāra* or *daś-āparādha*' (i.e. fines realised for ten minor offences); 'with things recovered from thieves' (*sa-caur-oddharaṇa*); 'with exemptions from all oppressions'; 'not to be entered by *cāṭas* and *bhaṭas* (i.e. royal agents; probably, policemen and peons)'; 'nothing to be taken [by way of tax, etc.]'; 'together with all revenues such as *bhāga* (i.e. royal share of the produce), *bhoga* (i.e. periodical supply of fruits, etc.), *kara* (taxes), *hiraṇya* (tax to be paid in coins), etc.'; 'according to the maxim of *bhūmicchidra* (i. e. the custom of allowing one bringing a piece of fallow or jungle land under cultivation to enjoy it without paying rent)'; 'to last as long as the moon, the sun and the earth endure.'[2]

In some cases, the donees were required to observe certain conditions such as that the land should not be sold or mortgaged, prostitutes should not be given quarters there, the donees should not form into an armed band, gambling should not be permitted on the land, etc.[3] A condition was sometimes added to the effect that nonfulfilment of the specific conditions including loyalty to the king and good

1. *Select Inscriptions*, pp. 414, 417, 422.
2. See *Ep. Ind.*, Vol. XXIX, p. 5 and note 3. See also below, Chapter VIII, Section v.
3. See *Ep. Ind.*, Vol. XXV, p. 218:

Ā-candr-ārkam=idaṁ bhojyam=ebhir=eṣāṁ ca vaṁśajaiḥ ।
n=ādheyaṁ na ca vikreyaṁ sadā sanmārga-vartibhiḥ ॥

Paṇy-āṅganānāṁ sadanaṁ na deyaṁ
dyūta-pracāro='pi nivāraṇīyaḥ ।
śastr-ādikaṁ v=āpi na dhāraṇīyaṁ
sat-karma-niṣṭhair=bhavitavyam=ebhiḥ ॥

relations with the neighbouring localities by the donees would lead to the confiscation of the gift land.[1]

5. *Conclusion*

The concluding part of a charter is important for it often contains the date. As indicated above, its items are: (1) an exhortation, (2) the names of the officials responsible for the preparation of the document, and (3) the date and authentication, though there may be difference in different records in respect of details and some of the items may be omitted in some charters as in the other cases.

The notification of a grant is often followed by an exhortation or admonition which was addressed by the donor to the future kings of the land whether of his own or of any other royal house, to the contemporary rulers and those who might replace him or his descendants and to his own officials, dependants and subjects including the villagers of the area where the gift land was located. It was requested that the addressees should respect the grant made by the donor. The residents of a gift village were then generally advised to pay all their dues in cash and kind regularly to the donee and to obey him. The appeal for the preservation of the grant was sometimes accompanied by passages in prose and verse referring to the transitory nature of wealth and worldly existence, to the permanent character of meritorious deeds like the gift of land, to the merit accruing to the grant of land and to the maintenance of such a grant, and to the suffering that would befall the confiscators or violators of it. Some benedictory and imprecatory verses are usually quoted in this context often as the sayings of the sages or of a particular sage or as occurring in one of the religious texts.[2] The number of such stanzas may be as small as one[3] and as high as more than a

1. Cf. *Select Inscriptions*, pp. 423-24 : *rājñāṁ sapt-āṅge rājye a-droha-pravṛttānāṁ brahmaghna-caura-pāradārika-rājāpathyakāri-prabhṛtīnāṁ saṅgrāmaṁ kurvatām=anya-grāmeṣv=anaparāddhānām=ā-candr-āditya-kalīyaḥ; ato='nyathā kurvatām=anumodatāṁ vā rājño bhūmi-cchedaṁ kurvataḥ a-steyam=iti.*

2. See below, Appendix, pp. 169 ff.

3. See, e. g., Majumdar, *Ins. Beng.*, Vol. III, p. 21, text lines 49 ff.

score.[1] A commonplace among these is a saying to the effect that the maintainer of a grant derives as much merit as the donor. The grants in the South Indian languages often end in a passage like the following: 'the kings ruling over the area should protect this righteous deed; those who do not do so will incur the sin of slaughtering a thousand cows at Vāraṇāsi (i. e. Vārāṇasī).'[2]

Some early documents like the Damodarpur plates[3] have no exhortation as such, while many charters of the early period have a simple exhortation. Thus in the Ipur plates, the king advises his own officials to collect no rent from the gift village and to see to the protection of the gift. Only one customary verse is quoted in this connection. The item is not elaborate also in records like the Sasanakota plates, in which we have a prose passage threatening the violators of the grant with the commitment of the five major sins,[4] though this is reinforced by three benedictory and minatory stanzas ascribed in this case to Manu. The more elaborate exhortation in Dadda's grant covers about 9 lines of writing out of the total of 30. A long passage in ornate prose in this case is followed by four of the customary verses, here ascribed to Vedavyāsa.[5] The prose passage first states that nobody should interfere with the donee who was entitled to enjoy the gift land in whatever way he pleased, by cultivating it himself or by leasing it out to others. After this, the donor addresses the future rulers of his own lineage and others requesting them to approve of the grant and to maintain it in view of the fact that the merit of the grant is to be shared by the donor of land and the protector of the donor's grant and that fortune is fickle and life

1. See, e. g., *Ep. Ind.*, Vol. XII, pp. 324-25, text lines 24 ff. ; Vol. XXV, p. 59, text lines 79 ff.; cf. lines 44 ff.; *IHQ*, Vol. XX, pp. 243-44; etc.

2. Cf. *Ep. Ind.*, Vol. XXXII, p. 174.

3. Ibid., Vol. XV, pp. 113ff. But they have a few benedictory verses.

4. Often the minor sins are also added to this. Ancient Indian works on law recognise five major sins (*mahāpātakas*) and fiftyone minor sins (*upapātakas*). The five major sins are : killing a Brāhmaṇa, drinking liquor, theft or robbery, incest, and the company of persons guilty of such crimes. Cf. *Manusmṛti*, XI, 54; *Yājñavalkyasmṛti*, III, 227 ff.

5. *Ep. Ind.*, Vol. XXVII, p. 201.

impermanent. The violator of the grant is next threatened with the commitment of the five major sins.

The royal order regarding the grant of a village or land was not always issued by the king himself, but was often conveyed through an intermediary who was generally a high officer, sometimes even a prince. He is generally called *Dūta* or *Dūtaka* (literally 'the messenger') in North Indian records and *Ājñā*, *Ājñapti* or *Ājñāpti* (literally, 'the order') in the charters of South India. When the order emanated from the king himself, the fact is indicated in passages like *ājñā svayam*, 'the order is [from] the donor himself', *sva-mukh-ājñā*, 'the order [is] from the [donor's] own mouth', etc. The words *dūta*, *dūtaka*, *ājñā*, *ājñapti* and *ājñāpti* are generally translated by the word 'executor [of a grant]',[1] though it is believed that the dignitary in question merely carried the king's order relating to the grant to the officials by whom the charter was later drawn up and delivered to the donee.[2] The interpretation is supposed to be suggested by the passage *sva-mukh-ājñayā utkīrṇam*, 'engraved at the verbal order of [the king] himself', found in some records,[3] and the passage *svayam=ājñā* noticed in certain charters is believed to mean the same thing.[4] But, in some cases, the *Dūtaka*'s function is indicated by the expression *praveśita* suggesting that he also looked into the entry of the charter into the donee's possession.[5] It

1. See, e. g., *SII*, Vol. I, p. 33, note 1.
2. *Corp. Ins. Ind.*, Vol. III, p. 100, note 3; *Ind. Ant.*, Vol. VIII, p. 79.
3. *Corp. Ins. Ind.*, Vol. III, p. 194, text line 23.
4. In the same sense, we have sometimes *svayam=ājñāpanā* also (*Ep. Ind.*, Vol. XXVII, p. 36, text line 19). It may be pointed out that the designation *Ājñā-dāpaka* was wrongly created out of the passage *svayam=ājñā dāpakāś=c=ātra śrī-Rudrādityaḥ* in the Ujjain plates of Paramāra Vākpatirāja (*Ind. Ant.*, Vol. XIV, p. 160, p. 161 and note 28). Similar passages are found in many of the Paramāra charters. The designation *Dāpaka* is sometimes believed to stand for *Dūtaka*. This is, however, impossible in view of the fact that sometimes the same person is represented both as the *Dāpaka* and the *Dūta* (*Ep. Ind.*, Vol. XXII, p. 76, text line 68). The word *dāpaka* possibly means the real donor whose grant was ratified by the king, as already suggested above, p. 118.
5. See, e. g., Bhandarkar's List, No. 1501, stating that the grant was taken to the donee's home (*praveśita*) by Keśava as *Dūtaka*. See also ibid., No. 1502. These records come from the Ganjam region of Orissa. Cf. also the passage *svayam=ādiṣṭo rājñā dūtako='tra śrī-Bhaṭṭa-Stambhadevaḥ* (*Ep. Ind.*, Vol. XXVIII, p. 278, text lines 33-34; cf. Vol. XVIII, p. 29, text lines 38-39).

is also interesting to note in this connection that the Jethwai plates[1] (786 A. D.) represent Śaṅkhayya as the *Dūtaka*, but state at the same time that Vasudeva, the minister of foreign affairs, wrote the document at the order of the donatrix of the grant. It therefore appears that the *Dūtaka* was the real executor of the grant at least in some areas of the country in certain ages of history.

The item is omitted in some records like Dadda's grant, while the Sasanakota plates have : 'by the order from the king's own mouth.'[2] The Ipur plates mention the donor's son as the agent : 'its order (*ājñā*) is [from the king's] dear son, Mañcaṇṇa-bhaṭṭāraka.'[3] The Svalpavelura grant[4] has the illustrious *Mahāsāmanta* (i.e. a subordinate ruler) Aśokadeva as its *Dūtaka*.

While many charters bear no date at all, in some of them only the year is quoted. When a detailed date is given, it may come at the beginning, in the middle or at the end of a charter. Thus the date of a grant may form the part of any of the three broad divisions of a charter, referred to above. Sometimes a date expressed in words is quoted again in figures. In certain cases, the date mentioned in the Notification in words is repeated in the Conclusion in figures. The year mentioned may be according to a regnal reckoning or to an era prevalent in the area and age in question. The month, fortnight and day, and sometimes also the week-day, are often mentioned in later charters. Occasionally, the date contains additional details such as the *nakṣatra*, etc. The specification of the week-day is helpful in verifying the details of a date and finding out its equivalent in a known calendar. The date of the actual grant is sometimes earlier than that of the issue of the plates on which it was recorded.[5]

To quote a few illustrations, the Ipur plates[6] were

1. *Ep. Ind.*, Vol. XXII, p. 109, text lines 66-68.
2. Ibid., Vol. XXVII, pp. 197 ff. ibid., Vol. XXIV, p. 238.
3. Ibid., Vol. XVII, p. 336.
4. Ibid., Vol. XXIV, p. 136.
5. See below, Chapter VII.
6. Ibid., Vol. XVII, p. 337.

issued 'in the thirtyseventh year of [king Mādhavavarman's] reign of increasing victory, the 15th day of the 7th fortnight of the hot season.' This date refers to an old practice of dividing the official year into three seasons instead of twelve months.[1] The date of the Sasanakota plates is given as the first regnal year of the donor and the details quoted indicate the 10th *tithi* of the bright fortnight of the month of Phālguna. These dates cannot be verified owing to the want of the week-day and a known era. The date of Dadda's grant[2] is quoted as the year 427 apparently referable to the Kalacuri era and corresponding to 675 A. D., the day being the Rathasaptamī or the 7th of the bright fortnight of the month of Māgha.

As indicated above, the occasions regarded as specially auspicious for purposes of making grants of land, etc., recorded in a large number of copper-plate inscriptions, were the full-moon, the new-moon, the solar or lunar eclipse, the vernal or autumnal equinox (*viṣuva*), the *saṅkrānti*, the *vyatīpāta* (when the new-moon falls on a Sunday and the moon is in certain *nakṣatras*, or when the full-moon falls on a Monday), *ayana* (the beginning of the sun's southerly or northerly course, i.e. the sun's appearance on or crossing of the equinoctial or solstitial point), etc. Certain grants are known to have been made on particular holy *tithis* like the Śiva-caturdaśī (14th day of the dark half of Māgha), Damanaka-caturdaśī (the 14th day of the bright half of Caitra), etc.

A high officer was generally entrusted with the task of drafting or writing out a charter. His name is mentioned in many cases and occasionally also his designation and his father's name. By way of illustration, reference may be made to the Sasanakota plates which simply record: 'this *tāmra-paṭṭikā* (i.e. copper-plate [charter]) has been written by Somaśarman',[3] while Dadda's grant has: '[this] has been written by Durgabhaṭa's son Saṅgulla, the *Mahāsāndhivigrahika* (i.e. chief officer in charge of peace and war or the minister

1. See below, Chapter VII, Section i, Subsection 4.
2. *Ep. Ind.*, Vol. XXVII, p. 201.
3. Ibid., Vol. XXIV, p. 238.

of external affairs)'.[1] The mention of the names of the officer and his father is sometimes helpful in the determination of the chronology of their masters when the order of succession of the latter is otherwise uncertain. Reference may be made in this connection to the help rendered by such details to the elucidation of certain knotty problems in the genealogy and chronology of the Gaṅgas of Śvetaka and the Somavaṁśīs of South Kosala.[2]

Often it is difficult to interpret with certainty whether the word *likhita*, 'written', used in a copper-plate grant, refers to the drafting or composition of the charter or to the copying of the draft on the plates for the guidance of the engraver. This is because, besides the composition of a document and its incision on the plates, the function of writing it on the plates with ink or a pointed instrument in order to help the engraver is sometimes referred to.[3] A calligraphist was entrusted with this work, though the engravers must have incised the documents without such help, in a large number of cases, directly from the drafts. Sometimes the correct position can be inferred. Thus the Salem plates of Śrīpuruṣa end with the passage: 'this charter has been written by Guru-śiṣya, an expert in the art of painting which is the basis of all arts',[4] even though the names of the composer and the engraver are not mentioned in this case.

In many records, the name of the person who engraved a document on the plates of copper is mentioned occasionally with that of his father and an epithet indicating his skill or profession. Thus the Bahmani plates[5] of Bharatabala state: 'and [it] has been engraved (*utkīrṇa*) by the goldsmith (*suvarṇakāra*) Īśvara's son Mihiraka'. The engraver of copper plates was generally a goldsmith or brazier whose profession is indicated by epithets like *suvarṇakāra*, *kāṁsyakāra*,

1. *Ep. Ind.*, Vol. XXVII, p. 201.
2. Ibid., Vol. XXV, p. 240; *IHQ*, Vol. XX, pp. 76 ff.
3. In rare cases, we have references to the composer, the writer and the engraver (cf. Bhandarkar's List, No. 156).
4. *Ep. Ind.*, Vol. XXVII, p. 150.
5. Ibid., p. 143.

taṭṭhakāra, *sekyakāra*, *akṣaśālin* (*arkaśālin*, *agasālĕ*), *pitalahāra*, etc. In some cases, an engraver is described as a *tvaṣṭṛ*, *śilpin* or *vijñānin* and is endowed with high-sounding epithets indicating his skill such as *varṇa-ghaṭanā-vaidagdhi-viśvakarman*.[1] In certain records of the Eastern Gaṅgas and Coḷas, the writer and the engraver are stated to have received each a share in the land granted, no doubt as fees for their services.[2]

Some charters like the Neulpur plate[3] of Śubhākara state that the record 'was written by the *Mahākṣapatalika* (chief officer in charge of accounts and records) *Bhogika* (*Jāgīrdār*) Brahmadatta; heated by the *Peṭṭapāla* (keeper of the record-boxes) Nārāyaṇa; and incised by the *Taṭṭhakāra* (brazier) Eḍadatta.' The expression 'heated' refers to the process of heating the plate or the ring holding the plates together for affixing the seal to it. An additional function, viz. that of authentication, is referred to in this connection in records like the Ganjam plates[4] of the Bhañja king Vidyādhara-bhañja Amoghakalaśa, in which we have: 'registered with a seal (*lāñchita*) by [the queen] Trikaliṅga-mahādevī, *Mantrin* Bhaṭṭa-Keśavadeva and *Vārgulika* (bearer of the king's betel-box) Cācika; written by *Sāndhivigrahika* Stambha; engraved (*utkīrṇa*) by *Akṣaśālin* (goldsmith) Kumāracandra.' The Nidhanpur plates[5] of Bhāskaravarman mention the designations *Ājñā*, *Sīmā-pradātṛ*, *Śāsayitṛ*, *Lekhayitṛ* and *Sekyakāra* respectively meaning the executor, the demarcator of the boundaries, the composer of the document, the writer on the plates and the brazier (engraver).

In the copper-plate charters of some medieval dynasties, such as the Bhauma-Karas of Orissa, there is often a stanza in the concluding part praying for the permanence of the

1. See, e. g., ibid., Vol. XXXII, p. 124.
2. See, e. g., ibid., Vol. XXVIII, pp. 189, 193.
3. Ibid., Vol. XV, p. 5.
4. Bhandarkar's List, No. 1500; cf. Nos. 1501-02. Some other functions are sometimes indicated in this connection by the expressions *anujñāta* which probably means 'witnessed', *anumata* probably meaning 'approved' and *praveśita*, 'executed' (*Ep. Ind.*, Vol. XXVIII, p. 279; Vol. XXIX, pp. 191-92).
5. P. N. Bhattacharya, *Kāmarūpaśāsanāvalī*, p. 26, text lines 132 ff. The passage seems to be wrongly interpreted by Bhattacharya.

grant or the donor's fame resulting out of it.[1] Such a verse is sometimes also found in the eulogies engraved on stone.[2]

Copper-plate charters usually bear some indication as regards their validity and genuineness. Generally this authentication is indicated by the royal seal affixed to the top or left of single plates and to the copper ring on which the plates of multi-plate records are strung. In some cases, the donor's signature on the original document, later incised on the plates, is also copied at the end. Thus Dadda's grant[3] concludes with the passage: *sva-hasto mama śrī-Daddasya*, '[This is] the own sign-manual of me, the illustrious Dadda.' Sometimes the words *mataṁ mama*, 'approved by me', are used. The word *mata* here may also mean the same thing as *sva-hasta*. But the records of the Candella king Madanavarman, e.g., have *sva-hasto='yaṁ śrīman-Madanavarmadevasya mataṁ mama*.[4] To such a sentence is in some cases added two others stating that the donor made his decree public through the language of the charter as drafted by the scribe and that the authoritative character of the grant could not be challenged on the basis of mistakes of omission and commission creeping into the text.[5]

With reference to the representation of the donor's signature on the copper-plate grants, it may be pointed out that, in most cases, the signature on the original record later engraved on plates was omitted, while, in certain medieval documents, it is not actually the donor's name that was engraved. The copper-plate grants of the Vijayanagara kings, which are generally written in Nandināgarī, have the name *Virūpākṣa* written in bold Kannaḍa characters at the end, Virūpākṣa probably being the family deity of the kings in question.[6]

1. See, e.g., *Ep. Ind.*, Vol. XXVIII, p. 216, text lines 27-28.
2. Cf., e. g., ibid., Vol. XXXII, p. 342, text lines 19-20 (verse 21); p. 346, text line 19 (verse 26); etc.
3. Ibid., Vol. XXVII, p. 201.
4. See, e. g., ibid., Vol. XXXII, p. 123, text lines 40-41.
5. See, e. g., ibid., p. 65.
6. Ibid., Vol. III, Plate facing p. 157.

In many late medieval documents, we have the word *śrī* or *sahī* in place of the donor's signature.[1] In the grants of the Sūryavaṁśī Gajapatis of Orissa, there is the curious representation of a dagger or sword in its place.[2]

We have referred above to some documents containing the expression *lāñchita* which really means 'endowed with the *lāñchana* or emblem', i.e. 'stamped with the royal seal'. This is generally noticed in the inscriptions of the Ganjam-Srikakulam region on the borders between Orissa and Andhra Pradesh such as the Ganjam plates[3] of Vidhyādhara-bhañja referred to above and the Svalpavelura grant[4] which was attested or registered by the king's seal (*lāñchita*) by the queen (*mahādevī*) Śrīvāsa-bhaṭṭārikā.[4] The same process is referred to in the East Indian records of the early medieval period, which speak of the stamping of the original document, later copied on a copper plate, by a seal bearing the representation of the royal family's emblem.[5]

The metallic representation of the seal used in stamping the original document is generally found, as indicated above, affixed to the top or left margin of single plates or to the ring holding several plates of a charter together. These seals sometimes exhibit the representation of one or more emblems forming the royal crest or insignia or coat-of-arms. Sometimes legends take the place of the emblem, the seals of some royal families having a metrical legend without any emblem. Most of the royal seals affixed to charters, however, contain both a legend and one or more emblems.

At the end of certain early medieval copper-plate grants of East India, e. g. those of the Senas, we have abbreviated endorsements like *śrī-ni*, *śrī-ni mahāsā-ni*, *śrī-ni mahāsāṁ-karaṇa-ni*,

1. Above, p. 125; *Or. Hist. Res. Journ.*, Vol. V, No. 1, p. 120; etc.

2. *Ep. Ind.*, Vol. XXXIII, Plate facing p. 20; *JAS*, Letters and Science, Vol. XXIII, p. 13 and Plate.

3. Cf. *Ep. Ind.*, Vol. XXVIII, pp. 335-36.

4. Ibid., Vol. XXIV, p. 136.

5. Cf. the expressions *śrīmad-Dharmacakra-mudrayā*, *Sadāśiva-mudrayā mudrayitvā*, etc., in the early medieval charters from Bengal (Majumdar, *Ins. Beng.*, Vol. III, p. 5, text line 31; p. 125, text line 56; etc.).

etc.[1] In these endorsements, *ni* is generally taken to stand for *nibaddha*[2] meaning 'registered', though the intended expression may also be *nirīkṣita* meaning 'seen' (i.e. 'approved'). *Śrī* is a contraction of *śrī-hasta* or *śrī-caraṇa* meaning 'the king' conventionally, while *mahāsā* or *mahāsāṁ* stands for *mahāsāndhi-vigrahika* (minister for peace and war) and *mahāsāṁ-karaṇa* for *mahāsāndhivigrah-ādhikaraṇa* (the office of the minister for peace and war). The mention of other officers is also noticed in such endorsements by their designation. Sometimes we have the endorsement as *ni anu makākṣa-ni* which seems to stand for *śrī-hasta-nirīkṣitaṁ tad-anu mahākṣapaṭalika-nirīkṣitam*, '[It has been] seen by the king and then by the *Mahākṣapaṭalika* (officer in charge of records and accounts).' Here *ni* at the beginning may also be the same as the contraction *śrīmat-karaṇa-ni* (i.e. seen by the palace staff of the king).

6. *Seals*

We have seen how, in order to assure the authenticity of copper-plate grants issued by kings, royal seals were attached to them. These seals are of various kinds and shapes. They are of small, medium or big size and generally round or elliptical in shape.[3] The seals of the early kings of Assam had the peculiar shape of a laddle.[4] Some of the royal seals are shaped like a lotus.[5]

The small seals generally contain only the representation of the emblem that was the crest of the family to which the issuer of the grant belonged. Often, however, the name of the king is found in addition to the emblem. Such emblems were generally associated with the religious persuasion of particular royal families. As Śaivism was the dominant

1. Cf. Majumdar, *Ins. Beng.*, Vol. III, pp. 21, 75, 88, 103, 126, etc.; above, pp. 125, 127.

2. The word *nibaddha* actually occurs, e. g., at the end of grants like the Barah plate of Bhoja (*Ep. Ind.*, Vol. XIX, Plate facing p. 18).

3. Cf. ibid., Vol. XXIX, Plate facing p. 37; Vol. XXVIII, Plate facing p. 85.

4. Ibid., Vol. XXIX, Plate facing p. 155; Vol. XXX, Plate facing p. 207.

5. Ibid., Vol. XXVIII, Plate facing p. 257.

religion in different parts of the country in all the ages of history, the representation of the bull (Śiva's *vāhana* called Nandin) is very often noticed on the seals of royal as well as private personages. The boar (representing an incarnation of Viṣṇu), Garuḍa (Viṣṇu's *vāhana*), Lakṣmī, Śiva, Viṣṇu, Dharma-cakra (the Buddhist wheel of Law), etc., are found on many seals. A number of seals also bear emblems without obvious religious association. Thus animals like the elephant and tiger figure on the seal of certain royal families,[1] while on some seals we have representations like a gate-way, a pair of fish, etc.[2]

In many cases, the royal seals are large in size. The legends on such seals often mention the name of the king and those of his ancestors reigning before him. Of some of the large seals, the upper half is generally covered by the emblem or emblems and the lower half by the legend.

The emblem on the seal of a family of rulers represented its crest or coat of arms, often called the *lāñchana*. In many cases, the same emblem is also found on the coins of the kings in question, both seals and coins being called the *mudrā*. Often the banner of the rulers of a particular family, generally called the *dhvaja*, bore a different emblem sometimes called *cihna*. Thus the Raṭṭas of Saundatti and Belgaum had the *Suvarṇa-garuḍa-dhvaja* (i. e. the banner of gold-colured Garuḍa) but the *Sindhura-lāñchana* (i.e. the elephant crest) and the Kadambas of Banavasi and Goa the *Śākhācarendra-dhvaja* or *Vānara-mahādhvaja* (i. e. the monkey banner) but the *Siṁha-lāñchana* (i.e. the lion crest).[3] The seal of the Pāla kings of Bengal and Bihar bore the representation of the Buddhist wheel of law and was mentioned in the charters of the family as the *Dharmacakra-mudrā*.[4] But

1. *Ep. Ind.*, Vol. XXVII, Plate facing p. 151; Vol. XXII, Plates facing pp. 213, 277.
2. Ibid., Vol. XXVIII, Plate facing p. 85; Vol. XXII, Plate facing p. 213.
3. *CII*, Vol. III, p. 151, note 4.
4. Other Buddhist rulers of Bengal, e. g., the Candras, had the same seal. The Sena seal bearing the figure of the god Sadāśiva was called the *Sadāśiva-mudrā* in the Sena epigraphs. See N. G. Majumdar, *Inscriptions of Bengal*, Vol. III, p. 5 and Plate facing p. 12; p. 125 and Plate facing p. 116.

the Nesari plates of Rāṣṭrakūṭa Govinda III suggest that the banner of the Pāla king Dharmapāla bore the figure of the Buddhist goddess Tārā.[1] The Nanda or Nandodbhava kings of Orissa had the bull crest on their seals, but are stated to have had *Sitadhātumaya-godhā-śikharīkṛta-lohitalocan-āmbara-dhvaja*, probably meaning a piece of cloth having the representation of a white alligator above that of a snake or of two eyes in red.[2] There were, however, cases where the same emblem was represented on the seal and banner of the kings of a family. The Nesari plates quoted above show that the Pallavas, Gaṅgas, Cālukyas, Coḻas and Pāṇḍyas had respectively the bull, elephant, boar, tiger and fish represented on their banners. But the bull also occurs on the seals of the Pallava kings.[3] The elephant adorning the banner of the Western Gaṅgas is also found on their seal.[4] That

1. See *Ep. Ind.*, Vol. XXXIV, p. 137; also G. H. Khare, *Sources of the Medieval History of the Dekkan*, Vol. I, p. 21 (cf. pp. 82-84) and Plate; cf. *JAS*, Vol. XXII, p. 133. The stanzas read as follows after correction of scribal errors : *Pāṇḍyadeś-ādhipān=matsyaṁ vṛṣabhaṁ Pallav-eśvarāt* I *Colād=vyāghraṁ gajaṁ Gaṅgāc=cāpa-yaṣṭiṁ ca Keralāt* II *Andhra-Cālukya-Mauryebhyo varāhaṁ Gurjar-eśvarāt* I *phalakaṁ prātipad-dhāryaṁ vṛṣabhaṁ Pallav-eśvarāt* II *Kosal-Āvanti-nāthābhyāṁ Siṁhalād=api nāmakam* I *Tārāṁ bhagavatīṁ khyātāṁ Dharmād=Vaṅgāla-bhūmipāt* II The passage *vṛṣabhaṁ Pallav-eśvarāt* seems to have been repeated unnecessarily, although it may be that two different victories or the defeat of two Pallava kings are referred to. It is stated that Govinda III snatched away the *cihnas* (*cihnāni* occuring in the verse following the above and apparently meaning the emblems on the banners) of his ememies whom he had defeated: the fish from the Pāṇḍya king; the bull from the Pallava king; the tiger from the Coḻa king; the elephant from the [Western] Gaṅga king; the bow from the Kerala king; the boar from the Andhra (Eastern Cālukya), Cālukya and Maurya and the *phalaka* bearing *pratipad* and *hārya* from the Gūrjara king; the bull from the Pallava king; the *nāmaka* from the Kosala, Avanti, and Siṁhala kings; the goddess Tārā from Dharma, king of Vaṅgāla. The word *phalaka* means a board, *pratipad* a kettle-drum, *hārya* a serpent, and *nāmaka* the name of the kings in question. The Nalas had a peculiar banner called Tripatākā-dhvaja, the word *tripatākā* being explained as 'the hand with three fingers stretched out' or 'three pennons' (*Ep. Ind.*, Vol. XXVIII, p. 13).

2. *Ep. Ind.*, Vol. XXVII, p. 327.

3. See, e.g., *SII*, Vol. II, p. 342, 362. The bull-banner of the Pallavas is referred to in Tamil literature, although in their inscriptions the Pallavas are stated to have had the banner having the emblem of the Khaṭvāṅga (a club with a skull fixed on top). See Mahalingam, *South Indian Polity*, pp. 85-86. According to one of the Vaikuṇṭha Perumāl temple inscriptions, the marks of Pallava sovereignty were the *Videlviḍugu*, *Samudra-ghoṣa*, *Khaṭvāṅga-dhvaja* and *vṛṣabha-lāñchana*. See *JAS, Letters*, Vol. XIII, p. 77.

4. *Ep. Ind.*, Vol. XXVII, Plate facing p. 151.

the Eastern Cālukyas had the boar on their seal is well known.[1] The Coḷa and Pāṇḍya seals bear the representations of the tiger, double-fish and bow,[2] although it is difficult to say whether, on their banners, the same group appeared or only one of the three emblems.

It appears that, in some cases, the emblem was an image fixed at the top of the banner-pole; but sometimes it may have been painted on the flag-cloth. That the *dhvaja* was often an image on a pole is suggested by the statement of Curtius that an image of Heracles (i.e. Vāsudeva-Kṛṣṇa) was being carried in front of the army of Porus (i. e. the Paurava king) as it advanced against the Greeks led by Alexander the Great.[3] In this connection, it is interesting to note that some coins of the Imperial Guptas, who had the Garuḍa emblem on their *dhvaja* and seal, bear the representation of a standard surmounted by the figure of Garuḍa.[4] The epic and Puranic literature suggests that the image of the individual emblems of particular archers were fixed at the top of their chariots. In an excellent survey of this evidence, Hopkins has shown that *dhvaja* is sometimes used as a synonym of *ketu*, but that sometimes the former means the whole arrangement including the staff and image or banner, while the latter means only the symbol or banner. *Ketu* is sometimes also synonymous with *patākā* or flag, while *dhvaja* is the metalic top-piece of the staff or that together with the staff. It has also been shown that the staff bore flags beneath the emblem.[5]

Sometimes a dynasty had its *dhvaja* and *ketu* clearly distinguished or had more than one emblem for the *dhvaja*. We have already referred to the bull and Khaṭvāṅga *dhvajas* of the Pallavas. The Imperial Rāṣṭrakūṭas claimed to have

1. Cf. *CII*, Vol. III, p. 151, note 4.
2. See *Ep. Ind.*, Vol. XXII, Plate facing p. 213; Vol. XXVII, Plate facing p. 125.
3. Mc'Crindle ,*Invasion of India by Alexander the Great*, p. 208.
4. See Allan, *Catalogue* (Gupta), pp. 1ff., Plate I, Nos. 1ff.; *CII*, Vol. III, p. 255. For the Gupta seal called *Garutmad-aṅka*, see Allan, op. cit., p. xxv.
5. *Journ. Am. Or. Soc.* Vol. XIII, pp. 243 ff.

the *Pāli-dhvaja*,[1] the *Oka-ketu* and the *Garuda-lāñchana*. It may be that originally they had the Garuḍa emblem on their seal and the Oka or bird on their banner, while the *Pāli-dhvaja*[2] was acquired by them at a later date after defeating their enemies. This is suggested by the fact that, though the Cālukya kings of Badami had the figure of the boar on their seal, and also on their banner according to the Nesari plates, Vinayāditya claimed to have acquired the *Pāli-dhvaja* after defeating some northern enemies.[3] Hopkins has shown that a charioteer had at times at least two ensigns. One of the two may have been depicted on the flag. Bhīṣma had the *Tāla-dhvaja* (banner of the palmyra tree) and the ensign of five yellow stars and a blue silk flag. Similarly, Droṇa had a *kamaṇḍalu* (pot) and also a *vedī* of gold as his emblems.[4]

Some royal families preferred the engraving of their charters on single plates of copper, while others incised their records on a number of plates.[5] In the former case, the seal was soldered to the top or left margin of the plate. But, when a grant was engraved on several plates, they were strung together on a ring which passed through a hole in the left or top margin of each plate, and the seal was affixed to the ring. The seal, usually moulded in bronze, was placed on the joint of the copper ring, and its inner part was fixed with the ring with the help of a lump of molten metal completely covering that particular part of the ring. The rings were generally round in shape. But copper-plate grants of some kings of Kathiawar and Assam exhibit longish rings, the side of one end of which touches the side of the other end and not the face of one end the face of the other end as is usually the case.[6]

1. *Bomb. Gaz.*, Vol. I, Part ii, pp. 387, 402.

2. The expression *Pāli-dhvaja* is said to have denoted an arrangement of flags in the following kinds of rows: garland, cloth, peacock, lotus, goose, eagle, lion, bull, elephant and wheel. See *Ind. Ant.*, Vol. XIV, pp. 104-05.

3. *Bomb. Gaz.*, op. cit., p. 368.

4. Hopkins, op. cit., p. 245. The Guttas of Guttal had both the *Vaṭa-vṛkṣa-dhvaja* and the *Garuḍa-dhvaja* (*Bomb. Gaz.*, op. cit., p. 578).

5. See above, pp. 75, 121.

6. Cf. *Ep.Ind.*, Vol. XXXI, Plate facing p. 304; P. N. Bhattacharya, *Kāmarūpaśāsanāvalī*, Plate facing p. 56 (reprinted from *JASB*, 1840).

As to single plates, the seals were so made as to have one knob or a few of them on their back side. The plates had a projection with one or more holes, and the knob or knobs on the back of the seals had to pass through them. The back of the seals was then affixed to the projected part of the plates with a lump of molten metal which totally covered the projection. In some cases, such single plates had no projection and the holes, meant for the knobs on the back of the seal to pass through, were made on the border of the plate itself. In some multi-plate charters (e. g. the records of the Maitrakas of Valabhī),[1] the plates were strung on two rings, but the seal was soldered to only one of them.

We may describe here a few of the royal seals affixed to the copper-plate grants by way of illustration. Thus the seal of the Sasanakota plates shows only the figure of an elephant, standing, facing the proper left, and there is no legend.[2] As it is a multi-plate record, the seal is affixed to the ring holding the plates together. The seal of the rulers of some families, on the other hand, bears a legend without any emblem. Thus seals affixed to the charters of Vākāṭaka Pravarasena II has for its legend the following stanza in *Anuṣṭubh*:

Vākāṭaka-lalāmasya krama-prāpta-nṛpa-śriyaḥ ।

rājñaḥ Pravarasenasya śāsanaṁ ripu-śāsanam ॥

arranged in four lines.[3] The seal of Kāntideva's charter is more elaborate in design. It is soldered to the top of the plate above the writing and has a raised rim with pointed end. "It is divided into two panels. The upper one bears in relief the figure of a seated lion inside a temple. The temple is indicated, as in many sculptures in Bengal, by a trefoil arch with flagstaffs on both sides. The seated lion is represented with mouth open and all the four paws

1. *CII*, Vol. III, p. 164, etc.

2. *Ep. Ind.*, Vol. XXIV, p. 134-35, Plate facing p. 239.

3. Ibid., Vol. XXII, Plate facing p. 173. The legend means : "[This is] the order (or, charter) of king Pravarasena, the ornament of the Vākāṭakas (i.e. of the Vākāṭaka family), who has attained royal dignity by inheritance—an order (or, a charter) for the observance [even] of his enemies."

in front. Across the lower panel of the seal is the legend *śrī-Kāntidevaḥ*. The letters are engraved in bold relief on a raised space. The seal is supported, at its lower end, by two figures of serpents, with raised hoods, whose interlaced tails and parts of the bodies are soldered both to the raised rim of the seal and the plate."[1] The circular seal of the Ipur plates has been described in the following words: "It is divided by a cross-line into two sections. The lower section bears, in relief, the legend *śrī-Mādhavavarmā* in two lines. Above the line seems to be a figure of Lakṣmī or a *svastika* on a pedestal, flanked by two lamp-stands and surmounted by the sun and the crescent of the moon."[2] The seal of the kings of Śarabhapura has a double-line demarcation in the middle of the surface, the upper field being occupied by the representation of Gaja-Lakṣmī and the lower by a legend in a stanza in the *Anuṣṭubh* metre arranged in two lines.[3]

The seal of some royal families like the Imperial Gaṅgas of Orissa bear no legend but a large number of emblems. Thus the seal attached to the Nagari plates[4] of Anaṅgabhīma III (c. 1211-39 A. D.), which is 3½ inches in diameter, has the form of an expanded lotus, the centre of which is occupied by an embossed figure of a seated bull, caparisoned and bedecked with ornaments, facing the front and having raised neck and head. To the proper left of the bull, there are the representations of a conch, the crescent moon, a dagger pointed downwards, and a *damaru*. To the right of the bull, are similarly found a trident and a goad or flywhisk. In the front of the bull, there is an emblem representing the solar orb. In some cases, the royal emblem is separately made and later attached to the seal. This is the case with the figure of Garuḍa on the seal of the Banda plates[5] of Paracakraśalya.

1. *Ep. Ind.*, Vol. XXVI, pp. 313-14, Plate facing p. 317. The lion is the symbolical representation of the Buddha, 'the lion of the Śākyas'.

2. Ibid., Vol. XVII, p. 334, Plate facing p. 335. The sun and the moon indicated the permanency of the rule of the family to which the king belonged or to that of the grant made under the seal.

3. Ibid., Vol. XXII, Plate facing p. 23.

4. Ibid., Vol. XXVIII, p. 236, Plate facing p. 257.

5. Ibid., Vol. XXX, Plate facing p. 139.

We have some good specimens of the royal seal of the Coḷa kings of South India. Thus the seal of a copper-plate grant[1] of king Rājendra-coḷa is about $4\frac{1}{2}''$ in diameter and has 16 projections around the margin at about equal intervals, the whole of it apparently designed to give the appearance of an expanded lotus. The central area of the seal, which is flattened, is marked off by a circular line and exhibits the emblems, constituting the Coḷa coat of arms. The most conspicuous among these are a pair of fish with the scales, fins, gills, eyes and snouts clearly delineated and a tiger, seated like a dog, with its tail brought forward between the legs and touching one of the two fish which it faces. Above the figure of the tiger is a parasol which is flanked by two flywhisks. A miniature representation of the sun occupies the space between the parasol and the left flywhisk, while the crescent is seen to the left of this flywhisk. Two lamp-stands are also found among the emblems, one to the left of the fish and the other to the right of the tiger, in a straight row with them. Each of the stands has a piece of cloth tied round the middle of it, while a wick-lamp is shown burning on each. Below this row of emblems appears a strung bow, with its string forming the pedestal for the emblems. Around the circle which encloses all these symbols, is engraved the following metrical legend in Choḷa-Grantha characters :

Etad=Rājendra-coḷasya Parakesarivarmaṇaḥ ।
rājad=rājanya-mukuṭa-śreṇi-ratneṣu śāsanam ॥[2]

But the legend on the seals of some of the North Indian royal families was much bigger. Thus the seals of the Imperial Guptas exhibit the figure of Garuḍa, the emblem of the family, in the upper part and sometimes as many as eight lines of writing below the emblem.[3] The seal of king Harṣavardhana, measuring about $5\frac{7}{8}''$ by $6\frac{7}{8}''$ has the bull

1. See ibid., Vol. XXII, p. 213. Cf. the seals illustrated in Plates facing pp. 213 and 277.

2. The legend means : "This is an order (or, a charter) of Rājendra-coḷa *alias* Parakesarivarman, which [rests] on the crest-jewels of [all] the reigning kings."

3. Cf. *JASB*, Vol. LVIII, Part i, p. 89 and Plate.

emblem in the upper part and a legend containing no less than 13 lines of writing.[1] Similarly, the seals of the early kings of Assam exhibit th: elephant emblem occupying the upper part of the surface, the legend in the lower part being big in some cases but smaller in others.[2] The legend was fairly big in the cases where the king, to whom the seal belonged, was described along with all his ancestors beginning with the founder of his house. Thus the legend on the oval seal ($3\frac{2}{5}''$ long and $3\frac{1}{10}''$ broad) of king Bhāskaravarman of Assam containing 11 lines of writing mentions no less than 14 of his ancestors together with the queens of 9 of them. The regal title *Mahārājādhirāja* is applied to 4 of the rulers while one of them is called 'the lord of Prāgjyotiṣa' and two 'the performer of two horse-sacrifices.'[3]

The legend on the seals of some royal families does not bear the name of the king who issued the charter bearing the seal. Thus the seals of the Maitraka kings of Valabhī in Kathiawad has the legend *śrī-Bhaṭakkaḥ* (*śrī-Bhaṭārkaḥ*), Bhaṭārka being the name of the progenitor of the royal family in question.[4] Similarly, the seals of some Eastern Cālukya kings attached to their copper-plate grants bear the legend *śrī-Tribhuvanāṅkuśa* which seems to have been a *viruda* of one of the earlier rulers of the dynasty.[5] It is difficult to say whether the Maitraka and Eastern Cālukya kings enjoyed the general name Bhaṭārka and Tribhuvanāṅkuśa respectively, since there is no such indication in the epigraphic records of the two families.

Some kings preferred to engrave the royal emblem on the copper plate (or on the first or last of the plates when the grant was written on several plates) instead of affixing the seal on the plate or on the ring holding several plates together.

1. *CII*, Vol. III, pp. 231-32, Plate XXXII B. According to Bāṇa's *Harṣacarita* (Nirnayasagara Press ed., p. 227), the state seal of king Harṣavardhana was made of gold. That was probably smaller in size.

2. *Ep. Ind.*, Vol. XXIX, p. 146 and Plate facing p. 155; Vol. XXX, p. 288 and Plate facing p. 305.

3. Ibid., Vol. XXX, p. 288.

4. See ibid., Vol. XXXI, Plate facing p. 304.

5. *SII*, Vol. I, pp. 31, 37; etc.

Thus the Mandhata plates (1274 A.D.) of Paramāra Jayasiṁha-Jayavarman has the representation of Garuḍa on the reverse of the fourth plate at the end of the document,[1] while the two rings holding the four plates together do not bear any seal. Similarly, the charters of the Candella kings have the figure of Lakṣmī or Gaja-Lakṣmī engraved about the middle of the first few lines of the inscription on a single plate or on the first plate where there are more plates than one.[2]

In records like the Sobharampur plate[3] of Dāmodaradeva, the emblems are engraved on a projection at the top of the plate. But there is no legend. In late medieval documents like the copper-plate grants of the rulers of Chamba, the seal was engraved by the side of the writing in the shape of a rosette or some such ornamental design, the space in the centre being occupied by the legend containing the king's name.[4]

Large numbers of seals (of clay and other materials) of kings, royal officials and private individuals as well as administrative, mercantile and religious organizations have been discovered in different parts of North India.[5] Hundreds of seals and sealings have been found at places like Basarh,[6] Kasia,[7] Sahet-Mahet,[8] Bhita,[9] Nalanda,[10] Rajghat[11] and Kausambi,[12] not to mention innumerable minor hoards. Some of these belonged to rulers, royal officials, members of the royal household and other dignitaries. But

1. *Ep. Ind.*, Vol. XXXII, Plate facing p. 156.
2. Ibid., Plates facing pp. 122, 126, 127.
3. Ibid., Vol. XXX, Plates between pp. 186 and 187.
4. Chhabra, *Antiquities of Chamba State*, II, p. 2; above, p. 125.
5. It is interesting to note that such seals have not been discovered in large numbers in South India where the practice of using seals does not appear to have been popular.
6. *ARASI*, 1903-04, pp. 101 ff.; 1913-14, pp. 110 ff.
7. Ibid., 1905-06, p. 83; 1906-07, pp. 63 ff.
8. Ibid., 1910-11, pp. 19 ff.
9. Ibid., 1911-12, pp. 44 ff.
10. *Mem. ASI*, No. 66.
11. *JNSI*, Vol. III, pp. 73 ff.; Vol. XIX, pp. 168 ff.; Vol XX, 195 ff.
12. Cf. *Indian Archaeology — A Review*, 1954-55, p. 18.

a large number of them contain the names of private persons, deities, temples, monasteries, guilds, etc. They throw welcome light on many topics. Indeed, the most important epigraphical discovery of the present century in India is that of the prehistoric seals at Harappa, Mohenjodaro, etc., which have pushed back the history of Indian civilization to the 3rd millennium B. C.[1] The writing on the seals is usually positive, although we have many sealings with legends in negative writing as well, the latter being apparently used for sealing documents or for the preparation of seals.[2]

As indicated above, some of these seals served the purpose of letters of introduction. They were what was called *abhijñāna*. The carriers of letters from a king often carried a royal seal to be delivered to the addressee in order to prove his *bona fides* and the genuineness of the letter he carried. The bigger and heavier seals discovered in the ruins of Buddhist religious establishments as those of Nalanda appear to be of this kind. Some of the smaller seals discovered at such places may have been tied to the letters to be delivered to the head of the religious institutions.

The legends on the seals are generally in the sixth case-ending, but rarely in the first case-ending or without any case-ending. The same is the case with coin legends.

1. J. Marshal, *Mohenjo-Daro and the Indus Civilization*; *Annual Reports of the Archaeological Survey of India*, 1923-24 to 1929-30; M. S. Vats, *Excavations at Harappa*; etc. For similar seals from Lothal (Ahmedabad District, Gujarat) and Kalibangan (Ganganagar District, Rajasthan), see *Indian Archaeology*, 1958-59, Plate XVIII; 1960-61, Plate XLVIII.

2. Cf. the Rohtasgarh seal matrix of Śaśāṅka believed to have been used for casting metal seals in relief to be fixed to copper-plate grants (*CII*, Vol. III, p. 283).

APPENDIX I

MEANING OF 'UPAGATA', ETC.

Different versions of Minor Rock Edict I of Aśoka contain the Prakrit words corresponding to Sanskrit *upagata*, *upayāta* and *upeta* (derived respectively from *upa-gam*, *upa-yā* and *upa-i*) in the same sense which has been variously understood.[1] Elsewhere[2] we have suggested that *upagata=upayāta=upeta* in the said context means *saṅgata*, 'intimately associated'. In our opinion, the passages in question indicate Aśoka's intimate association with the Buddhist *Saṅgha*. The lexicons, however, do no bear out this meaning quite clearly. In this connection, a study of similar words, often used in copper-plate grants to indicate the relation of the subordinates and officers of a king with the gift land or the district in which it was situated, may be of interest. These words are generally understood in the sense of 'assembled',[3] though really some of them appear to support the above interpretation.

From the standpoint of the recording of grants of land, copper-plate charters can be primarily divided into two classes, viz. (1) those that merely announce that some land or a village was granted by the donor, and (2) those that contain an order of the donor in respect of the grant addressed to certain people. Among the records of the first category, mention may be made of a number of charters issued by the Imperial Gaṅgas of Orissa.[4] Copper-plate grants written in verse (e.g. many

1. Cf. *CII*, Vol. I, p. 228; see Bhandarkar, *Aśoka*, 1932, pp. 81 ff.

2. *Maski Inscription of Aśoka*, p. 24; *Ep. Ind.*, Vol. XXXII, p. 9, note 1.

3. Cf. *Ep. Ind.*, Vol. XXVI, p. 12 and note 3.

4. See ibid., Vol. XXXI, p. 21, lines 181 ff.; p. 260, lines 125-27; Vol. XXVIII, p. 190, lines 179-81; p. 194, lines 179 ff.; p.256, lines 122-28. For such records belonging to other dynasties or kings, see ibid., Vol. XXXI, p. 15, lines 8-16; p. 190, lines 14-16; p.321, lines 6-9; Vol. XXX, p.140, lines 11-16; p. 187, lines 17-18; Vol.XXVIII, p. 75, lines 3-6; p.210, verses 17-21; p. 266, lines 7-13; p. 291, lines 17 ff.; Vol. XXVII, p. 77, lines 17-22.

of the charters issued by the Vijayanagara kings)[1] and those written mostly in verse[2] generally fall in the same class. The passage *s-ānunayaṁ prāha bhūpālān* occurring in the versified part of a charter[3] from Orissa is one of the few exceptions.

The second category of copper-plate grants, in which the donor's order is addressed to certain people, is important for our enquiry as it is some of these that contain the words in which we are interested. Such records can be broadly subdivided into five classes: (1) those in which the addresees are vaguely and generally indicated; (2) those in which the order is primarily addressed to the inhabitants of the gift village or the village wherein the gift land was situated or the district wherein the gift land or village was situated; (3) those in which the order is primarily addressed to the royal officers or agents including also the subordinate rulers, *Jāgīrdārs*, etc., in some cases; (4) those in which both the inhabitants of the locality in question and the royal officers or agents, etc., are mentioned; and (5) those in which the donor addresses neither the inhabitants nor his officers but only the future kings.

The first and last of these subdivisions are simple. The first of the two is illustrated by the charters of the Cālukyas of Badami, in which we have the passage *sarvān=evam=ājñāpayati.*[4] The other is likewise illustrated by the passage *sarvān= eva bhāvi-bhūmipālān=samanubodhayati* occurring in the grants of the Rāṣṭrakūṭas of the Gujarat region.[5] The other cases are complicated.

The order addressed to the inhabitants of a locality is simpler in passages like the following : (1) *śrī-Skandavarmaṇo vacanena Kudrāhāra-Kompare grāmeyakā vaktavyāḥ;*[6] (2) *°grāme*

1. See ibid., Vol. XXXI, p. 144. For such records belonging to other families, see ibid., Vol. XXX, p. 75; Vol. XXIX, pp. 103, 198; Vol. XXVIII, pp. 153-54.

2. Ibid., Vol. XXIX, p. 32; Vol. XXX, p. 304.

3. Ibid., Vol. XXX, p. 225, text lines 15-16. In this section, we have quoted the epigraphic passages after removing scribal errors, etc.

4. Ibid., Vol. XXVII, p. 118, note 2; p. 130, text line 54.

5. Ibid., Vol. XXVI, p. 253, text lines 29-30.

6. Ibid., Vol. XXXI, p. 9, text lines 8-9.

sarva-samavetān=kuṭumbinaḥ samājñāpayati;[1] (3) *Goṣṭhavāda-nivāsinaḥ kuṭumbinaḥ samājñāpayati;*[2] (4) *Sunikāyāṁ prativāsinaḥ samājñāpayati;*[3] (5) *Prastaravāṭa-vāsinaḥ sarva-samavetān=kuṭumbinaḥ samājñāpayati;*[4] (6) *Reyūru-grāme grāmeyakān=ittham=ājñāpayati;*[5] (7) *Pherava-grāme yathā-nivāsi-janapadaṁ samājñāpayati;*[6] (8) *Āndoreppa-grāme sarva-samanvāgatān=kuṭumbinas=samājñāpayati;*[7] (9) *Pratiṣṭhāpura-nivāsinaḥ sarva-samupetān=kuṭumbinaḥ samājñāpayati;*[8] etc. But slight elaboration is noticed in such passages as follows : (1) *Brāhmaṇa-purogān=grāmāñ=charīr-ādi-kuśalaṁ pṛṣṭvā likhati;*[9] (2) *Kontinīka-grāme Brāhmaṇān=sampūjya prativāsinaḥ samājñāpayati;*[10] (3) *Keśavake Brāhmaṇa-purassarān=prativāsi-kuṭumbinas=samājñāpayati;*[11] (4) *uktavāṁś=ca rājā tad-grāma-nivāsino mahattama-jānapadān;*[12] (5) *Keselaka - grāme Brāhmaṇ-ottarān=kuṭumbinaś=śīrṣakañ=c=ājñāpayati;*[13] (6) *sarva-samavetān=kuṭumbino bhojakāṁś=ca samājñāpayati;*[14] (7) *Gudravāra-viṣaya-nivāsino rāṣṭrakūṭa-pramukhān=kuṭumbinas=samāhūy=ettham=ājñāpayati;*[15] (8) *°viṣaye Vardhamānake grāmakūṭa-droṇāgraka-nāyaka-devavārika-gaṇḍaka-pramukhān=sarvān=eva yathā-prativāsinaḥ samājñāpayati;*[16] (9) *Mehāra-grāma-nivāsi-yathā-pradhāna-janapadān=mahattarāṁś=ca samādiśanti;*[17] etc.

In the first group of these passages, the inhabitants of a village (*grāmeyaka, kuṭumbin, prativāsin, janapada*, etc.;

1. Ibid., p. 200, text lines 9-10; Vol. XXX, p. 27, text lines 13-14; p. 117, text line 5.
2. Ibid., Vol. XXXI, p. 203, text lines 24-25.
3. Ibid., p. 315, text lines 4-5.
4. Ibid., Vol. XXX, p. 277, text lines 2-3 (on first plate, second side).
5. Ibid., Vol. XXIX p. 96, text lines 12-13.
6. Ibid., Vol. XXVII, p. 113, text lines 8-9.
7. Ibid., Vol. XXVIII, p. 178, text lines 5-6.
8. Ibid., p. 219, text lines 8-9.
9. Ibid., Vol. XXXI, p. 92, text lines 5-6.
10. Ibid., p. 221, text lines 10-11.
11. Ibid., p. 265, text lines 3-4.
12. Ibid., Vol. XXX, p. 149, text line 18.
13. Ibid., Vol XXVIII, p. 16, text line 3.
14. Ibid., Vol. XXVII, p. 35, text lines 2-3.
15. Ibid., p. 45-46, text lines 15-16.
16. Ibid., p. 142, text lines 35-36.
17. Ibid., p. 188, text lines 15-16.

cf. *grāma*, *jānapada*, etc., in the second group) are referred to, while, in the second group, they are mentioned along with their social or administrative leaders and with several village officials in a few cases. Rarely, the villagers of a whole district are stated to have been ordered after having been summoned (*samāhūya*). The word used in some cases in respect of the villagers is *sarva-samaveta* which may mean 'assembled from all sides'. This seems to be supported by the expression *sarva-samanvāgata* rarely used in place of *sarva-samaveta.* As will be seen below, the expression *samupasthita* is used in some cases in a similar context in respect of the villagers and local officials. Sometimes *sarva-samupeta* is also found in place of *sarva-samaveta.* The reference may be to an announcement to the people summoned by the beat of drums in respect of the grant in the gift village or the village containing the gift land or at the headquarters of the administrative unit in which the gift land or village was situated.

There are some charters in which the order is addressed not to the villagers but to others such as the subordinates, officers and agents of the king often with reference to a district. Cf. (1) *śrī-Kāpālivarmaṇo vacanena Śivapura-viṣaye vartamāna-bhaviṣyad-bhojak-āyuktaka-sthāyy-ādayo vaktavyāḥ*;[1] (2) *sarvān=eva svān=āyuktaka-mahattara-drāṅgika-cāṭa-bhaṭa-dhruvasthānādhikaraṇa-daṇḍapāśik-ādīn=anyāṁś=ca yathā-sambadhyamānakān=anudarśayati*;[2] (3) *asmin=Koṅgoda-maṇḍale śrīsāmanta-mahāsāmanta-mahārāja-rājaputr-āntaraṅga - daṇḍapāśik-oparika - viṣayapati-tadāniyuktaka - vartamāna - bhaviṣya - vyavahāriṇaḥ sa - karaṇān=yathārhaṁ pūjayati mānayati ca*;[3] (4) *sarvān=ev=āgāmi-vartamāna-nṛpati-sāmanta-viṣayapati-bhogika-rāṣṭragrāmakūṭa-deśillaka- mahattar - ādhikārik-ādīn=samanudarśayati*;[4] (5) *sarvān=eva samupagata-viṣayapati-rāṣtragrāmamahattar-ādhikārikān=samanudarśayati*;[5] (6) *Uttamāloka-viṣaye samupāgatān=vartamāna-bhaviṣyan-mahāsāmanta-*

1. Ibid., Vol. XXXI, p. 233, text lines 1-3.
2. Ibid., p. 300, text lines 11-12; p. 303, text lines 16-18.
3. Ibid., Vol. XXX, p. 268, text lines 31-34; cf. p. 272, text lines 23-26.
4. Ibid., Vol XXVIII, p. 21, text lines 15-17.
5. Ibid., p. 201, text lines 12-13.

mahārāja-rājaputra-kumārāmāty-oparika-viṣayapati-tadāyuktaka-dāṇḍa-pāśika-sthānāntarikān=anyāṁś=ca cāṭa-bhaṭ-ādīn=adhikaraṇāṁś=ca pūjayati;[1] (7) *yato='smat-santakāḥ sarv-ādhyakṣa-niyoga-niyuktā ājñāsañcāri-kulaputr-ādhikṛtāḥ bhaṭāś=chātrāś=ca viśruta-pūrvay=ājñay=ājñāpayitavyāḥ*;[2] etc. In these, the expressions *vartamāna-bhaviṣyat* and *yathā-sambadhyamānaka*, used in several cases, show that the order was meant for the king's officers, etc., who were associated with the administration of the area containing the gift village or land for the time being and also those who would be so associated in future.[3] Sometimes the word *samupāgata* has been used in relation to 'the present and future' subordinates and officers of the donor in the district containing the gift village (No. 6). It is difficult to take *samupāgata* here in the sense of 'assembled' since the whole district seems to be too big a place for an assemblage, while it is not easy to understand how the 'future' subordinates and officers also assembled.

In a large number of copper-plate charters, the order regarding the grant is addressed to both the local people or people in general and the royal officers, etc. This is simply indicated in the records of some dynasties, while the charters of some areas have it in a somewhat elaborate form. But it is the most elaborate in the records of some of the early medieval ruling families of Northern India, especially those

1. Ibid., p. 334, text lines 3-6. Cf. *Kārttikeyapura - viṣaye samupāgatān=sarvān=eva niyogasthān=rāja-rājanaka*, etc. (ibid., Vol. XXXI, p. 280, text line 11; cf. p. 287, text line 10; p. 294, text line 13).

2. Ibid., Vol. XXVI, p. 160, text lines 20-22.

3. For *sambadhyamānaka*, see *Lalitapuravāla-sambadhyamānaka-Tauḍā-grāme* (ibid., Vol. XXXI, p. 312, text line 8). In the charters of the Bhauma-Karas of Orissa, a distinction is generally made between the subordinates and officers of the district or province and those of a village or a group of villages; e.g., *Dakṣiṇa-Tosalāyāṁ vartamāna-bhaviṣya-mahāsāmanta-rājasatka-rājaputra-kumārāmāty-auparika-viṣayapati-tadāyuktaka-dāṇḍapāśika-sthānāntarikān=anyān=api rāja-prasādina=ścāṭa-vallabha-jātīyān=Tamura - viṣaya-Paścima-khaṇḍe mahāmahattara-bṛhadbhogi-pustakapāla - kūṭakolas-ādy-adhikaraṇaṁ yathārhaṁ mānayati bodhayati samājñāpayati ca*. Here the local officers of the western sub-division of the Tamura district have been mentioned separately from the subordinates and officers associated with the province of South Tosalā in which Tamura-viṣaya was situated. See ibid., Vol. XXIX, pp. 88-89, text lines 26-30; cf. p. 217, text lines 23-26; p. 219, text lines 25-27; Vol. XXVIII, pp. 215-16, text lines 213-16.

of its eastern regions. The simple and semi-elaborate forms of indication are illustrated in the following quotations.

For simple indication, cf. (1) *Pḷaki-viṣaye viṣaya-vṛddhān=adhikāriṇaḥ Kundura-grāma-kuṭumbinaś=ca samājñāpayati*;[1] (2) *Kaliṅganagarāt......................samast-āmātya-pramukha-janapadān=samāhūya samājñāpayati*;[2] (3) *sarvān=eva svān=āyuktaka-viniyuktaka-cāṭa-bhaṭa-kuṭumbi-mahattara-drāṅgikān=bodhayati*;[3] (4) *Ramalava-viṣaya-Paścima-khaṇḍe yathā-nivāsi-sa-karaṇa-sāmanta-bhogy-ādi-janapadān=yathārhaṁ mānayati bodhayati samādiśati ca*;[4] etc.

For semi-elaborate indication, see (1) *Nāṭavāḍi-viṣaya-nivāsino rāṣṭrakūṭa-pramukhān=kuṭumbinas=samāhūya mantri-purohita-senāpati-yuvarāj-ādy- aṣṭādaśa - tīrth - ādhyakṣam = ittham=ājñāpayati*;[5] (2) *Maṁḍāura-grām-opagatān=Brāhmaṇān=anyāṁś=ca mānyān=adhikṛtān=kuṭumbi-kāyastha-dūta-vaidya - mahattarān=Meda-Caṇḍāla-paryantān=sarvān=sambodhayati samājñāpayati ca*;[6] (3) °*grāmeyakān=rājapuruṣa-talavara-daṇḍanāyaka-rāṣṭrika-dūta-bhaṭa-naṭa-ceṭaka-paricāraka-niyukt-ādhyakṣa-praśāstṛ-samāhartṛ-nāya - kāṁś=c=ājñāpayati*;[7] (4) °*bhūmau yathāyathaṁ samupasthita-viṣaya-karaṇa-vyavahārika-pramukha-janapadān=rāja-rājñī-rāṇak-ādhi-kṛtān=anyān=api rājanyaka-rājaputra-rājavallabha-prabhṛtīn=yathā-kāla-bhāvino=pi sarvān=mānanā-pūrvakaṁ samādiśanti*;[8] (5) *Jīloṇḍā-viṣaye bhaviṣyad-yathā-kāla-bhāvino rājanyakān=rāja-putrān=Brāhmaṇa-purogān = sāmanta-nivāsi-janapadān = adhikāriṇaḥ sa-karaṇān=anyāṁś=ca cāṭa-bhaṭa-vallabha-jātīyān=rāja-pād-opajīvi-naḥ sarvān=yathārhaṁ mānayati bodhayati kuśalayaty=ādiśati c=ānyat*;[9] (6) *Vaṭapadrake Brāhmaṇān=sampūjya sa-pradhā-nān=prativāsino yathā-kāl-ādhyāsinas=samāhartṛ-sannidhātṛ-pramu-khān = adhikāriṇas = sa-karaṇān=anyāṁś=c=āsmat-pād-opajīvinas=*

1. Ibid., Vol. XXXI, p. 135, text lines 12-13.
2. Ibid., p. 196, text lines 44-47; p. 308, text lines 40-41.
3. Ibid., Vol. XXX, p. 4, text line 1.
4. Ibid., Vol. XXIX, p. 192-93, text lines 13-15.
5. Ibid., Vol. XXXI, p. 42, text lines 31-34.
6. Ibid., p. 72, text lines 7-9.
7. Ibid., p. 78, text lines 22-24.
8. Ibid., Vol. XXX, p. 207, text lines 30-32.
9. Ibid., Vol. XXIX, p. 188, text lines 27-29. Cf. Vol. XXVI, p. 79, text lines 24-27; also Vol. XXVII, p. 330, text lines 25-27, where we have *yathā-kal-ādhyāsin* for *yathā-kāla-bhāvin*.

sarva-rājapuruṣān=samājñāpayati;[1] (7) *Māṇḍiḍḍā-viṣaye rāja-rājanaka-rājaputrān = viṣayapati - daṇḍapāśikān = yathākāl-ādhyāsino vyavahāriṇo Brāhmaṇān=karaṇa-purogān=nivāsi-janapadāṁś=ca yathārhaṁ mānayati bodhayati samādiśati ca sarvataḥ śivam=asmākam=anyat*;[2] etc.

In these instances, the word *upagata* has been used once in relation to the inhabitants and local officials of the gift village (No. 2 of Group II). In one case (No. 4 of Group II), the local people and officials are stated to have been *samupasthita* at the gift land, while the subordinates, etc., are separated from the said class by the epithet *yathā-kāla-bhāvin*. The same distinction is also made in another case (No. 5 of Group II) by using the expressions *bhaviṣyad-yathā-kāla-bhāvin* and *sāmanta-nivāsin*. Similar use of the expressions *prativāsin* and *yathā-kāl-ādhyāsin* are noticed in one case (No. 6 of Group II) and *yathā-kāl-ādhyāsin* and *nivāsin* in another (No. 7 of Group II). This distinction is made clear in the Gāhaḍavāla records in which, in the course of an elaborate indication, we have °*grāma-nivāsino nikhila- janapadān=upatatān=api ca rāja-rājñī*, etc.[3] Here the relation of the subordinates and officers of the king with the gift village is indicated by the word *upagata*. Some charters indicate the same distinction by enumerating the two classes as *sarvān=ev=ātmīyān=mantri-purohita*°, etc., and *tan-nivāsi-Brāhmaṇ-ottarān*, etc.[4]

The word found in the Gāhaḍavāla records as *upagata* is often found in the form *samupagata* or *samupāgata* in the same context in many other charters,[5] especially in the elaborate indication in the grants of the Pālas and Senas of Eastern India.[6] We have seen above how the 'present' and 'future' subordinates, etc., of a ruler are described as

1. Ibid., Vol. XXVII, p. 290, text lines 6-9; cf. p. 323, text lines 6-8.
2. Ibid., p. 339, text lines 11-14.
3. Ibid., Vol. XXVI, p. 73, text lines 12-14.
4. Ibid., p. 202, text lines 28-30.
5. Ibid., Vol. XXXI, p. 280, text lines 11-17; p. 287, text line 10; p. 294, text line 13.
6. Ibid., Vol. XXIX, pp. 7-8, text lines 31-41; pp. 11-12, text lines 29-38.

samupāgata with reference to a *viṣaya* or district. The question now is what the words *upagata*, *samupagata* and *samupāgata* in this context really mean. In our opinion, they mean the same thing as *sambadhyamānaka*, *yathā-kāla-bhāvin* and *yathā-kāl-ādhyāsin* as found in the same context in many records. This may be clear from the quotation of a few corresponding passages from the charters of the Gāhaḍavālas, Pālas and Senas.

The Gāhaḍavāla grant referred to above has : *upagatān=api ca rāja-rājñī-yuvarāja - mantri - purohita - pratīhāra-senāpati - bhāṇḍāgārik - ākṣapaṭalika - bhiṣag - naimittik - āntaḥpurika - dūta- karituragapattanākarasthānagokulādhikāri-puruṣān=ājñāpayati bodhayaty=ādiśati ca.* It is difficult to believe that all the said kinds of subordinates and officers of the king would have assembled in a gift land or village whenever a grant was made, especially in view of the fact that the Gāhaḍavāla kings are known to have often issued such charters. The number of the classes of people is much higher in the Pāla and Sena charters. It has also to be noticed that often the subject of the gift was a plot or several plots of land including tanks, etc., and the assemblage of subordinate rulers, their queens and sons and of all the officers (cf. *aśeṣa-rājapuruṣān*) therein becomes inconceivable. The list sometimes includes also, besides others, the mercenary soldiers of various nationalities such as Gauḍa, Mālava, Khasa, Kulika, Karṇāta and Lāṭa and even people performing menial services such as Meda, Andhra and Caṇḍāla. An assemblage seems to be physically impossible in such cases.

Thus the Belwa plate of Mahīpāla has : *°grāma-puṣkariṇīṣu samupāgat-āśesha-rājapuruṣān = rāja-rājanyaka-rāja-putra-rājāmātya- mahāsāndhivigrahika - mahākṣapaṭalika - mahāsāmanta - mahāsenāpati - mahāpratīhāra - dauḥsādhasādhanika - mahādaṇḍanāyaka - mahākumārāmātya - rājasthān - oparika - dāśāparādhika - cauroddharaṇika - dāṇḍika - dāṇḍapāśika - śaulkika - gaulmika - kṣetrapāla - prāntapāla - koṭṭapāl - āṅgarakṣa - tadāyuktaka - viniyuktaka - hastyaśvoṣṭranaubalavyāpṛtaka - kiśora-vaḍavāgomahiṣyajāvikādhyakṣa - dūta - preṣaṇika - gamāgamik -*

ābhitvaramāṇa-viṣayapati - grāmapati - tarika - Gauḍa - Mālava - Khasa - Hūṇa - Kulika - Karṇāta-Lāṭa-cāṭa - bhaṭa - sevak - ādīn = anyāṁś = c = ākīrtitān = rāja - pād - opajīvinaḥ prati-vāsino Brāhmaṇ - ottarān=mahattam-ottama - kuṭumbi - puroga - Med - Āndhra - Cāṇḍāla-paryantān=yathārhaṁ mānayati bodhayati samādiśati ca.[1]

Thus the words *upagata*, etc., in the above context seem to refer to the close relation of the king's officers and subordinates with the land as administrators or fief-holders.

1. Ibid., Vol. XXIX, pp. 7-8, text lines 31-41. In the Sena charters, the list of subordinates and officers is concluded with the passage : *anyāṁś= ca sakala-rāja-pād-opajīvino—'dhyakṣa-pracār-oktān=ih=ākīrtitān = caṭṭa-bhaṭṭa-jātīyāñ = janapadānkṣe=trakarān=Brāhmaṇān = Brāhmaṇ-ottarān = yathārhaṁ mānayanti bodhayanti samādiśanti ca.* Cf. ibid., Vol.XXVI, p.8, text lines 32-34. Some records make it clear that the grant was made at the capital of the donor in the presence of officers, etc. See ibid., Vol. XXXIV, p. 222; cf. Vol. XXVIII, p. 309.

APPENDIX II

STANZAS ON BHŪMI-DĀNA QUOTED IN RĀJA-ŚĀSANAS[1]

We have seen above how, while making grants of land, the donor often emphasized the virtue of giving such gifts, especially to Brāhmaṇas, and the sacred nature of rent-free holdings created by past rulers, by inserting one or more benedictory and minatory verses in the deeds of grant. The stanzas generally extoll the donor of gifts and affirm the merit accruing to those who respect the inviolability of grants made by others and denounce the inequity of those who deprive donees of the gift land, and declare the punishment which awaits those who resume such gifts. The verses are sometimes also quoted in connection with the sale of land since there was a tendency to represent a sale of land also as a gift by a sort of popular fiction.[2]

The verses are sometimes quoted without any introduction[3] and often without any reference to the source, merely introducing them by a passage like *uktañ=ca*, "It has also been

1. See *JRAS*, 1912, pp. 248 ff., p. 476; 1913, pp. 388-89; *IHQ*, Vol. III, p. 432; Vol. VI, pp. 775 ff. ; S. Lévi, *Le Népal*, III, pp. 122 ff.; P. V. Kane, *History of Dharmaśāstra*, Vol. II, pp. 1271 ff. G. H. Khare quotes, without references, a large number of stanzas in his Marāṭhī work *Saṁśodhakācā Mitra*, pp. 20-37. But many of the verses quoted by him have nothing to do with gift of land and are apparently not quotations from ancient works. By way of illustration, we may refer to the stanza *Karmaṇā manasā vācā*, etc. (p.24), quoted from the charters of Harṣavardhana (cf. *Ep. Ind.*, Vol. IV, p. 211, text lines 13-14) and the two verses *Yasy=ānvaye bhūpatir=eṣa jātaḥ*, etc. (p. 32), which really form part of an endorsement at the end of the Mahada plates (cf. ibid., Vol. XXVIII, p. 292, text lines 32-38). An early copper-plate grant quoting two of the stanzas, *Bahubhir=vasudhā dattā*, etc. (No. 23, note) and *Sva-dattāṁ para-dattāṁ vā*, etc. (No. 132), is the Gunapadeya plates (c. third quarter of the 4th century) of the time of Pallava Skandavarman (*Select Inscriptions*, p. 445). The inscription is in Prakrit and the quotation has not been referred to any source. For such verses in an early Śālaṅkāyana charter of about the same age, see *Ep. Ind.*, Vol. XXXI, p. 6.

2. See *Ep. Ind.*, Vol. XXVIII, p. 48, note 2; *Mitākṣarā* on *Yājñavalkya-smṛti*, II, 114; above, p. 111, note 1.

3. See, e. g., *Ep. Ind.*, Vol. XVIII, p. 257, text lines 149 ff.; p. 292, text lines 25 ff.; Vol. XXIX, pp. 156, 189. Many of them were so well known that they are sometimes quoted by the first foot only (cf. *Ep. Carn.*, Vol. XI, Dg. No. 68).

said".[1] But they are very often assigned to Vyāsa[2] and are sometimes attributed specifically to the *Mahābhārata*.[3] Some of the stanzas quoted in the inscriptions are actually found in the *Mahābhārata* (especially in the Dānadharma section[4] of the Anuśāsana-parvan) as well as in the Purāṇas. In some cases, they are stated to be the sayings of Manu,[5] Brahman[6] or Bṛhaspati[7] and often of the sages.[8] They are represented in a few cases as quotations from the *Mānava-Dharmaśāstra*[9] or *Vaiṣṇava-Dharmaśāstra*,[10] but often from the

1. See, e.g., *CII*, Vol. III, p. 289, text line 12. Other such passages are *api c=oktam*, *tathā c=oktam*, *api c=āpi ślokāḥ*, *bhavanti c=ātra dharm-ānuśaṁsinaḥ ślokāḥ*, *bhavanti c=ātra puṇya-ślokāḥ* (also *pūrva-ślokāḥ*), *bhavanti c=ātra prāg-abhihitāḥ ślokāḥ*, *bhavanti c=ātra bhūmi-dāna-sambandhāḥ ślokāḥ*, etc. See Lévi, op. cit., p. 132; *IHQ*, Vol. VI, pp. 775-76; *Ep. Ind.*, Vol. XI, p. 145; Vol. XII, p. 3; Vol. XXIX, p. 8; etc.

2 Vyāsa is mentioned in a large number of early inscriptions such as those of the Traikūṭakas, Maitrakas, Parivrājakas, Uccakalpīyas, Śarabhapurīyas, Pāṇḍuvaṁśis, Early Cālukyas, Gurjaras of Nāndīpurī, Vākāṭakas and others (Lévi, op. cit., pp. 130-31).

3. See, e.g., the inscriptions of Jayanātha and Sarvanātha of Uccakalpa (*CII*, Vol. III, p. 119, text line 13; p. 122, text line 15; p. 127, text line 22).

4. The section is in the form of a dialogue between Bhīṣma and Yudhiṣṭhira, while it contains smaller dialogues such as that between Bṛhaspati and Indra. A large number of stanzas from this section are quoted by Hemādri in the *Dānakhaṇḍa* (of his *Caturvargacintāmaṇi*), Banaras, Vol. II, pp. 477 ff. Some scholars think that the stanzas quoted in inscriptions belonged to a recension of the *Mahābhārata*, which is now lost (*IHQ*, Vol. III, p. 432). The *Itihāsasamuccaya* (cf. XIX, 38-39, 44, 52), stated to have been composed in verses taken from the *Mahābhārata*, has some of these stanzas (*IHQ*, Vol. VI, p. 777).

5. See, e. g., *Ind. Ant.*, Vol. VI, p. 29, text line 13; *Ep. Ind.*, Vol. VI, p. 18, text line 20; p. 97, text line 47 (*Manu-ādayo mah-arṣayaḥ*). For an explanation of Manu's mention, see *IHQ*, Vol. VI, pp 777-78. Sometimes people were not quite confident and ascribed the stanzas to both Manu and Vyāsa; cf. *Manu-Vyāsa-gītau ślokau* in *Ep. Ind.*, Vol. XXVIII, p. 179, text line 14. See No. 164.

6. *Ep. Ind.*, Vol III, p. 146; Vol. VIII, p. 235, 240; etc. It is difficult sometimes to say whether Brahman is the god of that name or the word means the Brāhmaṇa class (i. e. the sages) or a Brāhmaṇa *par excellence*.

7. Ibid., Vol. III, p. 146; Vol. XXII, p. 95, text lines 12-13. In medieval records, the grant is sometimes stated to have been made according to the recommendations of Bṛhaspati (ibid., Vol. XXVIII, p. 245).

8. See, e. g., ibid., Vol. XXIV, p. 303, text line 23; *Gauḍalekhamālā*, p. 36. See also *Ep. Ind.*, Vol. II, p. 219, where some of the stanzas are represented as the sayings of the sages Parāśara, Vatsa, Kutsa, Āṅgirasa, Gautama, Manu and Yājñavalkya.

9. See, e. g., *Ep. Ind.*, Vol. III, p. 45; p. 268, text line 40. Out of the stanzas quoted below, only No. 164 (*Yo='rcitam*, etc.) belongs to the *Manusmṛti*.

10. Cf. *Ep. Ind.*, Vol. XVII, p. 304, text line 150.

Dharmaśāstras and rarely from the Smṛtis and the Purāṇas.[1]

The subject of gifts of all kinds is dealt with more or less elaborately in the epics and the Purāṇas[2] as well as in the Dharmaśāstras.[3]

Since the *Mahābhārata* and the Purāṇas, both of which are regarded as *Dharmaśāstra,* are ascribed to the authorship of the sage Vyāsa, it is interesting to note that some of the imprecatory and benedictory stanzas generally quoted in the copper-plate grants have been traced to the said sources and also that some of these charters specifically mention Vyāsa as the author of the verses. Thus some records introduce a few of the stanzas with the words *Vyāsa-gītāṁś=c=ātra ślokān=udāharanti,*[4] while others have *uktaṁ ca bhagavatā param-arṣiṇā Vedavyāsena.*[5] The *Mahābhārata* is particularly mentioned in another group of early charters in which we have *uktaṁ ca Mahābhārate bhagavatā Vedavyāsena Vyāsena*[6] or more fully

1. See, e. g., ibid., Vol. XXVIII, p. 263 (text line 34: *dharmaśāstre*); p. 282 (text line 24: *dharmaśāstreṣu*). For reference to *Smṛti,* cf. ibid., Vol. XXXI, p. 248, text lines 35, 38, and to *Purāṇa,* see ibid., Vol. II, p. 360, text line 17; Vol. III, p. 68. *Ep. Carn.*, Vol. XII, Si. No. 95 speaks of *Itihāsa-Purāṇa* and quotes from Rāma, Āditya and Bṛhaspati. A particular verse (No. 117, *Sāmānyo='yaṁ.* etc.), found in the *Skanda Purāṇa* in a story associated with Rāma is sometimes attributed to him (*Ep. Ind.*, Vol. XXXII, p. 55, text line 42; *Skanda Purāṇa,* Brahma-Khaṇḍa Dharmāraṇya-khaṇḍa, Ch. 34, verse 40). In a few cases, it is wrongly ascribed to Vālmīki, the author of the *Rāmāyaṇa* (cf. *Ep. Carn.*, Md. No. 113). Similarly, the stanza *Bahubhir=vasudhā,* etc. (No. 23) is sometimes ascribed to Rāma (*Ep. Carn.*, Vol. XII, Si. No. 95). Certain medieval records speak of attainment of the fruits of making grants of land as described in the *Śiva Purāṇa* (N. G. Majumdar, *Ins. Beng.*, Vol. III, p. 137, text lines 46-47).

2. *Mahābhārata,* III, 199; XIII, 57-81; *Agni Purāṇa,* Chapters 208-13, 271; *Garuḍa Purāṇa,* Chapters 51, 98; *Kūrma Purāṇa,* II, Chapter 26; *Liṅga Purāṇa,* Chapters 28-44; *Matsya Purāṇa,* Chapters 82-91, 223, 274-89; *Padma Purāṇa,* III, 24; VI, 33; *Varāha Purāṇa,* Chapters 99-111; *Bhaviṣya Purāṇa,* IV (Uttara-parvan), Chapters 148-202; cf. also *Saura Purāṇa,* Chapter 10; etc. For gifts of land, cf. *Mahābhārata,* XIII, 62; *Agni Purāṇa,* 213; *Kūrma Purāṇa,* II, 26, 12-15; *Matsya Purāṇa,* 284; *Padma Purāṇa,* III, 24; VI, 33; *Bhaviṣya Purāṇa,* IV, 164; *Brahma Purāṇa,* 155, 5-9; etc. See also *Skanda Purāṇa,* op. cit., Chapter 34; *Bhār. Vid.*, Vol. VI, 1945, p. 237, note 4.

3. See, e.g., the *Saṁhitās* of Bṛhaspati, Saṁvarta, etc., quoted below. See also the numerous quotations from various sources in the *Dānakhaṇḍa* in Hemādri's *Caturvargacintāmaṇi,* Banaras, Vol. I, pp. 4. ff.; for grants of land, cf. Vol. II, pp. 477 ff. Cf. Ballālasena's *Dānasāgara,* Bib. Ind. ed., pp. 316-38.

4. *CII,* Vol. III, pp. 194, 198, 238, 247, 296. See also *Ep. Ind.*, Vol. VI, p. 358 (*Vyāsa-bhaṭṭāraka*); Vol. XXI, p. 81 (*Vedavyāsa-mahātman*); etc.

5. *CII,* Vol. III, pp. 96, 104, 108, 115, 167, 179.

6. Ibid., pp. 119, 122, 127.

uktaṁ ca Mahābhārate śata-sāhasryāṁ saṁhitāyāṁ param-arṣiṇā Parāśara-sutena Vedavyāsena Vyāsena.[1] As will be seen below, some of the stanzas are found in the *Mahābhārata* and the Purāṇas. The fact that all the stanzas specifically attributed to the *Mahābhārata* cannot be traced in the present texts of the work may be due to the confusion of the scribes or to the loss of the version that contained the verses. The second alternative is not improbable since some verses assigned to the *Mahābhārata* by Hemādri in the thirteenth century cannot be traced in the available versions.

The few stanzas ascribed to Vyāsa or his *Mahābhārata* in the earlier records were later quoted often along with various additional verses which were assigned to Vyāsa or any of the other sources referred to above.[2] The introduction of Bṛhaspati as the author of the verses is easily explained by the fact that the *Mahābhārata* puts some of the stanzas in Bṛhaspati's advice to Indra[3] and that they are also found in the *Bṛhaspatisaṁhitā*. This double authorship ascribed to some of the stanzas gradually led to further confusion. It seems that the word 'sage' as the author of the stanzas, which was originally intended for Vyāsa or Bṛhaspati or both of them, was later confused with a sage in general and therefore sometimes used in the plural. This may have also been due to the fact that some of the verses are found in works ascribed to various sages. Similarly, the expression *Dharmaśāstra*, originally intended for the *Mahābhārata* or the Purāṇas or a work of Bṛhaspati, was later confused with the *Mānava-Dharmaśāstra* and, as a result, the sage Manu was confused with the author of the stanzas in question. It is not impossible that the earlier inscriptions influenced the later compilations of the

1. Ibid., p. 137. As has been noticed by scholars, the epithet *śata-sāhasrī saṁhitā* applied to the *Mahābhārata* refers to the large text such as we have it today.

2 In a few cases, the verses are separately ascribed to Vyāsa and to the old sages (*Ep. Ind.*, Vol. XXV, p. 60, line 51; p. 62, line 79; p. 63, line 86).

3 Cf. op. cit., XIII, 62, 51 ff. See also *Ep. Carn.*, Vol. XII, Si. No. 95 for a number of stanzas ascribed to Bṛhaspati.

Purāṇas and Dharmaśāstras which themselves influenced the imprecatory section of the medieval inscriptions.[1]

While many records quote only one or a few of the stanzas, certain medieval charters quote 20 or more verses.[2] The most frequently quoted stanzas are the two in the *Anuṣṭubh* metre, viz., *Bahubhir=vasudhā bhuktā*, etc. (No. 23) and *Ṣaṣṭiṁ varṣa-sahasrāṇi* (No. 123), though they are often quoted with the addition of one or more of the other verses. The two stanzas beginning with *Sva-dattāṁ para-dattāṁ vā* (Nos. 131-32) in the same metre are equally popular, though they are not generally found together in the earlier epigraphs. Most of the other verses are also in *Anuṣṭubh*. Among these, some are found in the records of different parts of India, while some occur occasionally in those of a particular area. Certain royal families (e. g. the Imperial Gaṅgas of Orissa) generally favoured a group of stanzas, a few of which are not usually met with elsewhere. The stanzas such as Nos. 30 (*Bhūmi-pradā*, etc.) and 99 (*Niśamya doṣaṁ*, etc.) and others like Nos. 80-81 (*Kṣudra-paśv-anṛte*, etc.; *Hanti jātān*, etc.) are rarely quoted. Sometimes verses quoted from works other than the Dharmaśāstras are also noticed. Thus No. 88 (*Madhu-Kaiṭabha*°, etc.) is quoted from Murāri's *Anargharāghava* in an inscription of 1521 A. D. There are many other stanzas of this nature, which do not appear to be quotations, but were probably composed by the court poets of the donors, who were responsible for drafting the documents.[3] This seems

1. Of the stanzas quoted below, Nos. 3-6, 78,80-81, 93, 106, 119, and 155-59 have been traced in the *Mahābhārata*, while Nos. 127 and 150 are assigned to the *Mahābhārata* by Hemādri (cf. Nos. 93,96). Nos. 5, 20, 23, 29, 98, 106, 119, 123, 132 and 137 have been traced in the *Padma Purāṇa*. Nos. 20, 23, 43, 53, 90, 117, 123, 137 and 150 in the *Skanda Purāṇa*, and Nos. 103, 106, 131-32 and 150 in the *Bhaviṣya Purāṇa*. Nos. 4-5, 13, 20, 23, 29, 34, 55, 64, 100, 106, 119, 121, 123, 126, 132, 137, 142 and 158 have been traced in the *Bṛhaspatisaṁhitā*, Nos. 5, 121 and 161 in the *Saṁvartasaṁhitā* and Nos. 4, 29, 124 and 164 respectively in the works of Atri, Vṛddha-Hārīta, Laghu-Śātātapa and Manu. No. 132 occurs in the *Brahma Purāṇa* and No. 98 in the *Baudhāyana Dharmasūtra* and *Vasiṣṭhasmṛti*.

2. Cf. *Ep. Ind.*, Vol. XII, pp. 321 ff.; Vol. XXV, pp. 199 ff.

3. See, e. g., *Ind. Ant.*, Vol. V, p. 207, text lines 13-14; Vol. VI, p. 12, text line 14; p. 29, text lines 9-10; Vol. XIV, p. 73, text lines 112-13; *Ep. Ind.*, Vol. XIX, p. 45, text lines 32 ff.; p. 73, text lines 32-33, 38 ff.; Vol. XXII, p. 157, text lines 46-48; p. 191, text lines 28-34; *Ep. Carn.*, Vol. XI,

to be supported by the fact that a few of the stanzas are sometimes found outside the usual list of imprecatory and benedictory verses.[1]

In some cases, stanzas which look like the composition of the court poets are mixed up with the usual benedictory and minatory verses to create the impression that they are also quotations from ancient authors.[2] A number of pseudo-quotations of this kind have been omitted by us. They do not appear to be quotations from the Dharmaśāstras, although some of them may be quoted from poetical works. Stanzas not directly connected with gift have often been omitted.[3]

There are cases where two consecutive stanzas have to be read together in order to get the complete sense. We have kept them together, although the position of the second verse in the couplet has also been indicated in its proper place in the alphabetical order.[4] But there are a few instances where more than two stanzas have to be read together for the sake of sense and we have found it difficult to accommodate them in our scheme.[5]

Eg. No. 28 (*Upāyan-ārthaṁ*, etc.); Vol. XII, Tp. No. 28 (*Naṣṭaṁ*, etc.). Cf. below, Nos. 17, 30, 70, 86-87, 99, 108, 136, 138, 140, 153, 163, etc., a few of which are quoted in many records.

1. See, e.g., *Calā vibhūtiḥ*, etc. (No. 36). cf. No. 30.

2. Cf. the following stanza among those ascribed to Vyāsa (*Ind. Ant.*, Vol. VI, p. 209) : *Yātā yānti mahībhujaḥ kṣitim=imāṁ yāsyanti bhuktv=ākhilāṁ no yātā na ca yāti na yāsyati na ken=āpi sārdhaṁ dharā* I *yat=kiñcid=bhuvi tad=vināśi sakalaṁ kīrtiḥ paraṁ sthāyinī matv=aivaṁ vasudhādhipāḥ para-kṛtā lopyā na sat-kīrtayaḥ* II For another stanza in a similar position, see *Iha hi*, etc., ibid., p. 207. Cf. *Ep. Ind.*, Vol. XVII, p. 303, verse 19 (lines 144-46); Vol. XXII, p. 191. See also Chhabra, *Antiquities of Chamba State*, II, p. 177 : *Ye c=aitad=grāma-ratnaṁ*, etc.

3. See *Ind. Ant.*, Vol. XII, p. 186 :
N=āyam=atyanta-saṁvāsaḥ kasyacit=kenacit=saha I *asti svena śarīreṇa kim=ut=ānyaiḥ pṛthag-janaiḥ* II *Prāṇena dhāryate kāyaḥ sa ca prāṇaḥ samīraṇāt* I *samīraś=c=āti-capalaḥ kṛtam=apy=āyur=adbhutam* II *Sapta-lokaika-nāthasya Viṣṇor=api mahātmanaḥ* I *n=eyaṁ niyata-vāsā Śrīḥ kim=ut=ānyasya kasyacit* II See also *Ep. Carn.*, Vol. XV, HN. No. 123.

4. See, e. g., Nos. 37-38.

5. The following verses are often found in the inscriptions of the Kannaḍa-speaking area (cf. *Ep. Carn.*, Vol. III, Sr. No. 64; Vol. XI, Jl. No. 41; Vol. XIV, Gu. No. 148, Nj. No. 295):

Indraḥ pṛcchati Caṇḍālīṁ kim=idaṁ pacyate śubhe I
śva-māṁsaṁ surayā siktaṁ kapālena cit-āgninā II
kim=arthaṁ vada kalyāṇi carmaṇā pihitaṁ tvayā I
Brahma-svaṁ Brāhmaṇa-kṣetraṁ hārayanti haranti ye I
teṣāṁ pāda-rajo-bhītyā carmaṇā pithitaṁ mayā II

The following stanzas, quoted from epigraphic records and arranged alphabetically, may be divided primarily into two groups, viz. (1) those extolling the merit accruing to gifts in general and particularly to gifts of land especially those made in favour of the Brāhmaṇas, and (2) those denouncing the resumption of gift land in the possession of Brāhmaṇas in particular. Some of the stanzas have been quoted after removing the linguistic and metrical errors in their texts as found in the inscriptions, while a few could not be quoted because their full texts are either not decipherable owing to unsatisfactory preservation[1] or too erroneous to be reconstructed.[2] It is felt that some genuine quotations from the Dharmaśāstras and medieval poems in epigraphic records may have escaped our notice.

Adbhir=dattaṁ tribhir=bhuktaṁ sadbhiś=ca paripālitam |
etāni na nivartante pūrva-rāja-kṛtāni ca || 1[3]

Āditya-candrāv=anilo='nalaś=ca
dyaur=bhūmir=āpo hṛdayaṁ manaś=ca |
ahaś=ca rātriś=ca ubhe ca sandhye
dharmasya jānanti narasya vṛttam || 2[4]

Ādityā iva dīpyante tejasā divi mānavāḥ |
ye prayacchanti vasudhāṁ Brāhmaṇāy=āhit-āgnaye || 3[5]

We have *kāka-māṁsaṁ surā-siktaṁ* in op. cit., Vol. V, Arkalgud No. 9. For *Brahma-svaṁ*, etc., sometimes we have *Deva-Brāhmaṇa-vittāni balād=apaharanti ye* (ibid., Vol. III, Sr. No. 157; Tn. No. 64).

1. See, e.g., *Ep. Ind.*, Vol. XXII, pp. 156-57, verses 24-25, 32.

2. See, e. g., *Ep. Carn.*, Vol. IX, Dv. No. 15 (*Śivaṁ*, etc., and *Indrāś=ca*, etc.); Vol. XI, Cd. No. 14 (*Deva-svaṁ*, etc.) ; Vol. XI, Cd. No. 82 (*Catuḥ-sāgara°*, etc.). The following stanza quoted from the *Atrisaṁhitā* in Vol. XI, Cd. No. 82, does not give a complete idea :

Bhramanti suciraṁ kālaṁ kṣut-pipās-ādi-pīḍitāḥ |
aghora-narakaṁ yānti yāvac=candra-divākaram ||

The verse is not found in the work as incorporated in the *Ūnaviṁśati-saṁhitā*, Calcutta.

3. See, e. g., *Ind. Ant.*, Vol. VI, p. 26, lines 26-27.

4. *Ep. Carn.*, Vol. I, revised ed., p. 35; *Ind. Ant.*, Vol. IV, pp. 333-34. See below, Nos. 37-38.

5. *Ep. Ind.*, Vol. XXV, p. 218, verse 39. The *Mahābhārata* (XIII, 62, 46) has it with *dīpyanti tejasā bhuvi* in the first half and *dadāti vasudhāṁ sphītāṁ ye veda-viduṣi dvije* in the second. Ballāla's *Dānasāgara* (op. cit., p. 332) seems to attribute the stanza to the *Viṣṇudharmottara*.

Ādityo Varuṇo Viṣṇur=Brahmā Somo Hutāśanaḥ ।
Śūlapāṇiś=ca bhagavān=pratinandanti bhūmidam ॥ 4[1]
Agner=apatyaṁ prathamaṁ suvarṇaṁ
bhūr=Vaiṣṇavī Sūrya-sutāś=ca gāvaḥ ।
dattās=trayas=tena bhavanti lokā
yaḥ kāñcanaṁ gāṁ ca mahīṁ ca dadyāt ॥ 5[2]
Agniṣṭom-ādibhir=yajñair=iṣṭvā vipula-dakṣiṇaiḥ ।
na tat=phalam=avāpnoti yad=dattvā vasudhāṁ nṛpa ॥ 6[3]
Aho Rāghava rājendra sapta kalpāni jīvinam ।
na śṛṇomi na paśyāmi svayaṁ-datt-āpahāriṇam ॥ 7[4]
Akara-kara-kāras=tu, etc. See No. 8, note.
A-karasya kar-ādānaṁ go-koṭi-vadha ucyate ।
sa-karasya kara-cchedī prāpnoti paramaṁ padam ॥ 8[5]
Akareṣu, etc. See No. 8, note.
Ānandanti ca, etc. See No. 20, note.
Andhakaḥ, etc. See No. 9, note.

1. See, e. g., *Ep. Ind.*, Vol. VIII, p. 142, text lines 33 f. Often *abhinandanti* is found instead of *pratinandanti* and sometimes *Hutāśana-purogamāḥ* (*Ep. Ind.*, Vol. XXX, p. 278, text line 14) in the second foot. Sometimes we have *Ādityā Vasavo Rudrā* in the first and *Nārāyaṇaś=ca bhagavān* in the third foot (*Ep. Carn.*, Vol III, No. Sr.15). The stanza occurs in the *Mahābhārata*, XIII, 62, 48; *Atrisaṁhitā*, verse 330 (with *abhinandati*); *Bṛhaspatisaṁhitā*, 16 (with *abhinandati*, and *Vahni*° for *Viṣṇu*°). Ballāla's *Dānasāgara* (op. cit., p. 316) attributes the stanza to the *Dāna-Bṛhaspati*. A similar stanza is *Pitaraḥ pitṛ-lokasthā deva-loke divaukasaḥ । santarpayanti dātāraṁ bhūmeḥ prabhavatāṁ vara* ॥ (*Ep. Ind.*, Vol XII, p. 97, lines 28-29).

2. *CII*, Vol. III, pp. 194, 198, 296. Sometimes we have *loka-trayaṁ tena bhaved=dhi dattaṁ* (*Ep. Ind.*, Vol. XXV, p. 60, text lines 51-52). The same stanza occurs in the *Mahābhārata*, III, 199, 128, *Bṛhaspatisaṁhitā*, verse 31, and *Saṁvartasaṁhitā*, verse 74, with *lokās=trayas=tena bhavanti dattā*°, while the *Padma Purāṇa*, VI, 33, 32, has the quarter as *teṣām=anantaṁ phalam=aśnuvīta*. Ballāla's *Dānasāgara* (op. cit., p. 317) attributes it to Saṁvarta.

3. *Ep. Ind.*, Vol. XXV, p. 218, verse 41. The second half is sometimes read as *yaṣṭā bhavati rājendra yo dadāti vasundharām* (ibid., Vol. XXV, p. 278, text lines 12-13). Sometimes we have the stanza as *Agniṣṭoma-prabhṛtibhir=iṣṭvā yajñaiḥ sa-dakṣiṇaiḥ । na tat=phalam=avāpnoti bhūmi-dānād=yad=aśnute* ॥ (*Ind. Ant.*, Vol. XIV, p. 319, text lines 108-09) while the *Mahābhārata* (XIII, 62, 73) shows this reading with *ca sv-āpta-dakṣiṇaiḥ* in the second foot.

4. *Ep. Carn.*. Vol. IX, Dv. No. 15; Vol. X, Goribidnur No. 3; cf. Vol. XIV, Gu. No. 126.

5. *Ep. Carn.*, Vol. V, Belur No. 74. Sometimes we have : *Akara-kara-kāras=tu go-sahasra-vadhaḥ smṛtaḥ । nivṛtta-kara-kāras=tu go-koṭi-phalam=aśnute* (ibid., Vol. VII, Sk. No. 323). For slight variations, see ibid., Vol. XII, Tp. No. 28. Ibid., Vol. XII, Ck. No. 42 has : *Akareṣu karaṁ kṛtvā bhīṣayitvā ca go-vrajam । sva-vaṁśaḥ kāla-sūtre ca kramaśo bhuvi pātyate* ॥

Andho dvādaśa janmāni daśa janmāni śūkaraḥ ।
kuṣṭhī janma-sahasrāṇi bhūmi-dān-āpahārakaḥ ॥ 9[1]

Aṅgam=ekam, etc. See No. 132, note.

Anityāni śarīrāṇi, etc. See No. 12, note.

Anucintya śriyaṁ jīvyaṁ padma-patr-āṇu-binduvat ।
buddhv=ātr=odāhṛtaṁ sarvaṁ na lopyāḥ para-kīrtayaḥ ॥ 10[2]

Anudakeṣv=araṇyeṣu, etc. See No. 150, note.

Anya-gotra-samutpannam=api c=ānya-samudbhavam ।
mahāpātaka-yuktaś=cha yo dānaṁ parisaṁvaret ॥ 11[3]

Anyaiś=ca charditaṁ, etc. See No. 14, note.

Anya-kṣetre kṛtaṁ pāpaṁ puṇya-kṣetre vinaśyati ।
puṇya-kṣetre kṛtaṁ pāpaṁ vajralepena tiṣṭhati ॥ 12[4]

Anyāyena hṛtā bhūmir=hāritā v=ānumoditā ।
atīt-āgāmi-pāpānāṁ dahaty=ā-saptamaṁ kulam ॥ 13[5]

Anyeṣāṁ charditaṁ bhuṅkte śv=āpi sva-charditaṁ na tu ।
tataḥ kaṣṭataro nīcaḥ sva-dattasy=āpahārakaḥ ॥ 14[6]

A-pānīyeṣv=araṇyeṣu, etc. See No. 150, note.

Api Gaṅg-ādi-tīrtheṣu hantur=gām=athavā dvijam ।
niṣkṛtiḥ syān=na devasva-brahmasva-haraṇe nṛṇām ॥ 15[7]

1. Chhabra, *Antiquities of Chamba State*, II, p. 177. Sometimes we have *Andhakaḥ sapta janmāni* in the first foot and *svayaṁ datt-āpahārakāḥ* in the last.

2. *Ep. Ind.*, Vol. XIX, p. 45, text lines 31-32. See No. 71 below.

3. *Ep. Carn.*, Vol. XIV, Hg. No. 143.

4. *Ep. Carn.*, Vol. VII, Sk. No. 63. For *vajra-lepaṁ bhaviṣyati* in the last foot, see ibid., Vol. XII, Tp. No. 28. This stanza is not specially related to *dāna* as also the verse : *Anityāni śarīrāṇi vibhavaṁ n=aiva śāśvatam । nityaṁ sannihito mṛtyuḥ kartavyo dharma-saṁgrahaḥ* ॥ (*A. R. Ep.* 1946-47, No. B 208).

5. *Ind. Ant.*, Vol. XVII, p. 12 (text lines 25-26) reads the second and third feet as *anyāyena tu hāritā* and *harato hārayataś=ca.* The *Bṛhaspatisaṁhitā* (verse 36) has the stanza with: *yair=narair=apahāritā* in the second foot and *harato hārayantaś=ca hanyus=te saptamaṁ kulam* in the second half. Cf. *Padma Purāṇa*, VI, 33, 34. See below, No. 100.

6. *Ep. Carn.*, Vol. III, ML. No. 121. Sometimes we have : *Anyais=tu charditaṁ kṣudraiḥ śvabhiś=ca charditaṁ na tu । tataḥ kaṣṭas=tato nīcaḥ svayaṁ-datt-āpahārakaḥ* ॥ (*Ind. Ant.*, Vol. IV, p. 334).

7. *Ep. Ind.*, Vol XIII, p. 22. Cf. *Śāstreṣu pāpīnāṁ dṛṣṭaṁ prāyaśeittaṁ dvijottama । na dṛṭṣaṁ bhūmi-hartṛṇām prāyaścittaṁ dvija kvacit* ॥ *Śiva-putro jano dātā pālakah punja-bhāk=param । lopakṛc=ca mahāpāpī vicārya=aivam prapālayet* ॥ (Khare, op. cit., p. 34); *Aṣṭāviṁśati-kotyo yā narakāṇāṁ su-dāruṇāḥ । kramena tāsu pacyante deva-brahma-sva-hāriṇaḥ* ॥ (*Ep. Ind.*, Vol. XXXI, p. 110).

Api hasta-mitāṁ bhūmiṁ yo viprāya prayacchati |
ṣaṣṭiṁ varṣa-sahasrāṇi svarga-loke mahīyate || 16[1]
Ārāmāṇāṁ sahasreṇa, etc. See No. 137, note.
Ārya-saṅghāya dattāṁ yo vṛttiṁ rakṣati mānavaḥ |
sa divaṁ prāpya divy-ātmā kalpa-koṭiṣu modate || 17[2]
A-saṅkheyāni varṣāṇi, etc. See No. 123, note.
Asāre=pi ca saṁsāre jīvitasya phala-dvayam |
pālanaṁ para-kīrtīnāṁ svayaṁ-kartṛtvam=eva ca || 18[3]
Asmat-kula-kramam=udāram=udāharadbhir=
anyaiś=ca dānam=idam=abhyanumodanīyam |
lakṣmyās=taḍit-salila-budbuda-cañcalāyā
dānaṁ phalaṁ para-yaśaḥ-paripālanañ=ca || 19[4]
Asmin=vaṁśe, etc. See No. 90, note.
Āsphoṭayanti pitaraḥ pravalganti pitāmahāḥ |
bhūmido='smat-kule jātaḥ sa nas=trātā bhaviṣyati || 20[5]
Aṣṭāviṁśati, etc. See No. 15, note.
Aśvamedha-sahasrāṇi vājapeya-śatāni ca |
pauṇḍarīka-sahasrāṇi bhūmi-dān-ārdhikaṁ phalam || 21[6]
Aśvamedha-sahasreṇa, etc. See No. 137, note.
Aviṣaṁ viṣam=ity=āhu, etc. See No. 98, note.
Āyuḥ putrā dhanaṁ saukhyaṁ saubhāgyaṁ rājyam=
akṣayam |

1. *Ind. Ant.*, Vol. XIV, p. 73.
2. *Ep. Ind.*, Vol. XXVIII, p. 75.
3. *Ep. Ind.*, Vol. XIX, p. 45, text lines 30-31.
4. *Ep. Ind.*, Vol. XXVIII, p. 277, text lines 22-25; cf. Vol. XXXVI, p. 46.
5. *CII*, Vol. III, p. 119. Sometimes we have *nandanti tasya pitaraḥ* or *nṛtyanti pitaras=tasya* (*Ep. Ind.*, Vol. XXIX, p. 194, text line 35; Vol. XXV, p. 218, verse 38) in the first foot and *valgayanti* for *pravalganti*, or *valganti ca* and *sa naḥ santārayiṣyati* (ibid., Vol. XXV, p. 60, text lines 52-53; p. 218, verse 38). For *Ānandanti ca pitaraḥ* in the first foot, see *Ep. Ind.*, Vol. XXV, p. 164, text line 20. The stanza occurs in the *Padma Purāṇa*, VI, 33, 17 (with *pitaro varṇayanti* and *bhūmi-dātā kule*); *Bṛhaspatisaṁhitā*, verse 17 (with *praharṣanti pitāmahāḥ*); *Skanda Purāṇa*, op. cit., verse 24 (with *kathayanti pitāmahāḥ* and *so='smān=santārayiṣyati*). Ballāla (*Dānasāgara*, op. cit., p. 317, with *pravadanti* and *so='smān=santārayiyṣati*) and Aparārka (*Yājñavalkīya-Dharmaśāstra-nibandha*, Anandasrama Press, p. 370) assign it to Bṛhaspati and the *Viṣṇudharmottara* respectively.
6. *Ep. Ind.*, Vol. XII, p. 324, text lines 26-27. The second half is also given as *kṛtvā yat=phalam=āpnoti bhūmi-dānat=tad=aśnute* (*Ep. Carn.*, Vol. X, Malur No. 57).

ābhiśraiṣṭhyaṁ yaśaḥ svargaṁ bhūmido labhate phalam ॥ 22[1]

Bahubhir=vasudhā bhuktā rājabhiḥ Sagar-ādibhiḥ ।
yasya yasya yadā bhūmis=tasya tasya tadā phalam ॥ 23[2]

Bahun=ātra kim=uktena saṁkṣepād=idam=ucyate ।
svalpam=āyuś=calā bhogā dharmo lokadvaya-kṣamaḥ ॥24[3]

Bho rājānaḥ, etc. See No. 117, note.

Bhūmi-dānaṁ su-pātreṣu su-tīrtheṣu su-parvasu ।
agādh-āpāra-saṁsāra-sāgar-ottāraṇaṁ bhavet ॥ 25[4]

Bhūmi-dāna-samaṁ dānam=iha-loke na vidyate ।
yaḥ prayacchati bhūmiṁ hi sarva-kāmān=dadāti saḥ ॥ 26[5]

Bhūmi-dāna-samaṁ dānaṁ na, etc. See No. 28, note.

Bhūmi-dānasya yaḥ kartā yaś=ca kārayitā śuciḥ ।
pālakaś=c=ānumantā ca svargaṁ gacchati mānavaḥ ॥ 27[6]

Bhūmi-dānāt=paraṁ dānaṁ na bhūtaṁ na bhaviṣyati ।[7]
tasy=aiva haraṇāt=pāpaṁ na bhūtaṁ na bhavisyati ॥ 28

1. *Ind. Ant.*, Vol. XII, p. 127.

2. *CII*, Vol. III, pp. 96, 104, 108, 115, 119, 122, 127, 133, etc., where this stanza is found together with *Ṣaṣṭiṁ varṣa-sahasrāṇi*, etc. (No. 123), which is also noticed in some cases without this one (cf. ibid., pp. 238, 247). Sometimes *dattā* (ibid., p.296) appears instead of *bhuktā* and *bahubhiś=ānupālitā* (*Ep. Ind.*, Vol. XXXI, p. 80, text line 43), or *bhujyate ca punaḥ punaḥ* (ibid., p. 66, text line 32), or *rājabhiś=ca punaḥ punaḥ* (ibid., Vol. XV, p. 1-39, verse 13), or *bhujyate ca narādhipaiḥ* (ibid., Vol. XVII, p. 304, verse 23), or *bahudhā vasudh-ādhipaiḥ* (ibid., Vol. XXXI, p. 93; often *vasudhā* wrongly for *bahudhā*—ibid., Vol. XXI p. 25, text line 10) for *rājabhiḥ Sagar-ādibhiḥ*. Occasionally we have : *Rājabhir=bahubhir=dattā* (*Iyaṁ rāja-śatair=dattā*—ibid., Vol. XXII, p. 161, text line 22) *dīyate ca punaḥ punaḥ* (ibid., Vol. XX, p. 159) in the first half which sometimes also reads as *Manu-prabhṛtibhir=mānyair=bhuktā yady=api rājabhiḥ* (ibid., Vol. XXVIII, p. 75, text lines 11-12). For *pārthivaiḥ* instead of *rājabhiḥ*, see *Ind. Ant.*, Vol. XII, p. 267. The stanza occurs in the *Padma Purāṇa*, VI, 33, 26-27; *Bhaviṣya Purāṇa*, IV, 164. 22 (with *bhuktā*, for *dattā*); *Skanda Purāṇa*, op. cit., verse 25 (with *rājabhiḥ pṛthivī tv=iyam*); *Bṛhaspatisaṁhitā*, verse 26; also Vṛddha-Gautama, according to Aparārka, op. cit., p. 541. Ballāla (op. cit., pp. 316-17) attributes the stanza (with *dattā* for *bhuktā*) to the *Dāna-Bṛhaspati*. Cf. two analogous stanzas : *Yas=tu pālayate bhūmiṁ bhūmipālas=tath=etaraḥ । sa dātuḥ phalam=āpnoti samaṁ dīrghaṁ ca jīvati ॥ Yānti kālena rājāno mahī punar=avasthitā । tad=etāṁ yo yadā bhuṅkte sa tadā phalam=aśnute ॥* (*Ep. Ind.*, Vol. XXXVI, pp. 18, 46).

3. *Ep. Ind.*, Vol. XXVIII, p. 216, text lines 25-26.

4. *Ep. Ind.*, Vol. XXV, p. 60, text lines 53-54.

5. *Ep. Ind.*, Vol VIII, p. 303, text lines 23-24.

6. *Ep. Ind.*, Vol. IV, p. 170, line 121.

7. See, e. g., *Ep. Ind.*, Vol. VIII, p. 235, text lines 26-28. Sometimes we have *iha-loke na vidyate* for the second quarter and *yaḥ prayacchati bhūmiṁ hi sarva-kāmān=dadāti saḥ* in the second half (ibid., Vol. XXIV, p. 303, text lines 23-24). For *Bhūmi-dāna-samaṁ* at the beginning and *dānena yat=phalaṁ proktaṁ pālanena tato='dhikam* in the second half, see *Ep. Ind.*, Vol. XIX, p. 42, text lines 25-26.

Bhūmiṁ yaḥ pratigṛhṇāti yaś=ca bhūmiṁ prayacchati ।
ubhau tau puṇya-karmāṇau niyataṁ svarga-gāminau ॥ 29[1]

Bhūmi-pradā divi lalanti patanti hanta
hṛtvā mahīṁ nṛpatayo narake nṛśaṁsā ।
etad=dvayaṁ parikalayya calāñ=cha lakṣmīm=
āyus=tathā kurutha yad=bhavatām=abhīṣṭam ॥ 30[2]

Bhūmi-pradānān=na paraṁ pradānaṁ
dānād=viśiṣṭaṁ paripālanañ=ca ।
sarve='tisṛṣṭāṁ paripālya bhūmiṁ
nṛpā Nṛg-ādyās=tridivaṁ prapannāḥ ॥ 31[3]

Bhūṣv=aṭavīṣv=atoyāsu, etc. See No. 150, note.

Brāhmaṇebhyaḥ, etc. See No. 55, note.

Brahma-svaṁ dur-anujñātām, etc. See No. 32, note.

Brahma-svaṁ praṇayād=bhuktvā dahaty=ā-saptamaṁ kulam ।
vikrameṇa yo bhokṣyate daśa pūrvān=daś=āvarān ॥ 32[4]

Brahma-svaṁ putra-pautraghnaṁ, etc. See No. 98, note.

Brahma-svaṁ tu viṣam, etc. See No. 98, note.

Brahma-sva-paripuṣṭāni vāhanāni balāni ca ।
yuddha-kāle viśīryante saikatāḥ setavo yathā ॥ 33[5]

1. *Ep. Ind.*, Vol. III, p. 343, text lines 30-31; p. 348, text lines 24-25. Sometimes we have *yas=tu* for *yaś=ca* (ibid., Vol. XI, p. 312) and *niyatau* (ibid., Vol. XXVIII, p. 292, text line 26) or *dvāv=etau* (ibid., Vol. XXII, p. 194, text line 19) for *niyataṁ*. The stanza is found in the *Padma Purāṇa*, VI, 33, 35-36; *Vṛddha-Hāritasmṛti*, VII, 164; *Bṛhaspatisaṁhitā*, verse 33 (with *bhūmiṁ yasya* in the second foot). It is attributed to the *Dāna-Bṛhaspati* in Ballāla's *Dānasāgara* (op. cit., p. 317), to the *Kūrma Purāṇa* in the *Dānacandrikā* (with *tāv=ubhau puruṣau loke sūrya-maṇḍala-bhedinau*) and to Bṛhaspati in Halāyudha's *Brāhmaṇasarvasva* (*IHQ*, Vol. VI, p. 777). See also the *Mitākṣarā* on the *Yājñavalkyasmṛti*, II, 114. A verse modified from this stanza (cf. also No. 27) seems to be : *Upadeśī ca dātā ca niyatau svarga-vāsinau* । *upadeśī prathamaṁ yāti paścād=dātā Dhanañjaya* ॥ (*A. R. Ep.*, 1946-47, No. B 205). Another such stanza is *Dātā ca prerakaś=c=aiva ye dharma-pratipālakāḥ* । *te sarve puṇya-karmāṇo niyataṁ svarga-gāminaḥ* ॥ (*Ind. Ant.*, Vol. XI, p. 243, text lines 40-41).

2. *Ep. Ind.*, Vol. XXXI, p. 221, text lines 21-24. The stanza is sometimes quoted separately from the *Vyāsa-gīta* group of verses (ibid. Vol. XXXIV, p. 114).

3. *CII*, Vol. III, p. 115, text lines 22-23.

4. *Ep. Ind.*, Vol. VI, p. 102 text lines 33-34. Ibid Vol. XXV, p. 219, verse 52 has it as : *Brahma-svaṁ dur-anujñātaṁ bhuktaṁ hanti tri-puruṣam* । *prasahya tu balād=bhuktaṁ daśa pūrvān=daś=āparān* ॥ while the second half is given in *Ind. Ant.*, Vol. XV, p. 176, text lines 48-49 as : *tad=eva cauryarūpeṇa dahaty=ā-candra-tārakam.* For variations, see *Ep. Carn.*, Vol. X, Mulbagal No. 157.

5. *Ep. Carn.*, Vol. III, Sr. 12.

Brahma-sve mā matiṁ kuryāḥ prāṇaiḥ kaṇṭha-gatair=api ı
agni-dagdhāni rohanti brahma-dagdhaṁ na rohati ıı 34[1]
Calā lakṣmīś=calāḥ prāṇāś=calaṁ jīvita-yauvanam ı
cal-ācale hi saṁsāre dharma eko hi niścalaḥ ıı 35[2]
Calā vibhūtiḥ kṣaṇa-bhaṅgi yauvanaṁ
kṛtānta-dant-āntara-varti jīvitam ı
tath=āpy=avajñā para-loka-sādhane
nṛṇām=aho vismayakāri ceṣṭitam ıı 36[3]
Candr-ārkau ca tathā bhūmir=nabhas=tāpanam=anilaḥ ı
tārakāś=c=ānalaś=c=aiva Dharmarājas=tath=aiva ca ıı
tisraḥ sandhyās=trayo vedās=trayo devās=trayo='gnayaḥ ı
aho rātraṁ ca dānasya ete vai sākṣiṇaḥ smṛtāḥ ıı 37-38[4]
Dānād=viśiṣṭaṁ paripālanajaṁ purāṇā
dharmeṣu niścita-dhiyaḥ pravadanti dharmam ı
tasmād=dvijāya suviśuddha-kula-śrutāya
dattāṁ bhuvaṁ bhavatu vo matir=eṣā goptum ıı 39[5]
Dānaṁ vā, etc. See No. 40, note.
Dāna-pālanayos=tāvat=phalaṁ sugati-durgatī ı
ko nāma svargam=utsṛjya narakaṁ pratipadyate ıı 40[6]
Dātā c=aiv=ānumantā ca svargasy=opari tiṣṭhati ı
hartā hārayitā bhūmeḥ pacyate Raurave dhruvam ıı 41[7]
Dātā ca preraka°, etc. See No. 29, note.
Dātā daś=ānugṛhṇāti daśa, etc. See No. 42, note.

1. *Ind. Ant.*, Vol. XIX, p. 310, text lines 30-32. The first half of the stanza is found in the *Bṛhaspatisaṁhitā*, verse 45 (with *ratiṁ* for *matiṁ*).
2. *Ep. Ind.*, Vol. XXII, p. 194, text lines 17-18.
3. *Ep. Ind.*, Vol. XXXII, p. 70, text lines 9-11.
4. *Ind. Ant.*, Vol. XII, p. 121. See above No. 2.
5. *Ep. Ind.*, Vol. IX, p. 173, text lines 12-14.
6. *Ep. Ind.*, Vol. XXXI, pp. 221-22, text lines 24-25. We have *Rakṣā* for *Dāna* at the beginning in *Ep. Ind.*, Vol. XXIII, p. 121, line 20; cf. ibid., Vol. XXXIV, p. 114 (where the stanza has been quoted seperately from the *Vyāsa-gīta* group of verses). The second half is sometimes quoted as *dānāt=svargam=avāpnoti pālanād=acyutaṁ* (*śāṅkaraṁ* in *Ep. Carn.*, Vol. VIII, Tl. No. 73) *padam* and we have *madhye* for *tāvat* in the first foot (*Ep. Ind.*, Vol. XVI, p. 351). Sometimes we have *Dānaṁ vā pālanaṁ v=ātra* and *dānāc=chreyo='nupālanam* in the first and second feet (*Ep. Carn.*, Vol. II, Nos., 253, 327; Vol. III, My. Nos. 7, 32). The third foot sometimes reads *dānād=Indratvam=āpnoti* (*Ep. Ind.*, Vol. XIV, p. 104, text lines 103-105).
7. *Ind. Ant.*, Vol. XII, p. 127.

Dātā daś=ānugṛhṇāti yo hared=daśa hanti ca ।
atīt-ānāgatān=īha kulāni Kurunandana ॥ 42[1]

Dattāni yān=īha purā narendrair=
dānāni dharm-ārtha-yaśaskarāṇi ।
nirmālaya-vānta-pratimāni tāni
ko māma sādhuḥ punar=ādadīta ॥ 43[2]

Dattvā bhūmiṁ, etc. See No. 117, note.

Deva-dravya-vināśena brahma-sva-harṇena ca ।
tad=dhanaṁ kula-nāśāya bhaved=ātma-vadhāya ca ॥ 44[3]

Deva-dravy-opabhoktā ca deva-kārya-vighātakaḥ ।
devatā-nindakaś=c=aiva aputraś=c=opajāyate ॥ 45[4]

Deva-dvija-gatāṁ bhūmiṁ pūrva-bhuktāṁ hareta yaḥ ।
praṇaṣṭam=api kālena tam=āhur=brahma-ghātakam ॥ 46[5]

Deva-śāsana-loptāro, etc. See No. 45, note.

Deva-svaṁ tu viṣaṁ ghoram, etc. See No. 98, note.

1. *Ep. Ind.*, Vol. XVII, p. 303, verse 21. Sometimes we have : *Dātā daś=anugṛhṇāti daśa hanti tathā kṣipan । pūrva-dattāṁ haran=bhūmiṁ narakāy=opagachcati* ॥ (*Ind. Ant.*, Vol. XIV, p. 319, text lines 111-12).

2. *CII*, Vol. III, p. 180, text lines 73-74; *Ep. Ind.*, Vol. III, p. 322, text lines 25-26; Vol. XXII, p. 109, text line 63; p. 120, text line 60; etc. Sometimes we have *Yān=iha dattāni* and *dharmāya* (*Ep. Ind.*, Vol. XXXII, p. 134), *purātanāni* for *purā narendraiḥ* (*Ind. Ant.*, Vol. VII, p. 64), *Yān=īha dāridya-bhayān=narendrair°* and *dānāni* (*dhanāni* in *Ind. Ant.*, Vol. V, p. 207 text line 12) *dharmāyatanī-kṛitāni, nirbhukta* (*nirvānta*; ibid., Vol. VI, p. 16, text line 19)-*mālya-pratimāni tāni* (*Ep. Ind.*, Vol. I, p. 88; Vol. XXI, p. 211), etc. For *nirmālyavānti*, see *Ep. Ind.*, Vol. XVIII, p. 323, text line 21; for *nirmālyavat=tāni ca mānitāni*, cf. *Ind. Ant.*, Vol. VI, p. 56, text line 11, and *nirmālya-tulyāni bhavanti tāni*, ibid., Vol. XVII, p. 122, text line 49. The stanza is found in the *Skanda Purāṇa*, op. cit., verse 36, with *Yān=īha dattāni punar=dhanāni* in the first foot and *audāryato vipra-niveditāni* in the third.

3. *Ep. Carn.*, Vol. V, Belur No. 58.

4. *Ep. Carn.*, Vol. V, Hassan No. 115. Sometimes we have *Vipra-dravy-āpahartāro deva-dravy-āpahārakāḥ* । ....*n=ātra saṁśayaḥ* ॥ (ibid., Channarayapatna No. 259) or *Deva - śāsana-loptāro deva-dravy-āpahāriṇaḥ* । *pacyante narake rakte janma-janma na saṁśayaḥ* ॥ or *Devasya śāsanaṁ ye tu lumpanti pāpa-karmāṇaḥ* । *patanti narake ghore sa-putra-paśu-bāndhavaiḥ* ॥ (ibid., Sb. No. 191). A few similar stanzas are : *Vipra-grāmeṣu yaḥ kuryād=anyāyena karaṁ karaiḥ* ।.........*naro bhuṅkte narakān=kalpa-pañcasu* ॥ and *Vipra-grāme kar-ādāne yo='numantā sa pāpa-kṛt* ।.........*brahma-haty-āyutaṁ śatam* ॥ (ibid., Channarayapatna No. 259). See also *Yaṁ vināśayituṁ*, etc., in Vol. XII, Ck. No. 42. Cf. *Yath-oktaiḥ pañcabhir=ghorair=mahāpātaka-vahnibhiḥ* । *nirdagdhā narakaṁ yānti brahmadey-āpahāriṇaḥ* ॥ (R. S. Panchamukhi, *Karnatak Inscriptions*, Vol. II, p. 3).

5. *Ep. Ind.*, Vol. XIII, p. 173. Sometimes we have *gavāṁ* for *gatāṁ* and *praṇaṣṭāṁ* for *praṇaṣṭaṁ* (R. S. Panchamukhi, *Karnatak Inscriptions*, Vol. II, p. 102).

Deva-svatvaṁ yav-āṁśaṁ ca brahma-svatvaṁ til-āṁśakam
apekṣayañ=ca narakaṁ bhakṣayañ=ca kula-kṣayam ॥ 47[1]
Deva-svāni harant=īha narā naraka-nirbhayāḥ ।
brahma-svāni tu ye mohāt=pacyate narake tu te ॥ 48[2]
Devasya, etc. See No. 45, note.
Dharmād=vivardhate rājyaṁ dharmāt=kīrtiś=ca śāśvatī ।
dharmāt=tṛpyanti pitaro dharmāt=tuṣyanti devatāḥ ॥
tasmād=dharmaḥ prayatnena rakṣaṇīyo mahīkṣitā ।
sva-kṛto='nya-kṛto v=āpi loka-dvaya-hitaiṣiṇā ॥ 49-50[4]
Dharmāt=Paijavano rājā cirāya bubhuje bhuvam ।
adharmāc=c=aiva Nahuṣaḥ pratipede rasātalam ॥ 51[3]
Dhavalāny=ātapatrāṇi, etc. See No. 119, note.
Dvijāś=ca n=āvamantavyās=trailokya-miti-hetavaḥ ।
devavat=pūjanīyāś=ca dāna-mān-ārcan-ādibhiḥ ॥ 52[5]
Ek-āhany=api, etc. See No. 82, note.
Ek=aiva bhaginī loke sarveṣām=eva bhūbhujām ।
na bhojyā na kara-grāhyā vipra-dattā vasundharā ॥ 53[6]
Ekaviṁśat-kulasy=eva kaṣṭaṁ hi narake sthitam ।
bhūmi-pradāna-mātreṇa tvac=ev=āher=vimucyate ॥ 54[7]
Gām=ekāṁ ca, etc. See No. 55, note.
Gām=ekāṁ ratnikā°, etc. See No. 55, note.
Gām=ekāṁ svarṇam=ekaṁ vā bhūmer=apy=ardham=aṅgulam ।
haran=narakam=āyāti yāvad=ā-bhūta-saṁplavam ॥ 55[8]

1. *Ep. Carn.*, Vol. XII, Tm. No. 37.
2. *Ind. Ant.*, Vol. XII, p. 121.
3. *Ep. Ind.*, Vol. VI, p. 344, verses 45-46.
4. *Ep. Ind.*, Vol. VI, p. 343, verse 43.
5. *Ep. Ind.*, Vol. XIX, p. 213, text lines 34-35.
6. *Ep. Ind.*, Vol. XVI, p. 351, text lines 78-80; p. 318. Sometimes we have *bhogyā* (ibid., p. 253). The same stanza occurs in the *Skanda Purāṇa*, op. cit., verse 39.
7. *Ep. Ind.*, Vol. XII, p. 324, line 33. The same stanza occurs again in lines 27-28 of the same epigraph with *ūrdhvaṁ yānti mṛtā divi* in the last quarter.
8. *Ep. Ind.*, Vol. XXXI, p. 128, verse 111. *Ep. Carn.*, Vol. VI, Kp. No. 53 has *Brāhmaṇebhyaḥ pradattāyā°* at the beginning. Sometimes we have *ca* for *vā* and *Hiraṇyam=ekaṁ gām=ekām* (*Ep. Ind.*, Vol. XXVIII, p. 114, text line 28); *āpnoti* or *āyāti* (ibid., p. 292); *ā-hūta°* or *ā-bhūti* for *ā-bhūta°* (see, e.g., ibid., Vol. XXIX, p. 57, text line 44; Vol. XIX, p. 19, text line 33); also *Suvarṇam=ekaṁ gām=ekāṁ* (or *Gām=ekāṁ ca suvarṇaṁ ca bhūmer=apy=eka°*) and *haranto hārayanta==cha* (or *hṛtvā narakam=āyāti*, or *haran=naraka-vāsī syāt*—*Ep. Ind.*, Vol. XXIII, p. 212, text lines 56-57)

Gām=ekāṁ svarṇa-raktiṁ, etc. See No. 55, note.

Gaṇyante pāṁsavo bhūmer=gaṇyante vṛṣṭi-bindavaḥ ı
na gaṇyate Vidhātr=āpi dharma-saṁrakṣaṇe phalam ıı 56[1]

Gāvo bhūmiṁ tathā bhāryāṁ ākramya hara mā naya ı
śrāvayanti hi rājānaṁ Brahma-hatyā ca limpati ıı 57[2]

Gayā-Godāvarī-Gaṅgā-Prayāg-ādiṣu dānataḥ ı
yat=phalaṁ tat=phalaṁ sarvaṁ bhaved=bhūmi-prapālanāt ıı 58[3]

Go-hatyā brahma-hatyā ca bāla-hatyā tath=aiva ca ı
vipra-haty=ārṣi-haty=āvabhañjakas=tayā lipyate ıı 59[4]

Gṛṇhanti yāvataḥ pāṁsūn=krandatām=aśru=bindavaḥ ı
viprāṇāṁ hata-vṛttīnāṁ vadānyānāṁ kuṭumbinām ıı
rājāno rāja-kulyāś=ca tāvato='bdān-niraṅkuśāḥ
kumbhīpākeṣu pacyante Brahma-bhūmy-apahārakāḥ ıı 60-61[5]

Haṁsair=yutaṁ yānam=āruhya divyaṁ
bhūmer-dātā yāti lokaṁ surāṇām ı
tapte kumbhe prajvalat-taila-pūrṇe
tasyā hartā pācyate Kāla-dūtaiḥ ıı 62[6]

Hanti jātān=ajatāṁś=ca, etc. See No. 81.

Harasya prīṇan-ārthaṁ tu Śiva-bhaktāya dīyate ı
dānaṁ tad=vimalaṁ proktaṁ kevalaṁ mokṣa-dāyinam ıı 63[7]

dahaty=ā=saptamaṁ kulam (ibid., Vol. XXXI, pp. 248, 281; or *yāvac=candra-divākarau*—Vogel, *Antiquities of Chamba State*, I, p. 167). The first half is sometimes given as : *Kanyām=ekāṁ gavām=ekāṁ bhūmer=ardhārdham=aṅgulam* (*Ind. Ant.*, Vol. XII, p. 203). Sometimes we have *Gām=ekāṁ svarṇa-raktiñ=ca* (*Ep. Ind.*, Vol. XXVIII, p. 67, text line 38) or *Gām=ekāṁ ratnikām=ekām* (ibid., Vol. XIII, p. 251, text lines 232-33). The stanza is found in the *Bṛhaspatisaṁhitā*, verse 40 (with *rundhan* for *haran*). Caṇḍeśvara's *Gṛhastharatnākara* (Bibliotheca Indica, p. 514) assigns it to Yama while Viśvarūpa (*Bālakrīḍā*, Trivandrum Sanskrit Series, on the *Yājñavalkyasmṛti*, III, 252) quotes the second half as : *apahṛtya dvij-āgrebhyo na cirād=vadhyate dhruvam.*

1 *Ep. Ind.*, Vol. VI, p. 97. *Ep. Carn.*, Vol. VIII, Tl. No. 5 has *dharma-saṁsthāpane.*

2. *Ep. Ind.*, Vol. IV, p. 197, lines 31-32.

3. *Ind. Ant.*, Vol. VII, p. 121.

4. *Ep. Ind.*, Vol. XIII, p. 208, text lines 6-8.

5. *Ep. Ind.*, Vol. XXV, p. 219, verses 53-54. For slight variations, see *Ep. Carn.*, Vol. XI, Dg. No. 28.

6. Chhabra, *Antiquities of Chamba State*, II, p. 179.

7. *Ep. Carn.*, Vol. VIII, Tl. Nos. 6, 46, 47. This stanza is usually preceded by the verse : *Yatra yogīśvaraḥ kuryāc=Chiva-liṅg-ārcanaṁ sakṛt ı vasanti tatra tīrthāni sarvāṇi satataṁ* (or *saptakaṁ*) *Guha ıı*

Harate hārayed=yas=tu manda-buddhis=tamo-vṛtaḥ I
sa baddho Vāruṇaiḥ pāśais=tiryag-yoniṁ ca gacchati II 64[1]
Hareta, etc. See No. 64, note.
Hartā devasya yo bhūmiṁ Brāhmaṇa-guror=api yaḥ I
sva-dattāṁ para-dattāṁ vā sa yāti narakaṁ naraḥ II 65[2]
Hartā hārayitā bhūmeḥ, etc. See No. 64, note.
Hinasti viṣam=attāraṁ vahnir=adbhiḥ praśāmyati I
kulaṁ samūlaṁ dahati Brahmasv-āraṇi-pāvakaḥ II 66[3]
Hiraṇya-maṇi-muktāni vastrāṇy=ābharaṇāni ca I
tēna sarvam=idaṁ dattaṁ yena dattā vasundharā II 67[4]
Hiraṇyam=ekam, etc. See No. 55, note.
Hṛṇa-hartā bhūmi-hartā hārayitā hi te trayaḥ I
ete ca narakaṁ yānti yāvad=Indrāś=caturdaśa II 68[5]
Iha-loka-kṛtaṁ karma tat=paratr=opabhujyate I
tala-siktasya vṛkṣasya phalaṁ śākhāsu dṛśyate II 69[6]
Imaṁ dharmaṁ ca ye ghnanti ye ca tat-sahakāriṇaḥ I
Kirāta-Mleccha-Cāṇḍāla-Carmakār-ātmajās=tu te II 70[7]
Iti kamala=dal-āmbu-bindu-lolāṁ
śriyam=anucintya manuṣya-jīvitaṁ ca I
sakalam=idam=udāhṛtaṁ ca buddhvā
na hi puruṣaiḥ para-kīrtayo vilopyāḥ II 71[8]

1. *Ep. Ind.*, Vol. III, p. 343, text lines 32-33; pp. 348-49, text lines 26-27; p. 353, text lines 49-50; ibid., Vol. XXVIII, p. 50. Often we have *hārayante* or *hāryate* for *hārayed°*, *bhūmiṁ* for *yas=tu*, *subaddho* for *sa baddho* and *yoniṣu* for *yoniṁ ca*. The first foot is sometimes read as *Hartā hārayitā bhūmeḥ* (*Ind. Ant.*, Vol. XIV., p. 255, text lines 30-31). For *Hareta* at the beginning of the first, and *sa-vaṁśo* at that of the second half, see *Ind. Ant.*, Vol. V, p. 56. The *Bṛhaspatisaṁhitā* (verse 37) has the stanza with *hārayed°*, *sa vadhyo* and *°yoniṣu*. Cf. *Mahābhārata*, XIII, 62, 75.

2. *Ind. Ant.*, Vol. XII, p. 121.

3. *Ep. Ind.*, Vol. XXV, p. 219, verse 51. The first half is given sometimes as : *Vanaṁ vana-caro vahnir=dahan=mūlāni rakṣati* (cf. *Ep. Carn.*, Vol. VIII, Tl. Nos. 130 and 133).

4. *Ep. Ind.*, Vol. XXIII, p. 229, verse 17.

5. *Ep. Ind.*, Vol. XI, p. 313. The second half is sometimes read as: *narakān=na nivartante yāvad=ā-bhūta-saṁplavam* (ibid., Vol. XIII, p. 281).

6. *Ep. Ind.*, Vol. XXXIII, p. 213, verse 9.

7. *Ep. Carn.*, Vol. III, TN. No. 63; Sr. No. 64.

8. *Ep. Ind.*, Vol. III, p. 343, text lines 37-39; p. 349, text lines 32-34; etc. For the third foot, we have occasionally *ativimala-manobhir=ātmanīnair°* (ibid., Vol. XXII, p. 109, text lines 65; p. 186, text line 62; cf. *ātma-līnai°* in Vol. XXXII, p. 134). The sense of this popular stanza is rarely conveyed in the following verse : *Taḍit-taraṅga-bahulāṁ śriyaṁ matvā ca martyānāṁ* I *na dharma-sthitayaḥ sadbhir=yuktā loke vilopitum* II (*Select Inscriptions*, p. 364, text lines 23-24). See also No. 10 above.

Iṣṭaṁ dattaṁ, etc. See No. 126, note.

Iyaṁ rāja-śatair-dattā, etc. See No. 23, note.

Jñātv=aivaṁ mat-pradatto='yaṁ bhūmi-dāyo manīṣibhiḥ ।
n=occhedyo bhāvi-bhūpālaiḥ sarvair=ātma-hitaiṣibhiḥ ॥ 72[1]

Kalpa-koṭi-sahasrāṇi kalpa-koṭi-śatāni ca ।
nivased=Brahmaṇo loke dharma-dāyaṁ karoti yaḥ ॥ 73[2]

Kanyām=ekām, etc. See No. 55, note.

Karmaṇā manasā vācā yaḥ samartho='py=upekṣate ।
sa syāt=tad=aiva Caṇḍālaḥ sarva-karma-bahiṣkṛtaḥ ॥ 74[3]

Kartuḥ kārayitur=hetor=anumoditur=eva ca ।
karmaṇāṁ bhāginaḥ pretya bhūyo bhūyas=tu tat=phalam ॥ 75[4]

Kharo dvādaśa, etc. See No 128, note.

Khila-bhagnā tu yā bhūmir=yā ca bhuktā daś=āparā ।
śataṁ yāvat=tu yā bhuktā na rājā hartum=arhati ॥ 76[5]

Koṭis=tu vājapeyānāṁ lakṣaṁ viśvajitāṁ tathā ।
sahasram=aśvamedhānāṁ sva-hastaś=c=aiva tat-samaḥ ॥ 77[6]

Kṛśāya kṛśa-vṛttāya vṛtti-kṣīṇāya sīdate ।
bhūmiṁ vṛttikarīṁ dattvā sukhī bhavati kāmadaḥ ॥ 78[7]

Kṛta-Tretā-Dvāpareṣu, etc. See No. 97, note.

Kṣitir=iyaṁ kulaṭ=eva bahu-priyā
hata-śarīram=idaṁ ca vinaśvaram ।
sukṛtam=adya na cet=kriyate dhruvaṁ
vipadi dhakṣyati vo='nuśay-ānalaḥ ॥ 79[8]

1. *Ep. Ind.*, Vol. XXXII, p. 54, text lines 55-56.
2. *Ep. Ind.*, Vol. XXXII, p. 70, text lines 21-22.
3. *Ep. Ind.*, Vol. VI, p. 97, text lines 52-53. We have also *dharma* for *karma* (*Ind. Ant.*, Vol. IV, p. 276).
4. *Ep. Carn.*, Vol. VIII, Tl. No. 5.
5. *Ep. Ind.*, Vol. XXXIII, p. 213, verse 6.
6. *Ind. Ant.*, Vol. XII, p. 186. The word *sva-hasta* here seems to mean the donor's signature in approval of a grant.
7. *Ep. Ind.*, Vol. XXXI, pp. 65-66, text lines 31-32. Sometimes we have *bhṛtyāya* for *vṛttāya* and *chatrī* for *sukhī* and the following half verse preceding the stanza : *Santarpayati dātāraṁ bhūmeḥ prabhavatāṁ vara* (ibid., Vol. XXV, pp. 218-19). The stanza is found in the *Mahābhārata*, XIII, 62, 29 (with *mriyamāṇāya vṛtti-glānāya* for *kṛśa-vṛttāya vṛtti-kṣīṇāya* and *sattrī bhavati mānavaḥ*, for which Hemādri has *kliśyamānāya c=ātyarthaṁ vṛtti-glānāya*). Cf. *Mahābhārata*, XIII, 59, 11.
8. *Ep. Ind.*, Vol. XXV, p. 156, text lines 30-33.

Kṣudra-paśv-anṛte pañca daśa hanti gav-ānṛte ।
śatam=aśv-ānṛte hanti sahasraṁ puruṣ-ānṛtē ॥
hanti jātān=ajātāṁś=ca suvarṇasy=ānṛte prabhoḥ ।
sarvaṁ bhūmy-anṛte hanti mā sma bhūmy-anṛtaṁ vadet ॥ 80-81[1]

Kulāni tārayet=kartā sapta sapta ca sapta ca ।
adho-dhaḥ pātayed=dhartā sapta sapta ca sapta ca ॥ 82[2]
Lobhād=gṛhṇāti mand-ātmā yaḥ pumān=pāpa-mohitaḥ ।
narake pacyate ghore sa hi kalpān=anekaśaḥ ॥ 83[3]
Loha-cūrṇ-āśma-cūrṇaṁ ca viṣaṁ ca jarayen=naraḥ ।
Brahma-svaṁ triṣu lokeṣu kaḥ pumāñ=jarayiṣyati ॥ 84[4]
Mā bhūd=a-phala-śaṅkā vaḥ para-datt=eti pārthivāḥ ।
sva-dānāt=phalam=ānantyaṁ para-datt-ānupālane ॥ 85[5]
Mad-dāna-phala-siddhy-arthaṁ tad-rakṣā-phala-siddhaye ।
mad-dharmaḥ paripālyo='yaṁ bhūpair=ā-candra-tārakam ॥ 86[6]

1. *Mys. Arch. Rep.*, 1910, paragraphs 47-50. The second stanza is sometimes found as : *Hanti jātān=ajātāṁś=ca bhūmy-arthe yo='nṛtaṁ vadet* । *sa baddho vāruṇaiḥ pāśais=tiryag=yonyāṁ tu jāyate* ॥ (*Ep. Ind.*, Vol. XIX, p. 213, text lines 33-34). Cf. *Mahābhārata*, Udyoga-parvan, Calcutta ed., Chapter 35, verses 33-34; Kumbakonam ed., Chapter 35, verses 44-45, where the first foot of the first stanza and the second foot of the second read respectively as *Pañca paśv-anṛte hanti* and *hiraṇy=ārthe='nṛtaṁ vadan*, while the second stanza ends with *vadeḥ* instead of *vadet*. For the first verse, cf. *Rāmāyaṇa*, IV, 34, 9: *Śatam=aśv-ānṛte hanti sahasraṁ tu gav-ānṛte* । *ātmānaṁ svajanaṁ hanti puruṣaḥ puruṣ-ānṛte* ॥ See also *Bṛhaspatisaṁhitā*, verse 43 ff. : *Pañca kany-ānṛte hanti daśa hanti gav-ānṛte* । *śatam=aśv-ānṛte hanti sahasraṁ puruṣ-ānṛte* ॥ *hanti jātān=ajātāṁś=ca hiraṇy-ārthe='nṛtaṁ vadet* । *sarvaṁ bhūmy-anṛte hanti māsma bhūmy-anṛtaṁ vadīḥ* ॥ Sometimes we have *janiṣyān* for *ajātān*.

2. *Ep. Ind.*, Vol. VI, p. 97, text lines 50-51. Similar style is noticed in the stanza: *Ek-āhany=api Kaunteya bhūmistham=udakaṁ kuru* । *tāraya pūrva-kulāni sapta sapta ca sapta ca* ॥ (*A.R. Ep.*, 1946-47, No. B 205).

3. *Ep. Ind.*, Vol. XXVIII, p. 75.

4. *Ep. Ind.*, Vol. XII, p. 325, line 37. The second half has been given in *Ep. Carn.*, Vol. XII, Tp. No. 18 as : *deva-svaṁ triṣu lokeṣu na jīrṇam=iti viśrutam.*

5. *Ep. Ind.*, Vol. III, p. 343, text lines 25-26; p. 348, text lines 18-20; p. 353, text lines 44-45. Sometimes *mā bhūta°*, *para-dān-ānu°* and *°pālanam, te para-datt=eti parthiva* and *sva-dattād=adhikaṁ puṇyam* (ibid., Vol. XXVIII, p. 257, text line 150), etc. The second half sometimes reads as : *sva-dānāt=para-dānasya tasmāc=chreyo='nupālanam* (ibid., Vol. XXXIV, p. 49, text lines 16-18).

6. *Ep. Ind.*, Vol. XXVIII, p. 311, text lines 10-11; p. 257. This stanza is generally found in the grants of the Imperial Gaṅgas of Orissa. Sometimes we have *bhūmeḥ* for *bhūpaiḥ*.

Mad-dattaṁ sad-dvijātibhyo pāti ya iha daivikam ।
mac-chiro-mukuṭa-nyastaṁ tasya rājñaḥ pada-dvayam ॥ 87[1]

Mad-dattā putrikā jñeyā, etc. See No. 133, note.

Madhu-Kaiṭabha-dānavēndra-mēdaḥ-
plava-visrā-miśram=ēva mēdin=īyam ।
adhivāsya yadi svakair=yaśōbhiś=
ciram=enām=upabhuñjate narendrāḥ ॥ 88[2]

Mad-vaṁśajāḥ para-mahīpati-vaṁśajā vā
pāpād=apeta-manaso bhuvi bhāvi-bhūpāḥ ।
ye pālayanti mama dharmam=imaṁ samastaṁ
teṣāṁ mayā viracito='ñjalir=eṣa mūrdhni ॥ 89[3]

Mad-vaṁśe para-vaṁśe vā yaḥ kaścin=nṛpatir=bhavet ।
tasy=āhaṁ kara-lagnaḥ syāṁ yo mat-kīrtir=na lumpati ॥
90[4]

Mahatām=api pāpānāṁ dṛṣṭā śāstreṣu niṣkṛtiḥ ।
brahmadey-āpahartṛnāṁ na driṣṭā niṣkṛtiḥ kvacit ॥ 91[5]

Mama vaṁśe, etc. See No. 90, note.

Mā pārthiva kadācit=tvaṁ brahma-svaṁ manasā api ।
āneṣa dharma-bhaiṣajyam=etad=dhalāhalaṁ viṣam ॥ 92[6]

1. *Ep. Ind.*, Vol. XXXI, p. 191. See Nos. 89 and 90.

2. *Mys. Arch. Rep.*, 1912, paragraph 108. The stanza is quoted from Murāri's *Anargharāghava* as already indicated above.

3 *Ep. Ind.*, Vol. XXVIII, p. 312, text lines 17-18. A modified form of the last three feet of the stanza reads : *ye bhūmipāḥ satatam=ujjvala-dharma-cittāḥ । mad-dharmam=eva paripālanam=ācaranti tat-pādukā-dvayam=ahaṁ śirasā vahāmi ॥* (ibid., Vol. XVI, p. 96, text lines 41-44). The second half is sometimes also given as : *mad-dharmam=eva satataṁ paripālayanti tat-pāda-padma-yugalaṁ śirasā namāmi* (or *vahāmi*). Cf. *Ep. Carn.*, Vol. III, Mysore Nos. 1-3, 34, etc. The stanza is also found as : *Mad-vaṁśajā v=ānya-kul-odbhavā vā rakṣanti ye dharmam—imaṁ nṛipālāḥ । teṣāṁ tu nityaṁ sa Harir=dadātu santāna-vṛddhiṁ bhuvan-ādhipatyam ॥* (ibid., Vol. III, Sr. Nos. 64, 100; TN. No. 63). For similar variations, see *Ind. Ant.*, Vol. XII, p. 121; Vol. XVI, p. 256; *Ep. Ind.*, Vol. XVIII, p. 299, text lines 40-42; Vol. XX, p. 134, text line 19; Vol. XXI, p. 25, text lines 39-40. See Nos. 87 and 90.

4 *Ep. Ind.*, Vol. XXVIII, text line 18. Cf. *mama dharmaṁ na lumpati* or *na lopyaṁ mama śāsanaṁ* (ibid., Vol. XXII, p. 194, text line 23) and *Asmin=vaṁśe kṣaya-kṣīṇe yo='nyo rājā bhaviṣyati । tasy=āhaṁ pāda-lagno='smi mayā dattaṁ na lopayet ॥* (ibid., Vol. XXVIII, p. 283, text lines 36-37; for *Mama* for *Asmin* and *kara* for *pāda*, cf. ibid., Vol. XXII, p. 194). For *Mayi rājñi vyatikrānte* in the first foot and *śāsanaṁ na vyatikramet* in the last, see *Ind. Ant.*, Vol. XII, p. 155. The *Skanda Purāṇa*, op. cit., verse 41, has it as : *Asmin=vaṁśe kṣitau ko='pi rājā yadi bhaviṣyati । tasy=āhaṁ karalagno='smi mad-dattaṁ yadi pālyate ॥* See Nos. 87 and 89.

5 *Ep. Ind.*, Vol. XXVIII, p. 320. text line 13.

6 *Ep. Ind.*, Vol. XI, p. 101, text line 32; Vol. XII, p. 328, text lines 48-50; Vol. XX, p. 104, text lines 48-49.

Manu-prabhṛtibhir=mānyaiḥ, etc. See No. 23, note.
Mayi rājñi vyatikrānte, etc. See No. 90, note.
Mṛtyor=hi kiṅkarā daṇḍā hy=agni-pātā sudāruṇāḥ ।
ghorāś=ca Vāruṇāḥ pāśā n=opasarpanti bhūmidam ॥ 93[1]
Na dadāti pratiśrutaṁ dattaṁ v=āparet=tu yaḥ ।
tau baddhau Vāruṇaiḥ pāśais=tapyate mṛtyu-śāsanāt ॥ 94[2]
Na hi bhūmi-pradānād=vai dānam=anyad=viśiṣyate ।
na c=āpi bhūmi-haraṇāt=pāpam=anyad=vidhīyate ॥ 95[3]
Nandanti tasya pitaraḥ, etc. See No. 20, note.
N=āsti bhūmi-samaṁ dānaṁ n=āsti rājñaḥ samo guruḥ ।
n=āsti satya-samo dharmo n=āsti dāna-samo nidhiḥ ॥ 96[4]
Na tathā saphalā vidyā na tathā saphalaṁ dhanam ।
yathā tu munayaḥ prāhur=dānam=ekaṁ Kalau yuge ॥ 97[5]
Na viṣaṁ viṣam=ity=āhur=brahma-svaṁ viṣam=ucyate ।
viṣam=ekākinaṁ hanti brahma-svaṁ putra-pautrikam ॥ 98[6]
Nighnatāṁ, etc. See No. 149, note.
Nirjale prāntare, etc. See No. 150, note.
Nirjane prāntare, etc. See No. 150, note.
Niśamya doṣaṁ haraṇe mahāntaṁ
guṇaṁ ca bhūmer=anupālane tu ।
dattaṁ narendraiḥ pratipālanīyaṁ
śreyo hi dānād=anupālanaṁ tu ॥ 99[7]

1 *Ep. Ind.*, Vol. XXV, p. 218, verse 42. Cf. *Mahābhārata*, XIII, 62, 27 : *Mṛtyor=vai kiṅkaro daṇḍas=tamo vahniḥ sudāruṇaḥ*, etc. Ballāla (*Dānasāgara*, op. cit., p. 320) attributes the stanza to the *Mahābhārata*.

2 *Ind. Ant.*, Vol. XIV, p. 319, text lines 113-14.

3 *Ep. Ind.*, Vol. XVII, p. 303, verse 20.

4 *Ind. Ant.*, Vol. XIV, p. 319, text lines 107-08. Ballāla (*Dānasāgara*, op. cit., p. 320) quotes the stanza with *bhūmi°* for *rājñaḥ* and *vidhiḥ* for *nidhiḥ* and attributes it to the *Mahābhārata*.

5 *Ep. Ind.*, Vol. II, p. 219. The stanza is sometimes found as : *Kṛta-Tretā-Dvāpareṣu tapo='tyarthaṁ praśasyate । munayo='tra praśaṁsanti dānam=ekaṁ Kalau yuge* ॥ (ibid., Vol. XXXII, p. 75, text lines 21-22).

6 *Ep. Ind.*, Vol. XXII, p. 167, text lines 35-36. In some cases, the first half reads : *Deva-svaṁ hi viṣaṁ ghoraṁ kālakūṭa-sama-prabham* (ibid., Vol. IV, p. 345). Sometimes we have *Brahma-svaṁ tu viṣaṁ ghoraṁ na viṣaṁ viṣam=ucyate । viṣaṁ tv=ekā°* (ibid., Vol. XV, p. 252) and *deva-svaṁ* for *brahma-svaṁ* or for *Na viṣaṁ* (ibid., Vol. VI, p. 105) and *Aviṣaṁ* for *Na viṣaṁ* (ibid., Vol. VII, p. 324). The stanza occurs in the *Bṛhaspatisaṁhitā*, verses 46-47 (with *pautrakam* for *pautrikam*); *Vasiṣṭhasmṛti*, 17, 86; *Padma Purāṇa*, VI, 33, 45. The *Baudhāyana Dharmasūtra* (I, 11, 16) has the stanza as : *Brahma-svaṁ putra-pautra-ghnaṁ viṣam=ekākinaṁ haret । na viṣaṁ*, etc.

7. *Ep. Ind.*, Vol. XXII, p. 191, text lines 37-39.

Nyāyen=opārjitā bhūmir=anyāyen=āpahāritā ।
haranto hārayantaś=ca hiṁsanty=ā-saptamaṁ kulam ॥ 100[1]

Pālanāt=paramo dharmaḥ pālanāt=paramaṁ yaśaḥ ।
pālanāt=paramo svargo garīyas=tena pālanam ॥ 101[2]

Pañca paśv-anṛte hanti, etc. See Nos. 80-81, note.

Pāpaṁ nirmoka-vat=tyaktvā saupānād=bhūmi-dānataḥ ।
pade pade divaṁ yāti pitṛṇām=ekaviṁśatiḥ ॥ 102[3]

Para-dattāṁ sva-dattāṁ, etc. See No. 90, note.

Para-dattāṁ tu yo bhūmim=upahiṁset=kadācana ।
sa baddho Vāruṇaiḥ pāśaiḥ kṣipyate pūya-śoṇite ॥ 103[4]

Paratra saṁvalaṁ divyaṁ bhūmi-dānāt=paraṁ na hi ।
tasmāt=sarv-ādareṇ=āpi bhūmi-dānaṁ prapālayet ॥ 104[5]

Patanty=aśrūṇi rudatāṁ dīnānām=avasīdatām ।
Brāhmaṇānāṁ hate kṣetre hanti traipuruṣaṁ kulam ॥ 105[6]

Phāla-kṛṣṭāṁ mahīṁ dadyāt=sa-bīja-śasya-medinīm ।
yāvat-sūrya-kṛt-ālokas=tāvat=svarge mahīyate ॥ 106[7]

Phalasya kathito dharmaḥ phalān=niṣphal-āsambhavaḥ ।
bhūmi-hartā phala-cchettā phalān=niṣphalatāṁ vrajet
॥ 107[8]

Pitaraḥ, etc. See No. 4, note.

Prāg-dattāṁ bhūmiṁ viprebhyo, etc. See 131, note.

Prajā-hit-ārthaṁ sthitayaḥ praṇītā
dharmeṣu vidvān=pratipālayeta ।

1. *Ep. Ind.*, Vol. XI, p. 312, text lines 50-51. Cf. *Bṛhaspatisaṁhitā*, 35; *Padma Purāṇa*, VI, 33, 34. See above, No. 13.

2. *Ind. Ant.*, Vol. XVII, p. 12, text line 25; Chhabra, *Antiquities of Chamba State*, II, p. 177. Sometimes we have *tapaḥ* for *yaśaḥ* and *pālayet* for *pālanam*.

3. *Ep. Ind.*, Vol. XII, p. 234, lines 33-34.

4. *Ep. Ind.*, Vol. VI, p. 97. Sometimes we have *Pūrva-dattāṁ* at the beginning (*Ind. Ant.*, Vol. II, p. 301). The stanza is found in the *Bhaviṣya Purāṇa*, IV, 164, 33, and, with slight variations, in Govindānanda's *Dānakriyākaumudī* (Bibliotheca Indica ed., p. 41).

5. *Ind. Ant.*, Vol. XII, p. 121, text lines 42-43.

6. *Ind. Ant.*, Vol. XIV, p. 319, text lines 115-16. For slight variations, see *Ep. Ind.*, Vol. VII, p. 97, text lines 33-34.

7. Cf. *Ep. Ind.*, Vol. XXVIII, p. 328. *Mahābhārata*, XIII, 62, 31 has it with *mahīṁ dattvā sa-bījāṁ sa-phalām=api* । *udīrṇaṁ v=āpi śaraṇaṁ yathā bhavati kāmadaḥ* ॥ while Hemādri (op. cit., p. 480) reads *udyānaṁ śaraṇaṁ v=āpi tathā*. The stanza also occurs in the *Padma Purāṇa*, VI, 33, 6; *Bhaviṣya Purāṇa*, Uttara-parvan, Ch. 164, 16; *Bṛhaspatisaṁhitā*, verse 6 (with *Phālākṛṣṭāṁ mahīṁ dattvā sa-bījāṁ śasya-śālinīm* । *yāvat=sūrya-karā lokā°*). Ballāla (*Dānasāgara*, op. cit., p. 323) quotes the stanza with slight variations and attributes it to Bṛhaspati.

8. *Ep. Ind.*, Vol. XII, p. 324, lines 34-35.

yo lobha-mohād=dharate durātmā
so='ndho vrajed=durgatim=āśu kaṣṭām ॥ 108[1]
Prāpsyase vipulān=bhogān=pūrva-dattasya tat=phalam ।
punar=dadāsi dānād=dhi punar=bhogī bhaviṣyasi ॥ 109[2]
Prāsādā yatra, etc. See No. 127, note.
Prasṛty=āsampradānena datt-āpaharaṇena ca ।
janma-prabhṛti yad=dattaṁ tat=sarvaṁ niṣphalaṁ bhavet ॥ 110[3]
Prāyeṇa hi narendrāṇāṁ vidyate na śubhā gatiḥ ।
pūyante te tu satataṁ prayacchanto vasundhrām ॥ 111[4]
Pṛthivyā dīyamānāyā yāvanto madhya-reṇavaḥ ।
tāvad=varṣa-sahasrāṇi Brahma-loke mahīyate ॥ 112[5]
Pūrva-dattāṁ dvijātibhyo, etc. See No. 131, note.
Pūrva-dattāṁ narendraiś=ca, etc. See No. 131, note.
Pūrva-dattāṁ tu, etc. See No. 103, note.
Purvaiḥ pūrvataraiś=c=aiva dattāṁ bhūmiṁ haret=tu yaḥ ।
sa nitya-vyasane magno narake ca vaset=punaḥ ॥ 113[6]
Rājabhir=bahubhir=dattā, etc. See No. 23, note.
Rājāno rāja-kulyāś=ca, etc. See No. 61.
Rakṣā, etc. See No. 40, note.
Ratn-ānna-pāna-goṣṭh-ādyaṁ sarvaṁ bhūmau prajāyate ।
tasmād=bhūmi-pradānena naro bhavati sarvadaḥ ॥ 114[7]
Ṣaḍaśīti-sahasrāṇāṁ yojanānāṁ vasundharā ।
aho puṇyāya Kaunteya svargo grāma-pradāyinaḥ ॥ 115[8]
Sadyo-dānaṁ nirāyāsaṁ s-āyāsaṁ dīrgha-pālanam ।
ata ev=arṣayaḥ prāhur=dānāc=chreyo='nupālanam ॥ 116[9]

1. *Ep. Ind.*, Vol. XII, p. 214, verse 35.
2. *Ep. Ind.*, Vol. XXXIII, p. 213, verse 8.
3. *Ind. Ant.*, Vol. XII, p. 252.
4. *CII*, Vol. III, p. 119, text lines 16-17; p. 122, text lines 17-18; p. 128, text lines 24-25. Sometimes we have *n=āśubhā* (ibid., p. 117).
5. *Ep. Carn.*, Vol. XV, Arkalgud No. 106.
6. *Ep. Ind.*, Vol. VIII, p. 235, text lines 29-30.
7. *Ind. Ant.*, Vol. XII, p. 121.
8. *Ep. Ind.*, Vol. IV, p. 201, lines 25-27. Ballāla's *Dānasāgara* (op. cit., p. 317) reads *yojanāni* in the first half and *datta svalp==āpi rājendra sarva-kāma-pradāyinī* in the second and attributes the stanza to the *Dāna-Bṛhaspati*.
9. *Ep. Ind.*, Vol. XXXII, p. 67, text lines 22-23. Sometimes we have *tasya* for *dīrgha* in the first half and the second half as: *evaṁ tu munayaḥ prāhur=dānāt=tat=pālanaṁ varam* (*Ind. Ant.*, Vol. XVII, p. 122, text lines 51-52).

Sāmānyo='yaṁ dāna-dharmaḥ, etc. See No. 117, note.

Sāmānyo='yaṁ dharma-setur=nṛpāṇāṁ
kāle kāle pālanīyo bhavadbhiḥ ।
sarvān=etān=bhāvinaḥ pārthivendrān=
bhūyo bhūyo yācate Rāmacandraḥ ॥ 117[1]

Sāmānyo='yaṁ dharma-setuḥ sarveṣām=iha bhūbhujām ।
yato='taḥ pālanīyo='yaṁ kāle kāle mahātmabhiḥ ॥ 118[2]

Śaṅkhaṁ bhadr-āsanaṁ chatraṁ var-āśvā vara-vāraṇāḥ ।
bhūmi-dānasya puṣpāṇi phalaṁ svargaḥ Purandara ॥ 119[3]

Santarpayati dātāram, etc. See No. 78, note.

Sapta-janm-āntareṇ=aiva, etc. See No. 126, note.

Sarvaṁ ca bhūmi-haraṇād=dhṛtam=eva na saṁśayaḥ ।

1. *Ep. Ind.*, Vol. III, p. 343, text lines 55-57; etc. Sometimes the first half becomes the second and we have *Rāmabhadraḥ* (or the name of the donor—ibid., Vol. XXVIII, p. 283, text line 35) for *Rāmacandraḥ*, *krameṇa* (ibid., Vol. XXIX, p. 9, text line 55) for *bhavadbhiḥ*, and *dattvā bhūmiṁ* (ibid., Vol. XXXII, p. 76, text line 36) for *sarvān=etān*. We have also *prārthayaty=eṣa Rāmaḥ* in the last quarter (ibid., Vol. VI, p. 62, verse 34). In some cases, we have the first half as : *Bho rājānaḥ prārthayaty=eṣa Rāmo bhūyo bhūyo prārthanīyā narendrāḥ* followed by *sāmānyo='yaṁ*, etc. (ibid., Vol. XXXI, p. 288, text line 27) or as : *Sarvān=eva prārthayaty=eṣa Rāmo bhūyo bhūyo bhāvinaḥ pārthivendrān*, and *rakṣaṇīyaḥ* for *pālanīyaḥ* in the second half (*Ep. Carn.*, Vol. III, Md. No. 113). For *setur=narāṇām*, *sve sve kāle* for *kāle kāle*, and *bhūmi-pālān* for *pārthivendrān*, see Chhabra, *Antiquities of Chamba State*, II, p. 178. For *Sāmānyo='yaṁ dāna-dharmaḥ*, *sve sve kāle*, see *Ind. Ant.*, Vol. VI, pp. 195, 202. *Ep. Carn.*, Vol. V, Arsikere No. 90, gives *etān=sadyo* for *sarvān=etān*. In the Kalasan (Java) inscription of Śaka 700, the stanza reads *Sarvān=ev=āgāminaḥ pārthivendrān=bhūyo bhūyo yācate rājasiṁhaḥ* । *sāmānyo='yaṁ dharma-setur=narāṇāṁ*, etc. (Chatterjee and Chakravarti, *India and Java*, p. 46). The *Skanda Purāṇa*, op cit., verse 40, has it as : *Dattvā bhūmiṁ bhāvinaḥ pārthiveśān=bhūyo bhūyo yācate Rāmacandraḥ* । *sāmānyo='yaṁ dharma-setur=nṛpāṇāṁ sve sve kāle pālanīyo bhavadbhiḥ* ॥ See No. 118.

2. *Ind. Ant.*, Vol. XII, p. 186. See No. 117.

3. *Ep. Ind.*, Vol. XXXII, p. 123, text lines 34-35. Sometimes we have *Siṁhāsanaṁ tathā chatraṁ* in the first quarter (ibid., Vol. XXV, p. 218, verse 37), *gaj-āśva-varavāhanam* in the second foot, *cinhāni* or *puṣyāṇi* (cf. ibid., p. 128, text line 17; Vol. XXII, p. 166, text line 29) in the third foot, and *phalaṁ svargas=tath=aiva ca* in the fourth (ibid., Vol. XXV, p. 218, line 121). We have also *śaṅkho* and *phalam=etat* (ibid., Vol. X, p. 89). For the first half, sometimes we have : *Dhavalāny=ātapatrāṇi dantinaś=ca mad-oddhatāḥ* (or *mad-otkaṭāḥ*), to which is also added : *sudhā-dhautāni harmyāṇi yuvatyo ratna-bhūṣaṇāḥ*, and in the second half *dharma-dāyasya* and *phalam=anyad=bhaviṣyati* (ibid., Vol. XXV, p. 60, text line 54; Vol. XXXII, p. 70, lines 22-24). For *dṛśyante tāni Bhārata* or *phalaṁ svargam=anuttamam* in the last foot, see *Ep. Ind.*, Vol. XIX, p. 73, text lines 35-36; p. 213, text line 30. The stanza occurs in the *Bṛhaspatisaṁhitā*, verse 15 (with *cara-sthāvara- vāruṇāḥ* in the second foot and *puṇyāni* for *puṣpāṇi*) and the *Padma Purāṇa*, VI, 33, 15. The *Mahābhārata* has the first half in XIII, 62, 89 (with *vara-vāhanam*) and the second half in XIII, 62, 91 (with *puṇyāni*; Hemādri has *dhar-āśvā vara-vāraṇāḥ* and *puṣpāṇi*—op. cit., pp. 483-84). Ballāla's *Dānasāgara* (op. cit., p. 316) attributes the stanza to the *Dāna-Bṛhaspati*.

bhūmi-hartā vaset=tasmān=narake kālam=akṣayam ॥ 120[1]

Sarvān=etān, etc. See No. 117, note.

Sarvān=eva=āgāminaḥ, etc. See No. 117, note.

Sarvān=eva prārthayaty=eṣa, etc. See No. 117, note.

Sarva-sasya-samṛddhāṁ, etc. See No. 132, note.

Sarveṣām=ev dānānām=eka-janm-ānugaṁ phalam ।
hāṭaka-kṣiti-gaurīṇāṁ sapta-janm-ānugaṁ phalam ॥ 121[2]

Sarveṣāṁ tu pradānānāṁ bhūmi-dānaṁ praśasyate ।
kalpa-koṭi-gataṁ pāpaṁ sañcitaṁ jayate naraḥ ॥ 122[3]

Ṣaṣṭiṁ varṣa°, etc. See No. 137, note.

Ṣaṣṭiṁ varṣa-sahasrāṇi svarge modati bhūmidaḥ ।
ācchettā c=ānumantā ca tāny=eva narake vaset ॥ 123[4]

Śāstreṣu, etc. See No. 15, note.

Śatam=aśv-ānṛte hanti, etc. See Nos. 80-81, note.

Śatam=indu-kṣaye dānaṁ sahasraṁ tu dina-kṣaye ।
viṣuve śata-sāhasraṁ vyatīpāteṣv=anantakam ॥ 124[5]

Śatruṇ=āpi kṛto dharmaḥ pālanīyo mahīpate ।

1. *Ind. Ant.*, Vol. XII, p. 121.

2. *Ep. Ind.*, Vol. XI, pp. 312-13, text lines 47-48. For *naika-janm-ātmakaṁ phalam* in the last foot, see ibid., Vol. XXI, p. 145, text line 55. The stanza is found in the *Saṁvartasmṛti*, verse 78, and the *Bṛhaspatisaṁhitā*, verse 33. Ballāla's *Dānasāgara* (op. cit., p. 317) attributes it to Saṁvarta.

3. *Ep. Ind.*, Vol. XII, p. 324, text lines 32.

4. *CII*, Vol. III, pp. 96, 104, 238, 247, etc. Often we have *Ṣaṣṭi-varṣa°* or *Ṣaṣṭir=varṣa°*. Sometimes *modati* is found replaced by *nandati* (*Ep. Ind.*, Vol. XXVIII, p. 16, text line 12) or *tiṣṭhati* (*CII*, Vol. III, pp. 167, 180) or *vasati* (ibid., p. 194.), and *ācchettā* by *ākṣeptā* (ibid., pp. 108, 137, 296). The first quarter is sometimes found as *Kalpa-koṭi-sahasrāṇi* (*Ind. Ant.*, Vol. XX, p. 417, text line 48), the second quarter as *modate divi bhūmidaḥ* (*Ep. Ind.*, Vol. XVII, p. 333, verse 3), and the first half as : *A-saṅkhyeyāni varṣāni svarge modanti bhūmidāḥ* (*Ep. Ind.*, Vol. XXIV, p. 303, text line 29). We also have *ṣaṣṭiṁ varṣa-śatāni ca* for the second quarter and *gavāṁ koṭi-pradānena bhūmi-hartā na śudhyati* in the second half (ibid., Vol. IX, p. 6, text lines 26-27). The second half is sometimes given as *kṣiti-pātr-ānna-hartā tad=dvitayaṁ narakaṁ vrajet* (*Ind. Ant.*, Vol. V, p. 56). For *yāvad=ā-bhūta-samplavam* in the fourth foot, see *Ep. Ind.*, Vol. XVIII, p. 299, text lines 34-35. The stanza occurs in the *Padma Purāṇa*, VI, 33, 29-30 (with *ṣaṣṭi°*, *tiṣṭhati* and *āhartā*); *Skanda Purāṇa*, op. cit., verse 26 (with *vasati* and *narakaṁ vrajet*); *Bṛhaspatisaṁhitā*, verse 29 (with *v=ānumantā ca tam=eva* and the omission of the first half); *Viṣṇudharmottara* quoted by Hemādri, op. cit., p. 486, and by Aparārka, op. cit., p. 369. It is attributed to the *Kūrma Purāṇa* in Divākara's *Dānacandrikā* and to Bṛhaspati in Nīlakaṇṭha's *Dānamayūkha* (*IHQ*, Vol. VI, p. 776).

5. *Ep. Ind.*, Vol. XXXII, p. 70, text lines 12-13. This is *Laghu-Śātātapasmṛti*, verse 150. Hemādri assigns it to Yājñavalkya (op. cit., p. 75).

śatrur=eva hi śatruḥ syād=dharmaḥ śatrur=na kasyacit || 125[1]

Satyaṁ c=aiva, etc. See No. 126, note.

Satyaṁ yajña-hutaṁ c=aiva yat=kiñcid=dharma-sañcayaḥ |
ardh-āṅgulena sīmāyā haraṇena praṇaśyati || 126[2]

Sauvarṇā yatra prāsādā vasor=dhārāś=ca kāmadāḥ |
Gandarv-Āpsaraso yatra tatra gacchanti bhūmidāḥ || 127[3]

Siṁhāsanaṁ tathā chatraṁ, etc. See No 119, note.

Śiva-putro, etc. See No. 15, note.

Suvarṇam=ekaṁ, etc. See No. 55, note.

Sva-dattād=dvi-guṇaṁ puṇyaṁ para-datt-ānupālanam |
para-datt-āpahāreṇa sva-dattaṁ niṣphalaṁ bhavet || 128[4]

Sva-dattā duhitā, etc. See No 133, note.

Sva-dattā medinī, etc. See No. 133, note.

Sva-dattāṁ para-dattāṁ vā hareta sura-viprayoḥ |
vṛttiṁ sa jāyate vidrug=varṣāṇām=ayut-āyutam || 129[5]

Sva-dattāṁ para-dattāṁ vā pālayanti narāḥ prītāḥ |
koṭiṁ varṣa-sahasrāṇi Rudra-loke pratiṣṭhitāḥ || 130[6]

Sva-dattāṁ para-dattāṁ vā yatnād-rakṣa Yudhiṣṭhira |

1. *Ep. Ind.*, Vol. XXVIII, p. 312, text line 16; p. 258 (*manīṣibhiḥ* for *mahīpate*).

2. See, e. g., *Ep. Ind.*, Vol. XXIX, p. 193, text lines 32-33; Vol. XXVIII, p. 283, lines 29-30. The first half is sometimes found as : *Sapta-janm-āntareṇ=aiva yat=puṇyaṁ pūrva-sañcitam* (ibid., Vol. XIX, p. 73, text lines 36-37), or *Iṣṭaṁ dattaṁ hutaṁ c=aiva yat=kiñcid dharma-sañcitam* (ibid., Vol. XXII, pp. 166-67, text lines 34-35), or *Satyaṁ c=aiva hutaṁ c=aiva* (ibid., Vol. XIII, pp. 312-13). For *yaḥ kaścid=dharma-sañcayaḥ* in the second foot, see *Ind. Ant.*, Vol. XVII, p. 122, text lines 57-58. The second half of the stanza is found in the *Bṛhaspatisaṁhitā* (verse 41) with *ardh-āṅgulasya.*

3. *Ep. Ind.*, Vol. XXXII, p. 123, text line 35. We have also *Prāsādā yatra sauvarṇā°* and *tiṣṭhati dānadaḥ* (ibid., p. 70, text lines 20-21). *Ep. Carn.*, Vol. XII, Sl. No. 95 ascribes the authorship of the stanza to Bṛhaspati, while Hemādri (op. cit., p. 481) and Ballāla (op. cit., p. 316) assign it to the *Mahābhārata* (cf. XIII, 62) and the *Dāna-Bṛhaspati* respectively.

4. *Ep. Ind.*, Vol. XVI, text lines 75-77; p. 318. Sometimes we have *adhikaṁ* for *dvi-guṇaṁ* (ibid., Vol. XXXI, p. 261, text lines 147). This is followed by the stanza : *Kharo dvādaśa janmāni aṣṭa janmāni śūkaraḥ | śvā tu saptati-janmāni ity=evaṁ Manur=avravīt ||* in *Ep. Carn*, Vol. XII, Gb. No. 34.

5. *Ep. Ind.*, Vol. XXV, p. 219, verse 49.

6. *Ind. Ant.*, Vol. XII, pp. 257-58.

mahīṁ mahīmatāṁ śreṣṭha dānāc=chreyo='nupālanam ||
131[1]

Sva-dattāṁ para-dattāṁ vā yo hareta vasundharām |
sa viṣṭhāyāṁ kṛmir=bhūtvā pitṛbhiḥ saha pacyate || 132[2]
Sva-dattā putrikā dhātrī pitṛ-dattā sahodarī |

1. *CII*, pp. 119, 122, 127, 133, 194, 198, 296. The word *mahīmatāṁ* is altered in most cases to *mahimatāṁ* (*CII*, Vol. III, pp. 96, 104, 108, 115, 137, 167) and sometimes to *mahībhṛtāṁ* (*Ep. Ind.*, Vol. XI, p. 313), while the first and third feet are sometimes quoted respectively as *Pūrva-dattāṁ dvijātibhyo* (*CII*, p. 108) and *bhūmiṁ deva-dvijātīnāṁ* (*Ep. Ind.*, Vol. XXXI, p. 261, text line 148). *Yudhiṣṭhira* is sometimes replaced by *narādhipa* (ibid., Vol. XXII, p. 85, text lines 74-75). Sometimes the first foot reads *Prāg-dattāṁ bhūmiṁ viprebhyo* and the third reads *mahyāṁ mahībhṛtāṁ śreṣṭha* (*Ep. Ind.*, Vol. VII, p. 97, text lines 26-27). The first half in some cases reads *Pūrva-dattāṁ narendraiś=ca yatnād=rakṣa Śatakrato* (ibid., Vol. XI, p. 313). The stanza occurs in the *Bhaviṣya Purāṇa*, IV, 164, 38 (with *rakṣe* and *mahībhṛtām*).

2. *CII*, Vol. III, pp. 104, 108, 137. In some cases, the first foot is found as: *Sarva-śasya-samṛddhāṁ tu* (ibid., pp. 11, 122, 127, 133) and the second foot as : *yo hared=vasudhām=iha* (*Ep. Ind.*, Vol. XXVIII, p. 114, text line 27). In the second half, sometimes we find *śva-viṣṭhāyāṁ* (*CII*, Vol. III, pp. 119, 137) and *sva-viṣṭhāyāṁ* (*JASB*, Vol. VI, 1910, p. 436) instead of *sa viṣṭhāyāṁ*, and *majjati* or *majjate* (*CII*, Vol. III, pp. 108, 119, 137) instead of *pacyate*, and the last three words also as : *pacyate pitṛbhiḥ saha* (*Ind. Ant.*, Vol. XXXIX, 1910, p. 196). Sometimes the first half is given as : *Para-dattāṁ sva-dattāṁ vā yo harati nar-ādhamaḥ* (*Ep. Carn.*, Vol. VII, Tm. No. 51) and the second half is modified as : *ṣaṣṭi-varṣa-sahasrāṇi viṣṭhāyāṁ jāyate kṛmiḥ* (*CII*, Vol. III, p. 289) or as *gavāṁ śata-sahasrasya hantur=harati* (or *pibati*) *duṣkṛtam* (ibid., pp. 238, 247; sometimes *hantuḥ pibati kilbiṣam* in the last quarter,—*Ep. Ind.*, Vol. XXXI, p. 80, text lines 43-3), or *ṣaṣṭiṁ varṣa-sahasrāṇi narake pacyate tu saḥ* (ibid., Vol. XVI, p. 267; cf. *bhṛśam* for *tu saḥ* in *Ind. Ant.*, Vol. VI, p. 26, line 26), or *ṣaṣṭi-varṣa-sahasrāṇi Kumbhīpāke sa pacyate* (*Ind. Ant.*, Vol. VI, p. 25, text line 16; or *niraye sa vipacyate*—ibid., p. 30, line 16; or *ghore tamasi vartate*—*Ep. Ind.*, Vol. XIV, p. 335, verse 90), or *tena jātā janayitā narake pātitā dhruvam* (*Ep. Ind.*, Vol. XII, p. 203), or *śvāna-yoni-śataṁ gatvā Cāṇḍāleṣu=abhijāyate* (ibid., Vol. XX, p. 128, text line 21), or *narakān=na nivartante yāvac=candra-divākarau* (*Ep. Carn.*, Vol. VIII, Sb. No. 477), or *sa rūpī kula-saṁyuktaḥ kalpāntaṁ narakaṁ vrajet* (ibid., Vol. X, Malur No. 57), or *na tasya narakād=ghorād=vidyate niṣkṛtiḥ kvacit* (*Ep. Ind.*, Vol. XVII, p. 304, verse 10), or *kapilā-śata-ghātīnām*: *enasā pratipadyate* (ibid., Vol. XXXIII, p. 213, v. 5). For *brahma-vṛttiṁ haret=tu yaḥ* (*hareta yaḥ*—*Ind. Ant.*, Vol. II, p. 159) in the second foot, see Chhabra, *Antiquities of Chamba State*, II, p. 178. We have also *Aṅgam=ekaṁ padam=ekaṁ* in the first foot and *divyaṁ varṣa-sahasrāṇi jāyate Brahmarākṣasaḥ* in the second half (*Ep. Ind.*, Vol. XXIII, p. 143, text lines 12-13). For *divyaṁ varṣa-sahasrāṇi* in the third foot, see also *Ind. Ant.*, Vol. XII, p. 121. The second half is sometimes given as : *ākṣeptā c=ānumantā ca sarvathā narakaṁ vrajet* (*Ep. Ind.*, Vol. XVII, p. 337, text line 13). In the Tan Kran (Cambodia) inscription of about the 7th century A.D., we have the second half as : *Avīci-narake yāti pitṛbhiḥ saha bandhubhiḥ* (R. C. Majumdar, *Inscriptions of Kambuja*, p. 50). The stanza occurs in the *Padma Purāṇa*, op. cit., verses 28-29 (with *haret=tu* and *viṣṭhā-kṛmi*⁰), *Bhaviṣya Purāṇa*, op. cit., verse 34 (with the second half as *sa naro narake ghore kliśyaty=ā pralay-āntikam*), *Brahma Purāṇa*, 115, 67 (with *ṣaṣṭir=varṣa*⁰ and *viṣṭhāyāṁ jāyate kṛmiḥ*); *Bṛhaspatisaṁhitā*, verse 28 (with *harec=ca* and *sva-viṣṭhayāṁ*). In the *Viṣṇudharmo-*

anya-dattā sva-mātā ca datta-bhūmiṁ parityajet ‖ 133[1]
Svalpām=api mahīṁ yas=tu dadāti śraddhay=ānvitaḥ ।
sa yāti Brahma-sadanaṁ yasmān=n=āvartate punaḥ‖ 134[2]
Svaṁ dātuṁ sumahac=chakyaṁ duḥkham=anyārtha-pālanam ।
dānaṁ vā pālanaṁ v=eti danāc=chreyo='nupālanam ‖ 135[3]
Sva-sukṛta-paripālanāt=prabhūṇāṁ
para-kṛta-pālanam=eva lālanīyam ।
Harir=api Kamalāsanasya sṛṣṭiṁ
satatam=avañ=jagatām=abhūd=upāsyaḥ ‖ 136[4]
Taḍāgānāṁ sahasreṇa vājapeya-śatena ca ।
gavāṁ koṭi-pradānena bhūmi-hartā na śudhyati ‖ 137[5]
Taḍit-taraṅga-bahulām, etc. See No. 71, note.

ttara (Hemādri, loc. cit.), the first and second halves occur as the first and second halves of two consecutive stanzas with *harec=ca* and *viṣṭhāyāṁ kṛmitām=eti pitṛbhiḥ sahitas=tathā*). Cf. *Padma Purāṇa*, III, 24, 10. Aparārka assigns it to the *Āditya Purāṇa* (op. cit., p. 370). The stanza is also ascribed to Viśvāmitra in the *Dānacandrikā* and *Dānamayūkha*, to Bṛhaspati in Govindānanda's *Dānakriyākaumudī* and to the *Mahābhārata* in the *Dānakhaṇḍa* (*IHQ*, Vol. VI, p. 777). Cf. Coedès, *Inscriptions du Cambodge*, Vol. V, p. 76.

1. *Ep. Carn.*, Vol. I, revised ed., p. 36; Vol. V, Hassan No. 36 (*svayaṁ mātā dattāṁ*). Sometimes we have *Sva-dattā duhitā c=aiva para-dattā sahodarī । vipra-dattā svayaṁ mātā na bhojyā ca vasundharā ‖* (ibid., Vol. IV, Yedetore 19). The first three feet are sometimes read as : *Mad-dattā putrikā jñeyā pitṛ-dattā sahodarā । anya-dattā tu jananī* (*Ind. Ant.*, Vol., IV, p. 334). The first half is also given as : *Sva-dattā medinī putrī vipra-dattā sahodarī* (*Ep. Carn.*, Vol. V, Hassan No. 40) and the second half as *para-dattā para-strī syān=na hartavyā vasundharā* (ibid., Vol. X, Govibinur No. 3).

2. *Ep. Carn.*, Vol. XII, Si. No. 95 assigning the stanza to Āditya.

3. See, e.g., *Ep. Ind*, Vol. VI, p. 19, text lines 22-23; *Ind. Ant.*, Vol. VI, p. 87, text lines 34-35 (*anyasya* for *anyārtha*°). We have also *kleśam* for *duḥkham* (*Ep. Ind.*, Vol. XVI, p. 85, verse 92).

4. *Ep. Ind.*, Vol. VI, p. 4, verse 50.

5. *Ep. Ind.*, Vol. XXII, p. 166, text lines 33-34. For *Taṭākānāṁ*, cf. *Ep. Ind.*, Vol. XXVIII, p. 50, text line 23. We have also *sahasrāṇi* and *śatāni* and sometimes *gosahasra* (ibid., Vol. XXVIII, p. 50, text line 23) or *aśvamedha* (ibid., Vol. XI, pp. 382-83) for *vājapeya*. The first half is also found as : *Ārāmāṇāṁ sahasreṇa taḍāgānāṁ śatena ca* (ibid., Vol. XXXII, p. 68, text lines 28), or *Ṣaṣṭiṁ varṣa-sahasrāṇi ṣaṣṭiṁ varṣa-śatāni ca* (ibid., Vol. IX, p. 6, text line 26-27). For *Aśvamedha-sahasreṇa* in the first foot, see *Ind. Ant.*, Vol. XVII, p. 122, text lines 58-59. *Ep. Carn.*, Vol. VIII, Sb. No. 391 has *kanyā-koṭi-pradādena* in the third foot. The verse occurs in the *Skanda Purāṇa*, op.cit., verse 35 (with *aśvamedha* for *vājapeya* and °*pradānena bhūmi-hartā viśudhyati*); *Padma Purāṇa*, VI, 33, 37 (with *Vāpī-kūpa-sahasreṇa*); *Bṛhaspatisaṁhitā*, verse 39 (with *Vāpī-kūpa-sahasreṇa aśvamedha*°); *Parāśara-saṁhitā*, XII, 51 (with *Vāpī-kūpa-taṭāk-ādyair=vājapeya-śatair=api*).

Taḍit-tulyā lakṣmīs=tanur=api ca dīp-ānala-samā
bhavo duḥkh-aik-āntaḥ para-kṛtim=akīrtiḥ kṣapayatām ı
yaśāṁsy=ā-candr-ārkaṁ niyatam=avatām=atra ca nṛpāḥ
kariṣyante buddhvā yad=abhirucitaṁ kiṁ pravacanaiḥ ıı
138[1]

Tādṛk-puṇyaṁ na dadatāṁ jāyate no dharābhujām ı
bhuvam=anya-pratiṣṭhāṁ tu yādṛg=bhavati rakṣatām ıı
139[2]

Tapati na tapanaḥ prakharo marud=api no vāti śāsane
tīvraḥ ı
Brahmasva-steya-pātakam=atiśaya-bhīmaṁ samā-
locya ıı 140[3]

Tasmād=dharmaḥ, etc. See No. 50.

Taṭākānām, etc. See No. 137, note.

Tisraḥ sandhyā , etc. See No. 38.

Toya-hīneṣv=araṇyeṣu, etc. See No. 149, note.

Tṛṇ-āgra-jala-binduś=ca jala-budbuda-sadṛśam ı
sadṛśaṁ jīvitaṁ jñātvā kīrti-dharmaṁ na lopayet ıı 141[4]

Trīṇy=āhur=ati-dānāni gāvaḥ pṛthvī sarasvatī ı
ā-saptamaṁ phalanty=ete doha-vāha-nivedanaiḥ ıı 142[5]

Upadeśī ca dātā ca, etc. See No. 29, note.

Vācā dattaṁ mano-dattaṁ dattaṁ pāṇi-kuś-odakaiḥ ı
yo haret=trīṇi dānāni sa ghoraṁ narakaṁ vrajet ıı 143[6]

Vāk-dattaṁ ca, etc. See No. 143, note.

Vahniṁ vahni-sutaṁ c=āmbu pañca-kṛtvaḥ prajāyate ı
dattvā sarva-rasāṁ c=aiva na martyo jāyate punaḥ ıı 144[7]

1. *Ep. Ind.*, Vol. IV, p. 250, lines 59-60.

2. *Ind. Ant.*, Vol. XX, p. 310, text lines 28-29. For *grāsa-hartā* for *bhūmi-hartā*, see *Ep. Ind.*, Vol. XXXII, p. 76, text line 46.

3. *Ep. Ind.*, Vol. XXII, p. 166, verse 21.

4. *Ep. Ind.*, Vol. XII, p. 325, lines 38-40.

5. *Ep. Ind.*, Vol. XI, pp. 312-13, text lines 46-47. The first half is found in the *Vasiṣṭhasmṛti*, 29, 19, and *Bṛhaspatisaṁhitā*, verse 18; cf. *Padma Purāṇa*, VI, 33, 18.

6. Chhabra, *Antiquities of Chamba State*, II, p. 178. Sometimes we have *Vāk-dattaṁ ca mano-dattaṁ mati-dattaṁ na dīyate ı ṣaṣṭi-varṣa-sahasrāṇi viṣṭhāyāṁ jāyate kṛmiḥ* ıı (*Ep. Carn.*, Vol. IV, Hg. No. 98, text lines 31-33). For *dhārā-dattaṁ* instead of *mati-dattaṁ* and other variations in the second half, see ibid., Vol. VII, Sh. No. 45.

7. *Ep. Ind.*, Vol. I, p. 56, text lines 57-58.

Vanaṁ, etc. See No. 66, note.

Vāpī-kūpa°, etc. See No. 137, note.

Vāridas = tṛptim = āpnoti sukham = akṣayam = annadaḥ ।
tila-pradaḥ prajām = iṣṭāṁ dīpadaś = ca . Kurūttama ।
bhūmidaḥ sarvam = āpnoti dīrgham = āyus = tath = aiva
ca ॥ 145[1]

Vāri-hīneṣv = araṇyeṣu, etc. See No. 150, note.

Vāt-ābhra-vibhramam = idaṁ vasudh-ādhipatyam =
āpāta-mātra-madhuro viṣay-opabhogaḥ ।
prāṇās = tṛṇ-āgra-jala-bindu-samā narāṇāṁ
dharmaḥ sakhā param = aho para-loka-yāne ॥ 146[2]

Veda-vāk-smṛtayo jihvā vadanti ṛṣi-devatāḥ ।
bhūmi-hartā tath = ānye ca aho mohena mā hara ॥ 147[3]

Vidyud-vilāsa-taralām = avagamya samyag =
loka-sthitir = yaśasi sakta-manobhir = uccaiḥ ।
nityaṁ par-opakṛti-mātra-ratair = bhavadbhir =
dharm-ābhirādhana-parair = anumoditavyā ॥ 148[4]

Vighnatāṁ bhartṛ-go-vipra-bāla-yoṣid-vipaścitām ।
yā gatiḥ sā bhaved = bhūmiṁ harataḥ śāsan-āṅkitām ॥ 149[5]

Vindhy-āṭavīṣv = a-toyāsu śuṣka-koṭara-vāsinaḥ ।
kṛṣṇāhayo = 'bhijāyante pūrva-dāyaṁ haranti ye ॥ 150[6]

1. *Ep. Ind.*, Vol. XXV, p. 219, verse 46.

2. *Ind. Ant.*, Vol. VI, p. 56; *Ep. Ind.*, Vol. XXVI, p. 56, text lines 13-14. Sometimes we have °*madhurā viṣay-opabhogāḥ* (ibid., Vol. XXIV, p. 295, text line 34).

3. *Ep. Ind.*, Vol. XXVIII, p. 328. Sometimes we have *mā hara* for *mohena* (ibid., Vol. XII, p. 325).

4. *Ep. Ind.*, Vol. XXIX, p. 43, text lines 49-51. Sometimes we have °*modanīyā* for °*moditavyā*.

5. *Ind. Ant.*, Vol. XVI, p. 134, text lines 17-18. Sometimes we have *Nighnatāṁ* for *Vighnatāṁ*.

6. *Ep. Ind.*, Vol. XXII, p. 76, text line 63; p. 85. Sometimes we have °*śāyinaḥ* for °*vāsinaḥ* (ibid., Vol. XXV, p. 219, verse 50), *hi jāyante* for °*bhijāyante* (ibid., p. 137) and *maru-sarpā hi* or *kṛṣṇasarpā*° or *mah-āhayo* or *kṛṣṇasarpāḥ prajāyante* or *kṛṣṇasarpāś = ca jāyante* or *kṛṣṇāhayo*° (*Ep. Ind.*, Vol. XX, p. 128, text line 22; Vol. XXIV, p. 295, text line 31; Vol. XXV, p. 219, verse 50; Vol. XXVIII, p. 311, text line 14; Vol. XXXII, p. 76, text line 43). For the first foot, sometimes we have *A-pānīyeṣv = araṇyeṣu* (*CII*, Vol. III, p. 108), *Vāri-hīneṣv = araṇyeṣu*, *Anudakeṣv-araṇyeṣu*, *Nirjane* (or *Nirjale*) *prāntare deśe* (ibid., Vol. XXIV, p. 295, line 31; Vol. XXVIII, p. 257, text line 152; pp. 311-12, text lines 14-15), *Bhūṣı = aṭaviṣv = a-toyāsu* (*CII*, Vol. III, p. 180), etc., and, for the fourth foot, *deva-brahma-sva-hāriṇaḥ*, *brahma-bhūmy-apahārakāḥ*, *bhūmi-dāna-harā narāḥ*, *bhūmi-dānaṁ haranti ye*, *ye haranti vasundha-*

Vipra-dravy-āpahartāro, etc. See No. 45, note.
Vipra-grāme, etc. See No. 45, note.
Vipra-grāmeṣu, etc. See No. 45, note.
Yaḥ kriyāṁ dharma-saṁyutāṁ manas=āpy=abhinandati |
vardhate sa yatheṣṭena śukla-pakṣa iv=aṁśumān || 151[1]
Yaḥ svayaṁ kurute dharmaṁ yaś=ca pāti kṛtaṁ paraiḥ |
tayoḥ pālayitā śreṣṭha iti prāhur=manīṣiṇaḥ || 152[2]
Yair=vāñchitaṁ śiśiradīdhiti-śubhra-kīrter=
yaiś=c=āmara-praṇayinī-parirambhanasya |
te sādhavo na hi haranti pareṇa dattaṁ
dānād=vadanti paripālanam=eva sādhu || 153[3]
Yajño='nṛtena kṣarati tapaḥ kṣarati vismayāt |
kṣiti-hart=aikaviṁśati-kulena narakaṁ vrajet || 154[4]
Yaṁ vināśayituṁ, etc. See No. 45, note.
Yān=īha dāridya°, etc. See No. 43, note.
Yān=īha dattāni, etc. See No. 43, note.
Yānti kālena, etc. See No. 23, note.
Yas=tu pālayate, etc. See No. 23, note.
Yathā candramaso vṛddhir=ahany=ahani jāyate |
tathā bhūmi-kṛtaṁ dānaṁ sasye sasye vivardhate || 155[5]
Yathā janitrī puṣṇāti kṣīreṇa sva-sutaṁ nṛpāḥ |
evaṁ sarva-guṇair=bhūmir=dātāram=anupuṣyati | 156[6]
Yathā nirohanty=uptāni kīrṇāni ca mahītale |
evaṁ kāmā virohanti bhūmi-dāna-samārjitāḥ || 157[7]

rām (*Ep. Ind.*, Vol. XXIV, p. 295, line 31; Vol. XXV, p. 219, verse 50; Vol. XXVIII, p. 312, text line 15). The stanza occurs in the *Mahābhārata* as quoted by Hemādri, op. cit., p. 483 (with °*sarpās=tu jāyante ye haranti vasundharām*); *Bhaviṣya Purāṇa*, IV, 164, 39 (with *Toya-hīneṣv=araṇyeṣu* in the first and *narā brahma-sva-hāriṇaḥ* in the last quarter); *Skanda Purāṇa*, op. cit., verse 3 (with *kṛṣṇasarpāḥ prajāyante datta-dāy-āpahārakāḥ*).

1. *Ep. Ind.*, Vol. XXXI, pp. 92-93.
2. *Ep. Ind.*, Vol. VI, p. 343, verse 44.
3. *Ep. Ind.*, Vol. III, p. 367, lines 20-21.
4. *Ep. Ind.*, Vol. XII, p. 325, line 38.
5. *Ep. Ind.*, Vol. XXV, p. 278, lines 47-48. The stanza occurs in the *Mahābhārata*, XIII, 62, 33.
6. *Ep. Ind.*, Vol. XXV, p. 218, verse 40. Cf. *Mahābhārata*, XIII, 62, 26 : *Yathā sva-putraṁ jananī kṣīreṇa bharate sadā | anugṛhṇāti dātāraṁ tathā sarva-rasair=mahī* || Ballāla (op. cit., p. 320) quotes the same verse with slight variations and attributes it to the *Mahābhārata*.
7. *Ep. Ind.*, Vol. XXIV, p. 303, text lines 26-27. The stanza is found in the *Mahābhārata*, XIII, 62, 47 (with *śasyāni rohanti prakīrṇāni* and *tathā kāmāḥ prarohanti*).

Yath=āpsu patitaḥ Śakra taila-bindur=visarpati ।
evaṁ bhūmi-kṛtaṁ dānaṁ śasye śasye prarohati ॥ 158[1]

Yathā sva-putraṁ, etc. See No. 156.

Yath-oktaiḥ pañcabhir=ghorair=mahā°, etc. See No. 45, note.

Yat=kiñcit=kurute pāpaṁ naro lobha-samanvitaḥ ।
api gocarma-mātreṇa bhūmi-dānena śudhyati ॥ 159[2]

Yatra yogīśvaraḥ, etc. See No. 63, note.

Yāvad=dattā bhaved=bhumiḥ sama-cchedā suśobhanā ।
tāvad=yuga-sahasrāṇi Rudra-loke ca tiṣṭhati ॥ 160[3]

Yāvanti sasya-mūlāni go-romāṇi ca saṁkhyayā ।
naras=tāvanti varṣāṇi svarge tiṣṭhati bhūmidaḥ ॥ 161[4]

Yāvat=sūrya-śaśāṅkau ca yāvad=bhūdhara-sāgarān ।
tāvat=putra-prapautrako grāmaḥ pālyaḥ nṛp-ottamaiḥ ॥ 162[5]

Ye Brāhmaṇānām=ayathā haranti
pradeśa-mātrām=api bhūtadhātrīm ।
pūrīṣa-kūpe pitṛbhiḥ sametās=
te kalpa-koṭir=api yāpayanti ॥ 163[6]

Yo='rcitaṁ pratigṛhṇāti dadāty=arcitam=eva vā ।
tāv=ubhau gacchataḥ svargaṁ narakaṁ tu viparyaye ॥ 164[7]

1. *Ep. Ind.*, Vol. XII, p. 327, text lines 37-38. The verse is found in the *Mahābhārata*, XIII, 62, 84 (with *tathā* for *evaṁ* and *vivardhate* for *prarohati*); *Bṛhaspatisaṁhitā*, verse 12 (with *sadyas°* for *Śakra* and *prasarpati* for *visarpati*). Cf. *Mahābhārata*, XIII, 33. Ballāla's *Dānasāgara* (op. cit., p. 316) attributes the stanza to the *Dāna-Bṛhaspati* at one place and to Vṛddha-Vasiṣṭha elsewhere (p. 322; with *janma-prabhṛti mānavaḥ*).

2. *Ep. Ind.*, Vol. XXIII, p. 161, verse 7. Sometimes we have *janma-prabhṛti mānavaḥ* in the second foot and *etad°* at the beginning of the second half (Vogel, *Antiquities of Chamba State*, I, p. 163). The *Mahābhārata* (XIII, 62, 19) has it with *puruṣaḥ pāpaṁ kurute vṛtti-karśitaḥ*. Ballāla's *Dānasāgara* (op. cit., p. 316) attributes it to the *Dāna-Bṛhaspati*.

3. *Ep. Ind.*, Vol. XXVIII, p. 50, note 7. For slight variations, see *Ep. Carn.*, Vol. XI, Cd. No. 82.

4. *Ep. Ind.*, Vol. XI, p. 312. The stanza is found in the *Saṁvartasmṛti*, verse 73.

5. *Ind. Ant.*, Vol. XII, p. 121.

6. *Ep. Ind.*, Vol. XXII, p. 156, text lines 40-41.

7. *Ep. Ind.*, Vol. II, p. 360. The verse is found in the *Manusmṛti*, IV, 235.

CHAPTER VI

INDIAN EPIGRAPHY ABROAD

With the spread of Indian culture over various countries of Asia, the Indian languages and scripts were introduced into many regions especially of Central and South-East Asia. Epigraphic and literary records in Sanskrit, Prakrit and the regional languages, written in Kharoṣṭhī, Brāhmī and the derivatives of the latter have been found in Central Asia which was regarded as forming a part of the ancient Uttarāpatha division of Bhāratavarṣa. The current alphabets of most of the South-East Asian countries are derivatives of Brāhmī. The earliest inscriptions of these regions, with the exception of Burma and Ceylon, are in Sanskrit. While Prakrit and Pali inscriptions are more numerous in Ceylon, Sanskrit and Pali were both used in early Burmese epigraphs.

There is a general tendency among scholars to describe the alphabet used in the early inscriptions discovered in the countries of Indonesia and Indochina as Pallava-Grantha and to speak of the expansion of Indo-Aryan culture in those territories from the Coromandel Coast during the rule of the Pallavas.[1] These views are however wrong. In the first place, the alphabet, used in the Pallava inscriptions from the 4th to the 6th century A.D. as well as in most of the early epigraphs of the lands beyond the Bay of Bengal, cannot be called Pallava-Grantha. It is really the Late Brāhmī common to the southern and western parts of India. Secondly, the earliest inscriptions of Indochina and Indonesia are written in verse like the records of the Early Kadambas of the Kannaḍa-speaking area and unlike those of the Early Pallavas.[2]

1. See, e.g., *JRASB*, Vol. I, 1935, pp. 1 ff.

2. It is interesting to note that the name Kaṅgavarman found in the Phnom Bayang inscription of Bhavavarman II of Kambuja reminds us of such personal and geographical names as Kaṅgvarman, Koṅgaṇi, Koṅgu-deśa, Koṅgi-nagara found in the southern part of the Kannaḍa-speaking area and its neighbourhood. See *Journ. G. Ind. Soc.*, Vol. V, p. 156; *Suc. Sāt.*, pp. 249, 252; etc.

Thirdly, the box-headed alphabet used in certain epigraphs of king Bhadravarman of Campā (South Annam)[1] is not a characteristic of Pallava inscriptions but is generally found in the epigraphs of Central India and the Upper Deccan as well as in the Kannaḍa-speaking western regions of South India. Fourthly, the Śaka era introduced in Indochina and Indonesia about the 6th century A.D. was never used in the inscriptions of the Pallavas, the Cālukyas of Bādāmi (from the middle of the 6th to that of the 8th century A.D.) being responsible for the association of the name Śaka with the said era and the popularity of its use especially in the present Kannaḍa and Marāṭhī-speaking areas. Fifthly, a number of South-East Asian inscriptions, particularly those of the early ruling families of Arakan (Burma) and of the Śailendras of Śrīvijaya (Palembang in Sumatra), are written in the Late Brāhmī and Siddhamātṛkā alphabets of Eastern India.[2] Sixthly, geographical names like Irāvatī (the river Irawady in Burma; cf. the old name of the Rāvī in the Punjab), Ayuthia (city in Siam; cf. the ancient city of Ayodhyā in the Fyzabad District, U.P.), Candrabhāgā and Gomatī (canals or streams mentioned in the Tugu inscription of Pūrṇavarman of Java; cf. the celebrated North Indian rivers of these names), Campāpura (the old capital of South Annam; cf. the same name of the ancient capital of Aṅga or East Bihar), Kambuja (ancient name of Cambodia; cf. the name of the Kamboja people of North-Western Bhāratavarṣa), etc.,[3] appear to associate the people responsible for coining the names with various areas of Northern India even though some of them may be merely Indianised forms of local names. Seventhly, there are some records in these countries which definitely point to a contact especially with East India among territories outside South India.

1. Cf. *JRASB*, op. cit., Plate I, fig. 1 (facing p. 10).

2. *Ep. Ind.*, Vol. XXXII, pp. 103 ff.; cf. Chatterji and Chakravarti, *India and Java*, Part II, p. 5.

3. Some other similar names of towns and countries common to India (excluding the Far South) and the lands beyond the Bay of Bengal are Kauśāmbī, Dvārāvatī, Mathurā, Kaliṅga, Gandhāra, etc. Cf. R. C. Majumdar, *Champa*, p. xxiii. Note also the representation of *b* by *v*.

The above facts suggest that the responsibility for the spread of Indian culture to the lands beyond the Bay of Bengal cannot be assigned exclusively to the Pallava dominions on the Coromandel Coast. As a matter of fact, the peoples of various parts of India, especially of the coastal regions—both eastern and western, contributed to the spread, the contributions of the Coromandel Coast being only a part of the whole and those of the western areas of the Deccan as also of East India being quite considerable.

The name-ending *varman* generally found in the royal names of these regions is not only found in the Pallava family but is also noticed in the ruling dynasties flourishing in other parts of India, e.g. the Aulikaras of Mandasor, the Śālaṅkāyanas of Veṅgī and the Kadambas of Banavāsi, all of whom began to rule from the 4th century A.D., as well as the Gaṅgas of Kaliṅganagara (from the end of the 5th century) and the Maukharis of Gayā (5th century). Most of the Kaliṅga dynasties of the 5th century, e.g. the Māṭharas and Pitṛbhaktas, had royal names ending in *varman*. It has to be noticed that none of the Varman kings of the lands beyond the Bay of Bengal appear to have flourished earlier than the close of the 5th century A. D.

In this connection, attention may be drawn to the traditions regarding the Indian colonisers in the said countries, e.g., the Ceylonese story of the conquest of the island by Vijaya, a great-grandson of the king of Vaṅga (then Southern Bengal); the foundation of Ligor ascribed to one of Aśoka's descendants, who fled from Magadha (South Bihar) and embarked on a vessel at Dantapura lying near modern Srikakulam in the ancient Kaliṅga country comprising wide areas of the coast lands of Orissa and Andhra Pradesh; the story preserved in the Javanese chronicles as well as in the traditions of many other islands regarding the colonisation of the lands in question by the people of Kaliṅga (generally called Kling);[1] a tradition

1. The inscriptions of Andhra Pradesh and Orissa are, however, written in prose as in the case of those of the Coromandel Coast while the Śaka era was introduced in Orissa at a late date. The Orissan alphabet was not of the southern type.

of Pegu regarding the colonisation of the Irawady delta and the adjoining coast lands of Burma by the people of the lower valleys of the Kṛṣṇā and the Godāvarī in the eastern coast lands of the Deccan; the story in the Javanese chronicles regarding the colonisation of the island by a prince of Gujarāt in 75 A.D.; etc.

The same story is told by what we know about Indian trade with Indochina and Indonesia, vaguely called Suvarṇabhūmi or 'the Land of Gold' in Indian literature. Thus the Jātaka stories show how the people of Bengal, Bihar and Eastern U.P. came down to the port of Tāmralipti in the present Midnapur District in South-West Bengal, whence they sailed for the eastern islands. The *Periplus* and Ptolemey's Geography refer to the city of Gaṅgā near the principal mouth of the river of that name as the main port on the Bengal coast. There were similar ports in the Puri-Ganjam region of the Kaliṅga country as well as in the region about the mouths of the Kṛṣṇā and the Godāvārī. The Greek sources speak of certain ports in the coast lands of the Tamil and Kannaḍa-speaking areas. Bhṛgukaccha (modern Broach or Bharuch) and Sūrpāraka (modern Sopara in the Thana District) were the most famous ports in the coastal area of Western India.[1] There is some indication that all these ports had trade relations with the lands beyond the Bay of Bengal.

1. *Central Asia*

Aśoka's inscriptions discovered in the Peshawar and Hazara Districts of West Pakistan are written in the Prakrit language and Kharoṣṭhī alphabet, the latter being an Indian modification of the Aramaic script introduced in the region during the Achaemenian occupation. But an important inscription of the Maurya king discovered in Afghanistan is the Kandahar bilingual epigraph which is in two versions, one in Greek and the other in Aramaic.[2] Among later records from

1. Cf. R. C. Majumdar, *Champa*, pp. xi-xii.

2. *Journal Asiatique*, 1958, pp. 1 ff.; *Ep. Ind.*, Vol. XXXIV, pp. 1 ff. A few other Aramaic inscriptions have also been ascribed to Aśoka.

the Afghanistan area written in Prakrit and Kharoṣṭhī, mention may be made of the inscriptions of the times of Menander and Vijayamitra found in the Bajaur tribal territory and the vase inscription of Huviṣka's time from Khawat (Wardak) about 30 miles to the west of Kabul.[1]

But, before the 6th century A.D., the use of Kharoṣṭhī died not only out of the north-western regions of the Indian subcontinent but also out of Afghanistan. The latest Kharoṣṭhī inscriptions in India are two small Taxila records of about the 5th century A.D., though we have a Brāhmī inscription of about the 3rd century A. D. from the same area.[2] The Gardez (Afghanistan) Vināyaka image inscription in Sanskrit, now in the Dargah Pir Ratan Nath at Kabul, may be mentioned in this connection. It is written in the Late Brāhmī alphabet of the 6th century A.D. and is stated to have been installed by the Śāhī king Khiṅgāla in the 8th year of his reign.[3] A late medieval inscription in Nāgarī characters is noticed on the left side of the Central Mihrab of the rock-cut chamber near Chahil Zina (literally 'forty steps') in the vicinity of old Kandahar.[4]

A large number of manuscripts and documents written in Kharoṣṭhī with ink on wedge-shaped and rectangular tablets of wood have been found in Chinese Turkestan. They are usually assigned to dates ranging from the 3rd century A.D. There are also manuscripts like that of the Prakrit *Dhammapada* which is written in Kharoṣṭhī on birch-bark sheets and is assigned to the 2nd century A.D. Kharoṣṭhī continued to be used in the said area till the 7th century A.D. side by side with Brāhmī which seems to have been introduced in Central

1. *Select Inscriptions*, pp. 102 ff., 153-54.

2. Cf. Marshall, *Taxila*, Vol. I, pp. 274 ff.; *Ep. Ind.*, Vol. XXX, pp. 59 ff.

3. Cf. Ramachandran and Sharma, *Archaeological Reconnaissance in Afghanistan* (Preliminary Report of the Indian Archaeological Delegation 1956), 1956, pp. II. 1-2. See *East and West*, December 1958, pp. 327-28; *Ep. Ind.*, Vol. XXXV, pp. 44 ff.

4. Ramachandran and Sharma, op. cit., p. I. 19. For similar records from Baku (Ajerbaijan), see *A. R. Ep.*, 1956-57, Nos. B 547 ff. We have seen the photograph of an inscription of the same type from Samarkand (Ujbekistan).

Asia during the Gupta age. Among Sanskrit manuscripts in Brāhmī on palm-leaf, paper and birch-bark, reference may be made to Kumāralāta's *Kalpanāmaṇḍitikā* and the *Udānavarga*, both of which are assignable on palaeographical grounds to the 4th or 5th century A.D., and the Bower manuscripts, the date of which is about a century later. Other Sanskrit manuscripts in Brāhmī, discovered in Central Asia, include fragments of Aśvaghoṣa's drama entitled *Śāriputraprakaraṇa*. From about the 7th century A.D., we have records in the local dialects of Central Asia written in the derivatives of Brāhmī.[1]

The earliest epigraphs in Nepal are the Rummindei and Nigali Sagar pillar inscriptions of the Maurya emperor Aśoka (3rd century B.C.) written in the Early Brāhmī alphabet and Prakrit language.[2] Early Licchavi epigraphs like the Changunarayan pillar inscription (464 A.D.) of Mānadeva are written in Sanskrit and the Late Brāhmī of East India, while the characters of the Sanskrit records of the later members of the Licchavi family are Siddhamātṛkā.[3] Though most of the early medieval records of Nepal belonging to later dates, both epigraphic and literary, are written in Gauḍīya or the East Indian derivative of Siddhamātṛkā, some Buddhist manuscripts are written in Bhaikṣukī, while Buddhist Dhāraṇīs, etc., in Sanskrit were often written in a derivative of the Siddhamātṛkā alphabet called Rañjā or Rañjanā which was also used for that purpose in Tibet.[4] The Tibetan alphabet itself is a slightly modified form of Siddhamātṛkā. Buddhist Dhāraṇīs were written in China and Japan in the Siddhamātṛkā alphabet till quite recent times.

Early medieval manuscripts of a large number of works copied in East India have been found in Nepal and Tibet. Of these, the Tibetan collection contains mostly Buddhist works, while both Buddhist and Brahmanical works are found

1. See my *Indian Palaeography*, Chapter II, Section 6, and Chapter III, Section 5.

2. *Select Inscriptions*, pp. 70-71.

3. See Sylvain Lévi, *Le Nepal*, Part III, pp. 10 ff. and Plates. Cf. R. Gnoli, *Nepalese Inscriptions in Gupta Characters*, 1956.

4. See my *Indian Palaeography*, Chapter V, Section 3.

in the Nepalese collection in large numbers. The discovery of many manuscripts in Nepal, which were copied in the dominions and during the reigns of the Pāla kings of Bengal and Bihar, is explained by the fact that, during the early days of the Muslim occupation of Eastern India, many scholars, afraid of Turkish persecution, fled to the north, especially to the Nepal region, together with the books in their family libraries. There is also evidence to show that professional copyists of one area were often employed for copying manuscripts in the neighbouring regions.[1]

2. *Ceylon*

Among the countries of South-East Asia, Ceylon's cultural contact with India is the oldest. According to an old Ceylonese tradition, Prince Vijaya, son of the king of Siṁhapura in Rāḍha (in South-West Bengal; or less probably Lāṭa in Gujarat) and a great-grandson of the king of Vaṅga (then South Bengal), colonised Ceylon about the beginning of the 5th century B.C. About the middle of the 3rd century B.C. the Maurya emperor Aśoka of Pāṭaliputra (near modern Patna) is known to have maintained friendly relations with Tāmraparṇī or Ceylon. He is also stated to have sent to that country a Buddhist mission which converted Devānāmpriya Tiṣya, king of the island, to Buddhism together with his subjects. Ceylon's contact with the Tamil-speaking region of South India, just beyond the Palk Strait, has been very close throughout the ages and, during the major portion of the 11th century A.D., wide areas of the island formed parts of the empire of the Choḻas of Tañjavūr. It is therefore interesting to note that the Ceylonese language belongs to the Aryan (and not the Dravidian) group. Old Ceylonese traditions appear to suggest that the peoples of Eastern and Western India were mainly responsible for the spread of Aryanism in that land.[2] The Ceylonese royal house often contracted matrimonial

1. Cf. *IHQ*, Vol. XXX, pp. 382-87.
2. See *CHI*, Vol. I, pp. 605-606.

alliance with Indian ruling families such as the Pāṇḍyas of the South and the Kaliṅgas of the East.

The close contact of Ceylon with non-Tamil India in pre-Christian times seems to be indicated by another fact. We know that the early independent rulers of India were satisfied with the simpler title *Rājan* while the Indo-Greek kings of North-Western Bhāratavarṣa introduced the royal title *Rājā mahān* or *Mahārāja*, which was essentially a translation of the old Persian title *Kshāyathiya vazrka* enjoyed by the Achaemenian monarchs, about the middle of the 2nd century B. C. The earliest indigenous Indian monarch assuming the title *Mahārāja* is king Khāravela of Kaliṅga who flourished about the close of the 1st century B.C., while the same title appears in Ceylonese epigraphs which may be somewhat earlier in date.[1] This seems to suggest that the title was borrowed by Ceylon from Western or North-Western Bhāratavarṣa which came under the influence of the Greeks. Some of these early Ceylonese records have to be read from right to left in the Kharoṣṭhī fashion.[2] This also seems to point to Ceylon's contact with the Kharoṣṭhī-using areas of the said part of India. The letter ḻ in early Ceylonese epigraphs is not idicated by a diacritically marked *l* as used in the Early Brāhmī alphabet of the Tamil areas but by *ḍ* endowed with a diacritical mark as known from other parts of India.

The story of the introduction of Indianism in Ceylon is different from that of its spread in Indochina and Indonesia which came under the influence of Indian merchants, adventurers and priests about the beginning of the Christian era. In many of these countries Brahmanical Hinduism not only spread earlier than Buddhism but Śaivism seems to have been the dominating religious faith throughout the early period. This was not the case with Ceylon where Buddhism was always the predominant faith as it is now.

Sanskrit inscriptions are rare in Ceylon, the more popular Indian languages there being Prakrit and Pali. The Ruvana-

1. Cf. *Select Inscriptions*, pp. 206 ff., 232-33.
2. Ibid., p. 233.

valisäya pillar inscription in Late Brāhmī of about the 5th century A.D. and the Kuchchaveli rock inscription in a developed form of the same alphabet assignable to a date about the 7th century A.D. are two of the few early Ceylonese records in Sanskrit.[1] The Gäraṇdigala inscription of about the first half of the 8th century A.D. is one of the early epigraphs in Ceylonese while the Sanskrit inscription from the Jetavanārāma is written in the Siddhamātṛkā alphabet of Northern India and may be assigned on palaeographical grounds to a date in the 9th century A.D.[2] Many Tamil inscriptions, especially of the time of the Coḷa occupation of Ceylon during the 11th century A.D., have been discovered in the island.[3]

3. *Burma, Siam (Thailand) and Malay Peninsula*

Among the early inscriptions of Burma, there are epigraphs in Sanskrit and in Pali, records in the latter being mostly Buddhist tracts. The simple Sanskrit inscriptions in verse, belonging to the Candras of Arakan and assignable to the 6th century A.D., resemble in style the records of king Mūlavarman of Borneo. It is interesting to note that, unlike Mūlavarman's inscriptions, the alphabet of these records is the Late Brāhmī of Eastern India, while the said style seems to have been borrowed from South Indian epigraphs like those of the Early Kadambas of Banavāsi in the Kannaḍa-speaking region. Ānandacandra's inscription (8th century A. D.) from the same region of Burma is a rare instance of a Sanskrit epigraph of the *praśasti* type found in that country, elaborate eulogies in Sanskrit verse written in ornate *kāvya* style being common in the other lands of Indochina and Indonesia. The inscription of Ānandacandra is written in the Siddhamātṛikā alphabet of Eastern India.[4]

1. *Ep. Zeyl.*, Vol. III, pp. 120 ff., 158 ff.
2. Ibid., pp. 195 ff.; Vol. I, pp. 1 ff. The earliest record dated in the Buddha-nirvāṇa era is the Anuradhapura inscription of year 941 (=28th regnal year of Buddhadāsa's son Upatiṣya), Kuja-vāra, Pūrṇimānta-Pauṣa-badi 1=16th December 396 A. D. (*Univ. Cey. Rev.*, Vol. XVIII, pp. 129 ff.).
3. Cf. *SII*, Vol. IV, Nos. 1388 ff.
4. See *Ep. Ind.*, Vol. XXXII, pp. 103 ff.; *Sel. Ins.*, pp. 462 ff.

Most of the early inscriptions found elsewhere in Burma are however written in the Late Brāhmī alphabet of West and South India. There is also evidence to prove the contact of Tamil-speaking merchants with Burma during the early medieval period. But South-East Burma seems to have closer ties with the people of East India. The Śaka era was not popular in Burmese epigraphy as it is in the inscriptions of the other regions of South-East Asia.

The earliest inscriptions in the language of the Mons (Talaings), who lived in the Irawady basin with Hanthawady (Haṁsāvatī, i.e. Pegu) and Thaton (Sudharmapura) as their chief cities, were found on a stone slab discovered at Lopburi in Siam.[1] They are written in characters of about the 6th or 7th century A.D. and point to the cultural contact between the two countries. A large number of Pyu inscriptions assignable to dates between the 6th and 8th centuries A. D. were found at Hmawsa (Prome) and Halin in the Shwebo District.[2] The Myazedi (Myinkaba, Pagan) inscription of the 12th century A.D. contains 4 different versions, viz. Pali, Burmese, Mon and Pyu.[3] A Pagan inscription of about the 13th century A.D. is written partly in the Sanskrit language and Grantha characters and partly in the Tamil language and alphabet and records the grant of certain gifts by a Vaiṣṇava devotee of Cranganore in Malabar in favour of a Viṣṇu temple at Pagan.[4]

An early Sanskrit epigraph discovered in Siam is the Ban Bungke inscription (886 A. D.) of king Indravarman of Cambodia.[5] The Sukhotai (Sukhodaya) inscriptions (Śaka 1214) of king Rām Kham-heng of Siam are written in the Siamese language and early Siamese characters.[6]

The earliest inscriptions discovered in the Malay Penin-

1. *Rep. Dir. Arch. Surv., Burma*, 1956, pp. 19 ff.

2. Cf. *Ep. Ind.*, Vol. XII, pp. 127 ff.; *ASI, A.R.*, 1911-12, p. 142; 1926-27, p. 172; 1927-28, p. 145; 1929-30, p. 182; *ASB, A.R.*, 1942, p. 22.

3. *Ep. Birm.*, Vol. I, pp. 1 ff.

4. *Ep. Ind.*, Vol. V, pp. 101 ff.; Vol. VII, pp. 197-98.

5. *BEFEO*, Vol. XXII, p. 63.

6. D. Diringer, *The Alphabet*, p. 416.

sula are Buddhistic in nature.[1] A prose endorsement in one of them, besides the Buddhist creed, speaks of *Mahānāvika* (i.e. 'the great sailor') Buddhagupta of Raktamṛttikā which was a locality near modern Murshidabad in South-West Bengal.[2] The alphabet of these records is however the Late Brāhmī of West and South India assignable to the 5th or 6th century A.D.

The earliest epigraph dated in the Śaka era in the Malay Peninsula is the Vieng Sa (Ligor, South of the Bay of Bandon) inscription of Śaka 697 (775 A. D.).[3]

4. *Indonesia*

The earliest inscriptions of Indonesia are written in Sanskrit verse. Most of the early medieval records of the area are in the ornate *kāvya* style; but their size is not big as in the case of Cambodian inscriptions. Java developed an indigenous literature originated from an intimate acquaintance with Indian literary tradition. Although the people of the area are now Muhammadans, the Indian element is still prominent in their culture. The people of Bali may be regarded as Hindu in both religion and culture.

The inscriptions of Mūlavarman from Kutei in Borneo are written in Anuṣṭubh stanzas in the style of some of the inscriptions of the Early Kadambas of Banavasi, their alphabet being Late Brāhmī similar to that found in Buddhagupta's inscription discovered in the Malay Peninsula and referred to above.[4] Pūrṇavarman's inscriptions from Java are written in a similar alphabet and style, there being one stanza in *Sragdharā* besides others in *Anuṣṭubh.* They may be assigned to the 6th century A.D.[5]

Epigraphic records of Indonesia continue in an unbroken series from the 5th or 6th century down to the end of the

1. Chatterji and Chakravarti, *India and Java*, Part II, pp. 6-7.
2. *Select Inscriptions*, p. 365; cf. *Ep. Ind.*, Vol. XXVII, p. 2.
3. Chatterji and Chakravarti, op. cit., pp. 40 ff.
4. *Select Inscriptions*, pp. 446-47; Chatterji and Chakravarti, op. cit., pp. 8 ff.
5. *Select Inscriptions*, pp. 468 ff.; Chatterji and Chakravarti, op. cit., p. 20 ff.

Indo-Javanese period about the beginning of the 16th century. But the number of Sanskrit inscriptions found in Malay Peninsula and Indonesia is much smaller than that of those discovered in Cambodia and Annam. The Indonesian inscriptions generally record pious donations or the building of temples. They usually inform us as to when and by whom a temple or monastery or image was constructed or a donation made. When a gift of land was the subject of an inscription, its boundaries were indicated, and, when privileges were bestowed their nature was written down. Usually the inscriptions give some information about the kings in whose regnal reckoning they were dated as well as about the royal officers associated with the documents together with facts throwing light on the religious, administrative and social condition of the country.

The inscriptions are generally written on stone, either slabs or rocks. But there are some epigraphs on plates of copper, silver or gold. The earlier inscriptions are in Sanskrit in the Late Brāhmī alphabet of West and South India or its local modification; but later epigraphs are mostly in the Kavi or old Javanese language and the Kavi script which was a derivative of Brāhmī developed in the land itself. The Kavi language is an admixture of Sanskrit and the local Polynesian dialect. The Śailendra kings of Śrīvijaya used the Siddhamātṛikā alphabet of East India and the Sanskrit language for their inscriptions.

The use of the Śaka era became popular in Indonesian epigraphy, its earliest use being noticed in inscriptions of the 8th century. It was probably introduced by the merchants of the Western part of the Deccan. The earliest record of Java dated in the Śaka era is the Kelurak inscription[1] of Śaka 700 (778 A.D.). The Minto stone inscription[2] of Śaka 876 (954 A.D.) is in the Kavi language but has two Sanskrit stanzas at the beginning. The Pereng stone inscription (Śaka 785-863 A.D.), written in the Kavi language,

1. *India and Java*, II, pp. 44 ff.
2. Ibid., p. 48.

contains five Sanskrit stanzas in the Āryā metre.[1] Similar is the case with the Singasari inscription (915 A.D.) of king Daṣka written in both Sanskrit and Kavi.[2]

5. *Cambodia*

Unlike Java, Cambodia does not possess a literature influenced by Indian literary tradition. But the Sanskrit inscriptions, dating from the 5th to the 14th century, found all over Cambodia, exhibit a very flourishing state of Sanskrit learning. The number of such inscriptions written in ornate *kāvya* style is the largest in Cambodia than in any other land of South-East Asia and many of them are quite voluminous. The use of the Śaka era and of the decimal system in numbers is first noticed in Cambodia respectively in the 6th and the 7th century. The first of them appears to have been introduced in this region by the merchants of the western areas of the Deccan, and the second probably by those of the southern areas of the Gujarātī-speaking region. In India, the decimal system is noticed for the first time in the date of the Sankheda (in the old Baroda State in Gujarat) copper-plate inscription of 594 A.D.[3]

The study of Indo-Cambodian epigraphy began in 1879 with the decipherment of some Sanskrit records by H. Kern from the estampages prepared by J. Harmand. A collection of estampages of such epigraphs made by E. Aymonier was published under the name *Inscriptions Sanscrites du Cambodge* by A. Barth and A. Bergaigne, in two Parts with a volume of Plates, the first Part edited by Barth appearing in 1885 and the second edited by Bergaingne with notes by Barth in 1893. The inscriptions in the native Khmer language in Aymonier's collection were translated and summarised by himself in his *Le Cambodge*, Vols. I-III (1901-04). A large number of inscriptions in Sanskrit and Khmer, discovered at later dates were published by L. Finot, G. Coedès and others in the

1. Cf. ibid., p. 48, note 6.
2. Kern, *V. G.*, Vol. IV, pp. 279 ff.
3. Bhandarkar's List, No. 1205.

Bulletin de l'Ecole Francaise d'Extreme-Orient appearing originally from Hanoi. Coedès has also published a large number of Sanskrit and Khmer inscriptions in several volumes (1937 onwards) of his *Collection de textes et documents sur l'Indochine* with several volumes of Plates.

Late Brāhmī of West and South India, which was introduced in Cambodia, gradually underwent modification in the same way as in different parts of India. The orthography of the Sanskrit epigraphs of Cambodia exhibit the substitution of *ḍ* for *d* and *ṇ* for *n* and *vice versa* and sometimes even of *ṇd* for *ṇḍ*. The use of *ṅ* for *anusvāra*, the change of *visarga* before a sibilant to the same sibilant, the occasional reduplication of a consonant before and after *r* as well as before *v*, the use of *tv* for *ttv* and of *jihvāmūlīya* and *upadhmānīya* for *visarga* before the guttural and labial surds, the occasional use of *candrabindu* for *anusvāra* and the rarity of cases in which *v* is distinguished from *b*, etc., are some of the orthographical features of the Sanskrit inscriptions of Cambodia.[1]

The language of the records is mostly correct Sanskrit, irregularities and mistakes which are few being probably due to the scribe or engraver rather than the composer. The records, which are generally incised on stone are mostly engraved with great care. The majority of the inscriptions are written in beautiful language in the *kāvya* style exhibiting the authors' thorough acquaintance with the metres and the rules and conventions of Sanskrit rhetorics and prosody. The Vat Thipedi inscription[2] (Śaka 832=910 A. D.) of king Īśvaravarman II is composed in the flawless Gauḍī style of composition, and it has been suggested that the author was an inhabitant of Gauḍa in East India or lived there for a long time. A large number of the inscriptions contain 50 stanzas or more, while some contain more than 100 stanzas. The Mebon (Śaka 874) and Pre Rup (Śaka 883) inscriptions[3] of Rājendravarman contain no less than 218 and 298 stanzas respectively.

1. R. C. Majumdar, *Inscriptions of Kambuja*, pp. xiv ff.
2. Ibid., pp. 161 ff.
3. Ibid., pp. 193 ff., 232 ff.

The epigraphs are usually *praśastis* extolling the king and recording details of endowments created in favour of religious institutions. Unlike Indian inscriptions of the *praśasti* type, the Cambodian eulogies of the kings often give, besides other details of historical importance, the date of accession of the reigning monarch as well as his ancestors. But, as in the case of Indian epigraphs, the eulogies usually contain a great deal of what is conventional.

The details of religious endowments, which are the subject of most of these records, supply the names of deities (fairly large in number) worshipped in the country together with long lists of articles of daily or seasonal worship; the utensils and other necessaries of the temples including their personnel; the accounts of temple properties both movable and immovable and the method of their management and various other matters connected with temples and throwing light on the religious, social and economic life of the people. There are remains of a large number of temples all over Cambodia, the inscriptions relating only to some of them.

The Cambodian inscriptions are mostly of Śaivite character, although there are some Vaishṇavite and a few Buddhistic records. The inscriptions show how Indian culture was adopted in Cambodia by some of the local people who were semi-savages roaming about naked about the beginning of the Christian era when the Indians first came into contact with them. Some interesting facts about life in Cambodia, as revealed by the inscriptions, are the worship of Śiva, Viṣṇu and the Buddha side by side; the existence of different religious sects like the Bhāgavatas, Pāñcarātras and Pāśupatas; the adoption of the caste system dominated by Brāhmaṇas versed in the Vedas, Vedāṅgas and Upavedas as well as of Sanskritic names by the kings, noblemen and common people; the popularity of the Tantric religion and of well-known Tantric texts; the existence of Devadāsīs in the temples and of priests of the same family sometimes conducting religious rites of the royal families for centuries in succession; the creation of new castes by the king and admission of new members to a caste such as that of the goldsmiths; the popularity of the study of the works of Indian authors like Pāṇini, Patañjali, Manu, Vātsyāyana, Viśālākṣa, Pravarasena, Mayūra, Guṇāḍhya and Suśruta. King Yaśovarman is stated to have composed a commentary on Patañjali's *Mahābhāṣya*, while one of his ministers was an expert in the *Horā-śāstra*.[1] The same king is known to have founded 100 *āśramas* which were a sort of convents or monasteries. The Śaivas, Vaiṣṇavas and Buddhists had their own *āśramas* which were religious centres radiating Indian culture throughout Cambodia.

Some of the inscriptions of Yaśovarman, who flourished about the end of the 9th and the beginning of the 10th century A.D., are written in the Siddhamātṛkā alphabet while some of his other records giving regulations about *āśramas* are both in the said alphabet and in the Cambodian derivative of Brāhmī. This fact suggests that there were fresh arrivals apparently from North or East India, who were not familiar with the latter alphabet. Contact with South India during the early medieval period seems to be indicated by the Prasat Kandol Dom inscription[2] of king Indravarman who flourished about the end of the 9th century, according to which the king's *guru* Śivasoma studied the scriptures at the feet of *Bhagavat* Śaṅkara, apparently the great Indian philosopher of the same name who was born in the western coast of South India.

The Śaka era appears in Cambodia in inscriptions like one of Śaka 531 from Prasat Ak Yom while the decimal system of writing numbers is first noticed in a pillar inscription of Śaka 605 (683 A. D.) from Sambaur.[3] The Sambaur pillar inscription contains 21 lines written in the Khmer language which was used in Cambodian epigraphy from about this time side by side with Sanskrit.

6. *South Annam*

The number of Sanskrit inscriptions discovered in South

1. Ibid. p. xvii. 2. Ibid., pp. 57 ff.

3. See ibid., pp. 7, 564. For the Roban Romas inscription of Saka 520, see *BEJEO*, Vol. XLIII, pp. 1 ff.

Annam (ancient Campā) is fairly large; but the size of most of them is not very big. Many of the epigraphs are written in verse; but there are some written either in prose or in a mixture of prose and verse. They are generally on stone stelae, although some of them are engraved on rocks, stone images and metalic plates. The palaeography of the earlier records is similar to that of the Cambodian epigraphs. The Dong Duong inscription of Indravarman II, dated Śaka 797 (875 A.D.), is a fairly big record engraved on the four faces of a stelae containing respectively 24, 24, 23 and 31 lines.[1]

A collection of the Sanskrit inscriptions of Campā was prepared by A. Bergaigne in 1888. It was published after his death by Barth in 1893 in the *Notices et Extraits de Manuscripts de la Bibliothèque Nationale et autres Bibliothèques*, Vol. XXVII, Part 1, Fasc. 2. A large number of inscriptions in the Cham language were edited by Aymonier in the *Journal Asiatique*, 1891. Inscriptions in Sanskrit and Cham, discovered at later dates, have mostly been published in the *Bulletin de l'Ecole Francaise d' Extreme-Orient* by scholars like L. Finot, M. Huber, G. Coedès and others.

The earliest inscription discovered in Campā is the Vo-cañh epigraph of a king of the Śrīmāra family who flourished in the 4th or 5th century A. D.[2] The Mi-son and Cho Dinh inscriptions of king Bhadravarman, who flourished in the 5th or 6th century A. D., are written in the box-headed alphabet.[3] The Śaka era began to appear in the records of this area about the second half of the 6th century A.D.[4]

1. R. C. Majumdar, *Champā*, Part III, pp. 74 ff.

2. Cf. *IHQ*., Vol. XVI, pp. 484 ff.; Vol. XVII, pp. 107 ff.; *Journ. As.*, 1953, pp. 477 ff. Some scholars assign the inscription to an earlier date.

3. See *BEFEO*, Vol. XXXII, 1932, pp. 127 ff. and Table; *JRASB*, Vol. I, 1935, Plate facing p. 10.

4. Cf. R. C. Majumdar, *Champā*, Part III, pp. 9 ff.

CHAPTER VII
DATING AND THE ERAS

Section I
DATES IN INDIAN EPIGRAPHS

1. *Nature of the Dates*

As will be seen below, the dates in the earliest Indian epigraphs as well as a large number of later documents quote only a particular year of the reign of a king, the years of various eras being quoted in some records from about the beginning of the Christian era. In the earlier instances of the specification of a day in the dates, the number of the day is mentioned as belonging to one of the 8 fortnights of a season, of which three were regarded as constituting a year.[1] We have generally a reference to the month instead of the fortnight in the dates of the Kuṣāṇa epigraphs. I later nstances, the day is quoted as belonging to one of the 12 solar months of the year or to either of the two fortnights (e.g. the dark and the bright) of one of the 12 lunar months. The mention of the name of the week-day became gradually popular.[2] After the mention of the day, sometimes the date was referred to as the *pūrvā* which really means 'the above' (in the feminine gender) and apparently indicates the *tithi* or lunar mansion on the day in question,[3] although the *vāra* or week-day was

1. These were *grīṣma* (summer), *varṣā* (the rainy season) and *hemanta* (winter). See below, pp. 236-37.

2. The earliest mention of the week-day by name is found in the Eran inscription of the time of Budhagupta, dated 484 A.D. (*Select Inscriptions*, p. 326). But the word *vāra* probably referring to a week-day seems to be used in the Andhau inscriptions of 130 A.D. (ibid., pp. 167 ff.).

3. The expressions used are *etasyāṁ pūrvāyāṁ*, *asyāṁ divasa-pūrvāyāṁ*, *asyāṁ saṁvatsara-māsa-divasa-pūrvāyāṁ*, etc., in the earlier records (cf. Bhandarkar's List, Nos. 2, 1261, 1287, etc.; *Select Inscriptions*, pp. 120, 279, etc.) and, in some late cases (cf. Bhandarkar's List, Nos. 241, 438, 451, etc.), *asyāṁ saṁvatsara-māsa-pakṣa-divasa-pūrvāyāṁ tithau*. Sometimes the mention of the *tithi* is followed by such expressions (cf. ibid., No. 122). See also expressions like *daśamī-pūrvakam* (ibid., No. 1077). Instead of *pūrvā*, the words *anupūrvā*, *kṣaṇa*, *divasa*, *divasa-kṣaṇa*, *ghaṭikā*, etc., are used in some cases (cf. *Select Inscriptions*, pp. 127, 135, 136, 143, 149, 153, etc.). In one case, the expression used in an inscription dated in the Vikrama era is *asyāṁ Mālava-pūrvāyām* (Bhandarkar's List, No. 5).

reckoned from one sun-rise to another. The week-day of a *tithi* is generally the day on which the *tithi* ends. In some inscriptions, the *nakṣatra*, *yoga*, *karaṇa*, *lagna* and many other details are quoted in the dates besides the above.[1] Some epigraphs exhibit the mention of several eras in the date.[2]

A peculiarity of the dating of Indian records is the use of abbreviations. Indeed, the use of contractions is first noticed in the epigraphs in connection with dates. The words *varṣa*, *vatsara*, *saṁvatsara*, etc., meaning 'the year', was often contracted into *va*, *saṁ*, *saṁva*, *saṁvat*, etc. The word *saṁvat* and its numerous corrupt variants were later used in the sense of 'an era'. A few early records suggest a similar contraction of the word *kāla* meaning 'an era' into *kā*.[3] Of the seasons mentioned in early inscriptions, *hemanta* (i.e. winter) was often indicated by *he* or *hema*, *varṣā* (i.e. the rainy season) by *va* or *vā* (for Prakrit *vāsa*), and *grīṣma* as *grī* or *gi* (for Prakrit *gimha*). Likewise *di* or *diva* often stood for *divasa* and *ti* for *tithi*. In the commonly found expression *śu-di* or *su-di*, *śu* stands for *śuddha* (bight) and *su* seems to be its corrupt spelling. Similarly, in *ba-di* or *va-di*, *ba* stands for *bahula* (dark) and *va* is either a wrong spelling or stands for *vadya*. In the Kashmir region, *śu-ti* or *su-ti* and *ba-ti* or *va-ti* (i.e. *śudha-tithi* and *bahula-tithi*) are generally found for *śu-di* and *ba-di*. The names of the months were often abbreviated; e.g. *Phā* for *Phālguna*. Sometimes the expression *rājya-saṁvatsara* is contracted into *rā-saṁ*.[4] In the medieval records of South India, very often the names of the week-days are likewise contracted; e.g. *So* standing for *Soma-vāra*, *Ma* for *Maṅgala-vāra*, etc.[5]

The numbers of the years, etc., in the earliest historical records of India, e.g. the inscriptions of Aśoka,

1 See, e.g., Bhandarkar's List , No. 27.

2. Cf. ibid., No. 565.

3. Cf. *Select Inscriptions*, p. 131.

4. Cf. Bhandarkar's List, No. 1787.

5. See *Ep. Ind.*, Vol. XXXIII, pp. 108, 112, 115. In Telugu-Kannaḍa epigraphs, Saturday was often called Bṛiha-vāra or Vaḍḍa-vāra (ibid., Vol. XXXI, p. 100; Vol. XXXIII, pp. 125-26). Both the names were sometimes also applied to Thursday.

were written in words. In later times, the practice of writing them by numerical figures became gradually popular.[1] In many cases, they are expressed by both words and figures. In some inscriptions from Dwarahat in the Almora District, U. P., the months and *tithis* of the lunar months are given in numbers; e.g. *māsa* 10 (i.e. the tenth month of the year).[1]

The numerals were written by symbols in the early inscriptions in Brāhmī and Kharoṣṭhī, the signs of the Kharoṣṭhī system being borrowed from the Aramaic alphabet with slight modifications. The decimal system of writing numbers with the figures for 1 to 9 and the cypher with the application of the principle of space value, which is the most convenient system of writing numbers and is now popular all over the world, originated in India, probably in West India amongst the astronomers of the Ujjayinī school, about the 5th century A. D.[2]

There was also a convention according to which ordinary words of the Sanskrit language, that can be associated with particualr numbers, were used to indicate those numbers. Thus words meaning 'the hand' (i.e. *kara*, etc.) came to be used to imply 2 since man has only two hands. Such words indicating numbers were arranged according to the principle of *vāma-gati*, i.e. 'the turning round of the sum', i.e. reading the figures from right to left.[3] This system of expressing numbers is often noticed in the dates of inscriptions especially of the medieval age.[4] Another system of expressing numbers

1. Cf. *A. R. Ep.*, 1958-59, No. C 382 (V.S. 1081, Month 11, *tithi* 10, *Friday*=20th August 1025 A. D., the year being Kārttikādi and the month *Pūrṇimānta*); No. C 384 (Śaka 1136, month 11, Māgha su 7, Thursday= 8th January 1215 A. D., the year being Caitrādi).

2. It was borrowed by the Arabs from the Indians and gradually spread to the rest of the world. See our *Indian Palaeography*, the section on Numerals.

3. In a few cases, the *vāma-gati* principle is found to have been ignored. Cf. Bhandarkar's List, No. 620.

4. See, e.g., *ved-āṅk-ābdh-indu-varṣa* (Bhandarkar's List, No. 775) in which *veda*=4, *aṅka*=9, *abdhi* =4 and *indu*=1 and, since the words are arranged according to the *vāma-gati* principle, they give the year as 1494 [of the Vikrama-saṁvat]. See below, pp. 228 ff.

by particular letters of the alphabet is known since 499 A.D. when Āryabhaṭa composed his *Āryabhaṭīya*. Although Āryabhaṭa's system is not noticed in inscriptions, a similar system called Kaṭapayādi, which developed in South India, is sometimes found in South Indian epigraphs of the medieval period. According to this system, the 10 letters from *ka* to *ña* and from *ṭa* to *na* have the values respectively of the numbers 1 to 9 and 0, while the 5 letters from *pa* to *ma* indicate the numbers 1 to 5 and the values of the numbers 1 to 9 are assigned respectively to the letters *ya* and *ḷa*. In the formation of chronograms, vowels, without numerical value, are added to the consonants and the last consonants in the conjuncts used have alone numerical values, while the principle of *vāma-gati* is also observed. Thus the Kandiyur inscription[1] of Kodavarman is dated in the 1,511,564th day of the Kali-yuga era expressed by the Kaṭapayādi chronogram *viṣamampuṇyamekam* in which *va*=4, *ṣa*=6, *ma*=5, *pa*=1, *ya*=1, *ma*=5 and *ka*=1 and they are to be read from right to left. Similar other known systems, such as the Nannādi developed in Kerala, do not appear in inscriptions.

The dates in the earlier inscriptions generally do not give details enough for finding out their equivalents in known calendars. Mention of the week-day together with the name of the month or that of the month and the fortnight as well as of the year of an era with known epoch is very useful for this purpose. Such details are often found in later inscriptions. Gifts were generally made on auspicious occasions such as the eclipses of the sun and the moon, the full-moon and new-moon days, the sun's movement from the south to the north or *vice versa*, the vernal and autumnal equinoxes, the holy *tithis* and particular positions of the planets, etc., and these are often clearly indicated in the inscriptions recording royal grants. For the purpose of verification of dates, one requires

1. *Trav. Arch. Ser.*, Vol. I, p. 294. See also the Srirangam inscription (*Ep. Ind.*, Vol. XXIX, pp. 71 ff.) of Sadāśivarāya in which the Śaka year 1467 is expressed by the chronogram *setu-vandya* which gives *sa*=7, *ta*=6 *va*=4 and *ya*=1, i.e. 1467. See below, pp. 233 ff.

to have some knowledge about the nature of the Indian years, months, etc. The beginning of the years, which were either solar or lunar, was counted variously from the months of Kārttika, Caitra, Āṣāḍha or Śrāvaṇa while the months were counted differently as solar or lunar.

The ecliptic is divided into 12 *rāśis* or signs of the Zodiac, viz. (1) Meṣa, (2) Vṛṣa, (3) Mithuna, (4) Karkaṭa, (5) Siṁha, (6) Kanyā, (7) Tulā, (8) Vṛścika, (9) Dhanus, (10) Makara, (11) Kumbha, and (12) Mīna. The sun's passage from the beginning of Meṣa to the end of Mīna is called a *saura* (solar) year (*varṣa*, *saṁvatsara*, *vatsara*, etc.). Generally the length of the solar year is regarded as 365 days, 15 *ghaṭikās* or *daṇḍas*, 31 *palas* and 30 *vipalas*,[1] although there is some slight difference of opinion among astronomers on this point. The sun's passage from the beginning to the end of a *rāśi* is called a *saura-māsa* (solar month) and its entry into a new *rāśi* a *saṅkrānti* or *saṅkramaṇa*. The day on which the *saṅkrānti* falls is counted as the first day of the solar month in the Punjab while, if it falls in the night, the following day becomes the first day of the month. The system followed in the Tamil region is similar to that followed in the Punjab. But, in Bengal, the day following the *saṅkrānti* day is regarded as the first day of the month. This leads to considerable difference in the almanacs of various parts of the country.

The solar months are usually named after the particular *rāśi* through which the sun passes at the time, although the names of the lunar months are also often applied to them. The solar years are prevalent in Bengal and the Punjab and their neighbourhood as well as in the Tamil- and Malayāḷam-speaking areas. The solar month of Meṣa, with which the solar year begins, is called Vaiśākha in Bengal but Caitra (Cittirai) in the Tamil-speaking area.

There are generally between 29 and 32 days in a solar month and they are counted from 1 to 29, 30, 31 or 32 without

1. The *ghaṭikā* or *daṇḍa* is the one-sixtieth part of the day, i.e. about 24 minutes, while the *pala* is its one-sixtieth part and the *vipala* is one-sixtieth of the *pala*.

reference to a *tithi* or lunar day (i.e. one-thirtieth part of the whole lunation) of the dark or bright fortnight (*pakṣa*), even though the *tithis* are also counted for the observance of particular functions in the areas where the solar months are prevalent.[1]

A lunar month consists of two fortnights or *pakṣas*, viz. dark and bright. The fifteen *tithis* or lunar days of either of the dark or bright fortnight, called respectively the *kṛṣṇa* or *bahula* and the *śukla*, are counted from 1 to 15. In North India, the lunar month is generally counted as *Pūrṇimānta*, i.e. 'ending in the full-moon (i.e. sudi 15)' or lasting from Kṛṣna (i.e. badi) 1 to Śukla (i.e. sudi) 15, while, in the land to the south of the Narmadā, the lunar month is *Amānta*, i.e. it begins on Śukla (sudi) 1 and ends with the new-moon (i.e. badi 15).[2]

The twelve lunar months are named after the *nakṣatras* or lunar mansions on which the full-moon occurs in each one

1. The names of the solar months in Tamil and Bengali are as follows: (1) Meṣa—Cittirai, Vaiśākha; (2) Vṛṣabha—Vaikāsi, Jyaiṣṭha; (3) Mithuna—Āni, Āṣāḍha; (4) Karkaṭa—Āḍi, Śrāvaṇa: (5) Siṁha—Āvani, Bhādra: (6) Kanyā—Puraṭṭāśi (Purattādi), Āśvina; (7) Tulā—Aippaśi, Kārttika; (8) Vṛścika—Kārttigai, Mārgaśīrṣa; (9) Dhanus—Mārgaḷi, Pauṣa; (10) Makara—Tai, Māgha;(11) Kumbha—Māśi, Phālguna; (12) Mīna—Paṅguni, Caitra.

2.

Amānta	*Pakṣa*	*Pūrṇimānta*
Phālguna	Śukla	
	Kṛṣṇa	Caitra
Caitra	Śukla	
	Kṛṣṇa	Vaiśākha
Vaiśākha	Śukla	
	Kṛṣṇa	Jyaiṣṭha
Jyaiṣṭha	Śukla	
	Kṛṣṇa	Āṣāḍha
Āṣāḍha	Śukla	
	Kṛṣṇa	Śrāvaṇa
Śrāvaṇa	Śukla	
	Kṛṣṇa	Bhādrapada
Bhādrapada	Śukla	
	Kṛṣṇa	Āśvina
Āśvina	Śnkla	
	Kṛṣṇa	Kārttika
Kārttika	Śukla	
	Kṛṣṇa	Mārgaśīrṣa
Mārgaśīrṣa	Śukla	
	Krnṣa	Pauṣa
Pauṣa	Śukla	
	Kṛṣṇa	Māgha
Māgha	Śukla	
	Kṛṣṇa	Phālguna
	Śukla	

of them.[1] These are : (1) Caitra, (2) Vaiśākha, (3) Jyaiṣṭha, (4) Āṣāḍha, (5) Śrāvaṇa, (6) Bhādrapada, (7) Āśvina (also called Āśvayuja), (8) Kārttika, (9) Mārgaśīrṣa (also called Agrahāyana probably because the beginning of the year was once counted from it in some parts of the country), (10) Pauṣa, (11) Māgha, and (12) Phālguna.

The length of the lunar year made of twelve such months is regarded as 354 days, 22 *ghaṭikās* or *daṇḍas*, 1 *pala* and 24 *vipalas*, the year therefore being shorter than the solar year by 10 days, 56 *ghaṭikās* or *daṇḍas*, 30 *palas* and 6 *vipalas*. Thus 32 lunar months become roughly equal to 31 solar months. Since the *tithis* have considerable importance in the religious life of the people throughout the country, the lunar year is made equal to the solar year in the areas following the solar system by what may be called the luni-solar reckoning. According to this, the lunar month, in which the *saṅkrānti* (i.e. the sun's entry into a *rāśi*) does not occur, is called the *Adhika* or *Mala* month, while the lunar month witnessing two *saṅkrāntis* is regarded as the *Kṣaya* or *Nija* month. Medieval inscriptions sometimes mention *yogas* and *karaṇas* in the dates. The *yogas* (the word *yoga* meaning 'conjunction' used with reference to the astronomical association of the movements of the sun and the moon and noticed in some records)[2] are 27 in number; e. g. (1) Viṣkambha, (2) Prīti, (3) Āyuṣmat, (4) Saubhāgya, (5) Śobhana, (6) Atigaṇḍa, (7) Sukarman, (8) Dhṛti, (9) Śūla, (10) Gaṇḍa, (11) Vṛddhi, (12) Dhruva, (13) Vyāghāta; (14) Harṣaṇa, (15) Vajra, (16) Siddhi or Asṛja, (17) Vyātīpāta, (18) Varīyas, (19) Parigha, (20) Śiva, (21) Siddha, (22) Sādhya, (23) Śubha, (24) Śukla, (25) Brahman, (26) Aindra and (27) Vaidhṛti. The *karaṇas*, each of which indicate half of a *tithi*, are noticed in medieval inscriptions like

1. The *nakṣatras* are 27 in number, viz. (1) Aśvinī, (2) Bharaṇī, (3) Kṛttikā, (4) Rohiṇī, (5) Mṛgaśirā, (6) Ārdrā, (7) Punarvasu, (8) Puṣyā, (9) Aśleṣā, (10) Maghā, (11) Pūrva-Phalgunī, (12) Uttara-Phalgunī, (13) Hastā, (14) Citrā, (15) Svātī, (16) Viśākhā, (17) Anurādhā, (18) Jyeṣṭhā, (19) Mūlā, (20) Pūrv-Āṣāḍhā (21) Uttar-Āṣāḍhā, (22) Śravaṇā, (23) Dhaniṣṭhā, (24) Śatabhiṣā, (25) Pūrva-Bhādrapadā, (26) Uttara-Bhādrapadā, and (27) Revatī.

2. See, e. g., Bhandarkar's List, No. 27 dated Vikrama 898.

the Ajmer inscription of Vikrama 1210.[1] The *karaṇas* called (1) Bava, (2) Bālava, (3) Kaulava, (4) Taitila, (5) Gara, (6) Vaṇija and (7) Viṣṭi (Bhadrā or Kalyāṇī) make a cycle which are repeated for eight times covering 56 half *tithis* from the second half of śudi 1 to the first half of badi 14. The remaining four half *tithis* from the second half of badi 14 to the first half of śudi 1 are covered by the *karaṇas* : (8) Śakuni, (9) Catuṣpada, (10) Kintughna and (11) Nāga.

The conception of a week of seven days does not appear in very early Indian literature. As indicated above, the name of the week-day first occurs in an Indian epigraph of the last quarter of the 5th century A.D., and it is generally believed that the conception was borrowed by the Indians from Greek astronomers. As in the West, the Indian week-days are named after seven out of the nine *grahas* : (1) the sun (called Ravi, Āditya, etc.), (2) the moon (called Soma, Candra, etc.), (3) Mars (called Bhauma, Maṅgala, etc.), (4) Mercury (called Budha, etc.), (5) Jupiter (called Bṛhaspati, Suraguru, etc.), (6) Venus (called Śukra, Daityaguru, etc.), and (7) Saturn (called Śani, Śanaiścara, etc.). Thus Sunday is called Ravi-vāra, Āditya-vāra, etc.

From the nature of the Indian year and month discussed above, it will be seen that the verification of the dates of some records is beset with difficulties. By way of illustration, it may be pointed out that it is often difficult to determine whether the years quoted, even when they are referred to an era, are Kārttikādi, Caitrādi, Āṣāḍhādi or Śrāvaṇādi and whether the month is *Amānta* or *Pūrṇimānta*. It is also often unknown whether the regnal years of kings were counted exactly from the date of his accession or they were adjusted with the regular years of the almanac. Another difficulty is that the years were sometimes regarded as current though generally they were counted as expired.[2] But there is a greater difficulty which is the possibility of errors in the enumeration of the

1. See Bhandarkar's List, No. 289.

2. Sometimes the records use the words *pravartamāna* and *atīta* to indicate respectively the current and expired years of a reckoning.

dates. There is no doubt that such errors account for a large number of irregular dates in the inscriptions of various ages in different parts of the country.

Some of the errors in the dates of Indian records have to be ascribed to the astrologer at the villages and courts.[1] With the innumerable copies of printed almanacs, called *Pañjī*, *Pañjikā* or *Pañcāṅga*, of various types in each one of the numerous regional languages, available to the literate people in all parts of India, it is impossible in these days of advanced literacy in the country to realise the great importance of the astrologer in Indian social life before the 19th century.[2] There is epigraphic evidence to show that the office of the village astrologer was an institution recognised by the State during Hindu rule.[3] That the astrologers at the royal courts of ancient and medieval India were often not competent astronomers is also clearly shown by the Sarkho plates[4] of Kalacuri Ratnadeva II, dated 1128 A.D.

There is a tendency among a section of epigraphists to view the genuineness of an inscription bearing an irregular date with suspicion. But it seems to be a wrong approach to the problem since the irregularity in the dates may be due to factors absolutely unconnected with the question of the genuineness of the documents. Many cases of irregularity were no doubt due to mistakes in the calculation of incompetent astrologers and the erroneous method of calculation

1. See *IHQ*, Vol. XXVIII, pp. 342 ff.

2. See L. B. Day, *Bengal Peasant Life*, Chapter VIII; Dubois, *Hindu Manners and Customs*, 3rd ed., pp. 135-36. Cf. Kane, *History of Dharmaśāstra*, Vol. III, p. 126.

3. Cf. T. V. Mahalingam, *Administration and Social Life under Vijayanagara*, pp. 218-19. The Brahmanical family name Joṣī (Sanskrit *Jyotiṣin*), found in various parts of India, seems to speak of royal recognition for the families of the astrologers in question. The family name Praharāja (Sanskrit *Prahararāja*), found among Oriya Brāhmaṇas, was originally a title conferred on an astrologer by the king.

4. *Ep. Ind.*, Vol. XXII, pp. 159 ff. It is stated that the astronomers at the court of the Kalacuri king were following wrong methods of calculation, as a result of which their predictions relating to eclipses hardly came true. A good astronomer named Padmanābha discovered the mistakes in their methods, made the required *bīja-saṁskāra* and correctly calculated the exact time of a lunar eclipse. Padmanābha was rewarded by the king for his success.

followed in the preparation of the almanacs.[1] Varying local traditions regarding the astrological character of particular days, *tithis* or moments may have also contributed to the difference referred to. Another cause of irregularity in the dates of royal documents seems to have been the fact that, in some cases at least, the court astrologer had reason to fabricate an auspicious moment when really there was none. This was hardly difficult for him to do since his royal master and most of the latter's courtiers were blessedly ignorant of astronomy and had to depend entirely on the astrologer for the determination of an appropriate moment for a particular undertaking. Of course there may be other possible reasons for an irregularity creeping into the date of a royal charter.

2. *Numbers expressed by Words*

The Indian students of astronomy, mathematics and many other subjects generally composed their works in verse. The nature of the works in some of these subjects necessitated the repeated mention of numbers, e.g., in the setting and solution of the problems of an arithmetical sum. There was, however, generally only one word in Sanskrit to indicate a particular number. Since the repeated mention of a word in the same sense was regarded as a bad style of composition, and such a word would often not fit in the metre of a stanza, the authors required a large number of words for indicating the same number. A convention therefore gradually developed, according to which ordinary words that can somehow be associated with particular numbers were used to imply those numbers. Thus all the Sanskrit words meaning 'the hand' came to be used to indicate 2, since man has only two hands. Similarly words meaning 'the arrow' were employed in the

1. The almanacs now published in different parts of India or even in the same part of the country do not exactly tally with one another owing principally to the difference in the method of calculation followed or in the approach to particular astronomical problems. If the details of a date do not tally with those quoted by modern astronomers (e.g. L. D. Swamikannu Pillai in his *Indian Ephimeris*), it may be irregular technically speaking, even though it was quite regular according to a particular almanac from which the details were quoted in the inscription.

sense of 5 because Kāma, the Indian god of love, is represented in tradition as armed with five arrows of flowers. When there were more than one tradition regarding the number associated with a particular object, only one of them was adopted. Thus, even though traditionally the Vedas are regarded either as three or as four and the seas either as four or as seven in number, the early Indian astronomers and mathematicians used the words indicating both the Vedas and the sea to indicate 4 only. But uncritical authors of the medieval age are sometimes found to have violated this old convention and introduced an amount of confusion in the system. Thus, in some cases, we notice the use of a word for 'the sea' to imply both the numbers 4 and 7.[1] The name of a metre was often used to indicate a number according to the number of syllables in a foot of a stanza in that metre. Thus the word *anuṣṭubh,* the name of a metre with eight syllables in a foot, implied 8. But there was want of complete uniformity since in some cases the number of syllables in all the four feet of a stanza was counted; e.g., Jagatī, a metre with 12 syllables in a foot, was used by late authors in the sense of both 12 and 48. When such a word-numeral was a compound of two words, often either the first or the second member of the compounds was used to indicate the number in question.

In the early astronomical and arithmetical works, single such words are generally used to indicate particular number. Piṅgala, Varāhamihira and later authors use such words with numerical meanings as grouped in *Dvandva* compounds. But, while Piṅgala's *ved-artu-samudrāḥ* means '4 or 6 or 4',

1. The polygraphic (multiscriptal) inscription of king Jaya-Pratāpamalla of Nepal is dated in *Nepāl-ābde yug-ābdhau muni-gaṇa-sahite* given in figures as Saṁva (Saṁvat) 774, thus equating *abdhi* (sea) to 7. The exact date of the record is quoted as Friday, Māgha-sudi 1 (13th January 1654 A.D.). See *Journ. As.*, Tome CCXLV, 1957, p. 338 and Plate. Cf. Śaka 1748 = Bengal San 1233, the date of the composition of Jagaddurlabha's *Uddhavacamatkāra* given in the colophon of the work (*Bhāratavarṣa*, Bengali, Śrāvaṇa, 1365 B.S., p. 173) respectively as *aṣṭa-sāgara-payonidhi-candra* and *netra-Rāma-yuga-candra*. The word *netra* = 3 according to the Bengali convention and *yuga* = 2 (not 4 as usual). Indeed it would have been difficult to determine the date of the composition of the work, in spite of the years in both the eras being quoted, unless it was separately stated that the work was completed on the 12th Caitra, 1233 B. S. (24th March 1827 A.D.). The Bengal San has been referred to as *yāvanika* and *ādhunika*. See below, pp. 230 ff.

Varāhamihira's *kha-kh-āṣṭi-yamāḥ* would mean '0 and 0 and 16 and 2" to be read actually from right to left as 21600.[1] This principle of *aṅkānāṁ vāmato gatiḥ*, 'the movement of the numerals from right to left', is generally followed in the dates expressed in inscriptions in word-numerals although there are a few exceptions especially in late records.[2] Such numerical words are sometimes found also in the ordinary enumeration of a number in words; cf. Śaka 1172 indicated by *dvisaptaty-adhika-Śiva-śata*,[3] in which *Śiva* means 'eleven.'

We give below an indication as to the words that were used to express particular numbers.[4]

0=*śūnya*, 'the empty space of the sky' (*kha*, *gagana*, *ambara*, *abhra*, *viyat*, *nabhas*, *antarikṣa*, *Viṣṇupada*, *ākāśa*, *ananta*, *vyoman*, *dyu*, etc.), *pūrṇa*, *vindu*, etc. The word *randhra*, which generally means 9, is used to imply 0 (cypher) in a few cases by late authors.

1=*ādi*, 'the moon' (*śaśin*, *indu*, *vidhu*, *candra*, *śītāṁśu*, *śītaraśmi*, *soma*, *śaśāṅka*, *sudhāṁśu*, *kṣapeśvara*, *Atrinayanaja*, *mṛgāṅka*, *candramas*, etc.), 'the earth' (*bhū*, *bhūmi*, *kṣiti*, *dharā*, *urvarā*, *go*, *vasundharā*, *pṛthvī*, *kṣmā*, *dharaṇī* *vasudhā*, *ilā*, *ku*, *mahī*, *dhātrī*, *jagatī* *kṣoṇī*, *kṣauṇī*, *avanī*, etc.), *ajba*, *raśmi*, *rūpa*, *Pitāmaha* (but cf. *Brahman* meaning 9), *nāyaka*, *tanu*, *jana*, *Airāvata* (sometimes wrongly *hastin*, etc., which really mean 8), *Uccaiśravas* (sometimes wrongly *aśva*, etc., which really mean 7), 'the single eye of Śukra' (*Śukra-netra*, etc.), *Dhruva*, *ātman*, *Parabrahman*, *Mūlaprakṛti*, etc. *Jagatī* is sometimes used to mean 12 and 48 and *go* 9.

2=*yama*, *yamala*, *yugala*, *dvaya*, *yugma*, *dvandva*, *Aśvin* (sometimes also *Āśvina*), *Nāsatya*, *Dasra*, 'the eye' (*locana*, *netra*, *akṣi*, *dṛṣṭi*, *cakṣus*, *nayana*, *īkṣaṇa*, *ambaka*, etc.), the words meaning other limbs which are in pairs such as

1. Cf. Bühler, op. cit., p. 86.
2. See, e.g., Bhandarkar's List, No. 620.
3. *A.R. Ep.*, May 1890, p. 2.
4. See Bühler, op. cit., pp. 84 ff.; Ojha, op. cit., p. 120; Filliozat, op. cit., pp. 708-09; Sewell, *Eclipses of the Moon in India*, pp. 7-8. A few words have been added from other sources, especially epigraphic.

bāhu, kara, karṇa, kuca, oṣṭha, gulpha, jānu, etc., *pakṣa, kuṭumba, ravi-candra, grahaṇa, nadī-kūla, Rāma-nandana, viṣuvat, ayana,* etc. In the Bengal region, the word *netra,* 'the eye', is generally taken to stand for 'Śiva's eyes' and therefore in the sense of 3. Sometimes *yuga*=2 instead of 4, and *pakṣa*=15.

3=*Rāma, guṇa, tri-guṇa,* 'the world' (*loka, jagat, tri-jagat, bhuvana,* etc., some of which are sometimes also used for 14), 'the fire' (*agni, vahni, pāvaka, vaiśvānara, dahana, tapana, udarcis, hutāśana, jvalana, śikhin, kṛśānu, hotṛ, anala,* etc.), *kāla, tri-kāla, tri-gata,* 'Śiva's eyes' (*trinetra, Hara-nayana Śaṅkar-ākṣi, Īśa-dṛś,* etc.), *sahodara, doṣa, nāḍī, śūla, gaṅgā-mārga, viṣṭapa, mūrti, vacana,* 'Daśaratha's wives', etc. For *śakti*=3, see *Ep. Ind.,* Vol. XIX, p. 166, and *guṇa*=6 below. *Veda* rarely indicates 3, though it really stands for 4. *Tapana* in the sense of 'the sun' would mean 'twelve'.

4='the Veda' (*veda, śruti,* etc.), 'the sea' (*sāgara, arṇava, amburāśi, abdhi, jaladhi, jalanidhi, ambhonidhi, vārinidhi, ambudhi, jalāśaya, sindhu, vāridhi,* etc., later used also in the sense of 7), *kendra, varṇa, āśrama, yuga* (rarely 2), *turya, kṛta, aya, āya, bandhu, koṣṭha,* 'Brahman's faces' (*Brahm-āsya, Caturānana-vadana,* etc.),' Viṣṇu's arms' (*Hari-bāhu,* etc.), *vyūha, sen-āṅga, khaṭvā-pāda, go-stana, puruṣ-ārtha,* etc. For *gati* in the sense of 4, cf. *Ep. Ind.,* Vol. XXV, p. 336. The words *diś, diśā,* etc., meaning 10, are sometimes found in the sense of 4. *Jala* (for *jaladhi*), *dadhi* (for *udadhi*) and *vanadhi* (mistake for *vāridhi* ?) are also counted in the same sense.

5='the arrow' (*bāṇa, śara, sāyaka, iṣu, viśikha, kalamba, mārgaṇa,* etc.), *bhūta, mahābhūta, parvan, prāṇa,* 'Pāṇḍu's sons' (*Pāṇḍava,* etc.), *artha, viṣaya, indriya, ratna* (also 9 or 14), 'Śiva's faces' (*Rudr-āsya, Tryakṣa-mukha,* etc.), 'the sins' (*pātaka, mahāpāpa,* etc.), *Purāṇa-lakṣaṇa, pallava, gavya, tanmātra, kṣāra, lavaṇa,* 'the sacrifices' (*mahāyajña,* etc.), *tattva* (generally used to indicate 25), etc. Words meaning 'a son' (*suta, putra,* etc., probably meaning Pāṇḍu's sons) and *tata* (for *tattva* ?) are also counted in the same sense.

6=*rasa, aṅga, kāya, darśana* (meaning the 6 *darśanas* and not *dṛṣṭi*, 'the eye', meaning 2), *rāga*, 'the enemy' (*ari*, *ripu*, etc.), *śāstra*, *mala*, *tarka*, *kāraka*, *ṛtu*, *māsārdha* (cf. *māsa*=12; but *pakṣa*=2), 'Karttikeya's faces' (*Kumār-āsya*, etc.), etc. In late medieval records, the word *guṇa* is sometimes used to indicate 6 instead of 3. Cf. *A. R. Ep.*, 1957-58, No. B 68.

7='the hill or mountain' (*naga*, *aga*, *bhūbhṛt*, *parvata*, *śaila*, *adri*, *giri*, *bhūdhara*, *mahīdhara*, etc.), *ṛṣi*, *muni*, *Atri*, *vāra*, *svara*, *dhātu*, 'a horse' (*aśva*, *turaga*, *turaṅgama*, *vājin*, etc.), *chandas*, *dhī*, *kalatra*, *dvīpa*, etc. *Loka*, *pātāla*, *sāgara* and *Sagara* are also counted in the same sense.

8=*Vasu*, 'an elephant' confused with 'a snake' (*ahi*, *nāga*, *gaja*, *dantin*, *diggaja*, *hastin*, *mātaṅga*, *kuñjara*, *dvipa*, *sarpa*, etc.), *takṣan*, *siddhi*, *bhūti*, *Anuṣṭubh*, *maṅgala*, *Dikpāla*, *tanu*, *yāma*, etc. *naga* (really 7), *mūrti* (cf. *rūpa*=1) and *tanu* (really 1) are soemtimes also counted in the same sense. *Naga* is used in the sense of 'eight' in *Ep. Ind.*, Vol. XXXV, p. 140.

9=*aṅka*, *Nanda*, *nidhi*, *nidhāna*, *randhra*, *chidra*, *dvāra*, 'the planet' (*graha*, etc.), *go* (also 1), *pavana*, *Bṛhatī*, *varṣa*, *khaṇḍa*, 'the god Brahman' (*Aja*, *Abjagarbha*, etc.), *ratna* (also 5 or 14), etc.

10='the quarters' (*diś*, *diśā*, *āśā*, *kakubh*, etc.), *aṅguli* (also used to indicate 20), *paṅkti*, 'Rāvaṇa's heads' (*Rāvaṇa-śiras*, etc.) *avatāra*, *karman*, *la-kāra*, etc.

11='the god Rudra' (*Rudra*, *Śiva*, *Īśvara*, *Hara*, *Īśa*, *Bhava*, *Bharga*, *Śūlin*, *Mahādeva*, etc.), *akṣauhiṇī*, *lābha*, *Triṣṭubh*, etc.

12='the sun' (*ravi*, *sūrya*, *sahasrāṁśu*, *arka*, *mārtaṇḍa*, *dyu-maṇi*, *bhānu*, *āditya*, *divākara*, etc.), *māsa*, *rāśi*, *vyaya*, *saṅkrānti*, *Jagatī* (sometimes used also in the senses of 1 and 48), 'the eyes or arms of Kārttikeya' (*Senānī-netra*, *Ṣaṇ-mukha-bāhu*, etc.), etc.

13=*Viśvedevāḥ* (sometimes contracted to *Viśva*), *Kāma*, *Manmatha*, *Atijagatī*, *aghoṣa*, etc.

14=*Manu*, *vidyā*, 'the god Indra' (*Indra*, *Śakra*, etc.), *loka* (sometimes also used to indicate 3), etc. *Pūrva* [of the Jains] and *ratna* (also 5 or 9) are sometimes counted in the list of words of the same sense.

15=*tithi*, *ghasra*, *dina*, *ahan*, *pakṣa* (sometimes also used to imply 2), etc.

16='a king' (*nṛpa*, *bhūpa*, etc.), *Aṣṭi*, *kalā*, etc.

17=*Atyaṣṭi*.

18=*Dhṛti*.

19=*Atidhṛti*.

20=*nakha*, *aṅguli* (also used to indicate 10), *Kṛti*, 'Rāvaṇa's arms' (*Rāvaṇa-bhuja*, etc.), etc.

21=*Prakṛti*, *svarga*, *Utkṛti* (generally used in the sense of 26).

22=*Akṛti*, *jāti*, *Kṛtin*.

23=*Vikṛti*.

24=*Gāyatrī*, *Jina*, *Arhat*, *Siddha*, etc.

25=*tattva* (rarely used to indicate 5).

26=*Utkṛti* (rarely used to indicate 21).

27='the stars' (*nakṣatra*, *uḍa*, *bha*, etc.).

32='the teeth' (*danta*, *rada*, etc.).

33='the gods' (*amara*, *deva*, *sura*, *tridaśa*, etc.).

34=*tāna* (generally used in the sense of 49).

40=*naraka*.

48=*Jagatī* (sometimes used to indicate 1 and 12).

49=*tāna* (cf. its use in the sense of 34), *vāyu*.

100=*Dhārtarāṣṭra*, *puruṣ-āyus*, *abja-dala*, *Śakra-yajña*, etc.

1000='the mouths of the Ganges' (*Jāhnavī-vaktra*, etc.) 'Śeṣa's heads' (*Śeṣa-śīrṣa*, etc.), 'the Sun's rays' (*Ravi-bāṇa*, etc.), 'Arjuna's arms' (*Arjuna-kara*, etc.), 'Indra's eyes' (*Indra-dṛṣṭi*, etc.), etc.

3. *Numbers expressed by Letters*

The celebrated astronomer Āryabhaṭa, who wrote his Āryabhaṭīya at Pāṭaliputra in the Kaliyuga year 3600 (499 A.D.), used a system of representing numbers by letters of the alphabet.[1] The 25 consonants from *ka* to *ma* indicated respectively the numerals 1 to 25. The 8 letters from *ya* to *ha* similarly indicated the numbers 30, 40, 50, 60, 70, 80, 90 and 100 respectively. The vowels *i*, *u*, *ṛ* and *ḷ* (short or long) and the diphthongs *e*, *ai*, *o* and *au* were added to the letters to indicate the multiplication of a number by 10^2 to

1. Cf. Filliozat, op. cit., p. 188. See above, p. 222.

10^{16}, i.e. the addition of two, four, six, eight, ten, twelve, fourteen and sixteen zeroes after a number indicated by a consonant. Thus *ga*=3, *gi*=300, *gu*=30000, *ya*=30, *yi*=3000, *yu*=300000, *ri*=4000, *giri* (or *gri*)=4300 (300+4000), etc.

A system developed in South India was called Kaṭapayādi. In this, the 10 letters from *ka* to *ña* had the value respectively of the numbers 1 to 9 and 0. The same was the case with the following 10 letters from *ṭa* to *na*. The five letters from *pa* to *ma* indicated the numbers 1 to 5, and the 9 letters from *ya* to *ḻa* had the value of the numbers 1 to 9 respectively. In the formation of chronograms, vowels were added to the consonants without affecting the numerical value of the letters and two or more consonants could be combined in conjuncts in which only the last consonant of a ligature had the numerical value. But the principle of *vāma-gati*, i.e. the turning round of the sum, was observed in the determination of the value of a word. Thus *ga*=3 and *ja*=8; but the word *gaja*=83 and not 38. The chronogram *khago=ntyān=meṣam=āpa* would give *kha*=2, *ga*=3, *ya*=1, *ma*=5, *ṣa*=6, *ma*=5 and *pa*=1, i.e. 1565132.[1]

The Nannādi system popular in Kerala was based on the following lines :

na-nna-nya-ṣka-jhra-hā(ha)-gra-pra-dre-ma |
tha-li(la)-pla-ba-tra(tru)-tri-ca-ṇa-ña ||[2]

The 10 letters of the first line had the value respectively of the numbers from 1 to 10 while the others in the second line represented 20, 30, 40, 50, 60, 70, 80, 90 and 100. This system was generally employed in paginating manuscripts.

In a simpler system prevalent in South India, the letters of the alphabet from *ka* to *ḻa* represented respectively the numbers 1 to 34, *kā* to *ḻā* the numbers 35 to 68, *ki* to *ḻi* the numbers 69 to 102, and so on.

There was a similar system of paginating manuscripts prevalent in Ceylon. According to this *ka*, *kā*, *ki*, *kī* *ku*,

1. See Bühler, op. cit., p. 87; Ojha, op. cit., 122 ff. See above, p. 222.
2. Cf. *JRAS*, 1896, p. 790; *Trav. Arch. Ser.*, Vol. II, pp. 132. ff.

kū, kṛ, kṝ, kḷ, kḹ, ke, kai, ko, kau, kaṁ and *kaḥ* had the value respectively of 1 to 16. Similarly 16 *akṣaras* formed by *kha khā*, etc., had the value of the numbers from 17 to 32. The 16 *akṣaras* associated with *ḻa*, the last consonant of the alphabet, thus represented the numbers 529 to 544. Numbers beyond 544 could be expressed by beginning again as 2 *ka*, 2 *kā*, and so on. In Burma, the same system was used with the omission of *ṛ, ṝ, ḷ* and *ḹ*, so that *ka* to *kaḥ* would indicate the numbers 1 to 12.

4. *Regnal Reckoning and Connected Problems*[1]

The earliest documents of the indigenous kings of India bear no trace of the use of any era. Many of them contain no date at all. But some of the official records of the independent rulers as well as those belonging to their officials and subordinates and persons residing in their dominions are dated. The date is, however, always expressed in the king's regnal years. A few of the numerous instances may be cited.

(1) Rock Edict III of Aśoka (c. 272-32 B.C.) —*dbādasa-vās-ābhisitena mayā idaṁ āñapitaṁ* (Girnar text),[2] "I have ordered this when 12 years [have passed after] my installation [on the throne]."

(2) Besnagar inscription of the time of Bhāgabhadra (c. close of the 2nd century B.C.)—*raño Kāsīputrasa Bhāgabhadrasa trātārasa vasena catudasena rājena vadhamānasa*,[3] 'when king Kāśīputra Bhāgabhadra, the saviour, was prospering with his sovereignty (or, realm) for 14 years (i.e., when 14 years of his reign had passed).'

(3) Pabhosa inscription of the time of Udāka (c. close

1. See *Vikrama Volume*, ed. R. K. Mookerji, pp. 557 ff.; *Ep. Ind.*, Vol. XXX, pp. 5-6; above, p. 219.

2. *Select Inscriptions*, p. 19. Cf. the same date in Rock Edict IV (ibid., p. 22) and other dates similarly expressed in Rock Edict V (ibid., p. 23: Mansehra—*tredaśa-vaṣ-abhisitena maya dhrama-mahamatra kaṭa*); Rock Edict VIII (ibid. p. 28 : Girnar—*Devānaṁpriyo Piyadasi rājā dasa-vas-ābhisito saṁto ayāya Saṁbodhiṁ*); Rock Edict XIII (ibid., pp. 35-36: Shahbazgarhi—*aṭha-vaṣa-abhisitasa Devanapriasa Priadraśisa Kaliga vijita*); etc.

3. Ibid., p. 91.

of the 1st century B.C.)—*Ūdākasa dasama-savacchare,*[1] 'in the tenth [regnal] year of Ūdāka.'

(4) Hāthigumphā inscription of Khāravela (c. close of the 1st century B.C.)—*abhisitamato ca padhame vase,*[2] 'during the first regnal year of the installed [monarch].'

(5) Nasik inscription of Gautamīputra Śātakarṇi (c. 106-30 A.D.)—*savachare* 18 *vāsa-pakhe* 2 *divase* 1,[3] 'on the 1st day of the 2nd fortnight of the rainy season in the 18th [regnal] year.'

(6) Nagarjunikonda inscription of Ehuvula Śāntamūla (c. 280-335 A.D.)—*Ehuvula-Caṁtamūlasa saṁvacharaṁ bitiyaṁ gimha-pakkhaṁ chaṭhaṁ* 6 *divasoṁ dasamaṁ* 10,[4] '10th day of the 6th fortnight of summer in the second regnal year of Ehuvula Śāntamūla.'

A study of the above and numerous other instances of the kind would suggest that originally the Indian custom was to refer to the past or current regnal year of the king without specification of the day. A little later, the day is found mentioned in some parts of India with reference to the specific fortnight of a season. The year seems to have been divided into 3 seasons, viz., summer (*grīṣma*), the rains (*varṣā*) and winter (*hemanta*) each consisting of 8 fortnights.[5] The seasons ended with the *Cāturmāsī* which was usually identified with the full-moon *tithi* of the months of Āṣāḍha, Kārttika and Phālguna. According to pupular tradition, summer consisted of the *pūrṇimānta* months of Caitra, Vaiśākha, Jyaiṣṭha and Āṣāḍha; the rains of Śrāvaṇa, Bhādra, Āśvina and Kārttika; and winter of Mārgaśīrṣa, Pauṣa, Māgha and Phālguna.[6] A South

1. Ibid., p. 98.
2. Ibid., p. 207.
3. Ibid., p. 192. Cf. similar other dates in the other records of the time of the Śātavāhanas (ibid., p. 195 : *Pulumāvisa savachare satame* 7 *gimha-pakhe pacame* 5 *divase pathame* 1; etc.).
4. Ibid., p. 229. For other dates, cf. *Ep. Ind.*, Vol. XX, pp. 1 ff.; Vol. XXXV, pp. 1 ff.
5. Cf., e.g., Lüder's List, No. 1186: *hemaṁtāna pakho* 7 *divasa* 1.
6. *Select Inscriptions*, p. 63, p. 119 note, p. 134 note. The seasons are often counted as six as follows (cf. *Amarakoṣa*, Kālavarga, v. 21): (1) Vasanta or Madhu=Caitra-Vaiśākha; (2) Grīṣma or Śuci=Jyaiṣṭha-Āṣāḍha; (3) Varṣā or Nabhas=Śrāvaṇa-Bhādrapada; (4) Śarad=Āśvina-Kārttika; (5) Hemanta or Sahas=Mārgaśīrṣa-Pauṣa; (6) Śīta, Śiśira or Tapas= Māgha-Phālguna. But sometimes Vasanta is regarded as consisting of Phālguna and Caitra instead of Caitra and Vaiśākha, and the other seasons are counted accordingly.

Indian epigraph of c. 300 A.D.[1] suggests the later inclusion of *śarad*, autumn, in the list of seasons in some parts of the country.

The dates found in the earliest records of the indigenous kings of India thus point to the absence of the custom of dating royal documents in the years of an era and also to the non-existence of any popular era in ancient India. There are, however, some Indian eras which have their epochs falling before the 4th century B.C. These are the Kali-yuga era of 3102 B.C., the Śrī-Harṣa era of 457 B.C. referred to by Al-Bīrūnī and the Parinirvāṇa eras of the Buddhists and the Jains. Purāṇic passages like the one giving the intervening period between the birth of Parikṣit and the accession of Mahāpadma Nanda as 1015 or 1050 or 1500[2] years no doubt suggest that the chroniclers of ancient Indian historical traditions attempted to base their chronological scheme on such important events as the birth of Parikṣit (placed by some authorities immediately after the battle of Kurukṣetra and at the beginning of the Kali-yuga) and the accession of the great empire-builder Mahāpadma Nanda. But the facts that the chroniclers do not always begin their computation from a point near about the supposed beginning of the Kali-yuga and that there is no uniformity among the traditions go to show that the reckoning from the starting of the Kali age (which itself belongs to the domain of mythology, the *yuga* division being unknown to very early works) was not a regular, far less a popular, era. The contemporaneity of the last Nanda king with Alexander (336-23 B.C.) and the Puranic traditions regarding the predecessors of the Mauryas suggest that Mahāpadma Nanda is not to be assigned to a period much earlier than 400 B.C. Different versions of the Puranic tradition quoted above thus place the birth of Parikṣit (and therefore the beginning of the Kali age) 1015 or 1050 or 1500 years

1. Lüder's List, No. 1196. Cf. *sarada-pakkhaṁ bitiyam divasaṁ paḍamaṁ*; cf. also *Successors of the Sātavāhanas*, p. 223.

2. Pargiter, *Puranik Texts of the Dynasties of the Kali Age*, p. 58; Raychaudhuri, *Pol. Hist. Anc. Ind.*, 4th ed., pp. 25-26.

before that date, i.e., about 1415 B.C. or 1450 B.C. or 1900 B.C. According to the evidence of the Aihole inscription[1] (634 A.D.) and certain other sources, however, the first year of the Kali-yuga corresponds to 3102-01 B.C. Another tradition, supported by authorities including Varāhamihira[2] and Kalhaṇa,[3] says that the battle of Kurukṣetra (and therefore the birth of Parikṣit) occurred 653 years later than the beginning of the Kali age, i.e. about 2449 B.C. Thus, whatever may have been the value attached by Purāṇic chroniclers to the event of Parikṣit's birth, there was apparently no regular and uniform reckoning from that chronological point. As to the Kali-yuga era of 3102 B.C., scholars have satisfactorily demonstrated that it is not a real historical era, but was invented by Indian astronomers for the purposes of their calculations some 35 centuries after that date.[4] The use of Al-Bīrūnī's Śrī-Harṣa era of 457 B.C.[5] is unknown to Indian epigraphic and literary records; but the fact that its epoch is just 400 years earlier than that of the Vikrama-saṁvat may suggest that this reckoning also was probably invented by astronomers for the purposes of calculations, although Al-Bīrūnī's statement really appears to be based on a wrong information. The existence of a Maurya era starting from the fourth century B.C. was suggested by some scholars on the basis of a wrong reading and interpretation of a passage in the Hāthigumphā inscription[6] of Khāravela.

Al-Bīrūnī does not mention the Buddhist and Jain Parinirvāṇa reckonings apparently because he never heard of them. But there is evidence to show that the Buddhists had a sort of rough reckoning calculated from the Buddha's death. It is however to be remembered that, in ancient India, the dates of this reckoning were usually referred to not by individual years, but by centuries. A few instances may be noticed.

1. *Ep. Ind.*, Vol. VI, p. 7.
2. *Bṛhatsaṁhitā*, XIII. 3.
3. *Rājataraṅgiṇī*, I. 51-56.
4. Cf. Fleet in *JRAS*, 1911, p. 479.
5. Sachau, *Alberuni's India*, II, p. 7.
6. *Select Inscriptions*, p. 210 and note 15.

(1) The *Milindapañha*[1] on the date of Milinda usually identified with the Indo-Greek king Menander—*parinibbāṇato paṁca-vassa-sate atikkaṁte*, 'at a time when 500 years elapsed from the death of the Buddha,' i.e. in the sixth century (between 501 and 600 years) after the Buddha's Parinirvāṇa.

(2) The *Laṅkāvatārasūtra*[2] on the date of Vyāsa, the Bhāratas (viz. the Kauravas and Pāṇḍavas), and the Nandas—*mayi nirvṛte varṣa-śate*, '100 years [after] my (the Buddha's) death,' i.e. between 101 and 200 years after the Parinirvāṇa.

(3) Paramārtha's *Life of Vasubandhu* (6th century A.D.)[3] on the date of the Sāṅkhya philosophers Vṛṣagaṇa (or Vārṣagaṇya) and Vindhyavāsa, a rival of Vasubandhu's teacher Buddhamitra and a contemporary of king Vikramāditya of Ayodhyā—'in the 900 years' (i.e. between the years 901 and 1000) after the Buddha's Parinirvāṇa.

(4) The same work[4] on the date of Aśvaghoṣa—'in the 500 years' (i.e. between the years 501 and 600) after the Parinirvāṇa.

(5) Tradition recorded by Hiuen-tsang[5] about the date of Kaniṣka—'400 years (i.e. in the 5th century between the years 401 and 500) after my (the Buddha's) decease.'

(6) Tradition recorded by the same authority[6] about the date of Vasubandhu's teacher Manoratha and king Vikramāditya of Śrāvastī—'within the 1000 years (i.e. in the 11th century between the years 1001 and 1100) after the Buddha's decease.'

The indication of the dates of the Buddhist reckoning in ancient India only by centuries has to be coupled with the fact that a large number of different epochs of the Parinirvāṇa is recognised in different parts of the world[7] and with the

1. Trenckner, *Milindapañho*, p. 3.
2. *JRAS*, 1905, p. 835.
3. Ibid., p. 51 and note.
4. Ibid., p. 52.
5. Watters, *On Yuan Chwang's Travels in India*, Vol. I, p. 203.
6. Ibid., p. 211.
7. S. C. Vidyabhushan (*Buddhadeva*, p. xi) notices the Ceylonese tradition of 543 B.C. (or 544 B.C.), a Japanese tradition of 947 B.C., a Tibetan tradition of 433 B.C. and a Chinese tradition of 770 B.C. The Cantonese dotted record suggesting 486 B.C. is now usually relied on by scholars.

absurd chronological position created by such traditons as those assigning Kaniṣka to the 5th and Menander to the 6th century after the Buddha's death. These facts show that the use of the Parinirvāṇa reckoning was limited within the Buddhist church and that it was never used as a popular era in ancient India. The absence of any use of the reckoning in the records of the early Indian Buddhists also points to the same direction.[1] Some scholars, however, believe that the Minor Rock Edict I of Aśoka refers to year 256 of the Buddhist Parinirvāṇa era,[2] although they are unable to explain why Aśoka used the era only in one of his many records which are usually dated according to his regnal reckoning. The theory is based entirely on misunderstanding. There can hardly be any doubt about the interpretation of the passage in question, if only the different versions of the record are read together. The explanation of the number 256 is clearly given in the Sahasram version where we have *duve-sapaṁnā-lāti-satā vivuthā ti* 256[3] (=*dvi-ṣaṭpañcāśad-rātri-śate vyuṣitaḥ* [*aham*] = *iti*—256). It will be seen that 256 was the number of nights which, as the word *vivāsa* of the Rupnath version[4] proves beyond doubt, Aśoka passed away from the capital apparently in connection with a *dharma-yātrā* (pilgrimage). Thus the Buddha-Parinirvāṇa era is entirely unknown to the early period of Indian epigraphy. The Jain ecclesiastical reckoning has even less claim than the Buddhist one to be taken as anything like a regular era in the early history of India.[5]

The absence of any trace of the use of an era in the dated records of the early indigenous kings of India has to be considered along with the fact that the earliest use of the regular

1. The Chronicles of Ceylon use the reckoning as an era. In India, however, the Nirvāṇa reckoning is used as an era only in the medieval period; cf. the Gayā inscription of Aśokacalla (Bhandarkar's List, No. 1459).

2. Cf. Bhandarkar, *Aśoka*, 2nd ed., p. 372.

3. *Select Inscriptions*, p. 51 note; p. 52 note; *Maski Inscription of Aśoka*, pp. 29-30.

4. *Select Inscriptions*, p. 51.

5. There is really no mention of this era in the early Brāhmī inscription from Barli. Cf. Ojha, *Bharatiyā Prācīn Lipimālā*, p. 2; *JBRS*, Vol. XXXVII, Parts 1-2, pp. 34-38; Vol. XL, Part 1, pp. 8 ff.

era in India is noticed in the epigraphic and numismatic records of foreigners. The two facts together would doubtless point to the extraneous origin of the custom of dating records according to the years of an era. It seems very probable that the use of the era in royal as well as private records was introduced and popularised in India by kings belonging to non-Indian extraction such as the Scytho-Parthians and the Kuṣāṇas.

In connection with the question of regnal reckoning, it has to be pointed out that some royal families (e.g. the Coḻas and Pāṇḍyas of South India, the Pālas and Candras of Bengal, the Brahmapāla kings of Assam and many others) dated their records in regnal years even when the use of an era was quite popular in the neighbouring territories. The influence of local conservatism explains the fact that, in spite of the introduction of the Gupta era in Bengal and Assam, later ruling families of those areas resumed the practice of dating charters in the regnal reckoning.[1]

There is a peculiarity of the regnal years quoted in early Pāṇḍya inscriptions as they generally mention two numbers to indicate a particular year, e.g., 4+9, 6+4, etc.[2] At first sight, this system appears to be explained by the fact that the predecessor and his successor on the Pāṇḍya throne often ruled conjointly for some time and therefore the 13th regnal year indicated by 4+9 may show that the king in question was ruling conjointly with his predecessor till his 4th regnal year and the date in question actually belongs to the 9th year of his rule as the successor of his predecessor. But there are difficulties in accepting such a suggestion. Sometimes the

1. A few records of the Pāṇḍyas are dated in the Kali-yuga or Śaka eras. See, e.g., *Ep. Ind.*, Vol. VII, pp. 11-12 ff.; Vol. XXXII, p. 335; Vol. VIII, p. 320; *A.R.Ep.*, 1952-53, No. B 143. The Kandiyur inscription of Kodavarman gives the date as the 1,511, 564th day from the beginning of the Kali-yuga (*Trav. Arch. Ser.*, Vol. I, p. 294). Similarly a few private records of the Pāla age are dated in the Vikrama or Śaka era. See Bhandarkar's List, Nos. 114, 370; *Ep. Ind.*, Vol. XXVIII, p. 145; Vol. XXXVI, p. 42.

2. See, e.g., *SII*, Vol. XIV, Nos. 12, 12B; *Ep. Ind.*, Vol. XXI, p. 106; Vol. XXVIII, p. 38, note 3. In the language of the Tamil records, the date +9 is expressed as 'the year 9 opposite (*edir āṇḍu*) the year 4'.

same rulers' records appear to contain regnal dates not only in single numbers but also in different groups of double numbers. We may refer to the inscriptions[1] of Soḻantalai-koṇḍaṉ Vīra-pāṇḍya (whose first regnal year seems to be 946-47 A.D.),[2] some of which referring to the construction of a temple for the god Śrīkaṇṭhēśvara by Kaṇḍaṉ Śāttaṉ *alias* Teṉṉavaṉ Tamiḻavēḷ, are dated differently as in the year 4+5 and 5+5.[3] It is not possible to solve the mystery of such dates without further light being thrown on the subject by future discoveries. In certain double-year dates of the above type, the second number is given not in years but in days, e.g., year 4+day 4635.[4]

The records of the Coḻas are occasionally dated in both the Śaka era and the regnal reckoning.[5] Most of the Coḻa records are however dated in the regnal reckoning together with the names of the solar month, the fortnight, the *tithi*, the week-day and the *nakṣatra*.[6] In some cases, the number of the day in a particular year of the reign is specified in the dates.[7]

5. *Introduction of Reckoning in Eras*[8]

According to some scholars, "it is an indisputable axiom that nobody but an anointed king can initiate a Saṁvat of his own."[9] But the statement is rather misleading. An early era appears to have been nothing more than the regnal reckoning of an independent king (who was not bound to use the regnal date of his suzerain) continued by his successors.

1. *A.R.Ep.*, 1914, Nos. 420-21, 423-24, 426, 429; 1907, No. 87; 1908, Nos. 102 ff.; 1909, No. 474; 1926, Nos. 624-27, 548; 1927, Nos. 12-13; 1932-33, Nos. 79 ff.
2. See *Ep. Ind.*, Vol. XXV, pp. 35 ff.
3. *A.R.Ep.*, 1926, Nos. 624, 625 and 627.
4. *SII*, XIV, No. 15; *Ep. Ind.*, Vol. XXII, p. 11.
5. See *Ep. Ind.*, Vol. VII, pp. 6 ff.
6. See ibid., pp. 1 ff.
7. See, e.g., *Ep. Ind.*, Vol. XXII, p. 207 (the 158th day of the 9th year).
8. See *Vikrama Volume*, op. cit., pp. 564 ff.; cf. *JAS*, Letters, Vol. XIX, pp. 1 ff.
9. *Ind. Ant.*, Vol. XIII, p. 420.

When the successors of an early Gupta king counted the year of a record not from their own first regnal year but from that of a particular ancestor of theirs, the reckoning came automatically to be an era and the said ancestor of later Gupta kings became the founder of an era without proclaiming it himself. Years of the era are usually referred to just like regnal years and, for some time to come, without any specification at all.[1] Soon, however, the reckoning came to be distinguished as the era of the Guptas. Of course there is also evidence of the institution of an era by the beating of drums;[2] but, in the early cases, the above appears to have been the usual process. The causes leading to the continuation of the regnal reckoning of a king after his death may be different in diverse cases.[3]

The earliest historical era in the true sense of the term seems to be the Seleucid era of 312 B.C. prevalent in the Greek empire of Western Asia which lay just on the north-western borders of the Maurya empire of India. About the end of the 3rd century B.C., the Greek emperor had to acknowledge the practical independence of the province of Bactria (modern Balkh) and the subordinate territory of Parthia (modern Khorasan), both of which had revolted about the middle of the same century. The Parthians conquered many districts of the eastern part of the Greek empire and instituted an era that starts from 248 B.C.[4] The Graeco-Bactrians poured into North-Western India and established their sovereignty in the Punjab and the adjoining regions. No official document of the Indo-Greek kings has so far been discovered. The older Shinkot inscription[5] belonging to an Indian feudatory of Menander is dated, in the

1. The Mathura inscription which makes a distinction between the Gupta era and the regnal reckoning of Candragupta II simply calls the former a *kāla*, 'era' (*Select Inscriptions*, p. 270).

2. Cf. the case of the Cālukya-Vikrama era of 1076 A.D.

3. Cf. *Select Inscriptions*, p. 132, note.

4. The date of foundation of the Arsacidan house is generally referred to c. 250 B.C. (Smith, *Classical Dictionary*, s.v. Arsaces). According to some recent writers, the era started in 247 B.C. (*East and West*, Vol. 9, No. 3, September 1958, p. 155). See below, pp. 281-82.

5. *Select Inscriptions*, p. 102; *The Age of Imperial Unity*, p. 115, note 1.

Indian fashion, in the 5th regnal year of the Indo-Greek king. A large number of coins belonging to the Indo-Greek rulers, about 40 in number, have been discovered; but they do not bear any date. A unique silver tetradrachm of Platon, copied from the tetradrachm of Eucratides, is said to bear the date 147 of the Seleucid era corresponding to 165 B.C. But the letters of the date are not altogether clear,[1] and doubts may reasonably be entertained as to the existence of any date on it, especially in view of the fact that the absence of date on other Indo-Greek coins then becomes inexplicable. It is not impossible that the Graeco-Bactrian kings neglected the Seleucid era owing to its association with the hostile imperial house. As a matter of fact, Diodotus of Bactria might have intiated an era as Arsaces did in Parthia; but this Bactrian era would have died out owing to the dynastic revolution brought in by Euthydemus.[2] The Indo-Greek power soon declined as a result of internal dissentions and the rise of the Scytho-Parthians.

We have seen that the Parthians had an era of their own. It is interesting to note that several epigraphic records discovered in the north-western part of India appear to have been actually dated according to the Parthian era of 248 B.C.[3] The Scythians on the other hand lived for some time on their way to India in the eastern provinces of the old Greek empire where they must have been acquainted with both the Seleucid and Parthian eras. It is therefore not at all curious that documents of the time of the Scytho-Parthian rulers of North-Western Bhāratavarṣa are found to be dated in an era unlike the indigenous Indian records dated in regnal reckoning.[4] There is no doubt that the epoch of the Scytho-Parthian era

1. Cf. *Camb. Hist. Ind.*, Vol. I, p. 456.

2. Raychaudhuri, op. cit., p. 316.

3. According to Lüders (*D. R. Bhandarkar Volume*, pp. 281, 286), the Mathura inscription of the year 292 and the Girdharpur record of the year 270 are dated in the Parthian era. Sten Konow believes (ibid., p. 306) that the Charsadda, Loriyan Tongai, Hashtnagar and Skarah Dheri inscriptions with dates ranging between the year 303 and the year 399 have also to be referred to the same era.

4. Coins of the early Scytho-Parthian rulers do not bear any date.

falls later than that of the Parthian era. It also appears that its use became popular in the age of the Scytho-Parthians who succeeded the Indo-Bactrians, i.e. probably after the second century B.C. A few dates may be quoted from the documents of the Scytho-Parthian rulers of India.

(1) Mathura inscription[1] of the time of Śoḍāsa—*Mahākṣatrapasa Śoḍāsasa saṁvatsare* 72 *hemanta-māse* 2 *divase* 9, 'on the 9th day of the 2nd month of winter of the year 72 [during the rule] of the Great Satrap Śoḍāsa.'

(2) Taxila inscription[2] of the time of Moga (Maues)—*saṁvatsaraye aṭhasatatimae* 78 *maharayasa mahaṁtasa Mogasa Panemasa masasa divase paṁcame* 5, 'on the 5th day of the [Graeco-Parthian] month of Panemus (corresponding to Āṣāḍha-Śrāvaṇa) of the 78th year [during the reign] of the Great King Moga the Great.'

(3) Takht-i-Bahi inscription[3] of the time of Gondophernes —*maharayasa Guduhvarasa vaṣa* 26 *saṁvatsarae ti-śatimae* 103 *Veśakhasa masasa divase praṭhame*, 'on the 1st day of the month of Vaiśākha in the year 103 and in the 26th [regnal] year of the Great King Guduhvara (Gondophernes).'

(4) Panjtar inscription[4] of the time of the Kuṣāṇa—*saṁ* 122 *Śravaṇasa masasa divase praḍhame* 1 *maharaya - Guṣaṇa-rajami*, 'on the 1st day of the month of Śrāvaṇa of the year 122 during the reign of the Great King, the Kuṣāṇa.'

(5) Kalawan inscription[5] referring to the reign of Azes II—*savatsaraye* 134 *Ajasa Śravaṇasa masasa divase treviśe* 23,

1. *Select Inscriptions*, p. 118.

2. Ibid., p. 120. Some scholars believe that Patika (son of *Kṣatrapa* Liaka Kusuluka) of this record is identical with Kusulaa Padika mentioned at a later date as a *Mahākṣatrapa* in the Mathura Lion Capital inscription which is slightly earlier than Śoḍāsa's Mathura inscription of the year 72, referred to above. If such was the case, we have to assume the foundation of two different eras within a very short period of time. This does not very much appeal to us, and we think it more probable that Patika of the Taxila plate was the grandson of *Mahākṣatrapa* Padika of the Mathura inscription. The grandfather and the grandson having the same name is not an unusual feature in India even among the Śakas (cf. the case of Azes I and II).

3. Ibid., p. 122.

4. Ibid., p. 126.

5. Ibid., p. 127 and note 2. See also *The Age of Imperial Unity*, p. 131.

'on the 23rd day of the month of Śrāvaṇa of the year 134 [during the rule] of Aja (Azes II).

(6) Taxila inscription[1] referring to the time of Azes II—*sa* 136 *Ayasa Aṣaḍasa masasa divase* 15, 'on the 15th day of the month of Āṣāḍha in the year 136 [during the rule] of Aya (Azes II).'

Besides the use of an era, i.e. a continuous reckoning, there are some other interesting features in the dating of these records. We notice the month (*māsa*), but not yet the *tithi*, introduced into the date. It is sometimes seen in connection with the season exactly as the *pakṣa* or fortnight in some indigenous records. This no doubt proves the influence of the Indian system of dividing the year into seasons. It is not known if the introduction of the *māsa* in the date or at least its popularity was due to the foreigners; but the occasional use of the names of months of the Macedonian calendar possibly points to that direction. Many inscriptions of the early centuries of the Christian era, e.g., the Taxila inscription of the year 78, have a passage like *etasyāṁ pūrvāyām*, i.e. 'in the said *pūrvā*', immediately after the quotation of the date, and we have already seen that the word *pūrvā* (literally 'the above') in the feminine gender refers to the *tithi* pertaining to the day mentioned in the date.[2]

In this connection we have to take notice of another reckoning instituted by a foreign dynasty. It is the era of Kaniṣka I, i.e. the regnal reckoning of a Kuṣāṇa king of that name continued by his successors. The evidence of palaeography and the known facts of early Indian history suggest that the epoch of the Kaniṣka era, i.e. the first regnal year of Kaniṣka, has to be assigned to a date considerably later than the epoch of the Scytho-Parthian reckoning. Kaniṣka's era seems to have been founded in order to replace the older Scytho-Parthian era used by the Scytho-Parthians and the early

1. Ibid., p. 129.

2. Cf. *asyāṁ saṁvatsara-māsa-pakṣa-divasa-pūrvāyāṁ tithau* in later records (Bhandarkar's List, Nos. 241, 438, 451, 455, 478, 486, 490, 534, 1393).

Kuṣāṇas. A few dates from the records of the Kaniṣka group of Kuṣāṇa kings may be cited.

(1) Sarnath inscription[1] of the time of Kaniṣka—*mahārājasya Kaṇiṣkasya saṁ* 3 *he* 3 *di* 22, 'on the 22nd day of the 3rd [month] of winter in the 3rd [regnal] year of the Great King Kaniṣka.'

(2) Sui Vihār inscription[2] of the time of Kaniṣka—*Kaṇiṣkasya saṁvatsare ekadaśe saṁ* 11 *Daisiṁkasya masasya divase aṭhaviśe di* 28, 'on the 28th day of the [Greek] month Daesius (=June=Jyaiṣṭha-Āṣāḍha) in the 11th [regnal] year of Kaniṣka.'

(3) Zeda inscription[3] of the time of Kaniṣka—*saṁ* 11 *Aṣaḍasa masasa di* 20 *Utaraphaguṇe*, 'in the *nakshatra* Uttara-phalgunī, on the 20th day of the month of Āṣāḍha in the [regnal] year 11.'

(4) Sanchi inscription[4] of the time of Vāsiṣka—*Sāhi-Vāsiṣkasya saṁ* 28 *he* 1 *di* 5, 'on the 5th day of the 1st [month] of winter in the year 28 [during the reign] of Ṣāhi Vāsiṣka.'

(5) Mathura inscription[5] of the time of Huviṣka—*maharajasya Huvakṣasya savasare* 44 *gṛsya-masa* 3 *divisa* 2, 'on the 2nd day of the 3rd month of summer in the year 44 [during the reign] of Huviṣka.'

(6) Mathura inscription[6] of the time of Vāsudeva—*maharajasya Vāsudevasya saṁ* 80 *hamata* 1 *di* 12, 'on the 12th day of the 1st [month] of winter of the year 80 [during the reign] of the Great King Vāsudeva.'

Of the Scytho-Parthian and Kaniṣka eras, the founder of the latter is the earliest of the several Kuṣāṇa kings named Kaniṣka. The initiator of the earlier reckoning is not apparent from the Scytho-Parthian records themselves. We have not been able as yet to trace dates in the first half of the 1st century

1. Ibid., p. 132.
2. Ibid., p. 135.
3 Ibid., p 136.
4 Ibid., pp 144-45.
5 Ibid., p. 150.
6. Ibid., p. 156.

of the Scytho-Parthian era. It is interesting to note that the earliest extant historical reckonings of India, viz. the Vikrama and Śaka eras of 58 B.C. and 78 A.D. respectively, have epochs falling exactly in the Scytho-Parthian and Kuṣāṇa periods of Indian history. There is no doubt that these foreign dynasties established themselves in India considerably after the early Indo-Greek kings Demetrius and Eucratides who belonged to the first half of the 2nd century B.C. On the other hand, the rule of the later Kuṣāṇa kings who held Mathura has to be placed considerably earlier than 380 A.D., the date of the Mathura inscription[1] of Candragupta II, as the Purāṇic traditions assign seven generations of Nāga rulers to Mathura immediately before the Guptas.[2] The suggestion is not only supported by Kuṣāṇa and Gupta palaeography, but also by the fact that the Sanchi inscription of Vāsiṣka is palaeographically earlier than the Sanchi (Kanakhera) record[3] of the Śaka Śrīdharavarman probably dated 279 A.D.

Considering the facts that the early indigenous kings of India used no era, that the foreign kings who ruled in India between the 2nd century B.C. and the 3rd century A.D. are known to have used two different eras separated from each other by a considerable period of time and that the epochs of the earliest extant historical eras of India, viz. the Vikrama and the Śaka, separated from each other by 135 years, fall in the 1st century B.C. and the 1st century A.D., it is only natural to think that the Vikrama and Śaka reckonings may after all be identical respectively with the two foreign eras known from epigraphs. Of course it is easy to argue that the Scytho-Parthian and Kaniṣka eras have died out and that the Vikrama and Śaka eras are different from them. But the identification of the two with the two is certainly more logical, if the attested facts of Indian history can be reconciled with

1. Ibid., p. 269 ff.

2. Raychaudhuri, op. cit., p. 402; cf. *Vāyu Purāṇa*, 99. 382.

3. *Select Inscriptions*, pp. 180-81; *Ep. Ind.*, Vol. XVI, p. 232.

it.[1] As regards the Śaka era, moreover, the very name points to its foreign origin. The identification of the Scytho-Parthian era with the Vikrama-saṁvat is again supported at least by one evidence. The Takht-i-Bahi inscription, as we have seen above, is dated in the year 103 of this era and in the 26th regnal year of Gondophernes. It is interesting to note that a Parthian king named Gondopharnes, called the king of India in some versions, is represented in an old Christian tradition as a contemporary of Saint Thomas, the apostle (one of the 12 disciples of Jesus Christ, 4 B. C. —29 or 33 A. D.) who flourished in the 1st century A.D.[2] It will be seen that, if year 103 of the Tekht-i-Bahi inscription be referred to the Vikrama-saṁvat, the reign of Gondophernes falls exactly in the said period, i.e. in the period 21-46 A.D. It should be pointed out that no difficulty that may be supposed to stand in the way of the identification of the Scytho-Parthian reckoning with the Vikrama-saṁvat and the Kaniṣka era with the Śak-ābda is insurmountable.[3]

Some scholars point to the absence of inscriptions dated in the third century of the Scytho-Parthian era and suggest that the same era was used by the Kaniṣka group of the Kuṣāṇa kings with the omission of the symbol for 200.[4] The absence of inscriptions dated in the third century of the older era is unimportant as we have a few records dated in the fourth century of the same era,[5] and these point to the continued use of the era since it is difficult to believe that

1. Those who regard the Scytho-Parthian and Kaniṣka eras as different respectively from the Vikrama and Śaka eras do not take into account the obvious foreign origin of both the latter reckonings. They have also no satisfactory explanation of the origin of three out of the four eras, viz. the Scytho-Parthian, Vikrama and Śaka, and of the circumstances leading to the disappearance of two of them, viz. Scytho-Parthian and Kaniṣka, and the continuation of the use of two, viz. Vikrama and Śaka. The conclusion that as many as four eras were founded in the age of the Scytho-Parthians and Kuṣāṇas appears to be unrealistic.

2. Smith, *E. Hist. Ind.*, 4th ed., pp. 245-50, 260-62.

3. See *The Age of Imperial Unity*, pp. 123 ff., 141 ff.

4. *JAS*, Letters, Vol. XIX, p. 12.

5. *CII*, Vol. II, Part I, Nos. XL, XLV, LIII and LX.

people reverted to the old practice of mentioning the hundred after the lapse of a century. We do not believe in theories based on the omission of hundreds because the whole range of Indian epigraphy offers only a few instances of omitted hundreds excepting of course the popularity of such omission in the calculation of the years of the Laukika era in the Kashmir region since the early medieval period. Records dated in regnal reckoning such as the Abottabad inscription[1] of Kadambeśvaradāsa (c. 3rd century A.D.) and the Kabul inscription of Ṣāhi Khiṅgāla (c. 6th century A. D.)[2] suggest that the use of both the Scytho-Perthian and Kaniṣka eras was no longer very popular in North-Western Bhāratavarṣa. This fact may be compared with the total disappearance of the Gupta era from Bihar and U.P. with the fall of the Guptas. While in Bengal it was not used after the middle of the 6th century A.D. and in Orissa after the beginning of the 7th, we have a solitary instance of its use in a record of 829 A.D. from Assam[3] (which probably did never from an integral part of the Gupta empire) and, in Kathiawar, it was in popular use for several countries after the fall of the Guptas. This was because their erstwhile feudatories, the Maitrakas, continued its use. The continued use of the Gupta era by the Maitrakas seems to be specially comparable with that of the Kaniṣka era by the Śakas of Western India.

1. *Ep. Ind.*, Vol. XXX, pp. 59 ff.
2. Ibid., Vol. XXXV, pp. 44ff.
3. Bhattacharya, *Kāmārūpaśāsanāvalī*, p. 187.

SECTION II

SOME CURRENT RECKONINGS

1. *Vikrama Era*[1]

If the Scytho-Parthian era has to be identified with the Vikrama-saṁvat, we have to determine as to how it came to be associated with the name of Vikramāditya. The earlier records bearing dates in this era naturally do not call it by a specific name. The earliest epigraphs that have a name for the reckoning have been discovered in Rajasthan. Slightly later records associate the era with the Mālava tribe and afterwards with the lord or lords of Mālava or the Mālavas. Finally, in the 8th century A.D., the reckoning was connected with the name of king Vikramāditya. A few instances may be quoted to illustrate the different stages.

(1) Year 282—Nandsa (former Udaipur State, Rajasthan) inscription[2] of Śaktigaṇaguru—*Kṛtayor=dvayor=varṣa-śatayor=dvyaśītayoḥ* 282.

(2) Year 295—Badva (former Kotah State, Rajasthan) inscription[3] of the Maukharis—*Kritehi* 295.

(3) Year 428—Bijaygarh (former Bharatpur State, Rajasthan) inscription[4] of Viṣṇuvardhana—*Kṛteṣu caturṣu varṣa-śatesv=aṣṭāviṁśeṣu* 428.

(4) Year 461—Mandasor (former Gwalior State) inscription[5] of Naravarman—*śrī-Mālava-gaṇ-āmnāte praśaste Kṛta-saṁjñite । ekaṣaṣṭy-adhike prāpte samā-śata-catuṣṭaye ॥*

1. See *Vikrama Volume*, op. cit., pp. 579 ff.; *The Age of Imperial Unity*, p. 125, note; *Proc. IHC*, Gwalior, pp. 371 ff. For various references, see *The Age of Imperal Unity*, ed. Majumdar, pp. 679-80.

2. Bhandarkar's List, No. 1. The latest epigraph referring to the Kṛta era is the Mungthala (former Sirohi State, Rajasthan) inscription of the Kṛta year 894 (*JUPHS*, New Series, Vol. III, pp. 1 ff.).

3. *Select Inscriptions*, pp. 92-93. The word *kritehi* has been corrected to *kṛtaiḥ*.

4. Bhandarkar's List, No. 2.

5. *Select Inscriptions*, p. 377.

(5) Year 480—Gangdhar (former Jhalawar State, Rajasthan) inscription[1] of Viśvavarman—*yāteṣu caturṣu Kriteṣu śateṣu saumyeṣv=āśīta-sottara-padeṣv=iha vatsareṣu.*

(6) Year 481—Nagari (former Udaipur State, Rajasthan) inscription[2] of some Vaiśyas—*Kṛteṣu caturṣu varṣa-śateṣv=ekāśīty-uttareṣv=asyāṁ Mālava-pūrvāyām.*

(7) Year 493—Mandasor inscription[3] mentioning Kumāragupta and Bhandhuvarman—*Mālavānāṁ gaṇa-sthityā yāte śata-catuṣṭaye* । *trinavaty-adhike=bdānām=ṛtau sevya-ghanastane* ॥

(8) Year 524—Mandasor inscription[4] of the time of Prabhākara—*vikhyāpake Mālava-vaṁśa-kīrtteḥ* । *śarad-gaṇe pañca-śate vyatīte tri-ghātit-āṣṭ-ābhyadhike krameṇa* ॥

(9) Year 589—Mandasor inscription[5] of Yaśodharman Viṣṇuvardhana—*pañcasu śateṣu śaradāṁ yāteṣv=ekānnanavati-sahiteṣu* । *Mālava-gaṇa-sthiti-vaśāt=kāla-jñānāya likhiteṣu* ॥

(10) A number of epigraphs[6] from the 5th century of the era referring to the year simply as *śarat*, *varṣa*, *saṁvatsara* (or contracted to *saṁ* or *saṁvat*) and also as *rājya-saṁvatsara*.[7]

(11) Year 770—Chitorgarh (former Udaipur State, Rajasthan) inscription[8] of Māna—the year apparently of 'the lord of men, the king of Mālava' the original possibly having *Mālaveśa* or *Mālavendra*.

(12) Year 794—Dhiniki (former Okhamandal State, Kathiawar) inscription[9] of Jāikadeva—*Vikrama-saṁvatsara-śateṣu saptasu catur-navaty-adhikeṣv=aṅkataḥ* 794.

(13) Year 795—Kanaswa (former Kotah State, Rajasthan) inscription[10] of Śivagaṇa—*saṁvatsara-śatair=yātaiḥ sa-pañcanavaty-argalaiḥ* । *saptabhir=Mālaveśānām.*

1. Ibid., p. 382. The word *kriteṣu* has been corrected to *kṛteṣu.*
2. Bhandarkar's List, No. 5.
3. *Select Inscriptions*, p. 295.
4. Bhandarkar's List, No. 7.
5. *Select Inscriptions*, p. 391.
6. Bhandarkar's List, Nos. 10-15, 19, 21-23, 26, etc.
7. Cf. Mandasor inscription of Naravarman of the year 474 (*Ep. Ind.*, Vol. XXVI, pp. 131-32).
8. Bhandarkar's List, No. 16.
9. Ibid., No. 17. Some scholars think that the record is spurious.
10. Ibid., No. 18.

(14) Year 898—Dholpur (Rajasthan) inscription[1] of Caṇḍamahāsena—*vasu-navak-āṣṭau varṣā-gatasya kālasya Vikram-ākhyasya.*

(15) Year 936—Gyaraspur (former Gwalior State) inscription[3]—*Mālava-kālāc=charadāṁ ṣaṭtriṁśat-saṁyukteṣv=atīteṣu navasu śateṣu.*

(16) Year 973—Bijapur (former Jodhpur State, Rajasthan) inscription[4] of Dhavala—*rāma-giri-kalite Vikrama-kāle gate.*

(17) Year 1005—Bodhgayā (Bihar) inscription[4]—'year of the era of Vikramāditya' (cf. another record which has *Vikramādity-otpādita-saṁvatsara*).[5]

(18) Year 1086—Radhanpur (Gujarat) inscription[6] of Bhīma I—*Vikrama-saṁvat* 1086 (cf. other records[7] referring to king Vikrama as *Vikramendra* and *Vikramārka*).

(19) Year 1103—Tilakwara (former Baroda State) inscription[8] of Yaśorāja—*vatsarair=Vikramādityaiḥ śatair=ekādaśais=tathā* । *try-uttaraiḥ.*

It will be seen that the reckoning was at first known as the Kṛta era and was prevalent in Rajasthan and Malwa. Soon it began to be associated with the Mālava tribe and was styled 'era handed down by the Mālava Republic,' 'the year counted in accordance with the custom established by (or, from the foundation of) the Mālava Republic' and 'the *pūrvā*[9] of the Mālavas'. It was also known as the era 'that speaks of the glory of the Mālava race', and later as the era (*kāla*) belonging to the Mālava country or to the king or kings of

1. Ibid., No. 27.
2. Ibid., No. 37.
3. Ibid., No. 48; cf. also Nos. 67, etc.
4. Ibid., No. 63; cf. also Nos. 80, etc.
5. Ibid., No. 141.
6. Ibid., No. 117.
7. Ibid., Nos. 134, 169, etc.
8. Ibid., No. 128.
9. As we have seen above, the word *pūrvā* really refers to a *tithi*, though in this case it seems to be used in a wider sense of 'a date' or 'a reckoning'.

Mālava. Sometime later, the era was further associated with Vikramāditya.[1]

When Alexander invaded India in the 4th century B.C., the Mālava (Malloi) tribe lived on the Ravi in the Punjab which was under Scytho-Parthian domination in the 1st century B.C. and the 1st century A.D. Owing probably to foreign pressure, the Mālavas moved towards Rajasthan where their existence is proved by an inscription[2] of Ṛṣabhadatta (c. 119-23 A.D.) and by the discovery of thousands of coins with the legend *Mālavānāṁ jayaḥ* at Nagar (ancient Mālava-nagara)[3] in the former Jaipur State.[4] The Mālavas must have also later settled in the ancient *janapadas* of Avanti and Ākara which came to be known as Mālava by the 7th century A.D. It is possible to suggest that the Mālava Republic was subjugated by the early Guptas in the 4th century A.D. and that the Aulikara family which enjoyed the viceregal position in Malwa under the Imperial Guptas, but which used the Kṛta and not the Gupta era, was a Mālava family. Thus it appears that the Mālava tribe carried the Kṛta or Scytho-Parthian era to Rajasthan and Malwa from their original home in the Punjab. When the memory of the Mālava tribe and its Republic was dimmed and the name Mālava only indicated a particular *janapada*, the era came to be associated with the Mālava country or with the king or kings of Mālava. The whole of the Malwa region was annexed to the Gupta empire by Candragupta II Vikramāditya (376-414 A.D.) who extirpated the Śakas of Western India about the end of the 4th century. From this time, Ujjayinī in Malwa became a secondary capital of the Gupta emperors and Candragupta II gradually became famous in Indian tradition and folk-lore as Vikramāditya Śakāri, the lord of Ujjayinī, even though the achievements

1. According to medieval tradition, king Vikramāditya of Ujjayinī defeated the Śakas and founded his era in 58 B.C. But it is clearly against the known facts of history. See *Vikrama Volume*, pp. 483 ff.

2. *Select Inscriptions*, p. 162.

3. *Bhārata Kaumudī*, Part I, p. 272.

4. Smith, *Catalogue*, pp. 161-52, 170 ff.

of other Vikramādityas especially of the Imperial Gupta family contributed to the growth of the Vikramāditya saga.[1] Thus, in the early medieval period, 'the lord of Mālava' *par excellence* was no other than Vikramāditya (Candragupta II), and it was then quite natural to identify the Mālaveśa, with whom the Kṛta era came to be associated after the subjugation of the Mālava-gaṇa, with the great Vikramāditya of tradition. It must be remembered that there is no genuine evidence to prove the existence of a Vikramāditya, as a matter of fact, of any king having a title ending in *āditya*, before the 4th century A.D. and that the epoch of an era is never associated with Vikramāditya in records earlier than the 8th century A.D. It was only in the medieval period that, with the development of the Vikramāditya saga, the old Kṛta or Scytho-Parthian era introduced in Western India by the Mālavas began to be called 'the era of Vikrama', 'the era known as Vikrama or Vikramāditya' and later also 'the era founded by Vikramāditya'.[2]

We have seen that the Vikrama-saṁvat was earlier known as Kṛta. The word is sometimes taken to mean 'made', i.e. invented by astronomers. But the theory is improbable as the era, the years of which can be traced from its first century, was apparently the continuation of a regnal reckoning. According to another theory, Kṛta was the name of a king who founded the era.[3] It has also been conjectured that Kṛta was the name of a *gaṇa-mukhya* of the Mālava tribe or that it indicates an era supposed to have been handed down from the Kṛta-yuga or the Golden Age. These are, however, guesses that it is

1. For the development of the Vikramāditya tradition, see H.C. Raychaudhuri's 'Vikramāditya in History and Legend' in *Vikrama Volume*, pp. 483ff. Some writers of the medieval period, e.g., Kālidāsa, author of the *Jyotirvidābharaṇa*, and Harisvāmin, commentator on the Ṛgveda, tried to imply that their works were composed under the patronage of king Vikramāditya in the first century B.C. Cf. Ojha, *Bhāratīya Prācīn Lipimālā*, pp. 166, note 1; *Bhāratīya Vidyā*, Vol. IX, 1948, pp. 325-90.

2. Cf. the association of the Śaka era with Śālivāhana from the 13th century A.D.

3. For Kṛta as a personal name, see Penzer, *Ocean of Stories*, Vol. III, p. 19.

impossible to substantiate with any evidence in the present state of our knowledge. Sometimes the word is taken to be actually *krīta*,[1] 'purchased', pointing to the origin of the reckoning with the barbarian kings of North-Western India who, according to a Buddhist tradition recorded by Hiuen-tsang,[2] were known as 'the Purchased'. But, though we have early instances of spelling the word as *krita* which may be a mistake for *krīta*, the suggestion does not satisfactorily explain the substitution of *kṛta* for *krīta* unless it is supposed that the word is an Indian modification of a foreign expression. This however is not improbable since Krīta as the name of a foreign people is mentioned in an early medieval inscription.[3]

As regards the founder of the Kṛta-Mālava-Vikrama-saṁvat, we should naturally look for a powerful Scytho-Parthian king who began to rule in 58 B.C. Some scholars have suggested the name of Azes I.[4] But the probable identification of the era with the older Scytho-Parthian reckoning renders it untenable in view of the fact that Maues, the predecessor of Azes I in the Indian possessions of the Śakas, is known from the Taxila inscription of Patika to have been ruling in the year 78 of the era.[5] It is interesting to note in this connection that the earliest local Parthian ruler of East Iran, who is known from his coins to have assumed the imperial title 'Great King of Kings', was Vonones who must have flourished sometime after the Parthian emperor Mitridates II (123-88 B.C.) as the latter assumed the said title fort he first time. Since the name of the month mentioned in the date of the Taxila inscription is Graeco-Parthian, it has been rightly suggested that the era used in that record is of Parthian origin and that it marks the establishment of a new kingdom in East Iran.[6] It is thus quite probable that the first year of the reign of Vonones, the earliest independent Parthian ruler of East

1. Cf. *Select Inscriptions*, p. 288, note.
2. Watters, op. cit., Vol. 1, p. 265.
3. *Ep. Ind.*, Vol. XXXIII, p. 152.
4. *Camb. Hist. Ind.*, Vol. I, p. 576.
5. *Select Inscriptions*, p. 120.
6. Cf. *Camb. Hist. Ind.*, Vol. I, p. 570.

Iran, came to be regarded as the beginning of a new reckoning that was instituted to oust the Imperial Parthian era of 248 B.C. As Vonones seems to have flourished shortly after Mithridates II about the middle of the 1st century B.C., it is not unreasonable to place his accession in 58 B.C. which is the epoch of the earliest extant Indian reckoning of a historical character.[1] The use of the era seems to have been introduced in Sind and the adjoining regions by the Śaka feudatories of Vonones, and the Mālavas, who originally lived in the Punjab within the dominions of these Śakas, carried its use to Rajasthan and the neighbouring areas with their migration to those parts.

The earliest use of the Kṛta-Mālava era outside the western and north-western parts of India is found in the Haraha (Bara Banki District, U.P.) inscription of Maukhari Īśānavarman, dated in the year 611. The use of the era by the Maukharis of U. P. and Bihar is clearly explained by the Badva inscriptions of the third century A.D., found in the Kotah region of Rajasthan. These records belong to the Maukharis and are dated in the Kṛta-Mālava era. The Maukharis, therefore, appear to have carried the use of the above era from their home in Rajasthan to their new settlements in the east. There is no doubt that they were originally subordinate to the Mālavas, and it is probable that they really belonged to the Mālava stock.[2]

Another factor that contributed to the expansion of the era was probably the Ujjayinī school of astronomers who appear to have favoured both the Śaka and Vikrama eras, some of them specially favouring the era of 58 B.C., the foreign association of which had been long ago forgotten. Its use was continued in U. P. by the Malayaketus and the Gurjara-Pratihāras. That the era was introduced in Bihar as well seems to be suggested by the date Saṁvat 898, quoted in Maithila Vācaspati Miśra's *Nyāyasūci* as the year of its

1. See *The Age of Imperial Unity*, pp. 123, 125 note.

2. It is interesting to note in this connection that the Maukharis claimed king Aśvapati as their progenitor while the same epic ruler is represented in the *Mahābhārata* (III. 296. 59-60) as the progenitor of the Mālavas. See *Ind. Cult.*, Vol. I, pp. 298 ff.

composition and a manuscript of the *Rāmāyaṇa* known to have been copied in Tīrabhukti (Tirhut) in Saṁvat 1076.[1] With the gradual extension of the Gurjara-Pratihāra power over wide regions of Northern India, the popularity of the era of 58 B.C. increased considerably. Another contributing cause of its popularity was the development of the Vikramāditya saga.

The Vikrama-saṁvat is believed to have started after year 3044 of the Kali era, so that Kali 3045=Vikrama 1. One gets the years of the Śaka and Christian eras by subtracting 135 and 57 or 56 respectively from the years of the Vikrama. The beginning of the Vikrama is counted from Caitra-śukla 1 in North India but from Kārttika-śukla 1 in South India. Thus the years of the era now start seven months earlier in the South than in the North, although in medieval times the years of the Vikrama were counted as beginning from Kārttika-śukla 1 also in North India.[2] In the North again the months are *Pūrṇimānta* and begin from badi 1 and end in sudi 15, while the months in the South are *Amānta*, i.e. they begin from sudi 1 and end in badi 15. Though the bright fortnight is the same in both the systems, the dark fortnight of a month in the northern system is counted in the previous month in the South. Thus the dark fortnight of Vaiśākha in the North is regarded in the South as the dark fortnight of Caitra. In some parts of the Rājasthānī- and Gujāratī-speaking areas, the beginning of the years of the Vikrama is counted from *Amānta* Āṣāḍha-sudi 1, while in the Udaipur region of Rajasthan it is counted from *Pūrṇimānta* Śrāvaṇa-badi 1.[3] The years are thus variously called Caitrādi, Kārttikādi, Āṣāḍhādi and Śrāvaṇādi in accordance with their beginning in the months of Caitra, Kārttika, Āṣāḍha and Śrāvaṇa.

2 *Śaka Era*[4]

The Identification of the Śaka and Kaniṣka eras primarily involves two questions, viz., the date of Kaniṣka and

1. Cf. *Ep. Ind.*, Vol. XXIX, pp. 52-53.
2. Ibid., Vol. XXXII, p. 332.
3. See Ojha, op. cit., pp. 169-70.
4. See *Vikrama Volume*, op. cit., pp. 572 ff.; The *Age of Imperial Unity*, p. 144, note 1; *IHQ*, Vol. XXVII, pp. 174 ff.; Vol. XXIX, pp. 294 ff.

the attribution of the era to the Śakas and not to the Kuṣāṇas.

There is difference of opinion among scholars about the date of the Kuṣāṇa king Kaniṣka whose accession is assigned variously to the 1st century B.C., the 1st century A.D., the 2nd century A.D. and the 3rd century A.D. The first of these theories is however now generally believed to be erroneous. It appears that there were actually three Kaniṣkas, the first having begun to rule in the 1st century A.D., the second in the 2nd century A.D. and the third in the 3rd century A.D. and that, just as the activities of a number of kings styled Vikramāditya, especially those belonging to the Imperial Gupta dynasty, contributed to the dynamic growth of the Vikramāditya saga even though the original Vikramāditya was Candragupta II, the legends that cluster round the name of Kaniṣka similarly absorbed a good deal of the achievements of his different namesakes. It would therefore be unwise to attribute all the activities of the traditional Kaniṣka to a particular king of that name. There is no insurmountable obstacle in assigning Kaniṣka I, the founder of the era, to the 1st century A.D.[1]

As has already been pointed out, an era, which was practically the continuation of a regnal reckoning, did not get a name immediately after its institution. But a specific name was attached to it when it became popular and had to be distinguished from other reckonings. Even then, however, the years of the era could often be referred to without specification simply as *saṁvatsara* (contracted to *saṁ* or *saṁvat*) or *varṣa*, i.e. 'the year'. It is therefore not unnatural that a year of the Kaniṣka era was at first simply styled 'the year'. The earliest epigraphic records that connect this era explicitly with the Śakas belong to the Cālukyas of Bādāmi. The Cālukya inscriptions of the 6th and 7th centuries A.D. use expressions like *Śaka-varṣa* and *Śaka-nṛpa-rājy-ābhiṣeka-saṁvatsara* (cf. *samāsu samatītāsu Śakānām=api bhūbhujām*).[2] There can be no doubt that the Śaka

1. See *The Age of Imperial Unity*, pp. 141 ff.
2. Cf. *Ep. Ind.*, Vol. VI, p. 7. The earliest Śaka date in the Cālukya

kings referred to in these passages are those who held sway over Western India for about 3 centuries before their extirpation by Candragupta II about the end of the 4th century A.D. As a matter of fact, the Śaka Satraps of Western India are known to have used a continuous reckoning from the year 41 to the year 310,[1] and there is no doubt that this has to be identified with the so-called Śaka-kāla, Śak-ābda or Śaka-saṁvat, i.e. the era of the Śaka rulers. These Śakas styled them selves *Kṣatrapa* (literally, 'provincial governor') and *Mahākṣatrapa* (literally, 'great provincial governor') which point to their original subordinate position, although the title continued in use even when they reigned practically as independent rulers. We know that Nahapāna was ruling in the year 41-46 of the era with the titles *Rājan* and *Kṣatrapa* or *Mahākṣatrapa*.[2] The facts that his overlord is not mentioned in the records of his time and that he had an extensive coinage appear to suggest that Nahapāna was enjoying a certain amount of autonomy. He was overthrown from the southern districts of his dominions by the Śātavāhana king Gautamīputra who was himself ousted from most of the areas by another Śaka house. By 130 A.D., the date of the Andhau inscriptions[3] of the joint rule of Caṣṭana and Rudradāman of this new Śaka house, Kathiawar was reconquered by the new-comers. Reference in Ptolemy's Geography (c. 140 A.D.)[4] to Tiastenes (Caṣṭana) as the ruler of Ozéné (Ujjayinī) points to the recovery of Malwa, and the Junagadh inscription of Rudradāman dated year 72 (150 A.D.)[5] proves the re-occupation of territories as far south as the Northern Konkan and the Narmadā valley. In the same record Rudradāman calls himself *svayam-adhigata-*

records is 465 (543 A.D.) while the earliest association of the Śakas with the era is found in Siṁha-sūri's *Lokavibhāga* composed in Śaka 380 (458 A.D.). See ibid., Vol. XXV, pp. 4 ff.; *Mys. Arch. Rep.*, 1922-23, p. 23.

1. *Select Inscriptions*, pp. 157, 182.
2. Ibid., pp. 157-66.
3. Ibid., pp. 167 ff.
4. VII. I. 63.
5. *Select Inscriptions*, pp. 169 ff. Gautamīputra Śātakarni is represented in the Junargadh inscription as having been twice defeated by Rudradāman (ibid., p. 172).

Mahākṣatrapa-nāmā, 'one who has himself acquired the title of Mahākṣatrapa', i.e. one who did not owe his position to any overlord. This Śaka ruler thus appears to have become practically independent, though he still did not assume imperial titles.

The era used by the Śakas of Western India could hardly be of their own institution. Firstly, they were originally feudatories, as their Satrapal title shows, and therefore were required to use the reckoning of their overlords. Secondly, no record of any date in the first forty years of the era can be traced in the records of the Śakas of Western India. It is therefore very probable that the early West Indian Śakas used the reckoning of their overlords and that their successors simply continued its use. From the facts already considered, it appears that the suzerains of the Śakas were the Kuṣāṇa kings of the Kaniṣka group. The suggestion is strongly supported by the fact that the rule of Vāsiṣka, the immediate successor of Kaniṣka I, over East Malwa is established by the Sanchi inscription.[1]

Assuming the identity of the Kaniṣka and Śaka eras, we may, on the basis of the known dates of the Kuṣāṇa records, assign Kaniṣka I to 78-102 A.D., Vāsiṣka to 102-06 A.D., Huviṣka to 106-38 A.D., Kaniṣka II to 119 A.D., Vāsudeva to 152-76 A.D. and Kaniṣka III to the 3rd century A.D. On the other hand, the rule of Nahapāna has to be ascribed to 119-24 A.D., that of Caṣṭana to 130 A.D. and that of Rudradāman to 130-50 A.D. It appears that the Śaka Satraps of Western India were completely subordinate to the Kuṣāṇas during the vigorous rule of Kaniṣka I, but that they became semi-independent after his death owing possibly to the division of power between the successors of Kaniṣka. About the middle of the 2nd century A.D. when the central government of the Kuṣāṇas began to decline, Rudradāman became practically an independent sovereign without, however, com-

1. *Select Inscriptions*, pp. 144-145. Sanchi lies near ancient Vidiśā, the capital of the Ākara or Daśārṇa *janapada* in East Malwa.

pletely throwing off the Kuṣāṇa yoke, and his successors continued the use of the era till the year 388, i.e. sometime after Siṁha-sūri's *Lokavibhāga* had been composed in Śaka 380. The above facts would explain why the Kuṣāṇa reckoning of Kaniṣka came to be known as the era of the Śaka kings first in the south-western and southern parts of India. It should also be remembered in this connection that the family name Kuṣāṇa is unknown to Indian literary records, while the name Śaka is known to have been often applied to foreigners including the Muslims who were not Scythians. It is therefore not impossible that the Indians often confused the Kuṣāṇas with the Śakas, the Kuṣāṇa emperors being known to have ruled the provinces of their empire often through provincial governors of Śaka nationality.[1]

In medieval times, people tried to forget the foreign association of the Śaka era and the word *śaka* began to be used in the sense of 'an era.' The same tendency is apparently noticed from the 13th century when the era was often associated, especially in the southern and western regions of India, with Śālivāhana, famous in Indian tradition and folklore as a great popular hero. The earliest association of the era with Śālivāhana is found in the Kannaḍa work *Udbhaṭakāvya* by Somarāja composed in Śaka 1144 expired (1222 A.D.) and the Tasgaon plates (Śaka 1172=1251 A.D.) of the Yādava king Kṛṣṇa.[2]

This popular fiction seems to have rested on the memory of the great Śātavāhana (Śālivāhana) king Gautamīputra Śātakarṇi who claims to have been the destroyer of the Śakas and other barbarians.[3] The association of the Scytho-Parthian era with the name of another popular hero of Indian tradition

1. Cf. *Select Inscriptions*, pp. 132-33.

2. See *Journ. Or. Res.*, Vol. XVII, pp. 92-93; Vol. XVIII, p. 190. It is reported that a Marāṭhī inscription of Śaka 1110 (1188 A.D.) found in the Vithoba temple at Pandharpur associates the era with Sālāhaṇa (Śālivāhana). See *Journal of the Oriental Institute*, Vol. VI, pp. 132, 134. Sometimes Śālivāhana was regarded as belonging to the Śaka race (Bhandarkar's List, No. 1028).

3. Cf. *Select Inscriptions*, p. 197.

and folklore, viz. Vikramāditya, should not therefore be looked upon as a unique case in the history of India. The Śālivāhana tradition appears to have been developed in the Kannaḍa-speaking areas of the Deccan, which apparently also contributed to the Śakāri Vikramāditya saga.

We have to note that the date of the completion of the Siṁha-sūri's *Lokavibhāga* is given in the book as the 22nd regnal year of king Siṁhavarman, lord of Kāñcī, and as the 380th year of the Śaka era.[1] Thus the above Jain work, completed in the Śaka year 380 at Kāñcī, gives us the earliest instance of the use of the Śaka era in South India and the earliest reference to the Śaka association of the reckoning. The spread of the Śaka era in the south seems to be essentially associated with that of the Jains from their stronghold in the Gujarat-Kathiawad region forming a part of the dominions of the Śakas of Western India, who used the era in question till the close of the fourth century A.D. Many of the Jain scholars were apparently employed as astronomers and administrators at the courts of the various South Indian royal families. As already indicated above, the Jains have largely contributed to the development of the legends about Śaka-Śālivāhana and Vikramāditya who are traditionally associated with the Śaka-kāla (later Śālivāhana-śaka or °śāka, the word *śaka* or *śāka* here meaning 'an era') and the Vikrama-saṁvat. The Jain preference of the Śaka era is explained by the fact that, in their tradition recorded in works like the *Kālakācāryakathā*, the Śakas are represented as the defenders of the Jain faith.[2]

Another interesting fact is that the *Pañcasiddhāntikā* of the celebrated Maga-Brāhmaṇa astronomer, Varāhamihira of Ujjayinī, makes use of the Śaka era,[3] and this points to the

1. *A. R. Arch Surv. Mys.*, 1909, p. 31; 1910, pp. 45-47. The verse in question runs :

saṁvatsare tu dvāviṁśe Kāñcīśa-Siṁhavarmaṇaḥ ।
aśīty-agre Śak-āhvānāṁ siddham=etac=chata-traye ॥

2 *JRAS*, 1913, p. 993.

3 Cf. *Pañcasiddhāntikā*, I, 8: *sapt-āśvi-veda-saṁkhyaṁ Śaka-kālam* (i.e. Śaka 427). See also references to *Śakendra-kāla* and *Śaka-bhūpa-kāla* in the *Bṛhatsaṁhitā*, VIII. 20-21.

contribution of astronomers to the popularity of the reckoning. That, of all the historical and popular eras of ancient India, only the Vikrama-saṁvat (the Scytho-Parthian era originated in Drangiana) and the Śaka-kāla (the Kaniṣka era) are still in use is probably due, to a considerable extent, to the fact that both of them came to be used in the region about West Malwa where the city of Ujjayinī became one of the strongest centres of astronomical studies in India, presumably under the patronage of Śaka and Gupta rulers. The Guptas used their own era on their coins meant for circulation in Western India, but did not compel their feudatories in Malwa, viz. the Aulikaras of Daśapura, to discontinue the use of the Vikrama-saṁvat and adopt the Gupta era. The Persian priests (Magi), who migrated to India and were known as the Maga-Brāhmaṇas of Śaka-dvīpa (Seistan),[1] preferred the Śaka era and contributed to the growth of the Ujjayinī school of astronomy.

The Śaka era was used by the successive ruling families of the Kannaḍa-speaking area of the South-Western Deccan, which flourished after the Cālukya house of Bādāmi. During the age of the Cālukyas, the use of the era spread, apparently from the said region, to the lands beyond the Bay of Bengal, the earliest inscriptions of Indo-China and Indonesia dated in this era belonging respectively to the 7th and 8th centuries A.D. In the 10th century A.D., the use of the Śaka era was adopted by the Eastern Cālukyas of Veṅgī in the Telugu-speaking territory from their western neighbours, viz. the Rāṣṭrakūṭa successors of the Cālukyas of Bādāmi. About the same time, it was also adopted by the Eastern Gaṅgas of Kaliṅganagara (modern Mukhalingam near Srikakulam), who originally used the Gaṅga era, from their western neighbours, the Eastern Cālukyas of Veṅgī. These Eastern Gaṅgas later extended their power over the whole of Coastal Orissa and the south-western part of Bengal. But the popularity of the Śaka era in Bengal was mainly due to the growth of

1. Cf. Bhandarkar's List, No. 1105; also No. 30.

Sena power in the twelfth century, the Senas having hailed from the Kannaḍa-speaking area. Similarly, the spread of the use of the Śaka era in North Bihar was primarily due to the establishment of the Karnāṭa house of Nānyadeva in Mithilā about the end of the 11th century. From Bengal and North Bihar, the use of the era spread to Assam. There are a few instances of the use of the said era by the Bengalis and Biharis before the advent respectively of the Senas and the Karṇāṭas of Mithilā. Thus Śrīdhara, an inhabitant of Dakṣiṇa-Rāḍha in South-West Bengal, wrote his *Nyāyakandalī* in Śaka 913 (991 A.D.). But there is no proof that the work was written in Bengal and not in an area where the use of the Śaka era had already become popular.[1] The Valgudar (Monghyr District, Bihar) inscription is dated in Śaka 1083 (1161 A.D.). But it is a private record and the persons responsible for it may have settled in the locality from an area where the era was in popular use.[2] The same may be the case with the Govindapur (Gaya District) inscription[3] of Śaka 1059 (1137 A.D.), though the date of this record as well as that of the Valgudar inscription is later than the introduction of the Śaka era in Bengal and North Bihar.

In Eastern Uttar Pradesh and Bihar, the use of the Kaniṣka era (later known as the Śaka era) was continued for sometime by the Maghas of Kauśāmbī[4] and kings like Ārya-Viśākhamitra of the Kailvan inscription.[5] From the Bihar-U.P. area, the use of the Śaka era seems to have spread to Nepal where the dates of the Licchavi inscriptions should probably be referred to this era.[6] But the popularity of the Gupta era of 319 A.D., introduced by the Imperial Guptas of Magadha, soon led to its disappearance in the central and eastern areas of Northern India.

1. See *Ep. Ind.*, Vol. XXIX, p. 53 and note.
2. See ibid., Vol. XXVIII, pp. 143-44.
3. Bhandarkar's List, No. 1105.
4. Cf. *Select Inscriptions*, p. 365, note.
5. *Ep. Ind.*, Vol. XXXI, pp. 229 ff.
6. See *Select Inscriptions*, p. 366, note 1; below, pp. 271, 279.

The use of the Śaka era in some inscriptions of Madhya Pradesh and Gujarat[1] is explained by the fact that the areas came under the influence of the imperial dynasties of the Kannaḍa-speaking region while most of the rulers using it in Gujarat were of Karnāṭa origin. But there are some cases of the use of the Śaka era in areas outside its usual sphere, e.g. in the Deogarh (Jhansi District, U.P.) inscripton[2] of Śaka 784 (862 A.D.) and the Baijnath (Kangra District, Punjab) inscription[3] of Śaka 1126. These appear to be due to the influence of outsiders.

There are conflicting traditions about the origin of the Śaka era. Works like the *Muhūrtamārtaṇḍa* suggest that it started from the birth of Śālivāhana[4] while Jinaprabha-sūri's *Kalpa-pradīpa* (c. 1300 A.D.) states that Śātavāhana (Śālivāhana) started it after having defeated king Vikramāditya of Ujjayinī and having established himself as the king of Pratiṣṭhāna.[5] According to another tradition recorded by Al-Bīrūnī, Vikramāditya started the era after having defeated the Śaka king.[6] Such traditions have of course no historical basis at all. The association of king Vikramāditya, originally of North Indian tradition, with the Vikrama-saṁvat led the people of the South to fabricate the relation of Śātavāhana or Śālivāhana, a similar hero of South Indian tradition and folklore, with the other early era popular in the South.

To get the equivalent in the Christan era, one has to add 78-79 to the years of the Śaka era. The era is popular in the land to the south of the Narmadā, where the year begins on Caitra-sudi 1 and the months are *Amānta*. But, in the areas of the South where solar months are in use, the year begins from the Meṣa-saṅkrānti. The years of the Śaka era are generally counted as expired. The reckoning is commonly mentioned also in the North Indian almanacs, though there the months are regarded as *Pūṇimānta*.

1. Cf. Bhandarkar's List, Nos. 1082-83, 1086, 1088, 1089, etc.
2. Ibid., No. 1085.
3. Ibid., No. 1084. The date was wrongly read as 726.
4. Alaṅkāra, verse 3.
5. *JBBRAS*, Vol. X, pp. 132-33.
6. Sachau, *Alberuni's India*, Part II, p. 6.

The Christian era alone continued to be the official reckoning of the Government of India for about a decade after the achievement of independence in 1947. In November 1952, a committee was appointed to examine the different calendars in use in different parts of India and to submit proposals for an accurate and uniform calendar for the whole country. As a result of the committee's report submitted in 1955, the Government adopted the Śaka era in addition to the Christian era and introduced a reformed calendar from March 22, 1957. According to this calendar, the year begins on Caitra 1, and the 12 months have fixed numbers of days as in the Christian calendar. Thus the months of Caitra, Vaiśākha, Jyaiṣṭha, Āṣāḍha, Śrāvaṇa and Bhādra have each 31 days while Āśvina, Kārttika, Agrahāyana, Pauṣa, Māgha and Phālguna have each 30 days. Phālguna has 31 days in a leap year. According to this reformed calendar of the Government of India, the Śaka year 1881 began on Caitra 1 corresponding to March 22 (Sunday), 1959 A.D.

3. *Jupiter's Sixty-year Cycle*[1]

The duration of Jupiter's stay in a particular zodiacal sign is called Jupiter's year which lasts for 361 days, 2 *ghaṭikās* or *daṇḍas* and 5 *palas*. This year is thus shorter than the solar year by 4 days, 13 *ghaṭikās* or *daṇḍas* and 26 *palas*. That is why one Jupiter's year becomes suppressed in 85 solar years.

There is a name for each one of the 60 years of Jupiter's Cycle, and the years are mentioned by their names. But the 60 names are counted in North and South India in two different orders.

The sixty years of Jupiter's Cycle are as follows : (1) Prabhava, (2) Vibhava, (3) Śukla, (4) Pramoda (Pramodūta), (5) Prajāpati, (6) Aṅgiras, (7) Śrīmukha, (8) Bhāva, (9) Yuvan, (10) Dhātṛ, (11) Īśvara, (12) Bahudhānya, (13) Pramāthin, (14) Vikrama, (15) Vṛṣa, (16) Citrabhānu, (17) Subhānu, (18) Tāraṇa, (19) Pārthiva, (20) Vyaya,

1. Ojha, *Bhāratīya Prācīn Lipimālā*, pp. 188-89.

(21) Sarvajit, (22) Sarvadhārin, (23) Virodhin, (24) Vikṛti, (25) Khara, (26) Nandana, (27) Vijaya, (28) Jaya, (29) Manmatha, (30) Durmukha, (31) Hemalamba (Hemalambin), (32) Vilambin, (33) Vikārin, (34) Śārvarin, (35) Plava, (36) Śubhakṛt (Śobhakṛt), (37) Śobhana, (38) Krodhin, (39) Viśvāvasu, (40) Parābhava, (41) Plavaṅga, (42) Kīlaka, (43) Saumya, (44) Sādhāraṇa, (45) Virodhakṛt, (46) Paridhāvin, (47) Pramādin, (48) Ānanda, (49) Rākṣasa, (50) Nala or Anala, (51) Piṅgala, (52) Kālayukta, (53) Siddhārthin (Siddhārtha), (54) Raudra, (55) Durmati, (56) Dundubhi, (57) Rudhirodgārin, (58) Raktākṣa, (59) Krodhana, and (60) Kṣaya or Akṣaya.

Varāhamihira applies the name Vijaya (No. 27) to the first year of the Kaliyuga era while later writers like the author of the *Jyotiṣatattva* gives it as Prabhava (No. 1). In North India, Jupiter's year theoretically begins from the planet's entry into a particular zodiacal sign, though in actual practice Caitra-sudi 1 is regarded as its first day.

According to Varāhamihira,[1] to find out the name of a particular Śaka year after the North Indian system, one has to multiply the number of the expired Śaka year by 11 and the product again by 4; to the product 8589 has to be added, and the sum has to be divided by 3750; the quotient has then to be added to the number of the Śaka year and the product has to be divided again by 60. The remainder thus received would be the number of the expired year in the Cycle beginning with Prabhava.

In South India, Jupiter's year is regarded as the same as the solar year. The first year of the Kali era is Pramāthin (No. 13), and the year is taken to begin from Caitra-sudi 1.

The rule for finding out the name of a particular Śaka year according to the South Indian Cycle of Jupiter is as follows: 12 has to be added to the number of the expired Śaka year; the sum has then to be divided by 60; the remainder would be the number of the current year of the Cycle beginning from

1. *Bṛhatsaṁhitā*, VIII. 20.

Prabhava. Another rule is as follows 12 has to be added to the number of the expired Kali year; then the sum has to be divided by 60 and the remainder would be the number of the year of the Cycle beginning with Prabhava.

The names of the years according to Jupiter's 60-year Cycle are only occasionally met with in the records of North India. But they are very popular in the South even today. It was formerly believed that the earliest epigraph mentioning such a name is the Mahākūṭa pillar inscription of Cālukya Maṅgaleśa (597-610 A.D.) of Bādāmi, dated in the year Siddhārtha (Siddhārthin).[1] But recently the name of the cyclic year Vijaya has been traced in two Nagarjunikonda inscriptions, one of the time of the Ikṣvāku king Vīrapuruṣadatta (second half of the 3rd century A.D.) and another of his son Ehuvula Śāntamūla (close of the 3rd and the early part of the 4th century).[2] Vijaya was originally the first year of the Cycle.

4. *Kollam* (*Kolamba*) *Era*[3]

This era is called the Kollam-āṁḍu (literally 'the western year or reckoning') in Tamil and the Kolamba[4]-saṁvat in Sanskrit. It is sometimes referred to as the reckoning which started from the origin of Kollam (called Kolamba-pattana in Sanskrit) which is the real name of the Anglicised Quilon in the Travancore region of Kerala.

It is prevalent in the Malayāḻam-speaking area (i.e. in the present Kerala State) and in the contiguous Tamil regions of Tirunelveli and Kanyakumari. The Malayalis call it Paraśurāma's reckoning and imagine that the years of the era are counted in cycles of 1000, i.e. from year 1 to year 1000 and then again from year 1 without counting the hundreds. This is of course due to the people's eagerness to assign a respectable antiquity to the era and to connect it with the Puranic hero

1. *Ind. Ant.*, Vol. XIX, p. 18.
2. *Ep. Ind.*, XXXV, pp. 1 ff.
3. Ojha, *Bhāratīya Prācīn Lipimālā*, pp. 178 ff.; *Trav. Arch. Ser.*, Vol. II, pp. 36-39.
4. Cf. *Ind. Ant.*, Vol. II, p. 360.

Paraśurāma who is very popular in the tradition of the western coast land of India.

The Trivandrum inscription of Vīra-Ravivarman,[1] dated in the current Kali year 4702 and the Kollam year 776, suggests the difference of 3925 years between the two eras. According to Kielhorn, we have to add 824-25 to the years of the Kollam era to get those of the Christian era. L.D. Swamikannu Pillai adds 825 instead of 824-25.[2]

In the northern parts of Kerala or the Malayāḷam-speaking area, the beginning of the Kollam year is counted from the Kanyā-saṅkrānti, i. e. solar Āśvina 1, while, in the Tirunelveli and the adjoining regions, it is counted from the Siṁha-saṅkrānti, i.e. solar Bhādrapada 1. The months are named after the *rāśis* (e.g. Meṣa, etc.) in the North, but are given lunar names after the *nakṣatras* (e.g., Caitra, etc.) in the South. The year is solar and is generally regarded as current. The earliest epigraph dated in the era bears a date in the year 149.[3]

The circumstances leading to the foundation of the era are unknown, though its name suggests that it started from the date of the foundation of the city of Kollam (Quilon). It is however believed that the said city existed earlier than 824-25 A. D., the first year of the era. If this is true, we have to think of the reconstruction of a new city on the ruins or in the vicinity of the old one.

5. *Nevārī Era and other Reckonings of Nepāl*[4]

According to the Nepalese *Vaṁśāvalī* examined by Bhagwanlal Indraji, the Newārī or Nepāl era was introduced by king Jayadevamalla, son of king Abhayamalla of the second Ṭhākurī dynasty, though Cunningham speaks of king Rāghavadeva as the founder of the era. Jayadevamalla had his headquarters at Kāntipura and Lalitapaṭṭana while his younger brother Ānandamalla was ruling from Bhaktapura or Bhatgaon.

1. *Trav. Arch. Ser.*, Vol. II, p. 28.
2. *Ind. Ant.*, Vol. XXV, p. 54; Pillai, *Indian Chronology*, p. 43.
3. *Ep. Ind.*, Vol. IX, p. 234.
4. Ojha, *Bhāratīya Prācīn Lipimālā*, pp. 180-81; Cunningham, *Indian Eras*, p. 74; below, pp. 187-88.

They were both driven out by the Karṇāṭa chief Nānyadeva who conquered Nepal on Śrāvaṇa-sudi 7 in Śaka 811 corresponding to the year 9 of the Nevārī era.[1] The rulers of Nepal were at first using the Śaka era and then Aṁśuvarman's era,[2] and it appears that Jayadevamalla's regnal reckoning was given the character of an era by the people who did not prefer the Śaka era re-introduced by the Karṇāṭa conqueror.

The *Vaṁśāvalī* tradition referred to above, gives the difference between the Vikrama and the Nevārī era as 937 years, while Dāmodara-bhaṭṭa's *Navaratna*, completed on Monday, Maghā-nakṣatra, Mārgaśira-vadi 8, in Śaka 1607 and Nevārī 806?, gives the difference between the Śaka and Nevārī eras as 801 ? years.[3] According to Kielhorn's calculations, the Nevārī era started on the 20th October 879 A. D., i. e. Caitrādi Vikrama 936, Kārttika-sudi 1.[4]

The months are *Amānta* and the years are generally expired. If 878-879 is added to the years of the Nevārī or Nepāl era, we get those of the Christian era. The era is still prevalent in Nepal, though the Śaka era has also been popular since the Gorkha conquest of the country in 1768 A.D.

6. *Lakṣmaṇasena Era and Allied Reckonings*[5]

The era is associated with the name of a king called Lakṣmaṇasena, sometimes described as an emperor and also as the lord of Gauḍa.[6] This ruler is no doubt identical with king Lakṣmaṇasena (c. 1179-1206)[7] of the Sena dynasty of Bengal. The era (called La-saṁ, Lakṣmaṇa-saṁvat or Lakṣmaṇasena-saṁvat) is still popular in North Bihar (Mithilā) where it is known to have also been current during the late medieval

1. *Ind. Ant.*, Vol. XIII, p. 414.
2. The inscriptions of Mānadeva and his successors including the earlier records of Aṁśuvarman are dated in the Śaka era (*Select Inscriptions*, p. 866, note 1). But the later epigraphs of Aṁsuvarman and his successors bear dates in the Śaka era *minus* 500, i. e. Śaka 501 = year 1 of Aṁsuvarman's regnal reckoning, as we shall see below (p. 297)
3. H. P. Sastri, *Catalogue of Palm-leaf and Selected Paper Mss.*, p. 195.
4. *Ind. Ant.*, Vol. XVII, p. 246.
5. Cf. *IHQ*, Vol. XXXIV, pp. 21 ff.; Ojha, op cit., pp. 184-86.
6. Cf. *Ep. Ind.*, Vol. XXX, p. 80, note 3; *JASB*, N.S., Vol. XX, pp. 372-73.
7. *History of Bengal*, Dacca University, Vol. I, p. 231.

period. The year is now regarded as starting from Māgha-badi 1, and the months are *Amānta*.[1] The earliest records dated in this reckoning are, however, found in the Gaya region of South Bihar where it appears to have originated. The years of the era are generally associated with the *atīta-rājya* of Lakṣmaṇasena. The real meaning of *atīta-rājya* (i.e. the past sovereignty) can be determined from the records of another king named Govindapāla.

The date of the Gaya inscription[2] of Govindapāla is quoted as Vikrama 1232, Vikārin, Āśvina-sudi 5 falling in the 14th year of the *gata-rājya* of king Govindapāla. The date corresponds to the 22nd September, 1175 A.D. The colophons of several Buddhist manuscripts copied in the Patna-Gaya region of Bihar refer to the reign of Govindapāla; but, while only one of them mentions the 4th year of his *vijaya-rājya* and two others refer respectively to his 18th *atīta* year and the 38th year of his *vinaṣṭa-rājya* (i.e. lost sovereignty), three of the colophons speak of the years 24, 37 and 39 as belonging to that monarch but do not mention his *rājya* either as *pravardhamāna-vijaya* or as *gata*, *atīta* or *vinaṣṭa*.[3] Since the date of the Gaya inscription corresponds to the 2nd September 1175 A. D. and falls in the 14th year of Govindapāla's sovereignty which was then *gata*, i.e. a thing of the past, the 22nd of September in the year 1162 A.D. falls in the first year of this reckoning. Govindapāla is generally believed to have belonged to the Pāla dynasty of Bengal and Bihar and to have been the successor of the Pāla king Madanapāla whose inscriptions have been found in the Patna-Gaya region, the latest of them being dated the 11th of Jyaiṣṭha in his 18th regnal year and in Śaka 1083.[4] The date of the inscription corresponds to the 4th May 1161 A.D. The above facts show that Govindapāla succeeded Madanapāla in 1161 or 1162 A.D., that he ruled at least upto his 4th regnal year and that his sovereignty became *gata*, *atīta* or *vinaṣṭa*

1. Modern Maithil almanacs are stated to give the equivalent of La-saṁ 1 variously as Śaka 1026-27, 1027-28, 1029-30 and 1030-31, i.e. between 1104 and 1109 A. D.

2. Bhandarkar's List, No. 370.

3. See *JAS*, Letters, Vol. XVII, p. 28; *Ep. Ind.*, Vol. XXXV, pp. 233 ff.

4. *Ep. Ind.*, Vol. XXVIII, pp. 141 ff.

sometime before the 22nd September 1175 A. D.[1] His *gata*°, *atīta*° or *vinaṣṭa-rājya* reckoning was thus not counted from the end of his reign or *vijaya-rājya* (as is often wrongly believed) but was undoubtedly counted in continuation of his ordinary regnal or *vijaya-rājya* reckoning.

The similar case of Govindapāla would suggest that the Lakṣmaṇasena-saṁvat was originally counted from the accession of king Lakṣmaṇasena about 1179 A.D. and not from any other date such as that of the end of his reign about 1206 A.D. or of his defeat at the hands of the Muhammadans a few years earlier. The initiation and prevalence of the era in Bihar again suggest the expansion of the suzerainty of the Senas of Bengal over that region.

As indicated above, the beginning of the Lakṣmaṇasena era is supposed to fall in 1104-19 A.D. according to the records of Mithila, although it is generally believed to be 1108 A.D. But Kielhorn pointed out that, according to some dates quoted in certain medieval works, its first year was equivalent to 1119-20 A.D. Actually, however, calculation based on the years of this era in the late medieval records quoted with the corresponding Śaka years has shown its beginning to have fallen variously in 1108, 1109, 1110, 1113, 1115 or 1119 A.D., i.e. on some date between 1108 and 1119 A.D.[2] King Lakṣmaṇasena of Bengal, however, flourished much later than this period.

About the beginning of an excellent survey of the problem of the Lakṣmaṇasena era, R.C. Majumdar observes, 'The first point to remember is that no Sena king, not even the two sons of Lakṣmaṇasena, ever used the era, and that there is no evidence that it was ever known, far less used, in Bengal during the Sena period......... This raises grave doubts about the foundation of the era by Lakṣmaṇasena or any other Sena

1. Ibid., Vol. XX, pp. 43 ff.

2. *Hist. Beng.*, op. cit., pp. 233, 238. See also S. Jha's introduction to his *Songs of Vidyāpati*. For other cases of the kind, see S. Mukhopādhyāy, *Prācīn Bāṁlā Sāhitye Kāl-kram*, pp. 21 ff. Mukhopādhyāy has tried to show that the initial year of the La-saṁ varies between 1080 and 1129 A.D.

ruler of Bengal."[1] On the same grounds, H. C. Raychaudhuri[2] proposed to identify the founder of the era with some other ruler bearing that name and conjectured the existence of a Lakṣmaṇasena among the ruling chiefs of the Sena dynasty of Pīṭhī.[3] But the tradition referring to the founder of the era as an imperial ruler of Gauḍa undoubtedly points to his indentification with the only known Lakṣmaṇasena of East Indian history, viz. the Sena king of that name.

It is admitted that the *atīta-rājya* reckoning started as a result of the reluctance of the partisans or co-religionists of king Govindapāla of the Gaya region to change the mode of dating their records even after his overthrow. If the dominions of Lakṣmaṇasena of Bengal included the same area of Bihar, the overthrow of his rule from there could have likewise induced his partisans to follow a similar method of dating. It has to be noticed that the people of the Gaya region of Bihar had a liking for this kind of dating in the *atīta-rājya* reckoning of particular rulers as it was they who started the *atīta-rājya* reckonings of both Govindapāla and Lakṣmaṇasena.[4] But there is as yet no evidence of Lakṣmaṇasena's rule over the Gayā area of Bihar, though there are traditions regarding Sena rule in Mithilā or North Bihar and we have now an inscription[5] pointing to the inclusion of the Bhagalpur region of South Bihar within the dominions of Ballālasena (c. 1158-79 A.D.), father of Lakṣmaṇasena, in the 9th year of his reign, i.e. about 1166 A.D. The discovery of this record shows that Lakṣmaṇasena's rule over parts of South Bihar including the Gaya region at least for a short time can no longer be regarded as altogether impossible. His claim of victory over the Gāhaḍavālas becomes intelligible in that case.

1. Loc. cit. 2. *JASB*, N. S., Vol. XXII, pp. 385 ff.

3. The expression probably indicated the Buddhist religious establishment at Bodhgaya together with its landed properties. These rulers enjoyed the title *Ācārya* and appear to have been the precursors of the later Mohant Mahārājas of Bodhgaya.

4. The occasional reference to the Vikrama-saṁvat in Bihar as the *atīta-rājya* reckoning of Vikramāditya (cf. *JAS*, Letters, Vol. XX, p. 44) may be due to the influence of the popular Lakṣmaṇasena-saṁvat.

5. *Ep. Ind.*, Vol. XXX, pp. 78 ff.

Majumdar says, "It is probable that when the Pāla kingdom in Gaya was finally destroyed, the people, especially the Buddhists, continued for sometime to count their dates with reference to the last Buddhist Pāla king Govindapāla. Again when the Muslim invaders destroyed the Hindu kingdoms in Bihar and Bengal, the people unwilling to refer to the *pravardhamāna-vijaya-rājya* of the foreign conquerors, counted the dates with reference to the destruction of the last Hindu kingdom."[1] But this is possible only if Lakṣmaṇasena ruled over Bihar. Govindapāla appears to have been ousted from the Gaya region by the Gāhaḍavālas[2] who were probably themselves ousted from that area by the Senas. This possibility explains the introduction of the two *atīta-rājya* reckonings of Govindapāla and Lakṣmaṇasena in the said region and the latter's introduction thence to North Bihar by the people of that part, who fled to the north after the Muslim occupation of South Bihar. Lakṣmaṇasena's *atīta-rājya* reckoning thus seems to have come into existence on the extirpation of Sena rule from Bihar although the calculation must have been the same as the regnal reckoning of that monarch.[3]

We do not know whether Lakṣmaṇasena was ousted from the Gaya area by the Gāhaḍavālas or the Muslims. The silence of the Muslim historians on this point may of course suggest that it was probably the Gāhaḍavālas who re-occupied the area from the Senas no doubt for a short time to be themselves overthrown by the Muhammadans. The Sena inscriptions actually speak of Lakṣmaṇasena's struggle with the Gāhaḍavālas.[4]

1. Op. cit., p. 235.

2. Cf. *Ep. Ind.*, Vol. XXX, p. 82.

3. In such a possibility, the 35 years' rule of Palapāla in parts of South Bihar in the second half of the 12th century has probably to be explained by supposing that he was a subordinate of the Senas. Cf. *JBRS*, Vol. XL, Part 2, pp. 43-53; *Ep. Ind.*, Vol. XXX, pp. 81-82.

4. Lakṣmaṇasena's Madhainagar (N. G. Majumdar, *Ins. Beng.*, Vol. III, p. 111) and Bhowal (*Ep. Ind.*, Vol. XXVI, p. 6) plates, both issued in the later part of his reign, speak of his victory over the king of Kāśi, i.e. a Gāhaḍavāla monarch. He or his son Viśvarūpasena is also stated in the Sena records to have planted pillars of victory at Viśveśvara-kṣetra (Kāśī) and Triveṇī (Prayāga or Allahabad), both in the dominions of the

As to the confusion regarding the starting point of the Lakṣmaṇasena-saṁvat in Mithilā between 1108 and 1119 A.D., Majumdar says, "......instead of counting from the end of the reign [of Lakṣmaṇasena about 1200 A.D.] people of the later age counted from his birth [about 1120 A.D.].........The artificial character of the era, set up at a later time with reference to a past event perhaps explains the great discrepancy in the initial years of that era as calculated from the different instances of its use."[1] But the era was not 'an artificial reckoning associated with an event of remote past' as Majumdar puts it,[2] since, as a matter of fact, it was essentially the continuation of Lakṣmaṇasena's regnal reckoning just as the Śaka era seems to have been the continuation of the regnal reckoning of Kaniṣka I. Since moreover the earliest known date in the era is found to be the year 51,[3] its origin could not have been of a remote past at least to its early users.

The earliest use of the Lakṣmaṇasena era is found in three inscriptions[4] dated respectively in (1) year 51, Bhādra 29, (2) year 74, Vaiśākha-badi 12, Thursday, and (3) year 83, Kārttika-sudi 15. Of the three dates, only the second one is verifiable since the week-day has been mentioned. If the reckoning started with the accession of king Lakṣmaṇasena about 1179 A.D., the years 51, 74 and 83 would fall respectively about 1230, 1253 and 1262 A.D. The second date is therefore Thursday corresponding to Vaiśākha-badi 12 in 1253 A.D. In the said year, the 12th *tithi* of the dark half of *Pūrṇimānta* Vaiśākha began on Thursday the 27th March at 10 of the day.

The inscriptions of the years 51 (1230 A.D.) and 74 (1253

Gāhaḍavālas. See N. G. Majumdar, op. cit., pp. 122-23, etc.; *Ep. Ind.*, Vol. XXXIII, pp. 315 ff. If both the *atīta-rājya* reckonings of Govindapāla and Lakṣmaṇasena started as a result of the people's reluctance to refer to Gāhaḍavāla rule, they may have had bitter feelings against the Gāhaḍavālas and were partial to the Pālas and Senas of Bengal.

1. Op. cit., p. 236.
2. Ibid., p. 328.
3. Bhandarkar's List, No. 1467.
4. Ibid., Nos. 1467-69. They were all found in the Gaya region, two from Bodhgaya and the third from Jaṇibigha near Bodhgaya.

A.D.) mention *Mahārāja* Aśokacalla of the Khasa country in the Sapādalakṣa hills, while the record of the year 83 speaks of *Ācārya* Jayasena, the lord of Pīṭhī and the son of Buddhasena. Another inscription[1] from Gaya, dated in the year 1813 of the Buddha's Parinirvāṇa era, Kārttika-badi 1, Wednesday, mentions the said Aśokacalla, king of the Sapādalakṣa hills. According to the Ceylonese Buddha Parinirvāṇa era prevalent also in Burma and Siam and believed to have started from 544 B.C.,[2] the year 1813 would correspond to 1269-70 A.D. In 1270 A.D. the first *tithi* of the dark half of *Pūrṇimānta* Kārttika fell on Wednesday the 1st of October.[3]

According to the biography[4] of the Tibetan pilgrim Chos-rje-dpal or Dharmasvāmin who was born in 1197 A.D. and died in 1264 A.D., the pilgrim visited Bodhgaya where he met its ruler Buddhasena in 1235 A. D. We have seen that Buddhasena's son Jayasena was ruling in the year 83 of the Lakṣmaṇasena era corresponding, in our opinion, to 1262, A.D. The rule of the father 27 years before a date in the son's reign does not appear to be exceptional.

We may conclude therefore that the Lakṣmaṇa-saṁvat was originally counted from the date of the accession of king Lakṣmaṇasena of Bengal [and Bihar] about 1179 A.D., although its starting point was later suposed to be some date between 1108 and 1119 A.D. in North Bihar through confusion. This confusion appears to be associated with the fact that the era was initiated by the people of the Gaya region, but that it migrated, even in its infancy, to North Bihar with the migration of many people of South Bihar to the north as a result of the Muslim conquest of the former region at the close of the twelfth century. We know that in the late medieval period the people

1. Ibid., No. 1459.
2. Ojha, *op. cit.* p. 194.
3. The mention of Aśokacalla in 1230, 1253 and 1270 A.D. would suggest that he ruled for over 40 years from about 1230 A.D. to about 1270 A.D. This reign period does not appear to be exceptionally long.
4. *JBRS*, Vol. XLII, Part 1, pp. 76 ff. In 1234 A.D., he met king Rāmasiṁha of Simraongadh, who ascended the throne in 1227 A.D., and in 1241 and 1256 A.D., he was invited to the court of Kublai Khān.

of North Bihar assigned the commencement of the era to different dates ranging between 1108 and 1119 A.D., although ultimately 1108 A.D. came to be generally regarded as the starting point. But the real circumstances leading to this confusion is difficult to determine. The commencement of the era, synchronizing with Lakṣmaṇasena's accession in 1179 A.D., seems to have been later confused with the date of the said king's birth, about which the people's ideas were probably characterised by confusion owing to the absence of a unanimous tradition.

In this connection reference may be made to two eras prevalent in some parts of Bengal during the late medieval period. These are the Balālī San of 1199 A.D. and the Parganātī San of 1202-03 A.D. (or 1201-02 A.D.). They appear to be modifications of the same era, sometimes called by local names such as 'the San of Parganā Bhuluā.'[1] Probably these eras were counted from the time when the Senas lost wide areas of their dominions in West Bengal and the adjoining region just as the La-saṁ was counted from the time when they had lost their possessions in South Bihar.

7. *Christian Era*[2]

Dionysius Exiguus of Rome, invented the era about 532 A.D. The birth of Jesus Christ was assigned to the 753rd year after the supposed date of the foundation of the city of Rome and in the 4th year of the 194th Olympiad.[3] Thus the era is based on the supposition that Jesus Christ was born in 1 A.D. though

1. See *History of Bengal*, Vol. I, pp. 235-36; *Ind. Ant.*, Vol. LII, pp. 314 ff.

2. Ojha, *Bhāratīya Prācīn Lipimālā*, pp. 194-95; see *A. D.* or *Anno Domini* in an *Encyclopaedia*.

3. In ancient Greece, the period of 4 years between two consecutive Olympic games was called an Olympiad and was the basis of calculation of time. About 264 B.C., Timaeus of Sicily calculated the first Olympic game to have been played in 776 B.C. and since then the Olympiad reckoning gradually obtained the nature of a sort of era. There was at first no definitely accepted date for the foundation of Rome though it was generally placed about the middle of the 8th century B.C. Fabius Pictor (220 B.C.) placed the date in 747 B.C., Polybius (204-122 B.C.) in 750 B.C., Porcius Cato (234-149 B.C.) in 751 B.C., Varrius Flaccus in 752 B.C. and Terentius Varro (116-28 B.C.) in 753 B.C.

scholars now believe that he was born between 8 and 4 B.C. (on Friday, April 5, 4 B. C., according to some). It reached England in the 8th century and in France, Belgium Germany and Switzerland in the 8th and 9th centuries and became popular in all Christian lands by about 1000 A.D. It is now used all over the world.

This era follows the Roman calendar[1] which was reformed by Julius Caesar in 46 B. C.[2] and Pope Gregory XIII in 1582 A. D.[3] The days are counted from midnight to midnight

1. The Roman year was originally of 304 days divided into 10 months from March to December, the fifth month (July) being called Quinctilis and the sixth (August) Sextilis. Numa Pompilius (715-672 B. C.) added January at the beginning and February at the end of the year and introduced the year of 12 lunar months and of 355 days. From 452 B.C., the year was regarded as solar, though it continued to consist of 355 days, while 22 and 23 days were added respectively to the second and fourth years in four years. Thus the average year of $366\frac{1}{4}$ days had one day more than the ordinary solar year. The gradually increasing difference had to be rectified from time to time by the recognition of additional months.

2. In 46 B.C., Julius Caesar, who named the 5th month after himself (July), reformed the calendar by removing the difference of 90 days by regarding the year in question as consisting of 455 days. He introduced the year of $365\frac{1}{4}$ days and fixed the days of the 12 months as follows : January, March, May, July, September and November—31 days each; April, June, Sextilis (later August), October and December—30 days each; February 28 days for 3 years and 29 days in each fourth year. Augustus Caesar, who gave his name to the eight month, fixed the days of the months now prevalent, i.e. August—31 days; September and November—30 days each; December—31 days; February—28 days for three years and 29 days in every fourth year; other months—the same as in the Julian calendar.

3. The Julian year of $365\frac{1}{4}$ days was longer than the solar year by 11 minutes and 14 seconds so that a day came to be in excess in about 128 years. As years passed on, the Meṣa-saṅkrānti, which occurred on the 25th March in Julius Caesar's time, came to fall on the 21st March in 325 A.D. and on the 11th March in 1582 A.D. To remove this difference, Pope Gregory XIII passed an order on the 22nd February 1582 A.D. to the effect that the 5th October of the said year should be regarded as the 15th October and that the month of February should have 29 days in the year completing a century (e.g. 1600 A.D., 1700 A.D., etc.) when its figures are divisible by 400 and only 28 days when they are not so divisible. In this system, one day would be in excess in no less than 3320 years. The Pope's calendar was accepted by the Catholic countries (e.g. Italy, Spain, Portugal, etc), while the Protestant countries, originally reluctant to accept the Gregorian calendar, also ultimately accepted it. In Germany, the last ten days of the year 1699

and the year begins from January.[1] It became popular in India during the days of British occupation.

A.D. were omitted, i.e., the 21st December 1699 A.D. was followed by the 1st January, 1700 A.D. In England, 11 days were similarly omitted from the the year 1752 A.D. by regarding the day following the 2nd September as the 14th September. The countries under the Greek Church (e.g. Russia, Greece, etc.) adopted the Gregorian calendar at a much later date.

1. Down to the 16th century, most of the European countries regarded the 25th March as the first day of the year. France adopted the 1st January as the first day of the year in 1663 A.D. In England, the Christmas day (i.e. the 25th December) was regarded as the new year's day from the 7th to the 12th century A.D. and the 25th March was the first day of the year between the 12th and 17th centuries.

SECTION III

OBSOLETE RECKONINGS

1. *Parthian or Arsacid Era*[1]

The Asiatic possessions of Alexander the Great ultimately passed after his death to his general Seleucus Nicator whose era started from the date of his triumphant entry into Babylon on the 1st of October, 312 B.C. No Indian record is definitely known to be dated in this era. But the Macedonian names of the months were adopted along with the use of the era in the Greek empire of Western Asia, whence their use in dates spread to India.

The Parthian era, indicating the foundation of the independent Parthian kingdom by Arsaces I about 248 B.C. and meant for the supercession of the Seleucid era from the Parthian dominions, is found in a few Indian inscriptions.[2] These are the Mathura inscription[3] of the year 292, Girdharpur inscription[4] of the year 270, Charsadda inscription[5] of the year 303, Loriyan Tongai inscription[6] of the year 318, Jamalgarhi inscription[7] of the year 359, Hashtnagar inscription[8] of the year 384 and Skarah Dheri inscription[9] of the year 399. Some epigraphs of the Scytho-Parthians and Kuṣāṇas of India, which are dated in the Vonones (old Scytho-Parthian or Vikrama) and Kaniṣka (Śaka) eras of 58 B.C. and 78

1. See Ojha, *Bhāratīya Prācīn Lāpimālā*, p. 165; cf. Smith, *Classical Dictionary*, s.v. *Seleucus* and *Arsaces*; see also Lempricres' *Classical Dictonary*. The date is sometimes put as c. 250 B.C. and also as 247 B.C. (*East and West*, Vol. 9, No. 3, September 1958, p. 155).

2. See *D. R. Bhandarkar Volume*, p. 306. The dates are often wrongly assigned to the old Scytho-Parthian era.

3. Ibid., p. 281.

4. Ibid., p. 286.

5. Ibid., p. 306.

6. *CII*, Vol. II, Part i, pp. 106-07.

7. Ibid., pp. 110 ff.

8. Ibid., pp. 117 ff.

9. Ibid., pp. 124 ff.

A.D. respectively, use the names of Macedonian months adopted by the Parthians. The 12 months of this calendar are : (1) Hyperberetaeus (=October=Āśvina-Kārttika); (2) Dius (=November=Kārttika-Mārgaśīrṣa); (3) Apellaeus (=December=Mārgaśīrṣa-Pauṣa); (4) Audunaeus (=January= =Pauṣa-Māgha); (5) Peritius (= February=Māgha-Phālguna); (6) Dustrus (=March=Phālguna-Caitra); (7) Xanthicus (=April=Caitra-Vaiśākha); (8) Artemisius (= May=Vaiśākha-Jyaiṣṭha); (9) Daesius (=June=Jyaiṣṭha-Āṣāḍha); (10) Panemus (=July=Āṣāḍha-Śrāvaṇa); (11) Lous (=August=Śrāvaṇa=Bhādra); (12) Gorpaeus (= September=Bhādra-Āśvina). Of these months of the Graeco-Parthian calendar, Audunaeus, Apellaeus, Artemisius, Daesius, Panemus and Gorpaeus are mentioned in the dates of certain inscriptions of the Scytho-Parthians and Kuṣāṇas.[1]

2. *Kalacuri or Cedi Era*[2]

The era was used by the Kalacuris, who ruled over the ancient Cedi country with their capital at Tripurī near Jabalpur, and was called the Kalacuri- or Cedi-saṁvat.[3] These Kalacuris carried the use of the era to the Jabalpur region from their original home in the lower valley of the Narmadā. About the said region, the era was first used by the Traikūṭakas of the Northern Konkan area in the 5th century A.D., then by the early Kalacuris ruling over the Northern part of the Marāṭhī-speaking tract and Malwa in the 6th and 7th centuries A.D. as well as by the rulers of the Gurjara and some other dynasties ruling about the Gujarātī-speaking area from the 6th century onwards.[4] There is no doubt that the era originated in the region around the Northern Konkan. It

1. See Cunningham, *Indian Eras*, p. 41; *Select Inscriptions*, p. 120 (Taxila inscription of year 78 of the older Scytho-Parthian era, Panema= Panemus); p. 135 (Sui Vihar inscription of year 11 of the Kaniṣka era, Daisika=Daesius); p. 143 (Kurram inscription of year 21 of the Kaniṣka era, Avadunaka=Audunaeus); p. 146 (Mathura inscription of year 28 of the Kaniṣka era, Gurpiya=Gorpaeus); p. 153 (Wardak or Khawat inscription of year 51 of the Kaniṣka era, Arthamisiya=Artemisius); etc.
2. *CII*, Vol. IV, pp. i ff.; Ojha, *Bhāratīya Prācīn Lipimālā*, pp. 173-74.
3. See, e.g., *Ind. Ant.*, Vol. XX, p. 84; Vol XXII, p. 82.
4. See Bhandarkar's List, Nos. 1199 ff.

is impossible to believe that its use spread far away from the said area before the rise of the Later Kalacuris of the Jabalpur region. The attempt to trace the use of this era in early records such as the U.P. epigraphs like those of the Maghas[1] of Kauśāmbī, M.P. inscriptions like those of the *Mahārājas* of Uccakalpa,[2] and Orissan records like the Patiakela and Soro plates[3] of Śambhuyaśas is no doubt absolutely untenable. Its identification with the Kaniṣka era is no better than fantastic.[4]

The use of the expression *pravardhamāna-rājya-saṁvatsara*, with reference to the era by the Traikūṭakas[5] who used it earlier than the other dynasties of West India,[6] may suggest that it was started by them. But the earliest date of the era in the Traikūṭaka inscriptions is year 207 (455 A.D.), and very little of the earlier history of the family is known. It has been suggested that the Traikūṭakas were originally feudatories of the Ābhīras who probably became independent of the Śakas in the North Marāṭhā country about the middle of the 3rd century A.D., that the era started from the first regnal year of Ābhīra Īśvarasena mentioned in a Nasik inscription[7] and that it was continued by the erstwhile subordinate families like the Traikūṭakas and early Kalacuris. The suggestion may not be impossible and, although there is really little proof in support of the conjecture, it seems that the era was started from the foundation of an independent kingdom carved out of the dominions of the Śakas in order to oust the use of the Śaka era from the said area.

Kielhorn suggested, on the basis of a number of dates, that the expired year 1 of the era started on the 26th August 249 A.D.

1. Cf. *Select Inscriptions*, p. 365, note 1.
2. Cf. Bhandarkar's List, Nos. 1194-98 and notes.
3. See ibid., No. 1203; *Ep. Ind.*, Vol. XXIV, p. 199.
4. See *Ind. Ant.*, Vol. XLVI, pp. 69-70.
5. See Bhandarkar's List, No. 1202.
6. The suggestion that records like the charters of Svāmidāsa, Bhuluṇḍa and Rudradāsa (cf. Bhandarkar's List, Nos. 1259, 1266, 1861) are dated in this era is untenable. These epigraphs are no doubt dated in the Gupta era. See *IHQ*, Vol. XXII, pp. 51-52; Vol. XXIV, pp. 75 ff.
7. *Ep. Ind.*, Vol. VIII, p. 88.

=Vikrama 306, Āśvina-sudi 1.[1] By adding 248-49 to its expired years, we get those of the Christian reckoning, although it has to be admitted that this epoch does not suit all the dates in this era found in inscriptions.[2] The use of the era disappeared sometime after the fall of the Kalacuris of the Chhattisgarh region in the early part of the 13h century A.D.[3]

3. *Gupta or Valabhī Era*[4]

The era used by the Imperial Guptas of Magadha and their feudatories as well as some of the successors of both was called the year or reckoning of the Guptas from about the middle of the 5th century, i.e. more than a century after its start.[5] In the earlier records dated in the era, it is treated exactly as the regnal reckoning of particular kings, without giving it any specific name. This is indeed the nature of all eras developed from the regnal reckoning of a ruler continued by his successors.

The Mathura inscription[6] of Candragupta II is dated both in his 5th regnal year and in the *kāl-ānuvartamāna* year 61 (i.e. the year 61 counted according to the era); but it does not specifically associate the reckoning with the Guptas as in the later cases referred to above. Other records of the Imperial Guptas mention particular years of the era either without any specification[7] or as belonging to a particular monarch or to his

1. *Ind. Ant.*, Vol. XVII, p. 215; *Ep. Ind.*, Vol. II, p. 299; *Festgruss an Roth*, pp. 53 ff. Kielhorn suggests that the months were *Pūrṇimānta*. Cf. *IHQ*, Vol. XXV, p. 81.

2. Mirashi points out that the earlier dates coming from Gujarat and Maharashtra show the epoch of the era to be 248-49 A.D. while the later dates coming from Chhattisgarh and elsewhere in North India suggest the epoch 247-48 A.D. (*ABORI*, Vol. XXVII, pp. 1 ff.). He also suggests that the year began on Kārttika-sudi 1 and that the months were generally *Amānta* in Gujarat and Maharashtra and *Pūrṇimānta* elsewhere. In *IHQ*. Vol. XXV, pp. 81 ff., he sugg sts that the epoch of the era in some parts of Vidarbha was 250-51 A.D. Much of this confusion about the epoch of the era, however, appears to be due to errors in the enumeration of the dates.

3. See Bhandarkar's List, Nos. 1251 ff.

4. *CII*, Vol. III, Intr., pp. 16 ff.; Ojha, *Bhāratīya Prācīn Lipimālā*, pp. 174 ff.

5. *CII*, Vol. III, Intr., pp. 29-30, Text, pp. 60-61, 107; *R. G. Bhandarkar Com. Vol.*, p. 203; *Ind. Ant.*, Vol. II, p. 258; etc.

6. *Select Inscriptions*, pp. 269 ff.

7. Cf. *Select Inscriptions*, p. 271 (Udaygiri inscription of Candragupta II—*saṁvatsare* 82); p. 274 (Sanchi inscription of Candragupta II—*saṁ* 93); etc.

reign.[1] It was of course later specifically attributed to the Guptas.[2]

It is as yet unknown which early member of the Imperial Gupta dynasty founded the Gupta era, i.e. the regnal reckoning of which amongst them was continued by his sucessors. Since Candragupta I, father of Samudragupta and grandfather of Candragupta II, was the first imperial ruler of the family, the first year of the era is generally believed by scholars to be equivalent to the year of that king's accession. This is quite probable in view of the fact that his grandson ascended the throne in the year 57 of the era, but is by no means certain. It is not at all impossible that the era started from the first regnal year of Gupta, Ghaṭotkaca or Samudragupta who were respectively the grandfather, father and son of Candragupta I. If the spurious Nalanda[3] and Gaya[4] inscriptions of respectively the 5th and 9th regnal years of Samudragupta are believed to be forged copies of two genuine records of that king bearing the said dates, the era may have started from Samudragupta's accession. But the records appear to have been copied from those of his successors.

On the decline of the power of the Imperial Guptas, especially in Western India, their erstwhile feudatories,[5] the Maitrakas of Valabhī in Kathiawar, continued the use of the era, the earliest record of that family being the Bhamodra Mohota plates[5] of Droṇasiṁha, dated in the year 183.[6]

1. Cf. ibid., p. 279 (Bilsad inscription—*śrī-Kumāraguptasy=ābhivardhamāna-vijaya-rājya-saṁvatsare ṣaṇṇavate* (*vatitame*).

2. Cf. *varṣa-śate Guptānāṁ sa-catuḥpañcāśad-uttare* (Bhandarkar's List, No. 1281); see also ibid., Nos. 1283, 1285, 1329, 1339, 1376, 1378, etc.

3. *Select Inscriptions*, pp. 263 ff.

4. Ibid., pp. 264 ff.

5. Ibid., pp. 403 ff.

6. The identity of the Gupta and Valabhī reckonings is indicated by the fact that, of two records of the same age and also the area in question, one associated the era with the Guptas and the other with Valabhī. These are the Unā (Kathiawad) plate of Valabhī-saṁvat 574 and the Morbi (Kathiawar) plate of Gupta-saṁvat 585. See Bhandarkar's List, Nos. 1379 and 1378 (these numbers should have been 1378 and 1379). To get the equivalent Christian year, 318-19 requires to be added to the current Kārttikādi Valabhī year and 319-20 to the current Caitrādi Gupta year, according to some (S. Pillai, *Indian Ephemeris*, Vol. I, Part i, p. 54):

The continuous use of the era by Droṇasiṁha's successors for a few centuries led to the era being designated the Valabhī-saṁvat[1] in that region. This fact is also at the root of the confused tradition about the era, recorded by Al-Bīrūnī in the 11th century A.D. Thus Al-Bīrūni says, "As regards the Gupta-kāla, people say that the Guptas were wicked powerful people, and that when they ceased to exist this date was used as the epoch of an era. It seems that Valabha was the last of them, because the epoch of the Guptas fall, like that of the Valabha era, 241 years later than the Śaka-kāla."[2] Al-Bīrūnī is certainly right when he says that the Gupta and Valabhī eras are identical and that the said era started 241 years after the commencement of the Śaka era, i.e. in 319 A.D. But his conjecture that the era started from the end of the Guptas is obviously wrong since we know for certain that the Maitrakas of Valabhī did not start any new era but only continued the use of the era of their former masters, the Imperial Guptas. This is quite clear from the dates of the Girnar (near Junagadh in Kathiawar) rock inscription of Skandagupta, viz., the Gupta years 136 and 138, and the date of the Bhamodra Mohota plates of Droṇasiṁha, viz. 183, which are respectively the latest Gupta dates in Kathiawar and the earliest date of the Maitrakas. The confusion is apparently due to the fact that the Maitrakas of Valabhī ruled independently sometime after the end of Gupta rule in Kathiawar.

The Veraval inscription[3] of the time of Caulukya-Vāghelā Arjuna is dated on Sunday, Āṣāḍha-badi 13 of a year given as Hijrī (Rasūla-Mahammada-saṁvat) 662, Vikrama 1320, Valabhī-saṁvat 945 and Siṁha-saṁvat 151. The difference between the Vikrama and the Valabhī or Gupta eras is thus given here as 375 years while Al-Bīrūni quotes it as 376 years.

1. See *Ep. Ind.*, Vol. IX. p. 6.

2. Sachau, *Alberuni's India*, Part II, p. 7; *CII*, Vol. III, Intro., pp. 30-31.

3. *Ep. Ind.*, Vol. XXXIV, pp. 143 ff.

The Veraval inscription probably speaks of the month of Āṣāḍha in the Kārttikādi Vikrama year 1320 which would be the same as the Caitrādi Vikrama year 1321 with reference to the month in question.

The years of the Gupta era are believed to have started on Caitra-sudi 1, and the months are regarded as *Pūrṇimānta*. During the age of the Imperial Guptas, the use of the era spread over wide areas of North India, including Assam, Bengal and Orissa. As we have seen, the Maitrakas used it for a long time after the decline of the Guptas. The latest use of the Valabhī (i.e. Gupta) era in Kathiawar is found in the inscription[1] of the year 945 (1264 A.D.) referred to above.

The era used in the inscription of the Licchavis of Nepal has been identified by Fleet with the Gupta era and he assigns the Changunarayan inscription of Mānadeva (dated in the year 386, Jyaiṣṭha-sudi 1, Rohiṇī-nakṣatra, Abhijit) to the 28th April 705 A.D.[2] But Bhagavanlal Indraji identified the Licchavi era with the Vikrama-saṁvat and assigned the Changunarayan inscription to 329 A.D.[2] while Sylvain Lévi suggested that the Licchavi era started in 110 A.D.[4] Without taking the astronomical calculations into consideration since they do not appear to be completely satisfactory, the theory of Fleet does not appear to suit the palaeography of the Licchavi inscriptions. The Changunarayan inscription, as for instance, should be palaeographically assigned to a date about the 5th century A.D. and not in the 8th as suggested by Fleet. As regards Bhagwanlal Indraji's views, it has to be remembered that there was hardly any possibility of the spread of the use of the Vikrama-saṁvat in Nepal in the early centuries of the Christian era. It is equally difficult to accept Lévi's theory. The existence of a new era can be entertained only on definite evidence when the identification of an era with any other era prevalent in the neighbourhood of the area and age in question

1. Bhandarkar's List, No. 1384.
2. *CII*, Vol. III, Intr., p. 95.
3. *Ind. Ant.*, Vol. XVII, p. 210.
4. *Le Nepal*, Vol. II, p. 126.

is found to be impossible. We are inclined to identify the era used by the Licchavis of Nepal with the Kaniṣka or Śaka era of 78 A.D. which is known to have been continued in the Bihar-U.P. region by ruling families like the Mitras of Magadha and the Maghas of Kauśāmbī.[1] The Changunarayan inscription of the year 386 may thus be assigned to 468 A.D.[2]

After Fleet satisfactorily determined the epoch of the Gupta era about the end of the last century, there have appeared many suggestions regarding various other epochs. But they are not worthy of serious consideration.[3]

4. *Jupiter's Twelve-year Cycle*[4]

The reckoning is associated with Jupiter's movement. This planet sets when the sun comes near it and reappears between 25 and 31 days later. The year is named after the *nakṣatra* in which Jupiter reappears, the names being those of the lunar months such as Caitra, etc. Sometimes the word *mahā* is prefixed to the names of the month to indicate the years of the cycle, e.g., Mahā-Caitra, etc.

Jupiter's reappearance in particular *nakṣatras* leads to the naming of the years in the following order : (1) Kṛttikā or Rohiṇī—Kārttika or Mahā-Kārttika; (2) Mṛgaśirā or Ārdrā —Mārgaśīrṣa or Mahā-Mārgaśīrṣa; (3) Punarvasu or Puṣyā—Pauṣa or Mahā-Pauṣa; (4) Aśleṣā or Maghā—Māgha or Mahā-Māgha; (5) Pūrva-Phalgunī, Uttara-Phalgunī or Hastā—Phālguna or Mahā-Phālguna; (6) Citrā or Svātī—Caitra or Mahā-Caitra; (7) Viśākhā or Anurādhā—Vaiśākha or Mahā-Vaiśākha; (8) Jyeṣṭhā or Mūlā—Jyaiṣṭha or Mahā-Jyaiṣṭha; (9) Pūrv-Āṣāḍhā or Uttar-Āṣḍāhā—Āsāḍha or Mah-Āsāḍha; (10) Śravaṇā or Dhaniṣṭhā—Śrāvaṇa or Mahā-Śrāvaṇa; (11) Śatabhiṣā, Pūrva-Bhādrapada or Uttara-Bhādrapada—

1. Cf. *Ep. Ind.*, Vol. XXXI, pp. 229 ff.; *Select Inscriptions*, p. 365, note 1.

2. If there are astronomical difficulties in accepting this indentification, similar difficulties are there in the cases of all the other theories. Such difficulties are due to defective almanacs. See above, pp. 226 ff.

3. Cf. *Ind. Cult.*, Vol. III, pp. 47 ff.

4. Fleet, *CII*, Vol. III, pp. 105 ff.; Ojha, *Bhāratīya Prācīn Lipimālā*, p. 187.

Bhādrapada or Mahā-Bhādrapada; and (12) Revatī, Aśvinī or Bharaṇī—Āśvina (Āśvayuja) or Mah-Āśvina (Mah-Āśvayuja).

In twelve solar years, Jupiter's reappearance occurs eleven times. One of the solar years of the Cycle is therefore regarded as suppressed. Some inscriptions of about the 5th century A.D. mention the years of Jupiter's Twelve-year Cycle though they are even now mentioned in the almanacs in some parts of India. The earliest occurrence of the reckoning in North and South India can be traced in the Khoh copper-plate grant[1] of the Parivrājaka king Hastin dated in the Gupta year 163 (482-83 A.D.) called Mah-Āśvayuja-saṁvatsara and a grant[2] of the Kadamba king Mṛgeśavarman (second half of the 5th century A.D.) dated in his third regnal year styled Pauṣa-saṁvatsara. Among other records mentioning the said reckoning, reference may be made to the Majgaon plates[3] of Hastin (dated in the Gupta year 191=510-11 A.D. called Mahā-Caitra-saṁvatsara), the Khoh plates[4] of Saṁkṣobha (dated in the Gupta year 209=528-29 A.D. called Mah-Āśvayuja-saṁvatsara) and the Bhumara pillar inscription[5] (dated in the Mahā-Māgha-saṁvatsara) of the time of Hastin.

5. *Gaṅga or Gāṅgeya Era*[6]

The Eastern Gaṅgas of Kaliṅganagara (modern Mukhalingam near Srikakulam) used an era down to the rise of the Imperial branch of the family in the 10th century A.D. The early records of the Imperial Eastern Gaṅgas used both the

1. *CII*, Vol. III, p. 102.
2. *Ind. Ant.*, Vol. VII, p. 35.
3. *CII*, Vol. III, pp. 106 ff.
4. Ibid., pp. 112 ff.
5. Ibid., pp. 110 ff.; *Ep. Ind.*, Vol. XXXIII, pp. 167 ff.
6. Ojha (*Bhāratīya Prācīn Lipimālā*, pp. 176-77) quotes certain untenable views of earlier authors on the subject of this era. The era is sometimes wrongly mentioned as the Gaṅga-Kadamba era. The Kadamba and Tumburu feudatories of the Gaṅgas introduced the name of their dynasties in the specification of the date of their records without having really anything to do with the foundation of the era. There are other instances of this kind. Some of the untenable views on the initial year of the Gaṅga era are those of G. Ramadas (349-50 A.D., *JBORS*, Vol. XVIII, p. 291), R.D. Banerji (741 A.D., *History of Orissa*, Vol. I, p. 239), B.C. Mazumdar (772 A.D., *JBORS*, Vol. II, pp. 361-62), R. Sewell (877-78 A.D., *Hist. Ins. S. Ind*, p. 58), etc.

Gaṅga and the Śaka eras. But the use of the Gaṅga era was discontinued from about the time of Vajrahasta III who ascended the throne in 1038 A.D.

The earliest date of the era is found in the Jirjingi plates of Indravarman, dated in the year 39.[1] The record does not mention any predecessor of Indravarman and it is possible that this king's regnal reckoning was continued by his successors thus giving it the character of an era. But it is by no means certain that Indravarman of the Jirgingi plates did not himself continue the regnal reckoning of his predecessor.

There was formerly no clue for fixing the commencement of the Gaṅga era excepting the palaeography of Gaṅga inscriptions. The discovery of the Santa Bommali plates[2] (dated in the year 520 in the reign of Devendravarman, son of Anantavarman) and the Mandasa plates[3] (dated Śaka 917[4] in the reign of Anantavarman), both belonging to the Kadamba chief Dharmakheḍi, son of Bhīmakheḍi, has been of great help. As Anantavarman of both the records is apparently identical, Śaka 917=995 A.D. is some years earlier than the Gaṅga year 520. The era thus started some years later than 995—520=475 A.D., i.e. about the end of the 5th or the beginning of the 6th century A.D. On the basis of this clue, R. Subha Rao[5] fixed 494-95 as the initial year of the era, while J.C. Ghosh[6] calculated certain dates of the Gaṅga records and came to the conclusion that the era started in 496 A.D. Subba Rao accepted the view.[7] On astronomical grounds, B.V. Krishna Rao[8] suggested that the Gaṅga era started on *Amānta* Bhādrapada-badi 13 in Śaka 419 (497-98 A.D.), while V.V. Mirashi[9]

1. *Select Inscriptions*, pp. 458 ff.
2. *JAHRS*, Vol. III, pp. 171 ff.
3. Ibid., Vol. V, pp. 272 ff.
4. See *Select Inscriptions*, p. 458, note 1. The year is quoted as *Śakāvda-(bde) nava-śataka-saptara(da)śa-mata(mite)*. Some scholars suggest *sapta-rasa* and take the year to be Śaka 913 or 967.
5. *JAHRS*, Vol. V, pp. 272 ff.
6. *Ind. Ant.*, Vol. LXI, pp. 237 ff.
7. *Proc. 7th A.-I. Or. Conf.*, p. 519.
8. *JAHRS*, Vol. XI, pp. 19 ff.
9. *Ep. Ind.*, Vol. XXVI, pp. 326 ff.; Vol. XXVII, p. 192; Vol. XXVIII, pp. 171 ff.

concludes that it commenced on *Amānta* Caitra-sudi 1 in the expired Śaka year 420, i.e. the 14th March 498 A.D. Among other views based on the same clue mention may be made of those of M. Somasekhara Sarma[1] and R. C. Majumdar.[2] According to Sarma, the era started sometime between June and January in Śaka 426-27 or 504-05 A.D. Majumdar places the beginning of the era about the third quarter of the 6th century A.D.

We are inclined to support the view that the Gaṅga era started in the period between 496 and 498 A.D.[3] It is however difficult to be sure about the exact epoch owing to the conflicting nature of the data available at present.

6. *Harṣa Era*[4]

There are certain seemingly conflicting traditions regarding the date of the accession of king Harṣa of Thanesar and Kanauj. Hiuen-tsang says : "As soon as Śīlāditya (Harṣa) became ruler, he got together a great army and set out to avenge his brother's murder and to reduce the neighbouring countries to subjection. Proceeding eastwards, he invaded the states which had refused allegiance and waged incessant warfare until in six years he had fought the Five Indias. Then, having enlarged his territory, he increased his army bringing the elephant corps upto 60,000 and the cavalry to 100,000 and reigned in peace for thirty years without raising a weapon."[5] Watters points out in this connection, "We find two dates given for the death of king Śilāditya, Chinese history placing it in the year A.D. 648 and the *Life* [*of Hiuen-Tsiang* by Hwui Li] in 655. Taking thirty-six years as the duration of his reign, we thus have 612 or 619 as the date of his accession. The latter date agrees with a Chinese statement that the troubles in India which led to

1. *Ind. Cult.*, Vol. IX, pp. 141 ff.
2. Ibid., Vol. IV, pp. 179; *Ep. Ind.*, Vol. XXXI, pp. 46 ff.
3. See *Select Inscriptions*, p. 458 note 1; *Ep. Ind.*, Vol. XXXI, pp. 53 ff.
4. See *IHQ*, Vol. XXVII, pp. 321 ff.; Vol. XXIX, pp. 72 ff.
5. Watters, *On Yuan Chwang's Travels in India*, Vol. I, p. 343.

Śīlāditya's reign took place in the reign of T'ang Kao Tsu (A.D. 618 to 627). But the date 648, or rather 647, is perhaps the correct one. It must have been in 641 or 642 that, in conversation with our pilgrim as given in the *Life*, Śīlāditya stated that he had been sovereign for above thirty years. This also gives 612 for the year of his accession, and the addition of six years to the thirty gives 648 as the date of his death. But the Chinese envoy despatched in the early part of that year found, on his arrival in the country, the king dead and a usurper on the throne. Moreover, it was in 648 that Yuan Chwang submitted his records to T'ai Tsung, and Śīlāditya must have been dead before this work was drawn up in its present form."[1]

The statement of the *Life* that Harṣa Śīlāditya died in 655 A.D. and another Chinese statement that the king's reign followed some date in 618-27 A.D. have rightly been rejected, though Watters' supposition that Hiuen-tsang knew the date of Harṣa's death before submitting his *Records* to the Chinese emperor in 648 A.D. seems to be entirely unwarranted.[2] There is no reason to think that anybody in China knew the date of Harṣa's death before the return of Wang Hiuen-tse's mission considerably after that event. It seems therefore that the thirty-six years given by Hiuen-tsang as the duration of Harṣa's reign covers actually the period from his accession to 642 A.D. when the Chinese pilgrim was staying with him and not the period from his accession to this death. It thus appears that, according to Hiuen-tsang's statement in question, Harṣa ascended the throne thirty-six years before 642 A.D., i.e. in 606 A.D. According to the *Life*,[3] Harṣa told Hiuen-tsang on the eve of the religious assembly at Prayāga (Allahabad) about the beginning of 643 A.D. that he had 'been lord

1. Op. cit., pp. 346-47.

2. The *Records* were compiled from Hiuen-tsang's notes with the help of Pien-chi. The first draft of the work was presented to the Chinese emperor in 646 A.D. though the book as we have it was not completed until 648 A.D. See *IHQ*, Vol. XXIX, p. 72.

3. See Beal's trans., pp. 183-84.

of India for thirty years and more' and further that he had 'completed five of these assemblies' and was 'about to celebrate the sixth'. As the assembly was celebrated every five years, it has to be seen whether these statements agree in placing Harṣa's accession thirty years before 643, i.e. about 612 or 613 A.D. At his accession, neither was Harṣa a 'lord of India' (i.e. a *cakravarttin* or *sārvabhauma* monarch, an emperor) nor did the Allahabad region, where Harṣa's conversation with the Chinese pilgrim is said to have taken place, form a part of his dominions. With the death of his elder brother Rājyavardhana, only the small kingdom of Thanesar about the eastern part of the Punjab came into Harṣa's possession. The dominions of the Maukharis covering the major part of U. P. and Bihar were then under the occupation of the king of Mālava (Devagupta) and his ally Śaśāṅka of Gauḍa. Harṣa came to free the dominions of his Maukhari relatives from the Mālava and Gauḍa enemies, which work may have taken him no less than six years as suggested by a statement of Hiuen-tsang quoted above. That he formally declared himself lord of the erstwhile Maukhari dominions in U.P. and Bihar a few years later seems to be clear from the following statement in Hiuen-tsang's *Records* : "The Bodhisattva promised him secret help but warned him not to occupy the actual throne and not to use the title *Mahārāja*. Thereupon Harṣavardhana became king of Kanauj (i.e. the former Maukhari capital) with the title *Rājaputra* and the style Śīlāditya."[1] It is clear that Harṣa of Thanesar offered to drive the Mālavas and Gauḍas out of the Maukhari dominions at first as a relative and ally of the late Maukhari king Grahavarman, but that he formally declared himself master of the Maukhari empire after having freed it from the Mālava and Gauḍa enemies. A confused statement of Hiuen-tsang (who seems wrongly to represent Harṣa's elder brother Rājyavardhana as a king of Kanauj) says that 'the statesmen of Kanauj', on the advice of their leading man Bāṇī or Vāṇī, invited Harṣavar-

1. Watters, op. cit., p. 343.

dhana to become their sovereign and that the prince at first 'modestly made excuses and seemed unwilling to comply with their request'.[1] This at least shows that the formal occupation of the Maukhari throne by Harṣa took place some time after he had become king of Thanesar on his brother's death. This formal occupation of the Maukhari empire and the attainment of imperial dignity by Harṣa appear to have followed his success against the Gauḍas and Mālavas in a protracted war lasting for about six years. Hiuen-tsang says that Harṣa 'waged incessant warfare until in six years he had fought the Five Indias (or had brought the Five India's under allegiance)', that is to say that he became 'an emperor' six years after his accession. As he got the throne of Thanesar in 606 A.D., he thus seems to have obtained imperial dignity in 612 A.D. This is corroborated by the *Life* according to which Harṣa had ruled as 'lord of India', i.e. as an emperor, for over thirty years by 643 A.D. The first quinquennial assembly at Prayāga, the sixth of which took place about the beginning of 643 A.D. could have been celebrated only after Harṣa had become formally anointed as the emperor of the erstwhile Maukhari realm covering U.P. and Bihar, in which Prayāga was situated. As a king of the small kingdom of Thanesar about the eastern part of the Punjab, he had nothing to do with the Allahabad region.

According to Al-Bīrūnī,[1] 'an era of Harṣa is used in Mathurā and the country of Kanoj. Between Śrī-Harṣa (i.e. the Harṣa era) and Vikramāditya (i.e. the Vikrama era) there is an interval of 400 years as I have been told by some of the inhabitants of that region. However, in the Kashmirian calendar, I have read that Śrī-Harṣa (i.e. the Harṣa era) was 664 years later than Vikramāditya (i.e. the Vikrama era). In face of this discrepancy, I am in perfect uncertainty which to the present moment has not yet been cleared up by any trustworthy information." The passage clearly says that Al-Bīrūnī heard of one Harṣa era with its epoch 400 years before the start of the

1. Watters, op. cit., p. 343.
2. Sachau, *Alberuni's India*, Part II, p. 5.

Vikrama era (i.e. in 457 B.C.) and of another Harṣa era having its epoch 664 years after the commencement of the Vikrama-saṁvat (i.e. in 606 A. D.). He refers to the two conflicting traditions regarding the epoch of the Harṣa era as well as to his doubts about them and apparently rejects, at least tentatively, the 606 A.D. epoch in favour of the 457 B.C. tradition, even though he had found corresponding years of both the Vikrama era of 58 B.C. and the Harṣa era of 606 A.D. in the Kashmirian almanac. The passage unquestionably shows that Al-Bīrūnī knew of a Harṣa era starting from 606 A.D., no doubt the year of accession of an Indian monarch named Harṣa. Now the combined strength of the statements of Hiuen-tsang and Al-Bīrūnī discussed above supports the conclusion that king Harṣa, a contemporary of Cālukya Pulakeśin II (610-42 A. D.) and the Chinese pilgrim Hiuen-tsang who travelled in India in 629-45 A. D., ascended the throne in 606 A.D. and that an era, later called the Harṣa era, was counted from that date.

Harṣa's regnal reckoning, continued by this erstwhile feudatories who became independent rulers after his death, developed into an era. This is suggested by the inscriptions of the so-called Later Guptas. That the Later Gupta prince Mādhavagupta, son of Mahāsenagupta, was a subordinate of Harṣa is suggested by Bāṇa's *Harṣacarita*, according to which the Mālava princes Kumāragupta and Mādhavagupta (sons of Mahāsenagupta) took shelter at the Thanesar court during the rule of Harṣa's father Prabhākaravardhana (apparently after Mahāsenagupta's death when the throne of Mālava was usurped by Devagupta) as also by verse 18 of the damaged Aphsad inscription of Mādhavagupta's son Ādityasena, king of Magadha.[1] It is not impossible that Ādityasena, who later claimed imperial dignity,[2] began his life as a feudatory of

1. *CII*, Vol. III, p. 204. The fact that Mahāsenagupta was a *Mālava-rāja* while his grandson Ādityasena flourished in Bihar with the title 'lord of Magadha' seem to suggest that Harṣa had placed his protégé, Mādhavagupta, over some parts of Bihar. See *JRASB*, Letters, Vol. XI, 1945, pp. 69-74; *Ep. Ind.*, Vol. XXX, pp. 295 ff.

2. *CII*, Vol. III, p. 211.

Harṣa. Thus the use of the Harṣa era in the Shahpur inscription[1] of the year 66 falling in Ādityasena's reign is easily explained. Magadha formed a part of Harṣa's empire and was no doubt using the regnal reckoning of that monarch during his reign. The Shahpur inscription shows that the Later Gupta successors of Harṣa in that country continued to use the same reckoning at least for some years after the end of Harṣa's rule.

Among other inscriptions dated in the Harṣa era, the following are well known : (1) Kot (Bharatpur District, Rajasthan) inscription of year 48;[2] (2) Tasai (Alwar District, Rajasthan) inscription of year 183;[3] (3) Punjab inscription of year 184;[4] (4) Khajuraho inscription of year 218;[5] (5) Ahar inscription containing dates between the years 258 and 298;[6] (6) Pehoa (Karnal District, Punjab) inscription of year 276;[7] and (6) Pinjaur inscription of year 563.[8] None of these records can be reasonably assigned to any other era.[9] To the inscriptions dated in this era, we have now to add : (1) Dungarpur (Rajasthan) plates of Bhāvihita, dated year 48;[10] (2) Dhulev (Udaipur Division, Rajasthan) plate of Bhetti, dated year 73;[11] (3) Dungarpur plates of Bābhaṭa, dated year 83;[12] and (4) Khandela (Jaipur Division, Rajasthan) inscription of year 207.[13]

1. Ibid., p. 210.
2. Bhandarkar's List, No. 1392.
3. Ibid., No. 1405; *Ep, Ind.*, Vol. XXXVI, pp. 49 ff.
4. Bhandankar's List No. 1406.
5. Ibid., No. 1408.
6. Ibid., No. 1410.
7. Ibid., No. 1412.
8. Ibid., No. 1421.
9. Some scholars do not believe in the existence of the Harṣa era (cf. *IHQ*, Vol. XXVII, pp. 183 ff.; Vol. XXVIII, pp. 280 ff.). They will indeed find it extremely difficult to explain the dates of these epigraphs.
10. *Ep. Ind.*, Vol. XXXIV, pp. 171 ff.
11. Ibid., Vol. XXX, pp. 1 ff.; 5 ff.
12. Ibid., Vol. XXXIV, pp. 174 ff.
13. Ibid., Vol. XXXIII, pp. 161 ff. For the dates in the Kaman inscriptions ranging between the years 180 and 279, see Vol. XXXVI, pp. 52-53.

According to the Nepalese *Vaṁśāvalīs*, 'immediately before the accession of Aṁśuvarman, Vikramāditya came to the country (Nepal) and established his era there'.[1] It has been suggested that by Vikramāditya the chroniclers meant Harṣa Śīlāditya as at this period there was no other Indian monarch capable of extending his influence in Nepal. This suggestion could be supported by the fact that, in Indian tradition, Harṣa Śīlāditya was persistently confused with the legendary Śakāri Vikramāditya of Ujjayinī, probably because Harṣa was the founder of an era like the traditional originator of the Vikrama-saṁvat.[2] Thus Indian tradition seems to speak of Harṣa indirectly as the founder of an era exactly as the celebrated Vikramāditya.

Some inscriptions of the Nepalese rulers Aṁśuvarman (years 34, 39 and 45), Jiṣṇugupta (year 48), Śivadeva II (years 119 and 143) and Jayadeva Paracakrakāma (year 153) are thus supposed to be dated in the Harṣa era.[3] But the Chinese pilgrim Hiuen-tsang mentions Aṁśuvarman as a past ruler in 637 A.D. whereas the Harṣa years 34-45 would place his period in 640-51 A.D.[4] As indicated above, the said records of Aṁśuvarman and those of his successors probably bear dates in the Śaka era *minus* 500, so that Śaka 501 = year 1 of Aṁśuvarman's regnal reckoning.[5]

7. *Bhauma-Kara Era*.[6]

The beginning of the era used by the Bhauma-Karas of Orissa, eighteen of whom reigned for about two centuries,

1. Tripathi, *History of Kanauj*, p. 94.
2. Note that the *Bhāvabodhinī* of the 17th century author Madhusūdana says, *Mālava-rājasy=Ojjayinī-rājadhānīkasya kavi-jana-mūrdhanyasya Ratnāvaly-ākhyanāṭikā-kartur=mahārāja-śrī-Harṣasya* (*Ind. Ant.*, Vol. II, pp. 127-28; Tripathi, op. cit., p. 184). That the confusion is much earlier than the seventeenth century is proved by Kalhaṇa's *Rājataraṅgiṇī* composed about the middle of the twelfth century. Cf. III, verses 125, 128; also ibid., II. 7.
3. See Kielhorn's Northern List, Nos. 530 ff., 536 ff.
4. See Sylvain Lévi in *Journ. As.*, Juillet-Août, 1894, p. 62, suggesting 595 A.D. as the starting point of the era used in the Nepal records. See also Kielhorn's comments in his Northern List, p. 75, note 3.
5. See above, p. 271, note 2.
6. *IHQ*, Vol. XXIX, pp. 148 ff.

probably coincided with the first regnal year of the first king of the family while the latest known ruler, viz. Dharmamahādevī, ended her reign not long after the year 200 of the era.[1] The feudatory families using the same era must have originally owed complete allegiance to the Bhauma-Karas, but gradually became semi-independent with the growth of their power.[2] Unfortunately, there was so long no clue to determine with precision the date either of any of the Bhauma-Kara kings themselves or of their feudatories except on grounds of palaeography.

Kielhorn was inclined to assign the Ganjam plates of Daṇḍimahādevī,[3] one of which is dated in the year 180, to about the thirteenth century A.D. on paleographical grounds. But the imperial Gaṅga monarch Anantavarman Coḍagaṅga (1078-1147 A.D.) conquered the Puri-Cuttack region about the beginning of the twelfth century, and it is impossible to place the rule of the imperial Bhauma-Karas in the same region after that date. It is again certain that Anantavarman Coḍagaṅga conquered the Puri-Cuttack area from the Somavaṁśīs, and this fact proves that the Bhauma-Karas must have flourished before the Somavaṁśī occupation of lower Orissa. Thus Bhauma-Kara rule in the Puri-Cuttack region must be assigned to a date considerably earlier than 1100 A.D. Moreover, the Bhauma-Karas throughout used numerical symbols

1. For the Bhauma-Kara inscriptions, see B. Misra, *Orissa under the Bhauma Kings*; *IHQ*, Vol. XXI, pp. 213 ff.; *Ep. Ind.*, Vol. XVIII, pp. 211 ff.; Vol. XXIX, pp. 79 ff., 210 ff.; 220 ff.

2. In this connection we have to refer especially to the following inscriptions : (1) Dhenkanal plate (cf. Bhandarkar's List, No. 1756) of Jayasiṁha of which the date may be year 128; (2) Jandapir plate (ibid., No. 1487) of Raṇabhañja of Khijjiṅga-koṭṭa of the year 288 which seems to be a mistake for 188; (3) Adipur plate (*Ep. Ind.*, Vol. XXV, p. 157) of Narendrabhañja and Raṇabhañja of Khijjiṅga-koṭṭa of the year 293 which seems to be a mistake for 193; (4) Talmul plate (Bhandarkar's List, No. 2043) of Dhruvānanda of the year 293 (which is a mistake for 193 as is now clearly demostrated by the recently discovered Daspalla Plate of Devānanda II, dated 184), etc. Cf. *Ep. Ind.*, Vol. XXVII, p. 327, note 1; Vol. XXIX, pp. 183 ff. The confustion between the 100 (*lu*) and 200 (*lū*) symbols is due to that between the medial signs of *u* and *ū* in Orissan epigraphs (cf. Vol. op. cit., XXVII, p. 326).

3. *Ep. Ind.*, Vol. VI, pp. 137 ff.

instead of figures, and this fact suggests that their rule did not survive long after 1000 A.D.

Sylvain Lévi suggested that the Bhauma-Kara king Śubhākara I should be identified with the Buddhist (Mahāyānist) king of Wu-ch'a (Oḍra=Orissa), who sent, according to Chinese sources, an autographed manuscript to the Chinese emperor in 795 A. D.[1] The name of this Buddhist ruler of Orissa is given in Chinese translation as 'the fortunate monarch who does what is pure, the lion', which was believed to suggest an original *Śubhakarasiṁha* (or *°kesarin*). But there was no such name in the family in question. R. C. Majumdar is inclined to identify 'the fortunate monarch who does what is pure, the lion', flourishing in Orissa 795 A.D., with the Bhauma-Kara king Śivakara I Unmaṭṭasiṁha, father of the above Śubhākara I.[2] These identifications would place the two centuries of Bhauma-Kara rule roughly in the period 750-950 A.D. or 775-975 A.D. Bhandarkar[3] suggests the identification of the Bhauma-Kara era with the Harṣa era of 606 A.D. According to his suggestion, the Bhauma-Karas flourished roughly in the period 606-806 A.D. It must, however, be admitted that the palaeography of the Bhauma-Kara records clearly suggests a date later than that implied by Bhandarkar's theory[4] and there is now evidence to show that the Bhauma-Kara kings flourished in a later age.

The records of the Bhañja kings of Dhṛtipura and Vañjulvaka, who apparently owed allegiance to the Bhauma-Karas, bear dates generally in the regnal years of particular kings. We know that king Raṇabhañja of this family flourished about the third quarter of the tenth century A.D.[5] The

1. Ibid., Vol. XV, pp. 363-64.

2. Cf. *Ancient India*, Banaras, 1952, p. 410. The name of *Paramasaugata* Śubhākara III surnamed *Siṁhadhvaja* (i.e. the lion-banner) has so far not been mentioned in this connection.

3. Cf. Bhandarkar's List, Nos. 1404, 1413, 1416, etc.

4. Bhandarkar was conscious of this difficulty and that is why he read the symbol for 100 in the Bhauma-Kara records in most cases as 200. Misra accepted Bhandarkar's identification of the eras, but read the symbol correctly.

5. See *IHQ*, Vol. XXVIII, pp. 225 ff. Raṇabhañja's father-in-law was the Kadamba chief Niyārṇava or Niyārṇama who was the grandfather of Dharmakheḍi, known from his records dated in the Śaka year 917 (995 A.D.) and the Gaṅga year 520 (1016-18 A.D.).

successors of Raṇabhañja, viz. his sons, Neṭṭabhañja Kalyāṇakalasa I and Digbhañja, and Digbhañja's son Śilābhañja II and grandson Vidyādharabhañja, had all very short reigns, so that a Brāhmaṇa named *Bhaṭṭa* Stambhadeva is known to have served all the four kings, while a goldsmith named Durgadeva not only served all of them but also Neṭṭabhañja Kalyāṇakalasa II, son of Vidyādharabhañja. Considering the fact that the active period of the lives of Stambhadeva and Durgadeva probably covered about half a century, the reign of Neṭṭabhañja Kalyāṇakalasa II may be assigned to the first quarter of the eleventh century A.D. Raṇabhañja flourished earlier than, or was an earlier contemporary of, the Somavaṁśī monarch Mahāśivagupta Yayāti I (c. 970-1000 A.D.) who conquered the Dhṛtipura region and pushed the former's successors to the Vañjulvaka area.

The Daspalla plates[1] of Śatrubhañja of Vañjulvaka are dated in the year 198 of apparently the Bhauma-Kara era. This Śatrubhañja was the son of Śilābhañja (who may not have ruled) and the great-grandson (possibly a mistake for 'grandson') of Vidyādharabhañja. King Śatrubhañja ruling in the year 198 of the Bhauma-Kara era may be assigned roughly to the second quarter of the eleventh century A.D. The date of his inscription (written in numerical figures instead of symbols) does not appear to be later than the middle of the eleventh century. In the first place, certain dates in the ninth and tenth decades of the second century of the era in question are written with numerical symbols instead of figures and the use of such symbols does not appear to have survived long after the end of the tenth century. Secondly, lower Orissa comprising the major part of the dominions of the Bhauma-Karas, who ruled from Jajpur in the Cuttack District for about two centuries (i.e. down to about the year 200 of their era, so that the date of Śatrubhañja's charter in the year 198 fell about the latest days of Bhauma-Kara rule) was included in the empire of the Somavaṁśīs during the rule of Caṇḍīhara Yayāti Mahā-

1. *Ep. Ind.*, Vol. XXIX, pp. 189 ff.

śivagupta III (c. 1026-60 A.D.) and his son Uddyotakesarin Mahābhavagupta IV (c. 1060-80 A.D.).[1] There is little doubt that the Bhauma-Karas were supplanted by the Somavaṁśīs about the second quarter of the eleventh century A. D. and that the epoch of their era falls in the first half of the ninth century.

The above conclusion is supported by the two Baud plates of Pṛthvī-mahādevī *alias* Tribhuvana-mahādevī II, dated in the year 158.[2] The inscriptions show that this Bhauma-Kara queen was the daughter of king Svabhāvatuṅga of the Somavaṁśa of Kosala (South Kosala). The same Somavaṁśī king is mentioned in the Balangir Museum plates of Mahāśivagupta Yayāti I (c. 970-1000 A.D.),[3] which suggest that the said king enjoyed the additional name Svabhāvatuṅga. The Bhauma-Kara queen Pṛthvī-mahādevī *alias* Tribhuvana-mahādevī II ruling in the year 158 of the Bhauma-Kara era was thus the daughter of the Somavaṁśī king Mahāśivagupta Yayāti I Svabhāvatuṅga of South Kosala and flourished about the end of the tenth century A.D. Supposing that the queen was ruling more or less contemporaneously with her father, the beginning of the Bhauma-Kara era may be assingned roughly to the first half of the ninth century A.D.

It is clear from the Baud plates that queen Pṛthvī-mahādevī ignored the claims of the sons of her husband's brother and this probably led to a struggle between herself and her husband's relations who ultimately deprived her of the throne. There is some evidence to suggest that Pṛthvī-mahādevī succeeded in occupying the Bhauma-Kara throne with the active help of her father, Mahāśivagupta Yayāti I, whose success against the Bhauma-Karas' feudatories at Dhṛtipura has already been referred to above. The early Somavaṁśīs claimed to have been the rulers of Kosala and are known to have held sway over the Patna-Sonepur region in the upper valley of

1. *IHQ*, Vol. XXII, pp. 300 ff.
2. *Ep. Ind.*, Vol. XXIX, pp. 210 ff., 220 ff.
3. *JAS*, Letters, Vol. XIX, 1953, pp. 117 ff.

the Mahānadī.[1] But a charter of Mahāśivagupta Yayāti I is known to record the grant of a village in Dakṣiṇa Tosalā (the Cuttack-Puri-Ganjam region forming an integral part of the Bhauma-Kara dominions) in his ninth regnal year.[2] The village granted by this charter was Candagrāma in the Maraḍa-viṣaya, the names being identified respectively with those of modern Chandgan about 32 miles to the south-east of Cuttack and Marada-Hariharpur in the Cuttack District. The grant of a village in coastal Orissa by Mahāśivagupta Yayāti I seems to be connected with his daughter's accession to the Bhauma-Kara throne. It was probably made about the time when the Kosalan forces defeated the Bhauma-Kara antagonists of Pṛthvī-mahādevī and raised her to the throne. In that case, the ninth regnal year of Mahāśivagupta Yayāti I may not be far removed from year 158 of the Bhauma-Kara era, when queen Pṛthvī-mahādevī issued her charters. As the ninth regnal year of the Somavaṁśī king may be roughly assigned to 978 A. D., the Bhauma-Kara era seems to have started from a date not much later than 820 A. D., that is to say, about the middle of the first half of the ninth century A.D.

The Daspalla plates of Śatrubhañja give the following details of the date : year 198 [of the Bhauma-Kara era], Viṣuva-saṅkrānti, Sunday, Pañcamī, Mṛgaśirā-nakṣatra. The combination is rather rare and would suit very few dates in a century. Considering the period in question, the date would suit only the 23rd March 1029 A.D. The Bhauma-Kara era thus appears to have started from 831 A.D.

8. *Cālukya-Vikrama Era*[3]

This era was introduced by king Vikramāditya VI (1076-1127 A.D.) of the Later Cālukya dynasty of Kalyāṇa,

1. Cf. the places mentioned in the Somavaṁśī charter in Misra, *Dynasties of Medieval Orissa*, pp. 66 ff.

2. *Ep. Ind.*, Vol. III, pp. 351-55.

3. Ojha, *Bhāratīya Prācīn Lipimālā*, pp. 181-82; 'The Cālukya-Vikrama Era' by P. B. Desai in *Quart. Journ. Myth. Soc.* (Karnataka Number), pp. 1-10 of reprint. See also *Ep. Ind.*, Vol. XXXIV, pp. 193 ff.

from the year of his accession with a view to outsting the use of the Śaka era from his dominions. It was continued by his successors and their subordinates and ultimately disappeared about a century after its start.

Fleet believed that the first year of the reign of Vikramāditya VI, i.e. of the Cālukya-Vikrama era, began on Caitra-sudi 1 in the cyclic year Nala or Anala, corresponding to the 9th March 1076 A.D., while Kielhorn accepted this view and suggested that a year of this era could be converted to one of the Śaka era by adding 997 to the number.[1]

But the inscriptions dated in the era variously equate the following four years with its first year: (1) Śaka 997=Rākṣasa=1075-76 A.D., (2) Śaka 998=Nala(Anala)=1076-77 A.D., (3) Śaka 999=Piṅgala=1077-78 A.D., and (4) Śaka 1000=Kālayukti=1078-79 A.D.[2] This fact shows that there was a good deal of confusion in the people's minds as regards the initial year of the era. It is also not certain that Vikramāditya VI was crowned on Caitra-sudi 1, i.e. on the first day of a Śaka and cyclic year. A. Venkatasubbiah suggests that the king's coronation took place either in Śaka 997 (1075-76 A.D.) or in Śaka 998 (1076-77 A.D.) and that the exact date of the event cannot be determined.[3] He seems to be right. The confusion, referred to above, was apparently due to the fact that the authority of Vikramāditya VI was not recognised at the same time in all parts of the dominions of his brother and predecessor Someśvara II who is known to have ruled as late as the 1st September 1076 A.D.[4] Thus we may add 1076 to a year of the Cālukya-Vikrama year in order to get its approximate Christian equivalent.

P. B. Desai has drawn out attention to an inscription[5] equating the first year of the Cālukya-Vikrama era with the

1. *Bomb. Gaz.*, Vol. I, Part ii, p. 446; *Ind. Ant.*, Vol. XXII, p. 109. Sewell equates the date with the 8th March 1076 A.D. (*Hist. Ins. S. Ind.*, p. 85).

2. See *Quart. Journ. Myth. Soc.*, loc. cit.

3. *Some Śaka Dates in Inscriptions*, p. 91.

4. See *SII*, Vol. XI, Part i, No. 117.

5. *Quart. Journ. Myth. Soc.*, op. cit., p. 6. The date is given as Cālukya-Vikrama year 1, Piṅgala, Śrāvaṇa-sudi 15, Āditya-vāra, lunar eclipse, corres-

cyclic year Piṅgala (Śaka 999=1077-78 A.D.) and referred the coronation of Vikramāditya VI to the 26th February 1077 A.D. on the supposition that the coronation took place on Caitra-sudi 1. The suggestion is not supported by any evidence worth the name. There is no reason to believe that the king was crowned exactly on the first day of the Śaka or cyclic year and that his first regnal year was universally regarded as corresponding exactly to a single Śaka or cyclic year.

In immitation of Vikramāditya VI, Hoysaḷa Vīra Ballāla II started an era from Śaka 1114 current (Virodhikṛt)=1191-92 A.D. on his formal assumption of independence.[1]

9. *Siṁha Era*[2]

This era is used in a few epigraphs found in Kathiawar. An inscription[3] on the Soḍhḍī *vāv* (*bāvḍī*, step-well) at Mangrol bears the date : Monday, Āśvina-badi 13, in Vikrama 1202 and Siṁha-saṁvat 32. A grant[4] of Cālukya Bhīma II was issued on Thursday, Mārgaśira-sudi 14, in Vikrama 1266 and Siṁha-saṁvat 96, while the Veraval inscription of the time of Caulukya-Vāghelā Arjuna bears the date : Āṣāḍha-badi 13 in Siṁha-saṁvat 151, Vikrama (probably Kārttikādi) 1320, etc. These records suggest the difference between the Vikrama and the Siṁha-saṁvat to be 1170 years. Thus the equivalents

ponding to the 6th August 1077 A.D. The Wadageri inscription, dated in the Cālukya-Vikrama year 1, Nala, Phālguna-sudi 5, Thursday, records the performance of several *Mahādānas* in connection with the festivities related to the coronation of Vikramāditya VI (*Prog. Rep. Kan. Res. Inst.*, 1953-57, pp. 50-52). To reconcile the evidence of this record with the theory assigning the king's coronation on the 26th February 1077 A.D., it has been supposed that Phālguna-sudi 5 of the year Nala 'must be in accordance with the *Pūrṇimānta* reckoning, which is equivalent to Caitra-sudi 5 of the next *Amānta* year Piṅgala, Śaka 999'. This seems to be due to misunderstanding since the bright half of a month is the same in both the *Pūrṇimānta* and the *Amānta* schemes. Although the date of the Wadageri inscription is irregular (Phālguna-sudi 5 corresponds to the 31st January 1077 A.D., which was a Tuesday), it shows that the coronation of Vikramāditya VI took place before the Phālguna-pūrṇimā of the year Nala, i.e. before the 10th February 1077 A.D. It is pushed back earlier than Pauṣa-badi 3 and Caitra-sudi 6 of that year respectively by the Mattikote and Kuruva inscriptions (*Ep. Ind.*, Vol. XXXIV, p. 195).

1. *Bomb. Gaz.*, Vol. I, Part ii, p. 503.
2. Ojha, *Bhāratīya Prācīn Lipimālā*, pp. 182 ff.
3. Bhandarkar's List, Nos. 268 and 1461.
4. *Ind. Ant.*, Vol. XVIII, p. 112.

in the Christian era can be found by adding 1113-14 to the years of the Siṁha-saṁvat.

Nothing is known about the founder of the era. Bhagwanlal Indraji suggested that the Siṁha-saṁvat may have been introduced by the Caulukya king Jayasiṁha Siddharāja to commorate the annexation of Southern Kathiawar to his dominions, the event probably taking place in 1113-14 A.D.[1] If this view is accepted, we have to think that the name *Jayasiṁha* was contracted to *Siṁha* in the naming of the era and that it was introduced for use only in Kathiawar since the era is not known to have been used elsewhere even in the epigraphs of the Caulukyas. The suggestions of some scholars attributing the dates of a few inscriptions discovered outside Kathiawar to this era have been shown to be untenable by Ojha who regarded those dates as years of the Vikrama era without the mention of hundreds.[2]The years of the era began on *Amānta* Āṣāḍha-sudi 1.

10. *Puḍuvaippu Era*[3]

An island called Bīpīn, 13 miles in length and 1 mile in breadth, emerged out of the sea to the north of Cochin in the year 1341 A.D. To commemorate this event, an era called Puḍuvaippu (from Malayāḷam *puḍu*, 'new', and *vepa*, 'habitation') came into use in the Cochin area, although it is no longer heard of. The treaty between the State of Cochin and the Dutch East India Company, written on five copper plates, contains the date : Mīna 14 of the Puḍuvaippu year 322, which corresponds to the 22nd March 1663 A.D.[4] In the Malayāḷam-speaking area, there was a popular tendency in medieval times to start the counting of an era from the dates of such minor events as the construction of a temple or the consecration of a deity.[5]

1. *Bomb. Gaz.*, Vol. I, Part i, p. 176.
2. Ojha, op. cit., p. 182, note 6.
3. *Trav. Arch. Ser.*, Vol. I, pp. 31 ff.; Ojha, *Bhāratīya Prācīn Lipimālā*, p. 186.
4. *Trav. Arch. Ser.*, Vol. I, p. 29.
5. Ibid., Vol. VI, pp. 190, 193.

11. *Cochbihar* (*Kocavihāra*) *Era*

This era is supposed to have started from the foundation of the Coch kingdom by Candana in 1510 A.D. Its first year is given as corresponding to year 914 of the Bengali era. It was used in Cochbihar and the neighbouring areas of Bhutan, Assam, Cachar and Manipur. Its use is noticed in some of the Cochbihar records,[1] many of which are dated in the Śaka and Bengali eras.

12. *Ilāhī Era*[2]

After the introduction of Dīn-i-Ilāhī, the Mughal emperor Akbar started the Ilāhī era in order to oust the use of the Hijrī associated with Islām. It was actually introduced in the 29th year of Akbar's reign corresponding to Hijrī 992 and 1584 A.D., though its beginning was counted from the year of Akbar's accession. The emperor ascended the throne on the 14th February 1556 A.D. (the 2nd of Rabiuṣ Ṣānī, Hijrī 963). But the beginning of the Ilāhī era was counted from 25 days later, viz., from the 28th Rabiuṣ Ṣānī of that year, corresponding to the 11th March 1556 A.D., which was the first day of the Iranian new year. In order to get the Christian equivalents of the Ilāhī years, one has to add 1555-56 to the years of that era. The years of the Ilāhī era are solar and the names of months and days were adopted from the ancient Iranian calendar. The days of the month are specifically mentioned in the dates by their names and not by their numbers.

The twelve months of the Ilāhī era are : (1) Farwardīn, (2) Ardibahisht, (3) Khurdād, (4) Tīr, (5) Amrdād, (6) Shahrewar, (7) Mihr, (8) Abān, (9) Āzar, (10) Dī (11) Bahman and (12) Isfandārmaz. The following are the names of 32 days : (1) Ahurmazd, (2) Bahman, (3) Ardibahisht,

1. See S.N. Sen, *Prācīn Bāṅgālā Patra Saṅkalan*, Intro., p. 2, and p. 1, etc.

2. *'Ain-i-Akbarī*, translated by H.S. Jarrett, ed. J. N. Sarkar, Vol. II, pp. 29-30; op. cit., Vol. I, translated by H. Blochmann, ed. D.C. Phillott, pp. 204-05; Ojha, *Bhāratīya Prācīn Lipimālā*, pp. 193-94.

(4) Shahrewar, (5) Sfandarmad, (6) Khurdād, (7) Muredād (Amrdād), (8) Depadār, (9) Āzar, (10) Abān, (11) Khurshed, (12) Mah, (13) Tīr, (14) Gush, (15) Depmihr, (16) Mihr, (17) Sarosh, (18) Rashnah, (19) Farwardīn, (20) Bahram, (21) Ram, (22) Govad, (23) Depdīn (24) Dīn, (25) Ard (Asisvamg), (26) Astad, (27) Asman, (28) Zamiad, (29) Mihrispand, (30) Aniram, (31) Roz, and (32) Shab. Of these days, Nos. 1-30 were taken from the ancient Iranian calendar and Nos. 31-32 were newly added.

The Iranian year of 365 days was solar, in which eleven months had 30 days each while the twelfth had extra days. One month called Kavisa was added in 120 years. But the solar months of the Ilāhī era had between 29 and 32 days.

This era was in use during the reigns of Akbar and Jahāngīr. Shāh Jahān reintroduced the use of the Hijrī in its place.

13. *Śivājī's Coronation Era*[1]

An era starting from the date of the coronation of Śivājī the great founder of the Marāṭhā empire, viz., the 6th June 1674 A.D. (Jyaiṣṭha-sudi 13 of the year Ānanda=Śaka 1596 expired), was prevalent in the dominions of the Marāṭhās for some years. It was called the Rājyābhiṣeka Śaka or Rājaśaka.

1 Ojha, *Bhāratīya Prācīn Lipimālā*, pp. 186-87.

SECTION IV

HIJRĪ AND ITS INDIAN MODIFICATIONS

1. *Hijrī Era*[1]

The name of the era is derived from the Arabic root *hijr*, 'to be separated, to leave', and the reckoning is believed to have started from the time of the departure of Muḥammad, the great founder of Islām, from Mecca to Medina, viz. the evening of the 15th July 622 A. D. (Vikrama 679, Śrāvaṇa-sudi 2). The era was instituted by Khalifa Umr (634-44 A.D.) a few years after the death of Muḥammad. According to some authorities, its institution took place in the Hijrī year 17.

The years of the Hijrī era are lunar. The months are counted from the sight of moon after the new-moon (i.e. from the evening of the 2nd *tithi* of the bright fortnight). The days are counted from the evening of one day to that of another. The twelve months of the Hijrī era are the following : (1) Muharram, (2) Safar, (3) Rabi'ul Avval (i.e. Rabi' I), (4) Rabi'ul Akhir or Rabi'uṣ̤ S̤ānī (i.e. Rabi' II), (5) Jamadaul Avval (i. e. Jamada I), (6) Jamadaul Akhir or Jamadauṣ̤ S̤ānī (i. e. Jamada II), (7) Rajab, (8) Shāban, (9) Ramẓ̈ān, (10) Shavval, (11) Z̤ilqada, and (12) Z̤ilhijja. Since the duration of the lunar month is 29 days, 31 *ghaṭikās* or *daṇḍas* 50 *palas* and 7 *vipalas*, the lunar year is shorter than the solar year by 10 days, 53 *ghaṭikās* or *daṇḍas*, 30 *palas* and 6 *vipalas*. Thus in a century of solar years, we have 103 lunar years, 24 days and 9 *ghaṭikās* or *daṇḍas*. The lunar year may happen to begin from any date in any month of the solar year without any link with the seasons.

The Hijrī era was introduced in India by the Muslim conquerors. It is first used in the legend of the bilingual

1. *'Ain-i-Akbarī*, translated by H. S. Jarrett, ed. J. N. Sarkar, Vol. II, pp. 25-26.; Ojha, *Bhāratīya Prācīn Lipimālā*, pp. 190-91.

coins issued by Sultān Maḥmūd of Ghaznī from the Maḥmūdpūr (Lahore) mint in Hijrī 418 and 419 (1027 and 1028 A.D.).[1] The era is called, in the Sanskrit legend on the reverse of one of the specimens, the Tājikīya-saṁvat, i.e. the era of the Tājika people. The word *Tāzīk*, from *Tāzī* meaning 'Arabic', denotes 'one of the Arab blood, born and brought up in Persia.'[2]

A rule for finding out the Christian equivalent of a given Hijrī year is as follows : Multiply the Hijrī year by 970203, cut off six decimals, add 622.54 and the sum will be the year of the Christian era, and decimal of the day following, in old style. Thus Hījrī 1215 × 970203=1178.796645, leaving 1178+622.54=1800.54. Another system is: Multiply the Hijrī year by 2.977 (the difference between 100 solar and as many lunar years); divide the product by 100, and deduct the quotient from the Hijrī year; add to the result 621.569, and the quotient will be the Christian year from the date at which the Muhammadan year begins. Thus Hijrī 1269×2.977=37778; 37778÷100=37.778; 1269—37.778= 1231. 222+621.569=1852.791 (791 or 9 months 15 days indicating the commencement of Hijrī 1269 on the 15th October). The formula of finding the Hijrī equivalent of a given Christian year is as follows : Subtract 622 from the current year; multiply the result by 1.0307; cut off four decimals, and add 46; the sum will be the year which, when this is a surplus decimal, requires the addition of 1. Thus 1852—622=1230; 1230×1.0307=1267.7610+46=1268.22; add 1 and we have the Hijrī year 1269.[3]

The use of the Hijrī era is found not only in Arabic and Persian epigraphs, but sometimes also in inscriptions in Sanskrit and other Indian languages.

1. Thomas, *Chronicle of the Pathan Kings of Delhi*, p. 48; *JAS*, Letters, Vol. XIX, pp. 133 ff. and Plate. On one of the issues, the legend reads in the central part : *Avyaktam=eka(ṁ*) Muhammada(ḥ*) avatāra(ḥ*) nṛpati-(r*)=Mahamūda(ḥ*)*. Around the border, the legend runs: *ayaṁ ṭaṁkaṁ-(kaḥ) Mahamūdapure ghaṭita(ḥ*) Tājikīyena saṁvatā* 419. On another specimen, the marginal legend on the reverse seems to read *avyaktīya-nāme(mni) ayaṁ taṁkaṁ(kaḥ) hata(h*) Mahamūdapure saṁvatā* 418.

2. Steingass, *Persian-English Dictionary*, s.v. *Tāz*, *Tāzik*. The Arabs are generally mentioned in Indian epigraphic records as Tājika.

3. Cf. Wilson's Glossary, s. v. *Hijra*.

2. *Faslī Era*[1]

The months of the Hijrī era which was introduced in the dominions of the Muslim rulers of India were not linked with the crop seasons. As it was easy to collect revenue from the tenants during the seasons of the Rabi and Kharif crops, the Mughal emperor Akbar introduced the era called Faslī, i.e related to *fasl* or crop, by solarising the lunar Hijrī year 971 (1563 A. D.=Vikrama 1620). Unlike the Hijrī, the years and months of the Faslī are solar (luni-solar). Thus Faslī is another solar modification of the Hijrī like the Śuhūr era.

Originally the Faslī era was introduced in the Punjab and U. P. regions. With the gradual expansion of Akbar's empire, it was introduced in Bengal and other tracts at different later dates. It was introduced in South India during the reign of Shāh Jahān in Hijrī 1046=1636 A.D. This and some other local factors are reponsible for the variations of the era as prevalent in different regions. In the Punjab, U. P. and Bengal, the Faslī era starts from *Pūrṇimānta* Āśvina-badi 1, and 592-93 added to the years of the era gives the equivalent years of the Christian era. The later introduction of the era in the South has lead to a difference of about 2¼ years between the North and South Indian Faslī, the South Indian Faslī being 2¼ years in advance of the North Indian. One has to add 590-91 to the years of the South Indian Faslī era to get corresponding years of the Christian era. In the Marāṭhī-speaking areas, i.e. in Maharasthra, the Faslī year, like the year of the Śuhūr San, begins with the sun's entry into the Mṛgaśirā *nakṣatra* (i.e. between the 5th and 7th of June), and the months are of the Arabic calendar, viz. Muharram, etc. In the Madras region, its beginning was originally calculated from the Karkaṭa-saṅkrānti (solar Śrāvaṇa 1). From 1800 A. D., the year was calculated to begin from the 13th of July and, from 1855 A.D., from the 1st of July.

1. Ojha, *Bhāratīya Prācīn Lipimālā*, p. 192.

3. *Śuhūr, Shāhūr or Sur Era*[1]

This era, often used in the *firmāns* of the 'Adilshāhī kings of Bijapur, is a modification of the Hijrī and is also called the Arbī (Arabic) San and Mṛiga Sāl. The name Śuhūr or Shāhūr is probably derived from the plural form of Arabic *shahr* meaning 'a month'. It was prevalent in the Marāṭhī-speaking areas of the Deccan. *Sur* is probably a Marāṭhī modification of the Arabic name.

It is a solarised form of the Hijrī, its years and months being solar. Like the Faslī era, it must have been introduced for linking particular months of each year with the two crop seasons for the convenience of rent collection.

In order to get the equivalent of the Christian era, we have to add 599-600 to the year of the Śuhūr era and this shows that the solarisation of the Hijrī for the creation of this era took place on the 15th of May 1344 A.D. (Vikrama 1401, Jyaiṣṭha-sudi 2) when the sun was in the Mṛgaśirā *nakṣatra.* The name Mṛga Sāl applied to the era is due to the fact that its years begin with the sun's entry in the said *nakṣatra.*

The years of this era are not indicated by figures but by Arabic words which have been modified in Marāṭhī spoken in the region where it was prevalent. Thus 1=Ahad (Marāṭhī *Ahde, Ihde*); 2=Asana (Marāṭhī *Isanne*); 3=Salasah (Marāṭhī *Sallīs*); 4=Arba; 5= Khamsa (Marāṭhī *Khammas*); 6=Sitta (Marāṭhī *Sin*); 7=Saba (Marāṭhī *Sabbā*); 8=Samaniya (Marāṭhī *Sammān*); 9=Tasaa (Marāṭhī *Tissā*); 10=Ashar; 11=Ahad Ashar; 12=Asana Ashar; 13=Salasah Ashar; 14= Arba Ashar; 20=Asharin, 30=Salasin (Marāṭhī *Sallāsīn*); 40=Arabain; 50=Khamsin; 60=Sittin (Marāṭhī *Sittain*); 70 =Sabin (Marāṭhī *Sabbain*); 80=Samanin (Marāṭhī *Sammānīn*); 90=Tisain (Marāṭhī *Tissain*); 100=Maya (Marāṭhī *Mayā*), 200=Maatin (Marāṭhī *Mayātain*); 300=Salas Maya (Marāṭhī *Sallās Mayā*); 400=Arba Maya; 1000=Alf; 10000= Ashar Alf; etc.

1. See Date's *Mahārāṣṭra Śabdakoṣa*, s. v. *Śuhūr* and *Suru sanna* or *Sursan* ; Ojha, *Bhāratīya Prācīn Lipimālā*, p. 91.

As indicated above, the era was prevalent in the Maraṭhī-speaking area and, although it is no longer in use, it still finds mention in the Marāṭhī almanacs. Nothing is known about the founder of the era. But it is possible that it was introduced by Sultān Muḥammad bin Tughlak (1325-51 A.D.) after his conquest of Devagiri (Daulatabad), the old capital of the Yādavas, near modern Aurangabad.

4. *Vilāyatī Era*[1]

This era may be regarded as another name of the Faslī era prevalent in Bengal and Orissa, in some parts of which countries it is still current. Its years are solar and the names of the months are Caitra, etc. The year begins from the day on which the Kanyā-saṅkrānti takes place, i.e. on the 1st of solar Kārttika. To get the equivalent year of the Christian era, we have to add 592-93 to the years of the Vilāyatī era.

5. *Amlī Era*[2]

This era is the same as the Vilāyatī era, the only difference being that its year begins from Bhādrapada-śudi 12 instead of the Kanyā-saṅkrānti day. The era is prevalent among the mercantile and scribal classes of Orissa.

6. *Bengali Era*[3]

This era is prevalent in Bengal and Assam. It is the same as the Faslī, the difference being that it starts not from Āśvina-badi 1 but seven months later from the Meṣa-saṅkrānti (i.e. the commencement of solar Vaiśākha). The months are solar and the day following the day of the *saṅkrānti* is regarded as the first day of the month. We have to add 593-94 to the years of the era in order to get the corresponding

1. Ojha, *Bhāratīya Prācīn Lipimālā*, p. 192.

2. Loc. cit.

3. Ibid., pp. 192-93. Cf. Sylvain Lévi, *Le Népal*, Vol. II, pp. 147, 153-54; *JBORS*, Vol. XXII, p. 172.

years of the Christian era.[1] It is impossible to believe that the era has been in continuous use since 593-94. If such was the case, its use would have certainly been noticed in some of the numerous pre-Mughal records of Bengal.

We have already referred above to the existence of two other similar eras in some parts of Bengal during the late medieval period, e.g. the Balālī San and the Parganātī San, the epoch of the former falling in 1199 A.D. and that of the latter in 1202-03 or 1201-02 A.D.[2]

7. *Tripurā Era*[3]

The era prevalent in the kingdom of Tripurā (Sanskritised from the tribal name *Ṭiprā*) is 3 years ahead of the Bengali era. Thus year 1357 of the Bengali era would be 1360 of the Tripurā era. There can be no doubt that the Tripurā era was adopted from the Bengali era. The difference of 3 years may be due to an arbitrary innovation or to the solarisation of Hijrī 1074.

8. *Magī Era*[4]

This era is prevalent in the Chittagong area of East Pakistan, which was sometimes under the dominiation of the Arakanese called Mag in Bengal. The era is similar to the Bengali era, the only difference being that it starts 45 years later than the other. This difference of 45 years between the two eras may be due to an arbitrary innovation based on the supposed date of an event of the past.

9. *Malla Era*[5]

Just as the Tripurā and Magī eras are several years ahead of the Bengali era, the Malla era, which was prevalent

1. Some old records point to certain discrepancies. Thus two manuscripts are stated to equate Śaka 1638 (1716 A.D.)=Bengal Sāl 1124 and Śaka 1711 (1789 A.D.)= Bengal Sāl 1195 (cf. S. Mukhopādhyāy, *Prācīn Bāṁlā Sāhityer Kāl-Kram*, pp. 221-22). These would suggest the difference to be 592-93 in one case and 594-95 in the other.
2. *History of Bengal*, Vol. I, pp. 235-36; above, p. 278.
3. See *JAS*, Letters, Vol. XVII, pp. 79 ff.
4. Ojha, *Bhāratīya Prācīn Lipimālā*, p. 193.
5. See *IHQ*, Vol. III, pp. 180-81.

in the State of the Malla rulers of Bishnupur in the Bankura District of West Bengal, is 101 years behind the Bengali era. There is no doubt that it is an adaptation of the Bengali era. The difference therefore may be attributed to the whims of one of the Malla rulers of Bishnupur.

10. *Bhāṭika Era*[1]

The use of the Bhāṭika era is known from some medieval epigraphs of the Jaisalmer region. It is said that Bhaṭṭi or Bhaṭṭika was an ancestor of the rulers of Jaisalmer, who were therefore called Bhāṭī, and that this Bhaṭṭi or Bhaṭṭika must have founded the Bhāṭika or Bhaṭṭika era. The fact, however, that no date of the earlier centuries of the era is known renders the suggestion extremely doubtful. It seems that the era was really not of local origin and that it was called Bhāṭika owing to its adoption by the Bhāṭī rulers of Jaisalmer.

The Jaisalmer Viṣṇu temple inscription[2] equates Vikrama 1494 (expired), Māgha-sudi 6, Friday, Aśvinī-nakṣatra with the Bhāṭika year 813 (current), while an inscription[3] near the Mahādeva temple at the same place quotes the current Bhāṭika year 993 (Uttarāyaṇa in Mārgaśīrṣa) with Vikrama 1673 (expired) and Śaka 1538. The first date corresponds to the 31st January 1438 A.D. and the second to the 28th December 1616 A.D. According to the first, the epoch of the era falls in 624-25 A.D. and, according to the second, in 623-24 A. D. There is a clear discrepancy of one year since the inscriptions specifically mention both the Bhāṭika years as current and it cannot be suggested that one of them was expired and another current.

It is very probable that the Bhāṭika era was an Indian solarised modification of the Hijrī which started in 622 A.D. and was in popular use in the Sind region to the west of Jaisalmer

1. See Ojha, *Bhāratīya Prācīn Lipimālā*, p. 178; *Ep. Ind.*, Vol. XXX, pp. 2 ff., pp. 5 ff.; *IHQ*, Vol. XXXV, pp. 65 ff. 227 ff.

2. Bhandarkar's List, No. 775; Ojha, loc. cit. Ojha speaks of the shrine as the Lakṣmīnārāyaṇa temple. The Bhāṭika year has been read as 812 and 813; but the same date with the year read as Bhāṭika-saṁvat 813 is found in other two inscriptions in the Jaisalmer fort (see below).

3. Bhandarkar's List, No. 962.

since the Arab conquest of that area in the eighth century A.D. The calculation seems to have been based on the fact that Vikrama 679-80=622-23 A.D. was the first year of the Hijrī and Bhāṭika eras, the year of the Hijrī being lunar and that of the Bhāṭika solar. The discrepancy of a year or two between this epoch and the epochs suggested by the dates in the inscriptions discussed above may be due to confusion.[1]

The following inscriptions[2] containing dates in the Bhāṭika era have recently come to light :

(1) an inscription of Lodhrava dated Bhāṭika-saṁvat 534, Kārttika-badi 2, Monday (7th October 1157 A. D.);

(2) an inscription on a Govardhana about 10 miles from Jaisalmer—Bhāṭika-saṁvat 539, Bhādrapada-sudi 10, Sunday (11th August 1163 A.D.);

(3) three inscriptions on memorial pillars near Gogākītalāī, about 5 miles from Jaisalmer—Bhāṭika-saṁvat 685, Āṣāḍha-badi 3, Thursday (26th June 1309 A.D.);

(4) three inscriptions on memorial tablets at the foot of the Jaisalmer fort—Vikrama 1418=Bhāṭika-saṁvat 738, Mārgaśīrṣa-badi 11, Wednesday (24th November 1361 A.D.);

(5) an inscription on a pillar near a well in the Jailsalmer fort—Vikrama 1494=Bhāṭika-saṁvat 813, Māgha-sudi 6, Friday (31st January 1438 A.D.);

(6) an inscription on a slab built into the Lakshmīkānta temple in Jaisalmer fort—Vikrama 1494=Bhāṭika 813, Māgha-sudi 6, Friday (31st January 1438 A.D.);

(7) an inscription engraved on a slab built into the wall of Vyāsonkī-baiṭhak in the Jaisalmer fort—Vikrama 1494 =Bhāṭika-saṁvat 813, Māgha-sudi 10, Wednesday (iregular for the 5th February 1438 A.D.); and

(8) an inscription on a pillar near Īsarlālji's tank about a mile from Jaisalmer—Vikrama 1673=Śaka 1538=Bhāṭika-

1. Cf. *ABORI*, Vol. XXVII, p. 35; *Ind. Ant.*, Vol. XXV, p. 265; *Ep. Ind.*, Vol. XXX, p. 3. Note the difference between the Gupta and Valabhī eras as also among the various modifications of the Hijrī. Cf. the Mavlūdī era.

2. See *Annual Report of the Rajputana Museum* for the year ending 31st March 1936; *ARASI*, 1935-36, p. 111; *IHQ*, Vol. XXXV, pp. 65 ff., see also pp. 227ff.

saṁvat 993, Māgha-sudi 5, Friday (31st January 1617 A.D.).

These inscriptions also suggest that the epoch of the Bhāṭika era was either 624-25 A.D. or 623-24 A.D. The era was prevalent in the Jaisalmer area between the 12th and the 17th century. The Bhāṭika modification of the Hijrī seems to have become prevalent about the 12th century A.D. There is no reason to believe that it was in use from the first quarter of the 7th century A.D.

11. *Mavlūdī Era*[1]

This era was introduced by Tīpū Sultān of Mysore. Tīpū came to the throne on the 4th May 1783 falling in Hijrī 1117, Śaka 1705, Śobhana the 37th cyclic year. He adopted the numbers of the cyclic years, but gave them names of his own. Thus the first four years of his reign were called Zakī, Azal, Jalav and Dalav instead of Śobhana (37), Krodhin (38), Viśvāvasu (39) and Parābhava (40). These names were coined by Tīpū to indicate the numbers of the cyclic years according to the Abjad system,[2] in which numerical value was attached to each of the Arabic letters according to their order in the old Hebrew alphabet. Tīpū also invented the names of the months of the years in accordance with the same system (as No. 1, No. 2, etc.) indicated by the numerical value of the first one or two letters of the names. On the expiry of the Hijrī year 1200 on the 23rd October 1786, the Sultān introduced the Mavlūdī era counted in luni-solar years from the birth of Muḥammad in 572 A.D. in place of the Hijrī lunar years counted from the latter's departure from Mecca to Medina in 622 A.D. Thus the Śaka year 1709 (1787-88 A.D.)=Plavaṅga (41), called Shā in Tīpū's nomenclature, was regarded as the luni-solar Mavlūdī year 1215.

1. Cf. G. H. Khare, *Saṁśodhakācā Mitra*, pp. 101 ff.; *Ind. Ant.*, Vol. II, pp. 112 ff.

2. Alif=1, bey=2, jim=3, dal=4, he=5, waw=6, zey=7, hey=8, toey=9, yey=10, kaf=20, lām=30, mim=40, nun=50, sin=60, ain=70, fey=80, sad=90 qaf=100, rey=200, shin=300, tey=400, sey=500, khey=600, zal=700, zad=800, zoey=900, gain=1000.

He also changed the numerical value of the letters of the alphabet as recognised in the Abjad system and introduced the Abtas system based on the position of the same letters in the Arabic alphabet.[1] New names of the years and months had to be coined in accordance with the new system.[2] The names of the year according to the Abtas system are found on Tīpū's coins. Among records of Tipū's time, a Marāṭhī document in Moḍī script is stated to bear the date : Cha 14, Māhe Takī Sāl Sāhar San 1221. According to the Mavlūdī reckoning and the Abtas system, the year Sāhir (year No. 47) corresponds to the cyclic year No. 47 (Pramādin)=Śaka 1715 (1793-94 A.D.) while Takī is month No. 3(i.e. Jyaiṣṭha).[3]

1. Alif=1, bey=2, tey=3, sey=4, jim=5, hey=6, khey=7, dal=8, zal 9, rey=10, zey=20, sin= 30, shin=40, sad=50, zad=60, toey=70, zoey=80, ain=90, gain=100, fey=200, qaf=300, kaf=400, lam=500, mim=600, nun=700, waw=800, he=900, yey=1000.

2. The names of the months according to the Abjad system were Ahmadī, Bahārī, Ja'frī, Dāraī, Hāshimī, etc., while according to the Abtas system they were Ahmadī, Bahārī, Takī, Samarī, Ja'frī, Haidarī, etc.

3. Cf. Khare, op. cit., p. 104.

SECTION V

FABRICATED RECKONINGS AND DOUBTFUL CASES

1. *Kali-yuga Era*[1]

A Kalpa constituting a single day of the god Brahman is believed to consist of 14 Manvantaras and 6 Mahāyugas, or 1000 Mahāyugas, or 4,320,000,000 years. Each Mahāyuga (also called Caturyugin) is supposed to consist of 4 Yugas, viz. Satya or Kṛta, Tretā, Dvāpara and Kali. The Kali age consists of 432000 years, while Dvāpara, Tretā and Satya or Kṛita respectively two, three and four times that number.

The Kali-yuga era is also called the Yudhiṣṭhira[2] or Bhārata war[3] reckoning. Its beginning is counted from the 18th February 3102 B. C. The Aihole inscription of Cālukya Pulakeśin II of Badami was incised on the expiry of 3735 years after the Bhārata war and 556 years of the Śaka kings. Thus the expired Kali year is arrived at by adding 3179 to the expired Śaka year. Similarly, we have to add to the years of the Kali era 3044 and 3101 to arrive at the years respectively of the Caitrādi expired Vikrama year and the year of the Christian era.

According to Varāhamihira,[4] the Saptarṣi were at the *nakṣatra* Maghā when king Yudhiṣṭhira was ruling and [the beginning of] his reign was 2526 years earlier than [the beginning of] the *Śaka-kāla*. This tradition places the end of the Bhārata war, and the succession of Yudhiṣṭhira resulting from it, 3179—2526=653 years after the beginning of the Kali era.

1. Ojha, *Bhāratīya Prācīn Lipimālā*, pp. 161 ff.
2. Kielhorn's Southern List, No. 1077.
3. Cf. *Ep. Ind.*, Vol. VI, p. 7.
4. *Bṛhatsaṁhitā*, XIII, verse 3 : *Āsan=Maghāsu munayaḥ śāsati pṛthvīṁ Yudhiṣṭhire nṛpatau* । *ṣaḍ-dvika-pañca-dvi-yutaḥ Śaka-kālas=tasya rājyasya* (var. lect. *rājñaś=ca*) ॥

The same tradition is followed in Kalhaṇa's *Rājataraṅgiṇī* according to which the Bhārata war was not fought at the end of Dvāpara,[1] and the Kurus and Pāṇḍavas flourished in the expired year 653 of the Kali era.

There are other discrepancies in the tradition besides the above. There is a Puranic saying, that 1015, or 1050, or 1115, or 1500 years intervened between the birth of Prikṣit (an event that took place shortly after the Bhārata war) and the accession of Mahāpadma Nanda (who ruled some decades before Alexander's invasion, i.e. about 400 B.C.).[3] This would make the difference between the Bhārata war and the beginning of Nanda rule between ten and fifteen centuries. On the shaky basis of the dynastic lists in the Purāṇas, Pargiter placed the Bhārata war about 950 B.C.[4]

There is no doubt that the Kaliyuga era was fabricated by the astronomers just as the Saptarṣi era.[5]

2. *Saptarṣi Era*[6]

The Saptarṣi era, otherwise called the Laukika, Śāstra, Pahāḍī or Kaccā reckoning, is an imaginary cycle of 2700 years. Its calculation is based on the supposition that the Saptarṣi (Great Bear) stays for one hundred years at each one of the 27 *nakṣatras* or lunar mansions. The name Pahāḍī is due to the prevalence of the era in the hills of the Punjab and Kashmir

1. I. 49 : *Bhāratarh Dvāpar=ānte=bhūd=vārtay=eti vimohitāḥ* | *kecid=etāṁ mṛṣā teṣāṁ kāla-saṅkhyāṁ pracakrire* ||

2. Ibid., verse 51 : *Śateṣu ṣaṭsu s-ārdheṣu try-adhikeṣu ca bhūtale* | *Kaler=gateṣu varṣāṇām=abhavan=Kuru-Pāṇḍavāḥ* ||

3. *Matsya Purāṇa*, 273. 36 : *Mahāpadm-ābhiṣekāt=tu yāvaj=janma Parikṣitaḥ* | *evaṁ varṣa-sahasraṁ tu jñeyaṁ pañcāśad-uttaram* || Cf. *Vāyu Purāṇa*, 99. 415; *Brahmāṇḍa Purāṇa*, Madhyama Bhāga, Upodghātapada 3, ch. 74, verse 227; *Viṣṇu Purāṇa*, IV. 24. 32: *jñeyaṁ pañca-śat-ottaram* or *pañcadaś-ottaram* || *Bhāgavata Purāṇa*, XII. 2. 26 : *etad=varṣa-sahasraṁ tu śatam pañca-daś-ottaram* || The reading *pañcāśad-uttaram* has been accepted by some scholars. See Pargiter, *Purāṇa Text*, p. 58; cf. pp. 13-22, 67-69, 74; *Anc.Ind. His. Trad.*, p. 179; Raychaudhuri (*PHAI*, 1950, pp. 29 ff.) assigns the Bhārata war to c.850 B.C. on the basis of the Vedic lists of teachers, which appear to offer somewhat better evidence than the Puranic lists of kings. But the importance attached to the event is possibly unrealistic.

4. See Pargiter, *Ancient Indian Historical Tradition*, pp. 179-83.

5. See Fleet in *JRAS*, 1911, pp. 479 ff., 675 ff.

6. See Ojha, *Bhāratīya Prācīn Lipimālā*, pp. 159 ff.

regions, while the names Laukika and Kaccā refer to its use with the omission of the hundreds. Owing to its use mainly in the works pertaining to *jyotiḥ-śāstra*, it is called the Śāstra-saṁvat. The movement of the Great Bear, though mentioned in works like the *Bṛhatsaṁhitā*[1], *Bhāgavata Purāṇa*, etc.[2], is really imaginary and is also recognised as such by medieval astronomers.[3]

The name of the individual *nakṣatra* for particular centuries of the Saptarṣi era is not mentioned, the years being counted from year 1 to year 100 and again from 1 to 100 for the following centuries without mentioning the figures for the hundreds.[4]

In Kashmir, year 1 of the Saptarṣi era is considered equivalent to year 26 of the Kali era,[5] though the *Purāṇas* and astronomical works equate the first year of the one with the same of the other.[6] Kalhaṇa's *Rājataraṅgiṇī*[7] refers to the year 24 (current) of the Laukik-ābda as corresponding to the expired Śaka year 1070. Thus the difference between the current Laukika year and the expired Śaka year is 1070—24=1046, i.e. 46 years. The number of the Laukika year with the hundreds omitted, when added to 46, would give the number of the expired Śaka year without the hundreds. It would give the current Christian year when added to 24-25 and the Caitrādi Vikrama year when added to 81.

The year of the Saptarṣi era begins from Caitra-sudi

1. XIII. 4: *ek-aikasmin=ṛikṣe śataṁ śataṁ te (munayaḥ) caranti varṣāṇām.*
2. XII. 2, 27-28 : *Saptarṣīṇaṁ tu yau pūrvau dṛśyeta uditau divi* | *tayos=tu madhye nakṣatraṁ dṛśyate tat-samaṁ niśi* || *ten=aita ṛṣayo yuktās=tiṣṭhanty=abda-śataṁ nṛṇām* || Cf. *Viṣṇu Purāṇa*, IV. 24. 53-54.
3. Cf. Kamalākara-bhaṭṭa's *Siddhāntatattvaviveka*, verse 32 : *ady=āpi kair=api narair=gatir=ārya-varyair=dṛṣṭā na c=ātra=kathitā kila saṁhitāsu* | *tat=kāvyam=eva hi purāṇavad=atra taj-jñās=ten=aiva tattva-viṣayaṁ gadituṁ pravṛttāḥ* ||
4. In some of the Kashmir almanacs, the hundred figures are also quoted. Cf. *Ind. Ant.*, Vol. XX, pp. 150-51.
5. Bühler, *Kashmir Report*, p. 60 : *Kaler=gataiḥ sāyaka-netra-varṣaiḥ Saptarṣi-varyās=tridivaṁ prayātāḥ* | *loke hi saṁvatsara-patrikāyāṁ Saptarṣi-mānaṁ pravadanti santaḥ* ||
6. Cunningham, *Indian Eras*, p. 4.
7. I. 52 : *Laukik-ābde caturviṁśe Śaka-kālasya sāmpratam* | *saptaty-ābhyadhikam yātaṁ sahasraṁ parivatsarāḥ.* See *Ind. Ant.*, Vol. XX, p. 152.

1, and the months are *Pūrṇimānta*. The era seems to have been fabricated by the astronomers of the Punjab-Kashmir region.

3. *Jain Nirvāṇa Era*[1]

A reckoning from the date of the Nirvāṇa or salvation of the last Jain Tīrthaṅkara, Vardhamāna Mahāvīra (or Vīra), is prevalent among the Jains and is called the Jina-kāla or Vīra-nirvāṇa-saṁvat.

The *Vicāraśreṇī* (c. 1310 A.D.) of the Śvetāmbara author Merutuṅga gives the difference between the Vīra-nirvāṇa and Vikrama eras as 470 years[2] while another Śvetāmbara writer named Nemicandra, disciple of Ambadeva and author of the Prakrit poem entitled *Mahāvīracariaṁ* (1084 A.D.), quotes 605 years and 5 months as the intervening period between Mahāvīra's Nirvāṇa and [the beginning of the rule of] the Śaka king, i.e. the beginning of the Śaka era.[3] The same difference between the Vīra-nirvāṇa and Śaka eras isgiven also in Digambara works like Nemicandra's *Trilokasāra* (11th century A.D.)[4] as well as in the *Harivaṁśa Purāṇa* and Meghanandin's *Śrāvakācāra*.[5] But there are discrepancies in the traditional dates of Mahāvīra.[6]

Mādhavacandra, commentator on Nemicandra's *Triloksāra*, understood by the expression *Śaka-rāja* the Śaka king named Vikramāṅka (Vikramāditya).[7] This makes the difference between the Vīra-nirvāṇa and Vikrama eras 605 years and 5 months and therefore gives 740 years between the Vīranirvāṇa and Śaka eras. Some other Digambara writers have also

1. V.A. Smith, *E. Hist. Ind.*, 1924, p.49 and notes 2-3; Ojha, *Bhāratīya Prācīn Lipimālā*, p. 163.

2. Cf. *Vikkama-rajj-āraṁbhā paraü siri-Vīra-nivvuī bhaṇiyā* I *sunna-muṇi-vea-juto Vikkama-kālaü Jina-kālo* II *Jina-kālaḥ śūnya-muni-veda-yuktaḥ catvāri śatāni saptaty-adhika-varṣāṇi śrī-Mahāvīra-Vikramādityayor=antaram=ity=arthaḥ* II

3. Cf. *Chahiṁ vāsāṇa sachiṁ paṁcahiṁ vāsehiṁ paṁca-māsehiṁ* I *mama nivvāṇa-gayassa u uppajissaï Sago rāyā* II

4. Cf. verse 848 : *paṇachas=saya-vassaṁ paṇa-māsa-judaṁ gamia Vīra-nibbuido Saga-rājo.*

5. See *Ind. Ant.*, Vol. XII, p. 22.

6. See Smith, *E. Hist. Ind.*, 1924, p. 49, note 3.

7. Cf. *śrī-Vīra-nātha-nirvṛtteḥ sakāśāt paṅc-ottara-ṣaṭ-chata-varṣāṇi pañca-māsa-yutāni gatvā paścād=Vikramāṅka-Śaka-rājo='jāyata.*

followed this tradition.[1] Certain authors of the Digambara sect have moreover given various durations of the intervening period between the Vīra-nirvāṇa and the Śaka eras, such as 461, 9795 and 149793 years.[2] These conflicting traditions clearly show that the era was fabricated at a much later date. There is no literary or epigraphic record of the first millennium after Mahāvīra's *nirvāṇa*, which uses the era. The era was never a popular reckoning in regular use.

Some scholars have accepted the Śvetāmbara tradition giving the difference between the Vīra-nirvāṇa era on the one hand and the Vikrama and Śaka eras on the other as 470 years and 605 and 5 months respectively and suggesting the beginning of the era in 527 or 528 B.C. But this is untenable since, as now accepted by most historians, Mahāvīra, who was a contemporary of the Buddha, must have died in the first half of the 5th century B.C.[3]

4. *Buddhist Nirvāṇa Era*[4]

The Cantonese dotted record suggests that the Buddhist Clergy had a record in which each past year after the Buddha's death was represented by a dot and that the said event took place in 486 B.C.[5] But that there was no genuine, continuous and universally accepted tradition on the subject is clear from the different epochs of the Buddha-nirvāṇa era prevalent in different parts of the Buddhist world. Thus, according to the Ceylonese tradition, now also accepted in Burma and Siam, the era starts from 544 B.C. while the Chinese tradition places it in 638 B.C.[6] The Chinese traveller Fa-hien, who came to India in 399 A.D., speaks of 1497 years having passed after the

1. See the Sravanabelgola inscription equating the Vīra-nirvāṇa year 2493 with Vikrama 1888 and Śaka 1752 (*Ind. Ant.*, Vol. XXV, p. 346).

2. Cf. *Trilokaprajñapti* quoted by Ojha, op. cit., p. 163, note 6.

3. In the *Camb. Hist. Ind.*, Vol. I, p. 696, the probable period of Mahāvīra is given as 540-468 B. C.

4. See V. A. Smith, *E. Hist. Ind.*, 1924, pp. 48 ff.; Ojha, *Bhāratīya Prācīn Lipimālā*, p. 164.

5. Cf. *JRAS*, 1905, p. 51; Smith, *E. Hist. Ind.*, 1924, p. 49.

6. Cunningham, *CII*, Vol. I, p. 3; Prinsep, *Antiquities*, Vol. II (Useful Tables), p. 165.

Buddha's death, thus placing the beginning of the era about 1097 B.C.[1]

On the basis of the Cantonese dotted record and considering certain other factors, scholars now generally assign the Buddha's death to 483 B.C.[2] The Gaya inscription of the Buddha-nirvāṇa year 1813, Kārttika-badi 1, Wednesday, was believed by some scholars to suggest the epoch of the era in 638 B.C.[3] But the date seems actually to be referable to the Ceylonese Buddha-nirvāṇa era of 544 B.C.[4]

5. *Grahaparivṛtti Cycle*[5]

It is a ninety-year cycle supposed to start from the current Kali year 3076 (24 B.C.). It is prevalent in the Madurai region of the Tamil-speaking area. As in the case of the Saptarṣi cycle of 100 years, the years of this cycle are counted from 1 to 90 and then again from 1 without being continued after 90. We get the number of the year in this cycle by adding 72 to the number of the current Kali year and then dividing the result by 90. Another way of getting it is to add 11 to the number of the current Śaka year and then to divide the result by 90. The era was apparently fabricated by astronomers.

6. *Śrī-Harṣa Era of* 457 *B. C.*

As we have seen above, Al-Bīrūnī speaks of a Śrī-Harṣa era which is stated to have started from 457 B.C. and to have been prevalent in his time, i.e. in the 11th century A.D., in the regions of Mathura and Kanauj.[6] It is said that he received this information from some inhabitants of the Mathura-Kanauj area. There is however no reason to believe that such an era

1. Beal, *Si-yu-ki*, Vol. I, Intr., p. 75.
2. See *Camb. Hist. Ind.*, Vol. I, p. 696.
3. *Ind. Ant.*, Vol. X, p. 346; Bhandarkar's List, No. 1459.
4. Cf. *IHQ*, Vol. XXXIV, p. 27; above, p. 277.
5. Ojha, *Bhāratīya Prācīn Lipimālā*, p. 189.
6. Sachau, *Alberuni's India*, Part II, p. 5; above, pp. 294-95.

was actually current in the said region in the age in question, and it is doubtful whether such an era was ever instituted, since no such reckoning is known from literary and epigraphic records.[1] As we have seen, the Indians never used any era in dating their documents before the introduction of the old Scytho-Parthian era or Vikrama-saṁvat of 58 B. C. Al-Bīrūnī learnt from the Kashmirian almanacs that the Śrī-Harṣa era commenced in 606 A.D. and failed to understand how this fact could be reconciled with the information regarding the prevalence of a Harṣa era commencing from 457 B.C. in the Mathura and Kanauj regions. The persons from the Mathurā-Kanauj area, whom Al-Bīrūnī happended to meet, appear to have played a trick on the foreigner by giving this false information.[2]

7. *Maurya Era*

Some scholars read the expression *muriya-kāla* (Sanskrit *Maurya-kāla*, i.e. the Maurya era) in line 16 of the Hāthigumphā inscription of Khāravela[3] and suggested the existence of an era of the Mauryas started by Candragupta (c. 324-300 B.C.). There is however no evidence that Maurya Candragupta ever started any era. The correct reading of the passage in question is again *mukhiya-kala* (Sanskrit *mukhya-kalā*, 'the principal art', and not *Muriya-kāla*. Thus the suggestion about a Maurya era is entirely based on imagination.

8. *Nanda Era*

R. C. Majumdar[4] draws our attention to the Yedarave inscription of Cālukya Vikramāditya VI, which is said to contain the following statement, with reference to the foundation of the Cālukya-Vikrama era : "Having said, 'Why should

1. See *IHQ*, Vol. XXIX, pp. 76-77.

2. A similar but more serious trick played on foreign scholars is known from the story of the *Ezour-vedam* (cf. Winternitz, *A History of Indian Literature*, Vol. I, p. 13).

3. *Select Inscriptions*, p. 210 and notes 15-16.

4. *JBORS*, September-December 1923, pp. 1-2 of offprint.

the glory of the kings Vikramāditya and Nanda be a hindrance any longer ?', he (i.e. Vikramāditya VI), with a loudly uttered command, abolished that [era] which has the name of Śaka and made that [era] which has the Cālukya counting."[1] In Majumdar's opinion the passage refers to an era founded by the Nandas. But the reading *nanda* in the passage in question is avowedly doubtful and seems to be wrong. The word expected in the context is *Śaka*. In any case, there is no evidnece in Indian epigraphic and literary records of the existence of a Nanda era. As we have seen, the use of the reckoning in eras was introduced into India by the foreigners long after the Nandas.

9. *Era of Samprati*

The era of the Maurya king Samprati is sometimes referred to on the basis of Jain sources.[2] It is another fictitious reckoning.

10. *Āguptāyika Era*

The Gokak plates[3] of the Rāṣṭrakūṭa king Dejja-mahārāja has the following passage to indicate the year when the charter was issued—*Āguptāyikānāṁ rājñām=aṣṭāsu varṣa-śateṣu paṁca-catvāriṁśad-agreṣu gateṣu*, 'when 845 years of the Āguptāyika kings had expired.' There is no means to determine exactly the period when Dejja-mahārāja flourished excepting the fact that the plates may be assiged on palaeographical grounds to a date about the middle of the 7th century A.D. It is not improbable that he ruled in the Belgaum region during the interval between the death of Cālukya Pulakeśin II in 642 A.D. and the accession of Vikramāditya I in 655 A.D., when the Cālukya suzerainty was shadowed by the occupation of the southern part of the Cālukya empire by the Pallava king Narasiṁhavarman I.[4] If such was the case, the origin of the

1. Cf. *Bomb. Gaz.*, Vol. I, Part ii, p. 447.
2. Smith, *E. Hist. Ind.*, 1924, p. 202, note.
3. *Ed. Ind.*, Vol. XXI, p. 289.
4. *The Classical Age*, ed. Majumdar, p. 241.

Āguptāyika era may be roughly assigned to 845—645=200 B.C. But we are entirely in the dark about an era with this epoch, nor have we any information about a ruling family called Āguptāyika. The date portion of the Gokak plates will remain a mystery till further light is thrown on the subject. But we can scarcely accept the evidence of a single inscription regarding the existence of a genuine era starting from about 200 B.C. in the face of overwhelming negative evidence. The tradition about the era recorded in the Gokak plates seems to be based on a local story of Āguptāyika rule starting 854 years previously. The story may have been fabricated by the astronomer at Dejja-mahārāja's court.

CHAPTER VIII

TECHNICAL EXPRESSIONS

1. *Abbreviations*

From about the early centuries of the Christian era, contraction of words began to appear in the date portion of inscriptions. The Prakrit forms of the words *saṁvatsara, pakṣa, divasa, grīṣma, varṣā* and *hemanta* were contracted respectively as (1) *sa, saṁ, sava, saṁva* or *saṁvat*, (2) *pa*, (3) *di* or *diva*, (4) *gi, gṛ* or *gri*, (5) *va* or *vā* (for Prakrit *vāsa*) and (6) *he* or *hema.*[1] These abbreviations were used when the numbers of years, etc., were expressed in figures. The contractions *saṁvat* for *saṁvatsara, śu-di, su-di* or *śu-ti* for *śukla-pakṣa-dina* or °*tithi*, and *ba-di, va-di, ba-ti* or *va-ti* for *bahala-pakṣa-dina* or °*tithi* or *vadya-pakṣa-dina* or °*tithi* are popular even to this day.[2]

In later epigraphs also, we have *saṁ, saṁva* (sometimes spelt *samva* or *samba*), *saṁvat* (often spelt *samvat* and rarely *sambat*) and *samvacha* or *samvaccha* for the word *saṁvatsara.*[3] But in many medieval records the contraction is noticed in various corrupt forms such as *samata, samatta, samanta, samvatta, saṁvvat, samvata, samvatu, samvatū, samaṁthu, saṁvatuṁ, saṁmat, samat, samta, smat*, etc.[4] In medieval Orissa, the word was generally written as *samasta.*[5] When *saṁvat* came to be stereotyped in

1 See, e. g., *Select Inscriptions*, pp. 126, 129, 132-33, 148, 151, 203, 205, 220, 253, 283, etc. For *ka* for *kāla* and *va* for *vāra*, see ibid., pp. 131, 168.

2 The form *ti* for *di* is found in records of the north-western regions. For these contractions, see Bhandarkar's List, Nos. 21, 23, 38, 70, 316, 1072, etc. In many cases, we have *śu-di, su-di, ba-di* and *va-di* further contracted into *śu, su, ba* and *va* (see ibid., Nos. 39, 136, 208, 1295, etc.). The names of the months *Bhādrapada* and *Mārgaśīrṣa* were often abbreviated to *Bhādra* and *Mārga* (ibid., Nos. 92, 125, etc.), while occasionally we have *Phā* for *Phālguna, Śrā*, for *Śrāvaṇa, pra* for *prathama*, etc. (ibid., Nos. 842, 361, 1443, 1451). In medieval records in the South Indian languages, we have often *So* for *Somavāra, Ma* for *Maṅgalavāra, Va* for *Vaḍḍavāra* (Saturday or Thursday), etc.

3. See Bhandarkar's List, Nos. 578, 1271, 1272, 1291, 1307, 1375, etc.

4. Ibid., Nos. 49, 357, 360, 366, 599, 1097, 1632, etc.; *IHQ*, Vol. XXX, pp. 187, 383; *JAS*, Letters, Vol. XIX, Plate I; etc.

5. Bhandarkar's List, Nos. 1133, 1769, etc.

the sense of 'an era', it was occasionally used with case-endings, e.g., *saṁvalaḥ, saṁvalā, saṁvali* and *saṁvalām.*[1] The word was sometimes regarded as *saṁvala*, and we have in rarely *saṁvale* in the seventh case-ending.[2] The word *śrāhi* or *srāhi* is often found in the medieval inscriptions of Orissa and the Telugu-Kannaḍa area in the sense of *saṁvat*; but sometimes both the words are used together apparently through some sort of confusion. The word *srāhi* seems to be derived from Sanskrit *śaradi* through Prakrit *sarahi*.[3]

From about the 6th century, abbreviations like *dū* for *dūtaka*, *rū* for *rūpaka*, *dvi* for *dvitīya*, etc., occur in West Indian inscriptions,[4] while in later records contractions of titles, technical terms, etc., appear very often.[5] *Ni* for *nirīkṣita* (examined) or *nibaddha* (registered) is common in the early medieval copper-plate grants of Eastern India, which also show composite contractions like *mahākṣa-ni* in which *mahākṣa* stands for *Mahākṣapaṭalika*.[6]

In some cases, we have the contraction *śrī-ni*[7] in which *śrī* seems to stand for *śrī-hasta* or *śrī-caraṇa*, both of them being honorific expressions to indicate the king.[8] Sometimes the endorsement reads *śrī-ni mahāsā-ni*[9] which suggests that both the king and the *Mahāsāndhivigrahika* had occasion to examine the charter. In *ni anu mahākṣa-ni*,[10] the first *ni* seems to stand for *śrī-ni* while the endorsement means that the charter was first examined by the king and then by the *Mahākṣapaṭalika*. In the contraction *mahā-ni*,[11] it is difficult to determine whether

1. Ibid., Nos. 86, 262, 932, 1003, etc.; *Or. Hist. Res. Journ.*, Vol. I, No. 2, p. 8; etc. See above, p. 309, note 1.
2. Bhandarkar's List, No. 988.
3. Cf. *Ep. Ind.*, Vol. XXIX, p. 106.
4. See, e.g., *Ind. Ant.*, Vol. VII, p. 73, line 20; Vol. XIII, p. 84, lines 37 and 40; Vol. XV, p. 340, line 57; *Ep. Ind.*, Vol. XXX, pp. 175 ff.
5. See, e.g., *JAS*, Letters, Vol. XX, 1954, pp. 201 ff.; *Ep. Ind.*, Vol. XXX, pp. 55 ff.
6. See, e.g., N. G. Majumdar, *Ins. Beng.*, Vol. III, p. 21, text line 51; p. 64, text line 50; p. 75, text line 64, etc.
7. Majumdar, op. cit., p. 88.
8. *Ep. Ind.*, Vol. XXVIII, p. 304.
9. Majumdar, op. cit., p. 103.
10. Ibid., p. 21.
11. Ibid., p. 64.

mahā stands for the *Mahāsāndhivigrahika* or any other high officer whose designation begins with the word *mahā*. Sometimes we have *mahāsāṁ-karaṇa-ni*[1] indicating that the document was examined by the *karaṇa* (*adhikaraṇa*) or office (or clerk) of the *Mahāsāndhivigrahika*.

But that such abbreviations were popular in earlier times is not only indicated by the date portion of early inscriptions referred to above, but also by the use of *ga* for *gāthā* in the Khotanese manuscript of the Dhammapada and *ślo* for *śloka* and *pā* for *pāda* in the Bower manuscripts.[2] In the medieval inscriptions and manuscripts, often a *daṇḍa* and sometimes a globular mark are used to indicate contractions; e.g., *ṭha* and *paṁ* followed by such a mark would indicate *ṭhakkura* and *paṁḍita* respectively.[3] In the manuscripts of Prakrit works, the same mark seems to indicate reduplication of the following consonant.[4]

In some regions, especially in the Orissa area, a word like *pala* was often contracted to *pla*.[5]

In certain medieval inscriptions from Bengal, we have a large number of contractions such as *sāṁ* for *sāṁvatsarika* (i. e. annual), *hi* for *hiranya* (i. e. tax to be paid in cash), *vā-bhū* for *vāstu-bhūmi* (i.e. homestead land), *nā-bhū* for *nāla-bhūmi* (i. e. cultivated land), *dro* for the land measure called *droṇa* or *droṇavāpa*, *u* for the land measure called *udāna*, *ṭi* for *ṭikara* or *ṭikkara* meaning 'a mound' in some Neo-Indo-Aryan languages, *vyā-bhū* for *vyāmiśra-bhūmi* (i.e. mixed land of different categories such as homestead, fallow, cultivated, etc.) and others.[6] *Saṁ* for *sambaddha* noticed in these records is also found in inscriptions found elsewhere.

Instances of an interesting type of contraction are offered by the Midnapur plates of the time of Śaśāṅka, in which the

1. Ibid., p. 75.
2. Bühler, op. cit., p. 92.
3. See, e.g., *Ep. Ind.*, Vol. XXXII, p. 125, text line 12; p. 153, text lines 97, 99, 101, 103, etc.
4. See Bühler, loc. cit.
5. See, e.g., *Ep. Ind.*, Vol. XXVIII, p. 47. Cf. *prama* for *parama*.
6. See *JAS*, Letters, Vol. XX, p. 203; *Ep. Ind.*, Vol. XXX, p. 53.

words *adhi* (or *ādhi*) and *karaṇa* have been used in the senses respectively of *Adhikaraṇika* (or *Ādhikaraṇika*) and *adhikaraṇa*.[1] Abbreviations like *droṇa* for *doṇavāpa*, noticed in these records, are however quite common in the early medieval epigraphs of Eastern India.

2. *Royal Titles and Epithets*

The earliest Indian monarchs known from epigraphic sources enjoyed the simple royal title *Rājan*, 'the king.' Thus the Maurya emperor Āśoka (c. 272-232 B.C.), who ruled over the major part of India and Afghanistan, refers to his own self in his inscriptions as Devānāmpriya Priyadarśī Rājā.[2] The earliest use of the more dignified title *Mahārāja* (literally 'the great king') in Indian epigraphic and numismatic records is found in the coin-legend of the Indo-Greek rulers who flourished in the first half of the second century B.C. Thus certain bilingual coins of king Eucratides has on the overse the Greek legend *Basilêôs Mêgalou Ēukratidou*, '[the coin] of the great king Eucratides', which is translated in Prakrit on the reverse of the coins as *Maharajasa Evukratidasa* (Sanskrit *Mahārājasya Evukratidasya*, '[the coin] of the great king Eucratides').[3] Eucratides originally issued coins with the simpler Greek legend *Basilêôs Ēukratidou*, '[the coin] of king Eucratides', without any Indian translation, probably when his dominions did not yet include any part of India.[4] The word *Mêgalou* was added to the legend in certain issues which have also likewise no Indian translation.[5] These may have been issued shortly after the expansion of his dominions. It is interesting to note that the Greek legend *Basilêōs Mêgalou Ēukratidou* was originally translated into Prakrit as *Rajasa mahatakasa*

1. Cf. *Ind. Cult.*, Vol. IX, p. 121, note.
2. Cf. *Select Inscriptions*, pp. 16, 18, etc.
3. See Smith, *Catalogue*, p. 12, No. 17, etc. Demetrius, an older contemporary of Eucratides, or more probably a later king named Demetrius also used the title *Mahārāja* on some of his coins (cf. Whitehead, *Catalogue*, Vol. I, p. 14).
4. Smith, op. cit., p. 11, No. 1, etc.
5. Loc. cit., No. 7, etc.

Evukratidasa (Sanskrit *Rājñaḥ mahataḥ Evukratidasya*),[1] the expression *Rajasa mahatakasa* (Sanskrit *Rājñaḥ mahataḥ*) in it being later changed to *Maharajasa* (Sanskrit *Mahārājasya*). The modification of the original simpler title 'king' to the more dignified 'great king' was apparently done in imitation of the style of the Achaemenian monarchs of ancient Iran, who referred to themselves in their inscriptions as *Khshāyathiya vazrka*, 'the great king'.[2] The Indo-Greek kings assumed certain other titles, of which *Soter*, 'saviour', translated into Prakrit as *Tratara* (Sanskrit *Trātṛ*),[3] became popular with some of the foreign rulers who succeeded them in North-Western Bhāratavarṣa.

A feudatory of the Indo-Greek king Menander is known to have enjoyed the Prakrit title *Apracaraja*,which seems to stand for Sanskrit *Apratyagrāja*, 'the king having no rival or equal.'[4]

While the title *Mahārāja* was being used by the Greek rulers of North-Western Bhāratavarṣa, the title *Rājan* was still popular with the indigenous rulers of India in the second century B.C. The Besnagar inscription[5] of Heliodorus mentions the Indo-Greek king Antiacidas of Taxila as *Mahārāja*, but the contemporary Indian monarch Bhāgabhadra of Vidiśā as *Rājan*.

The earliest indigenous Indian ruler who used the title *Mahārāja* is king Khāravela of Kaliṅga, who flourished about the last quarter of the first century B.C.[6] But, in the north-western part of Bhāratavarṣa, foreign rulers of Parthian and Scythian extraction, who were gradually supplanting Greek rule from that area, began to adopt more dignified royal titles. Thus certain coins of Maues, Azes I and Azilises use the

1. Ibid., p. 13, No. 29.
2. See *Select Inscriptions*, p. 1, etc.
3. Cf. Smith, op. cit., pp. 16, 18, etc. Other such titles were *Dikaios* (Prakrit *Dhramika*), *Anikētos* (Prakrit *Apadihata*), *Nikēphoros* (Prakrit *Jayadhara*), etc.
4. *Select Inscriptions*, p. 103.
5. Ibid., pp. 90-91.
6. Cf. the Hāthigumphā inscription (*Select Inscriptions*, pp. 206 ff.) in which he is called both *Mahārāja* (lines 1 and 3) and *Rājan* (line 17). See op. cit., p. 214, for another ruler of Khāravela's family enjoying the title *Mahārāja*. Khāravela is also called *Cakravartin*. Cf. *Ep. Ind.*, Vol. XXXV, p. 67, note 6, on the suggestion about Śuṅga Bhāgavata being called *Mahārāja*.

epithet 'the great king of kings'. The expression *Basiléōs Basiléōn Mégalou* in Greek on the obverse of their coins has its Prakrit translation *Maharajasa Rajarajasa* (or *Rajadirajasa*) *mahatasa* (Sanskrit *Mahārājasya Rājarājasya mahataḥ* or *Rājātirājasya mahataḥ*) on the reverse.[1] This style was also an imitation of that of the old Achaemenian emperors who described themselves in their inscriptions as *Khshāyathiya Khshāyathiyānām* (modern Persian *Shāhān Shāh*, 'the king of kings').[2] In the Prakrit legend on certain coins of the Parthian king Gondophernes, the title used in *Maharaja-rajatiraja-tratara* (Sanskrit *Mahārāja-rājātirāja-trātṛ*, 'the great king, the supreme king amongst kings, the saviour'),[3] in which the word *tratara* is a translation of the Greek epithet *soter* used, as indicated above, by many of the Indo-Greek rulers. The coins of the early Kuṣāṇa kings called them *Mahārāja Mahān*, *Mahārāja Rājarāja* and *Mahārāja Rājātirāja*, while some of them also used the title *Devaputra* believed by some scholars to have been borrowed from the Chinese royal title 'the Son of Heaven.'[4] The later Kuṣāṇas of Kaniṣka's house also enjoyed the titles *Mahārāja*, *Rājātirāja* and *Devaputra*.[5] They assumed the Persian title *Shaonano Shao* (*Shāhān Shāh*)[6] and are mentioned in a Gupta inscription as *Daivaputra-Ṣāhi-Ṣāhānuṣāhi*.[7] The successors of Kaniṣka sometimes called themselves *Ṣāhi* (Persian *Shāh*) and rarely *Kaïsara* (from Roman *Caesar*).[8]

The viceroy of the Scytho-Parthian rulers sometimes enjoy-

1. Smith's *Catalogue*, pp. 38 ff.; *Select Inscriptions*, pp. 110-11.
2. *Select Inscriptions*, pp. 1-2, etc.
3. Ibid., p. 123. Gondophernes also enjoyed the title *Devavrata* which may be compared with the Kuṣāṇa title *Devaputra*.
4. *Select Inscriptions*, pp. 120 ff. Kadphises I was called *Dhramathida* (Sanskrit *Dharma-sthita*) or *Sacadhramathita* (Sanskrit *Satya-dharma-sthita*), possibly referring to his adherence to the Buddhist faith. He was also called a *Yavuga* which is believed to be a Scythian word meaning 'a prince' (ibid., p. 108). The Hūṇa king Toramāṇa enjoyed the same title in the form *Jauvla* (ibid. p. 399).
5. Ibid., pp. 135, 144, 149, etc..
6. Ibid., pp. 142 155.
7. Cf. the Allahabad pillar inscription (ibid., p. 258).
8. Ibid., pp. 144, 146, 149, etc.

ed the official designation *Strategos* (commander of forces).[1] The viceroys or subordinate rulers under the Kuṣāṇas enjoyed the titles *Kṣatrapa* (derived from old Persian *Kshathrapāvan* meaning 'a provincial governor') and *Mahākṣatrapa* (literally, 'the great *Kṣatrapa*'). The earlier Śaka subordinates of the Kuṣāṇas, who ruled in Western India, called themselves *Kṣatrapa* or *Mahākṣatrapa* and also often *Rājan* and *Svāmin.*[2] The inscriptions and coins of the Śaka rulers of Caṣṭana's house, who ruled in Western India almost as independent monarchs, represent the kings as *Rājan* and *Mahākṣatrapa*, although they were often referred to by their contemporaries as *Mahārāja.*[3]

The Imperial Guptas who extended their power over wide areas of Northern India in the 4th century A.D. at first called themselves *Mahārājādhirāja* or *Bhaṭṭāraka-Mahārāja-Rājādhirāja* the title being soon more or less stereotyped as *Paramabhaṭṭāraka Mahārājadhirāja,*[4] while the subordinate rulers under them as well as their viceroys enjoyed the title *Mahārāja.*[5] The Gupta emperors were also called *Rājarājādhirāja* but only in verses and this was probably not a formal title.[6] In private records, the Gupta emperors were sometimes referred to as *Mahārāja*; but there is no doubt that, in the Gupta empire, the official designation of the paramount ruler was *Paramabhaṭṭāraka Mahārājadhirāja* and that of a subordinate ruler *Mahāraja*, although there were still smaller feudatory rulers generally called *Rājan.* Sometimes the word *bhaṭṭāraka* was suffixed to the name of an independent or a semi-independent ruler of the Gupta age.[7]

1. *Select Inscriptions*, p. 111, note.

2. Ibid., pp. 157, 160, 164 ff. In one of the Nasik inscriptions (ibid., p. 162), the Śaka chief Ṛṣabhadatta refers to his overlord in the honorific expression *bhaṭṭāraka.* The reference may be to the Kuṣāṇa overlord of his immediate liegelord Nahapāna rather than to Nahapāna himself.

3. Ibid., pp. 175, p. 221 and note 5.

4. Ibid., pp. 259, 270-71. Kumāragupta I is sometimes called *Paramarājādhirāja* and *Adhirāja* on his coins (Allan, *Catalogue of the Coins of the Gupta Dynasties*, pp. 63, 81). See Bhandarkar's List, No. 341 for *Adhirāja* as a feudatory title.

5. *Select Inscriptions*, pp. 267, 271-72, 324, 327-28.

6. Ibid., p. 300.

7. *Ep. Ind.*, Vol. XXVIII, pp. 16, 84.

The Gupta emperor Candragupta II assumed the title *Vikramāditya*. His successors also assumed similar *āditya*-ending titles like *Mahendrāditya*, *Kramāditya*, etc., besides *Vikramāditya*. No name or title ending in *āditya* is known to have been assumed by any historical personage before Candragupta II, though names and titles of this type became gradually popular from the days of the Imperial Guptas.[1]

Gradually the title *Parameśvara* came to be intimately associated with *Paramabhaṭṭāraka* and *Mahārājādhirāja*. Thus king Yaśodharman Viṣṇuvardhana of West Malwa, who ruled about the second quarter of the 6th century A.D., claims to have obtained for hismself the title *Rājādhirāja-Parameśvara*[2] which is stated to have been difficult to attain, while the Alina plates[3] of Maitraka Śīlāditya VI, dated the Gupta year 447 (766-67 A.D.) represent the kings of this dynasty from Śīlāditya II (662-84 A.D.) as *Pramabhaṭṭāraka-Mahārājādhirāja-Parameśvara*. The order of the three designations in the compound was sometimes different.[4] Later on when the said imperial style was stereotyped, it was sometimes felt unneccessary to mention all the three titles and the combination of the three was indicated by a passage like *Paramabhaṭṭārakelyādi-rāj-āvalī-tray-opeta* (i.e. 'endowed with the three royal titles commencing with *Paramabhaṭṭāraka*') as in records like the Rewa plates[5] of Candella Trailokyavarman, dated 1230 A.D. Instead of *rāj-āvalī-tray-opeta* often we have *rāj-āvalī-pūrvavat* (i.e. 'the royal titles as before').[6] The contraction is also found as *Parameśvar-ādi-rāj-āvalī-pūrvavat* in many records[7] since, as indicated above, it has often its full form as *Parameśvara-Mahārājādhirāja-Paramabhaṭṭāraka*. The combination of the three epithets is

1. It is clear from this fact that the tradition regarding the existence of a king named Vikramāditya in the 1st century B. C. is not genuine. Cf. above, p. 255.

2. *Select Inscriptions*, p. 388.

3. *CII*, Vol. III, pp. 171 ff.

4. In the records of the Pālas and Senas of Eastern India, *Parameśvara* comes first in the compound.

5. *Ind. Ant.*, Vol. XVII, pp. 235-36.

6. *JASB*, N. S., Vol. XX, p. 372; *JAS*, Letters, Vol. XVIII, p. 71.

7. R. D. Banerji, *The Pālas of Bengal*, p. 111.

sometimes indicated in a still shorter form as *Parameśvar-ety-ādi*.[1] Similarly sometimes the king is introduced with the epithet *samast-ety-ādi* which stands for *samasta-supraśasty-upeta* noticed at the beginning of the string of imperial titles, e.g., in the charters of the later Senas.[2]

When the combination of the said three titles was stereotyped as the designation of imperial rulers, their feudatories were usually styled *Mahārājādhirāja*, although smaller subordinates were called *Mahārāja* and *Rājan*. In rare cases, a feudatory was also called *Mahārājādhirāja Parameśvara*.[3]

The above is, however, an indication of the modification of the imperial and feudatory styles in North India. The position was somewhat different in the South.

The Śātavāhana kings generally called themselves *Rājan* and sometimes also *Svāmin* which was adopted probably after their contact with the Śaka kings of Western India.[4] But king Gautamīputra Śātakarṇī is once called *Rājarāja* in his son's inscription.[5] In the same record, the mother of Gautamīputra Śātakarṇi and the grandmother of his son Vāsiṣṭhīputra Puḷumāvi is described as *Mahārāja-mātā* and *Mahārāja-pitāmahī*. This shows that the title *Mahārāja* was known in the South as early as the second century A.D., although it was not yet quite popular.[6]

The custom of mentioning royal and private personages with metronymics like *Gautamīputra*, 'the son of a lady whose paternal *gotra* is Gautama', was popular in the early centuries of the Christian era especially in the southern areas of the country. The purpose was to distinguish a person from his step-brothers and a king also from his predecessors bearing

1. See *Ep. Ind.*, Vol. XXX, p. 79.
2. Cf. *JASB*, N. S., Vol. XX, p. 374; N.G. Majumdar, *Ins. Beng.*, Vol. III, pp. 124, 136, 145.
3. See the Rajor inscription of Mathanadeva (*Ep. Ind.*, Vol. Vol. III, pp. 263 ff.).
4. See *Select Inscriptions*, pp. 184-85, 191, 193, 195, etc.
5. Ibid., p. 196.
6. The Velpuru inscription applies the title *Mahārāja* to a 2nd century ruler of the Guntur region. This king seems to have been related to the house of Khāravela who is known to have used the title at an earlier date. See *Ep. Ind.*, Vol. XXXII, pp. 82 ff.

the same name. It has to be noticed that some popular forms of marriage in ancient India did not involve *gotr-āntara* or the change of the wife's paternal *gotra* to that of her husband. At a later date, such a metronymic was conventionally applied to all the members of a ruling family. Thus the Kadambas of Banavasi and the Cālukya kings of Badami claimed to have been *Harītīputras*.[1] The practice of mentioning metronymics went out of fashion in the early medieval period. But from this time the popularity of mentioning a man's name jointly with that of his father began to increase in the southern areas of the country. Thus the Early Cālukya king Kīrtivarman II seems to be mentioned in an inscription[2] as Vikramāditya-Kīrtivarman, i.e. Kīrtivarman II the son of Vikramāditya II.

That the more dignified title *Mahārājādhirāja* was used in the South side by side with *Mahārāja* about the middle of the 4th century A.D. is indicated by the Mayidavolu and Hirahadagalli plates[3] of the Pallava king Śivaskandavarman, in the first of which he is called *Yuva-mahārāja* (a modification of the usual *Yuvarāja*, 'crown prince') and in the second *Dharma-Mahārājādhirāja*.[4] The second inscription refers to the unnamed father of Śivaskandavarman as *Mahārāja-bappa-svāmin* (i.e. 'the *Mahārāja*, the father, the lord'). But the kings of South India belonging to the period upto the 6th century, including the successors of the said Śivaskandavarman, called themselves only *Mahārāja* (sometimes *Dharma-Mahārāja*).[5] In the

1. See *Suc. Sāt. L. Dec.*, p. 155. It was later misunderstood as *Hāriti-putra*.
2. *A. R. Ep.*, 1958-59, p. 8.
3. *Select Inscriptions*, pp. 433 ff.
4. The Kadamba king of the Malavalli inscription also calls himself *Dharma-Mahārājādhirāja* while the same title was assumed by Gaṅga Nītimārga Koṅgunivarma-Permanaḍi and his successors (cf. *Bomb. Gaz.*, Vol. I, Part ii, p. 303, note 3; p. 288, note 5). The title *Dharma-Mahārāja* is supposed to mean 'a *Mahārāja* who, at the particular time of the record, was engaged in an act of religious merit'. The word *dharma* was sometimes affixed to the royal title by several kings of both North and South India. See *Select Inscriptions*, pp. 96, 211, 407, 437, 456. For its penetration into the land beyond the Bay of Bengal, see ibid., p. 473. Sometimes a crown-prince was called *Dharma-Yuvamahārāja* in South India (*Suc. Sāt. L. Dec.*, p. 207). We have also *Mahāyuvarāja* for *Yuvamahārāja* (*Ep. Ind.*, Vol, XXXII, p. 202, note 1).
5. See *Select Inscriptions*, pp. 443, 446, etc.

Penukonda plates,[1] the Pallava overlords have been called *Mahārāja* while the Gaṅga feudatories have been endowed with the title *Mahādhirāja*. The epithet *Adhirāja* is sometimes known to have been used as a subordinate title.[2]

The Cālukya emperors of Bādāmi, including the great Pulakeśin II (610-42 A.D.), called themselves *Mahārāja*, though they soon adopted the more dignified combination of the three titles *Mahārājādhirāja*, *Parameśvara* and *Bhaṭṭāraka* (usually not *Paramabhaṭṭāraka*).[3] In the records of the successors of Pulakeśin II, that king is stated to have assumed the title *Parameśvara* as a result of his victory over the imperial ruler Harṣavardhana of Northern India, though Pulakeśin's own Hyderabad plates state that he assumed the said title after defeating certain hostile kings by 612 A.D. apparently before his engagement with Harṣa.[4]

An interesting title of the Cālukya kings was *Śrī-Pṛthivī-vallabha* often contracted into *Śrī-vallabha* or *Vallabha*.[5] They were therefore known as *Vallabha-rājas*. The same title was later adopted by their Rāṣṭrakūṭa successors who were known to the Arabs as the *Balharā* (Sanskrit *Vallabharāja*). The epithet seems to suggest that these rulers claimed to have been the incarnation of Viṣṇu, the husband of Śrī and Pṛthivī. The usual style of the Rāṣṭrakūṭas was *Paramabhaṭṭāraka Mahārājādhirāja Parameśvara*.[6]

The combination of the three titles was not popular with the Pallavas who ruled further south contemporaneously with the Cālukyas and Rāṣṭrakūṭas, though sometimes they called themselves *Rājādhirāja Parameśvara*.[7] Similar is the case with the Coḷas and Pāṇḍyas.[8]

1. Ibid., p. 457.
2. See *Suc. Sāt. L. Dec.*, p. 113 and note.
3. *The Classical Age*, p. 235; cf. *SII*, Vol.I, p.146 (Vakkaleri plate). *Bhaṭṭāraka* is found in the form *Bhaṭāra* or *Bhaḷāra* in Kannaḍa epigraphs.
4. *The Classical Age*, p. 237.
5. Ibid., p. 213. Often a word meaning 'king' was suffixed to these.
6. See, e. g., *Ep. Ind.*, Vol. XVIII, p. 249, text lines 57-58.
7. Cf. *SII*, Vol. II, p. 350, text lines 71-72.
8. Cf. ibid., Vol. III, p. 423, note.

Early rulers of the Eastern Cālukya dynasty of Veṅgī enjoyed the title *Mahārāja*.[1] But the later members of the family called themselves *Mahārājādhirāja Parameśvara Bhaṭṭāraka* (or *Paramabhaṭṭāraka*).[2] Sometimes the paramount title *Paramabhaṭṭāraka* was used by the later Eastern Cālukyas together with the title *Samadhigata-pañca-mahāśabda*[3] which was generally assumed by subordinate rulers. In this, however, the Eastern Cālukyas appear to have imitated the Imperial Rāṣṭrakūṭas who are known to have rarely used that title.[4] There are a few such instances of an independent ruler claiming this title.[5]

In medieval times, the imperial rulers of North India were sometimes called *Aśvapati-Gajapati-Narapati-rāja-tray-ādhipati*.[6] The word *rāja* in this compound may be regarded as having the same meaning as in *rāj-āvalī-traya*, i.e. 3 of the groups of royal epithets. The Vijayanagara kings called them-

1. See, e.g., *Ep. Ind.*, Vol. XVIII, p. 4.

2. *SII*, Vol. I, p. 33, text line 16; p. 45, text lines 20-21. See also p. 40, text lines 42-43, where the king is called *Mahārāja*.

3. See, e.g., the Vemalurpadu plates (*Ep. Ind.*, Vol. XVIII, p. 231, text lines 47-48) of Amma II.

4. Cf. the Sirur inscription of Amoghavarṣa I in *Ind. Ant.*, Vol. XII, p. 218, text lines 6-7.

5. See the Chirawa inscription of Paramāra Devapāla (*JBBRS*, Vol. XVI, p. 108).

6. The title was assumed by Kalacuri Karṇa (1041-71 A.D.) and his successors, Gāhaḍavāla Govindacandra (1114-54 A. D.) and his successors, the Sena king Lakṣmaṇasena (1179-1206 A.D.) and his successors and the Candella king Trailokyavarman (1205-50 A.D.). Mirashi suggests that Karṇa assumed the title after subduing three kings regarded as *Aśvapati*, *Gajapati* and *Narapati* (*CII*, Vol. IV, pp. c-ci). The Gāhaḍavālas and Candellas appear to have assumed it after their success against the Kalacuris and the Senas as a result of their success against the Gāhaḍavālas. But, as regards Candella Trailokyavarman, his name may have been inserted in the place of that of a Kalacuri king in the ready-made introductory part of the grants of the Kaurava feudatories of Karkareḍi, since the typical Kalacuri title *Vāmadeva-pād-ānudhyāta* (i. e. meditating on or favoured by the Śaiva religious teacher Vāmadeva to whom the Kalacuri kingdom was dedicated by his disciple Gāṅgeya) and *Trikaliṅgādhipati* are also found to have been used along with his name. See the Rewa plates in *Ind. Ant.*, Vol. XVII. pp. 230 ff.; cf. *Ep. Ind.*, Vol., XXX, pp.46 ff. Rapson associates the title with the Allahabad region and suggests that its assumption indicates the possession of the said region (*Woolner Com. Vol.*, pp. 196 ff.). It is difficult to accept this view. We have to note that the same title was assumed by the Vijayanagara kings.

selves *Aśvapati-Gajapati-Narapati-mūvaru-rāyara-gaṇḍa* which is the Kannaḍa translation of the same epithet.[1] The expression seems to represent a king as the lord of threefold sovereignty, i.e. of the three wings of sovereignty, viz. the cavalry, elephant force and infantry. In an inscription of the 13th century,[2] the Yajvapāla king Āsalla of Nalapur is represented as *trividha-kṣitīśa-cūḍā-maṇi* (literally, 'the head-jewel of the three kinds of rulers') probably with reference to an idea of grouping kings as *Aśvapati*, *Gajapati* or *Narapati* according as they were strong in cavalry, elephant force or infantry. It appears that some of the medieval Indian kings considered themselves sufficiently strong in all the three wings of sovereignty and claimed the comprehensive title referred to above, while their neighbours were inclined to apply to them any one of the three epithets with reference to the wing in which they were regarded as especially strong. This is how the latest rulers of the Imperial Gaṅga dynasty of Orissa and their Sūryavaṁśī successors gradually became famous as *Gajapati*.[3]

Sometimes kings assumed titles with reference to their particular achievements. Thus the title *Gaṅgaikoṇḍa* assumed by the Coḷa king Rājendra I (1012-43 A.D.) refers to his success against the Gaṅgas or the land watered by the Gaṅgā. But, in certain cases, such a title was continuously used by the successors of a ruler who first assumed it. Thus the Sūryavaṁśī monarch Kapileśvara, who became king of Orissa in 1434-35 A.D., claimed to be *Gauḍeśvara* and *Navakoṭi-Karṇāṭa-Kalavargeśvara*, i.e. 'the lord of Gauḍa' and 'the master of the Karṇāta-nine-crores as well as of Kalavarga (Gulbarga)', although the claim is more or less vainglorious. But it is interest-

1. Cf. *SII*, Vol. VII, No. 202 (p. 95). They are said to have been specially known as *Aśvapati* because of the strength of their cavalry (Mahalingam, *Administration and Social Life under Vijayanagar*, p. 147).

2. *Ep. Ind.*, Vol XXXII, p. 340.

3. Ibid., Vol. XXXIII, p. 4, note 2. The Vijayanagara kings are believed to have been famous as *Aśvapati* just as the later Imperial Gaṅgas of Orissa and their successors became celebrated as *Gajapati* (*IHQ*, Vol. XXXIII, p. 275). For the conception of *Gajapati* in the south (India), *Ratnapati* in the west (Persia), *Aśvapati* in the north (Turk or Hun) and *Narapati* in the west (China), see P. C. Bagchi, *Twelve Years of Wand ring of Buddha*, offprint, pp. 19 ff.; Watters, *On Yuan Chwang's Travels in India*, Vol.I, pp. 35 ff.

ing to note that the same title was continued not only by his successors but also by later Oriya rulers who claimed to have been the successors of the medieval emperors of Orissa. Sometimes kings of a family, especially of the Kannaḍa region, represented themselves as the lord of a particular city or locality from which it claimed to have hailed. Thus the Imperial Rāṣṭrakūṭas often called themselves *Lattalūrapura-parameśvara*, 'lord of Lattalūrapura (modern Lāṭūr in the Osmanabad District of the former Hyderabad State).[1]

The name of a king generally had the word *śrī* prefixed to it. Particular epithets were also sometimes prefixed to royal names. Thus certain medieval rulers of the Kannaḍa-speaking area prefixed words like *Nūrmaḍi*, *Immaḍi* and *Mummuḍi* to their names probably to distinguish them from their predecessors bearing the same names.[2] But names like Kubja-Viṣṇuvardhana falls in another category in which a descriptive epithet was added to the name. The word *vīra* became a popular prefix to royal names in some families. Thus the later Gaṅga kings, alternately named Narasiṁha and Bhānu, are usually called Vīra-Narasiṁha and Vīra-Bhānu. The word *pratāpa* and sometimes the expression *Vīra-pratāpa* were similarly used as prefixes to royal names. The expression *prauḍha-pratāpa* was also used.[3]

Sometimes the king was indicated by expressions like *śrīhasta*, *śrīpāda*, *śrīcaraṇa*, etc.[4] The predecessor of the ruling monarch was often mentioned as 'the big king', and we have expressions like *bṛhan-nṛpati-caraṇāḥ*, *periya-devar* (Tamil), *Baḍa-Narasiṁha* (Oḍiyā), *Pedda-Narasiṁha* (Telugu), etc.[5]

1. *Ind. Ant.*, Vol. XII, p. 220; *Ep. Ind.*, Vol. XXX, p. 138.

2. *Bomb Gaz.*, Vol. I, Part ii, pp. 332, 428, 433, 459, etc. They mean 'hundred times', 'double' and 'three times' respectively. Cf. Savāi Jayasiṁha, 'one-and-a-quarter Jayasiṁha.'

3. The Yādavas of Devagiri, e.g., called themselves *Pratāpacakravartin*, *Prauḍhapratāpacakravartin*, *Bhujabalapratāpacakravartin*, *Bhujabalaprauḍhapratāpa-cakravartin*, *Yādavacakravartin*, etc. Among the Hoysaḷas, we have also *Niḥśaṅkapratāpacakravartin*. Cf. *Bomb. Gaz.*, Vol. I, Part ii, pp. 507, 523, 528-29.

4. See above, p. 328; also below.

5. *Ep. Ind.*, Vol. XXXII, p. 231 and note; *JAS*, Letters, Vol. XX, p. 212, etc.

With the advent of the Muhammadans in Indian politics, some of the titles of the Muslim rulers were Indianised. Thus the Arabic title *Amīr* was Indianised as *Hammīra* or *Hamīra*.[1] Although no Indian king is known to have assumed *Hammīra* or *Hamīra* as a title, there were a number of kings and princes who adopted it as a personal name.[2] Even princesses were sometimes named Hamīradevī or Hammīradevī.[3] Another Muslim royal title similarly Indianised was *Sulṭān* which is often found in the form of *Suratrāṇa*.[4] As a title, it was very rarely assumed by Indian rulers;[5] but it was often adopted by Indian princes as a personal name.[6] Sometimes it was written as *Sulutāna*, etc., along with *Pātiśāha*=*Pādshāh*, etc., in Sanskritic epigraphs referring to Muslim rulers.

The feudatories often claimed to have obtained the five great *śabdas* (usually *samadhigata-pañca-mahā-śabda* or *prāpta-pañca-mahā-śabda*) in which *śabda* means either 'a title' or 'a sound'. Kalhaṇa's *Rājataraṅgiṇī* (IV. 140-43, 512, 680) explains the five *mahā-śabdas* as the five official designations beginning with the word *mahā*, viz. (1) *Mahā-Pratīhāra* (superintendent of the king's chamber or of the gate and guards of the palace or capital city), (2) *Mahā-Sāndhivigrahika* (minister for peace and war, i.e. of foreign affairs), (3) *Mah-Āśvaśālā-dhikṛta* (superintendent of the stables), (4) *Mahā-Bhāṇḍāgārika* (treasurer) and (5) *Mahā-Sādhanika* (commander of the forces).[7] This seems to be the meaning of the expression *pañca-mahāśabda* as was current in most parts of North India although the designation may not have referred to the same group of five as mentioned above.[8] In some West Indian

1. Cf. *Rājataraṅgiṇī*, VII. 53. 64; Bhandarkar's List, No. 598, etc.
2. See Bhandarkar's List, Nos. 623, 702, etc. Cf. also *Hambīra* and *Ahaṁvīra* in *Ep. Ind.*, Vol. XXXIV, p. 178.
3. Bhandarkar's List, No. 615.
4. Ibid., Nos. 535, 579, etc.
5. Cf. the case of the Vijayanagara kings who called themselves *Hindurāya-Suratrāṇa*.
6. Bhandarkar's List, Nos. 919-20, etc. It was often spelt as *Suratāṇa* (ibid., No. 919).
7. Cf. *Ep. Ind.*, Vol. XXXII, pp. 141-42.
8. Ibid., Vol. XXX, p. 167, note 7.

records, the five titles appear to have been *Mahārāja*, *Mahā-sāmanta* (feudatory), *Mahākārtākṛtika* (probably, a royal agent or remembrancer), *Mahādaṇḍanāyaka* (commander of forces) and *Mahāpratīhāra*. In South India, however, the title seems to refer to the privilege allowed by the overlord to enjoy the sounds of five kinds of musical instruments. These five instruments are mentioned by some authorities as the trumpet, tambour, conch-shell used as a horn, kettledrum and gong.[1] The use of these was allowed as a special mark of distinction not only to feudatory rulers but also to other persons of high rank and authority.[2] That the distinction or privilege was often conferred on a subordinate by his master is indicated by passages like *tat-pradatta-pañca-mahāśabda* (i.e. [enjoying] the five *mahāśabdas* conferred by the master) in respect of a feudatory of Pratīhāra Bhoja I in the Deogadh inscription[3] of 862 A.D. Instead of *pañca-mahāśabda* sometimes we have *aśeṣa-mahā-śabda* ('all the *mahāśabdas*') or *aśeṣa-pañca-mahāśabda* ('all the five *mahāśabdas*').[4]

In medieval records, a subordinate ruler or viceroy was often described as 'conducting the entire business of the seal' (cf. *samasta-mudrā-vyāpārān=paripanthayati*).[5]

A common feudatory title is *Sāmanta*, of which *Mahā-sāmanta* and *Mahāsāmantādhipati* of latter records appear to indicate superior grades.[6] *Rāṇaka* (later *Rāṇā* in Rajasthan) is another popular feudatory title of the medieval period. It seems to have been derived from *Rājanaka*, *Rājānaka* or *Rāja-nyaka* found in the list of addressees in the early medieval

1. *CII*, Vol. III, 196, note 9. S. K. Aiyangar interpreted the *Rāja-taraṅgiṇī* stanzas referred to above in support of the musical sounds theory (*JBBRAS*, Vol. I, N.S. 1925, pp. 238-45). But Kalhaṇa's meaning is quite clear from op. cit., IV. 680. See *JBBRAS*, Vol. VII, pp. 48-51; P. N. Bhattacharya, *Kāmarūpaśāsanāvalī*, p. 42, note.

2. Cf. *Indian Linguistics*, Turner Jubilee Volume, I, pp. 302 ff.

3. *Ep. Ind.*, Vol. IV, p. 310.

4. Cf. *Ind. Ant.*, Vol. XII, pp. 126, 160; Vol. XIV, p. 199; *JBBRAS*, Vol. IX, p. 219; Vol. XII, p. 329.

5. *Ep. Ind.*, Vol. XXXII, p. 152, note 2; p. 166. Sometimes *śrī-śrī-karaṇ-ādi-samasta-mudrā-vyāpārān* (i.e. the entire business including the preparation of documents) is used. See below, p. 359.

6. For a feudatory ruler called both *Mahāsāmantādhipati* and *Mahā-maṇḍaleśvarādhipati*, see *Bomb. Gaz.*, Vol. I, Part ii, p. 543.

copper-plate grants of Northern India. In these lists, the *Rājanaka* is mentioned after the *Rājan* who was also a feudatory but of a higher rank. Rarely *Rājanaka* and *Rāṇaka* are distinguished, the distinction being no doubt based on their being stereotyped wihout regard to the original meaning of the designation.

Some of the feudatories enjoyed the designation *Maṇḍaleśvara*, i.e. ruler of a *maṇḍala* (a district of a kingdom) sometimes modified to *Mahāmaṇḍaleśvara*.[1] The same designation is also found in the form *Māṇḍalika* or *Mahāmāṇḍalika*.[2] The designation *Māṇḍalika* was sometimes adopted as a personal name, though it was often spelt as *Maṇḍalīka*.[3] It is, in some cases, difficult to determine whether a provincial governor was a viceroy or a feudatory of an imperial ruler. There was no great difference between these two classes of rulers since a post was often held by an officer heriditarily. Thus the son and sucessor of a viceroy became practically a feudatory. These feudatories or viceroys very often enjoyed one or more official designations. Thus Vijayasena, a subordinate of Vainyagupta, is known from the Gunaighar plate[4] to have enjoyed the designations *Mahārāja* and *Mahāsāmanta* as well as *Mahāpratīhāra* (chief of the door-keepers of the king's chamber or the royal palace or the capital city), *Mahāpīlupati* (master of elephants),[5] *Pañcādhikaraṇoparika* (head of five administrative offices or departments), *Pāṭyuparika* (probably, head of the accounts department) and *Purapāloparika* (chief amongst the governors of cities). It is difficult to say whether the different posts were held by Vijayasena at the same time or one after another.

In medieval times, *Rājan* was often spelt *Rāya* or *Rāva* and similar change is also noticed in respect of *Mahārāja*.[6] Sanskrit *Rājaputra* was likewise modified to *Rāvata* (spelt as *Rāutta*, *Rāuta*, *Rāhutta*, etc., in Orissa) which was used as a title of

1. Bhandarkar's List, Nos. 24, 133, etc., and Nos. 141, 265, etc.
2. Ibid., No. 454, and Nos. 180, 205, etc.
3. Ibid., Nos. 133, etc., and 751, etc.
4. *Select Inscriptions*, p. 333.
5. We have also *Pīlupati*.
6. Cf. royal names like Kṛiṣṇadeva-rāya, Kṛṣṇadeva-mahārāya, etc.

nobility. After the formal dedication of the Gaṅga kingdom to the god Puruṣottama-Jagannātha of Purī, the Gaṅga kings, who then regarded themselves as subordinates of the god, usually called themselves *Rāuta*.[1]

Sometimes particular feudatory titles were popular in particular areas. Thus a number of dignitaries in the dominions of the Ikṣvākus of the Krishna-Guntur region enjoyed the title *Talavara* or *Mahātalavara*, their wives being similarly called *Mahātalavarī*. Although the wife of an official like *Mahāsenāpati* is often found to enjoy the designation *Mahāsenāpatnī*,[2] the large number of persons enjoying the above designation would suggest that *Talavara* in these cases indicates a title of nobility and not merely an official designation. Vinayavijaya's *Subodhikā* commentary on the Jain *Kalpasūtra* explains it as *tuṣṭa-bhūpāla-pradatta-paṭṭa-bandha-vibhūṣita-rājasthānīya*, i. e. a subordinate ruler (or viceroy) favoured by a turban by his master, and this meaning is suitable here,[3] even though Hariṣeṇa's *Bṛhatkathākoṣa* (931-32 A. D.) uses *Talāra*, apparently the same as *Talavara*, to indicate the administrator of a city or the prefect of the city police.[4] In the age of the Śātavāhanas, certain feudatories enjoyed the title *Mahābhoja* (from *Bhoja* or *Bhojaka* meaning 'a Jāgīrdār') and their wives were called *Mahābhojī*.[5] Subordinate rulers of the Kannaḍa-speaking region often called themselves *Ammana* (or *Appana*)-*gandha-vāraṇa* ('the musk-elephant of the father'), *Ayyana-gandhavāraṇa* ('the musk-elephant of the grandfather'), *Ayyana-siṅga* ('the lion of the grandfather), *Aṇṇana-siṅga* ('the lion of the brother'), *Śaraṇāgata-vajrapañjara* ('the impregnable shelter for one who seeks for it'), etc.

Sometimes the titles assumed by subordinate rulers are found to be an admixture of both imperial and feudatory

1. *Ep. Ind.*, Vol. XXX, p. 19.
2. Cf. *Select Inscriptions*, p. 204.
3. *JUPHS*, Vol. XIX, pp. 79-83.
4. Hemacandra's *Deśīnāmamālā* (V. 3) gives *nagara-rakṣaka* as the meaning of *talāra*. In some cases, the *Talāra* or *Talāri* was called the *Kotwāl*. Cf. *Bhār. Vid.*, Vol. XVII, Nos. 3-4, pp. 127 ff.
5. Lüders' List, No. 1021, etc.

titles or an ambiguous admixture of the two elements.[1] This indicates their newly achieved semi-independent status. The Panchobh plate[2] represents king Saṅgrāmagupta of Jayapura and his grandfather and predecessor Rājādityagupta as *Parama-bhaṭṭāraka-Mahārājādhirāja-Parameśvara* as well as *Mahāmaṇḍalika* which is a feudatory title originally enjoyed by this family of rulers. In some cases, the subordinate title enjoyed by a family of feudatory rulers was continued even when they began to rule as independent monarchs. Thus the Śaka *Mahākṣatra-pas* continued to use the feudatory title even when they ruled as almost independent rulers.

In the inscriptions of Aśoka, a queen of the emperor is called *Devī*,[3] though they were apparently also called *Rājñī* and *Mahiṣī*. Later on the queens of imperial rulers were called *Mahādevī*[4] and apparently also *Mahārājñī*, while the chief amongst the queens was called *Agra-mahiṣī*,[5] *Paṭṭa-mahādevī*,[6] etc. When suboridinate rulers enjoyed the title *Mahārāja* or *Mahārājādhirāja*, their queens were also styled *Mahādevī*,[7] *Paramadevī*,[8] etc. Often the wife of a crown-prince or a subordinate ruler was called *Devī* or *Rājñī*[9] and their chief wife *Paṭṭa-rājñī*.[10] The word *bhaṭṭārikā* was sometimes suffixed to the name of the queen of both independent and subordinate

1. *Ep. Ind.*, Vol. XXIX, p. 186. For a ruler called both *Mahāmaṇḍaleśvara* and *Cakravartin*, see *Bomb. Gaz.*, Vol. I, Part ii, p. 555.
2. *JBORS*, Vol. V, p. 588.
3. *Select Inscriptions*, pp. 66, 72. Cf. also the case of *Devī* Nāgannikā, queen of Śātakarṇi I who flourished about the close of the 1st century B. C. (ibid., p. 185).
4. For *Mahādevī* Gautamī Balaśrī mother of Gautamīputra Śātakarṇi who flourished in the 2nd century A.D., see ibid., pp. 193, 198. For later instances, see ibid., pp. 278-79, etc.
5. *Mahādevī* Prabhāvatiguptā was the *Agra-mahiṣī* of Vākāṭaka Rudrasena II (ibid., pp. 413, 416). For *Piriyarasi* (for Sanskrit *Mahāmahiṣī*) and *Agramahāmahiṣī* in the inscriptions of the Kannaḍa area, see *Bomb. Gaz.*, Vol. I, Part ii, pp. 448-49.
6. *Gauḍalekhamālā*, p. 154.
7. Cf. the cases of the queens of the *Mahārājas* of Uccakalpa (*CII*, Vol. III, pp. 117 ff., Nos. 26 ff.).
8. *CII*, Vol. III, p. 288.
9. See *Select Inscriptions*, p. 433.
10. *Ep. Ind.*, Vol. XXX, p. 84.

rulers.[1] Ruling queens generally enjoyed titles corresponding to those of the rulers of the other sex. Thus queen Daṇḍimahādevī (first quarter of the 11th century) of the Bhauma Kara dynasty of Orissa called herself *Paramabhaṭṭārikā Mahārājādhirāja-Parameśvarī*.[2]

In the inscriptions of Aśoka, the king's son seems to be called *Āryaputra* while princes of the royal blood were probably called *Kumāra*.[3] The expression *Āryaputra* in this sense does not appear in later records, although *Kumāra* and its regional variants occur in numerous epigraphs. Some of the medieval Paramāra rulers called themselves *Mahākumāra*.[4] The epithet *Prāpta-pañca-mahāśabda* and the suffix *bhaṭṭāraka* were sometimes added to the names of the *Yuvarāja* or crown-prince.[5] The word *bhaṭṭāraka* was also suffixed to the name of a king's son who may not have been the crown-prince.[6] In South India, the *Yuvarāja* was sometimes called *Yuvamahārāja*.[7]

Sectarian epithets indicating the religious persuation of the rulers is often noticed in their records. We have referred above to the epithet *Dharmasthita* or *Satyadharmasthita* applied to the Kuṣāṇa king Kadphises I probably with reference to his adherence to the Buddhist faith. Kadphises II seems to be called *Māheśvara*, 'a devotee of the god Maheśvara or Śiva', on some of his coins.[8] Such sectarian epithets became popular from about the 4th century A.D.

The Imperial Guptas were followers of the Vaiśṇava faith; but the epithet *Paramabhāgavata* (literally, 'a devout worshipper or the Bhagavat or Viṣṇu)', indicating their adherence to the Bhāgavata form of Vaiṣṇavism, appears in epigraphic

1. *Ep. Ind.*, Vol. XXIV. p. 136; *CII*, Vol. III, p. 211.
2. Cf. *Ep. Ind.*, Vol. XXIX, p. 88. The Kākatīya queen Rudramma or Rudrāmbā was sometimes called Rudradeva and was endowed with epithets in the masculine gender.
3. See *Select Inscriptions*, p. 49, note 4; pp. 44, 66; *CII*, Vol. I, p. 97, etc.
4. Bhandarkar's List, No. 257, etc.
5. See *IHQ*, Vol. XXIII, p. 238.
6. *Ep. Ind.*, Vol. XVII, pp. 335, 337.
7. *Select Inscriptions*, p. 433, etc.; above, p. 336.
8. *Select Inscriptions* p. 125.

and numismatic records for the first time with reference to Candragupta II (376-414 A.D.).[1] A similar epithet of sectarian character used with the names of the Gupta emperors is *Paramadaivata*. Thus Kumāragupta I is called *Paramabhāgavata* in some epigraphic and numismatic records,[2] but *Paramadaivata* in certain grants issued by his subordinates.[3] The expression *paramadaivata* means 'a devout worshipper of the *devatā* or god', the word *devatā* here appearently indicating the god Viṣṇu. Similarly the Sendraka king Nikumbhāllaśakti is called *Paramamāheśvara* and *Paramabrahmaṇya* at the same time.[4] The expression *Paramabrahmaṇya* means 'a devout follower of the Brāhmaṇas' and not 'a devout worshipper of the god Brahman' since the king in question is specifically stated to have been a Śaiva. There are only a few instances representing a ruler as devoted to two different deities. The Eastern Gaṅgas were Śaivas. But Anantavarman Coḍagaṅga (1078-1147 A.D.) became a devotee of the god Puruṣottama-Jagnnātha (Viṣṇu) of Purī after his conquest of that region. It is interesting to note that Coḍagaṅga's earlier records represent him as a *Paramamāheśvara* and later epigraphs as a *Paramavaiṣṇava*, while an inscription of the intervening period calls him both *Paramamāheśvara* and *Paramavaiṣṇava*.[5]

Instead of *Paramadaivata*, sometimes we have *Paramadaivatādhidaivata*. Thus a sixth century ruler of Orissa, named Śambhuyaśas, is called both *Paramamāheśvara* (a devout wor-

1. *Ep. Ind.*, Vol. XXVI, p. 136.

2. Cf. *Select Inscriptions*, p. 313; Allan, *Catalogue of the Coins of the Gupta Dynasties*, p. 89.

3. *Select Inscriptions*, pp. 280, 283, 285; cf. *Atyanta-deva-Brāhmaṇa-bhakta* (ibid., p. 375). *Paramadaivata* is often wrongly taken to be an imperial title and interpreted as 'a great divinity'. See my note read at XXVI International Congr.ss of Orientalists, New Delhi, 1964.

4. *Ep. Ind.*, Vol. XXVIII, pp. 201, 204. For a ruler claiming to be *Paramamāheśvara* and *Mahābrahmaṇya*, see *Int. Ant.*., Vol. XVII, p. 226, text line 5. Cf. *Atyanta-deva-Brāhmaṇa-bhakta* in note 3 above.

5. *Ep. Ind.*, Vol. XXVIII, p. 240. Some of the successors of this king also claimed to have been devoted to both Śiva and Viṣṇu at the same time. See ibid., Vol. XXXIII, p. 43. For other rulers enjoying similar epithets, see *Ep. Ind.*, Vol. II, p. 353, text line 48; Vogel, *Antiquities of Chamba State*, Part I, p. 185, text line 18.

shipper of the god Maheśvara or Śiva) and *Paramadaivatādhidaivata* meaning 'one who is firmly devoted to the gods and the supreme god'.[1] Similarly the Pāṇḍava rulers of Mekalā called themselves *Paramagurudaivatādhidaivataviśeṣa* side by side with *Paramamāheśvara* and *Paramabrahmaṇya*.[2] The meaning of this epithet is 'one who is a great teacher [of his subjects] and devotee of the gods and the supreme god'. There are numerous instances of the Śaiva kings styling themselves *Paramamāheśvara* in all parts of India.

Instead of the epithets *Paramabhāgavata* for a Vaiṣṇava ruler and *Paramamāheśvara* for a Śaiva king, we have differently worded epithets in rare cases. Thus the Vākāṭaka queen Prabhāvatiguptā called herself *Atyantabhagavadbhaktā* (staunchly devoted to the Bhagavat or the god Viṣṇu) and *Bhagavat-pād-ānudhyātā* (meditating on, or favoured by, the feet of Viṣṇu),[3] while the epithet *Atyantamāheśvara* is found in the records of her son Pravarasena II.[4] A number of rulers including the Traikūṭaka kings of the 5th century A.D. preferred to call themselves *Paramavaiṣṇava* (a devout worshipper of Viṣṇu).[5] Probably they followed a school different from the Bhāgavata. The worship of the *Avatāras* (incarnations) of Vishṇu is reflected in eipthets like *Paramanārasiṁha* (a devout worshipper of the Narasiṁha or man-lion incarnation of Viṣṇu) adopted by king Lakṣmaṇasena of Bengal, though most of his records represent him as *Paramavaiṣṇava*.[6]

Sometimes the rulers of the same dynasty were worshippers of different deities. Thus the inscriptions of Harṣa represent some of the rulers of the Puṣyabhūti family in the following way : *Paramādityabhakta* (a devout worshipper of the Sun-god) Rājyavardhana I; his son *Paramādityabhakta* Ādityavardhana, his son *Paramādityabhakta* Prabhākarvardhana; his son

1. *Ep. Ind.*, Vol. XXIII, p. 200. It is often wrongly taken to be *Paramadevatādhi°*.
2. Ibid., Vol. XXVII, p. 140, where the expression is wrongly interpreted.
3. *Select Inscriptions*, pp. 413, 416.
4. Ibid., p. 420.
5. *Bomb. Gaz.*, Vol. I, Part ii, p. 295, note.
6. N. G. Majumdar, *Ins. Beng.*, Vol. III, p. 95 and note 18.

Paramasaugata (a devout worshipper of the Sugata or Buddha) Rājyavardhana II; his younger brother *Paramamāheśvara* Harṣa.[1] Similarly, the Barah plate of Bhoja represents the kings of the Pratihāra dynasty as follows : *Paramavaiṣṇava* Devaśakti; his son *Paramamāheśvara* Vatsarāja; his son *Paramabhagavatībhakta* (a devout worhshipper of the goddess Bhagavatī) Nāgabhaṭa; his son *Paramādityabhakta* Rāmabhadra; his son *Paramabhagavatībhakta* Bhoja.[2] Instead of *Paramādityabhakta*, such devotees of the Sun-god as king Viśvarūpasena of Bengal, son of *Paramavaiṣṇava* or *Paramanārasiṁha* Lakṣmaṇasena, called themselves *Paramasaura*.[3] Similarly in place of *Paramasaugata*, Buddhist kings sometimes called themselves *Paramatāthāgata*.[4]

Very often the word *anudhyāta* and occasionally the word *parigṛhīta* are used in inscriptions from about the 4th century A.D. with reference to the relations between the predecessor and his successor on the throne, a king and his viceroy, an overlord and his feudatory, a god and his devotee, the father or parents and the son, etc.[5] We have already referred to queen Prabhāvatiguptā's epithet *Bhagavatpād-ānudhyātā*. The basic meaning of the root *anudhyai* is 'to consider or think of attentively', 'to meditate', etc. The *Mahābhārata*,[6] uses the word *anudhyāta* in the active in the sense of 'steeped in meditation' and this meaning is not unsuitable to the contexts, though in *bhagavat-pād-ānudhyātā*, the word seems to be used in the passive to give the meaning *bhagavataḥ pādau anudhyātau yayā sā*. But since the object of one's affection, favour or veneration demands one's constant thought or meditation, the verb soon came to

1. *Ep. Ind.*, Vol. IV, pp. 210-11.
2. Ibid., Vol. XIX, pp. 17-18.
3. N. G. Majumdar, *Ins. Beng.*, Vol. III, p. 145.
4. *Ep. Ind.*, Vol. XV, pp. 1 ff.
5. Cf. *Ep. Ind.*, Vol. XXXI, pp. 4, 9, 50, 72, 92, 107, 132, 135, 137, 221, 265, 280, 287, 293-94, 300, 315. A few rulers called themselves *vāvapād-ānudhyāta* in which the word *vāva* is used instead of the usual *bappa* meaning father (*Ep. Ind.*, Vol. XXX, p. 168). *Vāva* has been explained as an uncle or a relation of one's father's generation. Instead of *pād-ānudhyāta* sometimes we have *pāda-bhakta*, *pādapadm-opajīvin*, *pādapaṅkaja-bhramara*, etc.
6. XII. 127. 19.

be used in the sense of 'to wish well of', 'to bless', 'to favour' and Kālidāsa's *Raghuvaṁśa*[1] uses it in this sense.

That the word *anudhyāta* has been used in many cases in the inscriptions in the sense of 'meditating on' is indicated by the fact that occasionally we have *anudhyāna-rata* in its place. Thus the grant of Śilābhanja Tribhubhanakalasa mentions the king as *mātā-pitṛ-pād-ānudhyāna-rata* instead of the usual *mātā-pitṛ-pād-ānudhyāta*.[2] That however the expression was sometimes understood in the sense of 'favoured by' is also clearly indicated by some records. Thus verses 22-23 of the Talagunda inscription state that Ṣaḍānana (i.e. the god Kārttikeya-Mahāsena), together with the Mothers (i.e. the Mother-goddesses), anointed the *Senāpati* (i. e. Kadamba Mayūraśarman) [as king] after having favoured (*anudhyāya*) him,[3] while in many Kadamba records Mayūraśarman's family is described as *Svāmi-Mahāsena-Mātṛgaṇ-ānudhyāt-ābhiṣikta* (favoured and anointed by the lord Mahāsena and the Mothers)[4] obviously with reference to the same event.[5]

The word *parigṛhīta*, sometimes used instead of *anudhyāta* in a similar context, literally means 'accepted' and may suggest that the successor or subordinate so described was really selected, out of several candidates, for a post or position. Thus the description of Candragupta II as *Samudraguptasya putras=tat-parigṛhītaḥ*[6] may suggest that Samudragupta selected Candragupta II as his successor out of his many sons, or at least

1. XIV, 60, XVII, 36. Mallinātha explains *anudhyeya* and *anudadhyuḥ* in the second of the stanzas as *anugrāhya* and *anujagṛhuḥ* respectively. He also quotes the *Utpalamālā* explaining *anudhyāna* as *anugraha*.

2. *Ep. Ind.*, Vol. XXVIII, p. 277.

3. Cf. *Select Inscriptions*, p. 453 and note 3. The passage was misunderstood by Kielhorn (*Ep. Ind.*, Vol. VIII, p. 35).

4. *Ind. Ant.*, Vol. VI, p. 14, text line 2; p. 18, text line 3, etc.

5. See *JAHRS*, Vol. X, p. 229; *Ind. Cult.*, Vol. IX, pp. 115 ff.; cf. Lévi, *Le Nepal*, Vol. III, p. 64.

6. *Select Inscriptions*, pp. 313, 321. The viceroys of Puṇḍravardhanabhukti under Kumāragupta I and Budhagupta are represented as *tat-pāda-parigṛhīta* with reference to the kings (ibid., pp. 283, 285, 324, 328).

Candragupta II preferred to represent himself as such.[1] That seems to be the reason why *parigṛhīta* is used only rarely.

All kings, independent or subordinate, were often represented as the lord of the soil, the word for 'soil' also indicating 'the earth'. But independent monarchs were sometimes actually represented as the ruler or conqueror of 'the whole earth' meaning thereby the conventional *cakravarti-kṣetra* bounded by the Himalayas and the three seas, viz. the Bay of Bengal, the Arabian Sea and the Indian Ocean. This sphere of influence of a *cakravartin* or emperor was later conceived as two, the land between the Himalayas and the Vindhyas for North Indian rulers and the tract lying to the south of the Vindhyas for South Indian monarchs. This kind of representation of a king as the ruler or conqueror of the *cakravarti-kṣetra* is conventional and should not be regarded as historical.[2]

3. *Official Designations*

In the inscriptions of Aśoka, the highest class of officers in the Maurya administration is called the *Mahāmātra*.[3] The *Mahāmātras* were employed in various capacities such as the administrators or judicial officers of a city (*Nagara-vyavahārika*), the superintendent in charge of the matters

1. Lévi's suggestion that *parigṛhīta* in such cases means 'admitted in the family by adoption' (op. cit., p. 86, note 3) is palpably wrong, since Candragupta II was not an adopted son of Samudragupta, but is clearly stated to have been born of the latter's queen Dattadevī (*Select Inscriptions*, pp. 313, 321).

2. See my *Stud. Geog. Anc. Med. Ind.*, pp. 1 ff. The king is often represented as the husband of the earth or royal fortune conceived as a lady.

3. *Select Inscriptions*, pp. 46, 49, (note 4), 72-73. *Mahāmātra* as the designation of a high officer is rarely found in later epigraphs. In later times, it is known to have been used to indicate the driver of elephants (cf. *The Classical Age*, p. 193) possibly because for a time the officer in charge of the royal elephant corps enjoyed the designation more or less exclusively. The designation entered into Greek administrative vocabulary as *Mamátrai* meaning 'commanders or rulers among Indians' (Tarn, *The Greeks in Bactria and India*, p. 377, note 5; *Ind. Cult.*, Vol. VIII p. 408).

concerning the ladies of the royal household (*Stryadhyakṣa*), officers in charge of the bordering districts of the empire (*Anta-Mahāmātra*), etc.[1] Aśoka created a big department of religious affairs, which was conducted by certain officers of this class called *Dharma-Mahāmātra*.[2] The *Dūtas*[3] or envoys possibly belonged to the class of *Mahāmātras*. Other high officers mentioned in Aśoka's records are the *Prādeśika*, *Rajjuka* and *Rāṣṭrika*[4] who were all styled *yukta*[5] or officer and were probably the governor of a group of districts, of a single district, and of the sub-division of a district respectively. It is difficult to say whether some of these officers belonged to the *Mahāmātra* rank.

A class of high functionaries under Aśoka is merely referred to as 'the officer' (*Puruṣa*) probably meaning special agents of the king.[6] Among minor officers, mention is made of the reporters (*Prativedaka*) and scribes (*Lipikara*).[7] The officers in charge of the royal cattle and pasture lands (*Vraja-bhūmika*)[8] appear to have belonged to a higher class.

In the epigraphic and numismatic records of the Indo-Greek and Scytho-Parthian age, mention is made of the *Meridarkhes*[9] (meaning, 'a district officer') and *Strategos*,[10] literally

1. *Select Inscriptions*, pp. 34, 41, 55-56, etc. The *Stryadhakṣa-mahāmātra* was the same as the *Antaḥpur-ādhyakṣa* of the inscriptions of the Cālukyas of Kalyāṇa (*Bomb. Gaz.*, Vol. I, Part i, p. 451). The eunuchs guarding the royal harem apparently served under this officer. Cf. *Gopalakrishnamacharya Volume*, pp. 438 ff. The *Antamahāmātras* may also be regarded as officers stationed at outposts on the borders of the empire in order to deal with the peoples beyond the borders.

2. *Select Inscriptions*, pp. 23-24, 34, 66.

3. Ibid., p. 37, text line 10.

4. Ibid., pp. 20, 53, 59-60, 66. The official designation *Rajjuka* is rarely found in later records possibly in the sense of 'a surveyor' (cf. *Ep. Ind.*, Vol. XXIV, p. 54 and note). Megasthenes seems to refer to the *Rajjukas* as the *Agronomoi* who collected taxes of land, measured the land and superintended the irrigation works. They are the *Rajjugrāhak-āmātya* of the Jātakas. See Raychaudhuri, *Pol. His. Anc. Ind.*, 1938, pp. 241, 262-63.

5. *Select Inscriptions*, p. 20, note 2. Some scholars regard *Yukta* used in Aśokan records as the designation of a class of officers like *Āyukta*.

6. Ibid., p. 55. 59.

7. Ibid., pp. 25, 40.

8. Ibid., p. 34.

9. Ibid., p. 109 (*Meridarkha*).

10. Ibid., p. 111, note 1 (*Stratega*).

meaning 'commander of forces' but enjoying the status of the governor of a province.[1] In the epigraphs of the Scytho-Parthians and Kuṣāṇas, we have reference to the *Kṣatrapa* and *Mahākṣatrapa*,[2] both derived from old Persian *Kshathrapāvan* meaning 'a provincial governor', and also to *Daṇḍanāyaka* and *Mahādaṇḍanāyaka*.[3]

In the inscriptions of the Śaka rulers of Western India and of the Śātavāhanas of the Deccan, we have reference to officers like the *Amātya*[4] (in the capacity of the governor of a district or province), *Senāpati* (leader of forces)[5], *Mahāsenāpati*[6], *Matisaciva* (counsellor), *Karmasaciva* (administrator)[7] *Mahādaṇḍanāyaka*[8] (the great commander of forces), *Gañjavara* (treasurer or store-keeper)[9], etc. Early Śātavāhana inscriptions mention the official designation *Mahārāṣṭrin*[10]

1. *The Age of Imperial Unity*, p. 129. A feudatory of the Indo-Greek king Menander as well as his successor enjoyed the Prakrit title *Apracaraja* (Sanskrit *Apratyagrāja*), 'one having no equal or rival' (ibid., p. 103).

2. Ibid., pp. 112, 114-15, 118-20, 131, 133, etc.

3. Ibid., p. 138; *Proc. IHC*, 1958, Trivandrum, p. 63. The popularity of the designation *Daṇḍanāyaka* in Kuṣāṇa administration may tempt one to regard it as a translation of Greek *Strategos*. But, in that case, it would be the only title of foreign origin that became popular in South India. It may be noticed that other official disignations of foreign origin such as *Gañjavara*, *Pīlupati*, *Divirapati*, *Śarabhaṅga*, etc., are found in the records of the northern regions of India and did not become popular in the South. See *Ep. Ind.*, Vol. XXXV, pp. 95ff. Of course it may be said that the administration of the Śakas of Western India influenced to some extent the western areas of the Deccan and that the Ābhīra king Vasuṣena of the North-Western Deccan conquered as far as the Guntur District of Andhra Pradesh, whose Nagarjunikonda inscription of the year 30 [probably of the Ābhīra era of 248 A.D.] mentions an officer enjoying the designations *Mahāgrāmika*, *Mahātalavara* and *Mahādaṇḍanāyaka* (ibid., Vol. XXXIV, pp. 197 ff.). But the fact cannot be ignored that a *Daṇḍanāyaka-Balādhikṛta* is mentioned in the Gunji (Raigarh District, Madhya Pradesh) inscription of about the first century A.D. (*Ep. Ind.*, Vol. XXVII, pp. 48 ff.; *JAS*, Letters, Vol. XIX, pp. 59 ff.).

4. Ibid., pp. 174, 192-93. Sometimes we have also *Rājāmātya* (Lüder's List, Nos. 1053, 1141) and also *Mahāmātya* (*Bomb. Gaz.*, Vol. I, Part ii, p. 527, also called *Mahāpradhāna*). For an *Amātya* called *Sarvādhikārin*, see ibid., p. 527.

5. *Select Inscriptions*, p. 176. There is also *Mahāsenāpati* (Lüders' List, Nos. 1124, 1146).

6. *Select Inscriptions*, p. 204.

7. Ibid., p. 174.

8. Ibid., p. 181.

9. Ibid., p. 119.

10. Ibid., pp. 185, 187. I do not think it possible to take the designation as *Mahārathin* (cf. ibid., p. 195).

which is proabably the same as the *Rāṣṭrika* of the inscriptions of Aśoka and the *Rāṣṭriya* or *Rāṣṭrīya* of a Śaka inscription.[1] Originally, he was no doubt the governor of a territorial unit called *Rāṣṭra*. But sometimes the designation seems to have been used as a title of nobility. Among the royal officers of this age, inscriptions also mention *Bhāṇḍāgārika* (store-keeper or treasurer), *Rāja-vaidya* (physician to the king), *Rāja-lipikara* (the king's scribe), *Pratīhāra-rakṣī* (a female gate-keeper of the royal harem), etc.[2]

That in later times official designations did not always indicate the same responsibility and may have indicated merely a rank in many cases is suggested by the mention of the *Daṇḍa-nāyaka* (sometimes modified to *Daṇṇāyaka*) and *Mahādaṇḍa-nāyaka* in the medieval records of the Kannaḍa area. Often he is the governor of a territory and, in some cases, the collector of particular taxes.[3] In many cases, he enjoyed several other official designations at the same time, e.g. (1) *Mahāsāmantādhi-pati* and *Mahāpradhāna*; or (2) *Mahāpradhāna*, *Antaḥpuravĕr-gaḍĕ*[4] and *Mahāpasāyita*;[5] or (3) *Sarvādhikārin* and *Senāpati*; or (4) *Mahāpradhāna* and *Senāpati*; or (5) *Mahāpradhāna*, *Hĕri-(Mahā)sandhivigrahin* and *Maṇĕvĕrgaḍĕ* (superintendent of the royal household); or (6) *Mahāpradhāna*, *Hĕrisandhivigrahin*, *Senādhipati* and *Kaḍitavĕrgaḍĕ* (superintendent of accounts and records);[6] or (7) *Mahāpradhāna*, *Antaḥpur-ādhyakṣa*, *Hĕri-Lāḷa-Kannaḍa-sandhivigrahin* (Sanskrit *Mahā-Lāṭa-Karṇāṭa-sandhivi-grahin*) and *Manĕvĕrgaḍĕ*; or (8) *Mahāsāmantādhipati*, *Mahā-*

1. *Select Inscriptions*, pp. 53, 171.

2. Cf. Lüders' List, Nos. 1141, 1190-91, etc., 271, 1126. For *Mahāmātra* in later records, see No. 1144 and *Ep.Ind.*, Vol. XXIV, p.276.

3. An officer is described as the *Daṇḍanāyaka* of the southern part of his master's kingdom and as governing many districts. See *Bomb. Gaz.*, Vol. I, Part ii, p. 523.

4. Sanskrit *Antaḥpurādhyakṣa*. The word *vĕrgaḍĕ* or *vĕggaḍĕ* is also found in the independent official designation as *Pĕrgaḍĕ* or *Hĕggaḍĕ* often given in Sanskrit as *Adhikārin* meaning a governor (*Bomb. Gaz.*, Vol. I, Part ii, pp. 450, 485).

5. The word *pasāyita* may be Sanskrit *prasādita* and the designation possibly indicated a *Jāgīrdār* of a particular type.

6. For the *Śānabhoga* or village accountant, see ibid., p. 449.

pradhāna, *Bhānasavĕggaḍĕ* (Sanskrit *Mahānasādhyakṣa*, 'superintendent of the royal kitchen') and *Accupannāyadadhiṣṭhāyaka* (superintendent of revenue from mints); or (9) *Mahāpradhāna*, *Sarvādhikārin* and *Hiriya*(*Mahā*)*bhāṇḍārin*, etc.[1] It is not known whether the different responsibilities associated with particular disignations were held by an officer at the same time; but it will be seen that a distinction is sometimes made between the *Daṇḍanāyaka* and the commander of the army (*senā*, *sainya*), the latter officer being often mentioned in these records as the *Senāpati*, *Sainyādhikārin*, *Sainyapāla*, *Camūpati*, *Dala-adhikārin*, *Dalavāy*, etc.[2] Sometimes military and civil designations are applied to the same person. Thus the inscriptions of the Yādavas of Devagiri describe the same officer as *Mahāpradhāna* (chief minister), *Bāhattaraniyogādhipati* (superintendent of appointments of the 72 kinds of officers), *Paṭṭasāhanādhipati* (chief officer in charge of the army) and *Senāpati* (leader of forces).[3] In one case, an officer called *Mahāpradhāna* and *Bāhattaraniyogādhipati* is described as the *Sarvādhikārin* (apparently, 'governor' or 'chief administrator') of Hagaraṭṭagĕ 300.[4]

1. Mahalingam, *South Indian Polity*, pp. 118-119; *Bomb. Gaz.* Vol. I, Part ii, pp. 443, 451-52, 501. Nagaṇṇa-daṇṇāyaka is mentioned as the Prime Minister of a Vijayanagara king in the same record mentioning Cāmanṛpāla as the king's *Sarvasainyādhikārin*. The designation *Accupannāyadadhiṣṭhāyaka* may be compared with *Suṅkapannāyadadhiṣṭhāyaka* in which *suṅka* stands for Sanskrit *śulka* (*Bomb. Gaz.*, op. cit., p. 485), *Lāḷakhaṇḍeyakāraradhiṣṭhāyaka*, 'superintendent of the revenue from Lāṭa' (ibid., p. 487), etc.

2. Mahalingam, loc. cit. That there were various kinds of military officers is suggested by designations like *Manĕyasamastasainyādhipati* 'leader of all the troops in the royal household' (*Bomb. Gaz.*, op cit., p. 529).

3. *Bomb. Gaz.*, Vol. I, Part ii, pp. 520, 524. A feudatory of the Cālukyas of Kalyāṇa is called *Mahāsāmanta*, *Sen-ādi-bāhattara-niyog-ādhiṣṭhāyaka*, *Mahāpradhāna*, *Sarvādhikārin*, *Mahāpasāyita* and *Daṇḍanāyaka* (ibid., p. 485).

4. Ibid., p. 521. That sometimes kings had in their service more than one person enjoying the same designation is suggested by the Lucknow Museum plate of Kīrtipāla who is stated to have made a grant in the presence of all his *Pātras* apparently including (1) a *Mahāpurohita-ṭhakkura* (the head of the chief priests), (2) a *Mahāpurohita* (priest), (3) a *Dharmādhikaraṇika* (judge), (4) a *Daivāgārika* (priest in charge of the shrine probably within the palace), (5) a *Śaṅkhadhārin* (conchshell-blower), (6) *Paṇḍitas* (i.e. court Pandits), (7) three *Upādhyāyas* (teachers), (8) one *Daivajña* (astrologer), (9) one *Ṭhakkura* (fief-holder ?), (10) one *Mahākṣapaṭalika* (accountant and record-keeper), (11) one *Āṣṭavargika* (superintendent of eight departments ?), (12) one *Karaṇa-Kāyastha* (scribe), (13) one *Mahārthaśāsanika* (officer in charge of gifts ?), and (14) one *Mahāsādhanika* (commander of forces). See *Ep. Ind.*, Vol. VII, p. 97.

The practice of addressing a number of officers in connection with grants of land gradually came into vogue and the lists of officers furnished in many of the copper-plate charters give us a clearer picture of the administrative set up of some of the kingdoms. Sometimes it was specifically stated that the address was meant for present and future officers and subordinates who were then and might be later associated with the gift land.[1] The earliest copper-plate grant giving such a list of officers is the Hirahadagalli plates[2] of Pallava Śivaskandavarman. The royal order in respect of a grant of land was addressed in this case to the following categories of the king's subordinates: *Rājakumāra*, *Senāpati*, *Rāṣṭrika*, *Māṇḍapika*, *Deśādhikṛta*, *Grāmāgrāmabhojaka*, *Vallava*, *Govallava*, *Amātya*, *Ārakṣādhikṛta*, *Gaulmika*, *Tairthika*, *Naiyogika* and other servants like the *Sañcaratka* and *Bhaṭamanuṣya*.[3] Of these, the *Rājakumāras* were of course princes of the royal blood and the *Senāpati* the commander of the royal forces. The *Rāṣṭrika* seems, as in the earlier inscriptions referred to above, the governor of an administrative or territorial unit called *Rāṣṭra*, while the *Deśādhikṛta* was likewise the ruler of a similar unit called *Deśa*. The *Māṇḍapika* was the officer in charge of the *maṇḍapa* or customs-house, called *māṇḍavī* in Marāṭhī and Gujarātī.[4] *Grāmāgrāmabhojaka* refers to the Jāgīrdārs enjoying various rent-free villages in the kingdom. The *Vallava* and *Govallava* were respectively 'the keeper of horses' and 'the keeper of cows.' The *Amātya* was a minister or an administrative officer.[5]

1. Cf. expressions like *vartamāna-bhavishyat*⁰, *yathā-kāla-bhāvi*⁰, etc., and also *samavetān* or *samupāgatān* in the sense of 'associated' rather than 'assembled.' See above, pp 161 ff.

2. *Select Inscriptions*, pp. 437 ff. The order in respect of the Mayidavolu plates of Śivaskandavarman was issued to the *Vyāpṛta* who seems to have been the governor of the province of Andhrāpatha with his headquarters at Dhānyakaṭa (ibid., pp. 433 ff.). Like *Yukta*, *Āyukta* and *Niyogin*, *Vyāpṛta* essentially means 'employed' or 'an employee'.

3. See *Suc. Sāt. L. Dec.*, p. 191. The Prakrit words in the record for *Tairthika* and *Naiyogika* are *Tūthika* and *Neyika* respectively. The second designation is found in some other early Pallava charters as *Naiyyoka* and *Naiyogika*.

4. See Wilson's Glossary, s. v. *māṇḍavī*.

5. We have seen above that some *Amātyas* were governors of a district or province. Although the word is often used as a synonym of *Mantrin* or minister, Rāmavarman's commentary on the *Rāmāyaṇa*, I. 7. 4, makes the following distinction between the two : *amātyā deś-ādi-kārya-nirvāhakā mantriṇo vyavahāra-draṣṭāra iti bhedaḥ* (*Ind. Cult.*, Vol. VIII, p. 121).

The *Ārakṣādhikṛta* was either a magistrate looking after the watch over villages or towns, or an officer responsible for the protection of the king's person. The *Gaulmika* was in charge of a *gulma* or out-post,[1] and the *Tairthika* the officer in charge of a ferry or the ferries.[2] The designation *Naiyogika*, derived from *niyoga*, 'an appointment', may indicate officers in charge of small administrative units or offices. The *Sañcaratka* was a spy while the *Bhaṭamanuṣya* was apparently a constable, called *Pāik* (from Sanskrit *Padātika*, 'foot-soldier') or *Piāda* inmany parts of North India.[3] At the end of the Hirahadagalli plates, it is stated that the writer of the document was Bhartṛśarman who was the *Rahasyādhikṛta* (private secretary) and the *Bhojaka* (Jāgīrdār) of Kolivāla. The official designation *Rahasyādhikṛta* is noticed in several other records sometimes as *Rahasya*, *Rāhasika*, *Rahasiniyukta*, etc.[1] He seems to be the same as *Vaiśvāsika*, *Paramaviśvāsin* or *Mahāparamaviśvāsin* of other records.[4]

There is no such list of officials addressed in the few copper-plate grants of the Imperial Guptas so far discovered. But a number of official designations of the Gupta administration are known from their epigraphs and the records of their subordinates. Hariṣeṇa, author of the Allahabad pillar inscription of Samudragupta, is called *Khādyaṭapākika* and *Sāndhivigrahika-Kumarāmātya-Mahādaṇḍanāyaka*, while his father was also a *Mahādaṇḍanāyaka*.[5] The formation of the designation *Khādyaṭapākika* is obscure, and it may be a mistake for *Khādyakūṭapākika* meaning the superintendent of the preparation of the king's food. The *Sāndhivigrahika* was the minister of

1. Cf. *Manusmṛti*, VII. 190.

2. The word *tīrtha* in this designation may also be taken to mean 'a holy place of pilgrimage'.

3. See Wilson's Glossary, s. v. *Pāik* and *Piāda*. The second of these is a Persian word introduced by the Muhammadans. Cf. also *Barkandāz*.

4. Cf. *Ep. Ind.*, Vol. XXVIII, p. 17 and note 5; Vol. XXX, pp. 26, 275, etc.

5. See ibid., Vol. XXVIII, p. 329; *Bomb. Gaz.*, Vol. I, Part ii, pp. 505, 523 (the same officer is called here *Mahāpradhāna*, *Sarvādhikārin* and *Paramaviśvāsin* or *Mahāparamaviśvāsin*).

6. *Select Inscriptions*, pp. 259-60.

peace and war, i.e. of foreign affairs.[1] The *Kumārāmātya* was probably an *Amātya* enjoying the status of a prince of the royal blood.[2] We had occasion before to refer to the Gunaighar plate (507 A.D.) of Vainyagupta, which speaks of a feudatory ruler enjoying the designations *Mahārāja* and *Mahāsāmanta* side by side with *Mahāpratīhāra*, *Mahāpīlupati*, *Pañcādhikaraṇoparika*, *Pāṭyuparika* and *Purapāloparika*.[3] Since the word *pratīhāra* means 'a gate-keeper', the *Mahāpratīhāra* may have been the superintendent of the troops in charge of the defence of the gates of the palace and capital and probably also of the king's body-guards. He may also have been the officer attending on the king at the door of the royal bed chamber. In *Mahāpīlupati*, which means 'the master of elephants', the word *pīlu* is derived from Arabic and Persian *fīl* meaning 'an elephant'. The popularity of this semi-foreign designation in Eastern India about the beginning of the 6th century A.D. cannot be explained unless it is believed that the Imperial Guptas adopted it from the Kuṣāṇas. *Pañcādhikaraṇoparika* seems to mean 'the head of five administrative offices,[4] while *Pāṭyuparika* may be 'the head of the department of accounts,' the word *pāṭī* being known to mean 'arithmetic'. *Purapāloparika* seems to mean 'the chief amongst the governors of cities.'

We know from certain charters issued by the subordinate officers under the Gupta emperors that the Gupta viceroy

1. Sometimes such an officer is mentioned in medieval records with reference to a particular territory, e.g., *Gauḍa-mahāsāndhivigrahika*, *Kannaḍa-sandhivigrahin*, *Hĕri-Lāṭa-Karṇāṭa-sandhivigrahin*, *Hĕri-Lāḷa-sandhivigrahin* etc. See N. G. Majumdar, *Inscriptions of Bengal*, Vol. III, p. 138, etc.; *Bomb. Gaz.*, Vol. I, Part ii, pp. 451-52, 457-58.

2. The Karamdanda inscription of 436 A.D. mentions a *Kumārāmātya* who was also a *Mantrin*, but later became a *Mahābalādhikṛta*. His father was likewise a *Mantrin* and *Kumārāmātya*. Cf. *Select Inscriptions*, pp. 282-83. A similar designation is *Kumāramahāpātra* known from a medieval inscription of Orissa (*Ep. Ind.*, Vol. XXVIII, p. 187).

3. *Select Inscriptions*, p. 333; above, p. 343.

4. This designation seems to be the same as *Pañcakaraṇoparika* applied to the *Dūtaka* of one of Śailodbhava Dharmarāja's grants, who is also styled *Vaiśvāsika* (privy councillor) and *Bṛhadbhogin* (the principal Jāgīrdār). See *Ep. Ind.*, Vol. XXIX. p. 40. For *Vaiśvāsika* in other records, cf. ibid., Vol. XXVIII, p. 329.

or provincial governor was often called *Uparika* or *Uparika-Mahārāja*[1] and that the *Āyuktaka* was often the governor of a district (*Viṣayapati*) and that the *Pustapāla* or record-keeper was an important district officer.[2] In many cases, a district officer is referred to in the inscriptions as *tad-Āyuktaka* or *tad-Viniyuktaka* after the mention of the provincial governor in order to indicate that the said officer was employed by the viceroy and not directly by the crown.[3] In later times, *Tadāyuktaka* and *Tanniyuktaka* or *Tadviniyuktaka* appear to have become stereotyped official designations to indicate certain grades of subordinates and assistants of a high officer.

In the Gupta inscriptions of the Bengal region, sale of government land for the creation of rent-free holdings is represented as having been conducted by a board of administration, called *adhikaraṇa* such as *adhiṣṭhān-ādhikaraṇa* (administrative board of the city), *aṣṭakul-ādhikaraṇa* (administrative board consisting of members from eight communities), etc. In many cases, such a board consisted of the *Nagara-śreṣṭhin* (literally, 'the city banker'), *Sārthavāha* (literally 'the tradesman') *Prathama-Kulika* (literally, 'the chief Kulika or astisan') and *Prathama-Kāyastha* (literally, 'the chief Kāyastha or scribe'). There is little doubt that they formed what is now called a Pañcāyat Board. Such four-member Pañcāyat Boards were called Cauthiyā in late medieval Rajasthan and were headed by the *Nagar-Seṭh* (*Nagaraśreṣthin*), the Paṭel (the village headman) and Paṭvārī (the accountant clerk) being two of the members. In early medieval inscriptions and literally works, the *Cauthiyā* is called *Caturjātaka*. Five-member administrative boards of the same kind are known from the early medieval epigraphic and literary records of Western India as *Pañcakula*.[4]

1. In medieval records, the governoror viceroy was sometimes said to have been conducting the *mudrā-vyāpāra*, i.e. affairs associated with the royal seal. See *Ep. Ind.*, Vol. XXXIII, p. 71, etc.; above, p. 342.

2. *Select Inscriptions*, pp. 283-86, 324, 328.

3. For *Āyukta* and his subordinate, sometimes we have *Yuktaka* and *Upayuktaka*. See *Ep. Ind.*, Vol. IV, p. 285, text line 56.

4. See *Proc. IHC*, Ahmedabad, 1954, pp. 52 ff.; *Ep. Ind.*, Vol. XXXIII, p. 193; Vol. XXXIV, p. 142.

The Mallasarul plate[1] of the time of Gopacandra, who ruled over considerable parts of Bengal about the middle of the 6th century, gives the list of the following officers in connection with a grant of land : *Kārtākṛtika*, *Kumārāmātya*, *Cauroddharaṇika*, *Uparika*, *Audraṅgika*, *Āgrahārika*, *Aurṇasthānika*, *Bhogapatika*, *Viṣayapati*, *Hiraṇyasāmudāyika*, *Pattalaka*, *Āvasathika* and *Devadroṇīsambaddha*. The *Kārtākṛtika* seems to have informed the king about the progress made by officers in special undertakings. *Cauroddharaṇika* was a police officer reponsible for collecting fines for theft. The *Audraṅgika*, *Āgrahārika* and *Aurṇasthānika* were apparently superintendents respectively of *Udraṅga*, *Agrahāra* (rent-free lands granted to Brāhmaṇas) and *Ūrṇāsthāna* (wool factory). The word *udraṅga* is used in many records according to which the donee was entitled to enjoy the gift land together with *udraṅga*, possibly meaning the principal tax.[2] The *Bhogapatika* was probably the superintendent of *Bhogas* or *Jāgīrs*. The *Hiraṇyasāmudāyika* may have been the collector of taxes in cash (*hiraṇya*) and the *Pattalaka* the officer in charge of a territorial unit called *Pattalā*, while the the *Āvasathika* was apparently superintendents of *Avasathas* probably meaning colleges or *Dharmaśālās*.[3] *Devadroṇīsaṁbaddha* reminds us of the officer called *Devadroṇyadhikṛta*, taken to mean 'a superintendent of thep rocession of idols', in the Talesvar plate (6th century) of Dyutivarman.[4]

The Bhamodra-Mohota plate[5] (502 A.D.) of the Maitraka

1. *Select Inscriptions*, pp. 359 ff.

2. Cf. *CII*, Vol. III, p. 97 and note. The Tripura plate of Bhavadeva seems to use *udraṅgīkṛtya* and *sodraṅgīkṛtya* in the same sense (*JAS*, Letters, Vol. XVII, p. 94). This possibly means that *udraṅga* had to be paid by the donees of this grant for the gift land in question.

3. The word *āvasathika* also means 'one who keeps the domestic fire (*āvasatha*) burning with daily offering' (D. Bhattacharya, *Halāyudha's Brāhmaṇasarvasva*, p. xx). But the inscription in question seems to mean an official.

4. *Ep. Ind.*, Vol. XIII, p. 117. But the expression *deva-droṇī* may possibly mean 'temple property'. Cf. *Śrī-Somanāthadeva-droṇī-pratibaddha-Mahāyaṇā(jan-ā)ntaḥpāti°*, etc., in the Veraval inscription, line 12 (*Ind. Ant.*, Vol. XI, pp. 242-43; *Ep. Ind.*, Vol. XXXIV, p. 147).

5. *Select Inscriptions*, pp. 433 ff.

chief Droṇasiṁha of Kathiawar offers a small list mentioning the *Āyukta*, *Viniyuktaka*, *Mahattara*, *Drāṅgika*, *Dhruvasthānādhikaraṇa*, *Cāṭa* and *Bhaṭa*.[1] Of these, *Mahattara* may refer to the headmen of the villages,[2] although in South Indian records the expression seems to indicate the *Mahājanas* or heads of the families or communities, who constituted the village councils.[3] *Drāṅgika* is derived from *draṅga* which is the same as *udraṅga* according to Sanskrit lexicons and appears to be the same as *Audraṅgika* discussed above. The *Rājataraṅgiṇī* uses the word *draṅga* in the sense of 'a watch station'.[4] If that meaning is applicable, *Drāṅgika* of the inscriptions may have been 'the officer in charge of a watch station'. *Dhruvasthānādhikaraṇa* was the office of the *Dhruvasthāna*.[5] The officer in its charge is no doubt the same as modern *Dhruva* of Kathiawar and Kachh meaning a person who superintended the collection of the royal share of the produce from the farmers on behalf of a Rājā.[6] The same officer is sometimes called *Dhruvādhikaraṇika*, i.e. superintendent of the office of the *Dhruva*. The *Cāṭa* and *Bhaṭa* noticed here are a regular occurrence in the list of addressees in North Indian grants of the medieval age. Of the two, the *Bhaṭa* is no doubt the same as the *Bhaṭamanuṣya* known from certain South Indian epigraphs and referred to above. We are inclined to take *Bhaṭa* to mean a constable or a Pāik or Piāda, while the *Cāṭa* seems to have been the leader of a group of them. *Cāṭa* is also found in the form *Caṭṭa* and *Cāḍa* in later epigraphs and is apparently the same as the *Cāḍ* of modern

1. The charter of Viṣṇuṣeṇa of Kathiawar, dated 592 A.D., mentions a few more designations, one of them being *Vailabdhika* (*Ep. Ind.*, Vol. XXX, p. 167). This desingation, derived from *vilabdhi*, seems to indicate the custodian of presents offered to the king or of stolen property recovered from thieves.

2. Cf. Wilson's Glossary, s. v. *Mahto*, etc.

3. The *mahājana-sabhā* is often mentioned in the records of the Kannaḍa area.

4. VII. 1352; VIII. 1578, 2507, etc. *Draṅga* may be also taken to mean a station for revenue collection.

5. This probably means the station for the collection of the *dhruva* or the fixed royal share of the produce.

6. Cf. *Ep. Ind.*, Vol. XXX, p. 168.

Chamba where he was the head of a Pargana.[1] Since however the *Cāṭa* and *Bhaṭa* are mentioned in most of the epigraphic records as belonging to the lowest rank of royal servants, the meaning of *Cād* as prevalent at present in Chamba cannot be applied to *Cāṭa* in the early and medieval inscriptions. This is further suggested by the fact that the Vākāṭaka inscriptions generally mention *Chātra* ('an umbrella-bearer', a peon) instead of *Cāṭa* in association with *Bhaṭa*.[2] Sometimes we have *Cāra* (spy) instead of *Cāṭa*.[3]

Among other charters of West Indian rulers, mention may be made of the small list of addressees in the Kavi plates[4] (736 A.D.) of the Gurjara king Jayabhaṭa III. The list consists of the *Rājan*, *Sāmanta*, *Bhogika*, *Viṣayapati* and *Rāṣṭra-grāma-mahattara*. The *Sāmanta* was apparently a smaller feudatory than the *Rājan*. *Bhogika*, derived from *bhoga*, 'a *Jāgīr*', means a Jāgīrdār, while *Bhogapati*, found side by side with it in certain records, may be an officer in charge of *Jāgīrs*. *Bhogika* is the same as *Bhogin* of other records, to both of which the word *bṛhat* is sometimes prefixed. An early inscription from Orissa speaks of *Aṁśabṛhadbhogika* probably meaning 'partner of a *Jāgīr*'.[5] The last item includes *Rāṣṭramahattara* and *Grāma-mahattara* who may be the same as the *Rāṣṭrakūṭa* and *Grāmakūṭa* of certain records of the rulers of Kannaḍa origin and were the headmen respectively of villages and of the groups of villages called *Rāṣṭra*. If the expression *mahattara* is taken to mean the head of a family or community, who was the member of the local council, we have to think of a *Mahājana-sabhā* for *Rāṣṭra* also.

The charters of the early medieval kings of South India generally do not contain any big list of addressees. Thus while the Ellora plates[6] (742 A.D.) of Dantidurga are addressed to

1. See Vogel, *Antiquities of Chamba State*, Part I, pp. 130-32.
2. See *Select Inscriptions*, pp. 414, 417, 422. For *Chātra*, cf. also *Ep. Ind.*, Vol. XXX, pp. 373-74.
3. *Ep. Ind.*, Vol. XXVI, p. 199.
4. *Ind. Ant.*, Vol. V, pp. 114 ff.
5. *Ep. Ind.*, Vol. XXVIII, p. 329.
6. *Ep. Ind.*, Vol. XXV, pp. 25 ff.

the *Rājan*, *Sāmanta*, *Bhogika*, *Viṣayapati*, *Rāṣṭrakūṭa*, *Mahattara* and *Adhikārika*, the Sanjan plates[1] (871 A.D.) of Amoghavarṣa I were addressed to the *Rāṣṭrapati*, *Viṣayapati*, *Grāmakūṭa*, *Yuktaka* or *Āyuktaka*, *Niyukta*, *Adhikārika* and *Mahattara*. In these, the *Rāṣṭrakūṭa* of the one is the same as the *Rāṣṭrapati* of the other. *Niyukta* is the same as *Tanniyuktaka*, etc., of other records. *Adhikārika* seems to be the same as the *Niyogika* or *Naiyogika* of the early Pallava inscriptions. The *Viṣayapati* was the ruler of a *Viṣaya* or district.

The Saindhava plates[2] from Ghumli offer a slightly bigger list of addressees, one of them being *Vaikṣepika* who may have been the dispatcher of messengers like the *Preṣaṇika* of other records.[3] The word *janapada* is also used in the lists of addressees in these records possibly in the sense of *Jānapada* or the people of the countryside. Instead of the usual *Cāṭa*, these records use *Cāra* meaning 'a spy'.

But from about the 8th century A.D.,[4] the list of addressees was fairly big in the charters of the rulers of some of the North Indian monarchs. Thus the Khalimpur plate[5] of Dharmapāla who flourished about the end of the 8th and the beginning of the 9th century, is addressed to the following : *Rājan*, *Rājanaka*, *Rājaputra*, *Rājāmātya*, *Senāpati*, *Viṣayapati*, *Bhogapati*, *Ṣaṣṭhādhikṛta*, *Daṇḍaśakti*, *Daṇḍapāśika*, *Caurodharaṇika*, *Dauḥsādhasādhanika*, *Dūta*, *Khola*, *Gamāgamika*, *Abhitvaramāṇa*, *Hastyaśvagomahiṣājāvikādhyakṣa*, *Naukādhyakṣa*, *Balādhyakṣa*, *Tarika*, *Śaulkika*, *Gaulmika*, *Tadāyuktaka*, *Viniyuktaka*, *Cāṭa* and *Bhaṭa*

1. Ibid., Vol. XVIII, pp. 235 ff.
2. Ibid., Vol. XXVI, p. 199.
3. Although the expression *dūtapreṣaṇika* occurring in many East Indian records is taken to indicate *Dūta* and *Preṣaṇika*, sometimes *Dūta* and *Dūta-preṣaṇika* are mentioned together in the list of officers (cf. N. G. Majumdar, *Ins. Beng.*, Vol. III, p. 153, text lines 18-19).
4. The addressees in the grants of Harṣa (606-47 A.D.) are not too many. Cf. *Ep. Ind.*, Vol. IV, p. 211. The Deo-Baranark inscription of Jīvitagupta II (about the second quarter of the 8th century A.D.) is one of the earliest records containing a big list which the Pālas appear to have imitated. See *JAS*, Letters, Vol. XI, pp. 73-74.
5. *Gauḍalekhamālā*, pp. 9 ff.

as well as the district officers like *Jyeṣṭhakāyastha*, *Mahāmahattara*, *Mahattara*, *Dāśagrāmika* and *Viṣayavyavahārin* whose *Karaṇas* or offices are also specially mentioned.

The *Rājanaka* was apparently a smaller feudatory than *Rājan*. *Rājaputra* is the same as *Rājakumāra* of the Hirahadagalli plates, although the intention here may be to refer to the sons of the feudatories since the following *Rājāmātya* possibly indicates the ministers or administrators of the subordinate rulers. *Senāpati* (leader of forces), *Viṣayapati* (ruler of a district) and *Bhogapati* (superintendent of *Jāgīrs*) have already been discussed above. It is however interesting to note that, in the present case, the *Senāpati* is distinguished from the *Balādhyakṣa*. We have to remember in this connection that, according to some authorities, the smallest leader of the forces of an Indian king was a *Pattika*, ten of whom served under a *Senāpati*, while the *Senānāyaka* or *Balādhyakṣa* led ten *Senāpatis*.[1] Thus the *Balādhyakṣa* was a higher officer than the *Senāpati*, while the *Mahādaṇḍanāyaka* was probably a still higher military officer or a governor. The *Ṣaṣṭhādhikṛta* was no doubt the collector of the king's grain share from the farmer and was practically the same as the *Dhruvādhikaraṇika* or *Dhruvasthānādhikaraṇika* of the Kathiawar inscriptions. The designation shows that the king's share was one sixth of the produce at least originally. The *Daṇḍaśakti* is apparently the *Dāṇḍika* of later epigraphs and may have been a sort of police magistrate, while the *Daṇḍapāśika* was probably a smaller police officer. The expression *Daṇḍapāśika* still survives in Oḍiyā *Daṇḍuāsi* meaning 'a village watchman'. *Dauḥsādhasādhanika* seems to have been a leader of expeditionary

1. Cf. Kullūka's commentary on the *Manusmṛti*, VII. 189. The *Pattika* led the smallest division of an army called a *Patti* which consisted of one chariot, one elephant, three horsemen and five foot-soldiers. The word *patti* also means 'a foot-soldier'. In Kashmir, the Commander-in-chief was called 'the lord of *kampana*' (*Rājataraṅgiṇī*, VII. 154, 267, 365, 399, 579, etc.) and another commander was called the lord of the *dvāra* or gate' (ibid., verses 216, 223, 364, etc.). The latter seems to have guarded the passes leading to the heart of the Kashmir valley. Sometimes an officer was stated to have been appointed the *Senāpati* (apparently, 'a military governor') over a particular district (Bhandarkar's List, No. 245).

forces requisitioned on occasions of emergency. The word *sādhanika* forming a part of this designation is the same as Prakrit *Sāhaṇia* and means 'the commander of an army'. The designation *Sādhanika* in a Paramāra inscription and *Mahāsādhanika* in Merutuṅga's *Prabandhacintāmaṇi* are used to indicate a chieftain or military governor.[1] The *Dūta* (envoy) is distinguished from the *Abhitvaramāṇa* whose designation seems to mean a messenger or carrier of letters meant for quick delivery of the message, etc. *Khola*, also known from the Ramganj plate to be discussed below, is unintelligible if he was not a special type of messenger, while *Gamāgamika* seems to have been the officer regulating the entrance in and departure from towns. *Hastyaśvagomahiṣājāvikādhyakṣa* was no doubt the officer or officers in charge of the king's elephants, horses, cows, buffaloes, goats and sheep and may be compared with *Vallava* and *Govallava* of the Hirahadagalli plates and the *Vrajabhūmika* of the inscriptions of Aśoka. The *Naukādhyakṣa* was probably the admiral in charge of the royal fleet. The *Tarika* (superintendent of a ferry or the ferries) is the same as the *Tairthika* of the Hirahadagalli plates and the *Tarapati* of later records, while the *Śaulkika* was the collector of *śulka* or customs, similar to the *Māṇḍapika* of the Hirahadagalli plates. *Jyeṣṭhakāyastha* was the chief scribe or the representative of the scribal class on a board of administration. Since *Mahattara* was the head of a village or community and the member of a *Pañcāyat*, the *Mahāmahattara* appears to have been the head of a group of villages or the chairman of its council of administration, while the *Dāśagrāmika* was similarly

1. See *Ep. Ind.*, Vol. XXXII, pp. 141-42. The designation *Mahāsādhanika* may be compared with *Paṭṭasāhaṇādhipati* of South Indian records, sometimes called *Senāpati* separately (*Bomb. Gaz.*, Vol. I, Part ii, p. 520). *Sādhanika*, derived from *sādhana* or an army, is the same as the modern family name Sāhnī. *Sāhaṇi* occurring in a Rajasthan inscription has been supposed to indicate 'the master of the royal stables' (Bhandarkar's List, No. 395). See also designations like *Gajasāhiṇi*, i.e. *Gajasādhanika* or leader of the elephant corps (*Ep. Ind.*, Vol. XXVII, p. 310). For *Sāhaṇi* or *Sāhiṇi* in the inscriptions of the Kannaḍa-speaking area, cf. Kundangar, *Inscriptions of Northern Karnatak and Kolhapur*, p. 139, No. 16, etc.

the head of a group of about ten villages, or the chairman of the administrative council of the group.[1] These officials were apparently similar to the *Grāmakūṭa*, *Rāṣṭrakūṭa* and *Deśādhikṛta* of South Indian records.

The above list may be compared with that in the Manahali plate of Madanapāla (c. 1143-61 A.D.) who was one of the latest rulers of the Pāla family. In this list, we have *Rājan*, *Rājanyaka*, *Rājaputra*, *Rājāmātya*, *Mahāsāndhivigrahika*, *Mahākṣapaṭalika*, *Mahāsāmanta*, *Mahāsenāpati*., *Mahāprathīhāra*, *Dauḥsādhasādhanika*, *Mahākumārāmātya Rājasthānīya* and *Uparika*, *Cauroddharaṇika*, *Dāṇḍika*, *Dāṇḍapāśika*, *Śaunika*, *Kṣetrapa*, *Prāntapāla*, *Koṭṭapāla*, *Aṅgarakṣa*, *Tadāyuktaka*, *Viniyuktaka*, *Hastyaśvoṣṭranaubalavyāpṛtaka*, *Kiśoravaḍavāgomahiṣājāvikādhyakṣa*, *Dūta*, *Preṣaṇika*, *Gamāgamika*, *Abhitvaramāṇa*, *Viṣayapati*, *Grāmapati*, *Tarika*, *Śaulkika*, *Gaulmika*, Gauḍa, Mālava, Coḍa, Khasa, Hūṇa, Kulika, Karṇāṭa, *Cāṭa* and *Bhaṭṭa*. There are some new designations in this list while a few of them are found in slightly modified form. *Mahāsāndhivigrahika* is found in earlier inscriptions though not in the Khalimpur plate. The prefix *mahā*, which was probably used to distinguish the chief officer in a particular group, has been added to some of the designations found without it in the Khalimpur plate and earlier inscriptions. The *Mahākṣapaṭalika* was the keeper of records according to some but the chief accountant according to others, though he seems to have acted in both the capacities at least in some parts of the country. Amongst the new designations, the *Rājasthānīya* seems to be a subordinate ruler according to the *Subodhikā* commentary on the *Kalpasūtra* quoted above, though the designation is no doubt the same as the *Rājasthānādhikāra* mentioned in the *Rājataraṅgiṇī*[2] as one of the highest judicial officers of ancient Kashmir. But the explanation of the *Lokaprakāśa* that the *Rājāsthānīya* was 'one

1. The *Manusmṛti* (VII, 115-19) mentions the heads of one village, ten villages, a hundred villages and one thousand villages. The Tripura plate of Bhavadeva was addressed to the *Viṣayapatis* and the *Karaṇikas* (scribes or *Paṭvārīs*) and *Dāśagrāmikas* (*JAS*, Letters, Vol. XVII, p. 93).

2. See VII. 601; VIII. 181, 573, 1046, etc.

who carries out the object of protecting the subjects and shelters them'[1] and the Mandasor inscription[2] of Yaśodharman Viṣṇuvardhana representing a viceroy of the king as a *Rājasthānīya* appear to support the *Subodhikā*, although different functions may have been attached to the designation in different regions and ages. The *Śaunika* was apparently the superintendent of slaughter-houses and the sale of meat and the *Kṣetrapa* the superintendent of the lands of the king's Khās Mahāl. The *Prāntapāla* was the warden of the marches and the *Koṭṭapāla* the governor of a fort.[3] The *Aṅgarakṣa* was the king's body-guard. Instead of the *Hastyaśvoṣṭragomahiṣājāvikādhyakṣa* of the Khalimpur plate, we have here *Hastyaśvoṣṭranaubalavyāpṛtaka* (i.e. the military officers in charge of the elephant and camel corps and the navy) and *Kiśoravaḍavāgomahiṣājāvikādhyakṣa* (superintendent or superintendents of the young mares, cows, buffaloes, goats and sheep). As indicated above, the *Preṣaṇika* may have been the officer in charge of the despatch of messengers. The peoples of Gauḍa and other countries mentioned in the record appear to refer to the mercenary soldiers of various regions serving in the armies of the Pāla emperors. Among the peoples, the Kulikas appear to be the same as the Kulyas of the Purāṇas, who may probably be identified with the people of Kulait in the upper valley of the Ravi.

A similar comparison may likewise be made between the list of addressees in the charters of Lalitaśūra (middle of the 9th century) and Padmaṭa (middle of the 10th century), both of the Kumaun-Garhwal region.

Lalitaśūra's charters are addressed to the following subordinates and officers : *Rājan*, *Rājanaka*, *Rājaputra*, *Rājāmātya*, *Sāmanta*, *Mahāsāmanta*, *Ṭhakkura*, *Mahāmanuṣya*, *Mahā-*

1. *Ind. Ant.* Vol. V, p. 207; cf *CII*, Vol. III. p. 137, note. Fleet prefers to call him a political agent or regent.

2. *Select Inscriptions*, p. 390, verse 19.

3. Cf. the later *Kotwāl* generally regarded as a Persian word meaning 'the chief officer of police for a city or town, a superintendent of the markets' (Wilson's Glossary). The commnander of a fort seems to be called *Viśiṣa* (a word of uncertain derivation) in certain early medieval records of the central areas of India (cf. *Ep. Ind.*, Vol. XXX, p. 89).

kārtākṛtika, Mahāpratīhāra, Mahādaṇḍanāyaka, Mahārājapramātāra, Śarabhaṅga, Kumārāmātya, Uparika, Duḥsādhyasādhanika, Dāśāparādhika, Cauroddharaṇika, Śaulkika, Gaulmika Tadāyuktaka, Viniyuktaka, Paṭṭakāpacārika, Āsedhabhaṅgādhikṛta, Hastyaśvoṣṭrabalavyāpṛtaka, Dūta, Preṣaṇika, Dāṇḍika, Dāṇḍapāśika, Gamāgamin, Khāḍgika, Abhitvaramāṇaka, Rājasthānīya, Viṣayapati Bhogapati, Tarapati, Aśvapati, Khaṇḍarakṣa, Pratiśūrika Sthānādhikṛta, Vartmapāla, Koṭṭapāla, Ghaṭṭapāla, Kṣetrapāla, Prāntapāla, Kiśoravaḍavāgomahiṣyadhikṛta, Bhaṭṭa, Mahattama, Ābhīra, Vaṇik, Śreṣṭhin, such peoples as the Khaśa, Kirāta, Draviḍa, Kaliṅga, Gauḍa, Hūṇa, Uḍra, Meda, Andhra and Cāṇḍāla, and such servants as *Cāṭa* and *Bhaṭa*.[1]

The list has some new items not found in the Pāla grants discussed above. *Rājan* and *Rājanaka* have been distinguished from *Sāmanta* and *Mahāsāmanta* probably belonging to slightly lower grades of feudatories. Among the new entries, *Ṭhakkura* and *Mahāmanuṣya* are difficult to explain, but may mean noblemen and the chief attendant. *Mahārājapramātāra* is the same as *Pramātṛ* or *Pramātāra* of some records,[2] and may have been the king's counsellor on judicial matters. The function of the *Śarabhaṅga* cannot be determined; but the designation seems to be derived from Persian *Sarhang*, 'a commander', later modified in India to *Sāreng*.[3] *Duḥsādhyasādhanika* is the same as *Dauḥsādhasādhanika* of the Pāla charters. The *Dāśāparādhika* was probably the judge dealing with the ten offences including theft, murder, adultery, use of abusive language to others, desire to do wrong, tenacity for doing wrong, etc. The *Paṭṭakāpacārika* was the officer investigating offences against the royal edicts and charters, while the *Āsedhabhaṅgādhikṛta* was the officer in charge of the prevention of flight from prison or legal

1. *Ep. Ind.*, Vol. XXXI, pp. 282-83. The mention of the Andhras along with the Meda and Cāṇḍāla in many medieval records appears to refer to the low class people of the present Telugu-speaking area, who migrated to the territories in question and worked as sweepers, etc. For another suggestion, see *IHQ*, Vol. XVI, pp. 560 ff.

2. See ibid., Vol. IV, p. 211; Vol. XXVI, p. 199. He may have also been the superintendent of the measurement of the royal share of grains.

3. For *Sarhang*, see Wilson's Glossary. The word occurs as *Sarāṅgha* (a military governor) in the Hatun inscription (*Ep. Ind.*, Vol. XXX, p. 228). See ibid., Vol. XXXIV, pp. 95 ff.

restraint. The *Khāḍgika*, literally 'swordsman', was probably the palace guard. *Tarapati* (superintendent of a ferry or the ferries) was the same as *Tarika* or *Tairthika* of other inscriptions. In *Khaṇḍarakṣa*, sometimes found as *Khaḍgarakṣa*, the word *khaṇḍa* is the same as Bengali *khāṇḍā* and Oriya *khaṇḍā*, 'a heavy sword', and the expression means 'the king's sword-bearer', or a body-guard of the king,[1] since *Khāḍgika*, possibly meaning 'a palace guard', is mentioned separately. *Pratiśūrika* is difficult to interpret, but may have been the superintendent of gladitorial combats. The *Sthānādhikṛta* (modern *Thānādār*)[2] was the officer in charge of a police or military outpost similar to the *Gaulmika*. The *Vartmapāla* was the superintendent of roads and the *Ghaṭṭapāla* the superintendent of landing places on the river banks or of passes. Both these may have been customs officers. The *Kṣetrapāla* is the same as the *Kṣetrapa* of other epigraphs. In *Kiśoravaḍavāgomahiṣyadhikṛta*, *mahiṣī* in the feminine has been used instead of *mahiṣa* in the masculine. The *Mahattama* is apparently the same as the *Mahattara* of other epigraphs. The list includes the *Ābhīras* (cowherds), *Vaṇiks* (merchants) and *Śreṣṭhins* (bankers or foremen of guilds).

Padmaṭa's grant was similarly addressed to the *Rājan*, *Rājanaka*, *Rājaputra*, *Rājāmātya*, *Sāmanta*, *Mahāsāmanta*, *Mahākārtākṛtika*, *Mahādaṇḍanāyaka*, *Mahāpratihāra*, *Mahāsāmantādhipati*, *Mahārājapramātāra*, *Śarabhaṅga*, *Kumārāmātya*, *Uparika*, *Duḥsādhyasādhanika*, *Dāśāparādhika*, *Cauroddharaṇika*, *Śaulkika*, *Gaulmika*, *Tadāyuktaka*, *Viniyuktaka*, *Paṭṭakāpacārika*, *Āsedhabhaṅgādhikṛta*, *Hastyaśvoṣṭrabalavyāpṛtaka*, *Dūta*, *Preṣaṇika*, *Dāṇḍika*, *Dāṇḍapāśika*, *Viṣayavyāpṛtaka*, *Gamāgamika*, *Khāḍgika*, *Abhitvaramāṇaka*, *Rājasthānīya*, *Viṣayapati*, *Bhogapati*, *Kāṇḍapati*, *Tarapati*, *Aśvapati*, *Khaṇḍarakṣa*, *Sthānādhikṛta*, *Vartmapāla*, *Ghaṭṭapāla*, *Kṣetrapāla*, *Prāntapāla*, *Ṭhakkura*, *Mahāmanuṣya*, *Kiśoravaḍavāgomahiṣyadhikṛta*, *Bhaṭṭa*, *Mahattama*, *Ābhīra*, *Vaṇik* and *Śreṣṭhin*, the peoples including Khaśa, Kirāta, Draviḍa, Kaliṅga,

1. Cf. the Khaṇḍāit community of Orissa (Wilson's Glossary, s.v.).
2. Cf. Wilson's Glossary, s.v.

Gauḍa, Hūṇa, Uḍra, Meda, Andhra and Caṇḍāla as well as *Cāṭa*, *Bhaṭa* and other servants.[1]

In this list, *Mahāsāmantādhipati* is a more dignified title than *Mahāsāmanta*. *Viṣayavyāpṛtaka* is distinguished from the *Viṣayapati* or ruler of a district and may have been an officer associated with the administration of a district. In *Kāṇḍapati*, the word *kāṇḍa* seems to mean 'an arrow'. The designation may therefore refer to an officer in charge of the armoury. The *Aśvapati* seems to have been the keeper of horses or the leader of the cavalry while the *Bhaṭṭa* was apparently 'a minstrel'.

Among the records from the north-western parts of India, we may refer to the Sungal plate[2] of king Vidagdha of Chamba, who flourished about the first half of the 11th century A.D. The charter is communicated to the *Rājan*, *Rājānaka*, *Rājaputra*, *Rajāmātya*, *Rājasthānīya*, *Pramātṛ*, *Sarobhaṅga* (*Śarabhaṅga*), *Kumārāmātya*, *Uparika*, *Viṣayapati*, *Nihelapati*, *Kṣetrapa*, *Prāntapāla*, *Hastyaśvoṣṭrabalavyāpṛtaka*, *Dūta*, *Gamāgamika*, *Abhitvaramāṇa*, Khaśa, Kulika, *Śaulkika*, *Gaulmika*, *Khaṇḍarakṣa* (sometimes called *Khaḍgarakṣa*), *Tarapatika*, *Chattracchāyika*, *Veṭakila*, *Vīrayātrika*, *Cauroddharaṇika*, *Dāṇḍika* *Dāṇḍapāśika*, *Bhogapati*, *Viniyuktaka*, *Bhāgika*, *Bhogika*, *Cāṭa*, *Bhaṭa*, etc., and the householders and country people including the Brāhmaṇas at the top down to the Medas, Andhrakas, Dhīvaras (fishermen) and Caṇḍālas. *Nihelapati* is found as *Nihilapati* in the Nirmand plate.[3] But the meaning is uncertain. The *Chatracchāyika* was the king's parasol-bearer and the *Veṭakila* probably the betel-bearer of the king. The latter officer is called *Vārgulika* in the early medieval inscriptions from Orissa.[4] The *Bhāgika* was probably the collector of the king's share of the grains from the farmers and was the same as the *Ṣaṣṭhādhikṛta* and *Dhruvādhikaraṇika* or *Dhruvasthānādhikaraṇika* of other inscriptions.

1. *Ep. Ind.*, Vol. XXXI p. 289.
2. Vogel, *Antiquities of Chamba State*, Part I, p. 166.
3. *CII*, Vol. III, pp. 289, 291.
4. Cf. Bhandarkar's List, Nos. 1497, 1500.

The charters of the Bhauma-Kara dynasty of Orissa generally have two small lists of addressees making a distinction between the officers of the kingdom and those of the district in which the gift land was situated. Thus the Santiragrāma grant[1] of queen Daṇḍimahādevī includes the *Mahāsāmanta*, *Rājasatka*, *Rājaputra*, *Kumārāmātya*, *Auparika*, *Viṣayapati*, *Tadāyuktaka*, *Dāṇḍapāśika* and *Sthānāntarika* in the first list and, in the second, the *Mahāmahattara*, *Bṛhadbhogin*, *Pustakapāla* and *Kūṭakolasa*, to whose *adhikaraṇas* or offices the royal order is stated to have been addressed.

Among these, *Rājasatka* literally means 'those belonging to the *Rājan*' and may be the same as *Rājāmātya* of other records, meaning the subordinates of the feudatories. *Auparika* is of course the same as *Uparika* of earlier epigraphs. The *Sthānāntarika*, derived from *sthāna* or *sthān-āntara* may have been a particular type of *Sthānādhikṛta* or *Thānādār*. *Bṛhadbhogin* is a more dignified form of *Bhogika* (Jāgīrdār)[2] while *Pustakapāla*, called *Pustapāla* in earlier records of Eastern India, was a keeper of records. The expression *Kūṭakolasa*, not found outside Orissa, cannot be explained.

The Terundia plate[3] of Śubhākara II, a predecessor of Daṇḍimahādevī, has : *Mahāsāmanta*, *Mahārāja*, *Rājaputra*, *Antaraṅga*, *Kumārāmātya*, *Uparika*, *Viṣayapati*, *Tadāyuktaka*, *Dāṇḍapāśika*, *Sthānāntarika* and other dependants like *Cāṭa*, *Bhaṭa* and *Vallabha* in the first list and the offices of the *Mahāmahattara*, *Bṛhadbhogin*, *Pustapāla*, *Kuṭakolasa*, etc., in the other. In these, *Antaraṅga* seems to be the king's personal physician or private secretary[4] and *Vallabha* a courtier.

The Madhainagar plate[5] of Lakṣmaṇasena (1179-1206 A. D.) has the following list : *Rājan*, *Rājanyaka*, *Rājñī*, *Rāṇaka*,

1. See *Ep. Ind.*, Vol. XXIX, p. 85.

2. An earlier inscription from Orissa mentions *Aṁśabṛhadbhogin* probably meaning 'the partner of a *Jāgīr*' (*Ep. Ind.*, Vol. XXVIII, pp. 329-30).

3. Ibid., Vol. XXVIII, pp. 215-16.

4. Cf. *Ind. Cult.*, Vol. I, pp. 684 ff. There is an instance of the same physician being called both *Antaraṅga* and *Rājavaidya* (court physician). Some scholars interpret *Antaraṅga* as the privy councillor.

5. Majumdar, *Ins. Beng.*, Vol. III, p. 111.

Rājaputra, *Rājāmātya*, *Mahāpurohita*, *Mahādharmādhyakṣa*, *Mahāsāndhivigrahika*, *Mahāsenāpati*, *Mahāmudrādhikṛta*, *Antaraṅga*, *Bṛhaduparika*, *Mahākṣapaṭalika*, *Mahāpratīhāra*, *Mahābhogika*, *Mahāpīlupati*, *Mahāgaṇastha*, *Dauḥsādhika*, *Cauroddharaṇika*, *Naubalahastyaśvagomahiṣājāvikādivyāpṛtaka*, *Gaulmika*, *Daṇḍapāśika*, *Daṇḍanāyaka*, *Viṣayapati* and *Caṭṭa* and *Bhaṭṭa*.

In this list, *Rājñī*, probably meaning the queens of the subordinate rulers, has been added, and *Rājanyaka* and *Rāṇaka*, though the second is derived from the first, are distinguished. The *Mahāpurohita* was the chief priest and the *Mahādharmādhyakṣa* the superintendent of religious affairs. The *Mahāmudrādhikṛta* may have been the keeper of the royal seal, although it may be noted that a viceroy is sometimes described in medieval records as *mudrāvyāpārān=paripanthayati*, 'is conducting the affairs of the seal.'[1] *Bṛhaduparika* is a dignified form of *Uparika* comparable to *Bṛhadbhogika* of some records. The *Mahāgaṇastha* was probably the head of a *gaṇa*, i.e. guild or corporation, or the royal agent supervising the work of such guilds. *Dauḥsādhika* is the same as *Dauḥsādhasādhanika* or *Duḥsādhyasādhanika* of other epigraphs. In *Naubalahastyaśvagomahiṣājāvikādivyāpṛtaka*, the word *uṣṭra* is omitted and the designation seems to refer to certain military and civil officers in charge of the royal navy and cattle. The expression looks like a combination of *Hastyaśvanaubalavyāpṛtaka* and *Hastyaśvoṣṭragomahiṣājāvikādivyāpṛtaka* of earlier records. *Caṭṭa* and *Bhaṭṭa* are different spellings of the words *Cāṭa* and *Bhaṭa*. *Bhaṭṭa* used here in the sense of *Bhaṭa* should not be confused with *Bhaṭṭa* in the Pandukeswar plate of Padmaṭa, in which *Bhaṭa* is separately mentioned.

Curiously enough one of the biggest such lists comes from the charter of a small chief of Ḍhekkarī in North Bengal. *Mahāmāṇḍalika* Īśvaraghoṣa, who flourished about the 12th century, has the following list in his Ramganj plate[2] : *Rājan*, *Rājanyaka*, *Rājñī*, *Rāṇaka*, *Rājaputra*, *Kumārāmātya*, *Mahāsāndhi-*

1. Cf. *Ep. Ind.*, Vol. XXXII, p. 152 and note 2.
2. Majumdar, *Ins. Beng.*, Vol. III, p. 153.

vigrahika, *Mahāpratīhāra*, *Mahākaraṇādhyakṣa*, *Mahāmudrādhikṛta*, *Mahākṣapaṭalika*, *Mahāsarvādhikṛta*, *Mahāsenāpati*, *Mahāpādamūlika*, *Mahābhogapati*, *Mahātantrādhikṛta*, *Mahāvyūhapati*, *Mahādaṇḍanāyaka*, *Mahākāyastha*, *Mahābalākoṣṭhika*, *Mahābalādhikaraṇika*, *Mahāsāmanta*, *Mahākaṭuka*, *Ṭhakkura*, *Āṅgīkaraṇika*, *Dāṇḍapāṇika*, *Koṭṭapati*, *Haṭṭapati*, *Bhuktipati*, *Viṣayapati*, *Autthitāsanika*, *Antaḥpratīhāra*, *Daṇḍapāla*, *Khaṇḍapāla*, *Duḥsādhyasādhanika*, *Cauroddharaṇika*, *Uparika*, *Tadāniyuktaka*, *Ābhyantarika*, *Vāsāgārika*, *Khaḍgagrāha*, *Śirorakṣika*, *Vṛddhadhānuṣka*, *Ekasaraka*, *Khola*, *Dūta*, *Gamāgamika*, *Lekhaka*, *Dūtapraiṣaṇika*, *Pānīyāgārika*, *Sāntakika*, *Karmakara*, *Gaulmika*, *Śaulkika*, *Hastyaśvoṣṭranaubalavyāpṛtaka*, *Gomahiṣājāvikavaḍavādhyakṣa* and *Cāṭa* and *Bhaṭa*.

In this list, *Mahākaraṇādhyakṣa* may have been the head of the department of records. *Mahāpādamūlika* was the king's chief personal attendant. *Mahātantrādhikṛta* seems to have been an administrator or the superintendent of religious affairs and charities. He is the same as the *Tantrapāla* and *Mahātantrādhyakṣa* of other inscriptions.[1] An officer called *Tantrapati* is mentioned in the *Rājataraṅgiṇī* (VIII. 2422) without any indication regarding his function. But a Kashmirian author explains *Bṛhattantrapati* as *Dharmādhikārin*.[2] The *Mahāvyūhapati* was a military officer and the *Mahākāyastha* the chief scribe. *Mahābalākoṣṭhika* and *Mahākaṭuka* cannot be explained. If the first of the two is really *Mahābalakoṣṭhika*, he was apparently a treasurer of the military department. The *Mahābalādhikaraṇika* was probably the superintendent of the office of the commander-in-chief. The *Āṅgīkaraṇika* was the officer in charge of administering oaths in the courts of law. *Daṇḍapāṇika* and *Koṭṭapati* are the same as *Dāṇḍapāśika* and *Koṭṭapāla* respectively, while *Haṭṭapati* may be the superintendent of markets and *Bhuktipati* the governor of a *bhukti* or province or a *Jāgīrdār*. *Autthitāsanika*, found as *Utthitāsanin* in a Somavaṁśī record from Orissa, cannot be explained.

1. *Ep. Ind.*, Vol. XIV, p. 185; Vol. XXVIII, p. 55.

2. Ibid., Vol. XXVIII, p. 339. In South Indian records, *Tantrapati* would indicate a military officer.

He may have been the chief nobleman of the king's court.[1] *Antaḥpratīhāra* was probably the chief attendant and guard of the king, who waited at the gate of the harem when his master was there. *Daṇḍapāla* seems to be the same as *Dāṇḍika* and *Khaṇḍapāla* the same as *Khaṇḍarakṣa*. *Tadāniyuktaka* is apparently the same as *Tadāyuktaka*. *Ābhyantarika* was the officer-in-charge of guarding the inner apartments of the palace, while *Vāsāgārika* was in charge of the king's bed chamber.[2] *Khaḍgagrāha* is the same as *Khāḍgika* and *Śirorakṣika* a special body-guard of the king. *Vṛddhadhānuṣka* was the chief archer and *Lekhaka* the scribe. *Ekasaraka* and *Sāntakika* cannot be explained. *Dūtapraiṣaṇika* is the same as *Preṣaṇika*. *Pānīyāgārika* was in charge of the water-chamber, called *abdār-khānah* in Persian. The *Karmakāra* was probably the chief artisan. *Gomahiṣājāvikavaḍavādhyakṣa* is a modified form of *Kiśoravaḍavāgomahiṣājāvikādhyakṣa*.

A few of the new designations mentioned in this record are found in East Indian epigraphs like the Belabo plate[3] of Bhojavarman and the Rampal plate[4] of Śrīcandra.

Besides those mentioned in the lists quoted above, certain royal officers are mentioned about the end of copper-plate grants in connection with the preparation of the charters. The most important among these, as already indicated above, are the executor of a grant and the writer of the document. The executor, called *Dūtaka* in North Indian records and *Ājñā*, *Ājñapti* or *Ājñāpti* in the South Indian charters, although there may have been some difference between the functions of the two, was usually a person of high status, a high officer or a prince of the royal blood. The person responsible for the drafting of the grant was also an officer of high rank. But the

1. N. G. Majumdar, *Ins. Beng.*, Vol. III p. 183; *JAS*, Letters, Vol. XIX, p. 119. The expression suggests that he was a courtier of special rank provided with a special seat at the court.

2. See *Ep. Ind.*, Vol. XXX, p. 83.

3. Ibid. Vol. XII, p. 90. This record mentions in the list of officers one called *Pīṭhikāvitta* whose function is unknown.

4. Ibid., p. 139. It mentions the *Maṇḍalapati*.

designations of these officers are generally found in the lists quoted above.

Many other official designations are known from inscriptions. The lists of addressees of the kind quoted above is not found in the charters of the Imperial Gaṅgas of Orissa. But some of their grants are stated to have been made in the presence of a number of officers. Thus the second set of the Puri plates of Narasiṁha IV (1378-1402 A.D.) records grants which were made in the presence of certain officers enjoying the designations *Pātra*, *Mahāpātra*, *Sandhivigraha* or *Sāndhivigrahika*, *Dvāraparīkṣā*, *Mahāsenāpati*, *Puro-Śrīkaraṇa*, *Vāhinīpati*, *Senādhyakṣa*, *Buḍhāleṅkā* and *Bhitara-Bhaṇḍāra-adhikārī*.[1] Among these, *Pātra* indicates a minister and *Mahāpātra* a minister of a higher rank. Sanskrit *Parīkṣaka* is given here as *Parīkṣā* (Oḍiyā *Poricha*) meaning superintendent or governor. *Dvāraparīkṣā* was probably the old *Pratīhāra* or gate-keeper of the king's chamber, palace or city.[2] *Śrīkaraṇa* indicates a scribe or scribe-accountant and may be compared to *Śrīkaraṇādhipa* or *Śrīkaraṇaprabhu*, the designation of Hemādri who superintended the business connected with the drawing up of documents in the service of Yādava Mahādeva and Rāmacandra.[3] *Puro* prefixed to it is difficult to understand. It may be Sanskrit *Paura*, 'pertaining to a city or the capital' or *puras* indicating the front rank the person in question held among the officers of his class. The second alternative is preferable since it is probably the same as the first part of the Orissan official designations like *Paṭṭa-Nāyaka*. *Bhitarabhaṇḍāra-adhikārī* is Oḍiyā for Sanskrit *Abhyantarabhāṇḍārādhikārin*, officer in charge of the inner store-house or treasury (i.e. one inside the palace or the harem).' *Buḍhāleṅkā* is an Oḍiyā designation indicating 'the chief servant', comparable with the *Mahāpādamūlika* of the Ramganj plate. Similar other offi-

1. *Ep. Ind.*, Vol. XXVIII, pp. 304-05.

2. There was a military officer called 'lord of the *dvāra*' in medieval Kashmir. He was engaged in defending the passes through which enemies could enter into the Kashmir valley. See above p. 364, note.

3. *Bomb. Gaz.*, Vol. I, Part ii, pp. 248, 530 and note. 1

cial designations in the regional languages are found in the medieval epigraphs of different parts of the country, although most of the official designations were in Sanskrit or at least of Sanskritic origin.

Such designations, which sometimes involved different functions in different areas and ages with or without any change in the wording, are too numerous to be discussed here, though a large number of them have been noticed in our *Glossary*.

In ancient and medieval India, official designations were often stereotyped as family names. The most well-known instances of this amongst royal families are those of the Pratīhāras and the Rāṣṭrakūṭas. Official designations of the medieval age, such as Majumdār or Majmudār (from Perso-Arabic *Majumdār*[1]), were also similarly stereotyped.

4. *Administrative and Territorial Divisions*

The meaning of the geographical names found in the records of different parts of the country is not intelligible in many cases. A word indicating a particular kind of territorial or administrative unit (e.g. words meaning a village, a town, a city, a district, a province, etc.) was often suffixed to place names. Very often geographical names were coined by suffixing a word meaning a village or town to the names of persons who were generally associated with their foundation. Territories were often named after peoples.

An inscription[2] of Aśoka mentions a locality called Lumbinīgrāma, a name ending in the word *grāma*, 'a village'. The names of hundreds of villages mentioned in later inscriptions have the same ending. Often the name of a village or its part ended in words like *padra* or *padraka*, *pallī*, *pāṭaka*, etc., which are recognised in Sanskrit lexicons in the sense of a village or a part of it. The name-ending *pāṭaka* is also found in the modified form of *vāṭaka* even in early inscriptions, while, in

1. Wilson's Glossary, s.v.
2. *Select Inscriptions*, p. 70.

medieval records, we have its various modified forms like *vāḍa*, *vāḍā*, *paḍā*, *pāḍā*, etc., as the word was adopted in the different regional languages. Similar local modification also characterises the words suffixed to the names of localities. In the southern regions of India, *ūr*, a Dravidian word for 'village', was often suffixed to the names of localities.[1] Various other explanatory words were likewise suffixed to the names of villages in all parts of the country. Thus the words *sthāna*, *sthala*, *sthalī*, etc., are sometimes found at the end of names of places having a *deva-sthāna* or shrine of a deity, and the word *tīrtha* is found suffixed to the names of holy places.[2] Rent-free villages in the possession of gods and Brāhmaṇas had often names ending in the word *śāsana* especially in the Bengal-Orissa region. In the Tamil-speaking area, the names of such villages under Brāhmaṇas, generally called *agrahāra*, often ended in the expression *caturvedimaṅgalam*. In many cases, the names of cities and townships ended in words meaning a village. But very often the names of such localities had suffixes like *nagara*, *pura*, *purī*, *paṭṭana*, etc., meaning a city or town. The towns and villages were often named after persons or gods.

As regards the provinces, districts and subdivisions of a kingdom, it may be pointed out at the outset that it is sometimes difficult to use these terms for the words found in inscriptions. Their sizes may have varied cosiderably with reference to an empire like that of the Mauryas and a small kingdom, sometimes smaller than a District of today. The same territorial unit may have been a kingdom in one age and only a district of an empire in another. It is usually difficult to form an idea about the extent of a district, which may have varied in different ages. Such territorial units were very often named after their chief cities. Sometimes the districts and provinces in the Tamil-speaking area were named after royal personages.

1. Cf. *halli* for *pallī* in the Kannaḍa-speaking area, and numerous similar instances.

2. *Sthala* and *sthalī* were also used in the sense of the subdivision of a district.

The Sarnath pillar edict[1] of Aśoka mentions *Āhāra* and *Koṭṭaviṣaya* (a *Viṣaya* around a *koṭṭa* or fortress, or a *Koṭṭa* and a *Viṣaya*).[2] In later epigraphs, both *Āhāra* and *Viṣaya* are used to indicate 'a district'. It is difficult to say whether they were the names of the same kind or of two different kinds of territorial or administrative units of the Maurya empire. The official designations *Prādeśika* and *Rāṣṭrika* found in some records[3] of Aśoka mean respectively 'the head of a *Pradeśa*' and 'the head of a *Rāṣṭra*'. Of these, *Pradeśa* appears to have been a bigger unit like a province and *Rāṣṭra* a smaller unit like a district or its subdivision. It is again difficult to say whether *Rāṣṭra* was just another name of an *Āhāra* or a *Viṣaya* or all the three indicated different types of districts. In certain later records especially from South India, *Rāṣṭra* appears to have indicated a group of villages.[4]

Some other expressions of geographical significance used in Aśoka's records are *Pratyanta* and *Anta*, both meaning a state beyond the borders [of Aśoka's empire],[5] *Nāga-vana*, 'elephant-forest',[5] *Kaivarta-bhoga*, 'fishermens' preserve',[6] etc. The word *nagara*, 'a city', and *vraja-bhūmi*, 'grazing land', are mentioned respectively in the official designations *Nagaravyavahārika* and *Vrajabhūmika*.[7]

In the inscriptions of the Śātavāhanas of the Deccan and the Śakas of Western India, the district is generally indicated by the name *Āhāra*.[8] Often a *grāma*, sometimes having its name ending in the word *padra*, was made the subject of a grant and it was specifically stated that the place was situated in an *Āhāra* of a particular name.[9] But, in such cases, ins-

1. *Select Inscriptions*, pp. 51, 76.
2. Cf. *koṭṭam* meaning a district or province in Tamil inscriptions.
3. Ibid., pp. 20, 53.
4. Passages like 'the cultivators headed by the *Rāṣṭrakūṭa* or headman of the *Rāṣṭra*, dwelling in Pennātavāḍi-viṣaya' (*Ind. Ant.*, Vol. VII, p. 16) suggest that *Rāṣṭra* was a smaller subdivision of a *Viṣaya*.
5. *Select Inscriptions*, pp. 18, 37, 50. Cf. also p. 257. In the *Divyāvadāna* (ed. Vaidya, p. 13), *anta* means a tract near the borders but within the country, and *pratyanta* the land outside. Aśoka seems to have used *anta* in this sense also.
6. Ibid., p. 62.
7. Ibid., pp. 34, 41.
8. Cf. districts called Śātavāhanīy-āhāra in a Śātavāhana epigraph and Śātavāhanīya-rāṣṭra in a Pallava record. See *Select Inscriptions*, pp. 205, 439.
9. Ibid., pp. 158, 200-01.

criptions of the central and eastern parts of North India, of the time of the early Gupta emperors, generally speak of villages situated in particular *Viṣayas* which are stated sometimes to have formed parts of a *Bhukti* or province.[1] In Western India, however, *Āhāra* occurs sometimes in later records such as the Maitraka inscriptions. Thus the Alina plates (766 A.D.) of Śīlāditya VI speak of the grant of a village situated in a *Pathaka* which formed part of an *Āhāra*.[2] Here *Pathaka* is the designation of the subdivision of a district.[3] It was something like a Pargana of later times, which is called Pratijāgaraṇaka in the inscriptions of the Paramāra kings of Malwa.[4] The word *paṭṭa* occurs in some early inscriptions in the sense of a similar territorial unit.[5] The names *Golla* and *Khampaṇaka* are used in a similar sense in certain early medieval epigraphs of the Deccan.[6]

In the Gupta inscriptions, the name *Deśa* is occasionally applied to the district.[7] But the use of *Viṣaya*, found in the same sense and referred to above, is noticed in all parts of the country. Another popular name applied to a district in the Gupta records is *Maṇḍala* which, like *Viṣaya*, is also found in the epigraphs of other dynasties ruling in various parts of India.[8] The Paharpur plate of 479 A.D. represents a *Maṇḍala* as the subdivision of a *Vīthī*.[9] The Khoh plates[10] (529 A. D.)

1. Ibid., pp. 283 ff. The Junagadh inscription of 150 A. D. seems to use *Viṣaya* in the sense of 'a province' (ibid., p. 172).

2. *CII*, Vol. III, p. 189. The word *āharaṇī* occurs in Hastavapr-āharaṇī found in the Bhamodra-Mohota plates of Droṇasiṁha (*Select Inscriptions*, p. 404).

3. For the popularity of this subdivisional name in Western India, cf. H.D. Sankalia, *Stud. Hist. Cult. Geog. Ethn. Guj.*, pp. 185 ff.

4. *Ep. Ind.*, Vol. XXXII, p. 140.

5. Cf. *Ep. Ind.*, Vol. XXXIII, p. 304.

6. M. G. Dikshit, *Selected Inscriptions from Maharashtra*, pp. 111-12, 114.

7. *Select Inscriptions*, p. 273.

8. Ibid., p. 332. Sometimes we have *Mahā-maṇḍala* in medieval records (*Ind. Ant.*, Vol. X, pp. 159-60).

9. *Select Inscriptions*, p. 346. The word *pārśva* used in the record may not be taken to indicate a subdivision of *Maṇḍala*. It may be describing the situation of one village as abutting on another. Sometimes the word *prāveśya* is likewise used in indicating the relations between two localities. The description of a locality as *Siviḍi-prāveśya* seems to suggest that its revenue was assessed together with another locality called Siviḍi so that it was a part of Siviḍi from the official point of view. See *JAS*, Letters, Vol. XVIII, p. 78 and note.

10. *Select Inscriptions*, p. 375.

of Saṁkṣobha speak of a village situated in a *Peṭha*.[1] Sometimes a *Viṣaya* is mentioned as a subdivision of a *Maṇḍala*.[2] In the East Indian inscriptions of the Gupta age, a group of districts is called *Bhukti*[3] which seems to have indicated a smaller territorial unit in South Indian records.[4] In the early medieval records of Bengal, the subdivision of a tract in a *Bhukti* is called a *Bhāga*. Thus the *Bhāga* of Vikramapura was a part of Vaṅga within the *Bhukti* of Pundravardhana.[5] Bengal records also mention such small territorial units as *Khaṇḍala*,[6] *Caturaka*,[7] *Āvṛtti*,[8] etc.

There are several interesting aspects of the above territorial divisions. In the first place, sometimes in medieval inscriptions the words *deśa*, *maṇḍala* and *viṣaya* are used in a wider sense. Thus the kingdom of the Eastern Cālukyas is called Veṅgī-deśa in some records and Veṅgī-maṇḍala in others while certain *Viṣayas* are stated to have formed parts of it.[9] The Coḷa kingdom is often referred to as a *Deśa*, *Maṇḍala*, *Nāḍu* and *Viṣaya*.[10] Similarly, Bhārata-khaṇḍa or Bhārata-kṣetra is called both a *Deśa* and a *Viṣaya*.[11] Sometimes a *Khaṇḍa* is mentioned as the subdivision of a *Deśa*.[12]

Another interesting fact is that often a territorial or administrative unit enjoying a particular designation was represented as having another designation even without obliterating its earlier character. Thus names like Karma-rāṣṭra-viṣaya[13] and Gopa-rāṣṭra-viṣaya[14] show that the units called Karma and Gopa had been *Rāṣṭras* formerly but that they

1. In the inscriptions of the Kannaḍa-speaking area, we have *veṭe*, *veṭhe* or *venṭhe* (*Ep. Ind.*, Vol. XXX, p. 154, note 2).
2. *Ind. Ant.*, Vol. XV, p. 112.
3. *Select Inscriptions.*, pp. 284-285, etc.
4. *Bamb. Gaz.*, Vol. I, Part ii, p. 398.
5. N. G. Majumdar, *Ins. Beng.*, Vol. III, p. 137, etc.
6. Ibid., p. 20.
7. Ibid., p. 96.
8. Ibid., p. 112.
9. *Ind. Ant.*, Vol. VII, p. 16; Vol. VIII, pp. 74, 79; Vol. XIII, p. 213.
10. The same is the case with such other territorial units as Banavasi. Sometimes a territory comprising wide areas had composite names like *Mālava-Kānyakubja-viṣaya* (Sankalia, *Stud. Hist. Cult. Geo. Ethn. Guj.*, p. 186).
11. *Ind. Ant.*, Vol. XIV, p. 16.
12. *CII*, Vol. III, p. 32, note 7.
13. *Ind. Ant.*, Vol. VII, p. 187.
14. Ibid., Vol. IX, p. 124.

later became *Viṣayas*. There are similar other names like Kheṭak-āhara and Kheṭak-āhāra-viṣaya.[1]

The word for a district in the records of the southern areas of India is usually *nāḍu* and a district named Karma would generally be called Karma-nāḍu or Kamma-nāḍu.[2] In the Tamil inscriptions of the early medieval period, often a kingdom or its province called *Maṇḍalam* was divided into divisions called *Koṭṭam* or *Vaḷanāḍu*, which were subdivided into *Kuṟṟams* or *Nāḍus*, although the *Kuṟṟam* was sometimes represented as the sub-division of a *Nāḍu*.[3] In the records of the Vijayanagar period, the subdivision of a district called *Kuṟṟam* or *Nāḍu* was often called *Uśāvaḍi* or *Sāvaḍi* (*Cāvaḍi*) which was divided into smaller units called *Paṟṟu*.[4] The word *sīma* was often used in South Indian epigraphs in the sense of a subdivision of the district.[5] But Tamil inscriptions sometimes use the expressions *śīmai* or *rājyam* to indicate provinces of a kingdom. In Kannaḍa inscriptions, we have such other small territorial units as *Sthala, Bhukti, Kampaṇa, Bāḍa, Hobali, Vaṇita*, etc.[6]

Apart from the fact that words like *deśa*, *maṇḍala*, *viṣaya*, etc., were sometimes employed to indicate a kingdom or territory instead of a district of it, it is often difficult to determine which one indicated a district and which one its subdivision, even when the expressions are used in the restricted sense and the areas refer to a particular region of the country. Thus, in the early medieval inscriptions of Bengal, we have reference to several *Maṇḍalas* and *Viṣayas* forming parts of the *Bhukti* or province of Puṇḍravardhana. Among these, there were : (1) Vyāghrataṭī-maṇḍala in which Mahantāprakāśa-viṣaya was included; (2) Samataṭa-maṇḍala in which Paranāyi-viṣaya was included; (3) Sthālīkkaṭa-viṣaya in which

1. *Bomb. Gaz.*, Vol. I, Part ii, p. 382.
2. Cf. Wilson's Glossary, s. v. The word *nāḍu* was sometimes Sanskritised as *nāḍaka* or *nāḍuka* (*Ep. Ind.*, Vol. XXX, p. 154, note 2).
3. Cf. *A.R. Ep.*, 1906, No. 66; 1909, No. 395; etc.; T.V.Mahalingam, *South Indian Polity*, pp. 302 ff.
4. *A. R. Ep.*, 1913, No. 272.
5. T. V. Mahalingam, *South Indian Polity*, pp. 308.
6. Cf. ibid., pp. 308-09.

Āmraṣaṇḍikā-maṇḍala and Uḍragrāma-maṇḍala were included; (4) Koṭivarṣa-viṣaya in which Gokalikā-maṇḍala and Halāvarta-maṇḍala were included; (5) Khāḍī-viṣaya which was also called Khāḍī-maṇḍala.[1] It will be seen from these instances that in some cases a *Maṇḍala* included a *Viṣaya* and in others a *Viṣaya* included a *Maṇḍala*, while, in a third group of cases, the same district was called sometimes a *Maṇḍala* and sometimes a *Viṣaya*. A number of *Vīthīs* are known to have formed parts of Kaṅkagrāma-bhukti about the borders of Bihar and Bengal; but in the neighbouring Vardhamāna-bhukti the *Vīthīs* were included in *Maṇḍalas*.[2] According to the Ghugrahati plate[3] of Samācāradeva, the *Uparika* or provincial governor in charge of Suvarṇa-vīthī was the immediate superior of the *Viṣayapati*, i.e. the governor of the *Viṣaya* or district called Vāraka-maṇḍala. Sometimes we have names like Daṇḍabhukti-maṇḍala[4] showing that Daṇḍa was originally the name of a *Bhukti* and later that of a *Maṇḍala*.

In connection with the territorial unit called *Bhukti* (literally, 'enjoyment', i.e. a *Jāgīr*), we have to mention another such unit called *Bhoga*, literally meaning the same thing. While *Bhukti* is found in the sense of a province especially in East Indian inscriptions, *Bhoga* is found in various other parts of the country as a sub-division of a district. We may refer in this connection to a few such cases as (1) Gorajjā-bhoga in Bharukaccha-viṣaya in the Sarsavani plates[5] of Buddharāja; (2) Sātināla-bhoga in Palayaṭṭhāna-viṣaya in the Jejuri plates[6] of Vinayāditya; and (3) Āvaraka-bhoga in Hūṇa-maṇḍala in the Gaonri plates[7] of Vākpati Muñja. These *Bhogas* were parts of a district called *Viṣaya* or *Maṇḍala*. It is also interesting to note that the same unit called Eḍevoḷal-bhoga in the Sorab

1. *History of Bengal*, Dacca University, Vol. I, pp. 24-25.
2. Ibid., p. 28. *Vīthī* is supposed to be a district on the bank of a river.
3. *Ep. Ind.*, Vol. XVIII, pp. 74 ff.
4. *History of Bengal*, op. cit., p. 27.
5. *Ep. Ind.*, Vol. VI, pp. 297 ff. The term here may be *ābhoga*.
6. Ibid., Vol. XIX, p. 64.
7. Ibid., Vol. XXIII, p. 108.

plates of Cālukya Vinayāditya is called Eḍevoḷal-viṣaya in the Harihar plates of the same king.[1]

Monier-Williams recognises the word *bhoga* in the sense of possession, property, wealth, revenue, etc., while Wilson's Glossary mentions two kinds of *bhoga* or possession, viz. with or without obstruction. We have also inscriptions speaking of a *vīthī* (a shop or stall) in a market-place as *bhog-ādhīnā* with reference to its lying in the possession of an individual. From the sense of 'possession', the word *bhoga*, as also *bhukti*, came to be used in the sense of 'the property under one's possession'. We have instances in which expressions like *Mahārāja-Sarvanātha-bhoga* and *Mahāsāmantādhipati-śrī-Śrīdhara-bhoga* respectively mean 'a *Jāgīr* (*bhoga*) in the possession of *Mahārāja* Sarvanātha' and 'a *Jāgīr* in the possession of the illustrious *Mahāsāmantādhipati* Śrīdhara.'[2] The use of *bhoga* and *bhukti* in the sense of a territorial unit seems to be due to a further expansion of this meaning of the words.[3]

An interesting feature of the names of certain units is the mention of a number along with them. This is occasionally found in the inscriptions of various parts of the country, but is a popular feature of the names of kingdoms, provinces, districts and subdivisions in the medieval records of the Kannaḍa-speaking area of the South.

In an inscription[4] of 812-13 A.D., the village of Vaṭapadraka (modern Baroda in Gujarat) is stated to have been situated in Aṅkottaka-caturaśīti, i.e. Aṅkottaka-84. There are similar other instances of the number 84 being attached to the name of a territorial unit in medieval inscriptions, while Corāsī or Caurāsī (Sanskrit *caturaśīti.*, 'eightyfour') happens to be the name of several territorial units in various parts of India. Thus while Kārpaṭavāñjya-84 and Ratnapura-84 are known from inscriptions,[5] Caurāsī is the name of a

1. Ibid., Vol. IX, p. 16.
2. Ibid., Vol. XXX, pp. 212-13; Vol. XXXIII, pp. 169 ff.
3. Cf. *āhāra* (food, maintenance), *viṣaya* (sphere, jurisdiction), etc.
4. *Ind. Ant.*, Vol. XII, pp. 156 ff.
5. H. D. Sankalia, *Stud. Hist. Cult. Geo. Ethn. Guj.*, pp. 27, 198; *Bhavnagar Inscriptions*, p. 206.

Pargana in the Mirzapur District of U.P. and Corāsī is a subdivision of the Surat District of Gujarat. There is likewise a village called Caurāsī, probably the headquarters of a Pargana originally, in the Puri District of Orissa. A group of villages in the Ajmer District of Rajasthan is called Bhinaikī Caurāsī (i.e. Bhinai-84). There are similarly territorial units with names associated with numbers other than 84.

As already indicated above, in the medieval inscriptions of the rulers of the Kannaḍa-speaking area, territorial units are very often mentioned along with a number as in Aṅkottaka-caturaśīti, Bhināikī Caurāsī, etc. Thus we have Raṭṭappāḍi seven lakhs and a half, Gaṅgavāḍi ninetysix thousands, Nolambavāḍi thirtytwo thousands, Banavāsi twelve thousands, Alande one thousand, Harṣapura seven hundreds and fifty, Purigere three hundreds, Kuknūr thirty, Nirugundagi twelve, Puriddha ten, Tamba six, Koṇḍavaṭi two,[1] etc., etc.

Some inscriptions specifically state that these numbers refer to *grāmas* or villages forming parts of the territorial units in question. Thus the Aihole inscription[2] (634 A.D.) speaks of the three Mahārāṣṭras constituting the dominions of Cālukya Pulakeśin II as *navanavati-sahasra-grāma-bhāj*, i.e. having ninety-nine thousands of *grāmas*, while the Malkapur inscription[3] (1261 A.D.) refers to a *bhikṣā* or grant of three lakhs of *grāmas* in Ḍāhala-maṇḍala lying between the Bhāgīrathī and the Narmadā, made in favour of the Śaiva saint Sadbhāvaśambhu, founder of the Golakī-maṭha, by the Kalacuri king Yuvarāja-deva (probably Yuvarāja II). We have also reference to Veṅgīpura-sahasra sometimes as Veṅgīpura-viṣaya-grāma-sahasra.[4] Considering the abnormally high numbers of the *grāmas* mentioned in connection with the dominions of

1. For Tamba and Koṇḍavaṭi units, cf. transcripts of *A.R. Ep.*, 1933-34, B. K. No. 159; ibid., B. K. No. 42. For similar units in West India, which once came under the influence of the rulers of Kannaḍa origin, see Moḍherā-7½ and Ghaḍahaḍikā-12 in *Ind. Ant.*, Vol. VI, pp. 191, 193.

2. *Ep. Ind.*, Vol. VI, pp. 1 ff.

3. *JAHRS*, Vol. IV, pp. 156-57.

4. *Suc. Sāt. L. Dec.*, p. 402.

Pulakeśin II and a grant made by a Kalacuri king and the facts that the district of Gaṅgavāḍi could actually claim not more than a small fraction of 96000 *grāmas* and the whole kingdom of the Kalacuri ruler only a negligible fraction of 300000 *grāmas*, if *grāma* or village is understood in its usual sense, we were formerly inclined to interpret *grāma* as a landed property which was the subject of an assessment.[1] There is however some evidence to show that the word was used in such cases in the sense of a village whatever its size and nature may have been. Thus, in the Aland (ancient Alande) inscription[2] of Mallikārjuna, Alande itself is mentioned as the *modala-vāḍa* (i.e. 'foremost *vāḍa* or village') of Alande-sāsira or Alande-1000, and it is clear that the geographical and administrative unit of Alande consisted of one thousand *vāḍas* or villages, of which the village of Alande was the foremost, i.e. the head-quarters of the territorial unit in question. Sometimes a similar group of villages is mentioned without specifying its geographical name which remains understood. An inscription speaks of Kheḍa (modern Agarkhed in the Bijapur District of Mysore) as the *rājadhānī* of 'the thirtysix villages' included in Tardavāḍi-nāḍu, elsewhere called Tardavāḍi-1000.[3] The name of the said subdivision consisting of 36 villages was apparently Kheḍa. The people of Kuknūr even now quote an old list, traditionally handed down, of the thirty villages which formed the ancient administrative unit called Kuknūr-30, and all these villages can be traced in the area around Kuknūr even today.[4] It is interesting to note that the same village is mentioned in an inscription as *triṁśad-*

1. *Suc. Sāt. L. Dec.*, p. 400. For this question, see J. F. Fleet in *JRAS*, 1912; also V. S. Agrawala in *Sir Jadunath Sarkar Presentation Volume*, II, pp. 16 ff. Our original interpretation of *grāma* as a unit of revenue assessment (elaborated by Agrawala as 'one plough-measure of land assessed at one silver *Kārṣāpaṇa*') cannot be true in respect of many of the cases involving small numbers specified in this section. The number of such units of assessment or income, in coins, of a tract of land may of course have been confused with the number of villages in it in cases which speak of very big numbers.
2. *Ep. Ind.*, Vol. XXVIII, pp. 31 ff.
3. *A.R. Ep.*, 1937-38, Nos. 1 and 3.
4. See *JBRS*, Vol. XL, p. 12.

grām-ādhipati śrī-Kukkunūru, i.e. 'the illustrious Kukkunūru, the most important among thirty *grāmas*'.[1] We have also to note such names as Tamba-6 and Koṇḍavaṭi-2. It is difficult to believe that Tamba and Koṇḍavati respectively contained only 6 and 2 units of assessed landed property.

That the word *grāma* in such cases was understood in the sense of a village is also clear from a section of the *Skanda Purāṇa*, apparently interpolated in the work sometime in the medieval period.[2] This section says how the *nava-khaṇḍa* Bhārata, i.e. Bhāratavarṣa consisting of nine divisions, was subdivided into seventytwo *vibhedas* (apparently indicating 'countries' or 'tracts') and quotes a list of seventytwo (actually, seventyfive owing to confusion) countries together with the number of *grāmas* in each one of them. This list is introduced by the stanza : *Teṣāṁ nāmāni grāmāṁś=ca pattanāni ca Phālguna* | *velākūlāni saṁkhyāṁ ca vakṣyāmi tava tattvataḥ* || and ends with the following passage : *dvāsaptatir=amī deśā grāma-saṅkhyāḥ prakīrtitāḥ*. The latter is followed by the statement that the entire Bhārata-khaṇḍa had 967200000 *pattanas* (townships) and 36000 *velākūlas* (harbours). It can hardly be doubted that the word *grāma*, used in the context of *pattana* and *velākūla*, has to be understood in this case in the sense of a village. But the fact that the list speaks only of *grāmas* and not of *pattanas*, etc., seems to suggest that, for the purpose of enumeration, the latter also were counted as *grāmas*. This seems also to be supported by the fact that the concluding passages mention only *pattanas* and *velākūlas* and not *grāmas*. The list further shows that the traditional or conventional number of *grāmas* in a country as given in it could hardly have been true if the word *grāma* is taken exactly in its modern sense.

We quote below the names of some of the countries mentioned in the *Skanda Purāṇa* list together with the number of *grāmas* in them; (1) Nepāla—1 lakh; (2) Kānyakubja—36 lakhs; (3) Gauḍadeśa—18 lakhs; (4) Kāmarūpa—9 lakhs;

1. *JBBRAS*, Vol. XII, 1876, p. 43, text line 33.

2. See Maheśvara-khaṇḍa, Kumārikā-khaṇḍa, chapter 39, verses 127 ff. Cf. my *Stud. Geog. Anc. Med. Ind.*, pp. 198 ff. For the date of the Purāṇa, cf. *JAS*, Letters, Vol. XIV, p. 25.

(5) Ḍāhala or Cedi—9 lakhs; (6) Raṭṭa-rājya (the Rāṣṭrakūṭa country)—7 lakhs; (7) Mālava—118092; (8) Śākambhara-deśa—1¼ lakhs; (9) Mevāḍa—1¼ lakhs; (10) Gurjaratrā—70 thousands; (11) Kāśmīra—68 thousands; (12) Kauṅkaṇa (Konkan)—1422; (14) Sindhu—20 thousands; (15) Kaccha-maṇḍala (Kutch)—1422; (16) Surāṣṭra (Kathiawar)— 55 thousands; (17) Lāṭa (the Nausari-Broach region of Gujarat)—21 thousands; (18) Karṇāṭa—1¼ lakhs; (19) Kāmboja—10 lakhs; (20) Kośala (probably South Kośala in the Raipur-Bilaspur-Sambalpur region) — 10 lakhs; (21) Bāhlika—4 lakhs; (22) Vidarbha—5 lakhs; (23) Magadhadeśa—66 thousands; (24) Mūlasthāna (Multan)—25 thousands; (25) Yavana—40 thousands; etc.

It may be pointed out that the text of the Puranic section is not free from errors. Some of the names are redudant and many of them doubtful. There is however epigraphic support in favour of some of the traditional number of *grāmas* quoted in the list. Thus the Śākambhara or Śākambharī country is actually known to have been otherwise called Sapādalakṣa or 'one lakh and a quarter'.[1] Such traditional numbers of villages in particular countries are also referred to in some other works. Thus Vinayacandra's *Kāvyaśikṣā* mentions : (1) Surāṣṭra—9 thousands; (2) Lāṭadeśa—21 thousands; (3) Gurjaradeśa—70 thousands; (4) Pārata—70 thousands; (5) Ḍāhala—9 lakhs; (6) Mālava—9 lakhs and 92; (7) Kānyakubja—46 lakhs, etc.[2] There is apparently considerable exaggeration in the cases speaking of very big numbers. But we have no doubt that the reference is to villages which may have been in many cases very small or even nominal. Whether the inflation of the number of villages in a particular country or kingdom was due to a special method of

1. Cf. Bhandarkar's List, Nos. 279, 356. This was the name of the Cāhamāna kingdom with its capital at Śākambharī. Another country called Sapādalakṣa lay in the Nizamabad-Karimnagar region of Andhra Pradesh (cf. Sircar, *Maski Inscription of Aśoka*, p. 1). The Yajvapāla kingdom with its capital at Nalapura was similarly called Pādonalakṣa or 'one lakh *minus* a quarter' (*Ep. Ind.*, Vol. XXXIII, p. 68).

2. *Kāvyamīmāṁsā*, G.O.S. ed., pp. 248-49.

calculation cannot be determined without further evidence on the subject.

In this connection it may be pointed out that sometimes numbers mentioned in connection with the name of a tract do not refer to the villages but groups of them, although a distinction is made between the two classes. Thus an inscription[1] of 1173 A.D. from Udaypur in the former Gwalior State speaks of a village in Bhṛṅgārikā-catuḥṣaṣṭi-pathaka which formed a part of Bhailasvāmi-mahādvāśaka-maṇḍala. It appears that the *Pathaka* or subdistrict called Bhṛṅgārikā—64 consisted of sixtyfour villages while the *Maṇḍala* or district called 'Bhailasvāmin great-12' consisted of 12 such sub-districts. The speciality of the second case has been indicated in the record by prefixing the word *mahā* to the number (cf. *Mahāgrāma*).

It has also to be noticed that the tendency of forming this kind of geographical names can be traced in the Kannaḍa-speaking area even in early times. Thus an Early Kadamba inscription of the 6th century A.D. mentions Kiṟū-Kūḍalūr-pallī as one of the twenty-four *pallīs* of the *Mahāgrāma* called Tagare situated in Tagare-viṣaya.[2] Earlier still, a Malavalli inscription of about the 3rd century A.D. refers to Sahalāṭavī as a *Grām-āhāra*, literally 'a village-district', i.e. a group of villages, while a slightly later epigraph at the same place seems to suggest that the said *Grām-āhāra* consisted of twelve villages.[3] In later terminology, Tagare and Sahalā would have been called Tagare-24 and Sahalā-12.

5. *Royal Prerogatives and Taxes*

While creating rent-free holdings in favour of gods, Brāhmaṇas, etc., the king usually surrendered some of his prerogatives in respect of the gift land. Such surrendered rights are more or less clearly stated in a large number of charters. It may be pointed out that some of the privileges were enjoyed

1. *Ind. Ant.*, Vol. XVIII, pp. 344 ff.
2. *Suc. Sāt. L. Dec.*, p. 305.
3. Ibid., pp. 249-50; cf. Lüders' List, Nos. 1195-96.

by the king not directly but only indirectly. Thus according to the *Manusmṛti* (VII. 115-19), the heads of one thousand, one hundred, and ten villages enjoyed respectively a town, a village and five *Kulas* of land while 'the headman of a village (*Grāmika*) should get all of what is daily payable by the villagers to the king in the shape of food-stuff, drinks, fuel and other things'. As will be seen below, some of the exemptions allowed to be enjoyed by the donees of rent-free holdings relate to the free supply of articles that the villagers had to make to the royal officials when the latter visited their villages on tour.

The Rummindei pillar inscription[1] of Aśoka states that, on the occasion of the emperor's visit to Lumbinīgrāma the birth-place of the Buddha, the holy place was made free from the obligation of paying *bali* (*udbalika*) and liable to pay only one-eighth of the produce of the fields (*āṣṭabhāgika*). The word *bali* has been used here apparently in the sense of land tribute excluding *bhāga* or the king's grain share. The normal rate of the king's share of grains seems to have been one-sixth for certain crops and one-fourth for others.[2] The income resulting from these exemptions was probably meant for being utilised for the maintenance of the holy place or the Buddhist religious establishment existing there.

The Junagadh inscription[3] of the Śaka king Rudradāman speaks of *kara* (taxes)[4], *viṣṭi* (free labour) and *praṇaya-kriyā* which is the *praṇaya* of Kauṭilya's *Arthaśāstra*[5] and means behevolence or emergency imposts. The taxes are enumerated in the inscription as *bali*, *śulka* (tolls) and *bhāga*.

Some charters[6] of the Śātavāhana king Gautamīputra

1. *Select Inscriptions*, pp. 70-71.
2. According to Megasthenes, the husbandmen of the Maurya dominions paid a fourth part of the produce of the soil (*bhāga*) and a land tribute apparently in cash (*bali*). Other state dues included tribute and prescribed services from traders and cattle from hardsmen while in urban areas the main sources of revenue were birth and death taxes, fines and tithes on sales. See Raychaudhuri, *Pol. Hist. Anc. Ind.*, 1938, pp. 240-41. Indian sources generally speak of the king's grain share as one-sixth.
3. *Select Inscriptions*, p. 174.
4. The word *kara* has been explained by a commentator as *kṛṣi-paśucāraṇ-ādi-kṛta-rājakīya-bhūmy-upabhoga-hetuko raja-grāhyo bhāgaḥ* (cf. A. K. Majumdar, *The Chaulukyas of Gujarat*, p. 252).
5. Cf. V. ii.
6. Cf. *Select Inscriptions*, pp. 192, 194.

Śātakarṇi (c. 106-30 A.D.) records grants of land together with all the *Parihāras* (exemptions to be enjoyed by the donees) including the following : *a-prāveśya* (i.e. freedom from the entry of royal agents), *anāvamarśya* (i.e. freedom from troubles associated with the visit of royal agents), *a-lavaṇa-khātaka* (i.e. freedom from the land being dug out or the trees being pierced for salt) and *a-rāṣṭra-sāṁvinayika* (i.e. freedom from the administrative control to which the district was subject). The king's officers in charge of administration of the area in which the gift land was situated were instructed to exempt the land with all the usual exemptions including the above. There are also references to the grant of a village together with *kara* (tax) and *utkara* (probably, minor tax) and with *deya* (periodical offerings to be offered to the king) and *meya* (the king's share of grains) or with the renunciation of all kinds of the rights of the king (*sarvajāta-bhoga-nirasta*) in the Śātavāhana records.[1]

The Mayidavolu[2] plates of Pallava Śivaskandavarman (middle of the 4th century) mention the following *Parihāras* : *a-lavaṇa-khātaka*, *a-rāṣṭra-sāṁvinayika*, *a-paramparā-balīvarda*, *a-bhaṭa-prāveśya* and *a-kūra-cullaka-vināśi-khaṭvā-saṁvāsa*. Of these, *a-bhaṭa-prāveśya*, i. e. freedom from the entry of the *Bhaṭas*, is the same as *a-prāveśya* of the Śātavāhana epigraphs. The word *Bhaṭa* here means *Bhaṭamanuṣya* (constables or Pāiks and Piādas) mentioned in the Hirahadagalli plates of the same Pallava king.[3] *A-paramparā-balīvarda* (i. e. freedom from the supply of bullocks in succession) refers to the obligation of the villagers to supply bullocks to the royal officers when they visited a village for official work in a bullock cart from a neighbouring village. *A-kūra-cullaka-vināśi-khaṭvā-saṁvāsa* indicates freedom of the inhabitants of the gift village from the obligation of supplying to the touring royal officers such articles as *kūra*, *cullaka*, *vināśin*, cot and shelter. *Kūra* and *cullaka* have been explained as 'boiled rice' and 'pot' respectively; but they may really mean 'unboiled rice'

1. *Select Inscriptions*, pp. 195, 198. *Sakarukara* may be *sa-kar-otkara* or *sa-kārukara* (together with the tax on artisans).
2. *Ibid.*, p. 435; cf. *Suc. Sāt. L. Dec.*, pp. 186-87.
3. *Select Inscriptions*, p. 438.

and 'a fire-place for cooking'. *Vināśin* is 'fuel' or 'attendant'. The Hirahadagalli plates records the grant of land with the libation of water for so long as the moon and stars would endure together with the eighteen kinds of exemptions including the following: *a-kūra-cullaka-vināśi-khaṭvā-saṁvāsa*, *a-dughdha-dadhi-grahaṇa*, *a-rāṣṭra-sāṁvinayika*, *a-lavaṇa-guḍa-kṣobha*, *a-karaviṣṭi-koñjalla*, *a-paramparā-balīvarda-grahaṇa*, *a-tṛṇa-kāṣṭha-grahaṇa* and *a-harītaka-śāka-puṣpa-grahaṇa*.[1] The word 'eighteen' in the expression 'eighteen kinds of exemptions'[2] really means 'all'. *A-lavaṇa-guḍa-kṣobha* (i.e. freedom from the trouble in respect of salt and sugar) is similar to *a-lavaṇa-khātaka* of the earlier records referred to above and seems to refer to the practice of piercing trees for sugar. *A-dugdha-dadhi-grahaṇa*, *a-tṛṇa-kāṣṭha-grahaṇa* and *a-harītaka-śāka-puṣpa-grahaṇa* refer to the freedom of the donees from the occasional supply of milk, curds, grass, wood, myrobalan, vegetables and flowers. The reference is both to the periodical supply to be made to the king when demanded as well as to the touring officers. *A-kara-viṣṭi-koñjalla* speaks of the freedom from the payment of *kara* (taxes), *viṣṭi* (free labour) and *koñjalla* which may be *kauñjalya* meaning the obligation of free supply of *kuñjala* (sour gruel) to the king's labourers working in the neighbourhood.

The Basim plates[3] of Vākāṭaka Vindhyaśakti II (end of the 4th century A.D.) mention the following *Parihāras* usually going with land granted to Brāhmaṇas learned in the four Vedas : *a-rāṣṭra-sāṁvinayika*, *a-lavaṇa-klinna-khātaka*, *a-hiraṇya-dhānya-praṇaya-pradeya*, *a-puṣpa-kṣīra-grahaṇīya*, *a-paramparā-balīvarda*, *a-vāra-siddhika*, *a-carm-āṅgāraka*, *a-bhaṭa-prāveśya*, *a-khaṭvā-cullaka-vaināśika*, *a-karada*, *a-vaha*, *sa-nidhi*, *s-opanidhi*, *sa-kṛta-prānta* and *sa-mañca-mahākaraṇa*. It will be seen that, while the records discussed above refer directly to exemptions, the present epigraph mentions them together with certain previleges which involve exemptions. In *a-lavaṇa-klinna-khātaka*

1. *Select Inscriptions*, pp. 439-40; *Suc. Sāt. L. Dec.*, pp. 192-93.
2. Cf. *aṣṭādaśa-jāti-parihāra*.
3. Ibid., pp. 408-09.

klinna seems to mean a moist substance like sugar which, as indicated above, were obtained by boring certain trees like the palmyra palm. It may be toddy, sugar, etc. *A-hiranya-dhānya-praṇaya-pradeya* refers to freedom from the obligation of payment of tax in cash and in crops and of occasional supplies of fruits, etc. *A-puṣpa-kṣīra-grahaṇīya* speaks of the obligation of supplying flowers and milk. *A-vāra-siddhika* seems to refer to the obligation of offering free labour in turn. *A-carm-āṅgāraka* indicates freedom from the obligation of supplying hide-seats and charcoal to the touring royal officers when they camped in a village. *A-khaṭvā-cullaka-vaināśika* is similar to *a-kūra-cullaka-vināśi-khaṭvā-vāsa* of the early Pallava grants. *A-karada* means that the village was exempted from payment of taxes and *a-vaha* refers to the obligation of supplying horses to or carrying loads of the touring officers. *Sa-nidhi* and *s-opanidhi* indicate the privilege of enjoying treasures hidden in the earth and deposits or finds on the soil, without surrendering them to the king. *Sa-kṛta-prānta* suggests that the gift village was granted together with its demarcated boundaries. *Sa-mañca-mahākaraṇa* may mean that the grant was made together with the platforms used for the collection of tolls and important records in the custody of the local officials.

The normal privileges going with the rent-free holdings in the possession of Brāhmaṇas proficient in the four Vedas are enumerated in the Chammak plates[1] of Vākāṭaka Pravarasena II (middle of the 5th century A.D.) as follows : *a-kara-dāyī*, *a-bhaṭa-cchātra-prāveśya*, *a-paramparā-go-balīvarda*, *a-puṣpa-kṣīra-sandoha*, *a-cār-āsana-carm-āṅgāra*, *a-lavaṇa-klinna-kreṇi-khanaka*, *sarva-viṣṭi-parihāra-parihṛta*, *sa-nidhi*, *s-opanidhi*, *sa-klpt-opaklpta*, *ā-candrāditya-kālīya* and *putra-pautr-ānugamaka*. In this list, *a-kara-dāyī* is of course the same as *a-karada* (free from tax) of the earlier record. In *a-bhaṭa-cchātra-prāveśya*, the word *chātra*, literally 'an umbrella-bearer [of the king]' but actually a Pāik or Piāda like a *Bhaṭa* or the leader of a group of them, has been added. In *a-paramparā-go-balīvarda*,

1. *Select Inscriptions.*, p. 422; cf. p. 414 notes.

go, 'a cow', has been similarly added to *balīvarda* 'bullock', suggesting that cows were sometimes requisitioned by the officers on tour. In *a-cār-āsana-carmāṅgāra*, *pāra*, i.e. ferrying of rivers, is sometimes found instead of *cāra* which thus seems to mean 'movement' or 'passage'. This thus seems to refer to the free passage, free camping and free supply of hide-seats and charcoal usually offered by the villagers to the touring royal officers. In *a-lavaṇa-klinna-kreṇi-khanaka*, the expression *klinna-kreṇi*, 'moist commodity (sugar, liqour, etc.)', is more explicit that *klinna* in the earlier epigraph. *Sarva-viṣṭi-parihāra-parihṛta* refers to the freedom from the obligation of supplying free labour of all kinds. *Sa-kḷpt-opakḷpta* seems to mean 'together with the fixed and unfixed [imposts]'. The word *kḷpta* is used in Kauṭilya's *Arthaśāstra* (II. vi) in the sense of one of the seven principal sources of the king's income,[1] while the Motupalli inscription of Kākatīya Gaṇapati mentions *kḷpta-kara* and *kḷpta-śulka* apparently in the senses of 'fixed tax' and 'fixed tolls' respectively.[2] The last two privileges refer to the permanent nature of the grant to be enjoyed by the donees and their descendants in succession. Sometimes *a-paśu-medhya* (i.e. free from the obligation of supplying goats, etc., for sacrifice) is added to the above list of exemptions.[3]

Among early records from North India, the Khoh plates[4] (575 A.D.) of Hastin record the grant of land together with *udraṅga* and *uparikara* but without the entry of the *Cāṭa* and *Bhaṭa* as well as without *cora* which no doubt means fines from thieves. The *Śāśvatakoṣa* explains *udraṅga* as *uddhāra* and *udgrantha* which seem to mean the share of the produce payable to the king.[5] *Uparikara* appears to be the same as Marāṭhī

1. In the *Arthaśāstra* (II. xxviii), *kḷpta* is stated to have been payable by harbours and villages or villages near harbours.

2. *Ep. Ind.*, Vol. XII, p. 193 (text line 85), p. 195 (text lines 149-50).

3. *Select Inscriptions*, p. 414.

4. *CII*, Vol. III, p. 96 : *s-odraṅgaḥ s-oparikaraḥ a-cāṭa-bhaṭa-prāveśyaḥ cora-varjjaṁ.*

5. *CII*, Vol. III, p. 97, note 6.

upari, 'a tax levied on cultivators having no proprietory right on the soil' (Wilson's Glossary).

In many cases, the grant was made with the statement that the land was given as a property of the gods or of the Brāhmaṇas so that the customary privileges going with such lands remained understood. Thus the Banskhera plate[1] of king Harṣa (606-47 A.D.) simply mentions that a village was granted in favour of two Brāhmaṇas as an *agrahāra* (rent-free holding usually under the possession of Brāhmaṇas) according to the custom governing its acceptance by Brāhmaṇas, and the addressees were requested to approve of the grant and the people of the locality were asked to be obedient to the donees and to pay them the usual dues called *pratyāya* including *tulyameya* (tolls on commodities sold in the markets), *bhāga* (king's share of the grains), *bhoga* (periodical offerings), *kara* (tax in kind) and *hiraṇya* (tax in cash), etc.[2] But most medieval records of North India quote the donees' privileges elaborately.

In the Sungal plate[3] of king Vidagdha (first half of the 11th century) of Chamba, the land is given 'as far as its limits, grass, pounds and pasture ground; together with fruit-trees and with the water-courses and channels; with approaches, ingress and egress; with fallow land and cultivated land; with [the fines for] the ten offences; to be enjoyed by the succession of sons, sons' sons and so forth; uncurtailable; unopposed; not to be entered by the *Cāṭas* and *Bhaṭas*; free from tax; inalienable; for as long as the moon, the sun, the ocean and the earth endure'. It is further stated, 'Having understood this, he (i.e. the donee) should freely enjoy and make [others] enjoy

1. *Ep. Ind.*, Vol. IV, pp. 210 ff.

2. *Bhāgabhogakara* may also be *kara* in the shape of *bhāga* and *bhoga*.

3. Vogel, *Antiquities of Chamba State*, I, pp. 167-69. Cf. *sva-sīmā-tṛṇa-goyūthī-gocara-paryantā sa-vanaspaty-udak-āsīhāra-kullaka-pānīya-sametā s-āgama-nirgama-praveśā sa-khila-potācyā sa-daś-āparādhā putra-pautr-ādy-anvay-opabhogā anācchedyā a-paripanthyā a-cāṭa-bhaṭa-praveśā a-kiñcit-karā anāhārā*........... *yathā-samucita-bhāga-bhoga-kara-hiraṇy-ādi-sarva-rāja-bhāvya-pratyāyam=asy=opad-eyam=asya c=āsmadīya-cāṭa-bhaṭ-ānyatar-ādinā gṛh-āvataraṇa-harita-pakvasa-syekṣu-cāraṇa-lavan-opamardana-rocika-ciṭolā-grahaṇa-gokṣīragrahaṇa-pīṭhaka-piṭhikā-khaṭv-āpaharaṇa-kāṣṭh-endhana-ghāsa-bus-ādikaṁ na kenacit=pragrāhyam*, etc. The expression *gṛh-āvataraṇa* seems to be the same as *umbara-bheda* explained below.

[this grant] on the authority of our charter. The subjects, residents in the gift land, in obedience to our command, will have to deliver to him the regular share of [the produce], the periodical offerings, taxes in kind and cash, and every other tribute due to the king. And, of our *Cāṭas* and *Bhaṭas* and others, no one will be allowed to get into his house, to let his vegetables be grazed on, to cut his ripe crops and to crush his sugarcane, to take *rocika* and *ciṭolā* [from him], to take cow's milk [from him], to carry off his stools, benches or couches, and to seize his wood, fuel, grass, chaff and so on. Not even the slightest oppression or vexation should be caused to him or to his ploughmen, cowherds, maids, servants and all other people dependent on him'.

The Semra plates[1] of Candella Paramardin states : "Be it known to you that the above-mentioned villages, with their water and land, with their movable and immovable belongings, defined by their boundaries, with that which is below and above the ground, with all past, future and present imposts (*ādāya*), entrance into them being forbidden to the *Cāṭas* and the rest...... have been given, for the sake of the increase of our own and our parents' merit and fame......with a libation of water from our hand purified by stems of *kuśa* grass, the wish for prosperity having been duly recited......to the Brāhmaṇas......the grant having been made in connection with the intended ground which is to descend to the sons, grandsons and further descendants [of the donees] for a period equal to the duration of the moon and the sun.........Knowing this, you must bring to the donees the [royal] share [of the crops], the [periodical] offerings [payable to the king] and everything else. There-

1. *Ep. Ind.*, Vol. IV, pp. 155-56. Cf. *grāmāḥ sa-jala-sthalāḥ sa-sthāvara-jaṅgamāḥ sva-sīm-āvacchinnāḥ s-ādha-ūrdhvāḥ bhūta-bhaviṣyad-vartamāna-niḥśeṣ-ādāya-sahitāḥ pratiṣiddha-cāṭ-ādi-praveśāḥ.........mātā-pitror=ātmanaś=ca puṇya-yaśo-bhivṛddhaye.........Brāhmaṇebhyaḥ kuśa-latā-pūta-hast-odakena svasti-vācana-pūrvakaṁ putra-pautr-ādy-anvay-ānugāminyāḥ saṁkalpita-bhūmeḥ saṁbandhe śāsanīkṛtya pradattāḥ.........iti matvā bhavadbhir=bhāga-bhog-ādikaṁ sarvvam=ebhyaḥ samupanetavyam | tad=etān=grāmān=amīṣāṁ sa-mandira-prākārān=sa-nirgama-praveśān=sa-sarv-āśan-ekṣu-karpāsa-śaṇ-āmra-madhūkādi-bhūruhān=sa-vana-śvabhra-nidhānān=sa-loh-ādy-ākarān=sa-gokulān=aparair=api sīm-āntargatair=vastubhis=sahitān=sa-bāhyābhyantarādāyān bhuñjānānāṁ karṣatāṁ karṣayatāṁ dān-ādhāna-vikrayaṁ vā kurvatāṁ na kenacit=kācid=vādhā kartavyā*, etc.

fore nobody shall cause any hindrance to them (i.e. the donees) if they enjoy, cultivate, cause to be cultivated, give away, mortgage or sell these villages, together with their houses and walls, together with their gates of exit and entrance, together with all their plants, viz. *aśana*, sugarcane, cotton, hemp, mangoes, *madhūkas*, and so forth, together with their forests, hollows and treasure-troves, together with their mines of metal and so forth, together with their cow-houses, together with all other objects found within their boundaries, and together with the external and internal incomes."

In the passage referring to the imposts payable by the villagers to the donees, the Gāhaḍavāla charters read : *yathā-dīyamāna-bhāga-bhoga-kara-pravaṇikara-kūṭaka-prabhṛiti-samastādāya*,[1] in which the real nature of *pravaṇikara* and *kūṭaka* cannot be determined. In some records, *turuṣkadaṇḍa* and *kumāragadyāṇaka* are mentioned instead of *kūṭaka*[2] while other taxes like *hiraṇya*, *jalakara* (once wrongly read *jātakara*), *gokara*, *nidhi-nikṣepa*, *yamalikambali*, etc., are also occasionally introduced in the list[3], the taxes being sometimes characterised as *niyat-āniyata*, i.e. regular or fixed and occasional.[4] Of these imposts, *turuṣka-daṇḍa* may have been a tax levied on the Muhammadans or for the maintenance of special forces for defending the subjects from Muhammadan attacks. This tax is comparable with those called *āndhra-daṇḍa* and *tiguḷa-daṇḍa* associated respectively with the Āndhra and Tiguḷa (Tamil) peoples and mentioned in the epigraphs of the Kannaḍa-speaking area.[5] *Kumāra-gadyāṇa* was probably a tax of one coin called

1. *Ep. Ind.*, Vol. IV, pp. 101, 103, etc.Cf. *sa-jala-sthalaḥ sa-loha-lavaṇ-ākaraḥ sa-matsy-ākaraḥ sa-parṇ-ākaraḥ sa gart-oṣaraḥ sa-madhūka-cūta-vana-vāṭikā-viṭapa-tṛṇa-yūti-gocara-paryantaḥ ś-ordhv-ādhaś=catur-āghāṭa-viśuddhaḥ sva-sīmā-paryantaḥ ... . yathā-dīyamāna-bhāgabhogakara-pravaṇikara-kūṭaka-prabhṛti-samast-ādāyān .... Parṇ-ākara* probably means 'fields producing betel leaves' and *pravaṇikara* 'a tax on merchants'.

2. Ibid., pp. 106, 109, 120, etc.

3. Ibid., pp. 114, 116, 117, 120, 124, 129.

4. Ibid., Vol. IV, p. 120, etc.

5. Cf. *A.R.Ep.*, 1934-35, B. K. Nos. 153-54.*Tiguḷa-daṇḍa* may be the same as *tiguḷa-ghali* or the Tamilian measuring rod (*Ep. Carn.*, Vol VII, Ci. 21, text line 35). B. K. No. 154 of 1933-34 records the grant of 25 coins for feeding the assembly of *āndhra-daṇḍa*, the nature of which is uncertain. Of *bhoṭṭa-viṣṭi*, 'free carriage of loads to Tibet'.

Gadyāṇa or *Gadyāṇaka* payable in honour of a newly born prince, while *jalakara*, literally 'water-tax', was paid for fishing rights, etc., in tanks, lakes, rivers, etc. The *Gokara*, literally 'cow-tax', may have been a grazing levy. *Nidhinikṣepa* refers to the hidden treasure in the ground or deposits or finds on the soil occasionally discovered. *Yamalikambali* is really *yamalakambalin* payable for the possession of race bullocks.

In the copper-plate grants of the Pālas of Eastern India, we have usually the following specifications: "up to its boundaries, grass and pasture land (*sva-sīmā-tṛṇayūti*[1]*-gocara-paryanta*); with its ground (*sa-tala*); with the space above the ground (*s-oddeśa*); with its mango and *madhūka* trees (*s-āmra-madhūka*); with its waters and dry land; with its pits and saline spots or barren lands (*sa-gart-oṣara*); with the tax from temporary tenants (*s-oparikara*); with *daśāpacāra* or *daśāparādha* (*sa-daś-āparādha, sa-daś-āpcāra*; power to punish and realise fines for the ten offences); with fines realised from thieves (*sa-caur-oddharaṇa*); with exemptions from all oppressions (*parihṛta-sarva-pīḍa*); not to be entered by the *Cāṭas* and *Bhaṭas* (*a-cāṭa-bhaṭa-praveśa*); nothing to be taken [by way of tax, etc.] (*a-kiñcit-pragrāhya*); together with all imposts such as *bhāga, bhoga, kara, hiraṇya,* etc. (*samasta-bhāga-bhoga-kara-hiraṇy-ādi-pratyāya-sameta*); according to the maxim of *Bhūmi-cchidra* (*bhūmi-cchidra-nyāyena*); to last as long a time as the moon, the sun and the earth shall endure (*ā-candr-ārka-kṣiti-sama-kālam*)".[2] The *Bhūmi-cchidra-nyāya* referred to here is mentioned in a large number of records. It speaks of the old custom, according to which a person who brings a piece of fallow or jungle land under cultivation for the first time was allowed to enjoy it without paying rent. The custom was based on the principle that the hunted deer belonged to him who hit it first.[3] The word *chidra* in this case seems to have originally referred to the furrowing of the land. Gradually however the expression *bhūmi-cchidra* acquired the meaning of 'uncultivable

1. The word *yūti*, wrongly read as *pūti*, means 'a preserve'.
2. *Ep. Ind.*, Vol. XXIX, p. 5, note.
3. Cf. Jolly, *Hindu Law and Custom*, pp. 196-97.

(*kṛṣy-ayogyā*) land', and that is why some early medieval inscriptions from Orissa, e.g. the charters of the Bhauma-Karas, speak of the same maxim as *Bhūmi-cchidra-pidhāna-nyāya* literally 'the maxim of covering up the hole in the land', probably referring to the reclamation of fallow land for the first time.[1] These Orissan records usually speak of the grant of land together with the *uddeśa* (space above the ground called *tala*), with the tenants such as the weavers, milkmen (*gokuṭa* or *gauḍa*) and vintners (*śauṇḍika*) and with the *gulmakas* (outposts) at the *kheṭa* (village or hamlet), *ghaṭṭa* (harbour or pass) and *nadītara-sthāna* (ferry).[2]

South Indian charters of the early medieval period such as the Paithan plates[3] (794 A.D.) of Rāṣṭrakūṭa Govinda III record the donee's privileges as : together with *udraṅga*; together with *parikara* (*sa-parikara*, the same as *s-oparikara* of many records); together with *daśāparādha*; together with *bhūta-pāta-pratyāya*; together with *viṣṭi* that may be due (*s-otpadyamāna-viṣṭika*); together with the dues in *dhānya* (crops) and *hiraṇya* (cash); free from the entry of the *Cāṭas* and *Bhaṭas*; not to be interfered with by any royal officer (*sarva-rājakīyānām=a-hasta-prakṣepaṇīya*); to last as long as the moon, the sun, the ocean, the earth, the rivers and the mountains endure; to be enjoyed by the sons, grandsons and descendants [of the donee] ; excluding the property of the gods and Brāhmaṇas (*deva-brahma-dāya*) that was previously granted; together with *abhyantara-siddhi* (i.e. internal income or revenues, or the local taxes); and according to the principle of *Bhūmi-chhidra*. In these, *sarva-rājakīyānām=a-hasta-prakṣepaṇīya* is the same as *samasta-rājakīyānām= apravesya*, 'not to be entered

1. *Ep. Ind.*, Vol. XXIX, p. 86.

2. Cf. *s-oddeśaḥ sa-tantuvāya-gokuṭa-śauṇḍik-ādi-pra'ṛtikaḥ sa-kheṭa-ghaṭṭa-nadītara-sthān-ādi-gulmakaḥ sarva-pīḍā-varjitaḥ a-lekhanī-praveśatayā bhūmicchidra-pidhāna-nyāyena*, etc. The passage *sa-tantuvāya-gokuṭa-śauṇḍik-ādi-prakṛtika* seems to suggest that, sometimes, when a village was alienated, the taxes realisable from certain classes of tenants were reserved by the king or landlord.

3. *Ep. Ind.*, Vol. III, p. 109. Cf. *s-odraṅgaḥ sa-parikaraḥ sa-daś-āparādhaḥ sa-bhūta-pāta-pratyāyaḥ s-otpadyamāna-viṣṭikaḥ sa-dhānya-hiraṇy-ādeyaḥ a-cāṭa-bhaṭa-prāveśyaḥ sarva-rājakīyānām=ahastaprakṣepaṇīyaḥ ā-candr-ārk-ārṇava-sarit-parvata-sama-kālīnaḥ putra-pautr-ānvaya-kram-opabhogyaḥ pūrva-pratta-deva-brahma-deya-rahitaḥ abhyantara-siddhyā bhūmicchidra-nyāyena*, etc. For *bhūtapāta* cf. *infra*.

by any of the king's people', as in records like the Ilao plates[1] of Dadda II, and *rāja-sevakānāṁ vasatidaṇḍa-prayāṇadaṇḍau na staḥ*, 'no tax or contribution for the camping and passage of the king's officers', in the Paithan plates[2] of Rāmacandra.

In the medieval copper-plate inscriptions of the Sena kings of East India, the gift land usually carried with it the following privileges : together with *jhāṭa* and *viṭapa*; together with the land and waters; together with pits and barren lands; together with betelnut and coconut palms; with the ten sins tolerated (*sahya-daś-āparādha*); exempt from all troubles (probably meaning forced labour); not to be entered by the *Caṭṭas* and *Bhaṭṭas* (i.e. *Cāṭas* and *Bhaṭas* of earlier epigraphs); exempt from all dues (*a-kiñcit-pragrāhya*); including *tṛṇayūti-gocara* (grass land as well as grazing fields).[3] In the first item, Sanskrit *viṭapa* means 'a bush', while *jhāṭa* (Bengali *jhāḍ*) also means the same thing. The expression *jhāṭa-viṭapa* thus means all kinds of bushes. *Sahya-daś-āparādha* seems to suggest that the fines for the ten offences were not to be levied from the gift village. In some cases, 'together with *khila* (fallow land) and *nāla* (cultivated land)' is added to the list, and it is further stated that the donees were entitled to raise temples and excavate tanks in the gift land as well as to plant betelnut and coconut palms.[4] The grants of the Candras of Bengal usually add 'together with mango and jack fruit trees.'[5] The privileges of the donees in regard to the enjoyment of particular trees, indicated in these cases, were not enjoyed by ordinary tenants. There is a case in the Vaṅgīya Sāhitya Parishad plate of Viśvarūpasena, in which a Brāhmaṇa purchased a plot of land from certain rent-paying

1. *Ind. Ant.*, *Vol.* XIII, p. 117, text line 17.

2. Ibid., Vol. XIV, p. 318.

3. N. G. Majumdar, *Ins. Beng.*, Vol. III, p. 104, etc. Cf. *sa-jhāṭa-viṭapaḥ sa-jala-sthalaḥ sa-gart-oṣaraḥ sa-guvāka-nārikelaḥ sahya-daś-āparādhaḥ parihṛta-sarva-pīḍaḥ a-caṭṭa-bhaṭṭa-praveśaḥ ā-kiñcit-pragrāhyaḥ tṛṇa-yūti-gocara-paryantaḥ.*

4. N. G. Majumdar, *Ins. Beng.*, Vol. III, p. 147. Cf. *sa-jala-sthalā sa-jhāṭa-viṭapā sa-gart-oṣarā sa-khila-nālā sa-guvāka-nārikelā a-caṭṭa-bhaṭṭa-praveśā ā-candr-ārka-kṣiti-sama-kālaṁ yāvat devakula-puṣkariṇy-ādikaṁ kārayitvā guvāka-nārikel-ādikaṁ laggāvayitvā putra-pautr-ādi-santati-krameṇa svacchand-opabhogen=opabhoktum*, etc.

5. Ibid., p. 8.

tenants who had no right to the betelnut plantation on it; but, when the king made the plot rent-free in favour of the purchasing Brāhmaṇa, the ownership of the plantation automatically passed to him. This is because the possession of such plants was a monopoly of the kings, Jāgīrdārs and privileged tenants.[1]

Among medieval records of the Deccan, mention may be made of the Kalegaon plates[2] (1261 A.D.) of Yādava Mahādeva, which refer to the grant of land together with the eight *bhogas* or enjoyments including *śulka*, *daṇḍa*, *dāṇa*, *kāruka*, *maulika*, *śrotra*, *nidhi*, *nikṣepa*, *jala*, *pāṣāṇa* and *tejaḥ-svāmya* and state that the gift land was not to be pointed out even by a finger by the subordinate rulers and royal officers (*rāja-rājapuruṣair=apy=anaṅguli-nirdeśyam*) and that the grant was made with the libation of *hiraṇy-ākṣat-odaka* (water with gold and rice) in place of the usual libation of water only. Although the *bhogas* or privileges are specified to be eight in number, the items included in the category are eleven. *Aṣṭa-bhoga*, mentioned in many other records of the Deccan, thus indicates privileges roughly grouped in eight classes. In some inscriptions of the Vijayanagara kings, the eight *bhogas* appear to be enumerated as *nidhi* (treasure trove), *nikṣepa* (the same as *upanidhi*, i.e. deposits or accumulation on the soil), waters (i.e. fishing rights), *pāshāṇa* (hills, i.e. quarrying rights), *akṣiṇin* (actual income) *āgāmin* (future income), *siddha* (income from land under cultivation) and *sādhya* (income from land that may be brought under cultivation).[3] *Śulka* and *dāṇa* of the Kalegaon plates appear to indicate different kinds of customs duties and *daṇḍa* fines apparently for the ten offences mentioned in many records. In connection with *dāṇa*, it may be pointed out that *Dāṇī* is a family name in many areas and the *Mahārāṣṭra Śabda-koṣa* explains it as 'the officer collecting the tax or corn' or 'the

1. *JAS*, Letters, Vol. XX, p. 205.

2. *Ep. Ind.*, Vol. XXXII, p. 42; cf. pp. 35-36. Cf. *śulka-daṇḍa-dāṇa-kāruka-maulika-śrotra-nidhi-nikṣepa-jala-pāṣāṇa-tejaḥsvāmyam = ityādy = aṣṭa-bhoga-sahitam*, etc.

3. See *Ep. Ind.*, Vol. III, p. 123, verses 26-27; p. 245, verse 47.

officer to store the corn collected as tax from the farmers'. *Maulika* means the principal or main tax and *kāruka* seems to be a tax on artisans and craftsmen. *Maulika* may also mean 'perquisites of hereditary officers'. It included in that case the receipt of the headman of a village who enjoyed a share of most of the articles produced or sold in the village. *Śrotra* has been explained as the same as Marāṭhī *śilotarā*=*śilotarī*=*śilotrī* meaning a tax in kind collected from the cultivators by a lessee of State land. The same word seems to be used in another epigraph[1] as *śrotaka* in the sense of a kind of rent. *Tejaḥ-svāmya*, which is often mentioned separately from the *aṣṭa-bhoga*,[2] possibly means 'ownership with complete control'. Some inscriptions speak of *āvāta*, *vāt-ādeya*, *a-kara-vāt-ottara*, *bhūt-opātta-pratyāya*, etc., in the list of the donee's privileges.[3] This seems to refer to any income resulting from changes caused by nature and her agencies, e.g. storms, earthquakes, etc.

While discussing the rent-paying grants discovered in Orissa, we had occasion to refer to certain taxes called *tṛṇodaka*, *khaṇḍapāla* and *muṇḍamola*.[4] Of these, *tṛṇodaka* literally means 'a tax for grass and water' and may have been a sort of grazing tax. *Khaṇḍapāla* seems to be a tax levied for the maintenance of certain troops of that name. The official designation *Khaṇḍapāla* means swordsmen maintained by the king and they appear to be responsible for the development of the present day Khaṇḍāit community of Orissa. *Muṇḍamola* reminds us of Marāṭhī *muṇḍabandī* meaning a collective rate of rent for land partitioned among cultivators.[5]

Certain medieval Orissan records like the Balijhari plates[6]

1. *Ep. Ind.*, Vol. XXXII, p. 57.
2. Khare, *Sour. Med. Hist. Dec.*, Vol. III, pp. 63, 90, 98.
3. Altekar, *The Rāshṭrakūṭas and their Times*, p. 228; above, p. 398.
4. *JRAS*, 1952, pp. 4-10.
5. See Wilson's Glossary, s. v.
6. *JBORS*, Vol. XVII, p. 1 ff. Cf. *sa-gart-oṣaraḥ......catuḥsim-āvacchinnaḥ sīsu-madhūka-tāla-prabhṛti-nānā-vṛkṣa-(sametaḥ*) sa-nidhiḥ s-opanidhiḥ hasti-daṇḍa-varabalīvarda-coṭāla-andhānuvā (arthāruvā?)-pratyandhāruvā (pratyarthā-ruvā?)-adattā-padātijīva (or jīvya)-ahidaṇḍa-anta (ātu) rāvaḍḍi-bandhadaṇḍa-vijayavandā-panā-mārgaṇika-prabhṛti-bhaviṣyat-kara-sahitaḥ sa-pratihāraḥ sarva-vādhā-vivarjitaḥ sarv-oparikar-ādāna-sahitaḥ* etc.

of the Somavaṁśī king Uddyotakesarin and the Kelga plates[1] of *Kumāra* Someśvara of the same dynasty mention a number of interesting taxes. The Kelga plates have *suvarṇadaṇḍa*, *ahidaṇḍa*, *vartmadaṇḍa*, *vandāpanā*, *vijaya-vandāpanā*, *tṛṇodaka*, *śāsanārdhika*, *varabalīvarda*, *arthāruvā*, *pratyarthāruvā*, *padātijīvya*, *ādattā*, *āturāvaḍḍi*, *gogauḍa* and *khaṇḍapālīya*, while the Balijhari plates have such new items as *hastidaṇḍa*, *coṭāla*, *bandhadaṇḍa*, *mārgaṇika*, *pratīhāra* and *uparikara*. Of these, *tṛṇodaka* has been discussed above and *khaṇḍapālīya* is the same as *khaṇḍapāla* already referred to. *Vartmadaṇḍa* of the Kelga plates is apparently the same as *mārgaṇika* of the Balijhari plates. It was a sort of customs dues payable at the outposts on roads. *Suvarṇadaṇḍa* was a tax payable by professional goldsmiths, while *ahi-daṇḍa* was the tax payable for the maintenance of snake-charmers. *Vandāpanā* was the same as Persian *nazrāna* payable at the time of visiting the king, while *vijaya-vandāpanā* was the *nazrāna* payable on the king's return from a victorious campaign. *Śāsanārdhika* may be an additional share of the produce payable by the tenants engaged in cultivating rent-free lands. *Varabalīvarda* was a tax for bullocks meant for prize-fights and *padātijīvya*, called *pāikā* in Oḍiyā inscriptions,[2] was a tax for the maintenance of *Pāiks*. *Gogauḍa* literally means 'cow and cowherd' and appears to have been a grazing tax or a tax on the milkmen. *Hastidaṇḍa* was a tax payable for the possession of elephants, while *bandhadaṇḍa* may be the ransom payable in lieu of imprisonment, and *pratīhāra* a tax for entry into the royal palace or the maintenace of *Pratīhārīs*. *Arthāruvā* and *pratyarthāruvā* appear to indicate collection from the money-lenders for the amounts loaned out and those realised

1. *Ep. Ind.*, Vol. XXVIII, p. 323. Cf. *prasiddha-catuḥ-sīm-āvacchinnaḥ sa-jala-sthalaḥ sa-matsya-kacchapaḥ sa-viṭap-āraṇyaḥ sa-nidhiḥ s-opanidhiś=ca s-āmra-madhu-van-ākīrṇaḥ suvarṇadaṇḍa-ahidaṇḍa-vartmadaṇḍa-vandāpanā-vijaya-vandāpanā-tṛṇodaka-śāsanārdhika-ca* (*va*)*rabalīvarda-ārthāruvā-pratyarthāruvā-padā-tijīvya-ādattā-āturdāvaḍḍi-bhaviṣyat-kar-ādi-sahitaḥ gogauḍa-sametaḥ sa-khaṇḍapālīyaḥ*, etc. See also another inscription from the same place (ibid., p. 327) : *catuḥ-sīmā yāvat nidhy-upanidhi-hastidanta-vyāghracarma-nānāvanacara-sametaḥ sa-jala-sthalaḥ sa-matsya-kacchapaḥ sa-kheṭa-viṭapaḥ sa-khalla-unnataḥ sa-padr-āraṇyakaḥ sa-gulma-latākaḥ s-āmra-madhūkaḥ sa-tantalikaḥ sa-tālakaḥ nānāvṛkṣa-sametaḥ*, etc. Cf. *alīyaka* or *ālipaka*, 'income from bees' (wax, boney, etc.) in Vol. XXXVI, p. 14.

2. *Ep. Ind.*, Vol. XXIX, p. 107.

with interest. *Āturāvaḍḍi* seems to mean 'pellets for the sick' and may have been a levy for the treatment of the king when sick. The expressions *coṭāla* and *ādattā* cannot be explained though the former may be the same as *ciṭolā* mentioned above and the latter may mean 'interest or fine on the arrears of taxes'. Some inscriptions of the same area mention among the donees' privileges : 'together with fish, tortoises, etc.; together with bushes and jungles; together with the right to enjoy the property left by people dying without son'.[1] When the gift land was situated in a forest area, the privileges of the donees sometimes included his right to enjoy *hasti-danta* (ivory), *vyāghra-carman* (tiger's skin) and various animals as well as trees including tamarind and palmyra.[2]

An Oḍiyā inscription[3] of 1394 A.D., speaks of taxes like *ohoru, pāukā, pāikā, bheṭa, vodā* and *paridarśanā*. Of these, *ohoru* is the same as *daṇḍoāsi-ohora*, i.e. the watchman-tax, of another Oḍiyā record, while *pāukā* may be Oḍiyā *pāuseri* and mean a tax on the money realised by the creditors from the debtors. *Pāikā* is the same as *padātijīvya* and Oḍiyā *pāikāli*. *Bheṭa* is the same as *vandāpanā* or the occasional offering of money or presents, while *vodā* (Oḍiyā *vadāi*) is a similar offering of uncooked food. *Paridarśanā* may be a supervision tax, the nature of which is uncertain. It will be seen that most of the expressions belong to the local dialect. Such names of taxes in the regional languages are quite common in the medieval inscriptions from different parts of the country and a number of them have been noticed in our *Glossary*. Certain high officers of the Cālukya kings of Kalyāṇa are often described as managing the *vaḍḍāravula* and other taxes, the *vaḍḍāravula* and *pejjuṅka* taxes, the *pannāya* tax, or the *melviṭṭiya-vaḍḍāravula*, *eraḍu-bilkode* and *perjuṅka* taxes.[4]

The Hitnahebbagilu plates[5] of Kadamba Mṛgeśvarman (c. 470-90 A.D.) mention a number of privileges to be enjoyed

1. *Ep. Ind.*, Vol. XXVIII, p. 291. Instead of 'bushes and jungles', sometimes we have 'trees and jungles' (ibid., p. 311).
2. Ibid., p. 326.
3. Ibid., Vol. XXIX, p. 107.
4. *Bomb. Gaz.*, Vol. I, Part ii, pp. 450-51.
5. *Ep. Carn.*, Vol. IV, p. 136, Hunsur No. 18 : ***parihṛta-paṅg-otkoṭa***.

by the donee, the most interesting of them being the exemption from *paṅga* and *utkoṭa*. *Paṅga* or *pāṅga* is also mentioned in other records of the Kannaḍa-speaking area such as the Kapoli plates[1] of Aśaṅkitavarman (6th century A.D.), the Goa plates[2] of Satyāśraya Dhruvarāja Indravarman, a grant[3] (1107 A.D.) of Kadamba Tribhuvanamalla and the Panjim plates[4] of Jayakeśin I. The word *paṅga*=*pāṅga* found in the said inscriptions is no doubt the same as Telugu *paṅgamu* recognised in Brown's *Telugu-English Dictionary* in the sense of 'a tax in the shape of one-fourth of the produce collected in olden times by the government on lands in the possession of gods and Brāhmaṇas'. But expressions like *sarva-paṅga-parihṛta*, 'exempt from all the *paṅgas*', suggests that sometimes the word was used to indicate a tax in general. And this is supported by the use of the word *paṅga* (rarely *paṅgā*) in a large number of medieval Telugu inscriptions[5] sometimes in the sense of a group of levies. In these records, we have, besides *paṅga-tappu* and *paṅga-śulka* or *paṅga-tappu-śulka* in a single compound, the word used along with other levies called *āya-śulka*, *pannu*, *kāṇika*, *darśana*, *upakṣiti*, *puṭṭi* and *māḍalu*. Both *āya* and *śulka* mean 'tolls, tax, customs', etc., and the compound *āya-śulka* may mean 'customs duties'. Wilson's Glossary recognises *pannu* as a Tamil word meaning 'tax, tribute, custom, rent' and it is also recognised by Brown as a Telugu word meaning 'a tax'. *Kāṇika* may be Kannaḍa *kāṇike-kāṇe* or *kāṇike-kappa* (or *kappa-kāṇike*) recognised by Wilson in the sense of 'a present from an inferior to a superior, a subscription, a donation'. Brown recognises Telugu *kānika* or *kānuka* in the same sense. *Darśana* is the Tamil *pāvai* and Persian *nazrāna*. *Puṭṭi* reminds us of Telugu *puṭṭidosillu* recognised by Wilson in the sense of 'a fee of two handfuls from each *puṭṭi* of grain paid to the village servants'. *Māḍalu* reminds us what Wilson says under

1. *Ep. Ind.*, Vol. XXXI, pp. 234 ff.
2. *JBBRS*, Vol. X, pp. 348 ff.
3. *Ep. Ind.*, Vol. XXX, pp. 77 ff.
4. See ibid., Vol. XXXIII, p. 54.
5. See ibid., p. 55-56.

māḍa : 'a half pagoda; where it is applied to a rate of rent, payment of 50 per cent'. The expression *paṅgatappu* may indicate interest or fine on arrears of *paṅga*. *Upakṣiti* probably means the tax on a particular kind land such as *khajjana*.

The word *utkoṭa*, mentioned in the Hitnabebbagilu plates, is not known from Sanskrit lexicons. But there is no doubt that it is the same as Prakrit *ukkoḍa* meaning 'things to be offered to the *rājakula* (i.e. the king, royal officers and members of the royal family)', and 'presents made to the king and others'.

In earlier records, the rent-free holdings in the possession of gods and Brāhmaṇas were usually called *devadeya* or *devadāya* and *brahmadeya* or *brahmadāya* respectively. Gradually the word *agrahāra* became popular in South India in the sense of a rent-free village in the possession of Brāhmaṇas, although occasionally the word was used in a wider sense since we have also reference to *dev-āgrahāra*, *vaiśy-āgrahāra*, etc. Other expressions for rent-free holdings, noticed especially in South Indian inscriptions, are *mānya*, *namasya*, *sarva-mānya*, *sarva-namasya*, *namasya-vṛtti*, etc.[1] In modern documents of Bengal, the rent-free holding in the possession of a god is called *devottara* (Sanskrit *devatrā*) and that of a Brāhmaṇa *bhogottara* (possibly Sanskrit *bhogatrā*) or *brahmottara* (probably Sanskrit *brahmatrā*), while the rent-free holding in the possession of non-Brahmanical communities was sometimes called *mahātrāṇa*, etc.

There are a few inscriptions which supply us with informations that are not generally found in other records. Thus the Anjaneri plates[2] (709 A.D.), recording the grant of eight

1. Sometimes we have reference to *ardha-namasya-vṛtti* which refers to gift land taxed at half the usual rate. In some epigraphs of the Kannaḍa area, a person is mentioned as governing or managing an *agrahāra* according to the *tribhāg-ābhyantara-siddhi* which means that he took one-third of the revenues, the other two-thirds going in equal shares to the gods and Brāhmaṇas (*Bomb. Gaz.*, Vol. I, Part II, p. 440). Likewise we have reference to *pannasa* in Kannaḍa records (*Ep. Ind.*, Vol. XV, p. 336, note 3), which may be a corruption of Sanskrit *pañcāśat* and indicate a tenure in which the donnee enjoyed fifty per cent of the revenue.

2. *Ep. Ind.*, Vol. XXV, pp. 232-33. Cf. *ādānāni* I *āpaṇeṣu āvārāḥkaraṇe koveraṁ* I *sārtha-vahitreṣu praveśe nirgame ca pratyekaṁ rūpakaḥ devasya yātr-otsave dātavyaṁ* I ......*mūṭakaḥ ghṛta-setikā ca*......*sarv-ādāna-viṣṭi-prātibhedikā-parihīnāḥ a-cāṭa-bhaṭa-praveśyāḥ abhyantara-siddhikāḥ ā-candr-ārk-ārṇava-kṣiti-sthiti-sama-kālīnāḥ*, etc.

villages in favour of a deity, specifically mention the *ādānas* or receipts from the gift lands as follows : the *āvāra* [taxes, probably stall-taxes] to be levied from shops (*āpaṇeṣu*); the *kovera* [tax] in respect of the *karaṇa* (probably, an official document); one *rūpaka* on the occasion of the god's *yātr-otsava* to be levied at the entry and exit of each caravan of merchandise (*sārtha-vahitreṣu*); one *mūṭaka* (probably a small weight) [of corn] and one *setikā* (Prakrit *seiā* or *setikā* meaning 'two handfuls') of clarified butter to be levied from certain villages probably from each household; specified amounts of money in silver coins called *Kṛṣṇarāja-rūpaka* to be levied from some districts; the eight villages should be free from all imposts (*ādāna*), free labour (*viṣṭi*) and *prātibhedikā* (probably, the same as *bheṭ* or presents); they should be free from the entry of the *Cāṭa* and *Bhaṭa* and also *abyantara-siddhika* (enjoying the right of internal income or revenue). The inscription also mentions a *sthiti* or regulation in respect of the town where the god's temple was situated and of its merchants to whom the temple as well as the god's worship and the *yātrā* festival were entrusted. According to it, the merchants were made immune from *śulka* (customs duties) and *jemaka* (the feeding expenses of officers on duty). Another inscription[1] of the same king granted the following privileges to the merchant of a town : they should have to pay no *śulka* anywhere in the kingdom; there should be no *aputra-dhana*[2] and no *umbarabheda* for them; and they should pay no *āvāsaka* (camping expenses) and *jemaka* (food expenses) for royal officers. *Aputra-dhana* refers to the custom of confiscation of the pro-

1. Ibid., p. 237. Cf. *Somagiri-vāstavyānāṁ vaṇijāṁ candr-ārka-kālikaṁ śulkam=ādeyaṁ samasta-rājye n=āsti* I *aparaṁ ca aputra-dhanaṁ n=āsti* I *umbara-bhedaḥ rājapuruṣāṇām=āvāsako jemakaś=ca nāsti* I *kumārī-sāhase rūpakāṇām=aṣṭottara-śatam* I *saṁgrahaṇe dvātriṁśad=rūpakāḥ* I *karṇa-tṛoḍaṇikāyāṁ ṣoḍaśa-rūpakāḥ* I *śira-sphoṭane catvāri rūpakāḥ* I *bhārikāyāṁ vaṇik-putrasy=āṣṭo-ttara-śataṁ rūpakānām* I *naṅge gṛhītasya yac=c=āṣṭau ṣodaśa vā nagara-mahallakā vicārya vadante tad =eva pramāṇam.* Some of the words in the latter part of the passage are unintelligible. *Karṇa-troḍanikā* is the same as *Karṇa-troṭana.*

2. Cf *aputrā-sahitaṁ* (ibid., Vol.XXVIII, p. 291) and *nidhi-nikṣep-āputraka-dhana-daṇḍ-opajātaka-sahitaḥ* (loc. cit., note 13) in some records.

perty of one dying without sons and *umbara-bheda* (from Prakrit *ummara* meaning 'threshold', i. e. door) apparently suggests that no dues should be collected from the houses of the merchants when they were abroad. The charter[1] (592 A.D.) of king Viṣṇuṣeṇa of Kathiawar, called a *sthiti-pātra*, *ācāra-sthiti-pātra*, *anugraha-sthiti-pātra*, *sthiti-vyavasthā* or *sthiti-pātra-vyavasthā*, contains a large number of similar regulations made in favour of a group of merchants. These regulations (*ācāras*) contain a good many technical expressions not generally found in epigraphic and literary records and the Sanskrit lexicons. The Motupalli inscription[2] (1244-45 A.D.) of Kākatīya Gaṇapati is 'an edict assuring safety' to foreign traders whose vessels might be wrecked on the coast of his territories. It is stated that the cargo would not be forfeited to the State as before, but only the fixed customs duties would be levied on it. These duties are clearly specified in the inscription.

6. *Land Measures*

Although often entire villages were granted by charters, in many cases the gift land consisted of smaller plots of land, the areas of which were usually indicated in the records. The measurement of the plot was sometimes entrusted to a high officer of the king.[3] The unit of measurement was the cubit which was often measured by the length of the forearm of a particular individual in the king's service[4] and the measuring rod made of wood, bamboo, etc., had the length of a recognised number of such cubits.[5] Sometimes particular measuring

1. Ibid., Vol. XXX, pp. 169 ff.

2. Ibid., Vol. XII, pp. 188 ff.

3. Cf. the records of the Imperial Gaṅgas of Orissa (*Ep. Ind.*, Vol. XXVIII, pp. 188, 192, etc.)

4. Cf. *Śivacandra-hasta* in the Faridpur plate of Dharmāditya (*Select Inscriptions*, pp. 352, 356, 358). The cubit is indicated by a word like *hasta* (*kai* in the South Indian languages). In Kannaḍa inscriptions, sometimes we find *geṇu* (i.e. span) and *kālu* (i.e. foot) as units of measurement. The same units are also known from Tamil records (see below); cf. also the land measure called *Pādāvarta* referred to below.

5. Ibid., p. 344 and note 7; cf. *infra*.

rods (i.e. rods of particular lengths) are mentioned in inscriptions. Thus the inscriptions of the Senas of Bengal mention *Samataṭīya-nala* (the measuring rod prevalent in the Samataṭa country),[1] *Vṛṣabhaśaṅkara-nala* (the measuring rod introduced by *Arirāja-vṛṣabha-śaṅkara* Vijayasena),[2] 'the measuring rod 56 cubits in length prevalent in the district around the gift land',[3] etc. The 'measuring rod of the Samataṭa country' may be compared to *Eḍenāḍa-daṇḍa* (the measuring rod of the district of Eḍenāḍu),[4] *Palṭiyamattavurada daṇḍa* (the measuring rod of the village of Palṭiyamattavura),[5] etc., of Kannaḍa inscriptions which also refer to particular measuring rods like *Māṇikeśvarada kolu* (the rod of the god *Māṇikeśvara*),[6] *Gaṅgana ghaḻe* (the rod of a person named Gaṅga),[7] *Dharaṇidevana kolu* (the rod of a person named Dharaṇideva),[8] etc.[9] Measuring rods like *Gaṅgana ghaḻe* are comparable to *Śivacandra-hasta* referred to above. Sometimes the gift land is stated to have been measured according to the *rāja-māna*[10] indicating apparently the standard unit of measurement recognised by the government. Numerous measuring rods of this kind are known from Tamil epigraphs of the time of the Co̤ḷa and Vijayanagara kings, two of them being the *Śrīpāda-kkol* (the rod of the king's foot with reference to Kulottuṅga I) and the *Māligai-kkol* (the rod of the palace). The varying length of the rods is given in the records as 4, 12, 13, 16 or 18 spans, 36 or 48 steps and 12, 14, 16 or 20 feet.[11]

1. N. G. Majumdar, *Ins. Beng.*, Vol. III, p. 63.
2. Ibid., pp. 74, 87.
3. Ibid., p. 96.; cf. p. 102.
4. *Ep. Ind.*, Vol. III, p. 216, text line 9.
5. Ibid., p. 234., text line 45.
6. *A. R. Ep.*, 1933-34, B. K. No. 177.
7. Ibid., 1932-33, B. K. No. 152.
8. Ibid., 1958-59, Nos. B 661 ff. (transcripts).
9. In Kannaḍa inscriptions, the length and breadth of house-sites are often indicated in *kai* or the cubit instead of referring to the measuring rod.
10. *Ep. Ind.*, Vol. XXVII, p. 207; Vol. XXXIII, p. 91; *Ep. Carn.*, Vol. XI, Hiriyur No. 77; *A. R. Ep.*, 1932-33, B. K. No. 124; etc.
11. See Mahalingam, *South Indian Polity*, pp. 151, 156, 158-59, 160 note. There are also references to measuring rods 24, 32 or 34 feet long.

There is uncertainty about the exact area of most of the land measures prevalent in different parts of ancient India.

The Śātavāhana inscriptions of the second century A.D., discovered in the north-western part of the Deccan, mention a land measure called *Nivartana*[1] which is also known from later epigraphic records especially of the southern areas of India.[2] According to Śātātapa and Bṛhaspati, a *Nivartana* had the area of 300×300 square cubits (about 4¾ acres)[3] while a variant reading of Bṛhaspati's text gives its area as 210×210 square cubits (about 2¼ acres) only.[4] The Kauṭilīya *Arthaśāstra* (II. 20) speaks of the *Nivartana* as 240×240 square cubits in area (about 3 acres), though one of its commentators makes it 120×120 square cubits (about ¾ acre).[4] Bhāskarācārya's *Līlāvatī* speaks of the *Nivartana* as 200×200 square cubits in area (about 2 acres) which is supported by Hemādri's *Caturvargacintāmaṇi*.[5] The *Śukranītisāra* speaks of the *Nivartana* as 112×112 or 140×140 square cubits in area (about ⅗ of an acre and about 1 acre respectively), while Vasiṣṭha mentions it as 100×100 square cubits[6] (about ½ acre). The uncertainty about the exact area of a *Nivartana*

1. See *Select Inscriptions*, pp. 192, 194.

2. Telugu inscriptions sometimes refer to *Nivartana* as the same as *Maṟuturu* (P. Sreenivasachar, *Corp. Ins. Tel. Dist.*, pp. 206-08). On the strength of the Kasakudi plates, Hultzsch points out that 'the Sanskrit *Nivartana* (40,000 square *hastas*) and the Tamil *Paṭṭi* (a measure of land sufficient for a sheep-fold) are synonymous' (*SII*, Vol. II, p. 350, note 12). Medieval Kannaḍa records also often mention the *Nivartana* as the same as *Mattar* or *Mattaru* (Telugu *Maṟuturu*). See *SII*, Vol. XI, Part ii, No. 136, text lines 52 and 56.

3. See *Ūnaviṁśatisaṁhitā*, Vaṅgavāsī ed., p. 480 (*Śātātapasaṁhitā*, I. 15); p. 346 (*Bṛhaspatisaṁhitā*, verse 8) : *daśa-hastena daṇḍena triṁśad-daṇḍaṁ* (or °*daṇḍā*) *nivartanam*. The stanza is quoted in Ballāla's *Dānasāgara* (Bib. Ind. ed.), p. 323, and in a 13th century inscription from Andhra Pradesh (see *Nel. Dist. Ins.*, Vol. I, p. 147, C. P. No. 17, verse 28).

4. Cf. the Mitākṣarā on the *Yājñavalkyasmṛti*, I. 210 (*sapta-hastena deṇḍena triṁśad-daṇḍair=nivartanam*). See also the *Śabdakalpadruma*, Pariśiṣṭa, p. 160. The *Prāṇatoṣaṇītantra*, Vasumatī ed., p. 106, ascribes the verse to the *Svarodaya-ṭīkākāra*.

5. *Līlāvatī*, Calcutta ed., I. 6 (*tathā karāṇāṁ daśakena vaṁśaḥ* । *nivartanaṁ viṁśati-vaṁśa-saṁkhyaiḥ kṣetraṁ caturbhiś=ca bhujair=nibaddham* ॥). See also Hemādri referred to by M. Somsekhara Sarma, *History of the Reḍḍi Kingdoms*, pp. 366-67.

6. See P. Sreenivasachar, op. cit., pp. 206-07. Vasiṣṭha's text runs: *daśa-hastena vaṁśena daśa-vaṁśān=samantataḥ*.

in a particular region and age is also noticed in regard to most other ancient land measures.

Many of the authorities cited above mention the *Nivartana* as one-tenth of the *Gocarman* which is also mentioned in some inscriptions.[1] Originally, the *Gocarman* may have indicated that area of land which could be covered by the hides of cows slaughtered in a sacrifice and was granted to the priests as sacrificial fee. But the expression is differently interpreted by later authorities. Thus while many of the writers explain it as ten times a *Nivartana* which is however given various areas,[2] others offer quite vague indications regarding the area of the *Gocarman*. Nīlakaṇṭha's commentary on the *Mahābhārata* suggests that a piece of land large enough to be encompassed by straps of a single cow's hide was called a *Gocarman*,[3] while the *Parāśarasaṁhitā* and *Bṛhaspatisaṁhitā* appear to suggest that it was the area of land where one thousand cows could freely graze in the company of a hundred bulls.[4] According to the *Viṣṇusaṁhitā*, the area of the land, sufficient to maintain a person for a whole year with its produce, was called *Gocarman*.[5] Ballāla's *Dānasāgara* quotes a stanza from Vṛddha-Vasiṣṭha according to which a plot of land measuring 10 rods square, a rod being ten cubits long, is one *Gocarman* in area; or its area is 15×15 such rods. The passage indicating the second alternative is however explained by Ballāla differently and he says that a *Gocarman* may be 10 rods by 15 rods of the above length.[6]

1. Cf. *Ep. Ind.*, Vol. XXVIII, p. 245.

2. Loc. cit.; see the texts cited in the notes. While explaining Bṛhaspati's stanza quoted in the *Dānasāgara*, Ballāla says that the length and breadth of a *Gocarman* are 3000 and 300 cubits respectively (op., cit. pp. 323-324).

3. Vaṅgavāsī ed., I. 30. 23 (*vadhrī eka-tantukā carma-rajjuḥ...ekena gocarmaṇā kṛtayā rajjvā ākrānta-bhūr=gocarma-mātrā*).

4. *Parāśarasaṁhitā*, Calcutta ed., XII. 43; *Bṛhaspatisaṁhitā*, Vaṅgavāsī ed., verse 9. The stanza is attributed to Vṛddha-Vasiṣṭha in Ballāla's *Dānasāgara* (Bib. Ind. ed.), p. 322.

5. Vaṅgavāsī ed., V. 179.

6. See *Dānasāgara* (Bib. Ind. ed.), p. 322 : *Daśa-hastena vaṁśena daśa vaṁśān=samantataḥ* । *pañca v=āpy=adhikān=dadyād=etad=gocarma uchyate* । *pañca v=āpy=adhikam=ity=ekasmin pārśve pañca-vaṁś-ādhikaṁ vā.*

Another land measure of the same type is the *Hala*, literally 'a plough'.[1] It may have originally indicated an area of land that could be cultivated by a pair of bullocks during a year. Its area is now different in different parts of the country. In Rajasthan, it is regarded as equal to 50 *Bīghās*;[2] but 'the plough' (indicated variously in the regional languages) has different areas in other parts of the country.

Even in areas where the ancient names of land measures are still current, we cannot escape similar uncertainty. In the age of the Guptas, the popular units of the measurement of area in Bengal are known to have been the *Kulyavāpa*, *Droṇavāpa* and *Āḍhavāpa*.[3] These words are derived from *vāpa* (from the root *vap*, 'to sow') added to certain measures of capacity.

According to the Paharpur plate of 479 A.D., 4 *Āḍhavāpas* made 1 *Droṇavāpa*, and 8 *Droṇavāpas* made 1 *Kulyavāpa*.[4] Since the introduction of the unit of measurement called *Bīghā* (usually 80×80 square cubits, i.e. about ⅓ of an acre) in the medieval period, this land measure with its subdivisions has gradually ousted the older units and denominations from many parts of Bengal. But the *Kulavāy* (ancient *Kulyavāpa*), *Doṇ* (ancient *Droṇavāpa*) and *Āḍhā* (ancient *Āḍhavāpa*) are still locally known in the eastern regions of undivided Bengal and the adjoining western districts of Assam. It is however unfortunate that all the three denominations are not prevalent in the same locality, that the old relation of 1 *Kulyavāpa*=8 *Droṇavāpas*=32 *Āḍhavāpas* is totally forgotten, and that the *Doṇ* (*Droṇavāpa*) which is prevalent in various places is different in area in different localities.[5] Apparently the area of all of them has

1. Cf. *Ep. Ind.*, Vol. XXXIII, p. 197, text lines 8-9. In the Śātavāhana inscriptions, *hala* is used, in expressions like *bhikṣu-hala*, in the sense of a free-holding. An inscription refers to the area as a plot of land that could be tilled by one plough in a single day.

2. *Ep. Ind.*, Vol. XXV, p. 64 and note 2.

3. See *Bhārata Kaumudī*, Part II, pp. 943 ff.

4. *Select Inscriptions*, p. 347, note 5.

5. The *Kulavāy* known from Sylhet is equal to 14 *Bighās*, while the *Āḍhā* prevalent in several areas of the Mymensingh District is equal

changed in the course of time, especially owing to the difference introduced in different areas and ages in the length of the cubit and the measuring rod. Attention in this connection may be drawn to an early tradition regarding the practice of using a rod 4 cubits long for oridnary measurement but that of the length of 8 cubits for measuring *Brahmadeya* lands (i.e. rent-free lands granted to the Brāhmaṇas).[1]

The words *Kulyavāpa*, *Droṇavāpa* and *Āḍhavāpa* indicate the area of land that was required to sow seed grains of the weight respectively of one *kulya*, *droṇa* and *āḍhaka*.[2] Pargiter, who tried to determine the area of the *Kulyavāpa* as known from the Faridpur plates,[3] pointed out that the staple food of Bengal is rice and the most important grain is paddy and that, according to the *Raghuvaṁśa* (IV. 36-37), the usual practice especially in lower Bengal was to transplant in the cultivated land the seedlings taken out from a small plot of land where the paddy seeds had been originally sown. This is the system followed in rice cultivation in many parts of Bengal even today. Pargiter therefore suggested that the *Kulyavāpa* inidicated that area of land which was required to transplant the seedlings of paddy seeds one *kulya* in weight. Unfortunately he did not know the actual weight of a *kulya* of grain. He had moreover to explain the passage 'having measured with the rod of 8 and 9' used in the Faridpur plates in connection with the measure-

to about 4½ *Bighās*. The *Doṇ* is more widely distributed. In the Chittagong District, the *Doṇ* is equal to about 21 *Bīghās*; but, in the Noakhali District, it is equal to about 100 *Bīghās* in Sandvip and to about 144 *Bīghās* in the Shaistanagar Pargana. Hunter's *A Statistical Account of Bengal* shows this difference in the measurement of the same unit as due to the fact that the length of the measuring rod and also of the cubit is different in different localities. Usually a measuring rod was 14 cubits and a cubit 18 inches long. In Sandvip, however, the length of the cubit was 20¾ inches while, in the Shaistanagar Pargana, the measuring rod was 22 cubits long. Nowadays, 1 cubit=18 inches and 1 *nala* (measuring rod)=16 cubits, as standardised by the Government, have ousted the earlier lengths noticed by Hunter, and 1 *Doṇ* is now taken, according to the Government standard, to be equal to 76 *Bighās* in the Noakhali District. In the Rangpur Di trict, the *Bīghā* is known by the name *Doṇ*. In certain areas of the Mymensigh District, the *Doṇ* is equal to about 17 *Bīghās*, though elsewhere it is equal to about 51 *Bighās*.

1. *Suc. Sāt. L. Dec.*, pp. 186 note, 330 note.
2. Cf. *Amarakoṣa*, Vaiśyavarga, verse 10.
3. *Ind. Ant.*, Vol. XXXIX, pp. 195 ff.; *Select Inscriptions*, pp. 350 ff.

ment of a *Kulyavāpa*. He suggested that 1 *Kulyavāpa* of land was 9 rods in length and 8 rods in breadth, and further conjectured the length of a *nala* or measuring rod to have been 16 cubits and that of a cubit 19 inches. Accordingly, the area of a *Kulyavāpa* in Pargiter's calculation was a little above one acre ($3\frac{1}{40}$ *Bighās*). But the conclusion is not only based on several conjectures but also cannot be reconciled with the expression 'having measured with the rods of 6' used in connection with the measurement of a *Kulyavāpa* in thePaharpur plate, which would thus indicate an area of only 6×6 rods. It will be seen that a *Kulyavāpa* of 8×9 rods would be much larger than a *Kulyavāpa* of 6×6 rods, if the rods are regarded as of the same length.[1]

According to a persistent tradition followed by the Bengal authorities on S'mṛti, such as Kullūka-bhaṭṭa (15th century), Raghunandana (16th century) and Pañcānana Tarkaratna, 8 *muṣṭis* or handfuls=1 *kuñci*; 8 *kuñcis* or 64 handfuls=1 *puṣkala*; 4 *puṣkalas* or 256 handfuls=1 *āḍhaka*; 4 *āḍhakas* or 1024 handfuls=1 *droṇa*. That this refers to the measuring of paddy is clear from the fact that the verse in question is quoted by Kullūka to explain the expression *dhānya-droṇa* in the *Manusmṛti*, VII. 126. According to Pañcānana Tarkaratna, who translated the *Manusaṁhitā* into Bengali, and the Bengali compilers of the *Śabdakalpadruma*, 1 *āḍhaka*=16 or 20 modern Bengal seers,[2] and 1 *droṇa*=1 maund 14 seers, or 2 maunds. According to the lexicographer Medinīkara, 8 *droṇas* (8192 handfuls) =1 *kulya*. A *kulya* of paddy seeds would thus be equal to 12 maunds 32 seers, or 16 maunds. These are the traditional

1. Instead of *aṣṭaka-navaka-nalena* in the singular, we have sometimes *aṣṭaka-navaka-nalābhyām* in the dual and *ṣaṭka-naḍaiḥ* in the plural. See *Select Inscriptions*, pp. 281, 349. It is thus not impossible that the numbers refer to the length of the rods in cubits. Pargiter did not consider the price, viz. 4 gold *Dīnāras*=64 silver *Rūpakas*, at which a *Kulyavāpa* of waste land was sold (cf. *Select Inscriptions*, p. 343 note). If 6 Indo-British Rupees of 1912 were equal to one Akbarī Rupee (cf. Moreland, *India at the Death of Akbar*, p. 52), the purchasing power of a Gupta *Rūpaka* was more than 12 Rupees of 1912. The price of one *Bighā* of good land in most parts of the Faridpur District was even much less than Rs. 64 in 1912.

2. 1 seer=2 pounds, and 40 seers=1 maund.

weights of the *kulya*, *droṇa* and *āḍhaka* as recognized by the Bengali authors, especially writers on Smṛti who apparently relied on the authority handed down from old through a succession of teachers. The traditional weight can moreover be tested by a measurement of 8192 handful of paddy for a *kulya*. It should also be noticed that the scheme of 1 *kulya*=8 *droṇa*=32 *āḍhaka* perfectly tallies with the other scheme of 1 *Kulyavāpa*= 8 *Droṇavāpas*=32 *Āḍhavāpas*. It therefore appears that one *Kulyavāpa* of land originally required seeds or seedlings of 12 maunds 32 seers, or 16 maunds, of paddy.

Both the systems of planting seedlings and of sowing seeds are prevalent in Bengal, the first in some parts and the second in others, though, in certain localities like the Faridpur District, both the practices are followed. It is said that one maund of paddy seeds is required for 3 *Bīghās* for sowing, while seedling of the same weight of paddy require 10 *Bīghās* for transplanting. Seedlings of one *kulya* (12 maunds 32 seers, or 16 maunds) of paddy would thus require 128 *Bīghās* or 160 *Bīghās* of land for plantation. A *Kulyavāpa* would therefore appear to have been originally equal to 128 to 160 *Bīghās*, a *Droṇavāpa* to 16 to 20 *Bīghās*, and an *Āḍhavāpa* to 4 to 5 *Bīghās*. If the original calculation was based on the system of sowing seeds and not of transplanting seedlings, the position would be : 1 *kulyavāpa*=38 to 48 *Bīghās* ; 1 *Droṇavāpa* = $4\frac{1}{2}$ to 6 *Bīghās*; 1 *Āḍhavāpa*=$1\frac{1}{8}$ to $1\frac{1}{2}$ *Bīghās*. The original meaning of the root *vap*, 'to sow', seems to support the second alternative.

The *Droṇa* or *Droṇavāpa* was also known in certain regions outside Bengal and its neighbourhood. Thus the Pandukesvar plates[1] refer to its prevalence in the Kumaun-Garhwal area along with two other land measures called *Nālikāvāpa* and *Khārīvāpa*. The word *nālikā* is however not recognized in the Sanskrit lexicons in the sense of a measure of capacity. But Childers' *Pali Dictionary* seems to suggest that *nālī* or *nāḷī* (i.e. *nālikā*) was originally regarded as the same as *prastha* recogni-

1. *Ep. Ind.*, Vol. XXXI, p. 292.

sed in Sanskrit lexicons to be the one-sixteenth part of a *droṇa*. Thus the *Nālikāvāpa* appears to have been originally $\frac{1}{16}$ of the *Droṇavāpa* and $\frac{1}{4}$ of an *Āḍhavāpa*. Since the *khārī* was usually regarded as equal to 16 *droṇas*, a *Khārīvāpa* of land appears originally to have been sixteen times a *Droṇavāpa*. Another *vāpa*-ending land measure is the *Khaṇḍukavāpa* of the Penukonda plates of the Western Gaṅga king Mādhava, which record the grant of a plot of land measuring 65 *Kedāras* and 27 *Khaṇḍukavāpas*.[1]

Besides the *Kulyavāpa*, *Droṇavāpa* and *Āḍhavapa*, some other land measures are known from the post-Gupta inscriptions descovered in Bengal.[2] The Belwa plate[3] of Vigrahapāla III (third quarter of the 11th century A.D.) speaks of a locality which was divided into two parts, one of which measuring 1 *Kulya* 2 *Droṇas* 3¼ *Āḍhavāpas* and 3½ *Udamānas* was left out, while the second part measuring 3 *Kulyas* 7½ *Droṇas* and 11 *Udamānas* was made the subject of a grant. The land granted by the Amgachi plate[4] of the same king seems to have measured 6 *Kulyas* 2 *Droṇas* 1¼ *Āḍhavāpas* 2 *Udamānas* and 3 *Kākiṇīs*.

It may be pointed out that, in ancient Bengal, sometimes *Droṇa* (*Droṇavāpa*) and *Āḍhavāpa* were each regarded as the standard land-measure like the *Kulya* (*Kulyavāpa*) in the above record of Vigrahapāla III and in the other inscriptions referred to before. The Govindapur plate[5] of Lakṣmaṇasena (1179-1206 A.D.) gives the measurement of the gift land as 60 *Droṇas* and 17 *Unmānas*. It will be seen that 60 *Droṇas* would make 7 *Kulyas* and 4 *Droṇas*, or 7½ *Kulyas*. The Tarpandighi plate[6] of the same king speaks of a piece of land measuring 120 *Āḍhavāpas* and 5 *Unmānas*. Now 120 *Āḍha*-

1. *Select Inscriptions*, p. 457, note 7. For the land measures called *Khaṇḍuga*, *Śolaga* and *Kolaga* in medieval records of the Kannaḍa area, see *Ep. Carn.*, Vol. II, No. 335.

2. *IHQ*, Vol. XXVI, pp. 309 ff. Corrections have been suggested here in the reading and interpretation of some of the epigraphic passages referred to in the following lines.

3. *Ep. Ind.*, Vol. XXIX, pp. 9 ff.

4. Ibid., Vol. XV, pp. 293 ff.

5. N. G. Majumdar, *Inscriptions of Bengal*, Vol. III, p. 96.

6. Ibid., p. 102.

vāpas were actually equal to 30 *Droṇas* (*Droṇavāpas*), or 3 *Kulyas* (*Kulyavāpas*) and 6 *Droṇas* (*Droṇavāpas*). It is interesting to note that even the *Unmāna*, which is mentioned in these records as a subdivision of the *Āḍhavāpa*, is referred to as the standard land measure in the Vaṅgīya Sāhitya Pariṣad plate of Viśvarūpasena. In line 59 of this record,[2] the word *unmāna* has been used as a synonym of *udāna* which is mentioned in numerous places. Apparently the same *Unmāna* = *Udāna* is mentioned in the Amgachhi and Belwa plates referred to above as *Udamāna*.

The relation of *Udamāna-Unmāna-Udāna* and of its subdivision, the *Kākinī*, with the *Āḍhavāpa* is difficult to determine. The word *kākinī* seems to be the same as *Kāṇī* which is a land-measure even now prevalent in many parts of Bengal, although the area indicated by the *Kāṇī* is not the same in different places. According to Hunter,[3] a *Kāṇī* is a little above an acre in the Dacca and Mymensing Districts. It is regarded as $\frac{1}{6}$ of a *Doṇ* (*Droṇa*) in the Mymensingh District, while in the Faridpur District, 30 *Kāṇīs* are regarded as equal to a *Pākhī* (3622 square cubits) of land. This would make the *Kāṇī* about 120 square cubits. In Sandvip in the Noakhali District, 4 *Kaḍās* make 1 *Gaṇḍā*, 20 *Gaṇḍās* make 1 Kāṇī and 16 *Kāṇīs* make 1 *Doṇ* or *Droṇa*.[4] This scheme would suggest that the ancient *Kākinī* (modern *Kāṇī*) was $\frac{1}{16}$ of a *Droṇa* or *Droṇavāpa*. None of these indications is however supported by the inscriptions.

The Anulia plate[5] speaks of the area of a plot of land as 1 *Pāṭaka* 9 *Droṇas* 1 *Āḍhavāpa* 37 *Unmānas* and 1 *Kākinī*. According to the Gunaighar plate,[6] a *Pāṭaka* was equal to 40 *Droṇavāpas* (i.e. 5 *Kulyavāpas*). Thus here a land measure much bigger than the *Kulyavāpa* and *Droṇavāpa* is found in use.[7]

1. Ibid., pp. 143-48.
2. Cf. ibid., p. 179, note 8.
3. *A Statistical Account of Bengal*, Vol. V, pp. 95, 448.
4. See *Select Inscriptions*, p. 332.
5. Majumdar, op. cit., p. 87.
6. *Select Inscriptions*, p. 332.
7. The Saktipur plate (*Ep. Ind.*, Vol. XXI, pp. 216 ff.) of Lakṣmaṇasena uses the word *pāṭaka* both in the sense of a land measure and in that of a part of a village.

Another land-measure bigger than the *Kulyavāpa* and *Droṇavāpa* was the *Khārī* or *Khārikā* which is known from records like the Madhainagar plate of Lakṣmaṇasena.[1] This is no doubt the same as the *Khārikā°* or *Khārīvāpa* of the *Amarakoṣa.*[2] As 16 *droṇas* are known to have made one *khārī*, the *Khārīvāpa* was apparently equal originally to 16 *Droṇas* or *Droṇavāpas*, i.e. to 2 *Kulyas* or *Kulyavāpas*. In some records the *Hala* is mentioned as a bigger unit than the *Droṇa* or *Droṇavāpa*; cf. a plot of land measuring 2 *Halas* and 6 *Droṇas* in the Dhulla plate[3] of Śrīcandra.

The Anulia plate shows that an *Āḍhavāpa* was equal to more than 37 *Unmānas* (*Udamānas* or *Udānas*) and, since the *Kākinī* was a sub-division of the *Unmāna*, a much higher number of the former would have been regarded as equal to an *Āḍhavāpa*. That the number of *Unmānas* in an *Āḍhavāpa* was even bigger than that suggested by the above inscription is actually known from the Naihati (Sitahati) plate[4] of Ballālasena (1159-79 A.D.), which speaks of an area measuring 7 *Pāṭakas* 9 *Droṇas* 1 *Āḍhaka* (*Āḍhavāpa*) 40 *Unmānas* and 3 *Kākas*. Whether *Kāka* mentioned here is the same as *Kākinī* of the other records or whether the former was a sub-division of the latter cannot be determined; but it is known from the above inscription that more than 40 *Unmānas* made one *Āḍhavāpa*.

The Sundarban plate[5] of Lakṣmaṇasena seems to give the measurement of the gift land as 3 *Droṇas* 1 *Āḍhavāpa* 23 *Unmānas* and $2\frac{1}{2}$ *Kākinīs*. It appears from this epigraph that the area of the *Unmāna* was theoretically 32×32 cubits=

1. Majumdar, *Inscriptions of Bengal*, Vol. III, p. 112.

2. *Vaiśya-varga*, verse 10. As indicated above, *Khārīvāpa* is mentioned in some records like the Pandukesvar plates.

3. *Ep. Ind.*, Vol. XXXIII, p. 137.

4. Majumdar, op. cit., p. 74.

5. Ibid., p. 171. The inscription possibly also refers to the cubit (*hasta*) of 36 *aṅgulas* or 27 inches and to the measuring rod (*daṇḍa=nala*) of 32 cubits of the above length. Cf. Hunter's reference to the cubit of $20\frac{3}{4}$ inches as prevalent in Sandvip in the Noakhali District and of 34 inches in certain areas of the Faridpur District, and also the measuring rod of 56 cubits mentioned in the Anulia plate. Hunter refers to the measuring rod of 22 cubits of 34 inches each prevalent in the Naldi Pargana of the Faridpur District.

704 square cubits corresponding to about $\frac{1}{9}$ of a *Bīghā*, although actually, in the present case, it was 2304 square cubits, as the cubit is said specially to have been 36 *aṅgulas* in length instead of the usual 24 *aṅgulas*. This is not quite irreconcilable with the details gathered from other inscriptions discussed above. Since, as we have seen above, the *Āḍhavāpa* was originally equal to about 5 *Bīghās* and the *Unmāna* may have been about $\frac{1}{9}$ of a *Bīghā*, it is possible to suggest that 45 *Unmānas* made one *Āḍhavāpa*. But it is impossible to be sure on this point in the present state of our knowledge, especially because the records of Vigrahapāla III appear to suggest that the number of *Udamānas* in an *Āḍhavāpa* was divisible by 4 and was therefore an even number like 44, 48, 52, 56 or 60.

A passage in the unsatisfactorily preserved Bhowal or India Office plate of Lakṣmaṇasena[1] seems to give the area of the gift land as 1 *Droṇa* 1 *Āḍha* 28 *Gaṇḍās minus* 1 *Kāka* and therefore to mention *Gaṇḍā*, instead of *Udamāna-Unmāna*=*Udāna* as a subdivision of *Āḍha*, no doubt the same as *Āḍhaka* or *Āḍhavāpa*. It may be suggested that *Kāka* is the same as *Kākinī* and *Gaṇḍā* is no other than *Udamāna*=*Unmāna*=*Udāna*. But it is also possible that both *Gaṇḍā* and *Kāka* were smaller than *Kākinī*. The second suggestion seems to be supported by the relation between the *Gaṇḍā* and *Kānī* (i.e. *Kākinī*) as known in many parts of Bengal at the present time. The word *kāka* is now used in Bengal to indicate a denomination which is $\frac{1}{4}$ of a *kaḍā* (cowrie) and $\frac{1}{16}$ of a *gaṇḍā*.

Among other land measures mentioned in early inscriptions, we may refer to the *Pādāvarta* found in certain records from Western India[2] and the *Ṭimpīra*, *Timpīra* or *Timpira* noticed in some epigraphs of the Orissa region.[3] Nothing however is known about the exact area of the second of the two. Monier-Williams understood a *pādāvarta* as one square foot;

1. *Ep. Ind.*, Vol. XXVI, p. 9, text line 41.
2. Cf. ibid., Vol. XXXI, p. 299 and note 2.
3. Ibid., Vol. XXIX, pp. 39-40.

but the areas mentioned in inscriptions suggest a bigger unit.[1] Fleet therefore thought that '100 *Pādāvartas*' means 'a plot of ground measuring a hundred feet each way', i.e. 10000 square feet rather than 100 square feet.[2] In West Indian records of the early medieval period, we have often reference to fixation of the rent of a *Viṁśopaka* at 24 or 20 or 16 or 10 *Drammas* (coins probably of silver).[3] *Viṃśopaka* here no doubt means a land measure which was one twentieth of the standard measure of land in the area in question. The amounts of rent fixed for various grades of land would suggest that the *Viṁśopaka* was a fairly large area of land. The Caulukya records sometimes mention a land measure called *Pātha* which is regarded as equal to 240 square *cubits*.[4]

The inscriptions of the Imperial Gaṅgas of Orissa mention the *Vāṭī* (*Vāṭi* or *Vāṭikā*), *Māna* (*Māṇa*) and *Guṇṭha* which are even now prevalent in that region.[5] As at present times, 25 *Guṇṭhas* made one *Māna*, 20 of which made one *Vāṭī* also in the age of the Imperial Gaṅgas. A *Māna* is now regarded as equal to an acre, though its exact area in the medieval age cannot be determined.

In the records of the Kannaḍa-speaking area, we have mention, besides *Nivartana* or *Mattaru* referred to above, of the *Hāda* (i.e. Sanskrit *Pāda* really meaning one-fourth of the standard land measure) and *Kamma* (also found as *kamba*, *kambha*, *stambha*, etc.).[6] 4 *Hādas* were regarded as equal to 1 *Mattaru* (*Nivartana*) since an inscription of 1218 A.D. speaks of 2+2+1+1 (i.e. 6) *Hādas* as the same as 1 *Mattaru* and 2 *Hādas*.[7] The same inscription suggests that 100 *Kambas* or *Kammas* made 1 *Mattaru* since it equates 2 *Hādas*+35 *Kambas*+

1. Thus a *vāpī* or step-well is stated in a record to have covered an area of 32 *Pādāvartas* only (*Ep. Ind.*, Vol. XXXI, p. 303, text lines 19-20).
2. *CII*, Vol. III, p. 170, note 4.
3. Cf. A. K. Majumdar, *The Chaulukyas of Gujarat*, p. 244.
4. Ray, *DHNI*, Vol. II, p. 1008 and note 3.
5. *Ep. Ind.*, Vol. XXVIII, pp. 188-89, 192-93.
6. Cf. *Ep. Carn.*, Vol. VIII, Sb. 135; *Ep. Ind.*, Vol. XIII, p. 21, text line 44.
7. *Ep. Carn.*, Vol. VIII, Sb. 135.

1 *Hāda*+35 *Kambas*+35 *Kambas*+ 35 *Kambas* (i.e. 3 *Hādas* and 140 *Kambas*) with 2 *Mattarus* and 15 *Kambas*.

In the Tamil inscriptions, mention is made, besides the *Nivartana* or *Paṭṭi* referred to above, of the *Pāḍagam* (Sanskrit *Pāṭaka*) which consisted of 240 *Kuḻis*. But the largest popular unit was the *Veli* which was equal to $6\frac{1}{4}$ *Pāḍagams* and was divided into smaller units like *Mā* ($\frac{1}{20}$ of a *Veli*), *Kāṇi* ($\frac{1}{80}$ of a *Veli*; cf. *Mukkāṇi*=3 *Kanis*, *Araikkāṇi*=$\frac{1}{2}$ of a *Kāṇi*, etc.), *Muntirigai* ($\frac{1}{320}$ of a *Veli*), etc.[1] A number of other land measures, found especially in medieval records, are mentioned in our *Glossary*.

7. *Personal and Family Names*

The names of persons and families in different parts of India exhibit a great diversity so much so that many of them can be easily located in particular areas of the country. Thus personal names like Subrahmaṇya and Mahāliṅga and family names like Ayyar and Aiyangar are only found in the South,[2] while names like Rāsavihārī (pronounced *Rāśbihāri*) Harekṛṣṇa, etc., and cognomens like Mukhopādhyāya, Vasu, etc., are only expected in the East. Similarly, names with the suffixes *appa* and *amma* (*ambal* in Tamil) for males and females respectively can only be expected in particular areas of the South. In the West, family names are often formed by suffixing the word *kar* to the name of the locality from which the family in question originally hailed (e.g. Bījāpurkar, 'one whose family hails from Bījāpur'), while in the South the name of the locality itself is usually the family name which is placed before personal names. The name of the father is often added to one's name in these parts. But while, in Western names like Devadatta Rāmakṛṣṇa Bhāṇḍārkar, the first is the personal name, the second is the father's name and the last contains

1. Mahalingam, *South Indian Polity*, pp. 150-15, 156.

2. The South offers us some lengthy presonal and geographical names, e.g., *Viṣṇurudraśivalānandaśātakarṇi*, *Veṅkoṭanarasiṁharājuvaripeṭa*, etc. Note also—Mr. Rāmasvāmi's son Mr. Veṅkaṭarāman. For some personal and family names, see above, pp. 341-42, 376.

the name of a locality, in Southern names like Sarvepalli Rāmasvāmi Veṅkaṭarāmaṇ, the order is—first the family name which is the name of a locality, then the father's name and finally the personal name. Even the same name is pronounced and written differently in different parts; e.g. personal names—Gaṇapati=Gaṇpat, Kaṇabadi; Kṛṣṇa=Kiṣen, Kriṣen, Kruṣṇa and Kiruṣṇaṇ[1]; family names (professional)—Śreṣṭhin=Seṭh and Ceṭṭi, etc. Some such regional peculiarities are also noticed in inscriptions even of early times. Thus early inscriptions of South India, especially of the Telugu and Kannaḍa-speaking areas, often mention male and female names with the suffix *aṇṇaka* or *annaka* and *aṇṇikā* or *annikā* respectively. This peculiarity is not noticed in other parts of the country. Names like Saḍaiya-Māraṇ, i.e. 'Māraṇ, son of Saḍaiyaṇ', are also often found in South Indian records and not elsewhere.

Nāmakaraṇa or naming the child is a rite of considerable importance and we have copper-plate grants recording gifts made by kings on the occasion of the naming ceremony of the princes.[2] The Vedic literature often refers to two, three or four names of a person. Some authorities think that the four names were : (1) one derived from the *nakṣatra* on which the person was born,[3] (2) a secret name (after a *nakṣatra* according to some Gṛhyasūtras), (3) a popular name, and (4) one like *Somayājin* due to one's performance of a *Somayāga*. The three names are often taken to be (1) the ordinary name, (2) a name derived from the father and (3) one derived from the *gotra* or from the name of a remote ancestor; e.g., (1) Trasadasyu (ordinary name), Paurukutsya (son of Purukutsa) and Gairikṣita (descendant of Girikṣit); (2) Indrota (ordinary name), Daivāpa (son of Devāpi) and Śaunaka (belonging to the Śaunaka *gotra*). In the Vedic literature, a person is also often mentioned after a locality (e.g., Kaśu Caidya,

1. The Sanskrit name *Kṛṣṇa*, from which the Bengali name *Kānāi*, etc., are derived, was modified in the South as *Kannara*, *Kandara*, *Kandhara*, *Kannāra*, *Kandāra* and *Kandhāra*, sometimes re-Sanskritised as *Karṇa*.

2. Bhandarkar's List, No. 369.

3. Such names are rare in the Vedic literature probably because they were the secret names. They became quite common in later times.

'Kaśu of the Cedi country'; Bhīma Vaidarbha, 'Bhīma of the Vidarbha country'), while sometimes a metronymic was added to the personal name (e.g. Prahlāda Kāyādhava, 'Prahlāda, son of Kayādhū'; Mahidāsa Aitareya, 'Mahidāsa, son of Itarā'). The Gṛhyasūtras have a variety of rules regarding the formation of personal names though they are often conflicting, and we have names which do not conform to the rules. Some Sūtras prescribe names having two parts, e.g., Deva-datta, while others suggest names derived from a sage, a deity (the family deity according to some) or an ancestor, though giving the name of a deity itself is forbidden by others. Some authorities prescribe the naming of a boy after any of the ancestors excepting the father. It is interesting in this connection to note that there are innumerable epigraphical instances of the grandfather and grandson having the same name (e.g. the Gupta emperor Candragupta I and his grandson Candragupta II),[1] while some cases of the father and son having the same name are known from South India (e.g. Later Cālukya Someśvara I Āhavamalla and his son and successor Someśvara II Bhuvanaikamalla). According to some authorities, girls should not be named after *nakṣatras,* trees and rivers.

All the types of names referred to above, both prescribed and forbidden, are found in inscriptions belonging to different parts of India and different ages of history. People were often named after epic and Puranic pesonages as well as after persons famous in literature. The meaning of a large number of personal names (as also geographical names) is unintelligible apparently because they were often influenced by the local dialects.

A tendency to distinguish the names of persons belonging to the different *Varṇas* gradually developed. The *Manusmṛti* (II. 31-32), for instance, suggests that an *upapada* suggestive of *śarman* (happiness), *rakṣā* (protection), *puṣṭi* (prosperity) and *preṣya* (service) should be added to the names of Brāhmaṇas, Kṣatriyas, Vaiśyas and Śūdras respect-

1. Girls were likewise named after the grandmother (*Ep. Ind.*, Vol. XXXI, p. 102).

ively. This soon developed into the prescription of later authorities to the effect that the words *śarman* or *deva*, *varman* or *trātṛ*, *bhūti* or *datta*, and *dāsa* should be suffixed to personal names of the four *Varṇas* respectively.[1] Epigraphical evidence shows, however, that this custom was not popular long before the Gupta age, although it may be noticed in some cases in earlier records. The issuers of many coins who, flourished in several localities in North India shortly before and after the beginning of the Christian era, had names ending in *mitra*. Among ruling families, the name-ending *varman* is for the first time found popular in the Pallava dynasty of Kāñcī, which seems to have become powerful about the close of the third century A.D., although the Pallavas appear to have originally been Brāhmaṇas of the Bhāradvāja *gotra*.[2] The successors of Mayūraśarman, the Brāhmaṇa founder of the Kadamba dynasty of Banavāsi, assumed names ending in *varman*.[3] In the Mattepad plates of the 5th century A.D., the names of a number of Brāhmaṇa donees are mentioned with the suffix *ajja* (Sanskrit *ārya*; cf. the family name Ayyar and personal names like Rāmayya in particular areas of the South).[4]

The custom, referred to above, is intimately related to the development of family names out of name-endings. We have referred above to the coins of many North Indian kings having names ending in *mitra*. Most of the rulers of the Śuṅga dynasty, founded by Puṣyamitra about 185 B.C., had names ending in *mitra*. A large number of current family names in Bengal (e.g. Ghoṣa, Vasu, Mitra, Pāla, Datta, etc.) were no doubt derived in the same way. But the process was not complete in East India even in the early medieval period. The successors of Candragupta I (c. 319-40 A.D.), who was the son of Ghaṭotkaca and grandson of Gupta, all assumed names ending in *gupta* and thus led to the development of the

1. Kane , op. cit., pp. 250-51. See, however, Bodhiśarman of the mercantile community mentioned in a Nagarjunikonda inscription (*Select Inscriptions*, p. 225, text line 2).

2. Cf. *Suc. Sāt. L. Dec.*, pp. 390-91.

3. Ibid., p. 92-93.

4. Ibid., p. 62.

name of the Gupta dynasty. Similarly, the successors of Gopāla I (c. 750-70 A.D.), who was the son of Vapyaṭa and the grandson of Dayitaviṣṇu, all assumed names ending in *pāla* and thus gave rise to the name of the Pāla dynasty. But the popularity of framing family names even among ordinary people of Eastern India is attested by inscriptions like the Dubi and Nidhanpur copper-plate grants of king Bhāskaravaran (c. 600-50 A.D.), in which the Brāhmaṇa donees, belonging to particular *gotras* and *śākhās* and no doubt also to the same families, are found to have generally names ending in the same word such as *ghoṣa*, *soma*, *pālita*, *deva*, *kuṇḍa*, *nāga*, *bhūti*, *sena*, *mitra*, etc.[1] It may be noted that most of these Brahmanical names do not conform to the prescription of certain authorities regarding the name-endings, to which reference has already been made above. Another interesting fact is that no Brāhmaṇa family of the Bengal-Assam region is now known as Ghoṣa, Soma,etc., which are nowadays popular non-Brāhmanical family names. This apparently shows that a number of Brāhmaṇa families have been merged into the non-Brāhmaṇa communities in the area in question. Another fact to which attention may be drawn in this connection is that there are cases in which the uniformity of the name-ending is distrurbed by a few names. Thus the names of ten out of the eleven kings of the so-called Later Gupta dynasty of East Malwa and Magadha end in the word *gupta* with the exception only of the name of Ādityasena.

Inscriptions of the early centuries, especially of South India, often mention persons, of both royal and ordianary ranks, with metronymics like *Gautamīputra*, 'one born of a lady belonging to the Gautama *gotra*'. There is no doubt that the *gotra* mentioned in such cases is that of the father of a woman and not that of her husband. This shows that some of the popular forms of marriage in ancient India did not involve the *gotr-āntara* (i.e. the change of the wife's paternal *gotra* to that of her husband) at the time of her marriage.[2]

1. *Ep. Ind.*, Vol. XXX, pp. 290-91; *Kāmarūpaśāsnāvalī*, pp. 33 ff.
2. Cf. *Proc. IHC*, Annamalainagar, 1945, pp. 48 ff.; cf. above, pp. 335-36.

Family names derived from official or professional designations (e.g. Śreṣṭhin, Senāpati, etc.) are met with especially in medieval records. The original habitat of the family of the Brāhmaṇa donee is often indicated in the copper-plate grants. The South Indian type of family names which are generally those of the villages to which the families belong or originally belonged, is noticed in medieval inscriptions. Some medieval records of Bengal (e.g. the Mehar plate of Dāmodara[1]) mention the Brāhmaṇa donees often with reference to their original home, e.g. Kesarakoṇī 'one having the original home of one's family at Kesarakoṇā'. Such appelations are called *gāñī* (from Sanskrit *grāmīṇa*). In Mithilā, the localities known as *mūla-grāma* are mentioned, since the medieval age, along with personal names, as in *Sodarapura-saṁ-śrī-Rāmadevaśarmā*, in which *saṁ* probably stands for *sambhūta*, 'sprung'.

8. *Miscellaneous Terms*

Besides the categories discussed above, techinical expressions of various other kinds are often noticed in Sanskrit inscriptions. We have referred in the course of our discussion to words like *utkoṭa*, *umbara*, *setikā*, *paṅga*, etc. These are not recognised in Sanskrit lexicons. But the first three are found in Prakrit in the forms *ukkoḍa*, *uṁmara* and *seiā* or *seigā*, while the last is apparently borrowed from the Dravidian language. There are numerous other cases of these types. Besides there are many expressions of the Deśī class, the meanings of which are uncertain, to some of which reference has been made above. Again, we have sometimes expressions which are Sanskrit, though the meanings in which they are used in the inscriptions are not recognised in the Sanskrit lexicons. Only a few items of the various categories can be mentioned here.

Among words which can be traced in Prakrit but which are not recognised in Sanskrit lexicons, we may further refer to *varṇikā* and *chimpaka* used in Viṣṇuṣeṇa's charter.[2] They are respectively the same as Prakrit *vanniā* meaning 'a sample'

1. *Ep. Ind.*, Vol. XXVII, pp. 182 ff.
2. Ibid., Vol. XXX, pp. 177-78.

and *chimpaya* meaning 'a dyer of clothes'. Sometimes Prakrit words were wrongly Sanskritised. Reference may be made in this connection to *utkṛṣṭi* derived from Prakrit *ukkuṭṭhi* (Sanskrit *utkrośa*) meaning 'wailing'.[1] Similar is the case with *ḍheṅku-kaḍḍhaka* and *nīla-ḍumphaka* which appear to have been imperfectly Sanskritised.[2]

There are many words of Dravidian origin used in the Sanskrit inscriptions. An interesting word of this category is *pukkoli*, *pukkūli* or *pukkolli* found in certain Sanskrit inscriptions from the Kannaḍa-speaking area in expressions like *pukkoli-kṣetra* or *pukkoli-khajjana*. The word *khajjana*, also spelt *khajjaṇa*, *khajjāna*, *khajjaṇaka*, etc., is the same as Marāṭhī *khājaṇ*. It is a Sanskritised Deśī word meaning 'the area [near the sea-shore], on which a thin layer of sand accumulates after the ebb-tide coming through inlets' and 'a rice field created out of such an area near a hillock by erecting embankments on the three other sides', or 'a field created by reclamation of the river-bed'.[3] We were formerly inclined to regard the word *pukkoli*, *pukkūli* or *pukkolli* as derived from *poṁkalu* found in records of the Telugu-speaking area in the sense of Telugu *pokalu* meaning arecanuts[4] and *pukkoli-kṣetra* as a piece of land having an arecanut plantation on it.[5] It would then be the same as *guvāka-vāstu-bhū* or *kalana*, a Bengali word not found in Bengali lexicons, but mentioned in the Vaṅgīya Sāhitya Pariṣad plate[6] of Viśvarūpasena of Bengal. A recently published inscription however suggests that *pukkoli* and its variants mean 'land inundated by floods [of the ebb-tide]'. It would thus mean a kind of field similar to *khajjana*.

The number of Deśī words of uncertain meaning found in inscriptions is too many. Viṣṇuṣeṇa's charter uses such

1. Ibid., p. 171.

2. Ibid., p. 172. Cf. *āvedana* (tax) from Oḍiyā āvadānā (Vol. XXXIII, p. 292).

3. Ibid., Vol. XXXIII, pp. 53-54.

4. Ibid., Vol. VI, p. 238, text line 145; Vol. XII, p. 196, text line 165.

5. Ibid., Vol. XXXV, p. 152.

6. N. G. Majumdar, *Ins. Beng.*, Vol. III, p. 146 (text line 50), p. 147 (text lines 55 and 59).

expressions as *khovā*, *kelā*, *bharolaka*, *dosya*, *allavāṭa*, *lakaṭā*, etc., the meanings of which are not definitely known.[1]

Among Sanskrit words with modified meaning we may refer to the following expressions in Viṣṇuṣena's charter : *chātra* (literally 'an umbrella-bearer' but actually the leader of a group of Pāiks, Piādas or Peons), *karaṇa* (court), *vārika* (official), *atiyātrika* (tax for crossing the boundary), *vahitra* (wagon carrying merchandise), *viṁśopaka* (a particular coin), *avalokyā* (detection), *dhārmika* (a levy in the name of a religious festival), *prāveśya* (entry tax), *nairgamika* (exit tax), etc.[2] The word *vārika* is used in some records in the sense of a temple superintendent like the Paṇḍā of today.[3] The Midnapur plates of the time of Śaśāṅka not only uses the word *karaṇa* in the sense of *adhikaraṇa* but also *adhi* or *ādhi* for *adhikaraṇika* or *ādhikaraṇika* in a verse.[4] In medieval inscriptions from Orissa, the king is sometimes indicated in expressions like *śrī-hasta* and *śrī-caraṇa*.[5] The words *kīrti*, *kīrtana* and *kīrtanā* are sometimes used to indicate a performance (e.g., a temple, an image, a grant of land, etc.) calculated to render the person responsible for it famous.[6] The word *pūrvā* is often used with special reference to a *praśasti* (eulogy) or *tithi* (lunar day) even though essentially it means 'the above' i.e. the above-quoted or above-mentioned thing in the faminine gender.[7]

1. Ibid., pp. 171, 175-178.

2. Ibid., pp. 171, 173-76. Some interesting words in the same record are : *hrasita*, *śayanīy-āsana-siddhānna*, *abhyupāgama*, *rājārghikā*, *rājakule=dhikaraṇa*, *reṣa*, *āvedanaka*, *rāja-graha*, *prapāpūraka*, *arth-ābhiyukta*, *pratisamāsana*, *abhilekhitaka*, *grāhya*, *māna-pautava*, *peṭavika-vārika*, *vinaya*, *uttara-kulika-vārika*, *chala*, *mudrāpacāra*, *saṁvadana*, *jayika*, *bhāṣā*, *ullambana*, *karṇatroṭaṇa*, *tauṇḍika*, *caturtha*, *grahaṇaka*, *daṇḍaka*, *gañja*, *kalvapāla-vārika*, *śoṭī*, *nīla-kuṭī*, *yantra-kuṭī*, *varṣa-paryuṣita*, *bhāṇḍa-bhṛta-vahitra*, *śulk-ātiyātrika*, *mahiṣ-oṣṭra-bharaka*, *poṭṭalikā-saṁkācitaka*, *kaṇikkā*, *vara-yātrā*, *madya-vahanaka*, *khalla*, *pāda-ghaṭa*, *chimpaka*, *kolika*, *padakāra*, *paṭṭaka-dhārmika*, etc.

3. Ibid., Vol. XXXI, p. 164, note 1.

4. Cf. *Ind. Cult.*, Vol. IX, p. 121, note.

5. *Ep. Ind.*, Vol. XXVIII, p. 304. Such expressions were also used in other regions; cf. Tamil *Śrīpādakkol* meaning the measuring rod based on the length of the foot of the king (Kulottuṅgacoḷa I).

6. *CII*, Vol. III, pp. 212-13, note; *Ep. Ind.*, Vol. XXVIII, p. 184; Vol. XXXIII, p. 170.

7. Cf. *Ep. Ind.*, Vol. XXX, p. 123. Sometimes the word seems to be wrongly used as a synonym of *praśasti* or *tithi*.

We have referred above to the *Viṁśopaka* coin which is mentioned in Viṣṇuṣeṇa's charter along with the coin called *Rūpaka*. It seems to have been a copper coin, 20 of which made one silver coin called *Rūpaka*.[1] In this connection, it may be noticed that an interesting class of words found in inscriptions represents similar other names of coins.[2]

Some inscriptions of the time of the Śaka ruler Nahapāna (c. 119-24 A.D.) mention *Kārṣāpaṇa*, thirtyfive of which are stated to have been equal to the *Suvarṇa*. According to early Indian authorities, *Kārṣāpaṇa*, otherwise called *Purāṇa* or *Dharaṇa*, was a silver coin weighing 32 *Ratis* (58.56 grains) while Suvarṇa was a gold coin weighing 80 *Ratis* (146.4 grains), although the coins mentioned in the said inscriptions apparently refer respectively to the silver coins issued by Nahapāna and the gold coins of the Kuṣāṇa emperors.[3] The weight of the former was that of the Graeco-Persian *hemi-drachma* (43.2 grains) and of the latter that of the Roman *aurei* (124 grains).[4] A coin called *Dinārī-māṣaka* is known from the records of the Ikṣvākus of the 3rd and 4th centuries.[5] The word *dinārī* is derived from the name of the Roman silver coins called *Denarius* (124 grains) while *māṣaka* was an Indian coin which was one-sixteenth of the standard silver money. The *Dinārī-māṣaka* may have been the coins which were issued by the Ikṣvāku kings and were probably equal to one-sixteenth of the Roman Denarius in value at least theoretically.[6] The gold and silver coins of the Gupta emperors are called *Dīnāra* or *Suvarṇa* and *Rūpaka* respectively,[7] the weight of the former being originally

1. In some inscriptions of the Gujarat region, the word *viṃśopaka* is also used in the sense of a land measure which was apparently the 20th part of the standard measure of land. Cf. A.K. Majumdar, *The Chaulukyas of Gujarat*, p. 244.

2. Very often the designation of the standard coins also indicates 'money'.

3. *Select Inscriptions*, pp. 158-59, 162.

4. E. J. Rapson, *Indian Coins*, pp. 17, 21.

5. *Select Inscriptions*, p. 222. Cf. *dinnāra*(cowrie-shell) in the *Rājataraṅgiṇī*.

6. *Suc. Sāt. L. Dec.*, p. 27, note. Roman coins were in circulation in the Ikṣvāku kingdom and the neighbouring regions.

7. *Select Inscriptions*, pp. 273, 284, 286, 325, 330, 338-39, 344, etc.; *CII*, Vol. III, p. 265, etc. The Sanskrit part of an early Pāṇḍya inscription (*A.R. Ep.*, 1908, No. 136) records the gift of ten *Dīnāras* for a perpetual lamp, its Tamil counterpart using the word *Kāśu* for *Dīnāra*.

that of the Roman *aureus* and later that of the Indian *Suvarṇa*, while the latter followed the weight standard of the silver coins of the Śakas of Western India.

Sometimes coins were named after their issuer and remained in circulation for centuries after their actual issue. Thus the Anjaneri plates[1] (709 A. D.) of Sendraka Bhogaśakti refer to the currency of the coins called *Kṛṣṇarāja-rūpaka* in Western India. The *Kṛṣṇarāja-rūpaka* was the silver coin issued by the Kalacuri king Kṛṣṇarāja who ruled in the second half of the 6th century A.D.[2] Similar is the case with the *Ādivarāhadramma* and *Vigrahapāla-dramma* which were respectively silver coins issued by the Partihāra king Bhoja I Ādivarāha (c. 836-85 A.D.) and bearing the legend *śrīmad-Ādivarāha*, and those issued by a certain Vigrahapāla.[3] Similar names of coins issued by the Caulukyas of Gujarat are *Bhīma-priya-dramma* and *Vīsalapriya-viṁśopaka* known from some inscriptions.[5] The word *dramma*, found on certain copper coins issued by the Yaudheyas about the 3rd century A.D.,[4] was derived from Greek *drachma*, its old Attic standard being 67.5 grains although the Indo-Greeks adopted the Persian *siglos* standard of 86.45 grains.[6] Of the Muhammadan coin names *Dirham* and *Dām*, the first was derived from the Greek word and the second from its Indian form. Wilson's Glossary mentions the Dirham as a silver coin weighing about 50 grains. The Akbarī *Dām* (old *Dramma*) was a copper coin, 40 of which made a silver *Rūpīa* (Sanskrit *rūpya*, *rūpyaka*, i.e. Rupee) while $46\frac{1}{3}$

1. *Ep. Ind.*, Vol. XXV, p. 229; *The Classical Age*, p. 195.

2. The word *rūpaka* is found as *rūpa* in an early medieval epigraph from Orissa. *Rūpa* as a coin is found in Telugu.

3. V.A. Smith, *Catalogue*, pp. 239, 241, etc. The Siyadoni inscriptions mention *Pañciyaka-dramma* along with *Ādivarāha-dramma*, the former probably being a copper coin one-fourth of the latter in value (cf. *Ep. Ind.*, Vol. I, p. 178, text lines 37-38; Vol. XXX, pp. 212-13). Whether *Pañciyaka* was from *Pañca* (Pañcāyat) cannot be determined. The *Vigrahapāla-dramma*, probably also called *Vigrahatuṅga-dramma*, is mentioned in the Siyadoni inscriptions (cf. *Ep. Ind.*, Vol. I, pp. 167, 169).

4. A. K. Majundar, *The Chaulukyas of Gujarat*, pp. 269, 271. Caulukya inscriptions also mention the *Rūpaka* and *Kārṣāpaṇa* coins (ibid., p. 171).

5. *The Age of Imperial Unity*, p. 167; Smith, *Catalogue*, p. 182.

6. Rapson, op. cit., pp. 3, 6.

Alamgīrī *Dāms* made a Rupee. The proportionate rates varied in later times and were liable to great fluctuation. Another late medieval coin named *Dāmḍī*, sometimes regarded as equal to $3\frac{1}{8}$ or $3\frac{1}{4}$ *Dāms* or from 8 to 12 cowries, appears to have originated from the same source.[1] The *Dramma* is mentioned in medieval Tamil inscriptions as *Diramam*.[2] In the epigraphs of the Kannaḍa-speaking area, there are references to various kinds of *Drammas* such as *Gara-dramma*, *Dāya-dramma* and *Beḻḻiya-dramma*.[3] The expression *beḻḻiya-dramma* means 'silver *Dramma*'.

The medieval inscriptions of the Orissa region speak of a coin called *Māḍha* (sometimes called *Māḍhā*) which was of both gold and silver. Oḍiyā lexicons recognise the word in the sense of the weight of half a *Karṣa* or *Tolā*, i.e. 40 *Ratis*, although it is believed to have been regarded in later times to have been half this weight. The same name occurs in Telugu records as *Māḍa* which is explained in the lexicons as an old gold coin weighing about 25 grains.[4] Various kinds of *Māḍhas* or *Māḍas* are known from inscriptions, e.g. *Malla-māḍa*, *Malla-nandi-māḍa*, *Surabhi-māḍa*, *Gaṇḍa-māḍa*, *Kulottuṅga-māḍa*, *Gandhavāraṇa-māḍa* or *Gandhahasti-māḍa*, *Cāmara-māḍa*, *Uttama-gaṇḍa-māḍa*, *Padmanidhi-malla-māḍa*, *Rājarāja-māḍa*, *Rājendracoḻa-māḍa*, etc.[5] The *Gaṇḍa-māḍa* is sometimes also called *Kārṣāpaṇa*, *Niṣka* and *Gaṇḍa-niṣka*, although originally the weight of a silver and gold *Kārṣāpaṇa* was respectively 32 and 80 *Ratis* (i.e. 58.56 and 146.4 grains) and that of a gold *Niṣka* 4 *Suvarṇas* or 320 *Ratis* (585.6 grains). The epithet 'small' applied to the *Gaṇḍa-māḍa* in some records suggests that all the *Māḍaṣ* did not follow the same weight standard. The *Cāmara-māḍa* reminds us of the *Cāmara* coin of medieval Orissa, which weighed 4 *Ratis* and was probably also called *Cīnā*,

1. Cf. Wilson's Glossary, s. v. *Dām* and *Dāmrī*.
2. *SII*, Vol. IV, No. 813; Vol. VIII, No. 40.
3. See *A.R. Ep.*, 1933-34, B. K. No. 30; etc. Bhāskarācārya's *Līlāvatī* (I. 2), apparently referring to the Kannaḍa-Marāṭhī region of the 13th century, speaks of 20 Cowrie-shells=1 *Kākinī*, 4 *Kākinīs*=1 *Paṇa*, 16 *Paṇas*=1 *Dramma* [of silver], and 16 *Drammas*=1 *Niṣka* [of gold].
4. *JNSI*, Vol. XV, p. 139. The name is derived from Tamil *māḍa* or *māḍai* (Sanskrit *māṣa* or its modification *māṣā*).
5. Ibid., Vol. XVI, pp. 42-43.

ten of which were regarded as equal to a *Māḍa*. The *Rāja-rāja-māḍa* was probably issued by Cālukya Rājarāja I of Veṅgī and *Kulottuṅga-māḍa* or *Rājendracoḷa-māḍa* by the Coḷa-Cālukya king Rājendra Kulottuṅga I. Considering the meanings of the words in the names of the coins such as *malla* (a wrestler), *nandin* (Śiva's bull), *surabhi* (a mythical cow), *gaṇḍa* (a rhinoceros), *gandha-vāraṇa* or °*hastin* (an elephant in rut) and *cāmara* (a chowrie), it appears that these referred to particular representations on the coins. The word *padmanidhi* is sometimes used in inscripions in the sense of a sacred deposit made in the temple treasury and the *Padmanidhi-malla-māḍa* may have been a coin issued by the temples.

In Tamil inscriptions, the coins called *Kāśu* and *Māḍai* (the same as *Māḍa* of the Telugu epigraphs) are very often mentioned, sometimes in association with various names as in *Sambirānippalaṅ-gāśu*, *Rājarājaṉ-māḍai*, *Bhujabala-māḍai*, *Madhu-rāntakaṉ-māḍai*, etc.[1] An inscription[2] of 1050 A.D. equates one *Rājarājaṉ-māḍai* (i.e. *Maḍai* issued by the Coḷa king Rāja-rāja I, 985-1014 A.D.) with $1\frac{1}{8}$ *Kaḻañju* of gold, while another epigraph[3] speaks of one unspecified *Māḍai* as equal to $1\frac{3}{4}$ *Kaḻañjus*. Similarly two other inscriptions[4] of the 11th century equate one *Kaḻañju* of gold respectively with two *Kāśus* and one and six-twentieth *Kāśus*. The basis of the Tamil weight system was the *Mañjāḍi* which was regarded by medieval authors as $\frac{1}{20}$th of a *Kaḻañju* and equal to two *Ratis* of the North and has been equated with 4 grains in Wilson's Glossary.[5] The equation of the *Māḍai* and *Kāśu* with the *Kaḻañju* weight of gold in the above epigraphs shows that they were gold coins though there was difference either in the weight or in the metalic purity amongst different varieties of both the coins.[6] About the beginning of the 19th century, *Kāśu* (spelt

1. *SII*, Vol. V, Nos. 572, 520, 1361; *A. R. Ep.* 1915, No. 157.
2. Ibid., No. 520.
3. Ibid., No. 788.
4. Ibid., Vol. VIII, No. 737; Vol. V, No. 1356.
5. *JNSI*, Vol. XIII, p. 191.
6. Cf. ibid., Vol. XX, pp. 11-12. In recording the gift of gold coins to temples, Tamil inscriptions often specifically mention that they were not wanting in purity and weight and that the marks or impressions on them were in tact. Cf. ibid., p. 9; *Ep. Ind.*, Vol. XXX, p. 109.

Cash in English) was a small copper coin, 80 of which were taken as equal to a small silver coin called *Paṇam* (spelt *Fanam* in English), a name derived from Sanskrit *Paṇa* which was originally a copper coin weighing 80 *Ratis* (146.4 grains).[1] In the medieval period, *Paṇam* was the name of a small gold coin about 6 grains in weignt,[2] and was regarded sometimes as $\frac{1}{16}$ of a *Hūn* or *Varāha*, called Pagoda or Star Pagoda in English and weighing about 50 grains.[3] Ceylonese coins were called *Īḻa-kkāśu* in Tamil records and Chinese gold currency as *Cīna-kkanakam*.[4] The standard coin of the Koṅgu country in the north-western part of the Tamil-speaking area and in Kerala was called *Accu* which is supposed to have been a gold coin, one *Kaḻañju* in weight. In an inscription[5] of 1156 A.D., one *Accu* is equated with $9\frac{1}{4}$ *Kāśus*, *Kāśu* probably indicating a silver coin in this case. Inscriptions of the Koṅgu country mention various kinds of *Accus* such as *Ānai-accu*, *Nall-ānai-accu*, *Paḻamudal-accu*, *Paḻañjalāgai-accu*, *Paduccalāgai-accu*, *Amudan-accu*, *Uṇḍi-accu*, etc., with reference, in some cases,to the deviation from the standard fineness of their gold content. The word *ānai* suggests that the coins in question originally bore the representation of an elephant.[6]

We have referred above to the frequent reference to the *Dramma* in the medieval inscriptions of the Kannaḍa-speaking area. An equally popular coin of the same region was the *Gadyāṇa* or *Gadyāṇaka* (often contracted into *Ga* or *Gadyā*), various types of which are known from epigraphic records. Thus we have *Bhairava-gadyāṇa*, *Lokki-gadyāṇa*, *Aṅka-gadyāṇa*, *Gāva-gadyāṇa*, *Komarina-gadyāṇa*, *Priyaśrāha-Gajamalla-gadyāṇa*, *Ambili-gadyāṇa*, *Jagadaḻaṁ-gadyāṇa*, etc.[7] It is generally believed

1. Cf. Wilson's Glossary, s. v. *Kāśu*, *Pan*.
2. Hobson-Jobson, s. v. *Fanam*.
3. The word *pagoda* is now generally regarded as a corruption of *Bhagavatī*, i.e. the goddess Durgā. The coins often bore the representation of a deity or temple.
4. *JNSI*, Vol. XX, pp. 12-13.
5. *A. R. Ep.*, 1936-37, No. 68.
6. *JNSI*, Vol. XX, p. 14.
7. *Ep. Ind.*, Vol. XXXIII, p. 55; *SII*, Vol. XI, Part ii, No. 136, text line 55; *A. R. Ep.*, 1958-59, No. B 693 (transcript); Khare, *Sourc. Med. Hist.*

that the *Lokki-gadyāṇa* was the *Gadyāṇa* minted at Lokkiguṇḍi (modern Lakkundi in the Dharwar District). *Komarinagadyāna* reminds us of the tax called *Kumāra-gadyāna* mentioned in the inscriptions of the Gāhaḍavālas.[1] Gold coins were often called *Pon* or *Hon*, the word *ponnu* or *honnu* meaning 'gold' in Kannaḍa.[2] Probably the same coin was sometimes called *Niṣka*.[3] The Gadyāṇa was also called *Poṅ-Gadyāṇa* or *Gadyāṇa-ponnu* indicating that it was a gold coin. The said coin was in some cases called *Suvarṇa*. An inscription[4] of 1184 A.D. speaks of 2 *Paṇas* or *Haṇas* as the rate of annual interest on a *Gadyāṇa* or *Pon* and of 4 *Pons* accruing annually to 20 *Gadyāṇas*. One *Pon* or *Gaḍyāṇa* was therefore equal to 10 *Paṇas*. Coins called *Hāga* (*Bhāga*) and *Vīsa* and a particular variety of the latter known as *Lokkiya-vīsa* (possibly *Vīsa* minted at Lokki or Lokkiguṇḍi) are also known from inscriptions.[5] Five *Lokkiya-Vīsas* are stated to have been the interest on one *Pon* (*Gadyāṇa*) per month.[6] Mention is sometimes made of the 'big' and 'small' *Hāga* (*Bhāga*). The Brāhmaṇas of Salotgi (Bijapur District) were asked to pay to the local school, for the maintenance of its students, 5 *Puṣpas* (literally 'flowers') of good metal on the occasion of a marriage, half of the amount on that of an *upanayana* and half of the latter on that of a *cūḍākarman*.[7] Although the custom of offering gold and silver flowers to deities is known,[8] the *puṣpa* in the Salotgi records appears to mean a coin probably bearing the representation of a flower (cf. the *padmaṭaṅka*).

The inscriptions of the Senas of Bengal refer to the

Dek., pp. 27, 36; B. K. No. 154 of 1933-34. Bhāskarācārya's *Līlāvatī* (1.3) gives the weight of a *Gadyānaka* as follows : 2 *Yavas*=1 *Guñjā* or *Rati*; 4 *Ratis*=1 *Valla*, 8 *Vallas*=1 *Dharaṇa*, 2 *Dharaṇas*=1 *Gadyānaka*. A *Gadyānaka* was thus 48 *Ratis* in weight.

1. Cf. *Ep. Ind.*, Vol. IV, pp. 106, 109, etc. Cf. Tamil *Kumara-kaccāṇa*.
2. *A. R. Ep.*, 1933-34, B. K. No. 188.
3. Ibid., B. K. No. 153.
4. *SII*, Vol. XI, Part ii, p. 225 (No. 173, lines 55-56).
5. *A.R. Ep.*, 1933-34, B. K. No. 120.
6. Ibid., No. 185.
7. *Ep. Ind.*, Vol. IV, p. 58 and note 1.
8. Ibid., Vol. XXX, p. 86.

revenue-income of land in *Kapardaka-purāṇas*,[1] in which *kapardaka* means 'a cowrie-shell' and *purāṇa* the old silver coin 32 *Ratis* in weight, also called *Kārṣāpaṇa*. The expression *kapardaka-purāṇa* apparently means a *Purāṇa* counted in *Kapardakas*. This is because the Senas and other early medieval rulers of the Bengal region did not issue any coin and the transactions were carried on mostly in cowrie-shells. In the late medieval period, 80 cowries were usually regarded as equal to one *Paṇa* and 16 *Paṇas* as equal to one *Kāhaṇa* (Sanskrit *Kārṣāpaṇa*).

An inscription[2] from Nepal likewise mentions *Paṇa-purāṇa* which means 'a *Purāṇa* [of silver] counted in *Paṇas* [of copper]', the latter being the standard money of the land during the age in question.

1. N. G. Majumdar, *Inscriptions of Bengal*, Vol. III, pp. 63, 74, etc.
2. R. Gnoli, *Nepalese Inscriptions in Gupta Characters*, Part I, p. 122.

APPENDIX I

SPURIOUS EPIGRAPHS

Forgery of documents for the purpose of establishing one's title to a plot of land or some such object is well known throughout the ages. Students of Indian epigraphy are familiar with such records pertaining to the ancient and medieval periods, the earliest amongst them being the Nalanda and Gaya copper-plate grants[1] of Samudragupta (c. 335-76 A. D.). Similar records have been met with in all parts of India, though the southern part of the Kannaḍa-speaking area has been especially productive of them and has offered us some of the most bare-faced specimens purporting to have been issued by such legendary kings as Janamejaya of the *Mahābhārata*, whom tradition places about 5000 years ago.[2]

A rock inscription of 1169 A. D.[3] near Sasaram in Bihar records the interesting fact that the Brāhmaṇas of Svarṇahala secured a forged grant in respect of two villages by bribing an officer of the Gāhaḍavāla king Vijayacandra (c. 1155-70 A. D.) of Kanauj and that the local king Pratāpadhavala exhorted the future rulers of his family to be careful about the spurious document. The said copper-plate grant, issued in the name of Gāhaḍavāla Vijayacandra, was recently found in the possession of a Brāhmaṇa family of Sunahar (ancient Svarṇahala) near Sasaram.[4]

Although sometimes stone pillars were also used for engraving grants of land, etc., it was difficult to forge such documents in secret. Moreover, records of this type were expected to be set up near the gift land or in the compound of temples

1. *Select Inscriptions*, pp. 262-66.

2. Cf. *Bomb. Gaz.*, Vol. 1, Part ii, p. 301, note. For a fictitious grant of Rāma of Ayodhyā quoted in the *Skanda Purāṇa*, see *Bhār. Vid.*, Vol. VI, 1945, pp. 237 ff. See also Fleet's article in *Ind. Ant.*, Vol. XXX, pp. 201 ff.

3. *Ep. Ind.*, Vol. XXXIII, pp. 23ff.

4. Ibid., Vol. XXXV, pp. 153ff.

when the land, etc., were granted in favour of gods.[1] Forgery of stone inscriptions was therefore unusual. A few specimens of spurious lithic records are however known, though these were forged for a different purpose.

Sometime ago, a stone bowl bearing a small Kharoṣṭhī inscription was secured by the Bhārat Kalā Bhavan, attached to the Hindu University, Varanasi.[2] The writing is a palpable forgery since the persons responsible for it had apparently very insufficient knowledge about the forms of Kharoṣṭhī letters and the language expected in a Kharoṣṭhī document. With the partition of India in 1947, the zone where Kharoṣṭhī writing was prevalent now forms a part of West Pakistan. Kharoṣṭhī epigraphs have therefore a special demand in the Indian museums, and it is not very difficult here to pass spurious articles as genuine. Thus commercial motive lies at the root of the forgery of the said document.

Similar was the motive behind the forgery of the Rummindei pillar inscription[3] of Aśoka. About the beginning of the year 1928, Birendranath Ray of Purī, a well-known collector of antiquities and founder of the now-defunct Ray's Museum, was reported to have discovered a stone tablet (19″×12″×7″) bearing writing in Aśokan Brāhmī. It was said that Ray secured the inscription from a cultivator of Kapileśvara, about a mile to the south of the Liṅgarāja temple at Bhubaneswar, and that the stone had been fixed into the mud wall of the latter's house for generations. Haranchandra Chakladar of the University of Calcutta deciphered the writing and delivered a lecture on its identity with the Rummindei pillar inscription at a meeting of the Orissa Historical Association, Purī, on the 2nd Jyaiṣṭha, 1335 B. S., and its report appeared in the *Forward* of Calcutta. Since many of the edicts of Aśoka have been found in several versions scattered in different parts of his empire,

1. Sometimes votive inscriptions were engraved on walls or pillars in the temples or on stone tablets embedded in the walls or on plaques deposited in the temples.

2. *A. R. Ep.*, 1955-56, No. B 366.

3. *Select Inscriptions*, pp. 79-71; above, p. 389.

Chakladar regarded the Kapileśvara inscription as a genuine copy of the Rummindei epigraph. Unfortunately, he did not notice that the nature of the Rummindei inscription precludes the possibility of its having other versions. It records that Aśoka visited Lumbinī-grāma, sanctified by the birth of the Buddha, on a pilgrimage and that he not only raised a pillar and platform on the holy site but exempted the village from the payment of *bali* (land tax payable in cash) and made it *āṣṭa-bhāgika*, i.e. entitled to pay the royal share of the produce at the rate of $\frac{1}{8}$ instead of the normal rate which was much higher. It will be seen that such a record had no place outside Lumbinī-grāma (Rummindei) and that therefore no genuine copy of it required to have been displayed by the emperor in distant Orissa. We have little doubt that the Kapileśvara copy of the Rummindei inscription is a recent forgery.

Chakladar's erroneous views regarding the Kapileśvara epigraph being a genuine copy of the Rummindei inscription inspired uncritical writers to claim Orissa as the birth place of the Buddha. Some Oriyas believe that the Buddha was born at the headquarters of the former State of Baudh in Orissa while others speak of Baudapura in the Cuttack District. In a note in the *Pravāsī* (Bengali), Śrāvaṇa, B. S. 1335, pp. 626-27 Chakladar criticised such theories, but still regarded the Kapileśvara inscription as genuine and expressed his intention to publish the epigraph in English. But he does not appear to have done so probably because his friends in the field of Aśokan studies succeeded later in convincing him about the spurious nature of the record.

It is extremely difficult for a non-palaeographist to copy satisfactorily an old inscription in Brāhmī or Kharoṣṭhī because there are very few inscriptions in which all the letters are clearly visible to the unskilled eye. Moreover, books containing facsimiles of inscriptions are not easily available to the ordinary reader. It is therefore interesting to note that the Rummindei edict happens to be the only small inscription of Aśoka, in which almost all the letters are distinct and of which a clear representation appeared early in this century in text books meant for colleges and schools. V. A. Smith published a retouched facsimile of the record in his *Oxford History of India* and *Oxford School History of India*, prescribed respectively for the B.A. and Entrance (Matriculation) Examinations of the Indian Universities. The same facsimile became widely known in Eastern India with its reproduction in Haraprasad Sastri's History of India (in Bengali) meant for school children and later in some other text books of the kind. There can hardly be any doubt that the people responsible for the Kapileśvara inscription copied it from the said facsimile not much earlier than 1928.

The following news item emanating from New Delhi on the 19th June 1963 appeared in the newspapers : "Asokan Edict on Stone Bowl—A unique instance of an Asokan edict inscribed on a surface other than that of a pillar or a rock-face—the only two known so far[1]—has been recently brought to light, reports UNI. It is a short Kharoshthi inscription engraved around a stone bowl (diameter 20 cm) of Gandhara origin, recently acquired by the Prince of Wales Museum, Bombay. Studies have revealed that it is an exact copy of the major part of the seventh rock edict of Asoka, found at Shahbazgarhi of Peshawar District. The initial portion of the edict consisting of 18 syllables is missing and is probably engraved on the lid of the bowl, which is not available."[2] Unfortunately it has not been realised that the inscription is a recent forgery.

For a student of Aśokan records, it is difficult to believe that the Maurya emperor engraved his edicts on stone bowls. In the first place, Aśoka speaks of the incision of his records only on *parvata* (Rupnath and Sahasram), *śilā-stambha* (Rupnath, Sahasram and Delhi-Topra VII) and *śilā-phalaka* (Delhi-Topra VII) and never on stone bowls or any such thing. Secondly, Aśoka often refers to the purpose for which his edicts were engraved, viz. that they would be everlasting and that his officers, subjects and successors should hear them read so as to enable them to follow his instructions in regard to *Dharma*.[3]

1. The statement is rather misleading.
2. See *The Statesman* (Calcutta), dated 20.6.63, p. 8, column 4.
3. Cf. *Select Inscriptions*, pp. 24, 26, 38, 47, 57.

This purpose could scarcely have been served by a bowl which would easily break into pieces. Moreover the seventh Rock Edict belongs to a series of records which Aśoka engraved at various places together.

Another point to be remembered is that, if Brāhmī is difficult for a non-palaeographist to copy, Kharoṣṭhī writing is far more difficult, and the facsimile of the Shahbazgarhi version of Rock Edict VII is not likely to help even an ordinary student of palaeography. One may therefore wonder how the Prince of Wales Museum inscription could be forged, apparently by non-palaeographists, without help. But such help was provided by us in our small work entitled *Inscriptions of Aśoka*, published in 1957 by the Publication Division, Ministry of Information and Broadcasting, Government of India. In this book, meant for ordinary readers, an eye-copy of the Shahbazgarhi version of Rock Edict VII, prepared by us, was inserted for the purpose of illustrating Kharoṣṭhī writing just as the Rummindei edict was reproduced for illustrating Early Brāhmī. It will be seen that lines 2-5 have been copied in the Prince of Wales inscription, the first line consisting of 18 syllables being omitted. It is significant that the inscription was secured by the Prince of Wales Museum after the publication of the above work in 1957. There is hardly any doubt that the Prince of Wales Museum inscription was forged in the period between 1957 and 1963.

We have seen a few early or medieval images coming from the Orissa region and bearing inscriptions which are apparently incised recently though the engravers attempted to pass them as genuine old epigraphs. The motive is commercial since inscribed images are usually regarded as more valuable than uninscribed ones.

APPENDIX II

INTEREST IN EPIGRAPHIC STUDIES

We have referred to this subject in Chapter I of the present work.[1] In his recently published *Indian Archaeology Today*, 1962, p. 109, H. D. Sankalia says, "There are very few scholars who can read the ancient Brāhmī script.........Possibly epigraphy is a difficult subject and so people are not interested in it." This appears to be correct though it is unintelligible why 'the ancient Brāhmī script' has been singled out. Moreover, at the same time, Sankalia also observes, "Scholars as well as students do not get an opportunity to decipher inscriptions. The one reason is that, unlike the earlier volumes of the *Epigraphia Indica*, the recent volumes of this journal published by the Government of India are dominated by one person, viz. the Editor. It was formerly the practice of the Department of Epigraphy to send out inscriptions to other scholars in different parts of India and even outside. This has now been stopped and the result is that interest in the subject is fast decreasing, and I am afraid that, if this policy persist, then within 10 years there will be no scholars in India...... who will know anything of epigraphy."

These views are, we are afraid, based entirely on misunderstanding. In the first place, the knowledge of epigraphy and palaeography has to be acquired by an intensive study of numerous published inscriptions. A few inscriptions received from the Epigraphical Branch of the Archaeological Survey of India are not enough to make one an epigraphist. Secondly, the practice of sending impressions of inscriptions to students and scholars in India and abroad has certainly not been discontinued. The Editor of the *Epigraphia Indica*, referred to by Sankalia, is known to have sent out many records to people in India and outside. But very few of them succeeded in com-

1. See above, p. 11, note 1.

pleting their papers and submitting them for publication. Most of these scholars failed to submit their articles even after continuous goading for years. The few articles that were received were published in the *Epigraphia Indica* after revision. The Editor is also known to have encouraged many persons by making them joint authors of articles written by himself.[1]

Due to the dearth of articles worthy of publication, the *Epigraphia Indica* was suffering from chronic arrears for a long time. As is well known, the said Editor succeeded is bringing it up to date. He may probably be pardoned if he was compelled by circumstances to write too many articles for that purpose.[2]

1. Cf. *Ep. Ind.*, Vol. XXXIII, p. 269, note 1.

2. Cf. ibid., XXXIV, Appendix, p. v, note 8. We have often emphasised on the difficult nature of epigraphical research so little understood in our country (ibid., Vol. XXXIV, p. 209, note 3). A mutilated record cannot be read all at once, and the reading of a damaged passage baffling the decipherer for fifty times may occur to him in his fiftyfirst attempt or may not occur to him but to someone else (*JAS*, Letters, Vol. XVII, 1951, p. 84).

INDEX

A

B

C

M

O

P

S

T

U

V

ADDENDA ET CORRIGENDA

Page 8, foot-note 2, line 3.—*Add*—See also Fleet's article on Epigraphy in *Imperial Gazetteer of India*, Vol. II.

„ 9, foot-note 4.—*Add*—Vol. XIV has since been published.

„ 10, line 12.—*Read*—century (in 1904)

„ 11, line 5.—*Read*—work of reconstruction

„ „ line 13.—*Read*—like E. Burnouf, H. Kern, J.Ph. Vogel, R. Hoernle

„ 16, line 8.—*Read*—western standards

„ 19, lines 8 and 10.—*Read*—Āppāyika

„ 23, line 2.—*Read*—after (i.e. in the 6th century) the

„ „ line 3.—Read—*parinirvāṇa*

„ 26, line 3.—*Read*—Pāṇḍya, Dramiḻa, Coḻiya

„ 30, foot-notes 1 and 2.—*Add numbers to the foot-notes.*

„ 34, foot-note 1.—*Add*—For an inscribed brass tablet, see *Or. Hist. Res. Journ*, Vol. V, No. 1, p. 120.

„ 42, line 19.—*Read*—Śuṅga

„ „ line 28.—*Read*—Pāṇinian

„ 43, line 14.—*Read*—epic

„ „ foot-note 2, line 2.—*Read*—Vol. III

„ 46, foot-note 8, line 1.—*Read*—Pallankovil plates

„ 48, foot-note 4.—*Add*—where, however, 'Mṛgeśa' and 'who possibly figures in the Halsi grant of Harivarman (Sircar, *op. cit.*, p. 276)' are mistakes respectively for 'Kākustha' and 'who belonged to the Bhaṭāri dynasty and is known from the Talagunda Praṇaveśvara temple inscription (Sircar, *op. cit.*, p. 257)'.

„ 52, foot-notes 7 and 8.—*Rectify the mistakes in numbering.*

„ 53, line 17.—Read—*Marāṭhī*

„ 54, lines 21-22.—*Read*—several inscriptions in Persian and Marāṭhī

„ 56, line 13.—*Add note*—See below, p. 206 and note 4.

„ 57, line 22.—*Read*—Cambyālī

„ 59, line 7.—*Read*—the 13th century

Page 59, foot-note 9, line 2—*Add*—and already referred to above
,, 62, line 9.—*Read*—and it prevented
,, 62, line 21.—*Read*—writing material
,, 69, line 20.—*Read*—wooden objects
,, 70, line 7.—*Read*—covers, bowls, etc.
,, 71, line 22.—*Add*—The same is the case with many of the edicts of Aśoka.
,, ,, foot-note 6.—Read—*Lipimālā*
,, 73, foot-note 4, line 6.—Read—*Ep. Ind.*
,, ,, foot-note 5, line 2.—Read—*Indian*
,, 74, line 12.—For *mantras*, *read* inscriptions. *Add note*—See *JAS*, Letters, Vol. XV, 1949, pp. 101 ff.
,, 76, line 10.—*Read*—kalawan
,, 82, line 22.—*Read*—refers to the practice.
,, 94, line 1.—Read—*sdha* or
,, ,, foot-note 7, line 3.—*Read*—Vol. III
,, 107, line 18.—*Read*—Maharashtra State
,, 114, foot-note 3, line 2.—Read—*ṣaḍbhāgam*
,, 128, foot-note 4.—*Add*—The last of the three introductory stanzas in Bāṇa's *Kādambarī* is likewise quoted in one record, while another epigraph quotes the benedictory stanza from Kālidāsa's *Abhijñānaśakuntala*. See *Ep. Ind.*, Vol. XXV, p. 2; Vol. XI, p. 65; *Ind. Ant.* , Vol. XVII, pp. 231 ff.
,, 132, line 19.—Read—*ādiśati* or *samājñāpayati*
,, 133, foot-note 7, line 6.—*Read*—charge of the royal bed-chamber or
,, 136, foot-note 2, line 3.—Read—*c=ākṣayam*
,, 146, line 28.—*Read*—Bamhani plates
,, 161, line 6.—*Add*—In one case, the word *yāta* has been used at the same place (*Ep. Ind.*, Vol. XXXI p. 209).
,, 163, line 1.—Read—*Goṣṭhavāḍa*
,, 164, line 26.—Read—*daṇḍapāśik-oparika*
,, 165, foot-note 3, line 7.—Read—*prasādinaś=cāṭa*
,, 166, line 7.—Read—*cāṭa*
,, 167, foot-note 3.—*Add*—Cf. *sarvān=eva yathā-sambadhya-mānakān=āgāmi-grāmabhoktṛ-sāmanta-rāja-putr-ādhikāri-purapati-trivarga-sthāna-nagara*

prabhṛti-pradhān-āpradhā ıa-janān (Garde) *Imp. Ins. Baroda St.*, Vol. I, p. 52).

Page 169, footnote 1, line 4.—Read—=*kṣetrakarān*

,, 173, line 10.—*Add*—But this may also be due to the fact that the medieval authors sometimes borrowed the quotations from other works of the type of theirs.

,, 178, foot-note 7, lines 1 and 4.—Read—*pāpināṁ* and *koṭyo*

,, 179, foot-note 6, line 2.—Read—*dānāt*

,, 182, foot-note 6, lines 3-4.—*Read*—separately

,, 183, foot-note 5, line 2.—*Read*—for *praṇaṣṭaṁ*

,, 186, foot-note 8, line 2.—Read—*ativimala*

,, 194, line 4.—*Read*—ev=āgāminaḥ

,, 195, line 20.—*Read*—yatnād=rakṣa

,, 217, foot-note 3, line 1-2.—*Read*—Śaka 520, see *BEFEO*

,, 229, line 25.—*Read*—numbers

,, 235, last line—*Read* ūdāka

,, 241, foot-note 2, line 3.—*Read*—4+9

,, 250, line 18.—*Read*—never form

,, 271, foot-note 2, line 3.—*Read*—Aṁśuvarman

,, 299, line 13.—*Read*—in 795

,, 301, line 21.—*Read*—assigned

,, 303, line 26.—*Read*—known to have been ruling

,, 309, foot-note 1, line 7.—Read—*hata*(*ḥ**)

,, 319, line 7.—*Read*—Parikṣit

,, 325, foot-note 3.—Read—*Ep. Ind.*

,, 328, line 3.—*Read*—we have rarely

,, 338, foot-note 5, line 1.—Read—*JBBRAS*

,, 339, line 20.—Read—*Gaṅgaikoṇḍa*

,, 346, line 26.—*Read*—Vaiṣṇava

,, 355, foot-note 1, lines 3-4.—*Read*—Cāma-nṛpāla

,, 357, line 24.—Read—*Mahādaṇḍanāyaka*

,, 364, line 23.—*Read*—one-sixth

,, 365, line 22.—Read—*Māṇḍapika*

,, 370, lines 6-7.—Read—*Kāṇḍapati*

,, 371, line 16.—Add—*Sthānāntarika* may be the officer in charge of the shifting of the royal camp from one place to another.

,, 376, lines 14-15—*Read*—Perso-Arabic *Majmu'dār*

,, 380, line 8.—*Read*—Puṇḍravardhana

,, 381, line 12.—Read—*Śāvaḍi*
,, 385, foot-note 1, line 2.—*Read*—1912, p. 707
,, 389, foot-note 2, line 4.—*Read*—herdsmen
,, 390, line 1.—*Read*—record
,, 391, line 2.—*Read*—record
,, 396, foot-note 5, line 5.—*Read*—Cf. *bhoṭṭa-viṣṭi*
,, 397, line 3.—*Read*—etc. *Gokara*
,, ,, line 17.—*Read*—with power to recover stolen goods from thieves
,, 399, foot-note 3, line 3.—Read—*a-kiñcit*
,, 401, foot-note 4.—*Add*—above, pp. 111 ff.
,, 402, foot-note 1, line 4.—Read—*padātijīvya*
,, ,, ,, line 10—*Read*—wax, honey
,, 405, foot-note 2, line 4.—Read—*parihīnāḥ*
,, 406, line 8.—Read—*seiā* or *seigā*
,, ,, line 13.—Read—*prātibhedikā* (probably the dues realisable from merchants for the profits made during their absence from home on business trips; cf. *umbarabheda*)
,, 409, foot-note 4, line 2.—Read—*daṇḍena*
,, 410, line 26.—*Add*—According to the *Matsya Purāṇa* (283. 14-15), *Daṇḍena sapta-hastena triṁśad-daṇḍaṁ nivartanam* । *tribhāga-hīnaṁ gocarma-mānam=āha Prajāpatiḥ* ॥ so that *nivartana*=210×210 square cubits and *gocarman* is ⅔ of the same.
,, 413, line 18.—*Read*—1 *āḍhaka*
,, 419, line 9.—Add—*Viṁśopaka* is the same as modern *Biswa*.
,, 420, foot-note 2, line 1.—*Read*—personal
,, 423, line 19.—*Read*—community name Ayyar
,, 427, foot-note 2, line 6.—Read—*cāturtha*

Page 262, lines 2-3.—*Read*—year 310, i.e. sometime before

Page 261, line 19—*Add*—That the theories assigning the beginning of the Kaniṣka era to 248 A.D. or later are improbable and that it should better be ascribed to the second half of the first century A.D. and not to the second century is suggested by the Kailvan (Patna District, Bihar) inscription which is considerably earlier than the Gupta records but is dated in the year 108 no doubt of the Kaniṣka era (*Ep. Ind.*, Vol. XXXI, p. 230; Vol. XXXII, p. xiii). That the Kaniṣka era is indentical with the Śaka era is further suggested by the documents of the Chorasmian archives from Toprakkala in Central Asia, bearing dates between the years 207 and 231 of some era. Archaeological data suggest that the local palace and the archives were abandoned at the end of the third century and the begining of the fourth. The capital of Chorasmia was transferred from Toprakkala to the city of Kyat on the Amu Darya during the rule of the Chorasmian king Afrig who came to power in 305 A. D. according to Bīrūnī. Thus the era used in the documents started in the last quarter of the first century A. D. This must be the same as the Śaka era of 78 A.D. so that the years in the said documents referred to dates between 285 and 309 A.D. The use of the Śaka era in Central Asia can only be satisfactorily explained if it is identified with the Kaniṣka era (*ibid.*, Vol. XXXII, p. xiii; *Modern Review*, December 1959, p. 452; *Journ. Ind. Hist.*, Vol. XXXVIII, part i, April 1960, pp. 185 ff.).

PLATE I

1. Steatite Seal from Mohenjodaro

2. Steatite Seal from Mohenjodaro

3. Clay Seal from Nalanda

Courtesy : Archaeological Survey of India

PLATE II

1. Clay Seal from Nalanda

2. Clay Seal from Nalanda

3. Clay Seal from Nalanda

Courtesy : Archaeological Survey of India

PLATE III

1. Coin of Azes I

2. Coin of Spalyris (Śpalahora) and Śpalagadama

3. Coin of Vāsiṣṭhīputra Viḻivāyakura

Courtesy : Archaeological Survey of India

PLATE IV

1. Coin of the Yaudheya Republic

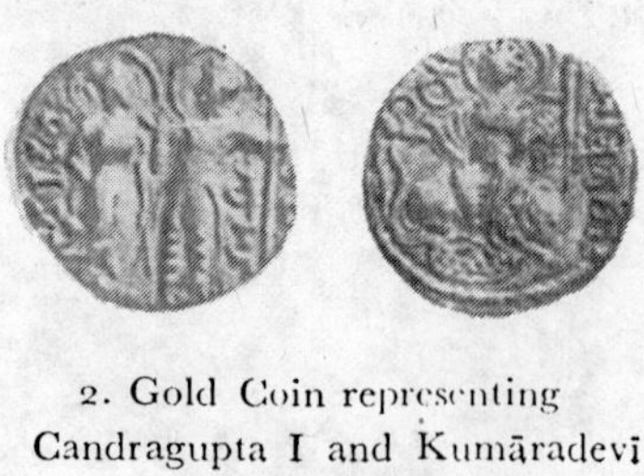

2. Gold Coin representing Candragupta I and Kumāradevī

3. Coin of Rājendra-coḷa I

Courtesy : Archaeological Survey of India

Plate V

Lauriya-Nandangadh Stone Pillar bearing Edicts of Aśoka

Courtesy : Archaeological Survey of India

PLATE VI

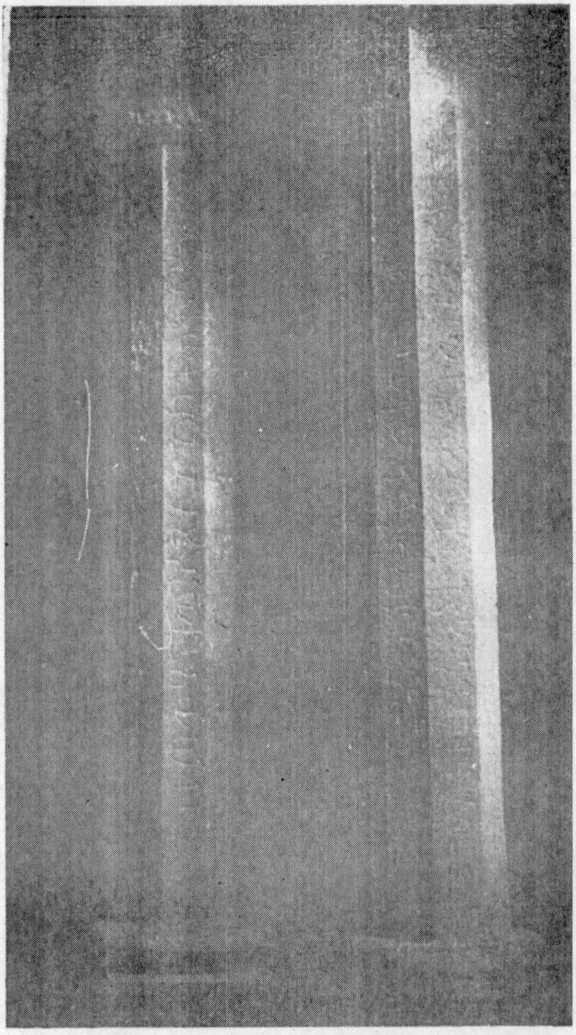

Nasik Stone Pillar bearing Inscription of Bhaṭapālikā

Courtesy : Archaeological Survey of India

PLATE VII

Inscribed Wooden Pillar from Kirari

Courtesy : Archaeological Survey of India

PLATE VIII

Meharauli Iron Pillar bearing Inscription of Candra

Courtesy : Archaeological Survey of India

PLATE IX

Mahakuta Stone Pillar bearing Inscription of Maṅgaleśa

Courtesy : Archaeological Survey of India

PLATE X

Stone Pillar Inscription from Sravanabelgola

Courtesy : Archaeological Survey of India

PLATE XI

Inscribed Stone Sculpture from Mathura
Courtesy : Archaeological Survey of India

PLATE XII

Nāga Inscription from Banavasi

Courtesy : Archaeological Survey of India

Plate XIII

Takṣaka-nāga Image Inscription from U.P.

Courtesy : Archaeological Survey of India

PLATE XIV

Inscribed Hero Stone from Tripurantakam

Courtesy : Archaeological Survey of India

Plate XV

Inscribed Satī Stone from Devagiri

Courtesy : Archaeological Survey of India

PLATE XVI

Inscribed Hero Stone from Kalukada

Courtesy : Archaeological Survey of India

PLATE XVII

Stone Inscription from Mallam recording Head-offering

Courtesy : Archaeological Survey of India

PLATE XVIII

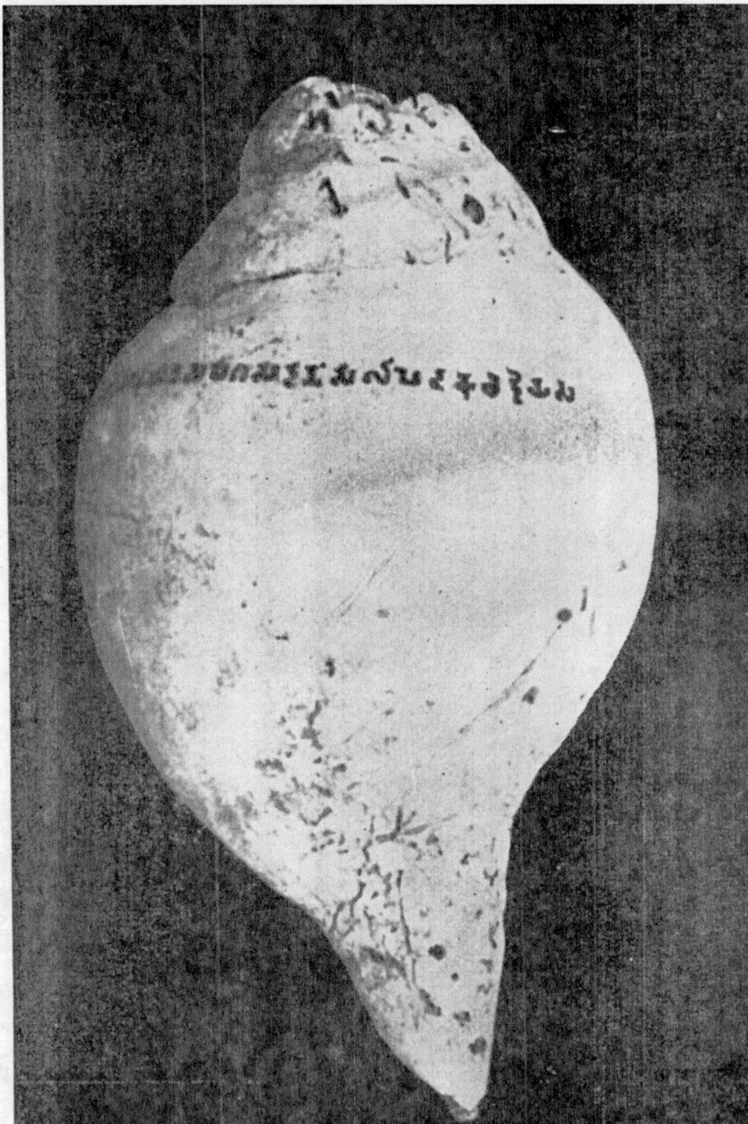

Inscribed Conch-shell from Ṣalihundam

Courtesy : Archaeological Survey of India

PLATE XIX

1. Inscribed Earthen Pot from Ponduru

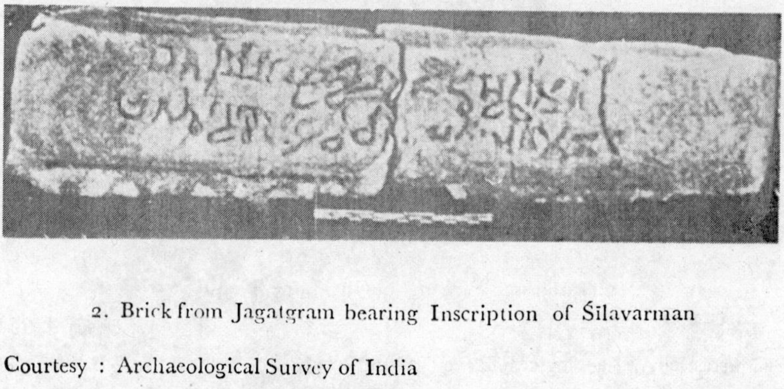

2. Brick from Jagatgram bearing Inscription of Śīlavarman

Courtesy : Archaeological Survey of India

PLATE XX

1. Inscription on Terracotta Plaque from Bihar

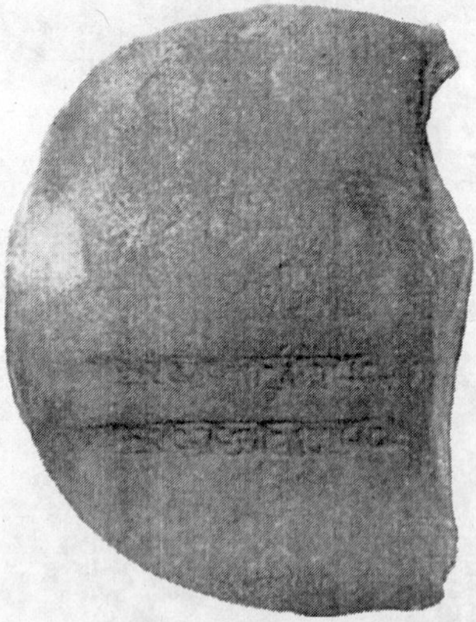

2. Embossed Writing on the same Plaque

Courtesy : Archaeological Survey of India

PLATE XXI

Sanokhar Copper Image-cover bearing Inscription of Ballālasena

Courtesy : Archaeological Survey of India

PLATE XXII

Pushpagiri Stone Slab bearing Inscription of Singhana

Courtesy : Archaeological Survey of India

PLATE XXIII

Inscribed Walls, etc., of the Saptarṣīśvara Temple at Lalgudi

Courtesy : Archaeological Survey of India

PLATE XXIV

Earthen Pot from Andhavaram containing Four Sets of Copper-plates

Courtesy : Archaeological Survey of India

PLATE XXV

Four Sets of Copper Plates inside Earthen Pot from Andhavaram

Courtesy : Archaeological Survey of India

PLATE XXVI

Tripura Plate of Lokanātha

Courtesy : Archaeological Survey of India

PLATE XXVII

A Set of Copper Plates from Andhavaram

Courtesy : Archaeological Survey of India

PLATE XXVIII

Udayendiram Plates of Hastimalla

Courtesy : Archaeological Survey of India

PLATE XXIX

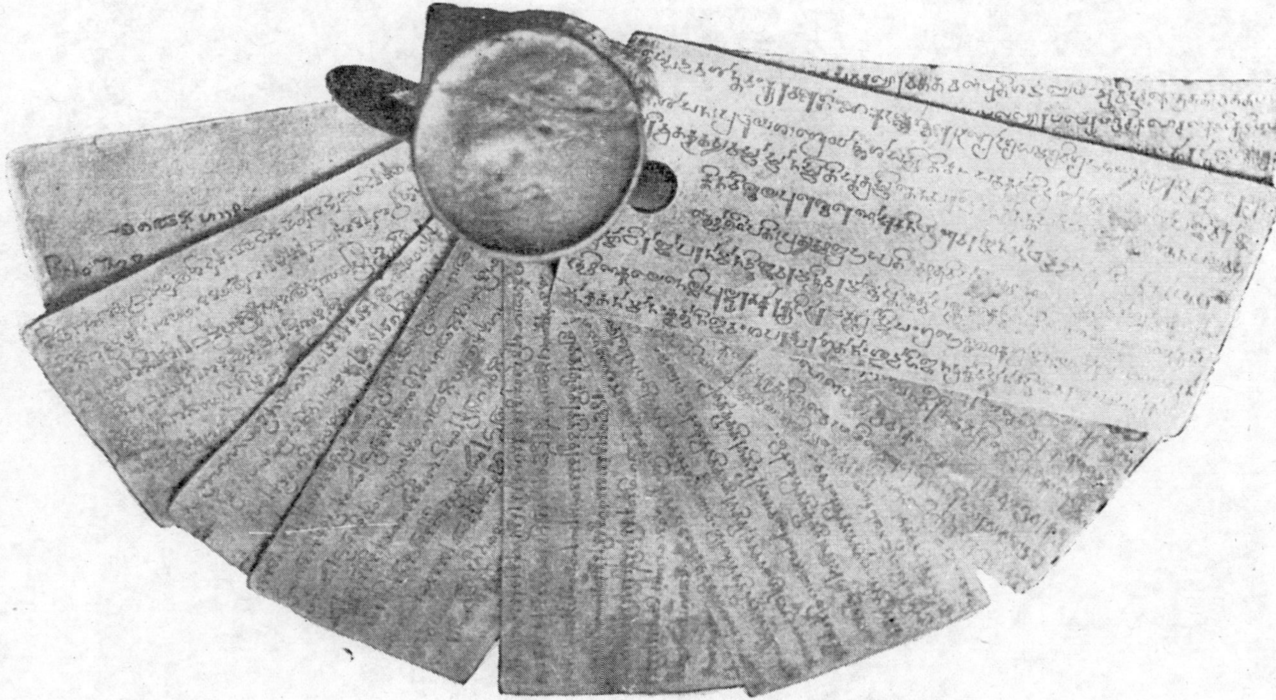

Pullur Plates of Nandivarman II

Courtesy : Archaeological Survey of India

PLATE XXX

Bronze Seal of Śarvavarma-maukhari

Courtesy : Archaeological Survey of India

PLATE XXXI

1. Bronze Seal of the Tandantottam Plat s of Nandivarman II

2. Bronze Seal of the Kolhapur Plates of Gaṇḍarāditya

Courtesy : Archaeological Survey of India

PLATE XXXII

Bronze Seal of the Nalanda Plate of Devapāla

Courtesy : Archaeological Survey of India

PLATE XXXIII

Bronze Seal of the Karandai Plates of Rājendra-coḷa I

Courtesy : Archaeological Survey of India

PLATE XXXIV

Bronze Seal of a Grant of Daṇḍi-mahādevī

Courtesy : Archaeological Survey of India

PLATE XXXV

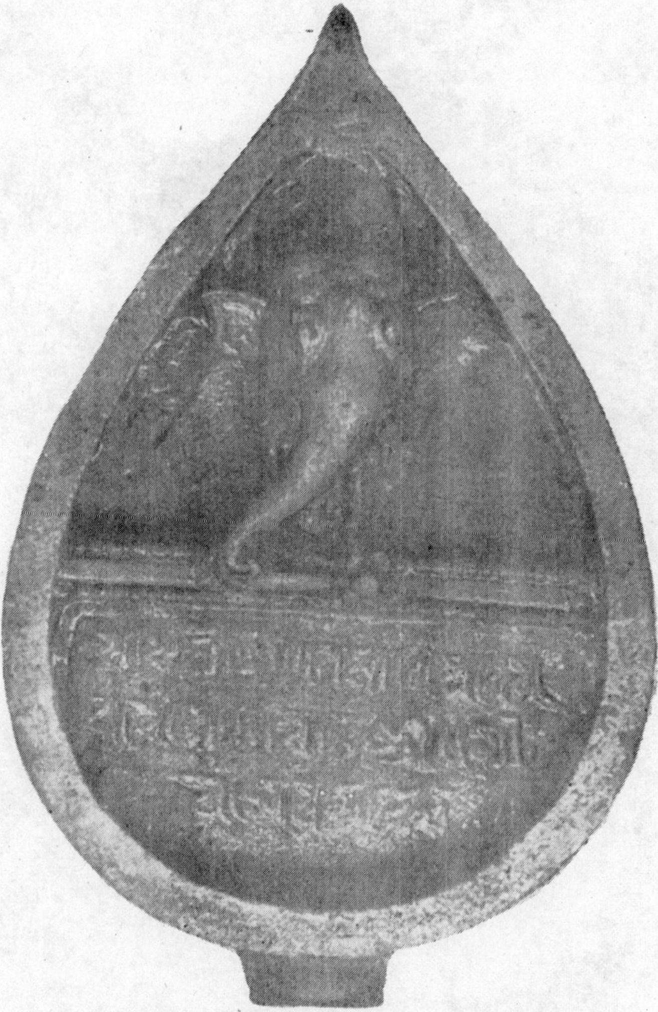

Bronze Seal of a Grant of Dharmapāla of Prāgyotiṣa

Courtesy : Archaeological Survey of India

PLATE XXXVI

Crystal Seal of Avarighsa

Courtesy : British Museum, London, and Archaeological Survey of India